British workers and the
Independent Labour Party
1888—1906

British workers
and the Independent
Labour Party
1888—1906

David Howell

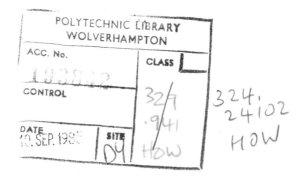

Manchester University Press

St. Martin's Press   New York

Copyright © David Howell 1983

Published by
Manchester University Press
Oxford Road, Manchester M13 9PL

British Library cataloguing in publication data

Howell, David
  British workers and the Independent Labour
  Party 1888—1906.
  1. Independent Labour Party — History
  I. Title
  324.24107   JN1129.I52
  ISBN 0-7190-0920-0

All rights reserved. For information, write:
St Martin's Press, Inc., 175 Fifth Avenue, New York, NY 10010
Printed in Great Britain
First published in the United States of America in 1983

ISBN 0-312-10568-1

Library of Congress Cataloging in Publication Data

Howell, David, 1945—
  British workers and the Independent Labour Party, 1888—1906.
  Bibliography: p.
  Includes index.
  1. Independent Labour Party (Great Britain) — History.
  2. Labor and laboring classes — Great Britain — History.
  3. Trade-unions — Great Britain — History. I. Title.
  JN1129.I52H68   1983   324.24107'09   82-24086
  ISBN 0-312-10568-1

Printed and bound in Great Britain by
Biddles Ltd, Guildford and King's Lynn

Contents

A summary of major events occurring during the period covered by this book is included as Appendix 1 on pp. 471—84.

Preface

Analyses of the early Independent Labour Party are few. The broader canvas portraying the emergence of the Labour Representation Committee has been the subject of much stimulating work by both scholars and polemicists, but the ILP as such has not been the subject of a detailed study for the early years. Instead, reliance has had to be placed on these wider works or on the often valuable biographies of ILP leaders. Yet the Party's importance is obvious. It furnished the political heart of the Labour Representation Committee, and it provided many of the first generation of Labour's political leadership, both national and local. It has been presented as an effective response to the problems facing socialists in Britain, proclaiming its flexibility through its Labour title which camouflaged its formal commitment to socialism.

This examination of the party's critical early years is intended not simply to deepen understanding of an important political organisation, but also to illuminate more fundamental debates about the development of working-class politics in Britain. The priority afforded to electoral politics, the search for a pragmatic understanding with the unions, the equivocal relationship with the Liberals — these helped to determine the agenda and the style of Labour politics for several years. Were they inevitable or did suppressed alternatives lurk beneath seemingly inexorable developments?

Readers concerned with such questions may wonder why they are impelled rapidly into the complexities of mining disputes, and of cotton mill hierarchies, or subsequently immersed in the various political traditions of Clydeside, Bradford and Blackburn. But the analysis of a political organisation's growth cannot begin with a study of its formal structure. It must start from an examination of the possible bases of support. In this case, this involves an exploration of the potential for ILP influence in trade unions, complemented by an assessment of the scope available in various communities for a new political organisation. Only when we grasp such bases in their unevenness and ambiguity is it possible to move forward to an appreciation of the party as a national organisation equipped with its own programme, principles and style.

It is a partial transformation of industrial and community particularisms into a wider identity built around a commitment to an organisation.

More is at stake than the important perception that explanation should proceed from the local and specific to the national and general. The creation of the ILP — and hopefully the argument of this book — stand as responses to those who see political action as the product of impersonal economic forces. ILP activists were constrained by a perplexing array of economic and cultural obstacles. Yet equipped often with very limited resources, they sought to innovate whilst working with the grain of their immediate industrial and political situations. No doubt, this led frequently to compromises of principle, but the emphasis should rest finally with the affirmation of a creative political response. This text can embody this as we begin with the exploration of local particularisms and responses, and then shift to an examination of national features.

This last emphasis is much more than a fine academic point. My research has taken me to the communities in which the early ILP was forged, when many of them are facing the horrendous consequences of long-term economic decline and of a government revelling in the tyrannies of the market and insensitive to its social consequences. To explore this past in this fashion offers some hope for the present, not so much through the substance of ILP politics as in the demonstration of workers' capacities to offer creative responses to the challenges of market forces, hostile authorities and corrosive fatalism.

My dependence on libraries and trade unions for access to manuscripts is documented in the list of references. The viability of this study owes much to my obtaining access to the ILP Archive. I am grateful to Barry Winters and Eric Preston for their help in this matter and also for their interest in the project, and also to Alastair Everitt for his hospitality whilst consulting this collection. Other collections of special value were consulted at the British Library of Political and Economic Science and at the University of Liverpool Library. I must express more general and long-standing debts to the University of Manchester John Rylands Library and the City of Manchester Reference Library.

Many friends and colleagues have argued with me, encouraged me and read earlier drafts. David Coates has undertaken the laborious task of reading the complete manuscript, amazing me with his endurance, encouraging me with his interest and stimulating me with his comments. David Beetham, Peter Lowe, Lewis Minkin and Dylan Morris have discussed the problems of this study over a long period, have read portions of the text, pointed out ambiguities, and reminded me that the topic mattered. Margaret Wagstaffe, Karen Hunt and Mike Tyldesley, all graduate students in the University of Manchester, have made valuable suggestions of methodology and of substance, whilst undergraduates and extra-mural students have listened to my involved monologues on the subject, and have encouraged me to clarify my ideas.

Other scholars have supported me with their suggestions and interest. My thanks go to David Clark, Jorgen Elkit, Arthur Lipow , Kenneth Morgan, Henry Pelling, Jack Reynolds and Philip Williams. Early ideas were tried out at the European Consortium for Political Research Workshop on Political Organisation at Grenoble in 1977, and then successively in seminars at Sheffield Polytechnic, Cambridge University, Manchester Polytechnic and Leeds University. I am grateful to all who contributed to these discussions.

This book would not have been completed easily without the grant of a sabbatical year from the University of Manchester. I am indebted for this, particularly to those colleagues who undertook extra duties during this period. Alec McAulay of Manchester University Press has shown infectious enthusiasm for the project. Lynn Dignan has typed successive and ever-expanding drafts with patience, interest, efficiency and humour and has played an indispensable part in its completion. Finally, Judith knows that the ILP was not so much a Party, more a way of life and provided the most vital encouragement of all, the confidence that it would be finished.

Manchester
October 1981

1

Images and emphases

The Independent Labour Party stood at the heart of the developments that produced those political structures that have dominated the British Left during most of this century. ILP members played leading roles at the foundation conference of the Labour Representation Committee in February 1900. This compromise of a separate political grouping, yet without ideological hostages reflected the ILP's predilection for a middle way between trade union sectionalism and socialist rectitude. The party provided the British left with several of its national leaders during the first three decades of the twentieth century. Keir Hardie, Phillip Snowden, and above all, Ramsay MacDonald were ILP members who rose to greater eminence in the wider labour movement. But the party was not just notable for providing political leaders. Many trade union officials served apprenticeships in the ILP. Some, such as Bob Smillie, the first socialist President of the Miners' Federation of Great Britain, were proud of their ILP connection. Other links were less publicised. J. R. Clynes, for many years the epitome of industrial moderation as President of the Gasworkers' and then of the General and Municipal Workers', served his time as a member of the Oldham ILP. Herbert Smith, 'the man in the cloth cap', leader of Britain's miners in the heroic struggle of 1926, had been an ILP activist in the Yorkshire coalfield, when the local trade union hierarchy was implacably Liberal. At a less elevated level, the early ILP provided training for many inter-war Labour backbenchers, for councillors who carried out the first Labour exercises in municipal administration, and for activists who staffed the upper echelons of local Labour Parties until well into the inter-war period. The ILP's emergence and early development involved much more than the creation of a new set of political structures. It also incorporated the start of a distinctive set of experiences encountered by a generation of Labour activists, and captured in a multitude of individual biographies. Their content, stretching from the street-corner oratory of the nineties to the dignities of Downing Street in the twenties implies much about the continuities and changes involved in Labour's advent to office. To encounter earlier passages in such careers is to confront a characteristic image, perhaps an appropriate method of introduction to the complexities of understanding the early ILP.

The socialist propagandist stands in the principal street of an industrial town in Scotland or the north of England in the mid-nineties. Typically he is in his late twenties or early thirties; his background seems to be that of the self-educated artisan or clerk. His appearance tends towards bohemianism; he sports a red tie. Sometimes the propagandist is a woman of similar age, probably from a more established middle-class background. In either case the oratory is emotional, sentimental and frequently effective. A crowd gathers. Some are merely curious, attracted to the rhetoric, as they would be to the hell-fire of a hot gospeller, or to the blandishments of a patent medicine salesman. Others are more serious. They listen to the speaker and possibly are converted.

Such is the image of the early propagandists of the ILP as they carried on their missionary campaigns, braving apathy and hostility, buoyed up by optimism, concerned not with the minutiae of political dealings but the broad uncomplicated advocacy of ethical principles. It is a sentimental and beguiling image to which hard-pressed ILPers would resort with longing during later difficulties. This retrospective vision was cultivated assiduously by later ILP publicists, as part of the creation of a party style. It was all the more effective for being based on a significant element of truth.

Yet this image needs to be offset by others. More than three decades later, the second Labour Government stumbled into its final disintegration, after more than two years' futile efforts to prevent a worsening economic depression through a dedicated devotion to orthodoxy. This government contained many who had been active in, or influenced by, the propagandising of the early ILP. Above all, it was two ministers concerned centrally with the ILP's early work — MacDonald and Snowden — who stood at the heart of Labour's 1931 agony. Their insistence on a cut in unemployment benefit, the rift with the TUC General Council, the split in the government, their involvement in a National Government led to their estrangement from Labour partisans. The tired faces of the old ILPers of 1931, trapped in the ranks of former opponents, provide a challenge. It is hard to see in this collapse the visionary orators of the 1890s. Yet any appreciation of the significance of the ILP must accommodate this contrast. Should it be attributed to the harsh impact of office and diminishing optimism — a verdict which carries implications for the quality of the initial vision — or were there significant continuities between the dreams of the nineties and the tragedy of 1931?

Several of the complexities of the ILP are captured in the careers of those four figures who dominated the party for much of its first twenty-four years. Keir Hardie towered over all others, symbolising the party's character both for its members and for a wider public.[1] Born illegitimate in a Lanarkshire hamlet in August 1856, he went down the pit in his eleventh year. His mining experiences left an indelible mark on his social perceptions which was reflected in much of his journalism. They led also to attempts to develop trade union organisation, a daunting task amongst the employees of powerful coal companies in the West of Scotland. Eventually the failure of the Lanarkshire coal strike of 1887 led to a political initiative. Hitherto Hardie had operated essentially within the broad Scottish Liberal coalition, accepting Gladstonianism as an appropriate creed for the working class, and voicing much of the self-respecting, self-improving morality that went along with it. Now there came a partial break symbolised by Hardie's candidacy in the Mid Lanark by-election of April 1888, and in the formation, four months later, of the Scottish Labour Party. Hardie's involvement in a separate political organisation and his acceptance of some socialist ideas did not entail a ready break with all Radical Liberal principles, nor with attempts to negotiate electoral arrangements with sympathetic Liberals.

Throughout his career, Hardie's strategy combined potentially conflicting elements, socialism and a Radical Liberal inheritance; staunch independence and the hope of particpating in a broader political realignment. Which elements predominated depended on the occasion. These complications, and the attendant subtleties of Hardie's strategy were masked frequently by a combative style. Here there were continuities from his celebrated 'Cloth Cap' entry into the House of Commons in 1892 through to his passionate criticism of Liberal Government attitudes to strikers in the years after 1910. It was a style frequently at odds with that of many parliamentary colleagues, and reached an appropriate climax in Hardie's outspoken response to the outbreak of war in 1914.

If Hardie symbolised the 'via dolorosa' of British socialism, his ILP colleague, Ramsay MacDonald combined platform rhetoric with the feline pursuit of influence.[2] His Scottish background was very different from that of Hardie. They shared illegitimacy and an early ethos of Radical Liberalism, but MacDonald's childhood in Morayshire was spent in a world remote from that of industrial Lanarkshire. In the landscape that MacDonald knew Radicalism was identified closely with the question of land reform. For him, Radicalism brought an attachment to the forces of Progress, together with a proud spirit of self-help; it was not pressurised by any industrial experience nor by attempts at trade union organisation. Instead, the search for a career rather than for mere employment took MacDonald first to Bristol in 1885, and then, after a brief return to Morayshire, south again to London early in 1886. The nineteen-year-old MacDonald experienced unemployment in that year's depression, but a clerical post led in 1888 to a secretaryship with a Radical politician, and increasing involvement in Radical London politics. He had been initiated into Bristol socialism, and this led to socialist activities in London. On the one side, a concern with the practicalities of socialism was reflected in Fabian Society involvements, but this was balanced characteristically by a preoccupation with the moral concerns of the Fellowship of the New Life. This dualism was accompanied by a belief that socialists could work productively with progressive Liberals. But eventual disillusionment experienced by

MacDonald in negotiations with Southampton Liberals over his proposed candidacy, plus further evidence from Sheffield of Liberal insensitivity to Labour claims, led to his joining the ILP in July 1894.

The pragmatic quality of this decision did not mean that MacDonald's attachment to his new political home was brittle, but it did lend it a distinctive quality. In MacDonald's view, the ILP must reach out to sympathetic elements in other parties. Such anti-sectarianism led in the short run to MacDonald becoming the Secretary of the Labour Representation Committee. He was committed perhaps more than anyone else in the difficult years after 1900, to making a success of this alliance of trade unionists and ILPers in which decision-making bodies were dominated by the unions, and the ILP refrained from pushing a socialist objective in order to develop a broader working-class unity.[3] Once again, it was MacDonald who negotiated with Herbert Gladstone the Liberal Chief Whip in 1902 and 1903 for some limited understanding in the next general election. This secret Gladstone—MacDonald pact, so often the object of suspicious comment, but never actually acknowledged, was fundamental in the LRC's eletoral breakthrough of 1906.[4] Only three of the party's seats were won against official Liberal opposition, two of these in Scotland where the pact did not apply. Less positively, MacDonald's strategy and style were expressed in heated attacks on critics within the ILP as they reacted against the perceived constraints of the alliance with trade unionists, or speculated about deals with the Liberals.

Some of these formative influences were shared by Phillip Snowden, another of the tired faces of 1931. This time the background was not the Radicalism of Scotland, but of a West Riding woollen village, Cowling, where Snowden was born in July 1864.[5] As a child he witnessed the vigour of nonconformity, its Radical politics, its temperance zeal, its emphasis on self-improvement. All left a profound mark on Snowden, a life-long temperance enthusiast, strongly attached to many Radical icons, most notably Free Trade. His pursuit of self-improvement led from a pupil-teaching post, through an insurance office to a career with the Inland Revenue. But in 1891, this was cut short by an illness which left him both unemployed and crippled. Now back at Cowling, Snowden became involved in the debates that followed the formation of the ILP in Bradford. Recruited by local Liberals to defend their cause in a debate with socialists, he was persuaded by the latter's case. He became a leading ILP propagandist, with a particular reputation for his evangelical style. This suggested a socialist incorruptibility, contrasting in the pre-1914 years with MacDonald's justifications of a more flexible approach. But behind the evangelical mask, there was an austere and implacable believer in Gladstonian economics.

Adherence to the precepts of self-help could be found also in the career of the last of the quartet, John Bruce Glasier. Like MacDonald and Hardie, he was an illegitimate Scot. Born probably in Glasgow and probably in March 1859, Glasier's politics were influenced heavily by his Glaswegian environment.

Once again, land reform with all its Radical associations was a formative element, although in Glasgow land agitations had their Irish dimension, and some of Glasier's early political activities were in association with Michael Davitt's Land League. But Glasier's politics had other inspirations which were revealed as he moved from early poetic aspirations, through the Social Democratic Federation into William Morris's Socialist League. His romantic style incorporated a rejection of parliamentary manoeuvres in favour of rhetorical performances at street corners. The oratorical style continued for many years, but his adherence to the ILP signalled a growing moderation on political strategy. Glasier alone of the 'Big Four' never became an MP, but he was a loyal supporter of the ILP's official policies, an opponent of the SDF and increasingly a defender of the compromises that he saw as inevitable milestones on the socialist road.

These important instances provide suggestive evidence of the complex sentiments which the ILP absorbed from the late-Victorian left. Dominant images do not only help to mould our thoughts at the level of individual biography. The significance of the early ILP, as reflected in the careers of its leading figures, lies also in its adoption of a specific strategy. It is necessary to come to terms with a dominant historiographical image of the party, which portrays it as an appropriate and effective vehicle for the political claims of both Labour and socialist partisans. Its pragmatism, its distaste for theoretical disputation, its general readiness to co-operate with Radical Liberals, and more importantly with trade unions, produced electoral success, firstly through the creation of the Labour Representation Committee, and then in 1903 through MacDonald's secret development of an electoral arrangement with the Liberals. These developments led to the electoral successes of 1906, in which seven ILP-sponsored MPs and several other party members who were sponsored by trade unions, secured election under LRC auspices, usually with Liberal good will. Thus the ILP can be presented as working with the grain of British politics. Socialists secured entry to parliament, an achievement that would have been unlikely if a more independent and more overtly socialist strategy had been followed. This successful progress by the ILP is typically contrasted with the narrow outlook and political sterility of the marxist Social Democratic Federation, and allegedly un-English appendage to the main direction of British Labour politics. This positive image has been countered by another which makes similar assumptions, but then characterises the outcome in very different terms. The ILP might have been suited to its environment, but it is all the worse for that. It can be condemned for its lack of theoretical sophistication, its obsession with parliamentary and electoral questions and its ready compromising with the prejudices of existing power-holders. From this counter-perspective, working with the grain involves the emasculation of socialist potential.

The positive portrait leaves unanswered questions posed by the ILPs accommodations with trade unionism and Liberalism. Did the creation of the LRC and the 1903 entente with the Liberals help to generate a Progressive

Alliance in which Labour politicians, let alone socialists, were a largely impotent and essentially incorporated minority? The sequence 1893—1900—1906 is often linked *sotto voce* with later Labour milestones — 1918—1924—1945. But this is simply to extend further and more flimsily a perhaps unpersuasive claim about natural or likely development. Similarly the negative image fails to deal with the complexities of constraint and agency. Understandable exasperation at the limitations of British Labour politicians is a poor substitute for a thorough examination of options and their feasibility. A sceptical characterisation of what actually happened does not necessitate a belief that — from the writer's viewpoint — some preferable alternative was readily available, but the value of such a characterisation must be enhanced by such an investigation.

Much of the examination which follows is located of necessity in highly specific terms — the politics of towns or regions, and the changing factional balances within specific trade unions. The ILP grew within a society where regional differences were expressed frequently in contrasting political attachments. The lack of political coherence in the labour movement only underlined the endemic sectionalism of the trade union world. From one important angle the emergence of the ILP and its later involvement in the wider Labour Party can be seen as an aspect of the erosion of such particularisms. Regional political divergences slowly gave way to a more national political argument based around class differences; trade union sectionalism diminished as small local unions gave way to larger national organisations. Yet the party grew in a world where local distinctiveness still mattered. Its own uneven growth was abundant testimony to this, and it carried the stylistic legacy of its own localised origins. Thus, the portrayal and explanation of specific points of growth and of failure, is a necessary condition for the presentation of an overall picture. As historical fact, the summation of the individual elements produced a picture that seemed coherent; whether an analytical account can generate a similarly coherent conclusion is questionable, and echoes earlier scepticism about the unique status of the early ILP.

The traffic within the ILP was never uni-directional. Some cohesion could be lent eventually to local initiatives because of the existence, at least in elementary form, of a national party organisation. Interventions from the top could help to develop some level of unity amongst local groups. It was not just a question of specific interventions from above. Activists, whilst still defending their local autonomy, came to see themselves as members of a national party. The growth of such beliefs itself constituted an aspect of the development of such an organisation. The picture could become more coherent in part because activists viewed the picture in increasingly coherent terms. Beyond beliefs, there lay other general factors. Those who attempted to promote or to deflect Independent Labour politics inevitably had to come to terms with certain phenomena which can be analysed at the societal level. These were presented in specific situations, through the veil of local sentiments, clothed in terms that rendered them intelligible within a particular communal or industrial experience. But at the beginning it is perhaps easiest to elucidate them in general terms.

The ILP emerged against a backdrop of economic difficulties. It has now become a commonplace to trace the problems of British capitalism back to the 1880s. The unique advantages of the first industrial nation were disappearing, as competitors emerged in fields where Britain had enjoyed a virtual monopoly, and newly industrialised nations took the lead in fields where technical innovations were fundamental. Much of the problem was the consequence of earlier exports of machinery which in time generated competitors. If contemporaries did not grasp the full dimensions of the deterioration, certain experiences inevitably left their mark. The impact of the Great Depression with particularly high unemployment in some years could deflate earlier optimism about the prospects for an essentially laissez-faire economy and lead some trade unionists towards collectivist responses. In particular trades, the shoe might pinch with particular sharpness. Increasing competition was biting deeply into sections of the engineering industry, into the boot and shoe trade, and in the woollen towns of the West Riding. Engineers and bootmakers faced the challenge of technical innovation, with its inevitable threat to established skills. The relationship between such experiences and industrial militancy or political radicalisation remains obscure. It is certainly true that many activists in such trades sharpened their economic and political beliefs, but many of their colleagues seem to have been little affected. Similarly the explosion of 'New Unionism' in the late eighties changed the topography of trade unionism, and arguably through organising those who allegedly lacked scarce skills, injected a bias in favour of collectivism into trade union debates. But once again, as we shall see, the legacy was ambiguous. Perhaps more significantly, the coal and cotton industries, important not just for the number employed, but also by the nineties for their relatively high levels of unionisation, seemingly remained more buoyant. Overseas markets were beginning to be a problem for the cotton trade, but as yet this did not seem to threaten the industry with ultimate collapse. Equally, difficulties loomed regarding the profitability of sections of the coal industry, especially in the predominantly exporting fields, but these rarely entered the prognostications of those employed in the industry. It is this absence which is perhaps the more important emphasis. Whilst some groups of workers felt themselves to be under increasing economic pressure, and some of these were likely to draw radical conclusions, many more remained largely committed to the liberal dream of progress. Occasionally it might threaten to turn into a nightmare, but hopefully the threats could be exorcised.

The myopia about long-term developments could be seen in areas that extended beyond the economic. In retrospect, it is clear how far social developments by the eighties and nineties had eroded the individualist basis of the liberal vision. The beginnings of amalgamations and cartelisations, and the emergence of large-scale national trade unionism pre-figured the advent of managed markets beneath the rhetoric of laissez-faire. The growth of conurbations presaged the development of a popular culture of mass entertainment, and led also to growing pressure for the municipalisation of utilities. Politics too became more collectivised. A widened franchise and attempts to build mass local parties meant that the significance of the 'Independent Member' was on the decline. In so many ways, a new world was being born; the liberal epoch was in decay, but the terms of the dominant arguments frequently failed to adapt.

One point at which the transmutation of liberal capitalism into a more collectivist variant might register for the individual was in the closing of avenues for social mobility. Artisans, often hard-pressed by technical change, had a diminishing hope of going it alone. The growth of large units of production, itself reflected in part the scale at which new technology was most advantageously applied, and presented a forbidding barrier. The bureaucratisation of the commercial world also left its mark in the growing army of white-collar workers, often performing routine tasks but regarding themselves as socially superior to the most skilled of craftsmen. This sector was protected increasingly by a formidable gatekeeper — the need to possess appropriate formal educational qualifications. This requirement had two significant consequences. In some senses, it increased the separation and the distinctiveness of the industrial working class, at a time when, for some of its members, standards were coming under pressure. It also led to frustrated expectations. The activists of the early ILP were often the early products of compulsory education. Such an experience could generate aspirations which were often disappointed, with dreams foundering on the reef of certificates. If individual hopes were blocked, then perhaps a collective solution should be sought.

The legacy of Britain's industrial supremacy was profound, engendering a feeling of security and high expectations, and blanketing more general modes of thought. Whilst the emergence of the ILP can be seen as one eruption of scepticism about the viability of the liberal system, it is crucial to remember that even the most sceptical gestures were encumbered with mementoes of the high noon of liberalism. If the pioneers of the ILP saw but dimly the full extent of the problems afflicting their society, they had even less awareness of its likely destination. The major consequence of economic competitiveness and nationalist rivalries was to be the cataclysm of August 1914. Today, it is easy to look at the working-class politics of the period with that hindsight which colours perceptions of Chekovian dramas. The dénouement is known, and the actions we survey are infused with tragic and ironic qualities. At least, for the British labour movement, this future was not a complete surprise; the fever of the South African War gave ILP members a pale foretaste of the later tragedy.

Beyond the bombastic or sentimental rhetoric of imperialism, there stood serious issues which related these dimly perceived developments to political debates. Slowly during the nineties and more rapidly after 1900, the questions of economic weakness, institutional obsolescence and modernising responses secured their places on the political agenda. One great milestone was Chamberlain's protectionist programme of 1903; the interventionist Liberal response emerged in the policies of the subsequent Liberal government. Here hindsight can be misleading. It is easy to see the Liberal victory of 1906 as a natural prelude to an intimate association between that party and policies of interventionist social reform. The counterpoint is the increasing connection of Conservatives with a range of reactionary causes. Yet this is a simplification that amounts to a distortion. Collectivists could be found in both parties, and so could many who clung to the chief planks of the old liberal vision. The post-1906 casting into 'Liberal Progressives' and 'Conservative Reactionaries' may be seductive Liberal historiography, but it generates an anaemic view of earlier controversies. This has had its impact on discussions about the emergence of Independent Labour.

The relatively effective integration of the British working class during the high noon of liberal capitalism had its partisan counterpart in the attachment to Radical Liberalism of many trade union officials and working-class activists. These phenomena have resulted in much of the discussion about the growth of Independent Labour sentiment focusing upon the increasing inappropriateness of Liberalism as a vehicle for working-class demands. Such an emphasis is valid from the viewpoint of the activists. For them in a period of economic optimism, individualist Liberalism with its emphasis on the removal of obstacles to political emancipation seemed an appropriate creed. There were always sharp discrepancies between promise and performance, supplemented eventually by some doubts about the viability of traditional economic prescriptions. In unions and in communities, the politics of working-class activists can be characterised frequently as a battle between a Liberal Old Guard, and younger advocates of independence. This emphasis on Liberalism is important not only in terms of the break, but also for continuities. Many of the critics carried much of the Liberal ethos with them; their additions were typically a special emphasis on labour questions, some sort of commitment to socialism, and perhaps most crucial of all, a strong attachment to an independent political organisation.

Such emphases on breaks and continuities with Liberalism are central, but inadequate. They must be supplemented by an awareness that in some regions — most notably Lancashire — a sizeable portion of the industrial working class had Conservative sympathies. This affected the political outlook of several Lancastrian trade union officials, and left a profound mark on the regional development of the ILP. But more fundamentally, the period of the ILP's emergence and early growth was one of a rare political plasticity. The Liberal split of 1886 helped to produce nearly two decades of Unionist domination and provided a prelude to recurrent debates about the future of the Liberal Party. Dreams of new political alignments occurred easily, and optimistic ILP leaders hoped to play a part in them. Such expectations seemed feasible in a world where Chamberlain's secession had redrawn the political map so dramatically. The implications of the secession were complex. The realignment symbolised by the dramas of 1886 was a result of a continuing shift away from Liberalism by the men of property — both landed and industrial. From this angle it is possible to talk about the first signs of a class-based party system, an interpretation which fits in neatly with the post 1906 classification noted earlier. But to analyse the political dialogues of the ILP's formative period through this distinction is misleading. The auguries in the nineties were much less decisive. Chamberlainite Unionism still held out some promise of social reform; the Liberal Party having lost its Radical hustler seemed stagnant. That in such a situation ILP leaders always stood closer to Radical Liberals than to any Unionist requires investigation. It should not be accepted instantly as a natural meeting of minds. Political arguments in the nineties had their own complex and distinctive qualities; to appraise them through the distorting prism of later alignments is to court misunderstanding.

The emergence of the ILP must be located also within arguments about explicitly socialist principles and strategy. We have already noted the prevalent image of the doctrinaire Social Democratic Federation. This was a claim propagated assiduously by some leading ILPers, and it did much less than justice to the flexibility shown by SDF members in several localities. ILP strategy and style form a contrast not so much on account of what happened, but for what many believed was the case. Other socialist experiences also provided themes to develop or warnings of pitfalls. Several individuals who were to become significant in the ILP enjoyed their first experience of the joys and frustrations of propagandists within the Socialist League. The League's eventual collapse combined with a desire to make more pragmatic connections with the labour movement shifted many away from a strict principled emphasis on the making of socialists to an initially cautious approval of electoral and parliamentary politics. This development hints at a more fundamental theme. The stabilisation of the ILP represented the success of a familiar brand of politics, centred on the pursuit of electoral success through a distinct party, and the defeat of a broader strategy tied neither to specific organisations nor institutional forms. Emphases upon making socialists and upon living as socialists provided attractive motifs within ILP propaganda, but were subordinated gradually to the harsh dictates of electoral strategy.

This contrast presents the ILP as offering a more precisely defined, narrower road to socialism. It must be balanced by the relationship between the positions of the ILP and the Fabian leadership. The overlaps were significant. At the beginning many individuals belonged to both, and provincial Fabian branches were often transformed into their ILP counterparts. Many assumptions about the nature of the progression to socialism were shared. But there was one fundamental distinction. ILP leaders sought power and influence on the basis of a separate party organisation. They sought the support of trade union activists, and the votes of electors, rather than concentrating on the intellectual consent of arrived or aspiring politicians.

The emphasis on socialist alternatives must be a continuing one. Contemporaries argued through the competing claims of 'making socialists' and a predominantly electoral emphasis, of the Labour Alliance and One Socialist Party, of a separate political organisation and permeation. Yet this could be the focus of the discussion only if it could be argued plausibly that the emergence of some kind of strong socialist presence could be safely assumed. Such a claim is perhaps particularly rash in a British context where industrial workers had been integrated to a considerable degree within existing economic and political arrangements. It would also skate too readily over the problems involved in characterising the political debates of the period. The legacy of debates between Gladstonian Liberalism and Conservatism blended with the consequences of the 1886 split and the beginnings of the debate over modernisation to raise the question of the relevance of traditional party distinctions. Location of the ILP must proceed from the recognition of widespread disagreement about what the defining contours of political debate should be.

Contemporary scepticism about the immediate appeal of socialism led many ILP propagandists to appeal for support on the terrain of labour representation. There had been some slight success in securing working class Lib-Lab MPs through the co-operation of local Liberal Associations. The 1885 election returned eleven Lib-Labs amongst the successful Liberal candidates. Six were miners' MPs; one of these, Thomas Burt had sat for the Borough of Morpeth since 1874, the other five were beneficiaries of the vast expansion of the mining vote resulting from the 1884 Reform Act.[7] The others included Henry Broadhurst, first elected in 1880, and appointed to a junior government post in February 1886. Yet even the slight improvement of 1885 was unlikely to be sustained. Few constituencies were as dominated by members of industry as most mining seats, and few groups of workers shared the commitment to Liberalism shown by many miners. Elsewhere these conditions of numerical dominance and political solidarity were generally lacking. More generally even those Lib-Labs who were successful were absorbed into the great Gladstonian Coalition, lost amongst the advocates of temperance, land reform, disestablishment, and the host of other causes competing for priority. An increasingly popular response in the years after 1885 involved the claim that labour's electoral strength could be expanded by independent organisation in the constituencies; similarly parliamentary influence could be maintained and strengthened by organising independently within the Commons. Some, such as the 'Tory Socialist', H. H. Champion, coupled such claims with enmity to the Liberal Party; others, such as Hardie, whilst determined to maintain independence still held many essentially Radical views, and argued usually that independence did not necessitate isolation from sympathetic sections of Liberal opinion.

Within this complexity, three themes can offer some analytical footholds: the first two cover the attempts by the ILP activists to secure support both in trade unions and in particular communities. The two processes could complement each other, and yet there were also tensions. Each exercise was constrained by its own institutional confines and inherited traditions. The appeals and compromises appropriate to growth in a union might diverge from those most relevant to a related community. The nature of the opportunities offered by an industrial base might differ radically from the space afforded by a configuration of political forces. Although there are always connections, each requires separate explanations.

These two facets can be approached profitably through an examination of specific local cases. Yet the development of a national party organisation, our third theme, meant that equivalent issues were debated amongst leading figures, and then solutions influenced local developments. Such national choices were constrained to some extent by local initiatives, but must be given an appropriate emphasis. Moreover, the fact of a national party emerging with a clear leadership group produced its own tensions between their preferences backed by expanding resources, and many activists' desire for local autonomy, and alternative policies. The industrial/political contrast must be supplemented by a local/national one.

Examinations of these elements, at the same time stressful and supportive, can be employed to understand what happened. Options were lived through locally and then ratified or quashed by national decisions. If the Labour/ socialist component is emphasised, then the critical date is 1900, the formation of the LRC. The critical question is why was there this type of alliance with the unions? If the broader plasticity of politics is emphasised, then the development of the ILP can be seen as one element in that rationalisation of political alignments that produced the electoral landslide of 1906, and the subsequent arguments. Here an emphasis on the complexities of the ILP and wider LRC relationship with the Liberals is fundamental. Both alliances must be emphasised, not just for what they involved, but also for what they excluded. One distinctive inclusion was the development of formal connections between ILP and unions in the national LRC and in local counterparts; and it is with ILP activities within individual unions that detailed analysis can begin.

Part 1

TRADE UNION BASES

Preliminary reflections

Explanations of the development of working-class and socialist political parties typically emphasise the prior emergence of trade union organisation, struggles and consciousness as bases for political growth. Such claims involve a more or less explicit belief in a learning process — a suggestion that workers are educated in the facts of life through their industrial activities and that these experiences can generate new political awareness and attachments. Contemporaty discussions of the early ILP demonstrated such beliefs. The right-wing publicist, J. L. Garvin, could depict the new party as a clear product of economic changes and industrial struggles: 'It grows with every strike; with every commercial disaster; with every new invention of labour-saving machinery; with every development of Asiatic competition.'[1] And this reflected closely the way that ILP propagandists liked to view their own progress. Pete Curran in his Barnsley by-election campaign of 1897 highlighted the bases for ILP growth as being 'the great struggle in the Engineering Trade, the gloomy outlook in the Textile Industry, the well-grounded discontent in the Mining Trade with its Low Wages and Tyrranical Rules and Bye-Laws. All tell of the growing power of Landlordism and Capitalism.'[2] Perhaps a ghost lurks here: the spectre of base and superstructure, a ghost whose exorcism has been attempted so often but still a recurrent and seductive spectre, often a travelling companion for a series of expectations about the 'normal' development of working-class political movements.

Any account of the ILP's early growth necessitates the excavation and examination of such assumptions. A distinction must be made between the ILP as it was in the nineties — a party lacking alliances with unions, but a party which individual trade unionists might be led to join through a political commitment evolving out of industrial experiences — and the post-1900 situation. Then, the ILP prospered, at least in electoral and membership terms, as a partner in the Labour Alliance. It became a natural organisation for rising trade union leaders to join.

Even the most cursory glance at the trade union world illustrates the hazards involved in attempts to generalise about the connection between trade union experiences and the emergence of support for the ILP. So many factors could be important. When were individual unions formed? Had a particular style of leadership established its ascendancy before the growth of Independent Labour politics? What types of workers did a union attempt to organise — workers within a specific trade distinguishable by their own skills, or a section of the less secure mass of unskilled and semi-skilled? How stable was the environment within which a union operated? Did craft privileges remain largely unchallenged, or were traditional distinctions being eroded by technical innovations? Many unions had distinctive political traditions typically involving some sort of attachment to the Liberal Party. This could serve as one more element in the union's identity, protected by a range of emotional attachments, but vulnerable when industrial strategies faltered.

The political end of any putative relationship was similarly complex. It is possible to ask how far changing industrial experiences generated ILP support, manifested through the development of strong branches or significant electoral support. But there was also the possibility of changes within a union. ILP activists could secure control of parts of the union machinery. Most characteristically, they could come to dominate local branches, generating thereby a stream of appropriate resolutions. Here there is a need to assess the forms in which conflict could be expressed within a union — possibly in overtly political terms, or perhaps through the medium of an aggressive industrial policy, or again through debates about procedural questions. ILPers could secure election as delegates to union conferences, or as members of union executives. Most symbolically, they could secure victories, or at least publicity, in contests for national posts. The possibilities for exerting influence or securing posts were affected by specific unions' structures. The facility with which union leaders could evade activists' demands varied with the frequency of delegate conferences, the terms of office of leaders, and whether officers tended to be elected or appointed. There were marked variations in the ease with which insurgent factions could come to dominate individual unions. In some instances, power was centralised, and the road to control required the capture of a few key positions. Elsewhere, power was more diffused, and this could present a major obstacle for those who sought to change union policies. Moreover, disputes and changes must be assessed with some awareness of other possible explanations. It was not all a matter of ideological divergence. This element must be disentangled from others such as the inter-generational conflicts characteristic of many unions. The case of mining trade unions offers an appropriate starting-point for an analysis of these issues. Their commitment to Independent Labour politics was significant because of their large, growing and geographically concentrated memberships. It also became a challenge, since the Miners' Federation of Great Britain as a whole was the last major union to commit itself to Labour politics. The varied industrial experiences of the coalfields, and their range of political trajectories, permit an appreciation of the complex connections between the two elements. The problems posed for the early ILP by coal, were matched for very different reasons by those raised by cotton. Analysis of the complexities of ILP involvement in the coalfields can be supplemented usefully with an account of the marginal role played by the party in the shift of the cotton unions towards political independence.

These two difficult areas can be contrasted with unions which moved more readily to political independence and which can illustrate the ambiguities of the ILP's role in ostensibly successful cases. Illumination is shed particularly perhaps by the Railway Servants, formally responsible for the crucial labour representation resolution at the 1899 TUC, but also retaining a Liberal General Secretary until 1909. The appeals of political independence and socialism for craftsmen threatened by fundamental technical changes are assessed for two groups: Engineers, and Boot and Shoe Operatives. Such industrial experiences and union traditions form a sharp contrast with the concluding case. The New Unions of unskilled and semi-skilled workers were often seen as related intimately to the growth of socialist sentiments.

Even an inventory hints at the complexities of the problem. In each case, received images of socialist influence within unions must be examined critically. So too must the more fundamental question of how far ILP growth can be explained by emphases upon experiences at the work-place and within unions.

2

Mining

The Federation ethos

The Miners' Federation of Great Britain symbolised the attachment of sections of the industrial working class to Labour politics during the inter-war years. Such a role came about only slowly. In its earlier years, the MFGB kept aggressively aloof from Independent Labour politics. The Federation had been established in November 1889, little more than three years before the formation of a national ILP. Such proximity in time might be thought likely to produce a sympathy in ideas as it did for some of the new general unions. But this proved not to be the case.

The MFGB emerged from more than a decade of falling coal prices which had destroyed most attempts at collective organisation.[1] In the late eighties prices rose in an expanding market, and miners sought to repair the ravages of the depression years. One exemplar could be found in the Miners' National Union dominated by the coalfields of the North-East, where traditions of class collaboration and sliding-scale wage bargaining had deep roots. Such sentiments were less attractive to workers in coalfields producing for the home market, who had been hit badly by falling prices. They sought improvement through a more aggressive wages policy and through the promotion of legislation for an eight-hour day. Between 1888 and 1890, wages in the English coalfields rose by 40 per cent and along with success went a drive for a more permanent organisation. The Federation was born at Newport in November 1889. It was dominated by the Yorkshire Miners' Association, who provided its President, Ben Pickard, whilst Lancashire provided the Secretary, Thomas Ashton. The other, smaller, constituents came predominantly from the Midlands. Early growth was explosive — 36,000 members at the start, 200,000 by 1893. The expansion occurred despite Scotland and South Wales remaining largely unorganised, and the North-Eastern coalfields retaining their separate structures.

The significance of the Federation's development could be seen in the rapid emergence of an employers' federation as a counterweight. Yet the distinctive conditions in the individual coalfields meant that the county unions retained much autonomy. Already in 1888 each federated coalfield had acquired a conciliation board, a development favouring industrial moderation, but one which institutionalised the union's presence in previously weak areas. The first optimism came to an end in 1890 when the rise in coal prices was reversed, and along with this an attempt to secure a legislative eight-hour day was defeated in the commons in 1892. The fall in coal prices led in 1893 firstly to sporadic attacks on miners' wages in the Federated coalfields, and then in June to a demand for a 25 per cent cut. The consequence was the Federated lockout lasting from July to November, leading in turn to the creation of a Conciliation Board covering the whole MFGB area.

The outcome strengthened the Federation's credibility, although by July 1894 the new procedures had produced a 10 per cent cut, and over the next few years short-time working served as a common method of limiting earnings. This enhanced credibility led to the affiliation of the Scottish Miners in 1894, and then following a defeat, the South Wales miners abandoned their sliding-scale associations in 1899. Only Northumberland and Durham remained outside, largely on the eight-hours question until 1907 and 1908 respectively. Membership rose to 360,000 in 1900 and nearly 600,000 a decade later.

ILPers clearly hoped that an experience such as the 1893 lockout would shift miners into sympathy with their cause. They expressed similar hopes about the Scottish lockout a year later and about the Welsh dispute of 1898. Perhaps in the latter cases there are traces of support for such a thesis, but more crucially the impact of 1893 was to strengthen a situation which afforded only limited scope for the party. The prestige of Federation officials such as Pickard, a belligerent critic of the ILP, was increased, and the stabilisation of collective bargaining appeared to suggest that trade union action could reap significant rewards. Yet over time, the limitations of this machinery became apparent. When coal prices rose during the Boer War, the system imposed constraints on wage rises. With the end of the boom, a series of wage cuts began. Employers demonstrated a more intractable attitude, bringing legal actions in South Wales and Yorkshire, and Pickard's death early in 1904 removed a symbol of the old Federation ethos. Consideration of the problems and opportunities facing the ILP necessitates a dual emphasis. Miners' organisations had — or hoped to have — political representation, an expectation aided by the geographical concentration of union members. Disputes about the political complexions of mining unions thus had an immediate practical relevance. Lib-Labs responded to the challenge of the LRC by developing a MFGB scheme for extending miners' parliamentary representation which could, it was hoped, draw on the pride of miners in their own organisational strength. By allowing properly-adopted miners' candidates to stand under any political label with Federation support, this could perhaps satisfy socialists and yet leave Lib-Labs free to continue in their old ways. Such a scheme itself reflected the diversities between coalfields. Controversies typically arose at the level of the individual coalfield, and it is there amongst industrial and political distinctiveness that attention must be focused.

The MFGB: the Lib-Lab coalfields

The hostility of several county unions towards Independent Labour, let alone socialist, politics was symbolised by the belated affiliation of the MFGB to the Labour Party.[2] In most of the coalfields that formed the heart of the MFGB in the nineties — Yorkshire, Derbyshire, Nottinghamshire, Leicestershire, Staffordshire and Warwickshire — Lib-Labism ruled. Now consigned to the dustbin of history, Lib-Labism still awaits its academic champion, but the attraction of such a position for many miners is clear. It was not just that from 1885, miners dominated some constituencies electorally, and could control, in principle, the selection and election of their own nominees under the Liberal banner. In fact, such resources were mobilised only tardily, as bourgeois-dominated Liberal associations fought lengthy rearguard actions. It was also that Liberalism — whether embodied in the shape of a local miners' leader or coal-owner — found a high level of acceptance in many mining communities. Relatively well-paid workers could accept the Liberal belief in shared interests across class lines, especially the alliance of industrial capitalists and workers against parasitic, royalty-drawing landlords. Such a commitment was strengthened perhaps by the religious nonconformity characteristic of several mining villages, although the culture of such villages was a complex of puritanical and hedonistic elements.[3]

The commitment to Liberalism did not necessitate industrial passivity. Lib-Lab leaders, especially Ben Pickard and Ned Cowey in Yorkshire, were tough negotiators who had built up their county unions often at personal risk. Past performance and a continuing espousal of miners' industrial claims generated a vast fund of loyalty which could be cashed at a moment of crisis. More broadly, the strategy of the early MFGB, with its espousal of the eight-hour day and the minimum wage, pre-empted much of the ground on which a socialist challenge to the Lib-Lab leadership might have been based. Here collectivism and industrial solidarity, as symbolised in the Federation's Rule 20, co-habited with political Liberalism.[4]

The strength of Liberalism did not flow solely out of political principle nor simply from industrial solidarity. Lib-Lab success bred further motivations. Union leaders could relax in the company of Liberal MPs; they had arrived and were determined not to be elbowed out by agitators who seemed to revel in insulting Liberal parliamentarians. Union bureaucracies gave birth to their own defences — a reputation for political soundness could be a passport to a minor union post. ILPers could be portrayed as a threat to the union, a tactic that could capitalise on the blend of principle, patronage and economic self-interest that united the bulk of the membership.

Lib-Labism in the coalfields presented a mighty challenge to the ILP. Nowhere was this more so in the nineties than in Yorkshire where Ben Pickard, the iron man of Barnsley, dominated the Yorkshire Miners' Association, gaining further credibility from his other roles as President of the MFGB and

Lib-Lab MP for Normanton. His place as MP had been the product of an 1885 deal whereby Liberals backed Pickard in return for YMA support of all other Liberal candidates in the coalfield.[5] The other leading officials were all committed Liberals, and the union's strength was impressive — more than 50,000 members by 1899. The leadership style was supported by a system of industrial relations which tended to limit conflict. Union recognition had come early, working conditions were comparatively acceptable, wages were relatively high. Employers in the nineties often responded in a conciliatory vein. The attitude of the Yorkshire leadership to ILPers had been demonstrated as early as the Attercliffe by-election of 1894, by Pickard's telegram favouring a Liberal employer against an ILPer backed by many Sheffield Trades Council delegates and by some YMA members.[6] So long as a Liberal supported the eight-hour day for miners, that was good enough for the YMA leadership; union solidarity ensured that it was good enough for most of their members as well.

The strength of the YMA's Lib-Labism was revealed above all at the Barnsley by-election of October 1897.[7] The ILP candidate Pete Curran was defeated heavily by Joseph Walton, a Durham coalowner. The story of the campaign has been described in detail, one of its most celebrated motifs being the possibly apocryphal claim that ILP campaigners had to face stone-throwing miners. The *Labour Leader* might express surprise at Liberal propaganda making 'every effort ... to make it appear that Pete Curran's candidature is in some mysterious way intended to injure the Yorkshire Miners Association'.[8] In fact, Pickard, not the Liberal candidate, was the ILP's principal antagonist. As one Curran supporter acknowledged, the miners 'have only one political belief — and that is a belief in Ben Pickard'. Whatever their reservations, this was 'quite strong enough to elect any possible candidate Pickard chooses to nominate'.[9] As the campaign reached its climax his comments became increasingly outspoken. The ILP's real objective was presented as the YMA's financial reserves — but miners were 'not going to share with the idle scamps of the country and the street corner loafers'. The socialists were attempting to wreck the YMA by unofficial action: they were trying to take control of the lodges. Pickard's remedy was cryptic — 'if any of them (i.e. the ILP) attended the miners' meetings, let the miners get rid of them not by violence but by preventing them from entering the doorway at all'.[10]

The ILP campaigners attempted to redress the balance by presenting their man as a trade unionist fighting a capitalist who had sent coal to Yorkshire during the 1893 lockout. More surreptitiously, they attempted to strengthen the case against Walton by uncovering evidence that he was involved with companies in the North-East that had engaged in victimisation.[11] But several trade unionists, including John Wilson of the Durham Miners, spoke from the Liberal platform; Robert Smillie was the only leading miners' official to back the ILP.

Curran's election post-mortem acknowledged the success of the Liberal tactics, adding that the role of the union machine went beyond a seemingly

inexhaustable supply of rhetoric. Rather Pickard did not shrink from employing his own brand of 'landlord politics'. Curran commented ruefully on how
the colliery deputy foremen,

Liberal almost to a man and in constant communication with Mr. Pickard ... in-
timidated the men while at work and in every possible form, and religiously attended our
meetings in the various mining villages, for purpose of watching who among their men
held up their hands in my favour.[12]

Barnsley was perhaps the nadir of the ILP's fortunes in the Yorkshire
coalfield. A dejected Hardie might refer to it privately as 'altogether ... the
worst thing we have done'.[13] But the message was not entirely negative.
Curran's candidature did meet with some support from YMA activists,
especially, so it was claimed in those villages where miners employed at the
South Kirkby Colliery lived. This was the scene of a dispute in which local
strikers lacked the sympathy of the County Officials. The latter saw the strikers
as having 'taken a bit into their own mouths', they 'would not be guided by
the rules and officials of the Association'.[14] The dispute and the reaction of
headquarters shattered the characteristic solidarity of the YMA and arguably
some of the critics could become more receptive to attacks on the officials'
Liberalism. As yet, such sentiments had only limited political significance. It
was simply a negative consequence of Pickard's dominance. Robert
Blatchford's *Clarion* acknowledged that such support for Curran arose, 'not
because the men are Socialist, but because they are so incensed with Mr.
Pickard for various reasons, that they would oppose anyone he chose to
support'.[15]

Here then was one basis for an ILP challenge to the Lib-Labism of the
YMA. In the long run — much longer than many ILP propagandists anticipated — changing economic conditions within the coal industry could
generate profitability problems and more abrasive industrial relationships. Lib-
Labism's credibility could be undermined by the failure of officials to deliver
on the industrial front. The assumed community of interest on which Lib-
Labism was based could begin to crack — and with an alternative leadership
beginning to emerge, the moral was perhaps obvious.

The coalfield began to harbour some ILP strongholds from an early date.
One of the most solid examples in the late nineties was at Rothwell; by April
1896 the ILP claimed two members on the local UDC and one on the School
Board.[16] The YMA lodge had 500 members and became a strong exponent of
the ILP position, backing Curran in 1897.[17] Early in 1900 Glasier found it
possible to hold a good meeting there at the height of Khakhi euphoria.[18] The
creation of the ILP village took place under the leadership of the Lunn family,
one of whose members rose from being local ILP activist and YMA radical,
to local MP and office in the inter-war Labour Governments. Once the decisive
change had been made by significant figures in a mining community then communal solidarity could work in favour of, rather than against, the ILP.

Rothwell was not unique. When Lunn moved to the Middleton Colliery, the lodge there became a critic of the Lib-Lab leadership, whilst in August 1896, a member of the Halton Lodge informed the *Labour Leader* that most of the elected positions were filled by ILPers. The informant suggested that 'all ILP and Socialist delegates to the Yorkshire Miners' Council meeting should either wear the red berry (*sic*) or tie so that we should know each other'.[19] This plea suggests perhaps an ill-organised weak opposition in contrast to the deeply rooted power of the Lib-Labs. Even a stronghold like Rothwell was not immune to pressures — by the summer of 1905 an ILP visitor could recall how: 'there used to be a branch here but trade has been so bad, and victimisation so rampant that nearly all the members have been driven from the place'.[20]

But it is possible to trace a small nucleus of lodges from the 1890s which were generally critical of the Association's leadership: Rothwell, Middleton, Glasshoughton and Hemsworth were amongst the most regular critics.[21] What was the basis of such opposition? Clearly it was likely to be a blend of industrial experiences, local patriotism and political conviction. Middleton and Rothwell both had associations with Will Lunn, and Glasshoughton with Herbert Smith.[22] Young ILPers could come to dominate the decisions of a local lodge as the result of a specific industrial question and could then attract support based on respect and patriotism.

Something of the atmosphere of the YMA debates at the end of the nineties survives in Lunn's reports to Keir Hardie. On one occasion, Pickard visited Middleton, but barely touched on the current dispute there; rather he 'spent his time in villifying the ILP and speaking favourably of Mr. Walton', — by then secure as Barnsley's MP.[23] At this time (May 1898) Lunn and other mining ILPers were attempting to supply Hardie with information demonstrating that Pickard milked union funds.[24] Such muck-raking hardly improved relationships within the YMA, nor did accusations (on some occasions, at least, well-founded) that ILP delegates leaked YMA Council deliberations to the press. Thus, in December 1899, Lunn commented to Hardie on a Pickardian onslaught over leaks to the *Labour Leader* — 'a paper which had always been antagonistic to them'. Ned Cowey's portrayal was more vivid, he 'called it *sparrow-gutter* press not gutter-sparrow'. In response, Lunn acknowledged that he read the *Leader* 'its principles were my principles'.[25] Such confrontations were no substitute for influence; by 1900 an ILP faction did exist in the YMA Council, but it was not extensive.

Beyond the slanging matches, changes were beginning that would erode the Lib-Lab position. The coalfield was expanding eastwards, new communities were being created and with an expanding workforce and a growth in absentee employers, the institutionalised industrial conflict on which Lib-Labism had been built became less stable. At the political level, a growing mining population made the bargain of 1885 seem increasingly unfair; any demand for more miners' MPs would test the flexibility of South Yorkshire Liberalism.

However, it was in the economic arena that the major changes occurred. In 1903 the YMA found itself involved in its own Taff Vale, the Denaby Main and Cadeby Case, which the Association eventually won before the Lords in 1906. But by then this protracted and bitter dispute had left a lasting imprint on the YMA. Cowey, Pickard and Parrott died during the dispute — all worn out, some writers have claimed, by the harsh, tortuous wrangles. The confrontation was an almost classic case of the impact of a large employer on a dependent community; camps of evicted families being one dominant motif. One Denaby man recalled:

You hadn't much trouble at the family pits — at little pits ... there were a stronger set of owner at Denaby, they could rule the roost ... Buckingham-Pope said he had a square yard of gold and he'd sink it before the miners would win. He had other collieries, you know, over in West Yorkshire.[26]

And yet neither Denaby nor Cadeby Lodges shifted to support the ILP faction as a result of the experience.[27] Perhaps this was not too surprising — the situation was one which enhanced the solidarity of *all* the union against a vindictive employer. What did make a significant difference was the need for a new Lib-Lab leadership. Those who emerged — men like Wadsworth and Fred Hall — found it difficult to fill Pickard's shoes. They could not draw on the respect accorded to a founding-father, and were more vulnerable in the face of a tough industrial challenge.

Such a situation developed during 1905 at Hemsworth. The origin of the dispute was a lengthy, complex disagreement over price-lists. The first lockout of some men took place in August 1904; a year later the number locked out or on strike was 1,600 and evictions had begun. The confrontation became a major interest of ILPers, with speakers being sent there and appeals for aid in the *Labour Leader*.[28] This dispute did radicalise many local people and John Potts the Hemsworth checkweighman and his colleague W. O. Bull became strong advocates of an ILP position. Hardie contrasted the contemporary position at Hemsworth with his previous visit in the ill-fated Barnsley campaign:

Mr. Pott (*sic*) ... was at that time a supporter of Liberalism. A slow, cautious, safe man is Mr. Potts, but even he has been driven to the conclusion that Labour has nothing to hope for, or expect from any political party until it has created a party of its own ... I do not know whether he has yet come to see the truth of Socialism but that will inevitably follow.[29]

The ILP propagandists claimed that the Barnsley officials were neglecting the Hemsworth people 'preferring the comfortable flesh pots of Liberalism to the stern realities of Labour representation'.[30]

Here then was an issue where local solidarities could work against rather than for the Lib-Lab leadership. This rift became wider during the 1906 election when Potts published, in the Conservative press, an appeal to oppose the two YMA Lib-Lab candidates. He claimed that the membership suffered due to the frequent absences of officials and argued against a link with 'the Liberal Party and capitalists'.[31] This brought a stern response from the Lib-Labs, an attack on Hardie 'and the extreme section' who aimed 'to capture the Union and dictate its policies'. The circular replicated the traditional Pickard tactic of contrasting solid trade unionism with the ILP — 'this man Hardie is not a friend to trade unionism'.[32] But Wadsworth was no Pickard — and the Yorkshire coalfield was now a different place. Old loyalties meant less to a growing workforce, especially perhaps when appealed to by new, relatively untried, leaders. Two attempts to expel Potts from the Association failed during 1906, an appropriate overture to the sizeable Yorkshire vote for LRC affiliation.[33]

Within less than a decade of the Barnsley defeat, the Independent Labour group had won major victories, another symbol being the election of Herbert Smith as YMA President in January 1906.[34] The transition can be placed intelligibly in the context of economic and demographic changes, growing political demands by the YMA and generational replacement at the top of the Association. All this is significant — yet two caveats must be entered.

The first is simply to note the limits of ILP influence. Even in June 1905, an ILP application for a platform at that year's Demonstration was thrown out at Council by more than three to one.[35] More significantly perhaps, down to 1906 political representation remained firmly in the hands of the Lib-Labs.[36] A Lib-Lab, Parrott, has succeeded Pickard as Normanton's MP,[37] but the YMA was now emboldened to consider further candidatures.[38] ILP activists were always pushing for such an expansion, the growth of union membership made the 1885 compact with the Liberals seem increasingly unfair, and the development of the Federation candidates scheme pointed in the same direction. ILPers hoped that the selection of further candidates would provoke a clash with local Liberals. Lunn felt that the Lib-Lab officials 'are now fighting for their very life', but such optimism was premature. The YMA left it to local lodges to reach deals with local Liberals; this approach to Labour representation provoked Lunn's scorn — 'we have the money, but the West Riding happens to be Liberal, so we are afraid to do anything'.[39] This discretion reaped a dividend in Hallamshire,[40] where the sitting Liberal was retiring. Wadsworth was selected late in 1904, and the threatened candidacy of a Liberal employer came to nothing. Here an understanding was relatively easy; as Lunn acknowledged, 'most of our local officials in that part are Liberals'.[41] Further east in Osgoldcross, matters proved more intractable.[42] Once again, there was a vacancy, which the Liberal caucus hoped to fill with Compton Rickett, the MP for Scarborough. The Miners failed to secure sufficient backing from other local labour organisations, but persisted with the claims of the Lib-Lab, Fred Hall. Lunn reported to MacDonald that Hall had been 'sorely touched by the treatment he has received from the Liberals',[43] but ILP hopes that this would lead to a decisive clash were disappointed. The Normanton seat became vacant for the second time in less than two years with Parrott's death in November 1905. Lunn had failed to prevent a continuation of Lib-Labism in February 1904, but now the ILPers were more hopeful.[44] The crucial decision was that of the YMA lodges over the choice of candidate and this produced a second ballot run off between Fred Hall and Herbert Smith, and a victory for the Lib-Lab by 652 to 435.[45] That was the vote that mattered — as John Penny, then active for the ILP in the coalfield, admitted: 'If Hall once gets in the field as a Liberal-cum-Labour candidate, it is all up. The miners generally will accept the position.'[46] The Liberals not only retained Normanton, but extricated themselves from the Osgoldcross problem. In the vote for candidate, Smith was viewed widely as the ILP representative, and his election two months later as YMA President could be seen as an important *quid pro quo*. But this leads to the second caveat.

Smith, although a veteran of the Curran campaign, placed his trade union interests first and his political aspirations very much in second place. He was prepared in the interests of union solidarity to become involved in the attacks on Potts. Thus, although he did not sign the circular attacking Hardie, he did support a further missive, condemning Potts as a disruptive influence within the Association.[47] Subsequently, Smith developed a reputation for industrial toughness complemented by hostility to left-wing critics within the MFGB. Should this be seen as a consequence of a lengthy period within a union bureaucracy, or as a salutary indication of the limits of the change from Lib-Labism to Independent Labour?

Yet, having entered such reservations, it does remain the case that by 1906, a change can be charted within the YMA — and given the size of the Yorkshire coalfield, this was of national significance. It afforded a sharp contrast with the situation in Derbyshire and Nottinghamshire, where Lib-Labism retained a hold through to 1914, with miners voting against LRC affiliation in both ballots. Although these were smaller coalfields than Yorkshire, together they provided a sizeable Liberal element within the MFGB. The Nottinghamshire Miners' Association rose from 15,000 members in 1898 to just less than 20,000 in 1900 and passed the 30,000 mark in 1905. Its Derbyshire counterpart had 24,000 members in 1900 and 38,000 eight years later. Further reinforcements for the Lib-Lab cause came from the other Midlands coalfields. In these counties, there were no Will Lunns nor Herbert Smiths and the 1909 affiliation to the Labour Party remained little more than a formality for some years.[48]

Here there was an almost classical combination of factors guaranteed to deflect Independent Labour propaganda. Relatively easy mining conditions produced profitable companies and paternalistic employers, who sometimes constructed model villages. Such paternalism went further than in much of Yorkshire, possibly because the slower rate of growth further south made the maintenance of such social relationships more straightforward. Sometimes coalowners doubled as Liberal MPs, and such representatives as Sir Arthur Markham of Mansfield showed a marked respect for miners' claims. Ironically, it was a Lib-Lab, Henry Broadhurst, who had provoked the opposition of the

Notts. Miners' Association in West Nottingham in 1892, because of his negative view on the legal eight-hour day.[49] Union leaders tended to be strong Liberals. By 1907 Haslam and Harvey of Derbyshire both sat in the Commons. Once again religious dissent provided one more close tie between several miners' officials and Liberalism. Spiritual and financial factors worked in the same direction. Consensual politics were fed by the consequences of industrial harmony. Peace led to sizeable financial reserves, loans to municipal authorities, and superannuation schemes. Could there be a better demonstration of common interests? Such factors were backed in Nottinghamshire by another. The tenacious survival of the 'butty' system of sub-contracting, and the strength of the butties within the NMA, was a force in favour of the existing order; when an ILP faction did develop eventually, it favoured abolition of the butty system. At a political level, the national debates of 1909—10 struck a significant chord. In the presence of ducal landlords waxing fat on coal royalties, it was possible for the People's Budget to unite industrious capitalists and workers in the way envisaged by its creator.

The officials were often strongly hostile to the ILP. In particular, W. E. Harvey had a long-running feud with Hardie. In 1897, he together with another Lib-Lab had refused to speak at a miners' meeting in Durham, after discovering that Hardie was also there as a speaker.[50] For Harvey, ILPers were 'wreckers and snatchers'[51] while for Hardie such a Lib-Lab was the epitome of the conformist trade union leader in 'a snug little office with rent and coal paid'.[52] The Derbyshire leader saw Taff Vale and its damaging consequences as the result of 'harum-scarum action on the part of the ILP and Socialist men'.[53]

Such industrial moderation and staunch Liberalism produced very limited opposition. The ILP in the Derbyshire coalfield was a slight presence until well after the affiliation ballots. Even in 1908, Harvey and Haslam could secure a vote of 61 to 19 from their council, for a resolution for the MFGB that affiliation be deferred on account of the pro-affiliation vote being less than 50 per cent of the national membership.[54] In Nottinghamshire, opposition to the leadership was, if anything, even less. There had been an ILP branch in Mansfield in the nineties,[55] but this had become moribund and was revived only in 1906. An attempt by George Spencer to propose affiliation to the LRC at the NMA's Council meeting in June 1904 had failed to find a seconder. A local ILPer dismissed the delegates as 'this Group of Party Hacks'.[56] Certainly, the NMA lodges in 1906 functioned as part of the Liberal machine and there seems to have been minimal rank and file criticism of this.[57] The Chairman of the Nottingham ILP claimed to MacDonald a few months later that 'there is a very strong movement amongst the rank and file in favour of independent action through the Labour Party'.[58] This was wishful thinking, as successive ballots demonstrated.

The growth of Independent Labour politics within the English Lib-Lab Federated coalfields was a complex matter and the place of the ILP within the growth raises further difficulties. The Yorkshire change — reservations and all — must be balanced by the much more static situation, not just in Nottinghamshire and Derbyshire but also in the other Midlands coalfiels. There, changes came eventually, perhaps as the consequence of national developments: the ILP contribution was minimal.

The opportunities and problems facing ILPers within a Lib-Lab coalfield were given a distinctive twist in South Wales.[59] Prior to 1898, the vast majority of South Wales miners were barely unionised. The rule of the sliding scale in an area where exports loomed large, and the strong localism resulting from the difficulties of communication between many mining valleys, led to a plethora of weak associations. Only the Cambrian Miners' Association under W. J. Abraham ('Mabon') could claim a mass membership. Such a lack of aggressive trade unionism could be seen readily as providing an opportunity for a breakthrough on the left. The established officials were associated closely with Lib-Labism — Mabon sitting as Lib-Lab MP for the Rhondda from 1885. What could be easier than for ILPers to outflank the Liberals by pushing for abolition of the sliding scale, the creation of real trade unionism and affiliation to the MFGB?

Credibility is given to this argument by recalling the impact of the 1898 lockout on the South Wales miners. This led to the creation of the South Wales Miners' Federation, to affiliation to the MFGB, to the eventual abandonment of the sliding scale — and with growing militancy, eventually to the Tonypandy riots and *The Miners' Next Step*. Beneath such evocative but not wholly representative images there lay growing mining difficulties and increasingly cost-conscious employers, who showed a strong tendency towards amalgamation. Welsh particularism was eroded by massive English immigration. Traditional ties between employers and workers were weakened: one had been that of Welsh nonconformity — 'the unholy trinity' of bishop, brewer and squire being a powerful unifying influence.

The power of this spectre wanted with economic and social changes. Once in Tredegar, a miner, David Bevan, had walked to Baptist Church twice on Sunday and back 'with the deacons and other mighty arguers, six or seven abreast across the road, debating the sermon and invoking his deep knowledge of the bible'. And then he went no more: as treasurer of his SWMF lodge, he became a *Clarion* reader. It was in this crucible, with a shift from radical nonconformity to Labour or socialist politics that the outlook of Aneurin Bevan was first moulded.[60]

These images are important, but illuminate only part of the truth. Set against such transition, with its moulding of future working-class leaders, there must be considered the continuing strength of Liberalism. This traditional dominance was distinct in quality because of the fusion between political Liberalism, religious nonconformity, and a sense of national identity. Here was a distinctive society with its own history, culture, self-awareness, and above all language, where Liberal politics could serve as one expression of that distinctiveness.[61] It was a political creed and style that could envelop most elements in Welsh society, a resource on which a Lib-Lab leader like Mabon could draw readily. In a rowdy meeting, his response was to strike up

a Welsh hymn or that magical melody, 'Land of My Fathers'. Hardly had he reached the second line, when, with uplifted arms ... he had the vast audience dropping into their respective 'parts' and accompanying him like a great trained choir ... When the hymn or song was finished, he raised a hand, and instantly perfect silence fell. The storm had passed.[62]

Economic changes might promote industrial conflict but such cultural attachments could retain a powerful force, especially for older miners. The Liberal electoral hegemony remained largely undisturbed in South Wales through to 1914.

The ILP did make great efforts in the Valleys, especially during the 1898 lockout. Hardie and other leading speakers held mass meetings; a Yorkshire ex-miner came in as organiser and new branches were reported to be springing up everywhere.[63] Hardie denounced Lib-Lab leaders — 'Mabon has ceased to lead'[64] — and attacked Liberal tenderness towards victims of persecution in other societies: 'A starving Welsh collier may not be so picturesque as a starving Armenian, but he is none the less human.'[65] He comforted himself with the thought that his audience 'like all true Celts ... are Socialists by instinct'.[66]

Eventually, thirty ILP branches were inaugurated — but even those eternal optimists at the head of the party did not expect many to survive, especially since recruits had been excused dues until the lockout ended. Several vanished almost immediately and by December 1899 the number had fallen to eleven.[67] Nevertheless, this represented a solid advance on the pre-1898 situation, when South Wales had contained only four ILP branches — and by 1905 the figure was back to 27. This solid nucleus began to spawn municipal representation, reaching a new level of achievement in November 1905, with the success of all twelve of Merthyr's Labour candidates. Such growing influence in local politics suggests a challenge to Liberalism at a level where the older party frequently lacked vigour. But in parliamentary contests, Hardie's success at Merthyr, building on traditional Radical sentiments, rather than Labour (let alone socialist) ones, was unique.

The ambiguous impact of ILP agitation can be found also within the SWMF itself. Lib-Lab dominance might have been challenged in 1898, and its prestige might have been dented, but Lib-Lab officials remained strongly influential for several years. The framework of industrial relations, crowned in 1903 by the formation of a Conciliation Board, was one in which Lib-Labs could feel comfortable. The degree of local autonomy within the Federation, in part a product of the coalfield's geography, left considerable local powers over funds and disputes. The local Miners' Agents could become significant figures in their communities; their responsibilities tended to ensure that they were prudent stewards.[68] One ILPer noted in May 1903 that the South Wales Miners' leaders were nearly all 'simply puppets of the Liberal Party'.[69] Similar views could be found more locally. Merthyr Miners' leaders moved only slowly to support Independent Labour after Hardie's 1900 success.[70]

Support for the Independent position gradually grew. One factor was the Federation's drive for more parliamentary representation. Under the MFGB scheme, they were entitled to eleven more candidates, whom they hoped to place as sitting Liberals retired.[71] This desire was strengthened by an adverse and costly legal decision on the practice of 'stop days' as a technique for maintaining the price of coal. The reactions of Liberal Associations were unsympathetic. The Lib-Lab, William Brace, was accepted by South Glamorgan Liberals only after arbitration by Herbert Gladstone. Another Lib-Lab, Tom Richards, won a by-election in West Monmouthshire in October 1904. The local Liberals had supported him narrowly, after much procrastination. He also had the sympathy of the LRC Executive. Hardie claimed that 'his sympathies are altogether with us',[72] Richards having misleadingly hinted that he would join the LRC Parliamentary Group. In January 1906, the SWMF had four successes; 'Mabon', Richards and Brace were supplemented by another Lib-Lab, John Williams, who defeated a Liberal tinplate manufacturer in Gower. In contrast, James Winstone, an ILP activist in the Federation, stood unsuccessfully as a LRC candidate in Monmouth Boroughs and received no union help. Although local Liberal stubbornness towards miners' political claims suggested future trouble, as yet a final rupture had been averted. Senior officials, the most likely parliamentary aspirants, held views that Liberals found sympathetic, and could still square loyalty to their union with their own political preference, but squabbles with the Liberals inevitably strengthened the argument for political independence. At the level of candidatures, this surfaced in claims that sitting Liberals should be opposed by younger Independent Labour men such as Vernon Hartshorn.

Most fundamentally, however, it was expressed in persistent demands that the Federation should join the LRC. A lead could be given by the SWMF's Delegates Conference, where younger men could make a mark, and could articulate claims based on economic pressures and shifting social mores. These delegates had some success in forcing the pace on LRC affiliation. In February 1904, the Conference requested the Executive Council to submit proposals on Labour Representation to a subsequent conference to be held in June.[73] The council were very divided between Lib-Labs and ILPers, and Lib-Labs attempted to avoid an immediate decision on the specifically South Wales question by suggesting that a motion be tabled at the next MFGB Conference, that the whole Miners' Federation should affiliate. This course was followed, but when it was ruled out of order the argument was inevitably reopened in South Wales. In the summer of 1905, a SWMF Conference backed affiliation,[74] but even now a divided Executive was able to procrastinate. When the MFGB held its first ballot on affiliation, the South Wales Executive divided evenly on whether to make any recommendation. Any advice would necessarily have reflected Conference policy. None was given, but ILP members engaged in an enthusiastic rallying of a 'yes' vote.[75] At least at the level of formal decisions the ILP case, supported by economic and cultural changes, and aided by local Liberal obduracy, was supplanting Lib-Labism.

But the political legacy tended to flow in directions other than that of the ILP. Younger activists in the SWMF such as C. B. Stanton and Noah Ablett carried ILP cards, but their primary attachments were given to other organisations and strategies. Direct Action and Syndicalism were the new watchwords: Ablett's verdict on parliamentarianism, seemed obvious — 'Why cross the river to fill the pail?' In contrast, the ILP seemed perhaps rather passé — damaged irretrievably for some activists by its involvement within the Labour Alliance. So here, there emerges an important question of timing. The late but then rapid unionisation and radicalisation of the South Wales activists led to a distinctive range of choices. On the one side, Welsh Liberalism, decaying perhaps, but still a powerful politico-cultural force, and on the other, aggressive industrial strategies. The ILP influence very marked in 1898 became less important, and the distinctive range of alternatives left a lasting mark on the coalfield's political tradition.

The challenges facing ILPers in the Lib-Lab coalfields within the MFGB varied and so accordingly did their responses and their success or failure. Economic conditions provided varying bases for a political initiative, but awareness of the opportunities provided by a Hemsworth or by the South Wales lockout needs to be balanced by an emphasis, even within this narrowly economistic sphere, on the appeal of Liberalism not just as a political, but also as a wider cultural, phenomenon. Clearly Liberalism depended in turn for its vitality on its ability to incorporate key aspects of miners' experiences. The appreciation of ILP successes and failures in Lib-Lab coalfields needs to be balanced by an analysis of its performance in those coalfields where institutionalised Lib-Labism offered no obstacle.

The MFGB: Labour's vanguard

Amongst the English coalfields the Lancashire miners took a distinctive path on the question of Labour Representation: the only major miners' organisation to send delegates to the LRC Conference, an independent affiliate to the LRC in 1903 and successful in returning two Labour MPs in 1906. Did this development indicate a distinctively socialist influence?[76]

A strong case can be developed, starting with the claim that working conditions were bad and hence profit margins tight. Faulted seams at great depth led to attempts by employers to keep down costs — working hours were long, rates of pay low and perks few. Not surprisingly, socialist propagandists were active in the coalfield in the nineties with some success. The SDF put down strong roots in Burnley, where relations in some local pits were bad, and local miners' leaders became SDF activists.[77] Similarly the ILP built up some centres of influence — Swinton and Pendlebury had a branch in which miners played a significant part, sending a delegate to the Bradford Conference and later achieving sizeable votes in local elections.[78] It is almost too neat that the first two ILPers to join the Manchester City Council were local miners elected following the 1893 lockout.[79] But this argument needs balancing by two other elements. Many Lancashire miners did not live in homogeneous communities where in favourable circumstances solidarity could aid the propagation of socialist ideas; and ILP strongholds (and SDF ones too) were few. Lancashire's ILP branches were to be found more in the textile centres than in coal areas.

More crucially, factors other than ideological conviction based on economic experiences served to drive Lancashire Miners towards Independent Labour politics. The Lancashire Federation records contain no socialist justifications for such a step, rather what emerges is a powerful pragmatic argument. The Federation wanted parliamentary representation and Independent Labour offered the only way forward. Political solidarity could not be achieved under a Lib-Lab banner. The workforce was divided between Liberals and Conservatives — a product of religious differences, and, more fundamentally, often of ethnic tension. Attempts had been made by officials to secure election as Lib-Labs. Sam Woods had succeeded in Ince in 1892 but had lost his seat three years later, and Thomas Aspinwall had fought unsuccessfully at Wigan in 1892 and 1895. The political division was replicated amongst the officials in the late nineties. Sam Woods' prominence as a Lib-Lab was balanced by Thomas Ashton's Conservatism, while there was at least one ILP agent, Thomas Greenall, plus some more pragmatic backers of Independent Labour.

Even when Woods was sitting for Ince, the officials felt that need to deflect possible critics; Ashton emphasised that:

the Federation does not recognise any politics except Labour ... although thousands of our members are Conservatives, what we require from Mr. Woods is constant watchfulness and adhesion to the Labour programme, and he has full political freedom afterwards.[80]

After 1895, the cost of the two defeats was a powerful incentive to try something new,[81] and it is not surprising that the Lancashire Federation decided to send delegates to the LRC Conference. Questions were asked at the preceding Lancashire Conference about the emphasis on '*Direct* Labour Representation' — a commitment which it was decided to accept after a speaker had made it clear that:

it did not mean independent, and what they advocated was that labour members should not only work together as a party, but should work also with either of the great parties in Parliament, on any question tending to the benefit of the working classes.[82]

Even this most diluted view of the Labour initiative did not persuade branches to back immediate affiliation: the rejection being 42 to 33 on a show of hands and 358 to 168 on a card vote.[83] But three years later the Lancashire men affiliated without much dissension.[84] In part, this can be seen as the aftermath of the Federation's final disillusion with official Liberalism. Woods' failure to capture the Dewsbury nomination in late 1901 had been a chastening experience.[85] ILPers were also active within the Federation over the issue. Greenall wrote to Ramsay Macdonald in April 1903 for material that would be beneficial in supporting the affiliation.[86]

The ILP ingredient was significant but so too was the pragmatic argument. Given the divided nature of the work-force, the LRC was the only political home open to the Federation — the only way in which industrial solidarity could be cashed in political terms. The weight of pragmatism had negative implications for committed socialists. Two years after affiliation, Hardie felt that the Lancashire leaders often did not grasp the consequences of the decision:

Even those of them who are candidates, and who are entitled to be endorsed by the LRC speak slightingly and disparagingly of that movement, and still regard themselves as what they undoubtedly are — Liberals first and Labour men a long way after.[87]

Certainly, the two successful candidates in 1906, Stephen Walsh in Ince and Thomas Glover in St Helens deserved these strictures. Their organisations owed much to the solidarity of local miners and little or nothing to pioneering work by the ILP. Both made gains from Conservatives in straight fights. Perhaps such victories reflected, to some extent, the viability in Lancashire of a straight 'Labour' ticket compared with a Lib-Lab one. But in 1906, the issues of Free Trade and trade union rights helped Lancastrian Liberalism to make sweeping gains, a tide from which Labour candidates benefitted. Little of substance distinguished these miners' members from their counterparts in other coalfiels.

Yet, political independence clearly meant something in a union where both ILP and Tory views had their supporters. The Federation had planned originally to run two other candidates.[88] One campaign, that of Sam Woods at Newton, was soon terminated because of Woods's ill health. The other raised sensitive issues. Greenall, an ILP supporter, had been adopted at Accrington, a seat with relatively few miners, where local socialists showed little sympathy with Liberalism. The seat had been retained by the Liberals in 1900, and although the sitting member, Sir Joseph Leese, had announced that he would not seek re-selection, a replacement Liberal had been chosen already — Franklin Thomasson, a sympathiser with Labour. Ramsay MacDonald, in pursuit of a Liberal/Labour concordat was anxious that Greenall should withdraw, but he remained immovable for more than a year. Perhaps this reflected more than Greenall's commitment to political independence; it was also necessary to persuade Conservative miners that Federation candidates would fight Liberals. Eventually Thomasson withdrew and the sitting member announced his intention to stand again. Greenall claimed that this would cost a thousand votes, and that there was little point in continuing.[89] Accrington activists opposed this, and Arthur Henderson and John Hodge were sent by the LRC to put its view. They addressed a Miners' Delegate Conference on

3 December 1904, and tried to persuade Greenall to move to the Newton vacancy. Henderson responded blandly to ILP and perhaps Conservative suspicions — 'they knew that neither him nor Mr. Hodge were in unison with the Liberal Party; he was surprised to hear either Liberal or Conservative Party mentioned in that meeting'. The Accrington delegate was unmoved; the proposal to shift Greenall was 'a political dodge'.[90] A Miners' Committee reviewed the case and indicted the hapless Greenall for a lack of energy. It found no evidence for accusations of collusion with the Liberals.[91] Greenall withdrew, and despite the traditional political split amongst the miners, there was no clash with any Liberal in 1906. The Lancashire miners' path to political independence was distinctive, but the political consequences were much less so. Indeed the earlier lack of ideological friction perhaps helped to diminish the distinctiveness of thef 1906 candidates.

This judgement would not be made conventionally about the other 'advanced' section, the Scottish miners. One authoritative work has categorised this as 'the one constituent association of the Miners' Federation in which the Socialists had won a clear victory by 1900'.[92] Such a judgement can be strengthened by a host of supporting images. The Scottish miners were associated with several prominent figures in the early ILP: Hardie first attracted attention within the wider British Labour Movement as the outspoken organiser of the Ayrshire miners; William Small, a Blantyre draper, became a miners' organiser in the mid eighties and moved through land reform agitation to socialism.[93] He was active in the Scottish Labour Party and was elected as one of the Scottish representatives on the first National Council of the ILP. He was joined there by Chisholm Robertson, organiser of the Stirlingshire miners, a volatile figure, secretary to the Glasgow Trades Council, and a bitter critic of Hardie.

But the most substantial link between the Scottish miners and the ILP was Bob Smillie.[94] Born in Belfast, of Scottish parents in 1857, he was orphaned early, had very limited schooling, and returned to Clydeside working in foundries and shipyards. Before his seventeenth birthday, he had moved into the Lanarkshire coalfield, and as early as 1879, he was elected a checkweighman at Larkhall. During the eighties, he played an important role in maintaining some trade union organisation in his village, and became a firm adherent to an independent political strategy. He was active in Keir Hardie's 1888 Mid Lanark campaign, and then in the work of the Scottish Labour Party. His importance in the trade union sphere was indicated by his election as the first President of the Scottish Miners' Federation in 1894. From his bailiwick in mining trade unionism, he explored strategies that could harness, he hoped, the potential power of trade unionism to Independent Labour politics. Within the MFGB he fought consistently for political independence against the implacable Liberalism of many English officials. As candidate or activist, he supported the Independent position in a series of Scottish elections. More successfully, he played a significant part in the early development of the

Scottish TUC and was involved in the negotiations leading to the creation of the Scottish forerunner of the Labour Representation Committee, the Scottish Workers' Parliamentary Elections Committee.* It was symbolically appropriate that Smillie should preside over its inaugural meeting in January 1900. Perhaps more than anyone else, Smillie epitomised the possibility of a rapport between the ILP and trade unionism. Personalities apart, the Scottish Miners supplemented their support for political independence with an early commitment to socialism. This seems to be a section of mining trade unionism that was politically advanced. Such a portrait constitutes an important part of the truth but requires elucidation and qualification.[95]

Analysis can begin with the state of trade union organisation. The Scottish coalfields in the late nineteenth century showed significant variations in the capacity of workers for collective organisation. At one extreme, the Fife coalfield had developed a stable county union by the 1880s, covering a majority of the workforce; but in the west, in Ayrshire and in the huge Lanarkshire coalfield, county organisation proved very difficult. The only really durable organisations were highly localised, for example those associated with Smillie at Larkhall and with Small at Blantyre. Western weakness could not be ascribed to workers' passivity; rather, attempts at trade union organisation faced two major obstacles. One was the strong position of many employers. Many mines were owned by giant iron companies, producing for their own use, and able to impose a harsh industrial regime in their 'company' villages. They had the motivation to depress wage costs, since Lanarkshire iron producers faced growing competition from English and continental producers. This hostile attitude to trade union organisation was aided by a second factor. Employers could circumvent threat of collective action by importing cheap Irish labour which could be used in the short term to break strikes, and in the long term might be more difficult to unionise. Certainly some union organisers identified the Irish influx as a source of weakness, a view which only served to strengthen ethnic stereotypes and could carry political implications.[96]

In these unpropitious circumstances, wages in the western coalfields were pushed very low during the Great Depression. Further downward pressures in 1886 produced new attempts to develop more inclusive organisation: Hardie became the Secretary of a new Ayrshire Miners' Union; Small acted as Secretary for a similar attempt in Lanarkshire; in October, a Scottish Miners' National Federation was created with Hardie as Secretary.[97] These new departures were soon tested. At the end of the year, coal prices rose and Lanarkshire miners struck for an increase. Hopes of concerted action by the Federation failed, but the Lanarkshire men remained impressively solid. In February 1887, with police protecting blacklegs, rioting erupted around Blantyre, followed by troops and police making over fifty arrests.[98] Already orators were presenting the struggle as one against capitalism[99] Now a mass

* An organisation which became the Scottish Workers' Representation Committee in 1902.

demonstration was held on Glasgow Green with speakers from the SDF and
the Socialist League, a reported audience of 20,000, and provocative attention from mounted police.[100] Although the strike failed, and the National
Federation became little more than a title, there were positive consequences.
Some local organisations survived, and at least for activists, the stoppage had
an educative effect. The Federation had hinted at the possibility of concerted
Scottish action; the problems encountered had suggested the need for legislative
action to compensate for industrial weaknesses. The legal eight-hour day
became a plank within the demands of many Scottish miners' activists. A
necessary condition for the securing of such a reform would be the election
of a Scottish miners' MP, a task which raised the question of miners' relationships with the Liberal Party. Except in Fife, union organisation was in no state
to bargain with the Liberals over parliamentary representation, and Scottish
Liberalism remained sufficiently confident of its hold over mining electorates
not to make concessions. Moreover, Liberal publicists had often shown scant
sympathy with the miners during the Lanarkshire stoppage. For Hardie and
often western activists, the moral was clear. The struggle for political representation must go outside official Liberal channels. By July 1887, Hardie was
attacking the Lib-Lab MPs:

What programme have they to put before the country, likely to be of benefit when
carried out to their constituents? Absolutely none. They are content to follow in the
train of the Liberal party, whithersoever it may lead ... Party be hanged. We are miners
first and partizans next.[101]

The road to the Mid Lanark by-election and the formation of the Scottish
Labour Party was signposted.

The enhanced political awareness of the activists was expressed through the
SLP over the next few years, as trade unionism remained limited except in Fife.
However, the success of the MFGB's 1893 action induced Scottish miners'
leaders to try and develop a more unified organisation, and in March 1894,
a Scottish Miners' Federation was formed, with an initial membership of
26,783. This affiliated immediately to the MFGB. The officials struck a
political balance. Smillie as President was balanced by the Treasurership of
the Fife Lib-Lab, John Weir, whilst Chisholm Robertson, supporter of Champion and an opponent of Hardie, gave an erratic flavour to the Secretaryship.
Employers reacted by attempting to break the Federation.[102] Wage cuts were
demanded, stoppages began, and for the first time, all Scottish coalfields acted
together, with many non-unionists stopping work. The link with the MFGB
produced acrimony amongst Scottish leaders, as under the Conciliation Board
arrangements further south, the English Federated coalfields accepted a wage
reduction. The Federation principle of equivalent wage movements implied
that Scottish miners should accept an appropriate reduction, sixpence instead
of the shilling demanded by the owners. Chisholm Robertson stood out against
this in characteristically abrasive terms, as did Shaw Maxwell, formerly

Secretary of the ILP, and, in less denunciatory terms, Hardie.[103] But Smillie, backed by a massive majority at a delegate conference, went along with the modified policy. The call of trade union solidarity was much more immediate than any other political sympathy.

The prospects of Scottish solidarity seemed limited in the years after 1894. The strike ended on the owners' terms, and although the Federation survived this time, its membership plummetted to less than 16,000 by the end of 1897, the nucleus being the traditionally strong Fife union. At the start of that year, the relative levels of unionisation were striking and carried significant political implications (see Table 1).

Table 1: *Scottish Miners' Federation by districts*

	Union membership	Number employed
Fife	7,000	11,000
Lanarkshire	3,000	31,000
Ayrshire	3,000	10,000
Mid Lothian	2,500	3,500
Clackmannan	750	1,000
Dumbarton	800	1,400
West Lothian	600	3,800
Stirlingshire	1,000	5,000

Source: MFGB Conference Report, January 1897

The vast Lanarkshire coalfield was the principal weakness, but union membership rose there in the late nineties, aided by the formation of a county union in 1896 and by buoyant demand for coal. The changing balance was captured in the breakdown of delegates at the 1901 Annual Conference, when 39 out of a total of 66 came from Lanarkshire.[104] Politically, this could be important, as the activists in such difficult virgin territory were likely to be alienated from Lib-Labism. More broadly, the Miners' Federation could hope to make more political claims as its membership rocketted to over 57,000 in 1900, and over 86,000 a decade later. With such growth, industrial relations developed along the lines of the English coalfields, with a Conciliation Board formed in October 1899. But relations were never easy and typically remained more polarised than in many English coalfields.[105]

Over time, the Scottish Federation became dominated by officials, most notably Smillie, but also David Gilmour, James Brown, John Robertson, Andrew McInulty and John Wilson of Broxburn, all of whom had served their time in the union-building efforts of the eighties and nineties and were disenchanted with official Liberalism.[106] They did not have to meet Liberal opposition within their county unions, and there was only the limited Fife presence within the Federation. Such leaders shared on many issues the views of Radical

Liberals, but their industrial experiences gave their view a distinctive flavour of miners' — perhaps of class — consciousness. Distinctiveness could be found also in the Scottish Miners' early attachment to a socialist objective. On October 5th 1896, the Federation Executive decided to submit a resolution to the Districts for instructions, with a view to having it debated at the MFGB's Annual Conference. The resolution proclaimed:

> That to secure the best conditions of industrial and social life, it is absolutely necessary that the Land, Minerals, Railways and instruments of production should be owned and controlled by the State for the People.[107]

Reservations about the position came only from Fife; the resolution was debated at the January 1897 MFGB Conference, causing much acrimony and with Weir separating himself from the other Scottish delegates.[108]

Such activist support for public ownership flowed from a variety of sources. Socialists had been involved in the industrial struggles in several western coal communities during the eighties, and their converts had frequently provided the heart of trade union organisation. The task of persuasion was facilitated possibly by two elements. Scottish Radicalism involved a central preoccupation with land reform, and by the eighties its content and fervour had been influenced by the tours of Henry George.[109] George evoked a warm response, particularly amongst the Highlanders and the Irish who had flocked into the urban centres of the west of Scotland. His message could be transmuted into support for land nationalisation. From there, it could be a ready progression to advocating the public ownership of mines and then of other means of production. A second element related more closely to the plight of the miner. One reaction to the growth of giant iron companies, with their regimented workforces was to recall a mythical past.[110] 'Independent colliers' had worked their own small pits, or had been employed by 'small masters' with whom they were on easy terms. They enjoyed considerable freedom in their work-practices, and could combine mining with agricultural work in the summer months. Desire for a lost arcadia was a frequent response to the disruption of traditional communities through the advent of industrial capitalism. The negative consequences for collective organisation were profound. It was a barrier to the development of class consciousness, since the myth did not incorporate those who could not claim a stake in the 'Independent' tradition. Irish immigrants could appear as a further threat to the status of the once-proud Scottish collier, rather than as fellow workers to be involved in collective action. The myth also inhibited acceptance of economic realities, and laid down for its subscribers a strategy that assumed a shared interest in output restriction between employers and miners that would produce 'fair' prices for all. The attempt to deny the allocative virtues of the market-place had another face. The notion of co-operative production could be used to mount a forward-looking criticism of industrial capitalism. It was a short step from notions of self-respect, co-operation and antipathy to large corporations, to the advocacy of the socialisation of the means of production. The formal socialist commitment of the Scottish Federation drew then on powerful elements in both the miners' own experience and the wider culture, but it was debatable how far such a commitment was shared by the wider mining population. Smillie showed some scepticism in his evidence to the Royal Commission ln Labour in 1892 — their views are sufficiently advanced to be called socialistic, but they would not like that you should call them socialists'.[111]

Such scepticism is supported by the limited ILP presence in the coalfields, notwithstanding the lead given through the SLP. The Scottish ILP was largely a party of the cities and large towns. In September 1905, Lochgelly was the only branch in the Fifeshire coalfield, and the party presence in Lanarkshire and Ayrshire was limited.[112] Attempts had been made. Glasier conducted a summer propaganda tour in Ayrshire in 1901, but initial enthusiasm rarely produced stable vigorous organisation.[113] Perhaps the most striking testimony to ILP weakness came from an activist in Smillie's Larkhall base. Writing in August 1899, he recalled that the previous meeting had been held in March 1898. Only three people had turned up for the next one, and since then, nothing had happened, 'the members evidently being more concerned about football and horse racing ... some of them used to say it was no use having meetings, unless Bob Smillie was present'.[114]

One hope for a wider conversion of miners to the independent position lay in the running of miners' candidates on an independent platform. Here, once again, the Fife miners were exceptional in that they had hopes of persuading the local Liberals to allow John Weir a free run. They could point to their strong membership as a bargaining resource, but when the seat became vacant in June 1889, they failed to capture the nomination. Some local Liberals were sympathetic but others were unprepared to guarantee that a Labour candidate would be adopted if the miners could produce one, and after considerable argument, the Liberals selected Augustine Birrell.[115] The miners supported him in 1892 and 1895, but when a further vacancy arose in 1900, Weir's claims were ignored in favour of an orthodox Liberal.[116] Once again the lack of socialists amongst the Fife miners prevented any immediate challenge, but by 1906, the disenchantment of the rank and file could be seen in the low poll. Eventually with all sections of the MFGB now affiliated to the Labour Party, the Fife miners nominated their own candidate, the right-wing official Willie Adamson. He ran second to the Liberal member in January 1910, and then won in a straight fight in December.[117] Two aspects of this development are significant. One is the unwillingness of the Fife Liberals to make any concessions to the miners, even when the auguries in terms of union strength and political colouration seemed favourable. The second feature is that this case was the only electoral success for a Scottish miners' candidate down to 1914. Elsewhere attempts on a more firmly independent, and perhaps more specifically socialist, platform came to nothing.

Candidates by Scottish miners' leaders in the nineties lacked strong union backing. Chisholm Robertson stood for the Scottish United Trades Councils Labour Party in Stirlingshire and John Wilson on an independent platform in Edinburgh in 1892, and Smillie as ILP candidate in a Glasgow seat three years later. In all cases the polls were small. A rather better performance came in April 1894 when Smillie stood for the SLP in Mid Lanark. Here local miners in some pits collected for his election fund,[118] and he doubled Hardie's 1888 vote. Trade union organisation remained weak, however, and this provided only a slight basis for a miners' candidate.

Union strength increased over the next few years, in the west. The involvement of the Scottish miners in the SWPEC and the development of the MFGB electoral scheme made a strong political challenge seem more feasible. The Scottish Federation began by endorsing Smillie's candidature in North-East Lanarkshire in September 1901. By late 1902, the Federation was considering a wider intervention.[119] Their first attempt came again in North-East Lanarkshire in August 1904, and they followed this by running five candidates in January 1906. All stood on firmly independent lines and all finished last in three-cornered contests. (See Table 2.)

Table 2. *Scottish miners' electoral interventions*

Date	Candidate	Constituency	Labour vote	Liberal vote	Unionist vote
9/01	R. Smillie	N.-E. Lanark	2,900	4,769	5,673
8/04	J. Robertson	N.-E. Lanark	3,984	5,619	4,677
1/06	J. Brown	N. Ayrshire	2,684	4,687	5,603
1/06	D. Gilmour	Falkirk Burghs	1,763	5,158	3,176
1/06	J. Robertson	N.-E. Lanark	4,658	6,436	4,838
1/06	J. Sullivan	N.-W. Lanark	3,291	4,913	5,588
1/06	R. Smillie	Paisley	2,482	5,664	2,594

Such failures were repeated in 1910. In part this record reflects the fact that despite union growth, many miners remained outside the union, but more crucially it demonstrates the centrality of elements beyond trade unionism.[120] Scottish Liberalism experienced a revival after 1900 in which it could tap the close association between radical sentiments and notions of 'Scottishness'. The contrast with traditional Liberal weakness in the Lancashire coalfield is significant. More weight should be attached however to an element present in Lancashire, but of much more importance in western Scotland, the conflict between Orange and Green. In the Lancastrian case, this had led to a successful Labour pragmatism. In Scotland, miners' candidates fell between two stools. They were typically former Liberals and supported Home Rule, thereby alienating working-class Unionists, but they could count rarely on the Green vote, which was normally promised to the Liberal. The Scottish miners' commitment to political independence grew in part out of weak trade unionism that could be attributed to some degree to ethnic rivalries within the workforce. But the same rivalries limited the scope available for the political expression of this formal independence.

In both Lancashire and western Scotland, the Irish presence had a significant but varied impact on the development of Independent Labour sympathies within the miners' unions. Yet it could be dangerous to assume a simple connection between the two elements. The case of the Cumberland Miners' Association shows how a determined official could block or limit political developments within a small union.[121] The West Cumberland coalfield was geologically difficult, experiencing stiff competition from Lancashire and western Scotland and with low unstable wages. It contained a sizeable Irish population, a significant ILP presence based largely on local metal workers, and an electorate whose attachment to Liberalism tended to be uncertain. This combination seemed to have little impact on the Miners' Association, which was dominated by its General Secretary, Andrew Sharp. He had been the only English miners' official present at the foundation conference of the ILP, but he remained a staunch Liberal, and was able to retain the support of his members. When the Cockermouth seat became vacant in the summer of 1906, the miners walked out of a selection conference when the other delegates pushed for Smillie rather than Sharp. This rebuff to the 'amour propre' of miners' officials led to the CMA supporting the Liberal, the Honourable Freddie Guest, and Smillie finished a poor third.[122] Within four years there had been a remarkable change. National developments and local deals allowed Cumbrian ILPers to score a notable first. The CMA was affiliated to the Labour Party along with the rest of the MFGB and in January 1910, Sharp fought Whitehaven as an orthodox Labour candidate. His intervention let in the Unionist, and by the December election a deal has been reached whereby Labour stood aside in Cockermouth, but was allowed a straight fight in Whitehaven. The successful Labour nominee was Thomas Richardson, a Durham miners' activist, and leading North-Eastern ILPer, sponsored by the party. Cumberland thus provided the only pre-1914 case of a miner as an ILP MP.

Exploration of the factors facilitating early moves towards political independence must emphasise the importance both of economic experiences and of wider political opportunities and constraints. The trade union dimension in which activists laid down critical terms for debate was important, but explanations must then extend into discussions of local politics, in particular into investigations of the space afforded to independent miners' candidates. But these formal political attachments of the Districts also fed back into political arguments within the MFGB, and the resolution of political conflicts had its inevitable consequences for the political development of specific coalfields.

MFGB politics

At the level of the MFGB, certain important decisions on industrial and political policy could be made — and Executive members and delegates might reflect political differences in a distinctive environment.[123] During the nineties the balance of forces within the MFGB conferences and on the Executive was affected by the adherence of the Scottish and South Wales Federations — high memberships, especially in South Wales, made the position of these coalfields on key issues extremely important. By the early years of this century Scotland and South Wales together with Lancashire could maintain a clear majority at MFGB gatherings.

Membership of the Executive was on a federal basis, with the larger districts being guaranteed places in proportion to their membership, and the smaller ones securing some representation on a rotating basis. This system meant that in the mid nineties the Scottish representation could have a socialist component, but that such a protagonist would often be isolated. Thus in 1895, the Executive's composition was as shown in Table 3.

Table 3. *The MFGB executive; political constitution in 1895*

Lib-Labs		Conservative
Pickard (Yorks.)	Aspinwall (Lancs.)	Ashton (Lancs.)
Woods (Lancs.)	Weir (Fife)	
Edwards (North Staffs.)	Hancock (Notts.)	
Cowey (Yorks.)	Johnson (Warks.)	
Parrot (Yorks.)	Chambers (Leics.)	*Socialist*
Haslam (Derbys.)	Peters (N Wales)	
Harvey (Derbys.)		Smillie (Scotland)

Source: MFGB Conference Report, January 1895, p. 2

Over time the balance shifted with the deaths of some of the toughest Lib-Labs, the adoption by the Lancashire men of an independent line, and the adherence of the politically uncertain South Wales representatives.

Typically, political divisions within the national movement did not find a ready reflection in industrial matters. Certainly, political differences could affect industrial arguments, but basically Federation membership necessitated the acceptance of certain industrial objectives and obligations — and this unity ensured that the political divisions within the national organisation expressed themselves only on specifically political questions.

During the nineties this was reflected most dramatically in attempts to secure the adhesion of the MFGB to a socialist objective. Pickard characteristically drew a sharp distinction between socialism and trade unionism — and at one stage declared his opposition to mines nationalisation.[124] This argument came to a head at the MFGB Conference in January 1897 when the Scottish delegation promoted their socialist resolution[125] Despite the promoters of the proposition[126] sticking to practical considerations, they provoked an instant dismissal by Pickard as 'word-painters' drawing 'self-evident contradictions'.[127] He became involved in a confrontation with Smillie over Hardie's supposed anti-trade union views[128] — for Pickard, the resolution was:

the core of the Independent Labour Party as enunciated by its leaders and we have had gentlemen saying in here yesterday that they will support that rather than support Trade Unionism ... if Trades Unionists assembled here don't know where Trade Unionism begins and ends, it is about time they studied Adam Smith (A Delegate, Oh) and John Stuart Mill.[129]

Yet Pickard's unbending approach was not emulated by all the Lib-Labs — both Harvey and Haslam backed the nationalisation of land, minerals and railways; it was the wider objective that they refused to accept.[130] So although the Scottish proposal was rejected by 137,000 to 18,000 and a Yorkshire amendment backing 'Trade Union ... not Socialistic lines' was carried by 134,000 to 21,000, this was not the end of the matter. There were also resolutions from Lancashire and Cleveland backing the nationalisation of land and minerals — and in the Lancashire case of railways as well. These were not socialist propositions, but suggestions that, as one Lancashire speaker put it: 'we shall extend the principle that has been adopted with regard to the Post Office and telegraph'. Both attracted Lib-Lab support and were passed easily with the Yorkshire delegates abstaining.[131]

Here, the uncertainties of any collectivist commitment produced a blurring of the line between socialists and some of the Lib-Labs. Subsequently, the public ownership of utilities, something quite compatible with some variants on the Liberal creed, became a fixed part of the MFGB programme, and argument shifted to the even more unstable terrain of Labour Representation.

Here the Federation's response to the formation of the LRC was crucial. Pickard's verdict was sharply sectionalist: why should they 'find money, time or intellect' to aid other unions to secure parliamentary representation?[132] The miners had been successful in this field — they now proposed to build on their success with their scheme for increasing the number of Federation candidates. The scheme, based on a 1s levy was prepared during 1901 and allowed for one candidate for each 10,000 members in a District.[133] An accepted candidate could run under any political label, and so in 1906 the Lancashire and Scottish ones ran under LRC and SWRC auspices. Nevertheless, Pickard and the other Lib-Labs remained firm in their own commitments. They lamented the 1900 election result,[134] but saw hope for Liberalism reborn, as the Free Trade and Chinese labour issues became central. Such attempts to sell Liberalism within the Federation provoked the anger of the ILPers. Smillie objected strongly to the use of the MFGB platform for Liberal propaganda over Chinese labour:

He would like to deny that the Tory Government have done what a Liberal Government would not have done. He protested against advantage being taken to put in a plea for Liberalism and Liberal Government ... with a few outstanding exceptions ... Liberals were as mad for the war as the Tories.[135]

It would 'only be changing from one capitalist party to another'. Faced with such Liberal enthusiasts, socialists and Independent Labour delegates sought to exploit the new scheme as an instrument for Labour Independence. By 1903, the Scottish delegation were attempting unsuccessfully to secure the retention of one-sixth of the political levy for local purposes — a device that in the Scottish context would have secured a significant sum for socialist propaganda.[136] The following year resolutions from Scotland, South Wales and Lancashire urging LRC affiliation were ruled out of order, on the grounds that the existing arrangements should be operated for at least one election. Nevertheless, a lively debate did occur on a Scottish resolution advocating political independence for Labour MPs.[137] Smillie's justification combined the various strands in Independent Labour agitation within the MFGB:

He wanted a Socialistic group in the House ... the advanced movement within the trade unions ... should not be dependent on capitalists either of the Liberal or Tory party ... he supposed the Lancashire Conservative men's convictions were as honest as those of any Liberal ... Therefore, if they wanted to make a scheme a success, they must be able to tell the men they were paying into that scheme to return Labour men to Parliament, not to support either a Liberal or Tory Party, or, at the same time, they did not ask them to pay towards a Socialistic Party, but to support an Independent Party.[138]

Here were displayed the various elements, socialist and pragmatic, against which the Lib-Labs were to fight a rearguard action. Here too was a clear presentation of the compromise made by socialists in the idea of 'Independent Labour'. Haslam might object to 'cutting adrift some of the friendships of half a life time'[139] but, in the end, changing industrial experiences in some coalfields, the fact of LRC successes in 1906, and the relative decline of the strong Lib-Lab fields in terms of MFGB votes pointed to only one conclusion. Yet it was an outcome achieved only after two ballots, and with a minority that remained sizeable. It was an outcome on which the socialist message of the ILPers had had an influence, but it was only one factor amongst many. Smillie's socialism needs to be balanced by the pragmatism of Thomas Glover the St Helen's LRC candidate: 'They must come out on the stronger Labour lines, as there were scores of men, working men on his Committees, who were Tories.'[140] The case for political independence had to be justified in terms of trade union solidarity; it could be sold as less divisive than traditional Lib-Labism.

The North-Eastern coalfields

These controversies did not find a direct echo in the coalfields of Northumberland and Durham.[141] These districts remained mostly outside the

MFGB until 1906—7 — and their distinctive trade union traditions and economic circumstances presented the ILP with a unique range of opportunities and problems. Both counties were Liberal strongholds, in which miners had had more success than elsewhere in returning their own representatives. In part, this dominant political ethos reflected the strength of nonconformity — a blanket term for varied experiences, leading perhaps to ultra-respectability and class collaboration, but also to class-conscious religious testimony and trade unionism. The contradictory pressures are important, but the dominant cultural legacy was most probably that enshrined in the ballad 'A Pitman Gan te Parliament' celebrating Tommy Burt's election as the first miner's MP for Morpeth in 1874. Here the enemy was no coalowner but the Bishops 'guslin' away on five thousand a year'. It proved to be a formidable cultural legacy.[142]

But it was the economic base that was most important. Both counties were exporting areas and experienced sliding-scale experiments in the 1880s. These failed to survive, but leaders tended to hope for their revival and much of the philosophy of the sliding scale continued. Union leadership was collaborationist and claimed a community of interest between capital and labour, exemplified in the nineties in finely tuned apparatus for conciliation. For one leading Lib-Lab: 'A strike is the harvest field of the agitator who cares not what is destroyed so long as he prospers'.[143]

Awareness of the vagaries of export markets and pride in a high level of unionisation led North-Eastern leaders to favour a distinctive style of trade unionism and to look sceptically at more nationally focused MFGB policies. This particularism, together with the leadership's zealous Liberalism, could be seen as a stimulant to rank and file agitation backing the more assertive MFGB position and generating support for the ILP.

Certainly, the North-Eastern leaders did leave such a space to their left, and Independent Labour partisans sought to capitalise on this; but the leaders also had a resource not available to Lib-Labs inside the MFGB. Agitation for the eight-hour day was regarded critically in the North-East. Already the Durham and Northumberland hewers who formed the majority of the membership in the nineties had negotiated a system of two seven-hour shifts. They were served by other workers who could be below ground from eight to ten hours. Any legislation promoting eight hours for all was seen as threatening the employment prospects of hewers — or as leading to the hated option of a three-shift system with its consequential disruption of family life. The eight-hour question was a trump card used by union leaders to safeguard the status quo — however attractive, other aspects of the MFGB programme might be, the eight-hours question made industrial independence acceptable as part of a package deal.[144] This issue also blended with a traditional Liberal position. The Durham Miners' Association Executive preached a proud self-help: 'We are not to set up a show of weakness, and sacrifice our manhood and independence by handing ourselves over to the supervision and control of the House of Commons.[145]

The two county unions were highly efficient testaments to collaboration. They were controlled by tough individuals — Crawford and, later, John Wilson in Durham; Burt in Northumberland — able to draw on massive reservoirs of loyalty. But first in the larger Durham coalfield, and then north of the Tyne, there came an ILP advance that changed the political direction of the county unions and left the Lib-Lab patriarchs isolated — dignified rather than efficient parts of their union machines.

In searching for the roots of change in Durham, due weight must be given to the ambiguities in Radical Liberalism. With the new electoral arrangements of 1885, the DMA had secured Liberal backing for Crawford and Wilson in Mid Durham and Houghton le Spring, and although Wilson was defeated the following year, he succeeded Crawford in Mid Durham in 1890.[146] This cosy relationship was equivalent to that of the YMA with local Liberals, but in Durham many miners had backed the old Owenite socialist Lloyd Jones, in Chester-le-Street in 1885. Moreover, Lloyd Jones had had a significant influence on Crawford who, loyal Liberal though he was, remained a strong critic of many aspects of the economic system.[147] These influences apart, socialism began to make its impact in the North-East in the late eighties — William Morris's speeches during the Northumberland coal strike of 1887 provided one expression.[148] The development needs to be located also within the growth of New Unionism on Tyneside, the agitations amongst the engineers of the North-East and the development of more aggressive industrial policies amongst the employees of the North-Eastern Railway. Here then was an environment within which radical initiatives could spread to the DMA and it is suggestive perhaps that several of the DMA lodges most critical of Lib-Labism were close to the Tyne, where miners were less isolated from other workers.[149]

Certainly in the early nineties, it could appear that Lib-Labism was on the way out in the DMA. Crawford has been succeeded by the already ailing William Patterson — he lacked his predecessor's ruthlessness and made little attempt to influence rank and file decisions.[150] The DMA became involved in a long disastrous strike in 1892 and then on the rebound joined the MFGB — a flirtation that ended abruptly in July 1893 with the DMA's expulsion on the eve of the great lockout.[151] Already, Wilson was the union's dominant figure, a position reaffirmed titularly in 1896 on Patterson's death. A more thorough Liberal than Crawford, he sought to rebuild after the debacle of 1892. His industrial watchwords were Conciliation, Independence, Eight Hours By Trade Union Effort. His method was to lead from the top. He fought a lengthy action against the advance of the ILP within the Association: an advance that could hope to capitalise on discontent with collaboration, with Liberalism and with Wilsonite authoritarianism, but which could be blunted by the periodic re-enactment of the eight hours argument.[152]

Wilson also developed a manipulative and obfuscatory style. One seasoned ILP delegate reported on a characteristic example:

Our friend J. W. played the game very low. It is quite a usual thing for him to do if there is any vital question he is opposed.
Act 1   As soon as he rises, pick a quarrel with some delegate.
Act 2   After which he will play the role of the martyr-hero.
Act 3   Make a piteous appeal to the sentiment and passions of the Council.
Playing so successfully upon the feelings and passions of a large number of the delegates as to make it impossible to get a reply to his twaddle.[153]

During the late nineties — a period of general ILP retrenchment — the progress of the party in the Durham coalfield was limited. By the middle of the decade, a few ILP branches had begun to develop close to the Tyne and by 1899 Keir Hardie could inform David Lowe that he had 'special designs in Durham'.[154] But, by the end of the decade, many parts of the coalfield had no acquaintance with ILP propaganda — one young miner who became later an ILP activist could recall how in 1900 'the ILP was little more than a rumour amongst us'.[155] However, the party, although thin on the ground, nevertheless had more of a presence than in many other coalfields.

Within the DMA the late nineties saw the consolidation of Wilson's rule as he used his monthly circular to preach Liberal politics and industrial harmony. Yet, although control of the union remained firmly in Lib-Lab hands, there were signs that some lodges were moving to a critical position. Resolutions were submitted to the DMA Council backing MFGB affiliation and the legal eight hours: there was a series of complaints against conciliation.[156] Critics began to oppose the control imposed by the Executive — Marsden Lodge, a centre of ILP activity, circularised lodges in an attempt to limit Executive power over motions submitted to Council, and portrayed the Executive as displaying 'unlimited wisdom supplemented by unlimited insolence.[157] By 1898, the opposition had crystallised, much to Wilson's annoyance, into the Durham Miners' Progressive Federation, later the Durham Miners' Reform Association, with a programme of industrial aggression and internal democratisation.[158]

Opposition also began to be expressed in overtly political terms: the Annual Council of December 1896 saw lodge resolutions to amend the rules on parliamentary candidates. One backed 'independent Labour candidates', another urged that any Durham vacancy be contested by 'a Labour candidate … in opposition to the two orthodox parties'. The theme was to become a familiar one; so was the Executive's opposition and, as yet, so was the defeat of the resolutions.[159] But Independent Labour supporters made a few gains. Tom Mann was invited by lodge votes to speak at the 1898 Gala. His sentiments on the Gala platform were criticised by Wilson.[160] Even the DMA Executive did not remain a purely Lib-Lab preserve. By 1899 Will House, later to be DMA President and a staunch Labour man, had been appointed Agent, whilst Tom Richardson, Washington checkweighman and later one of the ILP's standard bearers, had been elected to the Executive during the previous year.

Many of the Independent Labour initiatives of those years were clearly defeated by large majorities. Although no voting figures survive, records show that the attempts come from a relatively small number of lodges, often near the Tyne or on the Coast.[161] However, figures are available for the lodge voting on conciliation in 1899. Although the overall ballot showed acceptance by 20,149 to 19,569, some individual lodges cast high votes against (see Table 4). These too tended to be near the Tyne or the coast and to be critical of the Lib-Lab leadership on a wide range of issues.

Table 4. *Some votes against conciliation, 1899*[162]

Monkwearmouth	499— 97
Usworth	448—240
Washington	308—129
Marsden	627—173

Here pits tended to be newer and larger, and communities were much less stable than in West Durham. Jack Lawson recalled conditions at Boldon, later to become an ILP centre:

the great collieries were less settled in their personnel, and this fact, together with their large scale operations, produced a different type of people from those of the west, and a different spirit as well. They had many problems which did not trouble the older collieries. Union and mining officials have a different and far more difficult job in these new collieries.[163]

But overall by 1900 the ILP presence in the coalfield and in the DMA was an irritant rather than a threat. Lib-Labism seemed to be secure as the Boer War raised coal prices, and wages advanced accordingly.

But such dominance clearly rested on performance, and from 1901 Durham wages began to fall.[164] Decline increased the attractiveness of the demands for MFGB affiliation and independent political action; the latter argument was now given a further dimension by the existence of the LRC, and resolutions for affiliation soon began to appear.[165] Wilson's own view on the new organisation was clear — its inaugural meeting was notable for 'plenty of heroics and not a little slander and ignorance';[166] his main barrier to change remained the eight hours problem. Even in August 1903, he could secure a majority of 2½ to 1 for the *status quo*.[167]

Inevitably perhaps, industrial isolation was ceasing to be attractive as MFGB strength became more apparent and the disadvantages of isolation seemed to outweigh the advantages; ironically, the establishment of the legal eight hour day by the Campbell-Bannerman Government removed the Liberal trump card. By the Autumn of 1907 the DMA had voted substantially to affiliate to the MFGB, with many of the biggest majorities occurring once again on the Tyne and the coast.[168]

Now an objective that had provided a basis for ILP agitation in the DMA had been achieved, but how far had the controversy leading up to this strengthened the ILP's presence in the coalfield? In the early years of the century, progress remained slow — by early 1905, the party still claimed only eleven branches in the county, not all in coal communities.[169] But 1905 was a year of dramatic expansion, aided by the activities of Matt Sim, a Geordie propagandist. Branches were formed in several mining villages, often with the active encouragement of local leaders. One sample of Sim's numerous reports provided the essential flavour:

On Tuesday 10th (October) Councillor R. Richardson of Ryhope presided over a meeting held in the Miners' Hall, Ryhope ... Councillor R. Richardson is the local miners' leader, and the fact that he has undertaken to look after the men who promised to form a branch makes Ryhope safe for the ILP.[170]

It was not always easy; at Murton 'About ten present were willing to join a branch but only two could be induced to hand in their names for a start'.[171] But in the northern half of the coalfield, at any rate, the younger generation of activists were committing themselves to the ILP. By 1904, young Jack Lawson already a reader of the *Labour Leader* and the *Clarion* had become a founder member of the Boldon Colliery ILP.[172] Washington and Usworth had become ILP strongholds under the leadership of the Richardson brothers — Tom later to become ILP member for Whitehaven and W.P. to be MFGB Treasurer in the twenties.[173] Here too we find a characteristic interlocking of trade union positions, local government activity and ILP politics. Local ILPers trod carefully. They formed the Durham Labour Council in 1901 to contest local government elections, bringing together ILP branches, Co-operative Societies and DMA Lodges.[174] Its publications emphasised the need for political independence, but made strong allowance for the Liberal sensibilities of many miners — 'the working people of this great country hold the key that alone can unlock the golden gate to liberty. The great W. E. Gladstone knew this when he gave the people the franchise.'[175] The mould was being cast for a new generation of Durham miners' leaders and the ILP was a crucial part of the process.

Such activity within the coalfield was bound to have an impact on the DMA's deliberations. As more ILP-inspired resolutions were submitted to Council meetings, the representatives at such meetings became more receptive to ILP ideas and ILPers began to secure a few more Executive posts. One way in which pressure could be exercised effectively was on the question of increasing the number of parliamentary candidates — an issue which left the political status of the new men ambiguous but which could be seen as a challenge either to sitting Liberals, or to Liberal control of nomination processes.

Early in 1903, the Durham Federation Board, containing representatives not only of the DMA but also of three smaller bodies, the Enginemen, Cokemen and Colliery Mechanics, considered a possible increase in the number of parliamentary candidates, and passed the problem to a united meeting of delegates from all four sections.[176] It appears that at the united meeting there was a strong attempt by some ILP supporters to commit the delegates to political independence — one observer claimed that 'several delegates expressed their disapproval of the manner in which some of the workers' leaders hanker after the bosses of the Durham Liberal party — Joicey, Pease, Furniss and Co'.[177] Wilson commented laconically that there was 'some little diversity of opinion'.[178] Eventually, the leaders repeated their tactic of 1885, approaching the Northern Liberal Federation to negotiate on possible vacancies — a manoeuvre that failed to secure a positive response.[179]

The Lib-Labs appeared to secure a victory when one of the newly-selected candidates, J. Johnson the DMA's financial Secretary, was returned as a Lib-Lab in a by-election at Gateshead in January 1904. But this success only provoked criticism from some ILPers — the Hobson Lodge responded by forwarding an unsuccessful resolution that Johnson be denied financial support.[180] As yet, the Lib-Labs retained control of the DMA's political policy, despite the burgeoning strength of the ILP. Nevertheless by a most individualistic route, Durham, still under Lib-Lab leadership, was to return an ILP member at the 1906 election.

J. W. Taylor of the Colliery Mechanics had been selected as a future candidate in 1903, and there had been considerable pressure from ILP-dominated lodges in the Chester-le-Street constituency to run Taylor there against the sitting Liberal coalowner, Sir James Joicey.[181] At one stage, Taylor had been a member of the North West Durham Liberal Association, but by 1905 he was a member of the ILP and refusing to accept the Lib-Lab label.[182]

Delegates representing the four sections of the Durham Federation were ready late in 1905 to see Taylor run as Labour 'pure and simple', either in Chester-le-Street or North West Durham,[183] but when the lodges were ballotted, it was decided that he should wait for a vacancy.[184] As yet, the ILP could succeed at a delegate conference, but not when the issue was left to the wider membership. However, the granting of a peerage to Joicey created a vacancy in Chester-le-Street and the Federation Board now backed Taylor's claims, informed the Liberal Association, expressed the hope that he would have no Liberal opponent, but appointed the local ILPer Tom Richardson as Election Agent.[185]

Taylor had much to recommend him from the Liberal point of view: 'a staunch Home Ruler ... temperance advocate of a moderate type, and a broadminded Free Church man', but Richardson set out to conduct the campaign in strongly independent terms. He arranged a meeting of ILP and trade union branches — essentially an embryonic LRC.[186] Both Taylor and Richardson met the Liberal Association and remained firm on the independence question — the candidate stressed that he was an ILPer not a Liberal, he doubted whether he could have accepted a Lib-Lab label if the miners had insisted on it, and if elected he would 'in all probability' take the Labour whip. He was in effect a LRC candidate, although promoted too late for central approval.[187]

The Liberals responded by adopting a local Congregational Minister, but Taylor, backed by an impressive array of miners' lodges and by Fred Jowett, Walter Hudson and Ramsay Macdonald, won easily in a three-cornered fight, despite being ill for much of the campaign. His heartland was the ILP stronghold of Washington, and it is tempting to see Chester-le-Street 1906 as illustrating the ILP advance within the Durham coalfield.[188]

However, Chester-le-Street would be a misleading basis to such a general claim. In part, this is because the constituency was atypical: there remained the memory of Lloyd Jones's Independent challenge in 1885, and the ILP influence was unusually strong. At Usworth, a Liberal meeting was faced with the humiliation of a vote of confidence being defeated by 300 to 40. In other parts of the county the ILP was much weaker, and even after the DMA had affiliated to the Labour Party, Liberals could head off Labour challenges, even when the latter came in the guise of a DMA official. The ILP presence was distributed unevenly in geographical terms, but it was most concentrated amongst the union activists. Even in Chester-le-Street, the near-unanimity of the lodges was not matched by miners at the ballot box.

There is also a more fundamental point about Chester-le-Street, and by implication about the ILP/Lib-Lab argument in Durham. This was no confrontation between Liberal and socialist. Taylor argued that his first plank was 'Labour absolute Labour'.[189] He went on to claim support for the standard Radical items, securing Irish support en route. One supporting speaker responded to opponents' claims: 'The Liberals were going about whispering to them that Mr. Taylor was a rabid Socialist ... Mr. Taylor had been a consistent Radical ... not only ... a Liberal leader, but a Labour leader.'[190] The argument was much more one within radicalism, than between radicalism and socialism. Taylor with his free church background and Labour politics was to be a harbinger of generations of Durham Labour leaders — industrially tough, proud of their class, politically moderate. Early manifestations of this tradition came through the ILP: House, W. P. Richardson, James Robson, Lawson, Peter Lee, John Swan. It was an important transition of political allegiance, but many of their values could have been accommodated within a Liberalism more progressive than that of Durham. In the end, it was a question not of a massive ideological gulf, but of miners controlling political representation within their own districts, with the credibility of old approaches being undermined both by Liberal inflexibility and industrial problems.[191]

The Northumbrian change was much less protracted. There was little ILP activity in that coalfield in the nineties, and it was only with Sim's propaganda in 1905 that branches began to spring up in the smaller coalfield.[192] But when it happened, the change was rapid. By 1906, the Northumberland miners were backing the legal eight hours and that year's miners' picnic was dominated by Keir Hardie.[193] Once again we see the ILP carrying the new generation of leaders forward; the Northumbrian equivalent of W. P. Richardson was Ebby Edwards.

At one level then, it was an ILP/Liberal confrontation, but in several ways a continuity of idiom. Miners in both coalfields had deserted the industrial and to a lesser extent the political positions of the Lib-Labs. But Wilson, Burt and Fenwick were all permitted to remain as Lib-Lab MPs long after MFGB affiliation to the Labour Party.[194] No doubt this reflected in part a powerful emotion of gratitude for past services, and also the continuing attraction of Liberalism for sections of the rank and file. But possibly it should provoke once again the question, how great was the change? In the North-Eastern coalfields the ILP was given opportunities by the collaborationist strategy of union leaders, and the result was that it served as a vehicle for all those discontented with the existing order, including younger men fretting at the caution of the old. Such a basis aided expansion especially in Durham but reduced distinctiveness. The ILP played a key role in the defeat of Lib-Labism, but was then absorbed by a moderate Labourism.

It is easy to see the industrial—political relationships in the coalfields as a confusing mosaic. Particularism was important. It is possible to differentiate between coalfields, and within these, it is possible to distinguish between communities and indeed between individual pits. In the end, it was the coalfield that mattered, since it was there that formal political attachments were made. But such attachments were, at least in part, the product of more local loyalties. The range of relevant factors was immense: economic and demographic changes leading to shifts in industrial relationships and possibly the weakening of traditional methods of social control, variable divisions of labour at the work-place, competing conceptions of trade unionism, differing levels of unionisation, cultural divisions, generational changes, variations in the degree to which Liberalism would accommodate demands for miners' candidates. Equally, there were diverse political consequences: the socialism of Scottish activists, the aggressive industrial strategy of some South Wales militants, the moderate Labourism of Herbert Smith and the young generation in Durham, the largely formal Labour commitment of many Midlands leaders. At the one extreme, we see as the product of the agitations of these years A. J. Cook, the Labour Movement's 'Billy Sunday' with his messianic oratory, all of a piece with the South Wales of Tonypandy and *The Miners' Next Step*; at the other, we meet George Spencer, dark-suited, flexible, the inheritor of a traditional Nottinghamshire ultra-moderation. In 1926 they were to epitomise two different continents of experience. But at various times they both carried ILP cards. Do we then conclude that the ILP's involvement in mining trade unionism left no clear mark? The answer must be negative. In those coalfields where the party mattered most — as opposition to a Lib-Lab machine in Durham and Yorkshire, or as a vehicle for early leadership in western Scotland — the ILP served as the political schooling for a generation of miners' leaders and left a lasting although variable legacy. In Durham and Yorkshire, it was the moderate Labourism of W. P. Richardson and Herbert Smith; further north, it could take a more radical turn, although many older Scottish leaders had become pillars of the Labour establishment and dedicated anti-Communists by the early twenties. Elsewhere, the legacy was less dominant. In South Wales it is possible to trace a link between the ILP and the more cautious Labour activists of the inter-war years. But in parts of the coalfield, significant support developed for strategies and organisations that stood to the left of the ILP and later of the Labour Party.

But the role of a political party was only one factor amongst many. Changing political affiliation with all its ambiguities was in part a reaction to changing economic circumstances. A party faction could act as a creative force, but it was constrained by or sometimes encouraged by conditions within the industry. Of course, reactions to diverse economic developments were expressed through variegated cultural and political traditions — but these experiences were within a world where regional particularism within the coal industry was becoming less dominant. The logic of both MFGB organisation and Labour Party affiliation was towards a more universalistic frame of reference. Miners began to act more as men within a common industry, rather than as hewers, or as men of Durham and South Wales. The vision of the miners as the shock troops for a whole class was just over the horizon.

Table 5. *The decision to affiliate to the Labour Party*

District	1906 Ballot			1908 Ballot		
	For	*Against*	*Total Member-ship*	*For*	*Against*	*Total Member-ship*
South Wales	41,843	31,527	121,261	74,675	44,616	144,600
Yorkshire	17,389	12,730	62,182	32,991	20,793	78,300
Scotland	17,801	12,376	52,500	32,112	25,823	78,000
Lancashire	8,265	3,345	55,420	30,227	13,702	71,500
Derbyshire	1,789	11,257	29,480	5,811	16,519	38,475
Nottinghamshire	1,806	11,292	23,774	2,459	5,822	30,753
Midland Fed.	666	13,553	26,100	10,772	19,951	38,100
Cumberland	492	372	4,311	2,816	1,522	4,900
North Wales	295	2,428	9,232	2,467	6,017	13,200
Somerset	1,101	1,527	3,000	2,052	1,291	3,254
South Derbyshire	136	208	1,923	656	1,072	3,500
Leicestershire	60	747	3,693	194	675	5,000
Bristol	570	352	2,197	1,074	474	2,300
Northumberland	—	—	—	14,331	19,169	34,200
Total	92,222	101,714		213,137	168,446	

Durham voted to join MFGB by 47,986 to 18,963 at the end of 1907 but did not participate in the 1908 ballot — it appeared that such political involvement was contrary to its rules.

3

Cotton

The challenge posed for the early ILP by miners' organisations was equalled by that offered by cotton textile unions. In both cases, modes of industrial and political activity had been established which seemed to offer little scope for ILP initiatives. At the least in several coalfields ILP standard-bearers played important roles in the MFGB's shift towards the Labour Party. Although the affiliation of the cotton unions came earlier and was completed by February 1903, it is difficult to find much specifically ILP influence behind the taking of this decision. Yet, there is a paradox which requires elucidation. Several cotton towns developed a strong ILP or SDF presence during the nineties. Blackburn and Preston were prominent in 1900 for the candidacies of Snowden and Hardie; Burnley's strong SDF attracted Hyndman as candidate in 1895, 1906 and 1910; both organisations could point to some strength in Rochdale and Nelson. Other centres had their smaller ILP or SDF branches. But such sentiments are difficult to find within the cotton unions. Controversies in the coalfields during this period helped to produce a generation of leaders such as Robert Smillie and Herbert Smith who came throgh the ILP to achieve trade union leadership. There were no equivalents in the cotton unions. Cotton-town political developments often appear distant from trade union strategies and arguments. It will be necessary later to clarify the cultural and political factors that helped to precipitate an ILP presence in several cotton towns. For the moment, attention must be paid to a dog that barely barked.[1]

The inhospitable terrain offered to the ILP by the cotton unions can be approached best through an appreciation of union sectionalism. Broadly, the production process could be divided into three elements — preparatory work in the card and blowing rooms, spinning, and weaving. By the late nineteenth century, there was a great and increasing geographical division between spinning and weaving centres. The earlier processes had become concentrated in a crescent around Manchester, most prominently in Oldham and in Bolton. Weaving had its strongholds further north, in Blackburn, Burnley, Preston, Nelson, Colne and a host of smaller centres. Within this dichotomy, there was further specialisation: Bolton was celebrated for fine spinning, Oldham for coarser thread. Weaving communities tended to concentrate on particular types of produce, often for specific markets.[2]

These divisions were reflected in trade unions organisation.[3] In each centre, the three basic sections had their own local organisations, who might work together as a Town Textile Federation on some issues. But the important unity was in the federation of local units into sectional Amalgamations aiming to cover that section of the process throughout the whole industry. Thus, there had developed by the 1890s three principal industry-wide Amalgamations — the Spinners' Amalgamation, with a membership of 18,000—19,000; the Northern Counties Amalgamated Association of Weavers, with between 70,000 and 80,000 members, and the Cardroom Amalgamation, which had passed 30,000 members in the early nineties, but stood at around 10,000 fewer for the remainder of the decade. For the union members, it was the sectional organisations rather than the town federations that mattered. The local union played the fundamental role within the complexities of local bargaining, but the weight of the Amalgamation was needed for industry-wide problems and stoppages.

One further factor complicating the organisation of the workforce arose from the high proportion of women employed in the industry. They undertook monotonous, supposedly less-skilled jobs within the preparatory process, and were recruited readily into the Cardroom Amalgamation, although very rarely taking active roles. Mule spinning remained a male preserve, but from the eighties, women were employed on the new, quicker, simpler ring spinning machines. They were eventually admitted into the Cardroom organisation. It was in the weaving sector that womens' unionisation reached its strongest levels, both amongst weavers and their winders. Here, women union members formed majorities, although, once again, providing few activists.

This complex union structure provided major obstacles to change. Each Amalgamation was composed of so many constituents that it was difficult for a new faction to take control. A group could hope, perhaps, to win influence within a particular local union, but a rash of such victories would be needed for a decisive overall change. The structure provided few key posts where a change of incumbent could affect radically the direction of policy. Most local bodies had their own permanent officials, jealously guarding their rights against those of the Amalgamation spokesmen. A sectionalised structure was far from the only problem faced by socialists who wished to make headway within the cotton unions. Each of the three major blocs posed its own distinctive problems.

The spinners were the most thoroughly unionised group, organising at least 90, and perhaps 95 per cent of the mule spinners. Their distinctive strategy produced a reputation for tough sectionalism. Its success turned on their capacity to control the supply of recruits, thereby establishing themselves as a 'de facto' craft in a trade where the requisite skills could be acquired easily.

This capacity was founded on the exploitation of the spinners' assistants. Each mule was staffed typically by three workers: the spinner; the 'big piecer', an adult usually possessing the spinner's skills; and the 'little piecer', who was either a school-leaver or a half-timer. The first exploitative link was that wages were paid for the mule as a whole, and were then allotted by the spinner who kept the lion's share for himself, an arrangement not unlike the 'butty system' common in the Nottinghamshire pits. But more crucially, the 'big piecer' was tied in to his position through sentiments of envy, fear and hope. He could dream of one day becoming a spinner, and therefore felt reluctant to challenge the system that could benefit him in future. As piecers waited anxiously for vacancies in their mill, they cherished dreams of individual elevation, and saw risks in collective action.[4] Despite their dependent status, piecers posed a threat to the economic position of the spinners. They could perform the spinner's tasks and were a potential strike-breaking force. Spinners were torn accordingly between maintaining their exclusive organisation, and attempting to neutralise this threat. Sometimes, they ignored the danger; in other towns, they organised piecers, although not as full members of their organisations. Perhaps inevitably, the growth of new unionism led in the early nineties to an attempt to develop a separate Piecers' Union. The movement began in Bolton, it was abetted by local socialists, and received encouragement from the Oldham piecer and socialist, J. R. Clynes.[5] But it failed, frozen out by the spinners' hostility and the victim of the competitiveness built in to the piecers' predicament. It was hard to overcome this, particularly since those likely to be the most effective organisers were typically the first to be elevated to fully-fledged spinners.

The spinners provided a distinctive, strongly elitist element within cotton unionism. It is a portrait that appears to validate the frequently held view that the spinners were strongly Tory. This view has been fortified by an emphasis on the politics of James Mawdsley, Secretary of the Spinners' Amalgamation until his death in 1902, and Winston Churchill's unsuccessful running mate at the 1899 Oldham by-election.[6] Mawdsley typified the tough unsentimental ethos of the Spinners'. David Holmes, his counterpart in the Weavers' Amalgamation was credited with a pointed obituary: 'there wasn't a damned bit of sentiment about Jim; there wasn't an atom of sympathy in his bones'.[7] Mawdsley justified his candidacy on the grounds that on labour questions the Tories had proved easier to squeeze than the Liberals.[8] He had made the transition from Liberalism to Conservatism but whether this represented a considered judgement on the labour question is doubtful. In his 1899 campaign, he subscribed to Conservative views on licensing, Home Rule and church discipline. Whether Mawdsley should be seen as typical of spinners' politics is even more doubtful. Other local officials were Liberals. Whilst the Spinners' Amalgamation permitted Mawdsley to contest Oldham, his campaign was in no sense a trade union one, and some local Spinners' Associations condemned him for standing on a partisan platform.[9] A more feasible interpretation of the political significance of spinners' unionism would be a negative one. Their position and strategy were hardly conducive to political innovation. When differentials between spinners and weavers narrowed in the two decades before 1914, the spinners' principal response was a further retreat into exclusiveness.[10] The spinners were not a fertile soil for socialist propaganda, but they were not peculiarly addicted to Tory sentiments. In so far as spinners voted Conservative this indicated the considerable support for Toryism in towns where cotton-spinning was concentrated. Such support was attributable largely to cultural factors, and extended across much of the working class.

The Weavers' Amalgamation provided an organisational contrast. Strength was sought not through exclusiveness but through an ecumenical recruitment policy. The target was not the restriction of the labour supply, but the protection and raising of wage levels. They enrolled massive numbers of women workers, and developed links with other closed groups such as the overlookers. By the nineties, they had developed a system of collective bargaining that seemed to be paying dividends. Wage cuts were avoided after 1884, and until the first years of the new century, they reaped the benefits of rising wage levels and expanding productivity.[11] One source suggests that wages for four-loom weavers increased in Blackburn during the two decades down to 1906 by 24 per cent, and in Burnley in the same period by 33 per cent.[12] It was claimed frequently that weavers were also more likely to be radicals. Certainly their form of industrial organisation was less elitist than the Spinners', and David Holmes, the counterpart of Mawdsley was a staunch Liberal, who gave his blessing to Hardie and Snowden in their 1900 campaigns.[13] This was in the absence of Liberal candidates; on other occasions Holmes behaved as a conventional party man. Once again though, it must be queried how far the political position of a leading official mirrored that of the membership as a whole. Liberal sentiments were strong in largely nonconformist weaving villages; but the popular Toryism of Blackburn must have enjoyed support from many weavers. Once again, perhaps, political allegiances depended on elements other than specifically industrial experiences, and often in north-east Lancashire such elements tended to generate Radical Liberal sympathies.

Such Radical sentiments could provide a springboard in appropriate circumstances for a shift to a more independent — perhaps socialist — position. It is a shift that we shall find frequently in our survey of ILP growth. Amongst the weavers, however, the general economic buoyancy of the nineties helped to limit such changes. Nevertheless in north-east Lancashire there were groups of weavers who reacted to particular blends of economic and cultural experience by going beyond Radicalism to some form of socialist commitment. This was particularly the case in Burnley, Nelson and Colne.[14] The weaving section expanded relatively late, and employers often lacked the assured social status of older-established counterparts in centres such as Blackburn. Class-based politics could arise more easily. The late start meant that the cotton unions were less settled into a rhythm of collective bargaining that could help to contain and defuse conflict elsewhere. The workforce was swelled by an influx from rural districts, not only from northern Lancashire, but also from the West Riding. This led in material terms to overcrowding that was significantly worse than in older cotton towns. Housing conditions and child mortality rates were reckoned to be particularly dreadful. The cultural consequences of this demographic pattern could carry their own political implications. The Irish were, by Lancastrian standards, few, and nonconformity was strong. Therefore, both Burnley and the adjoining Clitheroe constituency were strongly Liberal. Yorkshire immigrants brought with them Radical and Chartist traditions that had been swamped in the more mechanised, more developed cotton communities.[15] These elements could combine to produce a political challenge to Liberalism that had much more in common with the woollen towns of the West Riding than with other cotton towns. A distinctive element in such challenges was provided by some women weavers. The acquisition of self-confidence and of raised expectations were necessary conditions for working-class women to participate in the growing suffrage agitation. Weavers were in an almost unique position to acquire them. The world of work at a trade where womens' wages came near to equality could provoke sceptical social enquiry; the path of union activism taken by a very few could lead to the development of organisational skills. Once the commitment had been made, joining one of the socialist groups, either ILP or SDF, was a natural next step.[16] The vast ranks of the Weavers' could conceal some socialist activists, few in number but nevertheless significant. Clearly industrial experiences played their part in such attachments, but other factors were perhaps more important.

The strength of the Spinners' and Weavers' Amalgamations contrasts with the relative weakness of the Cardroom Amalgamation. Dating only from 1886, its early growth was soon bedevilled by the inevitable interdependence with the much stronger Spinners' Amalgamation. A strike in one sector was bound to affect the other, and when the Spinners' found themselves involved in a twenty-week lock-out in the winter of 1892—3, the impact on the cardroom organisation was disastrous.[17] It might appear that here was a suitable area for socialist agitation, but it is difficult to find any supporting evidence. Potential members were difficult to recruit, the risk of blacklegging was ever-present. Such workers suffered not just from the lack of a scarce skill, but also because within the complex hierarchy of the industry, they stood near the bottom. The high proportion of women involved in the preparatory processes seemed to lack the self-confidence of some women weavers, and even fewer became involved in union or political activity.

If we stand back from this omnipresent sectionalism, it is possible to consider more general arguments for the failure of ILP agitation. One would be the bald claim that cotton workers were affluent and felt no need for radical alternatives. Such arguments can be bolstered by the image of the lordly spinner, with his own house, the piano in the parlour, watching Bolton Wanderers on Saturdays, and taking his family to Blackpool one week a year. Such a portrait is highly partial. As might be expected from the sectionalised structure of the industry, wages varied enormously. The average wage in the industry in 1906 has been calculated at 19s 11d — higher than in other textile trades — but such an average has little significance.[18] If males only are considered, then the average rose to 29s 6d. At the very top, a mule spinner could command 41s, rising to 45s 9d amongst the fine spinners of Bolton and 47s 6d in Leigh. Weavers' wages averaged about 25s for a male four-loom operative with women about half a crown below. Many in the preparatory processes received less than £1, as did the big piecers and the women ring spinners. Viewed as individuals, a few cotton workers were affluent, while some had expectations of future affluence; weavers by contemporary standards fared adequately; preparatory workers often toiled long hours in unpleasant conditions for low wages. Even the spinner's position was less desirable than it might seem. It was hard won and sometimes short-lived. Health hazards were considerable, the average working life of a spinner has been reckoned at no more than twenty years.[19]

Claims of cotton towns affluence were based significantly on aggregate of family income, reflecting the employment of unmarried daughters, and, less frequently, of wives. The average family income in a weaving town in 1900 has been calculated at 38s, but again such a figure is misleading. Inevitably within any specific family there would be a cycle of affluence and poverty as the number and earnings of its members fluctuated in a predictable pattern.[20] It is clearly impossible to account for cotton workers' lack of interest in independent Labour politics by citing wage levels. This impossibility is in part of course the product of the general inadequacy of narrowly economic explanations. Cotton workers were cemented into a particular community and a characteristic style of politics, not just because of certain economic experiences, but also because of a web of communal ties, incorporating the culture of the mill, the neighbourhood, Church and Chapel, townsfolk and outsiders.[21] All could be means of expressing employer paternalism. The disappearance of family firms and the expansion of the cotton towns could weaken many of the old ties. More centrally in terms of our present focus, a pattern of industrial relations had developed which usually integrated protest into established channels.

A symbol of this pattern is provided by the permanent local official with his facility in handling the industry's complicated price lists. Appointed often as the result of a competitive examination involving mathematical calculations, essay writing and a staged negotiating session, he was much more the adept bureaucrat than the propagandist for an interest. He could come to enjoy a reputation for expertise that could insulate him to some degree from rank and file criticisms.[22]

Such negotiators helped to produce a business unionism in which visions of fundamental change had little place. This characteristic was prominent in the great lockout of November 1892—March 1893. This arose after a series of disputes over compensation for 'bad spinning', and was precipitated by an attempt to impose a 5 per cent wage cut.[23] The dispute straddled the foundation of the ILP and, no doubt, party activists waxed optimistic about the possibilities for radicalising cotton workers. This did not happen. The dispute allowed the Spinners' to demonstrate their industrial solidarity. Their exclusiveness was an advantage, and there could be no doubting their militancy once their anger had been aroused. They could be incensed by employers' apparent breaches of rule or expectation, but this did not produce a questioning of existing rules. Such industrial strength was unlikely to have far-reaching political consequences. In part this was because in the nineties, the cotton operative's world remained a reasonably predictable place, with none of the attacks on work practices which carried political consequences for some craft unions. This stability was enhanced by the settlement of the great lockout. The Brooklands Agreement established a system of negotiation and conciliation for the spinning section paralleling that developed already by the Weavers'. Industrial relations were stabilised in a fashion that could outlast the economic conditions that had helped to generate the stability. The number of recorded disputes fell significantly during the decade, from 156 in 1891 to 44 in 1899.[24] The fall was not just in quantity — both the duration and the extent of disputes lessened.

This stable rule-governed basis for industrial relations did not mean that the cotton unions lacked all interest in political proposals. Superficially the regional concentration of workers suggested that they might emulate the miners and elect their own parliamentary representatives. This did not happen in the pre-Labour Representation Committee days, probably for a combination of two reasons. The pre-existing party political split amongst the cotton workers was the same as that amongst the Lancashire miners. In the latter case, it produced a pragmatic move to political independence. The very different world of cotton shared much of this pragmatism and arrived eventually by a different route at the same destination. But the cotton unions faced a second problem. The industry's workers rarely dominated electorates. Cotton towns, for all their dependence on one industry, were socially much more complex than mining villages, and the sexually mixed composition of the workforce served to blunt any electoral impact still further. Textile candidates needed a platform that went beyond union fidelity — and this, in politically-divided Lancashire, raised problems.

The fear of getting involved in partisan politics, together with the need to pursue certain legislative objectives had been reconciled through the formation of the United Textile Factory Workers Association.[25] This was the political mouthpiece of cotton unionism. It has a General Council, numbering in the early nineties about 200 delegates from the local unions, but the crucial power lay with the Legislative Council, a body of full-time officials. The efficacy of this organisation was debatable. The Webbs painted a positive portrait of cotton unionism on the political warpath:

Public meetings are organised, at which the local members of Parliament, or in default, the opposition candidates are impartially invited to preside ... It is no small help in this process that the Cotton Operatives have what is virtually their own organ in the press, and that their leading officials write ... much of the 'labour news' in the provincial newspapers ... No member for a cotton constituency, to whichever party he may belong, escapes the pressure.[26]

Such an exercise occurred in the 1895 election when unions worked with employers against Indian Cotton Duties, in a lobby that produced widespread support for Conservative candidates. Some success was also achieved on two other important questions, those of controlling 'steaming' in weaving sheds,* and of providing detailed wage statements to each operative.[27] But elsewhere the lobby system encountered difficulties. Agitation for an eight-hour day not only met with employer opposition but also with divided opinions amongst the membership. An 1894 ballot gave a majority for the proposal of only 2,000 out of a total poll of over 87,000. The Association also had to tread carefully on the half-time question, where the conservatism of members offended the instincts of social reformers. The difficulties of the lobbying method clearly increased when the demand provoked employers' opposition. This was the case with the agitation for the 'twelve o'clock Saturday', which had become, by 1900 a major issue. The vitality of the UTFWA was also questionable. It had a shadowy existence, it did not meet from 1896 to 1899, and its leading figures tended to revert back to sectional lobbying, pressurising particular candidates, and mobilising their own Amalgamations, rather than agitating on an industry-wide basis.

The shortcomings of the lobby method inevitably raised the issue of direct representation, either as adjunct or alternative. The Webbs had followed their eulogy of the lobby machinery by casting doubt on the political judgement of its members:

the political machinery is better than the material out of which it is made. Absorbed in chapels and co-operative stores, eager by individual thrift to rise out of the wage-earning class, and accustomed to adopt the views of the local millowners and landlord, the Cotton Operatives as a class are not remarkable for political capacity.[28]

A similar claim, although in more positive terms, was made by the *Cotton Factory Times* in the aftermath of the Tory victories of 1895:

if a workman votes for a man with a carriage and pair, it is because he believes that his views will be more adequately and efficiently represented by him than by his opponent who may have to do his business on foot.[29]

Such a choice did not just indicate a judgement about effective lobbying: it also incorporated prejudices central to the popular culture of many cotton

* Steaming is the practice of artificially raising the humidity of working areas to reduce the breakage of cotton thread.

towns. Already the alternative of direct representation had been considered. The membership ballot on the eight-hours question had been combined with one on labour representation. The result had been indecisive (see Table 6). Nevertheless, an UFTWA meeting decided to go ahead with a scheme,

Table 6. *1894 Ballot on Labour Representation*[30]

	For	Against
Cardroom Amalgamation	5,662	5,608
Spinners' Amalgamation	6,496	6,145
Weavers' Amalgamation	27,804	25,271
Overlookers	834	728
Total	40,805	37,752

proposing Mawdsley and Holmes as candidates, and approaching each party for one candidate. This scheme, balancing the dominant sections and partisan rivalries, was disrupted when Mawdsley refused to stand, and was subsequently abandoned.

A lack of ILP influence within this industrial and political climate is hardly surprising. Indeed, local textile unions often thwarted ILP hopes within cotton communities. The general ILP strategy of winning over local trades councils encountered a series of difficulties when the councils were dominated by cotton delegates. The Bolton Spinners', for example, dominated their trades council and their secretary, John Fielding, a committed Liberal, doubled as the Council Secretary.[31] Although a local ILP emerged in the early nineties, it received no encouragement from the trades council. Delegates rejected an ILP request for their prospective candidate to address them, and a council ballot decided against political involvement. This reflected the views of the dominant Spinners', who resolved in March 1895 that 'it is not advisable that trade unions in Lancashire should enter into Party politics'. This position indicated not only the industrial elitism and complacency of the Spinners', but also the strength of traditional sentiments in a town where the party battle was close. The consequence was that the ILP failed to take root in Bolton. A mediocre poll in 1895 was followed by decline. When the Spinners' brought out a candidate under LRC auspices in 1906, this was an essentially trade union affair with no significant ILP presence.[32] Similarly in Blackburn, a trades council dominated by cotton delegates ran its own municipal candidates, and refused to co-operate with the ILP and the SDF. This refusal extended into the parliamentary sphere in 1897, when the council refused to meet Joseph Burgess, then the ILP's likely candidate.[33] Such rebuffs could induce payment in kind. By May 1898, Blackburn socialists were attacking the local Spinners' as 'more selfish than so-called savages', because of their attitude on the half-time question.[34]

Episodes such as these highlight the difficulties facing the ILP during the 1890s in dealing with cotton unionism. Obviously, in Preston, Blackburn and, to a lesser degree, in other places, individual cotton workers must have voted for ILP candidates, but such attachments did not carry the weight that would be involved in a formal commitment of union organisations. Nevertheless, there were exceptions; the sectionalism and localism of the unions could enable socialists to secure a foothold where local conditions were peculiarly favourable. As might be expected from the earlier discussion of the Weavers', the exceptional cases were to be found in north-east Lancashire.

The political consequences were apparent in the nineties — Burnley with its strong SDF, Nelson and Colne both with branches of the ILP and SDF. This presence had its impact on the local Weavers' Associations. The Burnley Weavers' proclaimed their objective in 1892, as including the

socialization of the means of production, distribution, and exchange, to be controlled by a democratic State in the interests of the entire community, and the political and financial support of the Society shall be used toward the creation of an Independent Socialist Party.[35]

Such a declaration was too much for the union's Lib-Labs who fought back so strongly that in 1896 the committed socialists formed a breakaway union which survived for several years, although always with a limited membership.[36] Even in Burnley, many weavers remained committed to the older parties, and the SDF recruited far better amongst the miners.[37]

In nearby Nelson, the nineties were notable for a strong tradition of independent Labour initiatives in municipal politics, and a fluctuating relationship between the Weavers' and the ILP. The advent of Labour municipal candidates was aided by the fact that Nelson received its charter as a borough only in 1890, so that there was no legacy of municipal electoral attachments with which Labour candidates had to contend. A trades council was formed, also in 1890, dominated by the Weavers', and not surprisingly, it endorsed the Weavers' decision to run two municipal candidates.[38] They were successful and initiated a pattern of labour representation that continued for some years. By 1893, Nelson had both SDF and ILP branches and relations seem at first to have been harmonious. ILP representatives met trades council delegates, agreed to work together in School Board elections and then with the addition of the SDF operated as a combined force in the municipal elections of November 1893.[39] After this campaign, the trades council prohibited its officers and honorary members from supporting any candidates of the older parties: 'it would conduce to the Welfare of this Council if the members would generally support labour members only'.[40] Confidence now extended to the parliamentary arena. In February 1894, the trades council decided to sound out the ILP on the prospects for challenging the Liberals' monopoly in the Clitheroe Division.[41] These political attitudes had their impact on the UTFWA ballot on Labour representation, with the Nelson Weavers' voting strongly for such a scheme.[42] But difficulties soon arose over municipal candidatures. Council delegates in May 1895 discussed an ILP declaration that if a council nominee did not belong to either the ILP or the SDF, then he would be opposed. In the end the council decided not to run any candidates, and the tradition of labour representation was broken.[43] Even so, a distinctive political position lived on. A meeting of Nelson Weavers' instructed its 1897 TUC delegates to support 'Socialising the Means of Production, Distribution and Exchange'.[44] By then, their colleagues in the Colne Weavers' Association were making headway in municipal politics. A. B. Newall, their Secretary, a strong advocate of Independent Labour, had been elected to the Colne Town Council in 1898, and was followed by supporters under a variety of labels.[45] These bodies were far in advance of most sectors of cotton unionism, whose votes, combined with the miners, had provided much of the minority in the crucial TUC vote of 1899 on political representation. Yet lack of enthusiasm about the LRC gradually gave way to a more positive attitude.[46]

The industry, although still expanding, was beginning to encounter problems of profitability. Employers reacted by imposing a harsher regime. Work loads began to increase, the factory environment deteriorated, the 'driving' of weavers became more onerous, and, despite earlier legislation, complaints about steaming increased. Paternalism gave way to more impersonal hierarchies, symbolised by the disappearance of family firms and the growing number of limited companies.[47] The full impact of a deteriorating competitive position was disguised until 1914 by rising output, but even at the very beginning of the new century, an episode suggested that the old stability was being lost. The Taff Vale case seemed to cause relatively little alarm amongst cotton unions, but soon they faced their own legal battle, the Blackburn Weavers case. This involved an industrial dispute in the summer of 1901, when employers had taken legal action against the Weavers', not for intimidation, but simply for picketing. Eventually the weavers found themselves faced with a bill of £11,000 and a drastically weakened legal position. The expectations on which cotton unionism traditionally operated had been radically broken.[48]

This catalyst was critical. Initial responses to the creation of the LRC had continued the earlier scepticism. Ramsay MacDonald had attempted to build on the exceptionalism of Nelson and Colne, and had corresponded with Newall. The Colne Secretary had advised working through the Weavers' Amalgamation, but here the north-eastern Lancashire position was in a minority, and in January 1901 the amalgamation had decided against affiliation. Newall now advocated persuading local unions to affiliate separately and at the start of 1901 he brought the Colne Weavers into the LRC.[49] As yet, their Nelson counterparts did not follow suit, but later that year, they resumed their interest in local Labour representation.[50] The implications of the Blackburn case were now becoming clear. The Weavers' Amalgamation took up the cause of Labour representation in January 1902 and urged the UTFWA to follow suit.[51]

Such a shift was ambiguous in its political implications. Justification was essentially sectional:

it would certainly be advantageous for the cotton operatives to have representatives in the House of Commons who thoroughly understand the technicalities of their work, and have worked at the trade themselves.[52]

This was an argument for direct representation, maintaining a discreet silence on the question of political independence. Two developments early in 1902 suggested that the second question would be resolved in favour of Lib-Labism. Mawdsley, the leader most closely associated with Toryism, died in February. Three months later, with the Free Trade question beginning to influence political alignments, the cotton unions came out strongly in favour of the Liberal candidate in the Bury by-election. But a series of events in north-east Lancashire ensured that this would not be a resting place.

Sir Ughtred Kay-Shuttleworth had sat securely as Gladstonian Member for Clitheroe since the creation of the constituency in 1885. Even advocates of Independent Labour felt that a challenge to him held out little promise of success. Newall admitted that he was 'not one of the worst opponents to labour questions by far'.[53] Yet local Labour forces were growing in confidence. The November 1901 municipal results were in encouraging in both Nelson and Colne and the Colne Trades Council and local socialist bodies had begun to consider the possibility of a Labour parliamentary candidate. On 31 January 1902, Textile Workers' representatives met with socialists and other trade unionists, discussed the problem, and then adjourned for a month.[54]

The second conference was preceded by a public meeting whose principal speakers symbolised the Labour Alliance. Philip Snowden represented the ILP. He had been born only a few miles away across the county border, and had long-standing connections with north-east Lancashire. John Hodge of the Steel Smelters' represented trade unionism and pragmatic independence. They were supported by local textile leaders, one of whom moved a resolution for direct and independent representation. The second, formal conference, on 1 March brought together about 100 representatives of trade unions, co-operative societies, and the ILP and SDF. Hardie spoke, and his ILP colleagues took the opportunity to demonstrate their tactical flexibility. There was ready agreement on the principle of Labour representation, but more difficulty was encountered in defining its political complexion. ILPers supported a move for 'a labour and Socialist candidate' but when this was defeated, they accepted the position and supported a resolution simply for a Labour candidate. This willingness to fall in with the pragmatic concerns of many trade unionists was not shared by local SDF spokesmen who left their future actions undecided.[55] Nevertheless, in the spring of 1902, local textile activists seemed prepared for a political intervention against all comers. This heightened political tempo was reflected in the political development of the Nelson Weavers'. In March, the Weavers' executive recommended affiliation to the LRC, and six weeks later a members' meeting decided on a ballot.[56] The result was overwhelmingly in favour — 4,995 against 628 — and on 9 July the Nelson Weavers' formally affiliated.[56] By then, the situation had changed dramatically. On 26 June, it had been announced that Kay-Shuttleworth had received a peerage in the Coronation Honours. But the underlying trend is important. A movement for running an independent candidate was well-developed before the vacancy was declared. Newall's response to the announcement was unequivocal — 'Labour will fight for the seat'.[58]

Local activists met rapidly to consider possible candidates. They discussed the possibility of at least three Weavers' officials, and also of Philip Snowden.[59] The possibility that a prominent ILPer might stand raised the delicate question of relations between the party and the cotton unions. The ILP had shown flexibility at the March conference. Should this be taken further in an attempt to develop an alliance between these unions and the LRC?

Glasier, the Party Chairman, worked assiduously to develop an understanding. Immediately he saw the announcement of the vacancy he contacted Snowden and the local ILP secretary.[60] Hardie and MacDonald visited the constituency on 3 July, as participants in a LRC Executive meeting where local trade unionists assured national leaders of their determination to contest.[61] The following day, Glasier, Hardie and Snowden met in Leeds with their ILP hats on, and took a critical decision. Snowden's withdrawal was recommended in favour of the Darwen Weavers' official, David Shackleton, 'provided that the latter's position was clear on the question of independence'.[62] The nomination then went forward on the following day. Eighty-one delegates, representing about 18,000 trade unionists, mostly textile workers, plus local ILPers, adopted Shackleton, the sole nominee, unanimously.[63]

The Labour candidate was emphatically not a socialist. In party terms, he was a firm Liberal, and had been considered for Darwen's Liberal candidate in 1900.[64] His politics provoked the wrath of the local SDF. Dan Irving, the Federation's Burnley organiser attacked his respectability: 'if a man stood for his class against capital, that man would not be made a J.P. like Mr. Shackleton had been'.[65] The ILP responded on two levels. They courted local trade unionists. The party were supporting

a very able and earnest trade union official … it is believed that he will, if elected, most scrupulously respect the terms of independence of Liberal and Tory politics upon which his candidature is being prompted.

Local trade unions had shown 'a most cordial desire to act with the ILP'.[66] This must be reciprocated. The ILP's justification for its own members was a shade more Machiavellian:

one of the charges which is being levelled against the Labour Representation Committee is that it is but an annexe of the ILP, and had Mr. Snowden been the candidate there, the libellers would have had their case strengthened.[67]

The viability of the ILP strategy for wooing the textile unions depended on whether Shackleton could retain credibility as an independent candidate. Local Liberals were understandably eager to retain the seat, although there is some evidence that their organisation had stagnated during the years of easy dominance.[68] The Conservative challenge was never likely to be significant, and eventually failed to materialise. The critical factor for Liberals was, therefore, their relationship with Labour. One strategy would be to adopt a Liberal candidate who could make plausible claims for Labour support, a second would be to so compromise the Labour candidate that he ceased to be a plausible Independent.

The Liberals made a credible start on the first exercise by arousing the interest of Philip Stanhope, previously the Radical Member for Burnley, an opponent of the South African War and a an enthusiast for labour reforms. But Stanhope's political sentiments made him susceptible to the argument that he might be opposed by trade unionists. He reacted indencisively to Shackleton's adoption, but eventually withdrew.[69] Local Liberals had begun to follow the second strategy, before Shackleton was selected. On 2 July they had met their Labour counterparts in an attempt to thrash out a compromise, but encountered a dogged resistance on the question of independence. A Labour member would not accept the authority of the Liberal Whip, even if he were given a free hand on Labour questions.[70] Once Shackleton's candidature was announced, some Radicals began to make offers of assistance.[71] Most crucially, a meeting was held on 14 July in the Manchester Reform Club, between Shackleton, his supporters and local Liberals. Once again the Labour side proved adamant on the question of independence, and this precipitated the delayed announcement of Stanhope's withdrawal.[72] Other Labour comments at this meeting were more delphic. Shackleton refused to call himself a Liberal in his election address, but said he would clarify his principles. Labour spokesmen said they would use their influence to prevent Liberal/Labour clashes in other Lancashire constituencies. Local Liberal leaders subsequently went through the motions of seeking another Liberal candidate, but both they and several national leaders seemed prepared to accept the absence of an official standard-bearer.

These developments aroused some suspicions amongst the ILP leaders. They had conceded much, but they could not countenance a widespread belief that 'independence' was under threat. At first Glasier had comforted himself with the reassurance that those who were really committed to the party would accept the strategy, although the party must take care not to be pushed to the sidelines: 'it must be our campaign as well as that of the Trade Unionists'.[73]

But, he found the *Manchester Guardian*'s account of the Reform Club meeting disturbing: 'it would be a great pity were Shackleton to prejudice the independent attitude'.[74] When he met Snowden in Manchester on 17 July, the latter seemed less anxious. He was

confident that Shackleton and his committee will stand the ordeal. The Manchester meeting was ... due to a natural desire merely to avoid the expense and uncertainty of a contest — though of course, it was a distinct mistake.[75]

Glasier decided to concoct a warning against a compact with the Liberals. He wrote an interview with himself and succeeded in having it inserted in the *Manchester Guardian* on the following day.[76] This boosted Shackleton's claims as an independent, but hinted that in the 'fantastic' event of a deal with the Liberals, many ILP members and trade unionists would demand that Snowden take the field.[77] Such a suggestion was more fantastic than the possibility of a deal, but it symbolically protected the ILP's socialist credentials in a potentially embarrassing situation. In fact Shackleton remained pledged to the principle of independence: 'the trade unions whose candidate I am, are composed of men of all parties and if I were to declare myself a Liberal, it would mean the wrecking of the organisation'.[78] His election address began with a list of labour and welfare reforms which could be accommodated within this non-partisan stance, but these were followed by declarations on such topics as Free Trade, abolition of the Lords, international arbitration, licensing, education and Home Rule, all placing him firmly in the Radical camp. Such a combination was effective in Radical Clitheroe. His unopposed return indicated the weakness of local Toryism and disguised the significance of his LRC sponsorhip.

The flexibility of the ILP helped in the generation of profound consequences. Locally, a Clitheroe LRC was formed during the election, in which ILPers and textile representatives then worked together to expand municipal representation and to protect Shackleton's position. This represented a successful realisation of the Labour Alliance within a hitherto difficult industry. For the Nelson ILP this partnership proved fruitful as membership showed impressive growth.[79] Inevitably the extent of the concessions produced some criticism, and for some, a purely socialist alignment with the SDF seemed more attractive. But such critics could be answered by pointing to the coup of harnessing at least some of the cotton union's organisational strength to the Labour Alliance. It was this that had impressed Stanhope:

the real trouble is that the Labour movement springs from the Weavers' Unions, and they have funds, and a wonderful organisation. The whole thing is a great surprise to everyone.[80]

At least the Weavers' had a parliamentary representative. The LRC label seemed a solution to the problem of a politically divided working class. It could be sold to sceptics as an extension of the cotton unions' tradition of pragmatic responses to particular problems. The success of the Clitheroe venture, coupled with the Blackburn Weavers case, increased the likelihood of the UFTWA affiliating to the LRC. Already in June Labour partisans had urged affiliation of the Weavers' at the monthly General Council and had been blocked only by evidence that the UTFWA were going to reconsider the issue. The Association decided to take another ballot on Labour representation and the results formed a sharp contrast with those of 1894.[81] (See Table 7.) As the votes were being counted, Newall wrote excitedly to MacDonald in December 1902:

And now for a great secret! At the ½ yearly Conference of the Textile Factory Workers is on the agenda — 'Shall we join the Lab Rep Come?' A few of us who are on the exec of this body have got it put down.[82]

Table 7. *1902 Ballot on Labour Representation*

	For	*Against*
Cardroom Amalgamation	14,173	4,573
Spinners' Amalgamation	9,978	3,057
Beamers, twisters and drawers	2,509	377
Weavers	54,637	11,352
Overlookers	1,210	170
Bleachers and dyers	1,647	327
Total	84,154	19,856

When the UFTWA met, the decision was barely controversial. A warning that affiliation would be used by the socialists was answered by Shackleton, a reassuring barrier against such a risk. The vote was overwhelming, and the conference went on to select two more constituencies — Oldham and Bolton — both to be fought by Spinners' candidates.[83] 'What do you think of the Textiles now?' Newall inquired of Macdonald.[84]

The answer of any ILP member, however committed to the Labour Alliance, could only be ambiguous. Relief at such an important trade union affiliation had to be tempered by realism about why this had happened. It could not be ascribed to the growing influence of an ILP faction. Industrial and political factors conspired to produce unfavourable terrain, and this situation was compounded by the fragmented nature of union organisation. It was simply very difficult for any would-be insurgents to achieve dominance. Some significance must be attached to the Clitheroe vacancy in an area where cotton unions' support for independent politics was exceptional. Even here the ILP accepted the priority of union claims and did not emphasise its socialist principles. Clitheroe was significant for its espousal of pragmatic independence, and helped to spotlight, and probably to accelerate a trend that was emerging in many sections of cotton unionism. This position fitted readily with the earlier tradition of lobby politics, and could be seen as an extension to deal with a changed industrial situation.

The consequences of the affiliation occasionally benefitted the ILP. In Blackburn, Phillip Snowden's position was strengthened by the formation of a local LRC which brought together ILP and cotton unions. Elsewhere, however, where the ILP presence was less, the entry of the textile unions into Labour politics was hardly a radicalising influence. Labour politics in Oldham stagnated with the hardly inspiring prospective candidacy of Thomas Ashton of the Spinners', a stagnation revealed when the gap left by Ashton's withdrawal was not filled. In Bolton, the other Spinners' candidate, A. H. Gill fought successfully in 1906 on a platform that revealed his own — and the electorate's — moderation. He stigmatised recent attacks on trade unions as 'unfair and Un-English', and expressed scepticism about the possibility of raising piecers' wages through legislative action.[85]

For the future, some cotton workers would be radicalised by a deteriorating economic environment, but union structures and established practices meant that such shifts would have only marginal influence on the politics of the cotton unions. The contrast with the other big battalion — the miners — is significant. The difficulties facing the ILP in the pursuit of an alliance with the unions were to be revealed most acutely in the cotton towns. Frustrations arose not just in the initial process of persuasion, but also from the consequences of the affiliation. The hearts and minds of the great majority of textile union activists were never won for the policies of the ILP.

4

Railways

The railway industry had a unique position in the late Victorian economy, and railway trade unionism played a distinctive part in the gestation of Independent Labour politics. There has been a traditional tendency to emphasise the leading role of railwaymen in the formation of the LRC, centring on the initiation of the crucial TUC Resolution of 1899 by the ILP activists within the Doncaster branch of the Amalgamated Society of Railway Servants. This emphasis highlights an important part of the truth — but it requires clarification and qualification. ILP members and sympathisers did secure major influence inside the ASRS in the late nineties, but their legacy was profoundly ambiguous.

It was inevitable that railwaymen would develop an interest in political action. The central contribution of the railways to economic activity had led to a relatively high degree of state regulation, involving between 1889 and 1893 a sharp tightening of restrictions on railway rate increases. Such constraints were intensified at a time when railway companies had moved out of their earlier relatively competitive phase into a situation characterised by pooling agreements, the provision of elaborate facilities as a means of enhancing company-status, and later, suggestions of amalgamations. Costs tended to increase as coal prices rose, and technical developments and traffic growth required heavy injections of new investment. The problem could be captured in the proportion of working expenses to gross receipts — 52 per cent in the late eighties, but 57 per cent by 1893 and 62 per cent by 1900. The pressures to keep down labour costs were clearly increasing.[1]

Railwaymen had to respond to these developments in the face of the largest concentrations of private economic power in the country. By the 1890s, the major companies employed vast numbers in a bewildering range of grades. The position of the railway employees was distinctive. They were more secure than many late Victorian workers, although this security was threatened as companies became more cost conscious. Wages, however, tended to be low — even in 1906, they averaged only 24s 4d for a full week. This average enveloped massive variations, with porters perhaps five shillings below, but drivers £1 above. One factor facilitating low wages, as management spokesmen admitted, was the ease with which low-paid rural railwaymen could be recruited easily from an even worse-paid agricultural workforce. The wage relationship was buttressed by a range of paternalistic devices: company housing and pension schemes, clothing allowances, and an intricate and protracted promotional ladder. The full weight of 'the Company' could be seen above all in railway towns such as Swindon and Crewe. It was a rule-bound industry — within the almost suffocating embrace of the employer, a railwayman could achieve security and a degree of status, if he accepted the tempo of this most disciplined of occupations.[2]

Such an environment, with increasing managerial concern about labour costs backed by a tradition of almost military discipline, was hardly conducive to the easy growth of effective trade unionism. Railway companies evinced a rooted hostility to anything that smacked of union recognition. Sir George Findlay of the London and North Western Railway disarmingly informed the Royal Commission on Labour that trade unionism on the railways was an unthinkable as trade unionism in the armed forces.[3] Some companies gave practical expression to such sentiments by conducting purges of union activists.[4] Union organisation developed only slowly, gaining relative stability in districts such as the North-East, where trade unionism in other occupations was relatively well established. The Amalgamated Society of Railway Servants carried a title affording eloquent testimony of the paternalism and discipline endemic in the railwayman's situation. Founded in 1872, it bore in its early years more the character of a friendly society than of a combative trade union. The Associated Society of Locomotive Engineers and Firemen, an 1880 breakaway, remained small, while the General Railway Workers' Union — a product of socialist influence and New Unionist enthusiasm, a 'fighting' union with low dues — had only marginal significance.[5] Indeed, it was the older, largely Lib-Lab ASRS that became the vehicle for Independent Labour politics.

Within this organisation, the transition to a more assertive industrial policy took place under Lib-Lab leadership, and the beginnings of the shift pre-dated the emergence of London-centred New Unionism. Apart from the central aspects of the railway workers' changing situation, a complex blend of factors could facilitate or inhibit industrial militancy. On the one hand, there was the sheer complexity of the grading system, and the sedulously fostered inter-company rivalries. How could a national movement ever be organised? But, on the other side there were ways in which some railway workers could develop a level of consciousness that went beyond their immediate situation. Locomen and guards frequently met their colleagues from other depots and could acquire an awareness of common problems; signalmen, latterly, could discuss their grievances by telephone.[6] Their frame of reference could expand beyond their own community — they could become aware of their position as members of an industrial workforce within an extensive modern industry. For railway workers who had come perhaps from agricultural employment — and in rural settings, remained within an agrarian social structure — the contrast could be acute. But it could go even further. Traffic on the railway network reflected the ebb and flow of late Victorian prosperity. A trade boom could lead to exhaustingly long hours. A coal strike or lockout could lead to railwaymen working short time or being laid off. The revelations of such interdependencies could expand the consciousness of railway workers even further. They could come to see themselves as part of an industrial working class.

Such expansion of awareness could be abetted for locomen, signalmen and guards by their enjoyment of a degree of industrial space. Signal cabin, footplate and guard's van — all permitted workers to escape for a time from the onerous supervision of inspectors. They controlled part of their work-process under the very armpit of the discipline-conscious management — a control threatened increasingly by more intensive traffic, more 'scientific' management and the development on some railways after 1900 of centralised control.[7] For goods guards, grievances were perhaps particularly acute. The line of promotion from shunter was one in which the accident rate was particularly high and the earnings of goods guards were affected directly by changes in the general level of economic activity. There were, of course, more general grievances, especially over overtime payments and hours of work — but it was from these relatively well-paid grades with opportunities for an expanded consciousness, and some industrial space, that many of the ASRS industrial and political militants came.

Early agitation was centred in the North-East — until the early nineties by far the strongest region for railway trade unionism. The forward movement symbolised by the Darlington Programme of 1888 was led by such figures as Walter Hudson, a mineral guard on the North-Eastern Railway, later ASRS President, and from 1906, Newcastle's first Labour MP. The ASRS gained some economic advances from the NER but most significantly, between 1890 and 1897, the ASRS secured 'de facto' recognition from the company — the fourth largest in Britain. It was both a beacon for other sections of the ASRS, and a warning to other companies. In some ways, the North-Eastern's position was distinctive. It enjoyed a situation more nearly a monopoly than many other companies; although cost-conscious, there seemed no way that it could lose business. Moreover, the strength of local trade unionism in Durham and Northumberland not only produced a relatively strong ASRS, but also NER directors and managers who were aware that the recognition of trade unions could have a harmonising effect on industrial relations. Especially was this so, since the NER's directors tended to have close links with local coal and iron interests. They dealt with union officials elsewhere, and believed that both the NER and their other concerns would benefit from predictable industrial relations in the railway industry.[8]

But elsewhere, the growing readiness of at least some grades to back demands with organised industrial action met with obdurate employers sticking to a non-recognition policy. Growing optimism was reflected in ASRS membership — 19,589 in 1889, 26,360 a year later, then a gradual rise to 44,709 by the end of 1896.[9] By then the Society was moving towards its first All Grades Campaign, a shift which brought in a flood of new members from previously ill-organised sections. Much of this 1897 expansion was probably little more than formal, the programme was something of a patchwork quilt. The threat of growing union assertiveness produced a relatively united response from the companies, and the campaign achieved little except to demonstrate that the extent of union organisation was insufficient to justify such an ambitious exercise. Given such an anti-climax, the attraction of political action to redress some railwaymens' grievances was inevitably enhanced.[10]

The basic attraction was already there. Railwaymen were keenly interested in state action on some of their conditions of work. Apart from parliamentary involvement in rate regulation, safety legislation and, in the early nineties, victimisation had become questions of political concern. The safety aspect raised issues such as legislation for the eight-hour day, the prohibition of excessive overtime, and the compulsory introduction of automatic couplings to reduce fatalities and injuries in shunting operations. It was hardly surprising that direct parliamentary representation was seen as some compensation for the phalanx of railway directors who sat in the commons.

The ASRS had discussed parliamentary representation in the 1880s, and by 1892, an Annual General Meeting decision had decided narrowly to sponsor the Lib-Lab General Secretary, Edward Harford.[11] He was adopted subsequently at Northampton, where local Radicals were eager to deflect the challenge of a significant local SDF.[12] Such an adoption raised the question of Harford's political position — his personal Liberalism was clear, but was this acceptable to the ASRS? The majority of the Executive Committee certainly thought so, and endorsed his Northampton candidature in June 1894,[13] but critical resolutions, from some branches promised some controversy at that year's AGM. The opposition was mixed. Several of the critical resolutions were from Lancastrian branches, suggesting that Conservative railwaymen were perhaps unhappy at a sponsored candidate having links with the Liberals, but some resolutions emphasised the need for independence, and the consent of local labour organisations. One, from Liverpool Edge Hill, referred to 'independent Labour representation'.[14]

The Newport AGM of October 1894 saw the first appearance of some ILP activists at an ASRS forum. The most notable was Tom Peacock, a NER clerk from Tyneside,[15] whilst another North-Eastern activist, Walter Hudson, occupied the Presidency and set the tone of the proceedings in his opening address: there should be 'one common standard for the cause of labour ... alone, clear, and distinct from either of the two political parties'.[16] The funding of Harford's candidature was uncontroversial; the split came over political attachments. A Lib-Lab attempt to secure approval for Harford irrespective of either political party was lost by 26 votes to 17. Instead the delegates backed by 27 to 21 a motion moved by Peacock that endorsement of the candidature by the Executive was valid only 'providing he agree to hold himself independent of either of the political parties'. Peacock then built on this victory and the delegates accepted by 42 to 2 a resolution emphasising the independent character of all ASRS candidatures. These Newport decisions were undoubtedly significant — Liberalism could not secure unity amongst the Society's activists, and the second decision could be emphasised subsequently by precedent-hungry advocates of independent politics. The *Labour Leader* saw the Newport decisions as 'a great victory for the ILP',[13] but this was an exaggeration. It was a success for all those united on a negative proposition — opposition to a sponsored candidate being attached to Liberalism — and it was ignored by Harford in his July 1895 Northampton campaign. Here he acted as an orthodox Lib-Lab candidate in a two-member seat, failing narrowly as the result of both Independent Radical and SDF intervention. This posture evoked opposition from Hardie, but not, it seems from Society members. Harford was unrepentant, informing the 1895 AGM that:

While fully pledged to all the points in our programme with a perfectly free hand on labour questions generally, I secured the hearty support of the Radical party in Northampton, and the recent election clearly proves that direct Labour representation has nothing to gain by wantonly ignoring, much less repudiating, the political party willing to co-operate with us for a common object.[18]

This was really the zenith of Lib-Lab influence. At the 1895 AGM in the aftermath of electoral defeat, delegates debated the most basic political issue of all — the continuation of a parliamentary fund; they agreed by a narrow majority to carry on. On this, at least, Liberals and ILPers could be at one.[19] The argument was of a very different order from twelve months earlier; a clear ILP challenge seemed a long way off. But the story of internal ASRS politics for the remainder of the decade is one of increasing Independent Labour influence. In part this reflects the industrial context, but it would be misleading to restrict the analysis to this aspect. Method, issues and consequences are all important.

The structure of the ASRS was in some ways a peculiarly suitable one for a new tendency to make its influence felt. The Society's Executive met at least four times a year to administer the affairs of the union. Its membership of thirteen had to face election annually, and members could serve only for two consecutive terms. The elections were carried out on the basis of equal electoral districts, using a first-past-the-post voting system.[20] Here, then, was an attempt to have a wide representation of members' sentiments at the head of the union, with Executive members remaining at their jobs and travelling up to London periodically on union business. The rapid turnover of members of the Executive could be seen as a way of preventing elitism. It opened the Executive to shifts of opinion amongst the membership, whilst the voting system meant that a relatively small but self-aware group, perhaps organised through a large branch, could dominate a contest for an Executive place. The consequence of this structure in the nineties was that a number of Executive positions were captured either by ILP members, or by those sympathetic to Independent Labour representation. Tom Peacock served on the Executive in 1895 and J. Miller from Glasgow Parkhead in 1896—7. But the largest injection of Independent Labour Supporters came onto the Executive at the start of 1897 (see Table 8).[21]

Table 8. *Independent Labour sympathisers on ASRS EC, 1897*[22]

District	Name	Branch	No. of opponents	Vote	Total vote cast
No. 2	J. Miller	Glasgow Parkhead	Unopposed		
No. 5	T. R. Steels	Doncaster	3	1,260	2,591
No. 7	B. Kirby	Batley	7	735	2,275
No. 8	E. J. Perry	Stratford, West Ham	3	560	1,276
No. 10	J. Turton	Southport	11	775	2,014
No. 11	E. Bancroft	Stockport No. 1	6	664	1,488

This represented an important breakthrough, but qualifications must be entered. Most clearly there is no way in which this could be seen as indicating a major shift in rank and file sentiment. The five new members had been elected on minority votes within small turnouts. But more crucially, in terms of decision-making, the upsurge had a somewhat ephemeral quality. This was not just a question of ambiguities in the political positions of some EC members — or indeed that they might find union solidarity a priority. It was also that the structures which facilitated their emergence also ensured that it would be brief. With no continuity in Executive membership, the development of a strong Independent Labour tendency there was circumscribed. Raw Executive members had to face a General Secretary who was full time, knowledgeable and who could appeal directly to the membership. The same unequal relationship obtained between General Secretary and Annual General Meetings, since delegates could serve only two consecutive years. Processes designed to strengthen rank and file involvement, and to prevent the growth of an insulated caste at the top of the Society could lead in most cases to the augmentation of the General Secretary's power. The checks and balances normally lacked effectiveness. Yet the change in Executive outlook by the start of 1897 did have some importance in the specific industrial and political context — an impact strengthened by the falling prestige of the General Secretaryship during the next twelve months.

One issue in particular indicated a changed style within the Executive. In the summer of 1895, a majority of the Executive had decided to support the

TUC Old Guard over the Congress's new standing orders. In reaction to this, Independent Labour activists within the Society launched a campaign for the reform of the ASRS's TUC delegation. The Doncaster branch, in which ILP members including T. R. Steels were active, resolved as early as June 1895 that delegates to the TUC should be elected by the membership, not appointed by the Executive. A resolution from the Sheffield branch that the basis be one delegate per 10,000 members was defeated at the 1895 AGM by 30 votes to 20.[23] The agitation continued over the next two years, and in June 1897 the Executive's Independent Labour supporters succeeded in having a resolution passed by the EC that the TUC delegation be formed in the terms suggested by Sheffield — a proposal accepted, despite Liberal opposition, by the 1897 AGM.[24]

Clearly the lure of democratisation was attractive, as one supporter at the AGM affirmed: 'it was conceived on democratic principles, and he was surprised to see it opposed'.[25] But by October 1897, other developments had enhanced the influence of the ILPers. The All Grades campaign was evoking much enthusiasm amongst the activists, but more critically the AGM saw the censure and dismissal of Harford both for failure to push members' demands and for drunkenness during negotiations on the North-Eastern.[26] A prominent Liberal had been removed, one obstacle to Executive power had been temporarily lessened, and the atmosphere of revolt perhaps affected the delegates at the 1897 AGM. Nevertheless, the limited penetration of Independent Labour sentiments amongst the rank and file was highlighted by the election of the new General Secretary in June 1898. The Lib-Lab Richard Bell defeated the cautious backer of Independent Labour, Walter Hudson, by 22,671 to 14,518. Clearly regional loyalties — the South West and Wales for Bell, the North-East for Hudson — were an important influence, as was the fact that Bell had acted as General Secretary since Harford's dismissal.[27] But the result certainly does not indicate a membership reacting strongly against Liberalism. Bell, however, faced a more difficult prospect politically than his predecessor. The collapse of the All Grades Movement had implications for political action — and in the interim period since Harford's dismissal, the ILPers had captured a significant position, the editorship of the Society's Journal, *The Railway Review*.

This had been edited by the prominent Lib-Lab and hammer of the ILP Fred Maddison, who had been returned as Liberal member for Sheffield Brightside in the August of 1897, despite the opposition of Sheffield ILPers and also of some railwaymen. It was in this context that Hardie described Maddison as 'a blustering bully, ill-mannered and with the unscraped tongue of a fish-wife'.[28] Maddison's politics had been discussed by the Executive earlier that year, and the ILP sympathisers had succeeded in carrying a resolution leaving the AGM with power to instruct Maddison about the insertion of political material in the *Review*.[29] The question was debated with more heat at the 1897 AGM when Manchester area delegates attempted to secure

Maddison's resignation from the editorship on account of his election as a Liberal MP.[30] The seconder, A. E. Bellamy, an ILP sympathiser from Stockport, linked politics to industrial experiences:

The North Eastern dispute had been prominently before them, and the North Eastern men found among the directors both Liberals and Conservatives, but in the board room, those men were neither Liberals nor Conservative, but capitalists ... They considered that any person allied to a political party which was formed of capitalists could not fully represent their views ...[31]

But Maddison's impassioned defence carried the meeting, and the proposal was overwhelmingly defeated. Yet nemesis was at hand. Less than two months later, as the All Grades Campaign stood at its most critical point, Maddison wrote editorially of the prospects of success: 'With 90,000 members, it is within sight; 150,000 would make it a "certainty". It is all a question of the size of the battalions. Are they at present large enough? Candidly we think not.'[32]

This industrial caution — and perhaps realism — produced a sharp response from Bell, and an Executive decision expressing regret at the article, and asking for consultation with the General Secretary in similar future cases. Maddison resigned immediately. Significantly, it was a question of industrial solidarity that provided the occasion for his departure, although Liberals on the Executive did attempt to rescue him.[33]

It might have been an industrial question that produced the vacancy, but the consequences were heavily political. In March 1898, Steels and Turton succeeded in obtaining Executive support for George Wardle, a Keighley railway clerk, and more significantly an ILPer and editor of the *Keighley Labour Journal*. This was a major breakthrough. Wardle was certainly no firebrand — a highly respectable Methodist, he belonged very much to the worthy, diligent self-improving side of the ILP.[34] The *Review* in no sense became a pulpit for socialist propaganda, but Wardle did employ it to push the cause of Independent Labour representation.[35] He was supported from September 1898 by a series of articles from a 'Candid Friend' backing 'an independent Trade Union political party'.[36] This was the 'Keighley Connection' in operation — the candour being supplied by none other than Philip Snowden.

So, as the 1898 AGM approached, the ILP element could look forward with optimism. Industrial developments favoured them and they now had both a more established position, and faced a new Lib-Lab General Secretary. The impact of industrial confrontation could be seen in the effect of the South Wales coal lockout on the views of some of the Welsh delegates. Liberals MPs had often neglected the miners' case — a point made by the young Jimmy Thomas, then making his first appearance as the Newport delegate. Sympathy for South Wales colliers was one thing, following the argument through was quite another. One English delegate highlighted the central point:

One of the first things done by workingmen in York after the Engineers' dispute was to get one of the engineering employers as their candidate ... Passing a resolution of this kind was the beginning, the sticking to it, when an election came on was the finish

(Hear Hear) It was no use talking Trade Unionism in Trade Union company, if they were not prepared to 'face the music' when the necessity for strong action arose.[37]

In this atmosphere, renewed calls for independent political representation were bound to secure a sympathetic hearing. Already the Executive had suggested Bell and Hudson as the two ASRS candidates, and Hudson had been briefly involved with a possible contest at Darlington.[38] The AGM decisions restricted support to Bell, but reaffirmed that he should be politically independent. A resolution moved by the Leicester Liberal, Green, was carried, probably by one vote: 'That the time has now arrived when the ASRS should be directly represented in Parliament by the General Secretary, who shall be independent of either political parties ...'[39] Yet the speech of the mover revealed a different emphasis, arguing that it was essential: 'that a representative of the railwaymen should be independent of either party of the House on labour questions'.[40]

Possibly he believed that in practice the machinery of a major party, presumably the Liberals, would be essential for success. However, the wording of the resolution left open the possibility of three-cornered contests. ILP sympathisers representing South Yorkshire branches envisaged the possibility of Bell contesting a Liberal vacancy at Rotherham. The local delegate favoured a three-cornered fight there, and a snap vote produced a recommendation that Bell should contest.[41] This was a naive suggestion. Proponents of the candidature talked of Bell standing as a trades council nominee with that body able to mobilise 6,000 voters. The local ILP was in no position to give much support — a local activist admitted to John Penny that the party was not strong enough to fight on its own.[42] Bell and the ASRS soon abandoned the idea of a Rotherham candidature.

The decisions of the AGM did not go unchallenged by Liberals within the union. The London District Council was dominated by them, and this body decided to contact the organisers of the two major parties, regarding possible support for Bell. The Conservatives' lack of flexibility was predictable, but the Liberal spokesmen, Tom Ellis and Robert Hudson, were more accomodating. They accepted Bell's independence and said the Liberal machine would back him in a suitable seat.[43] No doubt Bell's views, taken with the readiness of other trade union members to come into the Liberal fold, reassured them that the independence pledge should not be taken too seriously.

This development provoked ILP wrath, and when the Executive met only three members backed the London Liberals. The majority condemned the action as 'unauthorised and irresponsible', a violation of AGM decisions, and reiterated that: 'Our representative must hold himself absolutely independent of both political parties, and no other attitude will be tolerated by this Committee.'[44]

The issue was complicated by Liberal allegations that Green's resolution had been tampered with on the Executive — the phrase 'independent of any political party' being changed to 'independent of both political parties'. (In fact, the term in the original draft was 'either'.) Dark murmurings also surfaced about ILP activists manipulating the union for political purposes, and one Executive supporter of political independence responded publicly.[45] Rather disingenuously be suggested his inability to recall 'any incident that has ever led to a revelation of a member's particular bias in politics or religion'.[46]

The dominance of Independent Labour activists was reaffirmed in March 1899 when the Executive backed T. R. Steels's celebrated Doncaster resolution on Labour representation. Its initiator was not now on the Executive, but only one member opposed its submission to the TUC.[47] Some Liberals were ready to support it, no doubt because of its pragmatic content. In part, this tone clearly reflected a search for maximum backing both within the ASRS and the TUC, but the objective 'to devise ways and means for securing the return of an increased number of labour members in the next parliament',[48] was in keeping with the style and strategy of the ILPers within the ASRS. Although silent on the vexed question of independence, the inclusion of 'socialistic' groups amongst those to be consulted was suggestive. Most crucially, the emphasis on 'representation' was precisely that of the ASRS ILP faction — they had kept away from discussions of socialism. They had won the Society's decision-making bodies for Independent Labour Representation by restricting the issue to precisely that.[49]

Even this commitment had to come to terms with surviving Lib-Labism within the union, and more crucially with the General Secretary's basic Liberalism. Eventually in August 1899, he had been adopted by the Derby Trades Council.[50] One local ILPer was satisfied by what he had seen at the Trades Council meeting:

Mr. R. Bell is the adopted Labour candidate ... fighting independent of both Liberal and Tory ... There was a sign of some one wanting to arrange with Liberals, but our delegates made it plain that if it was not a straight fight for Labour, we should go against any man, as we had had sufficient already, of place hunters and time servers.[51]

So the Derby ILP decided to back Bell. But there were forces operating in the opposite direction: it was a question of not only Bell's Liberalism but also that in this two-member seat, where the Liberals had suffered a humiliating defeat in 1895, they were anxious for success, and were likely to be sympathetic to a Liberal railwayman despite his pledge of independence. Such sentiments were expressed at the 1899 AGM where pressure came from Derby and Nottingham delegates for the removal of the independence criterion. This brought a fiery riposte from the ILPers: the decisions of earlier AGMs were cited; to adopt the Derby proposals would be 'simply insane'; it was an 'ignoramus recommendation'. The deletion proposal 'was negatived by acclamation'.[52] Yet the oratory of the advocates of independence was somewhat misleading. A writer (probably Wardle) in the *Railway Review* took a flexible, perhaps more cynical, view of the Derby situation: 'The adoption of Mr. Bell for Derby, and the decision of the Liberal party to be satisfied with only one candidate leaves the course open for the election of a genuine Labour candidate.'[53]

Within little over a year, the results of the ILP activities within the ASRS were apparent. Wardle on behalf of the union seconded Hardie's amendment at the LRC Conference defining the independence of the new organisation,[54] the ASRS affiliated almost immediately,[55] and seven months later Bell was elected for Derby as an LRC member.[56] Yet this picture of the Railwaymen as part of Labour's industrial vanguard is misleading. Bell's political position was very uncertain, and the Executive's attitude towards the new LRC was equivocal. At the meeting at which the decision to affiliate was taken, the ASRS Executive also regretted the failure to represent the Parliamentary Committee of the TUC within the LRC Executive.[57] This hardly suggests that the new organisation was viewed as a major new political initiative. These obscurities, produced perhaps in part by the strategy of the ILP activists, were to bedevil the ASRS relationship with the Labour Representation Committee until 1906.

Superimposed upon these political uncertainties, the ASRS relationship with the LRC — and indeed the prospects of the whole LRC enterprise — were affected by the legal consequences of the Society's Taff Vale strike in the summer of 1900. The impact of the judgment concerning ASRS liability on union affiliations to the LRC is well known;[58] what was less straightforward were the consequences of Taff Vale for political arguments inside the ASRS. It would have been easy to cash in on the internal conflict in a straightforward political fashion. On the one side stood the Liberal, Bell: cautious, flexible, anxious to avoid conflict whenever possible; on the other, the 'hero' of Taff Vale, the West of England Organiser, James Holmes, an ILPer, warm-hearted, impetuous, a passionate orator, who had moved the Labour Representation resolution at the 1899 TUC. But there were other nuances. In part, the dispute between Bell and Holmes was about union discipline, with Holmes breaking rules over the calling of industrial action. It was also about industrial policy. Bell remained in favour of a national programme, although a belief that progress on this must necessarily be slow fitted in with his temperament and general outlook. In contrast, Holmes backed a strategy of sectional claims against particular companies — a tactic that might highlight Bell's caution, but, in the longer run, an approach that could provide no basis for railwaymen's solidarity.[59] The issue of militancy on sectionalist issues obviously raised acute problems for ASRS socialists. More concretely, the censuring of Holmes by a Special General Meeting in January 1903 helped to strengthen Bell's position at the time when his political difficulties were increasing.

It had become apparent early in the 1900 parliament that Bell's view of Labour Representation was far removed from that of Hardie. By the spring of 1903, Bell's readiness to be involved with the Liberals was producing a sharp response from his 'colleague'.

I do not feel inclined to allow a Labour colleague of my own to be used as a cats-paw by men who are much more astute than himself to lead the Labour movement into the Liberal camp, and thereby bring about its destruction.[60]

By then, Bell's political position, and developments within the LRC, were producing considerable controversy inside his union. Early in 1902, he had appeared at a Liberal Federation meeting in Bradford, provoking a critical response from local ASRS branches, where ILP sentiment was strong, and leading to an expression of regret from the Executive.[61] But twelve months later, the position had become much more complicated. The Newcastle Conference of the LRC enacted a more stringent definition of political independence — a decision backed by the ASRS delegates, Palin, Holmes and Brodie (the first two at least being ILP members) since 'in view of the known policy and decisions of the governing body of the society for some years, we felt we had no option but to support a policy of complete independence'.[62]

Bell dissented from this, resigned from the LRC Executive, and refused to meet the new requirement that he sign the revised LRC Constitution. This development occurred very soon after the SGM of January 1903 had amended the ASRS rules to incorporate a political fund, in such a fashion that the union was tied by its own rules to support the LRC.[63] Bell's own position in the aftermath of Newcastle seemed strong. Many branches responded to criticisms of him in the socialist press by expressing support for their leading official, and first by implication, and then more overtly, querying the nature of the ASRS—LRC connection.[64] Yet even with Bell's cause apparently prospering, the logic of LRC affiliation meant that the main drift of union decisions was away from him. The 1903 AGM approved three more sponsored candidates, Hudson, Wardle and Holmes, all of whom were unequivocally committed to the LRC position. Now Bell seemed in a distinctly isolated position, although delegates perhaps attempted to limit the socialist as opposed to Labour element in future LRC delegations by insisting that they, like their TUC counterparts, should be elected by the membership.[65]

The most crucial milestone in Bell's divergence from the LRC came in January 1904 when he backed the Liberal candidate rather than the LRC one in the Norwich by-election. This intervention provoked the wrath of ILP journalists, and also of ILP trade unionists. Curran felt that a crucial point had been reached: 'the behaviour of Mr. Bell and a few others are making the position of the LRC seem absurd to outsiders and I fear there will have to be a sorting-out policy if the movement is to be kept on straight lines'.[66] Such reactions helped to provoke a crisis within the ASRS. Now Bell seemed to have separated himself from other non-socialists within the LRC, he was behaving in a fashion distinct from that of Henderson and Shackleton. It was, in fact, the Weavers' MP along with MacDonald who represented the LRC at a crisis meeting with the ASRS executive two months after the Norwich incident. Once again Branch opinion was divided, some condemning Bell, but others echoing the Birmingham Small Heath Branch's condemnation of 'vindictive attacks' by 'a few extreme socialists', and opposing 'the tyranny practised by the Labour Representation Committee'.[67] Clearly, opinion within the union was far more variegated than its record as a pioneer of independent representation might suggest. It was not a matter of the Executive being divided neatly between Liberals and socialists. This came out clearly in the discussion with Shackleton and MacDonald.[68] On the one side, there was Nathan Rimmer, who argued that although not a member of any socialist group he expected Bell to back the LRC.[69] The growth of the Committee carried its own attractions for such trade unionists: it was simply the place to be. But there were also considerations of the solidarity of the ASRS; these were articulated by Jimmy Thomas, a young Executive member of increasing influence. Unity must be maintained:

I bow to no one in my advanced thought and principle on this question, but I feel that we here today have a great and important consideration to weigh in the first place ... there is such a thing as statesmanship. We are here as representatives of the railway servants of the country.[70]

This meant that Bell had to be dealt with sympathetically, but on the other hand, the basic fact that the membership was politically divided led Thomas pragmatically to back 'a distinct Labour group'. Bell attempted to utilise these sentiments by driving a wedge between those who sympathised with the idea of labour representation, and those who were committed to the ILP: 'the controversy is not so much one between the LRC and myself, as it is ILP versus myself, and it is the ILP which has undertaken the endeavour to dethrone me from my seat in the House of Commons, and not the LRC'.[71] Unity was maintained by leaving the crucial decision on Bell's political attachment for the 1904 AGM.[72] Here the decisions narrowly favoured Bell. With the help of a Liberal chairman, an attempt by T. R. Steels to secure Bell's signature for the LRC Constitution was defeated, and then by one vote a resolution was carried giving the General Secretary much of what he wanted. It was acknowledged that 'certain of his actions may have been somewhat indiscreet', but not sufficiently to justify a withdrawal of confidence. There was to be no break with the LRC, but its constitution was 'too stringent' and proposals for constitutional modifications were to be submitted to the 1905 LRC Conference. Most crucially, it was agreed that 'Mr. Bell still act as at present without signing the Constitution and in the event of an election taking place he shall be allowed to stand as our representative on the same conditions as heretofore'.[73]

The Constitutional amendments came to nothing at the 1905 LRC Conference, and at that year's AGM, J. H. Thomas, now President, adopted a reconciling role, slapping down Bell's hints of the possibility of disaffiliation from the LRC but also blocking an ILP attempt to force Bell to sign the Constitution.[74] And so the ASRS, who had been responsible far more than anyone for the convening of the LRC, fought the 1906 election with four sponsored candidates — three endorsed by the LRC but Richard Bell standing effectively as a Lib-Lab. Now with the election of Hudson and Wardle, and the emergence of a sizeable Parliamentary Labour Party, Bell's position was clearly anomalous. Already, before the election, Joseph Cross of the Blackburn Weavers' had raised the anomaly of Bell's electoral position with MacDonald, who in turn had informed Walter Hudson. The response of this Railwaymen's parliamentary candidate was that success at the ballot box would settle the question 'after the General Election with a strong nucleus of a Labour Party in the House, the LRC can tell our Society to put itself in order or be expelled, there will then be a great deal to loose (*sic*)'.[75] At the 1906 AGM the ILPers succeeded in changing the Society's rules so that in future all sponsored candidates had to be members of the Labour Party. The significance of this was limited — the vote was far from unanimous (37 against 22) and it would take effect only at the next election. An attempt to make Bell join the Labour Party immediately was defeated heavily.[76] Even now a desire to maintain unity and a strongly pragmatic attitude towards parliamentary representation were apparent.

The reverberations of Bell controversy through the decision-making channels of the union for several years suggest major qualifications should be entered to the conventional portrait of the ASRS as a socialist or Independent Labour vanguard in the trade union world. Many of the activists were ready to back their General Secretary, through personal loyalty, or a feeling of union solidarity, or a distaste either for socialism, or for a staunchly independent political commitment. Equally, several on the ASRS Executive saw the question of political commitment in harshly pragmatic terms. It was a matter of which tactic would cause less disaffection amongst the membership and would maximise union influence. Before 1900, the first consideration tended to point to sponsored candidates being independent of established parties; from around 1903 and certainly from 1906 the second one pointed to an unequivocal commitment to the LRC or Labour Party. This pragmatism had been the hallmark of the agitation carried on by the ILP sympathisers inside the union in the nineties. The developments that led to the Doncaster resolution included practically nothing in the way of socialist propaganda.

This emphasis is important but it is not the whole truth. The pragmatism of many officials and activists has to be balanced against the enthusiastic role played by railwaymen in many local political initiatives. Frequently, ASRS stalwarts, often doubling as ILP enthusiasts, carried the Labour standard, acting as socialist nuclei amongst less committed workers. In the Erewash Valley on the border of Derbyshire and Nottinghamshire, an ILP signalman propagandised for several years amongst the predominantly Lib-Lab colliers.[77] It was not just amongst the Lib-Labs that ILP railwaymen could provide a taste of an alternative. In textile Lancashire, similar developments occurred. The staid deliberations of the supposedly apolitical Blackburn Trades Council were disturbed in the 1890s by the interventions of an ASRS ILPer; the opposition or indifference of many textile workers towards Fred Brocklehurst's

Bolton candidacy in 1895 was not shared by at least some employees of the London and North Western Railway.[78] Most significantly, the driving force behind the Stockport LRC came significantly from local railwaymen rather than the much more numerous textile workers. They received some reward in 1906 with Wardle's election as the town's first Labour MP.[79] Similarly, some railway centres developed significant ILPs. The party succeeded in developing a branch at Crewe in the nineties in the face of what one observer saw as the 'perpetual state of terrorism' engendered by the London and North Western. The Derby ILP also developed a sizeable membership, despite the hostility of the Midland Railway and the consequential unwillingness of Company employees to stand for office under ILP auspices.[80] The visibility of individual railwaymen as local socialist enthusiasts was aided perhaps by certain aspects of their work. The nature of much railway employment could develop many of the skills that were essential to the running of a political organisation; it was, after all, by late Victorian standards a most literate and rule-conscious industry.

Railwaymen did play a distinctive role in the drive to Labour politics, and the ASRS was in many ways an ILP union. It is easy to see how much developments fitted with economic changes and industrial relations within the industry. The attractiveness of political action is clear, as are the problems in agreeing on a Liberal parliamentary representative with a membership spread across districts with varying political traditions. Equally, it is apparent how an articulate minority could find the ILP position acceptable, and how their influence could be magnified by union structures. Yet the ASRS was in no sense a socialist union — individual members were committed socialists but in the making of union decisions they subordinated this commitment to a pragmatic drive for majorities where they mattered in the Executive and at AGMs. This meant that the watchword was Labour Representation. The ASRS's significance is, in fact, as a depiction in miniature of the ILP strategy towards trade unionism. Here the formal positive decisions came early — the negative implications followed. Formal support and a few socialist activists were one thing — conversion of the rank and file, as the complex arguments over Richard Bell showed, was quite another. As the commitment to Labour grew, the legacy of the strategy of the nineties was increasingly clear. Pragmatism begat pragmatism, individual socialists might strive for a better world in their own communities, but the politics of the ASRS were to become dominated increasingly by the staunch conformism and reconciling genius of Jimmy Thomas. It was but a short road from the socialist enthusiasts of the nineties, through an accommodation with existing trade union sentiment, to cigars and champagne leadership.

5

Two craft unions

Trade union weakness and oppressive management provided the context for the Railway Servants' ambiguous shift towards political independence. In contrast, craft workers had developed stronger organisations, but by the nineties both their unions' strength and their own status were threatened by technical innovations. Attempts to retain worlds that they were losing led some younger craftsmen towards aggressive industrial action, advocacy of direct political representation, and sometimes a commitment to socialism. Inevitably, there were tensions. Skilled workers could be portrayed as status-conscious defenders of traditional privileges, bearing some responsibility for working class divisions. Yet the protection hoped for, and sometimes achieved by craftsmen, hinted at an alternative to the rigours of the market. Such experiences had their impacts, especially upon the Amalgamated Society of Engineers and the National Union of Boot and Shoe Operatives. Results varied, in part because of the differences in union organisation and style of decision-making. But in both cases ILP activists left significant, yet sometimes disputable legacies for union politics.

The Amalgamated Society of Engineers

If any trade union epitomised the certainties of mid Victorian society, it was the Amalgamated Society of Engineers. Here was an organisation basing its power on the work-skills of its members, restricted to craftsmen proud of their status, thoroughly respectable, epitomising the world of the skilled artisan. It was hardly surprising that the politics of the ASE officials for the first four decades of its existence were Liberal, although political commitment was not a central part of the Society's involvements.[1] But in 1896, George Barnes, a member of the ILP, was elected General Secretary of the ASE — a socialist at the head of the 'Guards Brigade' of trade unionism.[2] To contemporaries, it seemed to symbolise a major growth of socialist influence within trade unionism. Why did it happen and what were the implications?

The world of the engineers was changing.[3] Foreign competition from Germany and the United States was beginning to have an impact, but more immediately methods of production were being revolutionised in British workshops. The last decade of the century saw the introduction of a wide range of new machines with specialised functions. They undermined the necessity for the all-round craftsman; specific tasks could be carried through by operatives who had served no apprenticeship, had no wide experience of the engineering industy, but who would learn a narrow range of techniques, and were willing to work for below established craft rates. Such developments threatened the basis of ASE influence, a threat deepened by the significant increase in unemployment during the early nineties.

Along with the threats resulting from new technology, there went changes in workshop organisation. Specialisation and standardisation meant the reduction of the skilled craftsman's traditional elbow-room. Improvisation was replaced by the ministrations of planners, rate-fixers and progress men. Supervision tightened, and along with this came frequently a speeding up of production based on payment by results.

Here was a massive challenge to the old order within the ASE. Inevitably some reactions involved a reaffirmation of traditional practices — opposition to piecework, the tight control of apprenticeships and the regulation of overtime. Most crucially, attempts were made to establish the principle that ASE members must follow the work to the new machines, being paid at established craft rates for operating the new technology. This was a classic demonstration of traditional craft responses to innovation.[4]

Even in the 1880s, however, it is possible to see a rather different development within some sections of the ASE, a development associated with younger activists, frequently socialists, and linked with New Unionist doctrines. John Burns, active in the ASE throughout the eighties, attempted in 1885 to interest the Society in independent political action.[5] Tom Mann found the ASE 'very respectable and deadly dull'; recalling that 'I conceived it my duty in addition to my Socialist propagandist efforts, to try and shake up the Engineers'.[6] Other Socialists such as Tom Proctor[7] and George Barnes were also active in the Society. Moreover engineering disputes could sometimes have political consequences. A lengthy dispute at Bolton in 1887 led to the election of eight 'Labour' candidates to the town council.[8] Although this gesture of independence was only short-lived, it was perhaps a harbinger of future developments. The critics also attacked the ASE's policies as lethargic and conservative. The Society should become much more aggressive and seek to exploit new machinery for the benefit of all working within the industry. Craft boundaries would inevitably be eroded and the rational response was to accept this. Industrial strategy and socialist principle both pointed in the same direction.

Hope of a more aggressive Society depended however on internal reform. The existing ASE structure was not suited to a forward policy. There was no strong central administration. As the Webbs noted, 'the Engineers ... clung tenaciously to every institution or formality which protected the individual member against the central executive'.[9] All officers were elected directly by members; executive control was located in a body elected only by the London district; there were no salaried office staff; administration seized up and the ability to respond to changing conditions was slight. So here was another string to the reformers' bow — not only industrial assertiveness but internal modernisation.

By the end of the eighties, Tom Mann was leading a campaign within the Society on these questions, and in 1891, the death of the General Secretary, Robert Austin, led to a contest between the old and new outlooks, a contest won narrowly by the champion of traditional responses, John Anderson, who defeated Mann by 18,102 to 17,152.[10] Here apparently, was a battle royal between Liberal and socialist, exciting wide interest both inside and outside the ASE. That was certainly how the victor viewed the contest. Speaking after the result he identified Tom Mann as 'the mouthpiece of what might be called the revolutionary party in their society, a party which was chiefly found in London', and implored his audience to 'cast away this new-fangled idea of piling up money for fighting the capitalists'.[11]

In fact, the voting patterns in this contest were complex.[12] Mann's greatest strength was in London, where a strong committee with George Barnes as Secretary worked on his behalf. Here the vote went to Mann by 2,797 to 1,721. He also secured sizeable victories in other leading centres — Sunderland, Sheffield, Glasgow and, to a lesser degree, Newcastle. Mann's weakest region was the North-West, where Anderson's local connections were clearly important — even in Bolton, where Mann had been active in the aftermath of the 1887 dispute, Anderson secured a decisive victory. Local links were important, and Mann's arguments clearly appealed to a wide audience as a response to the staid policies of the established leaders. Socialism versus Liberalism was not an adequate interpretation.

The pressures of reform surfaced once again at the Leeds Delegate Meeting of 1892.[13] Here, in discussions lasting ten weeks, major reforms were implemented. The old London-based Executive was abolished and replaced by an Executive Council of full-time officials chosen by eight electoral districts. There would now be six full-time Organising District delegates — in sum, the number of full-time officials increased dramatically to seventeen. The bases for membership were broadened and financial changes introduced to permit a more aggressive industrial policy, whilst some recognition of the impact of technical change was contained in a more liberal response to the piecework question.

Now the ASE, at least structurally, was much more adapted to a changing industrial environment. Partisans of a more forward political strategy were jubilant — one claimed that it was 'one of the most encouraging signs of the progress of Socialist thought and action in trades unionism'.[14] Yet, as with the contest for the General Secretaryship, such a verdict is too simplistic. Certainly, socialists amongst the ASE activists were well pleased with the reforms but clearly many members backed them simply because they wanted a more industrially effective organisation.

One decision at Leeds was directly political. By 34 votes to 28, it was decided to amend the rules so that:

If it should appear to the Executive Council, at any time desirable that the Society should be directly represented in Parliament, the Council shall have power, after submitting the question to a ballot of the members of the Society to cause a levy to be made ...[15]

It is difficult to imagine a commitment more limited than this, with discretion left to the officials and no reference to the political position that should — or should not — be adopted by any future MP.

Over the next five years, significant developments affected the politics of the ASE. On the industrial front, the introduction of new machinery became an increasingly acute problem. By late 1895, discontent was being expressed through stoppages of Clydeside and Belfast engineers in pursuit of pay increases. When the Clydesiders — numerically stronger but industrially weaker — accepted a compromise, the Ulstermen were highly critical.[16] Their dissatisfaction was supported widely at the 1896 Delegate Meeting where the Executive's action in using the combined Clydeside and Belfast vote to terminate the Belfast dispute ws censured as 'unconstitutional and injurious to our interests'.[17] The Society's leaders were not only harrassed by aggressive sections of the rank and file: they were also facing tougher employers' organisation. The Clydeside and Belfast employers had worked in harmony, and in June 1896, the Employers' Federation of Engineering Associations was formed. Now the lines for industrial battle were being drawn.

Political developments during the same period were less clear cut.[18] The Executive made very limited attempts to pursue the question of parliamentary representation. In June 1893, they responded to resolutions urging action on the issue by requesting a ballot of members,[19] the result being in favour by 7,080 to 3,775,[20] but there the matter rested, except for a decision later that year for a levy of 1d. per member and a grant of £100 to John Burns.[21] Indeed, the Executive declined to select candidates or pay election expenses, but would consider financial assistance for ASE members who became MPs.[22]

These halting steps by a largely Liberal Executive Council need to be placed in the context of the attraction of the newly formed ILP for some ASE activists. Their activities led to a tart response by the Executive late in 1894. They reacted to complaints that branch meetings were considering political matters by emphasising that 'our Society is purely non-political in its constitution and practice', so 'the Council are determined to discountenance the introducing of such topics'.[23]

The involvement of ASE members in ILP activities can be seen through their role as ILP candidates. In June 1894, the Executive Council had defeated a motion: 'that every facility be given to G. N. Barnes to contest a constituency as an Independent Labour candidate'. Instead it was decided that: 'so long as his candidature or election does not interfere with his official duties ... the Executive Council does not deem it necessary to interfere'.

In fact, in July 1895, four ASE men stood as ILP candidates — George Barnes at Rochdale,[25] Tom Mann in the Colne Valley,[26] Fred Hammill at Newcastle and A. Shaw in South Leeds. Yet such attempts were essentially the result of local ILPers adopting people who happened to have links with the ASE rather than following from the mobilisation of local ASE opinion. Indeed in the Colne Valley there was barely any ASE membership to mobilise. At this stage, it was difficult to find any basis for an ILP initiative within the Society. Although there were socialist nuances within the broader reactions on the new technology question, these were not sufficient. Moreover, the eight hours question was not one which divided socialist from Liberal. On this topic, there was agreement both as to the principle and also that industrial action was the appropriate tactic in dealing with private engineering firms. The growth of ILP influence was facilitated by a somewhat adventitious circumstance, the failings of John Anderson as General Secretary.

Such failings were particularly significant given the economic changes of the nineties. In 1895, Barnes resigned as Assistant Secretary to oppose Anderson and was backed by Tom Mann, now Secretary to the ILP. Mann attacked the ASE for a policy of drift, and brought an angry response from his former comrade, John Burns:

the object and tenor of Mr. Mann's speech were to disparage all other candidates, cast reflections on active, honest, non-political officers who will not subordinate the interest of our great Society to the shibboleths of the ILP and its intolerant leaders.[27]

Once again, it would be easy to see this as a set piece battle between Liberals and ILPers. But the election address issued by Barnes was a study in moderation. He backed the Leeds reforms with a few qualifications; his position on industrial policy showed little enthusiasm for confrontation: 'I am favourable to caution and negotiation as against precipitation and warfare', but the ASE's case should be presented: 'not only with the requisite intellectual capacity, but backed with the necessary force'. Politically, he made a minimal gesture for independence:

While I should oppose our identification with either political party, I am favourable to working through the public bodies because I believe that therein lies immense scope for the application of Trade Union principles.[28]

It hardly amounted to a clarion call for socialist politics or industrial assertiveness, but it provided a stark contrast with Anderson's self-pitying appeal to his past record, and present difficulties, and avoidance of any political comment. Despite trade unionists' characteristic reservations about removing office-holders, Barnes ran Anderson close, being defeated by 12,910 to 11,603.[29] Just over a year later, with the Executive under pressure in the aftermath of the Belfast and Clyde dispute, Anderson was removed from office, apparently owing to the discovery of financial irregularities.[30] He stood for re-election against Barnes, whose 1895 candidature now seemed vindicated. Barnes's address was much the same, except that he now reacted to the creation of the Employers' Federation by urging a similar combination on the trade union side. Support came in testimonials from members of the large engineering centres — but it did not have a political tone. Rather Barnes was recommended for his competence and 'high moral character'.[31] Now the result was decisive — Barnes with 17,371 votes led Anderson by more than 8,000. The ILP had captured the principal office in the most respectable of craft unions. The success must be placed in context however. The party had not set out systematically to capture the Society, and it had not made masses of converts amongst the members. The success of Barnes could be attributed to the pressures of industrial change, the unpopularity of Anderson and the enthusiasm of socialist activists within the rank and file. But even with these qualifications, it is arguable that Barnes's success could have led to major changes in the Society's political position. How much was Barnes the aggressive socialist militant, as his opponents loved to portray him? It is perhaps unfair to see in the newly-elected ASE leader of 1896 the super-patriot of 1914, the Lloyd George Coalitionist who broke with official Labour at the Armistice. And yet Barnes's politics even in the 1890s had a cautious quality, evinced in his Rochdale campaign of 1895 as well as in his campaigns for the ASE General Secretaryship. A Rochdale activist recalled that he 'was run on the lines of independent Labour, as much or more so than as a socialist by the ILP'.[32] He was a legitimate heir to the tradition of capable ASE officials. He was backed by the Webbs on account of 'vigorous energy ... great official experience, proved integrity and the strictest regularity of habits'.[33]

It was not just a question of Barnes's political preferences. Any General Secretary of the ASE faced very strict limits on the extent to which he could impose a political perspective on the Society. It was not simply that many members had no commitment to advanced politics; it was also that the scope for a political initiative by a leading official was restricted. The decision-making process was cast in a pragmatic mould. Delegate Meetings considered political issues, as they had in 1892, in terms of changes of the rules; therefore discussion was in terms of specific items, not principled political alternatives. Similarly, the Executive had some leeway in terms of implementation or perhaps interpretation — against a resolutely pragmatic decision. Beneath such items, political divergences might lurk, but the structure and style of decision-making inevitably generated a blurring of options. Such a process was furthered by the question of priorities. For any union, and for the ASE in the mid nineties more perhaps than most, industrial strategy and unity were paramount. Politics had to take second place.[34]

This was particularly so during Barnes's first two years in the office as the increasing tensions between ASE members and employers reached a climax in the thirty weeks' lockout of July 1897—January 1898. The occasion for the dispute was an attempt by the ASE to achieve the eight-hour day in London workshops, but the crucial issue was that of technical change, and the degree to which managements should be allowed to determine its rate and extent. Although the dispute was a major clash on a relatively novel issue, its direct impact on the ASE membership was restricted. No more than 27,000 of the Society's members were locked out at any one time.[35] At the beginning the Engineers were optimistic — in August 1897, the *ASE Journal*, grateful that the break had come over 'Eight-Hours', could raise enthusiasm:

A trial of strength with the federation was inevitable, and the present is as favourable an opportunity as was likely to be presented to us. Trade is brisk, the weather good, and the issue a popular one.[36]

But three months later, the tone was very different:

No break, no whimpering or complaining, although the fight has had to be sustained under what is generally most depressing circumstances ... we have been ever on the defensive.[37]

Funds were limited, and the tough unity of the Employers' Federation was not matched on the union side. The Boilermakers and the Patternmakers refused to back the ASE,[38] and the TUC Parliamentary Committee did little. It was perhaps not surprising that ASE officials began to look for a way out, urged to do so by the increasingly respectable John Burns.[39] Intervention by the Board of Trade late in November appeard only to underline the desire of the Employers' Federation for a thorough solution of the machine question, and the ASE membership threw out the employers' proposals by 68,966 to 752.[40] But now the lockout was extended, the shortage of funds became even more acute, and in January 1898 ASE officials agreed to a settlement granting collective bargaining on general wage levels but giving employers massive discretion on the machine question, and relinquishing the demand for an eight-hour day. It was esentially a defeat for the ASE — a defeat accepted by an embattled membership by 28,588 to 13,727.[41]

A craft union had taken on a determined and united group of employers on the machine question; they had challenged managerial prerogatives and they had been defeated. Did this chastening experience, demonstrating perhaps the limitations of industrial action, carry any political implications? In fact, the questions of ILP involvement within the ASE ran through the dispute. One Tyneside employer mourned the good old days, claiming that: 'the degrading doctrines of the new unionism have so poisoned the ASE as to make them as a class fully 20 per cent less valuable than they ought to be'.[42] This view was shared by organs of Establishment opinion: *The Times* lamented that the ASE: 'a body once regarded as comparatively conservative in its action ... has fallen under the domination of an extremely aggressive set of leaders'.[43]

Sometimes the criticism was more specific. The Engineers' opposition to the new technology was 'due to the success of the Independent Labour Party in this particular society'. In particular there had been: 'a marked change for the worse in the spirit and conduct of the Engineers since the election of Mr. Barnes as secretary'. He was, after all, 'a declared Socialist', engaged not just in 'abstract aspirations for a future millenium', but also in the advocacy of a policy to lower unemployment by cutting hours.[44]

Such claims of ILP influence were obviously heartening for a party facing a decline in membership and a loss of optimism. The *Labour Leader* gave continual coverage to the Engineer's case: local ILPs organised supporting demonstrations and collected funds.[45] As the situation became more critical, ILPers campaigned in the press, in local trade union branches and on trades councils for a special TUC to organise concerted aid.[46] Hardie directed his wrath at the Parliamentary Committee: 'For sheer, helpless imbecility, (their) inaction ... stands unequalled'.[47] And in the York by-election of January 1898, the ILP attacked the Liberal candidate, the North-Eastern industrialist Sir Christopher Furness, as a supporter of the Engineering Employers.[48] In the end, the ILP's moral was predictable: 'fifty stalwart Labour members in the House of Commons would make a lock-out like this impossible'.[49] Was this conclusion accepted within the ASE?

It depends on which groups within the ASE are being discussed. By the late nineties, the Society not only had an ILPer as General Secretary, but its delegates to the TUC, including such men as Tom Proctor and Isaac Mitchell, tended to favour any resolutions backing Independent Labour representation or public ownership.[50] Once again, there is evidence that the activists involved in the election of such delegates had moved beyond Lib-Labism. Proctor, a long-standing socialist, was arguing in the aftermath of the 1897 TUC that much of its work was wasted due to:

the need of a strong force of Trade Union Labour Members in the House of Commons, independent of political parties ... pledged to carry out the mandate of the Trades Union Congress.[51]

It was up to the TUC to produce a scheme. Here, there is a clear foreshadowing by an ASE ILPer of the project that emerged in February 1900. Yet the Society's involvement with this was at first tentative.

The Executive still had the Delegate Meeting decision of 1892 regarding parliamentary representation awaiting implementation; and in 1899, after much activist pressure, a ballot was held on the question of a parliamentary levy. The result showed that the question of Independent Labour politics evoked little reaction amongst the members, despite recent industrial experiences and despite the work of ILPers within the Society; 3,530 voted in favour, 842 against, but more than 80,000 members did not vote at all.[52] Apathy led to the Executive delaying any further action. Nevertheless, the ASE did send a delegation to the foundation conference of the LRC, although the speech of one of its members, John Burns, attempted to undermine the idea of independent working-class political action.[53] A ballot was held in March on the question of LRC affiliation, but interest here was even less than on the levy question. 2,897 voted for and 702 against. Barnes wrote pessimistically to MacDonald 'the members of the Society have evinced so little interest in the question of Parliamentary representation that I cannot see how we can take part'.[54] But some activists revived the issue at the 1901 Delegate Meeting. It was decided there that permanent officials should be eligible for financial support if they ran as parliamentary candidates, and also that the Executive could join the LRC with the sanction of a further membership vote.[55] The vote was held, and favoured joining the LRC by 5,626 to 1,070. It was hardly evidence of rank and file commitment to the idea of political independence, but it enabled the Executive to affiliate.[56]

The shift of the ASE was now apparently clear — the Executive had proclaimed that all ASE candidates should stand 'on independent lines and independent of all political parties'.[57] These developments formed a sharp contrast with the Society's traditional position; they were clearly a product of industrial change, and the influence of a relatively small number of socialist activists, aided by the uninterested position of the bulk of the membership. If socialists had been important in this development, it was not because they campaigned on any socialist ticket. The ASE position was expressed resolutely in terms of a trade union or labour commitment, a readily intelligible development given the craft tradition and highly pragmatic decision-making processes of the Society.

Eventually, five ASE candidates stood under LRC auspices in 1906 (see Table 9). All candidates took as primary the question of Labour representation

Table 9.

Candidate	Constituency	Opponents	Result
George Barnes	Glasgow Blackfriars	Cons and Lib	1st 29.5%
Isaac Mitchell	Darlington	Lib Un	2nd 48.3%
Charles Duncan	Barrow	Cons	1st 60.3%
Frank Rose	Stockton	Cons and Lib	3rd 23.1%
Tom Proctor	Grimsby	Lib Un and Lib	3rd 17.8%

separate from the established parties. This, after all, was what they were committed to by ASE policy. But beyond this there were significant divergences. Barnes remained a moderate ethical socialist, a member of the ILP; Proctor was much more a militant adherent to socialist principles. He had been identified as such ever since he had been involved in John Burns's Nottingham campaign in 1885. Rose, too, was clearly committed to socialism, although his individualism meant that he failed to develop a lasting relationship with any organisation. The other two candidates were rather different — Duncan's commitment seems to have stopped at the idea of a vague political independence. A disillusioned Barrow supporter poured out his doubts to MacDonald, after Duncan's 1906 victory:

amongst Socialists, and some who are not, Duncan is known here as the 'wobbler'. He conciliated every section but the Tories ... When asked if he was a Socialist, he said 'Yes a Socialist like John Burns'. He has only once in the whole of his visits to Barrow come to the ILP Rooms lest he should be thought a Socialist.[58]

Mitchell, a strong advocate of socialist policies in the nineties showed every sign of moving to a closer relationship with Radical Liberalism.[59]

Inevitably, these varying political positions provoked difficulties. Mitchell's desire to court the Darlington Liberals led to questions about Rose's involvement in nearby Stockton, and to tensions within the Society. Predictably, Rose and Proctor emerged as the defenders of complete independence, and no involvement at all with the Liberals. In contrast, Barnes certainly sought local Liberal support and in the end was opposed only by an idiosyncratic anti-Home Rule Liberal, whilst Mitchell and Duncan secured considerable support from local Liberals.[60]

It is easy to see this as the virtual collapse of any independent political identity. Yet there were limits to the Executive's willingness to compromise. Despite considerable pressure they went ahead with the Stockton candidature when it would have been relatively easy to have abandoned it, as an aid to Mitchell. And when Burns entered the Liberal Cabinet, his financial support from the ASE was discontinued.[61]

This severance reflected Burns's own alienation from the ASE whcih he now dismissed as 'dominated by a fanatical and vindictive' ILP clique.[62] This assessment is so partial as to be a grotesque misunderstanding. By 1906, ASE officials and activists were committed largely to political independence, in itself a major change which must be placed in the context of industrial developments and defeat. But the quality of the change also must be appreciated. It occurred through a series of pragmatic decisions over rules and their implementation — in so far as it had an overtly partisan form, it was that of Labour and trade union representation, not socialism. It was hardly surprising that the custodians of such a change, especially the flexible Barnes, responded readily to further constraints. The priority of industrial matters was one factor. Another was the question of relationships with Liberals. Closeness was facilitated by the rapport between their views and those of Barnes, Mitchell and Duncan; it was also fostered by a natural wish to use Society funds in successful election campaigns.

If the ILP influence was diluted when it came down to political tactics, this was also because it remained limited to a very small section of the membership. For many engineers political action had a low priority. This was evident not just in the minimal involvement in ballots on political matters; it could be discovered also in the reactions of ASE members where the local candidate was sponsored by the Society. The lack of interest could be due to rank and file dislike of Executive industrial policies — Barnes's candidature nearly came to an early end because of the Executive's failure to support Glasgow members in a local dispute. More fundamentally, perhaps, the ASE's Barrow District Committee seems to have remained aloof from Duncan's campaign, sceptical of any political solution to their problems.[63] ILP activists might have changed union policy on political matters, but they had had little impact on the rank and file. Despite the major technical changes of the nineties, many engineers continued to see the remedy for their difficulties in local industrial responses; the ASE was not yet an effective agent for political mobilisation.

The National Union of Boot and Shoe Operatives — a socialist union?

The Spring of 1895 witnessed a lockout in the boot and shoe trade — the climax to a period of increasing bitterness between employers and workers. One Leicester Liberal Alderman pointed out a moral:

On the surface this struggle might appear to be a quarrel between the employers and the workmen with regard to the wages being paid for work done. In reality, however, it was nothing of the kind (hear, hear). This was one of the first industrial fights on Socialism.[64]

A Leicester employer agreed: 'the union had been captured by Socialists and by the Independent Labour Party who were advocating doctrines not only inimical to the trade, but to the working men themselves'.[65] The same characterisation was suggested by the formal commitments of the union. By 1894, the NUBSO's objectives included: 'The Nationalisation of the Land, and the implements of Production and Distribution'.[66] A decade later the commitment had sharpened and now embraced:

The socialisation of the means of production to be controlled by a Democratic State in the interests of the entire community, and the complete emancipation of Labour from the domination of Capitalism and Landlordism, with the establishment of a social and economic equality between the sexes.[67]

This was a much more thorough socialist commitment than that of many other unions. It could lead to early support for the inclusion of a socialist objective within the Labour Party Constitution. Thus a prominent Northampton SDF member serving as one of the union's delegates supported such a change in both 1907 and 1908, justifying it on account of his own union's commitment.[68] The Boot and Shoe Operatives was one of the small minority of unions evincing a desire to change the original basis of the Labour Alliance. If this fact is complemented by an emphasis that the bootmaking centres of Leicester and Norwich had strong ILPs in which workers within the industry were prominent, that Northampton had a significant SDF and that links between Bristol socialists and the industry were close, then the claim that the union was a socialist organisation acquires further plausibility.[69] The connections and the commitment were important, and the influence of individual ILP members was significant. T. F. Richards, a prominent member of the Leicester ILP, was the union's successful parliamentary candidate in 1906 and later the union's President.[70] But the consequences of the early formal indentification with socialism were not clear-cut — the union moved steadily to the right in its political policies after 1906. In order to understand the role of the ILP within this 'socialist union', it is essential to begin with an analysis of the state of the industry in the last fifteen years of the nineteenth century.[71]

The NUBSO in the early nineties was a relatively strong trade union, with 44,000 members by the end of 1894. But such strength must be placed in the context of growing industrial problems. Mechanisation had started to have an impact on the trade in the eighties, and within a few years threatened even the most complex of hand operations. Innovations led to a sharp increase in the sub-division of labour, a growing tendency to employ boys, a threat to the position of traditional craftsmen from new, easily assimilated processes, and a drive towards more sub-contracted outwork. For employers, it was apparent that, as one of them expressed if, 'Humanity must make room for iron'.[72] The search for the benefits of mechanisation intensified as competition from American imports grew dramatically. This was a major challenge to the union, and in particular to its existing leadership.

The response was affected by union structures, by the style of existing leadership and by the nature of the workforce. Officials had always been identified closely with Lib-Labism, a commitment epitomised in the nineties by the beliefs and style of the General Secretary, William Inskip, a Leicester Alderman whose industrial toughness and tactical adroitness were combined with fervent Gladstonianism and a Smilesian outlook.[73] Inevitably, such a dominant full-time official could exercise major influence, although there were countervailing tendencies. Other union institutions were heavily democratic, with an Executive Council elected on a geographical basis, and a Biennial Conference laying down union policy.[74] Moreover, there was no restriction on repeated re-election to either body so that a nucleus of experienced opponents to Inskip could take root. Union structures were affected also by the location of the industry. The tendency for production to be concentrated in a few centres meant that some branches, most notably the Leicester No. 1 Branch, were very large. Not only did they — or at least their activists — play a predominant part in national union decision-making, but they also had significant local powers. They could elect their own permanent officials and played a major role in wage negotiations. Such localism reflected patterns of production and payment. Here was an industry in which piecework was the norm, with lists varying between towns and between classes of work. Units of production varied equally: there was factory production in Leicester, but in many smaller towns and villages, more traditional, small-scale units endured, with trade unionism barely known.[75] The union faced not only major technical challenges but had to organise in an industry where local sentiments tended to outweigh emotions of national solidarity. In such a setting, the achievement of such a large membership was a considerable one, but the tensions of the early nineties clearly suggested that scope existed for an alternative socialist leadership to outbid the cautious and established Lib-Labs.

This alternative leadership developed in some of the larger centres: in the London Metro Branch, in Northampton, and, perhaps most significantly, in Leicester, where an aggressive policy was associated with a group of young activists, especially T. F. Richards. Within the industrial field, the critics found abundant ammunition for campaigns against the Liberals. The tensions within the trade were revealed in the arguments over conciliation and arbitration.[76] The industry had developed an elaborate machinery for this purpose, with local boards, umpires, and industry-wide national conferences. The latter were the peak of an elaborate system, held in Leicester Town Hall, involving 'elaborate debates conducted with all the ceremony of a State Trial'.[77] Yet, this supposedly finely-tuned machinery rarely operated smoothly. There were recurrent complaints from groups of operatives that the machinery was ponderous and biased.[78] Critics of the union leadership began to argue that an aggressive strike policy would be more effective; in both London and Leicester, there was significant opposition to the established procedures. Here was an issue which generated a clear division inside the union. This was articulated sharply at a special Delegate Conference in Leicester in April 1893. For the arbitrationists, Inskip derived the policy of aggressive strikes: 'It was an appeal to the passions ... sensible men discussed and reasoned'.[79] Arbitration was particularly important given the current technical changes: 'they would be able to keep their men employed on that machinery at a fair rate of wages'.[80] Moreover, as another Liberal arbitrationist implied, many workers had much more to lose than their chains, for those 'thousands ... whose conditions had been vastly improved ... the resort to unnecessary strikes would mean untold misery and suffering to themselves and their families'.[81] The critics did not rest in every case with an appeal to the greater effectiveness of the strike weapon. Already some were prepared to draw a socialist conclusion from their industrial experience. One Northampton socialist argued that: 'the only hope of the masses of the people ... was getting control of the industries themselves',[82] or as a colleague expressed it succinctly: 'They must abolish the capitalists and ... obtain control of the means of production, distribution and exchange'.[83]

This extension of the argument is important as were other features of this meeting. Socialist delegates attacked the union leadership for inviting employers to address delegates on the merits of conciliation, and then for lunching with them. They condemned those ready to: 'waste time in drinking whiskey and champagne with those parasites who lived on the life blood of the nation'.[84]

The critics made an impact, but they were very much a minority at the Leicester Conference. In the end, a pro-arbitration resolution was carried by 74 votes to 9.[85] This dual emphasis is important. The changing circumstances of the industry were beginning to suggest a need for aggressive policies, a few drew a Socialist moral, but many were happy to back the established officials.

Despite the Liberals' easy victory on arbitration, the ever-growing effect of technical changes threw up issue after issue on which leaders had to declare an opinion that would satisfy their own activists, and permit continuing bargaining with employers who themselves felt subjected to tightening constraints.[86] Between these two millstones, it is hardly surprising that Liberal confidence began to waver. Urban workers clamoured about the growing tendency of employers to send lower-grade work out to cheaper village producers. Since this cost advantage owed much to the prevalence of out-working in rural district, the union response tended to be one of campaigning for the abolition of outwork, and the concentration of production in factories. But such agitation was seen as being against the immediate interests of many rural workers, whilst there was a more general ambivalence since the drives for factory production and a stronger union were yoked with problems of intensifying mechanisation. Rationalisation of production within factory units was met by union concern to maintain traditional methods of payment. When attempts were made to organise hitherto independent workers into teams, thereby increasing productivity, employers encountered a union vehemently defending the old methods of calculating wages. This defence inevitably meant that employers would gain nothing from such a rationalisation of production, and the idea was dropped.

This tactic of attempting to anull the advantages of any reorganisation for the employer was followed also in the most crucial area of all — that of the introduction of new machinery. By the early nineties, mechanisation was beginning to affect the lasting and finishing processes, two areas where the position of the traditional craftsman had been regarded as secure. Now the questions of job-security and of payment for operating the new machines became of central importance. These were basic issues on which the Liberal leadership had to respond, and where local socialist activists could hope to make much of the running. One response was to restrict output. In Leicester, where day-wages were the rule on recently introduced machinery, the strategy was to calculate how much output under the old piece-rate system would be needed to obtain the present day-wage — and then to produce only that amount. For employers fearful of foreign competition, such a restriction cut deep; for the union leadership, it posed problems.[87] Inskip and his allies risked alienating support in leading centres if they showed no sympathy, but they also wished to keep relationships with employers on a reasonable basis. In the end, it proved impossible to ride these two horses.

Crisis was precipitated by a Leicester initiative on the question of payment for machine work. Here was a question on which the Liberals had clearly failed to lead, perhaps fearing that piecework statements for machines would lead to workers increasing their productivity, thereby generating more unemployment. But now, the Leicester No. 1 Branch, under Richards's encouragement, sought to devise a piecework statement that would remove any advantage to employers from mechanisation. The Leicester men concentrated on the lasting and finishing processes, where mechanisation was a current threat. The result of their labours was to devise a piece-rate statement that preserved much of the old content of earlier statements for hand-work on these processes. The only change was to deduct from each price a percentage equivalent to the interest on the cost of the new machines. Thus employers would gain nothing from introducing them. Here was a device which sought to protect labour and also to secure the net advantage of any new invention. It could be seen as a characteristic response by what had been an industry of individual producers to the growth of mechanised factory production. It also fitted in with a socialist commitment to workers obtaining the whole product of their labour. Socialists could build on and gain inspiration from a desire for 'the world we have lost'.[88]

This response on payment, and the failure of the Liberals on the Executive Council to oppose it, clearly helped to produce a flight by employers towards a more aggressive position. Like the union leadership, they felt squeezed: in their case between foreign competition and union recalcitrance. They contrasted British and American reactions to new machines:

In America the men *work*, they run the machines to the utmost capacity, and vie with each other in their endeavour to get through as much work as possible. But in an English factory, they seem to loaf away their time in a manner which is perfectly exasperating.[89]

Now events within the industry moved inexorably to the Great Lockout of March 1895. This was a watershed in the union's development, the terms marking the final victory of mechanised factory production. From then on, the links between economic changes and political expressions take a different form. Until 1895, the agenda of industrial problems was placing the union's Liberals under pressure, and some critics were drawing socialist conclusions — but how far did these developments leave their mark on the political commitments of the union?

The most important vein of argument concerned the possibility of running a union-sponsored parliamentary candidate. Like other unions, the NUBSO had some objectives the furtherance of which clearly required political action, including the control of 'pauper immigration'.[90] By 1891, the issue of sponsoring a candidate, or Parliamentary Agent as he became designated, had become an important one. Interest in 'Direct' Labour Representation was expressed initially in a Northampton resolution,[91] but some members wished to push matters further. One Leicester correspondent, drawing on the Irish parallel, urged that improvements in working-class conditions could be secured:

'only by forming a Labour party independent of either of the great political parties'.[92] A second Leicester member asserted that: 'nothing can possibly be got for bettering the conditions of the masses by sending either Tory landlords or Liberal Capitalists to Parliament'.[93] The question of Independent — as opposed to simply Direct — Labour Representation was there from the beginning.

This distinction was raised in debate at the 1892 Conference.[94] Some, such as the London socialist William Votier, argued for independence since: 'Neither Liberal nor Conservative party cared for the welfare of the worker',[95] but Inskip, heavily involved in Leicester Liberalism, employed his own experience in municipal politics, as an argument:

I, myself, made my success such as it was by Liberal party aid, and I say we are justified in using both political parties so long as we attain the object we have in view — direct labour representation.[96]

But this position was opposed not just by socialists, but also by pragmatists — a Leeds delegate urged independence since: 'In Leeds fully half of their members were Tories';[97] and one committed Radical-Liberal urged that they be: 'labour men first — Conservatives, Liberals or Socialists afterwards'.[98] The requirement that the union candidate be 'independent of either political party' was carried by 42 votes to 4, despite Inskip's opposition.[99] No doubt the majority contained many divergent definitions of 'independence', but nevertheless the commitment had been made. Inskip remained unhappy, arguing that the independence requirement would prevent the success of any candidate, but he readily accepted nomination as Parliamentary Agent.

By February 1893, the General Secretary was appearing before a meeting of Northampton union members, as a possible local candidate. This initial meeting served to demonstrate the gulf between Inskip's old-style Liberalism and the socialism of some members.[100] The would-be candidate's programme included such standard Liberal nostrums as land reform, suffrage reform, an eight-hour day in dangerous trades, plus the union's concern to control immigration. On other areas of possible state intervention he was much more coy:

As for old age pensions, he did not believe in too much of that kind of business. He would sooner pay a man a sufficient wage that he could take care of himself than pander to him and make him a semi-pauper.[101]

Such an unadventurous Smilesian programme provoked a ribald response from Northampton socialists:

There was scarcely an old Whig in the House of Commons that would not agree to such a programme as Mr. Inskip's. It was nothing only political claptrap.[102]

Although the number of opponents in the meeting was small, the existence of opposition amongst union activists was undeniable. As in the industrial field, Inskip attempted to accommodate them by extending his programme over the next twelve months to include pensions, the nationalisation of land, mines, quarries, telephones, and direct employment by public authorities[103]

But given industrial differences within the union and the emergence of the ILP, it was clear that Inskip with his obvious unwillingness to relinquish a traditional Liberal standpoint would face a significant challenge in the 1894 Conference. An initial passage of arms occurred there when Richards moved as an addition to the union's objectives, the 'Nationalisation of the land and the implements of production and distribution',[104] citing both John Stuart Mill and the 1893 TUC as supporting authorities. Inskip, although clearly unhappy about the motion, had decided to save his arguments for the more immediate question.[105] The resolution then passed after little debate and with no votes against.

The discussion on the Parliamentary Agent was a much more contentious affair.[106] Initially, debate developed on a Stafford resolution that the candidate should accept the Labour Programme as laid down by the TUC. Inevitably this was carried without opposition, although it did imply one element that Inskip was unhappy about, namely the 1893 TUC decision on collective ownership of the means of production.[107] More crucially, this early discussion demonstrated the ambiguities, surrounding the commitment to independence. One Leicester Lib-Lab argued for the development of their own programme, but then for taking political support from whatever (presumably Liberal) source it was offered. In contrast, Frank Sheppard the Bristol Labour leader claimed that independence certainly involved isolation from other parties.[108]

Differences became much more apparent when an attempt was made to clarify the political position of the Parliamentary Agent — essentially a Liberal gambit for liberation from what they saw as the stultifying independence requirement passd two years earlier. Stanton, a Northampton Liberal, argued for the rescinding of the earlier decision on grounds of practicality — the idea that workers would oppose capitalists politically was naive:

In Northampton if they had a big strike, the workmen on the spur of the moment might combine against the capitalists and run a man in, but under ordinary circumstances they might take it from him that their chance at Northampton was damned through the 'independent' resolution.[109]

But opposed to this there were the committed socialists: Richards argued that he could not support candidates sponsored by Liberal Associations, citing the German Social Democrats as a positive example, and affirming that: 'those who opposed them industrially would oppose them politically'.[110] But unlike 1892, the pragmatic argument pointed towards rescindment, and the independence commitment was removed by 33 votes to 14.[111] It appeared that on the political issue of immediate importance, Inskip had secured a victory.

However, this was not to be. Throughout the discussion references had been made to the need for a political programme and a committee was appointed immediately to draft one. Its membership was certainly not dominated by socialists. Although Richards was a member, he was balanced by the Lib-Lab, Woolley, while Freak and Poulton were pragmatists, not socialists, but ready to go along with what they felt was the broad drift of trade union opinion.[112]

When the programme was presented to the Conference[113] most of it proved to be impeccably Radical — but one item evoked a sharp response from Inskip:

The Nationalisation of the Land, Mines, Quarries, and all means of Production and Distribution, and abolition of Mining Rents, Royalties, and Way Leaves.

The General Secretary wished to stick at the 'ultimate' nationalisation of land, mines and quarries.[114] But he met massive opposition. In part this was perhaps because the wider commitment was now formally part of the union objective, but it was clear in the debate that Inskip's austere economics were unacceptable to some who saw themselves as Liberals. Stanton justified public ownership as a means of alleviating unemployment, whilst from the 'Labour' viewpoint Poulton justified it as 'simply carrying out the theories of Trades' Unionism to the ultimate end, the emancipation of labour'.[115]

Perhaps the most significant contribution came from Freak the pragmatist:

If a man introduced a machine which made things much quicker than before, and cheaper, the patent should not be bought up by capitalists who could rig the market and make a big profit for themselves. Such patents ought to be bought by the Government, and worked for the good of the people.[116]

Here is a pragmatic trade union leader absorbing experience of technical changes, and producing a political conclusion. It was a conclusion acceptable to delegates, but not to Inskip who resigned as Parliamentary Agent refusing to place himself 'at the mercy of any hare-brained Members who choose to bring in a Bill of Confiscation'.[117]

The Liberals within the union had suffered major setbacks: there was now a public ownership commitment amongst the union objectives and within the political programme, and the candidature of the leading Liberal had been made subject to conditions that he would not accept. No doubt the Liberal position could have been defended better by some one more 'advanced' or flexible than Inskip, but the real basis for the Liberal retreat was economic, with grievances providing abundant bases for socialist agitation. But the decisions that have been examined were essentially the result of arguments between the activists. What reason is there to believe that economic experiences had generated any wider radicalisation of the union membership?

Evidence is sparse but suggestive. Even on the narrowly economic issues, the head of steam behind the socialist campaigns was not always very great. Thus, early in 1894 the Leicester members voted that the Executive Council should ballot members on the desirability of ending arbitration. But the number voting was very small — only 683 of a total membership of 7,000 — and the majority for the proposal was only 33.[118] Even militant Leicester on a crucial economic question was both passive and divided. These same traits can be found in political fields. Although the NUBSO was an organisation with frequent elections for officers and delegates, turnout was typically meagre. In the summer of 1893, the Lib-Lab Hornidge defeated the socialist Votier in a presidential election by 2,205 votes to 1,057. Moreover the supposedly socialist-dominated branches showed divided viewpoints — London Metro (Votier's base) voted 138 for him but 73 for his opponent. Northampton backed the Lib-Lab by 310 votes to 63, whilst Richards's Leicester No. 1 Branch split Votier 299, Hornidge 271.[119] The split between Liberals and socialists — or conciliators and militants — ran through the active minority.

It was not just a question of who was persuaded, but also what the commitment to a new political objective was considered to entail. It was easy to shift something like a union's formal commitment to public ownership of the means of production to a Never-Never Land of ideal aspirations, having minimal relevance to immediate issues. It could cohabit with harsh ideas about the undeserving poor. One delegate to the 1894 Conference reflected that although he had supported public ownership as a union objective: 'he did not mean to say that a man who would not work, should have equal food and clothing with those who did work'.[120] The significance of the Socialist advance was problematic. How far were the gains purely symbolic? Were they merely the sentiments of a few activists? There remains the question of how far the reaction of craftsmen to major technical changes can serve as the basis for a socialist politics. Certainly there were links, as had been made clear in the debates over political action, but how durable those connections would prove to be as technical changes proceeded was another matter.

The most important episode in this sequence of technical change and industrial polarisation was the lockout of March—April 1895.[121] The build-up to the lockout showed how far the events of the previous few years had led employers to take a stand against what they saw as 'extreme Socialistic doctrines encroaching upon the individual rights of manufacturers'.[122]

The negotiations centred around the so-called 'Seven Commandments' of the employers. These dealt with managerial powers over new machinery and more generally work discipline, including specific opposition to piece-payments on lasting and finishing machinery, and to restriction of output, plus freedom for employers to move work between towns.[123] Such a programme represented a basic attack on union policies, and particularly on the aggressive strategies associated with the socialists. Initially, the union leadership temporised, rejecting the proposals but backing a National Conference as opposed to the alternative of quitting the arbitration machinery forthwith. The membership vote on this policy revealed that even on such a crucial question there was a considerable amount of apathy. Detailed voting figures give a clear indication of the centres which favoured a more aggressive trade policy (see Table 10).[124]

Inevitably, the breakdown came. The Liberal officials found the employers

Table 10. *Voting on the 'Seven Commandments'*

	Whole Membership	Leicester, London, Bristol	Rest
For Executive	5,046	1,278	3,678
Against Executive	1,930	1,718	212
Total Vote		6,976	
Total Membership		33,379	

opposed to a Conference, and had to make a stand in order to avoid losing all initiative to their critics. The match was put to the gunpowder by the union making wage demands on behalf of worker in selected Leicester and Northampton factories; yet the explosive mixture was compounded of elements other than disagreements over wages. The machine question and managerial prerogatives were not all — for some employers the confrontation had a political purpose. One London employer claimed that:

The struggle is not with the men or with Trade Unionism as such, but ... against the pernicious and most outrageous doctrines that are being disseminated by the extreme Socialistic Party ... that section has managed to capture and lead the Executive at Leicester.

One of his colleagues affirmed quite simply that 'the Executive of the Union has been captured by the Socialists and the ILP'.[125] These assertions are not supported by the facts: although Liberals were under considerable pressure, they still held both Presidency and General Secretaryship and could usually block socialists on the Executive.

Nevertheless, the ILP did see the lockout as an opportunity for building support, encouraged in Leicester by their promising vote in a by-election the previous summer. It was there that the party's energies tended to be concentrated during the stoppage, with Fred Brocklehurst, Sam Hobson and Enid Stacy attempting to drive home the political significance of the dispute. Hobson portrayed it as 'a forcible example of the evils of modern private capitalism',[126] and argued that many of the employers involved were Liberals who; 'hate the Socialist-Labour movement with a bitter hatred. They are fighting because the National Union of Boot and Shoe Operatives is a Socialist society'.[127] So ILP propagandists took up the political claims of some employers and answered them in kind — this was standard propagandist practice. However, there was one aspect of the dispute that worried some visiting ILPers — the predominance of piece-rate payments in the industry. After all, such payments were seen by many socialists as one of the more obnoxious manifestations of capitalism, an effective technique of exploitation and a method of dividing workers. And yet here was a dispute where local socialists wished to hold fast to piece-rates on new machinery. Hobson was robustly practical:

Most of us have a lively horror of that method of industrial remuneration ... But the prominent ILP men in Leicester like Councillor Fred Richards are supporters of piece-work payment in their own trade. However much academic objections may be taken, it is surely right to regard local opinion in the matter.[128]

Did the brute factor of a lockout, in itself a failure for Inskip's basic outlook, lead to any radicalisation of the rank and file? The lockout ended after six weeks with most of the employers' proposals being accepted. It was a fundamental check to those who sought to counter mechanisation through an aggressive industrial policy.[129] But the fact of a settlement inevitably provoked criticism from the union's left wing. A mass meeting in Leicester produced considerable criticism of the national officials, with Richards alleging that the employers had obtained all but one-and-a-half of their seven demands. Political differences were clearly exhibited in this argument: Liberals strongly defended the terms, and hinted that opposition came from outside the union.[130] Even at this stage an ambivalence was beginning to appear in Richards's attitudes. Although he attacked the settlement, he had previously agreed that the Executive should settle on the best available terms. Sometimes critic and sometimes pragmatist, which role he played depended on the occasion.

After the initial hostile reaction from some workers, however, the union accommodated itself to the new order. Over the next decade membership declined almost continually. At the end of 1894, it had stood at almost 44,000; at the end of 1906, it had fallen to 24,000. This fall was a symptom of other more basic changes. The late nineties were years of depression, and there were particular difficulties in Norwich where a long, disastrous stoppage occurred in 1897. But above all, the pace of mechanisation increased still further, with a tendency for old trade unionists to be displaced by younger operatives, often with little attachment to the union. This development clearly was facilitated by the employers' victory of 1895. Loss of union funds, and increased bargaining freedoms for employers allowed mechanisation to go through with little resistance.[131]

The decade was clearly one in which tough industrial action was hardly a promising option. But the union already had a commitment to political action — moreover a commitment with a clear socialist slant. Did awareness of industrial weakness lead to a greater emphasis on political initiatives? On one level, that of the rank and file membership, any commitment to Independent Labour — let alone socialist — politics was very limited in the late nineties. Whether such an attachment had declined in the aftermath of the lockout is unclear, but when Inskip died in 1899, the resulting election for the General Secretaryship was fought on clear political lines. The two principal contenders were W. Hornidge, a Lib-Lab, and T. F. Richards of the ILP. It was a clear victory for Liberalism: on the second ballot, the margin was 4,501 to 3,139. Even in Leicester, Richards's stronghold, the Liberal had a majority of the votes. Although this contest was one in which only a minority of the membership participated, it is the most extensive measure of opinion where a choice with clear political overtones was offered. And here, despite all that had happened in this 'Socialist Union' the Liberals remained in control.[132]

In other areas of union decision-making, the degree of rank and file involvement was much less, and there Independent Labour influence could be more successful. This was particularly so in the case of the union's attempts to secure parliamentary representation. This issue emerged again at the 1896 Conference, with discussion centering around the union's failure to run a candidate at Leicester in 1895.[133] Independent Labour partisans alleged that there had been a compact with the Liberals there.[134] Inskip, whilst denying this, accepted that there was a 'mutual understanding' in municipal contests.[135] Such an argument, whilst demonstrating yet again the political division inside the union, led to no immediate development, although now the elections for the post of Parliamentary Agent were being contested on political lines. The lack of progress on the question was due in part to the union's financial situation, and the issue stagnated until 1900.[136] By then, however, one important development had occurred. On a very small poll, and after much mutual disqualifying of votes, Richards replaced Stanton as Parliamentary Agent. It was hardly the consequence of a mass mobilisation. After votes had been disallowed, the final totals were Richards 646, Stanton, the Liberal, 641.[137] Yet now the potential parliamentary representative of the union was for the first time someone firmly committed (or so it seemed) to Independent Labour politics.

This change was giving added bite by the TUC's Plymouth Resolution. The political decisions of the union inevitably led to support for this, with one London delegate speaking for the ASRS resolution. His argument suggests that perhaps industrial difficulties had made political action more attractive: 'Their efforts should be directed towards removing the fight from the industrial to the political field'.[138] The union's delegates to the LRC foundation conference — Freak and Richards were both sympathetic to the strategy for political independence — and their report on the proceedings suggested a more ambitious projection than that of some other delegates. The decisions could

be the means of establishing in this country a party that should include all Labour interests whether Trade Unionist — or Socialist ... As for the Official Liberal party who are simply working for self-interest, and who belong to companies, who have shares in all the circumstances of the world, who are owners of land, who have no sympathy with the workers, who are the proprietors of different combines or syndicates, it will ride them over to their unofficial associates, the Conservatives.[139]

Here there was a prognostication not just of a Labour Alliance, but of a long-term change in the party system, with Labour ultimately not a pressure group, but a serious contender for power. Such a vision was a testimony to the development of Independent Labour sentiments amongst some of the activists — but such enthusiasm was clearly limited to a few. The 1900 Union Conference had to face the question of affiliation to the LRC — a course urged in an introductory speech by MacDonald, the LRC candidate for Leicester.[140] Now the style of Richards was accommodating: 'they wanted unity on Labour questions ... in this new party there was no attempt to prevent a man being a Liberal, a Tory or a Socialist', and anyway the resolution 'would be furthering one of their objects'.[141] Not all speakers were so diplomatic, one claimed that: 'there was no difference between the advanced Radical and the moderate Tory'.[142] Many delegates must have been unhappy about this claim, but the resolution was for a membership ballot, a proposal difficult to oppose, and it passed unanimously.[143] The consequential ballot showed the overwhelming indifference of most members; affiliation was supported by 1,500 to 675 — enough for it to go forward. Much of the opposition came from the traditionally militant Leicester No. 1 Branch. Here the vote went for affiliation by 295 to 277. Probably it was here, where political divisions were well developed, that the decision was seen as one with possibly major political implications, and this perception led to a keen contest. Elsewhere, polls were favourable, but perhaps more as a reflection of a belief that most national leaders seemed committed to the idea than of any clear political choice. Certainly, amongst those interested enough to vote, Richards's hold on the Parliamentary Agency remained slim, being reaffirmed in the post over Stanton by only 1,360 votes to 1,148.[144] Thus, by the Autumn of 1900, the union was affiliated to the LRC and had an ILPer as parliamentary candidate — both developments reflecting the enthusiasm of the few, not the conversion of the many.

But even those actively involved in the union's political decisions differed over the implications of the LRC affiliation. This was demonstrated clearly at the 1902 Delegate Conference when the ubiquitous Richards attempted to secure the acceptance of a new union object — 'To use all legitimate means and funds to further Labour Representation independent of capitalistic parties'.[145] This produced strong opposition from Liberals, and even from Freak, a LRC supporter who claimed that the final phrase was contrary to the spirit of the LRC. The original resolution was dropped in favour of an anodyne proposition backing Labour Representation.[146] This Conference clearly did not adopt a radical interpretation of the LRC's role.

This was emphasised even more forcibly in a second debate, again initiated by the Leicester ILPers. Clearly the viability of the Labour Alliance was dependent upon the extent to which a trade union could cash industrial solidarity into a political currency. An attempt to induce such a transfer was expressed in a Leicester resolution that:

Branch officials shall not support candidates for public positions in opposition to the nominee of the Labour Representation Committee. Officers acting contrary to these instructions shall be deemed to be working against the interest of the Union.[147]

This attempt to specify one political commitment as in the union's interest provoked widespread opposition. In part this related to the specific Leicester situation. MacDonald's 1900 candidacy was presented by Liberals as having let in a Conservative. Surely the rational and proper tactic there was to support Henry Broadhurst.[148] But beyond this, the opposition demonstrated a deep-rooted distaste for introducing political matters into the union. Hornidge blamed industrial weakness on the fact 'that there was too much political trickery in the Union'.[149] Other speakers recalled how at branch meetings: 'they ignored politics altogether'.[150] What was wanted was 'trade unionism and not politics'.[151] The ILP response was to deny the distinction — the TUC was involved inevitably in politics — and to stress that it was a commitment simply to Labour that was being demanded: 'They did not ask their officials to join any of the Socialist organisations'.[152] But the Conference went along with a looser commitment recommending members to support the LRC candidates;[153] socialists had to hope that attachment to the union would be enough. They could gain limited encouragement perhaps from the 1904 Conference decision to insert a more detailed socialist objective into the rule book, despite Hornidge's reservations. He claimed that: 'by the insertion of these Socialistic definite ideals in their rule book, they were driving men away from their Union, and it was the reason of many men refusing to join them'.[154] However, the insertion of such an objective was far less crucial for many activists than attempts to pin down their freedom of political action. It might give legitimacy to socialists concerning the position the union delegation should adopt at the Labour Party Conference, but it did little to influence more immediate political developments.

The immediate question in the political field was now the parliamentary candidacy of T. F. Richards. On the eve of the 1900 election the Wolverhampton ILP had written to the Union's Executive Council, inviting Richards to stand for West Wolverhampton, but the Executive, after taking local soundings, decided not to take the matter further.[155] However, early in 1903, Richards was adopted as Labour candidate for the same seat.[156] From the very start, Richards, so long the hammer of Leicester Liberalism, attempted to unite all elements against the sitting Tory. Even before the MacDonald—Gladstone pact he informed union members that: 'We are doing our best to get the support of all Progressives',[157] and two days later he emphasised his attachment to Free Trade and his opposition to the Balfour Government.[158] This strategy had received an early endorsement from the Union's Executive. On 26 October 1903, it had passed a resolution expressing the belief that:

to ask for the support of any of the other parties will not contravene the objects of our Union or the principles of the Labour Representation Committee and trust that the local LRC will adopt and act upon this resolution.[159]

Eventually, his courting of the Wolverhampton Liberals grew too intense for many inside the ILP. During the election campaign Hardie cancelled an engagement to speak for him, observing ruefully that: 'I have had a few surprises in the world of politics during the past year or two, but yours is the greatest'.[160] MacDonald's criticisms were more circumspect, and he was perhaps embarrassed by Richards's use of his union influence in Leicester to bring the MacDonald—Gladstone pact to local fruition by urging members to split their votes between the Lib-Lab, Broadhurst, and MacDonald. Richards remained unrepentant — 'although I may have offended the ILP, I have not yet offended my Union'.[161] The Boot and Shoe Operatives might have secured an uncompromisingly socialist objective, but its parliamentary expression, in the dapper form of a once-militant ILPer, was the very model of Lib-Lab respectability.

Richards's growing conformism evoked a heated response from some socialists. By the 1907 Labour Party Conference, Gribble of the SDF, elected as a union delegate on a tiny poll,[162] was attacking the Parliamentary Agent:

Our friend, Richards, says the Conference refused to commit itself to a Socialist resolution. Yes, and he who claims to be a Socialist, and belongs to a union which is a political as well as an industrial organisation which has Socialism for its objective is pleased. Some day we shall understand why.[163]

The vociferous Gribble could claim NUBSO support for socialism drawing legitimacy from the union's formal commitment, but that commitment was a misleading indicator of rank and file opinion.

Here then, was a union in which the impact of technical change produced an effective socialist response. There were union activists who were led to a socialist commitment through their industrial experiences, becoming influential in large union branches and eventually in the national decision-making of the union. Moreover, they succeeded in leaving a lasting mark on the politics of the union through the early establishment of a clear attachment to political independence, and a detailed socialist objective. All of these must be important emphases — arguments inside this union were expressed in more overtly political terms than elsewhere. Yet there were limitations to the socialist penetration. It was restricted basically to activists — on most matters they could influence or determine policy, although the 1899 contest for the General Secretaryship showed limits to their influence — and such penetration could leave the mass of members largely unaffected. It was also limited geographically to a few centres where factory production was well-established. In the boot-making villages of Northamptonshire, Radical Liberalism remained firmly in control.[164] Moreover, even the socialist inheritance became increasingly weakened, as the young critics became middle-aged officials and the union accommodated itself to the dominance of mechanised production. T. F. Richards, the iconoclastic ILP critic of the nineties, became first the dandified politician of the Edwardian years, and then the harsh official of the late twenties, breaking up the Minority Movement within his union.[165] Here the impact of union bureaucracy, changing economic circumstances, and perhaps the fragility and ambiguity of ILP socialism, made the image of the 'Socialist Union' both partial and ephemeral.

6

New Unionism

Frederick Engels looked forward with optimism in January 1892, not because of the brittle enthusiasm of drawing-room socialists, but on account of the massive shift of opinion that he detected in the trade union world. The trajectory of events is widely known — discontent at the cautious policies of trade union leaders exacerbated by the depression of the eighties and revealed in the development of critical factions in some established unions and in the stirrings of organisataion amongst those typically labelled by officials as unskilled and unorganisable: the strike of the Bryant and May women in 1888; the dramatically successful organisation of gas workers and others, first in London and then elsewhere under the leadership of Will Thorne during 1889; more evocatively perhaps, the successful London Dock strike of August 1889. Labourers were showing levels of audacity and solidarity that some dismissive craft-union officials had regarded as impossible. This success led to a rash of 'New Unions' which, by the 1890 TUC, boasted impressive memberships: Will Thorne's Gasworkers' and General Labourers' Union claimed 60,000 members; Ben Tillett's Dock Wharf, Riverside and General Workers' Union had 56,000; a second dockers' organisation, the National Union of Dock Labourers, founded in Glasgow by two Ulstermen, McGhee and McHugh, but with its stronghold in Liverpool, had a further 50,000; Havelock Wilson's Sailors measured a precise 58,780, and the Tyneside-based National Amalgamated Union of Labour brought in another 40,000. Such bodies, claiming to speak for masses of hitherto unorganised workers, were a new and, to some, disturbing phenomenon in the previously staid world of the TUC. The old balance of forces there was disrupted; a challenge to the cautious Lib-Lab leadership was left no longer to a few faithful propagandists who could be treated with a blend of ridicule and tolerance.[1]

The optimistic prognostications of Engels were not focused on the hope of new alignments within trade union hierarchies. He saw the advent of the 'New Unions' as marking a watershed in the drive of the working-class towards socialism. Older craft unions were seen as thoroughly entangled within the capitalist order; they

preserve the traditions of the time when they were founded, and look upon the wages system as a once-for-all established final fact which they can at best modify in the interest of their members.

In contrast New Unions were

founded at a time when the faith in the eternity of the wages-system was severely shaken; their founders and promoters were Socialists, either consciously or by feeling.

Supporters also differed from those of the older organisations; they were 'rough, neglected, looked down on by the working class aristocracy'. Such recruits should be welcomed by socialist propagandists:

their minds were virgin soil, entirely free from the inherited 'respectable' bourgeois prejudices which hampered the brains of the better situated 'old' unionists.[2]

Similar contrasts were drawn by some New Union leaders. One active in Manchester New Unionism and in the ILP claimed that Old Unionists refused to acknowledge the existence of the class war. In contrast, he characterised New Unionists as seeing 'the wage-slave system itself, based as it is on class ownership and artificial inequality, as the parent of all the social evils from which labour suffers'. They therefore looked:

to the gradual replacement of the present arrangement by a Co-operative Commonwealth ... based upon the final emancipation of the workers from masterdom and monopoly in all their forms.[3]

Such claims and hopes seemed, from one angle, to be borne out to some degree by the formation of the ILP and the subsequent creation of the LRC. It seemed far removed from the limited, largely craft-based Lib-Lab unionism of the late eighties. Yet we have seen how groups of activists in older unions played significant, if often ambiguous parts in these developments. What then was the contribution of the New Unions, in particular their role in the development of the ILP?

The first task must be to characterise New Unionist developments. Membership reached a peak in 1890, and then declined sharply for some years. By 1896, the Gasworkers' had fallen below 30,000 and Tillett's Dockers' had shrunk to 10,000.[4] One hostile observer claimed that in London the organisation's membership had plummeted from 24,000 to 256 by 1894.[5] The NUDL fell to 8,500 in 1892, and subsequently perhaps to 5,000,[6] but then showed a slow recovery. Wilson's Sailors' Union had disintegrated by 1894. In contrast, the NAUL stabilised at around the 20,000 mark. Such declines reflected the operation of the trade cycle to a considerable extent. The unions had recruited well in conditions of labour scarcity, but then contracted as the depression bit. But the response of employers, especially in shipping and on the docks was of immense significance as they set out to break trade unionism, with notable success.[7] Divergent membership levels also reflected perhaps the varied talents of union officials. Thorne proved a prudent administrator and the NUDL showed more stability once Sexton had been appointed General Secretary. In contrast, Tillett proved a casual and inefficient officer, and much time was spent at early Dockers' conferences wrangling over administrative details as membership plummeted. But competence at the top did not seem to be essential. The relative stability of the NAUL owed little to a succession of negligent officials.[8]

The survival of New Unions depended on the organising of specific groups of workers who had some scarcity value and could be organised on a relatively stable basis. The Gasworkers' depended heavily on membership in large concerns; gasworks in East London and the provinces, metal trades in Birmingham; tinplate in South Wales; ships and engineering in the North East. Tillett's Dockers' came to depend heavily on the South Wales tinplate workers; the NAUL acquired much of its stability from its standing in the North-Eastern shipyards. Sexton's union was perhaps aided in its recruitment in the Irish Sea ports by the existence of pre-existing patterns of communal solidarity.[9]

Such frequent dependence on particular locations and distinctive groups of workers contrasted sharply with the original ecumenical hope of large-scale general unions which, it had been hoped, would mobilise across a wide range of occupations. The dream of 'one man, one ticket' — the interchangeability of union cards — advocated by Gasworkers' disappeared. From the start, Tillett's union attempted to establish fenced-off areas for its own recruitment, and over time, Gasworkers' branches, once having achieved a precarious recognition, were induced to follow the same path. A degree of labour scarcity could produce policies very like those of the craft unions. More broadly, industrial militancy was succeeded by prudence as a condition of survival, and officials became more conservative as they sought to stabilise their organisations, and as they grew away from their abrasive earlier struggles. Such mellowing was aided by the recruitment of some New Union spokesmen to the TUC Parliamentary Committee. Havelock Wilson moved quickly towards official Liberalism and aggressive anti-socialism; Tillett became an enthusiast for compulsory arbitration; Thorne remained loyal to the SDF but combined this with conventional attitudes inside the Parliamentary Committee.

Prudence at the top and the cultivation of scarcity within a diminished rank and file helped to produce a change in the *raison d'etre* of New Unions. The original justification had been stated clearly in an account of the formation of a New Union for railwaymen — the General Railway Workers' Union. Two socialists approached the Railway Servants' General Secretary in the autumn of 1889 to suggest a reduction in the Society's weekly dues of 5*d*; the Lib-Lab Harford refused. So the GRWU was born, one of the two 1889 supplicants claiming that the ASRS 'is evidently too much of a sick benefit and burial fee society, and insufficiently energetic to meet the requirements of the great mass of railway employees'.[10] No fringe benefits, a mass membership, an aggressive policy — these were the widely proclaimed traits of early New

Unionism. Yet some organisations paid fringe benefits from the start, and, as membership declined and an aggressive trade policy seemed impossible, so others moved towards the provision of the normal selective benefits. They might help to cement together the surviving membership, and perhaps to attract new recruits. They certainly indicated a significant adjustment to the existing economic order.[11]

Such emphases are important to prevent any misleading dichotomisation of Old and New Unions; but they represent only part of the story. The new organisations fused together a series of elements which could provoke consternation in respectable circles. The fear of working-class violence, never wholly dormant in the collective consciousness of the Victorian bourgeoisie, had been awakened by the London confrontations of 1886 and 1887; now the industrial tactics of many New Unionists stirred this further. The August 1889 Dock Strike, with its monster processions and meetings, had the support of much Establishment opinion and was a relatively demure affair. But this support was transformed rapidly into opposition to the tactics of the new organsations, with frequent acccusations of bullying and intimidation.[12] The abrasive mass picketing often associated with the New Unions reflected their members' industrial situation. The possibility of blackleg labour being introduced pointed to a vulnerability that skilled craftsmen and many textile workers and miners rarely suffered from; moreover, the substitution could sometimes be long-term rather than merely for the duration of the dispute. Here was an ever-present danger given the difficulty of developing unions strong enough to embrace the apathetic or the initially hostile. In the end, as in the celebrated Leeds gas strike of June and July 1890, the best antidote to blacklegging was a barrage of missiles, more than sufficient to offset the protection of police and military.[13] The assertiveness of the newly organised, shedding the inhibitions of many years, produced a vehement response from many employers and their assorted supporters in political, journalistic and academic circles. Such hostility survived the retrenchment of the New Unions, fused with conflicts over craft-union opposition to mechanisation and helped to shape trade union and socialist debate for more than a decade.

Bourgeois concern about methods was complemented by anxiety about objectives. Many leaders of, and sympathisers with New Unions were socialists. Thorne remained in the SDF; Mann shifted from the SDF to the ILP; Burns shifted to an uncertain position, but still counted himself as a socialist; Tillett was involved with the ILP in Bradford; Sexton was active in the Liverpool ILP and stood as an ILP candidate in 1895; Dipper, Secretary of the NAUL withdrew as ILP standard-bearer for Jarrow at the last minute.[14] Local union activists also showed socialist zeal. The Leeds Socialist Leaguers — Tom Maguire, Tom Paylor and Alf Mattison — energised and organised a diverse range of workers;[15] in Manchester, two SDF members organised a branch of the Gasworkers' in 1889. Nearby in St Helens, P J King organised a Chemical and Copper Workers' Union.[16] Along with Hardie he was to provoke the wrath of the TUC 'Old Guard' at the 1891 Congress through attempts to organise a slate for the Parliamentary Committee elections.[17] Later he was to represent his short-lived union at the ILP's foundation conference. There were also the *eminences grises* — Eleanor Marx sat on the Gasworkers' Executive, H.H. Champion had been involved in the London Dock Strike and opened the columns of the *Labour Elector* as official organ for Gasworkers', Dockers' and General Railway Workers'.

The equivalence of New Unionist activism to socialist or even Independent Labour sympathies was not absolute; but it was sufficiently common to lend its own edge to New Unionists' frequent advocacy of the legislative eight hour day. While this cause was far from a socialist monopoly, the linking of industrial violence, interference with the market and a commitment to socialism, could suggest that a fundamental change was occurring in British trade unionism. Such a prediction needs to be set against the long-term factors diminishing the distinctions between New Unions and their older, craft-based counterparts. The similarities are perceivable with hindsight — the contrasts, real or imagined, were apparent immediately.

The impact of these factors on the development of the ILP can best be appreciated through a study of the politics of individual unions. The Gas Workers' Union was the most ostentatiously committed to Independent Labour politics, although in its earliest months its advent had been hailed not just by the *Labour Elector* but also by the Radical journal, the *Star*. But the dominant personality, Thorne, was a committed socialist; there was a connection through Eleanor Marx with Engels and his circle.[18] This led in turn to contacts with the international socialist movement, especially perhaps with the luminaries of the SPD.[19] Domestically, the socialist quality of officials and activists was revealed in the union's strong involvement in the London Labour Movement's first May Day celebrations in 1890. Not surprisingly, Thorne's political pronouncements to the membership had a strongly socialist flavour. In preparation for the anticipated 1892 election, he argued that members should make the Eight Hours question the critical test and that from the labour standpoint, no distinction could be made between the existing parties.[20] A year later, he saw political methods as the way to solve the unemployment and Eight Hours questions. It required 'the capturing of all Local and Imperial Government machinery by the workers'.[21] By now, two elements were of wider importance. The shift to a stronger political emphasis was itself a reaction to economic depression, a substitute for an aggressive industrial policy. More specifically, the emphasis on local government representation was important. The union, recruiting as it did amongst municipal employees, was strongly interested from an organisational as well as a more broadly working-class viewpoint. It was a pioneer of Independent Labour slates in local London elections, and Thorne already sat on the West Ham Borough Council.[22] Sometimes union pronouncements emphasised the value of labour representation as such, but on other occasions, Thorne spoke specifically of his own and other officers' socialist beliefs:

To my mind, no *permanent* solution ... can be found so long as the trade of this and other countries is carried on for profit ... We are often twitted by the profit-seeking class and even by some old Trade Unionists, with being more of a Socialist organisation. True many of us are Socialists because we believe that only in the realisation of Socialism can be found the true solution of our social miseries.[23]

Trade solidarity should be carried through to the ballot box:

To be a trade unionist and fight *for* your class during a strike, and to be a Tory or Liberal and fight *against* your class at election time is folly.[24]

It was not just Thorne. Pete Curran, the National Organiser, certainly lived up to Engels' image of the New Unionist: 'the work of trades unionism is far from accomplished as long as the laws of competition guide all commercial and industrial transactions'.[25] The political ethos of the Gasworkers' was expressed formally in the 1892 preamble to the union rules, probably drafted by Edward Aveling and Eleanor Marx. This emphasised the opposed interests of workers and master, and, after emphasising the immediate material objects of the union, it concluded with an optimistic clarion call against sectionalism:

the interests of all Workers are one, ... a wrong done to any kind of Labour is wrong done to the whole of the Working Class ... victory or defeat of any portion of the Army of Labour is a gain or loss to the whole of that Army, which by its organisation and union is marching steadily and irresistably forward to its ultimate goal — the Emancipation of the Working Class. That Emancipation can only be brought about by the strenuous and united efforts of the Working Class itself. WORKERS UNITE![26]

Such views amongst officials, and such a statement within the union rule book, made later developments predictable. In July 1896, the ILP's National Administrative Council wrote to three unions in an attempt to secure the tabling of a resolution on a joint meeting of trade unionists and socialists for that year's TUC. The Gasworkers' were one of the selected unions, but were unable to help because the closing date for resolutions had passed.[27] Inevitably, the union was one of the first to affiliate to the LRC, having previously sanctioned the running of Thorne as a parliamentary candidate.[28] Although he lost in Hardie's old seat of West Ham South in 1900, he won very easily there in 1906.

Thorne's central role in the Gasworkers' political concerns serves as a reminder that enthusiasm for independent labour politics and for socialism need have nothing to do with the ILP. He remained in the SDF, apparently rejecting an invitation by Hardie to become involved in the arrangements for the Bradford Conference.[29] Yet, two other prominent members of the union were associated closely with the ILP: Pete Curran and J. R. Clynes. Curran, after a Glaswegian political apprenticeship in the Irish and Scottish Land Leagues and in the SDF, moved south and helped to form a Gasworkers' branch in the Woolwich Arsenal in 1889.[30] He soon became an organiser for the union, first in the West of England, and then nationally, and throughout the nineties was a prominent advocate of New Unionist and socialist positions at the TUC. His socialism was expressed most strongly in his ILP activities, although he was also a Fabian until the exodus over the South African War. He was closely involved in the party from the beginning, serving on the NAC until he resigned in 1898 because of union commitments.[31] During this period he stood twice for parliament. His first contest at Barrow in 1895 made little impact, but in October 1897, his role as ILP candidate in the bitter Barnsley campaign brought him to the centre of the arguments between socialist and Lib-Lab trade union officials.[32] He exemplified for many the links between socialism and New Unionism, links that were too readily presented as a general stereotype. In Curran's case, the commitments to socialism and political independence remained strong. He served as the union's first representative on the LRC Executive, and moved the important 'Newcastle resolution' on political independence at the 1903 LRC Conference.[33] Those who harboured doubts about official Labour links with the Liberals could be mollified perhaps by Curran's capture of the Liberal seat of Jarrow in July 1907.

If Curran suggested the combative face of the ILP, a less flamboyant link between party and union was found in J. R. Clynes, recruited by Thorne as the union's Lancashire Organiser. Although a member of the ILP from the start, and a persistent advocate of independence on the Oldham Trades Council,[34] his political interests were always subordinate to his trade union activities. Some Oldham party activists regarded him as a damper on the party's progress. One complained to Hardie that 'Clynes was ever over-cautious ... So much so that he should be called De Clynes'.[35] Certainly his electoral success in 1906 as an ILP-sponsored candidate gave a misleading impression of his priorities.

The Gasworkers' leadership included a range of Independent Labour enthusiasts — Thorne losing much of his early socialist enthusiasm and industrial sharpness on the way to becoming a conservative trade union MP; Curran a volatile partisan; Clynes carrying an ILP card but moderate in all things. This leadership was able to determine the basic elements of the union's political position. There were no wrangles with Lib-Labs, since they had no earlier traditions to contend with. As the first generation of officials, they had a wide area of discretion on the political front, and could inscribe commitments to independence and socialism on a *tabula rasa*.

At the level of the making of political policy, Engels' claim about the opportunities open for socialist propaganda had in the case of the union's officials its maximum plausibility. But there were major obstacles in extending this commitment to the rank and file. The occupational heterogeneity of the membership entailed a lack of common yet specific objectives that could be pursued unitedly through political action. The contrast with miners and railwaymen is significant. Similarly, the geographical dispersal of the membership meant that there was little chance of mobilising union members to capture particular constituencies or even particular wards. On the other hand, such dispersals could help to ensure that the union's political campaigns were free of the sectionalism that could mark equivalent efforts by unions with more concentrated and homogeneous memberships. Perhaps only in West Ham, where the union had begun, where numbers remained relatively numerous and Thorne was personally involved, was it plausible to claim that local gas workers formed a significant element in the support for Independent Labour initiatives at parliamentary and municipal levels.[36] These, of course, were individual cases of immense significance — Hardie's victory in 1892 and the creation of the first Labour municipal majority six years later. Otherwise the preferences and decisions of officials helped to commit the union to support for certain political objectives, but did not produce a clear mobilisation of the rank and file.

Yet the Gasworkers' were more of a force for Independent Labour politics than Tillett's Dock, Wharf, Riverside and General Labourers. In part, this reflected the latter's precipitate fall in membership during the early nineties; in part the union was hindered in all directions by Tillett's erratic style and lax administration. Although the Dockers' were not a major industrial force, they were firmly committed to Independent Labour politics. The causes were similar to those influencing the Gasworkers'. The socialist presence at the union's birth continued in the political allegiances of officials. Mann was initially the union's President, Tillett was closely involved with the early ILP; Tom McCarthy, a recruit from the stevedores, and a Dockers' organiser, stood as an ILP candidate in 1895; Harry Kay, the union Treasurer, later joined the ILP.[37] As with the Gasworkers', there was a strong interest in municipal politics, stimulated perhaps by a belief that water-front membership seemed to survive better in docks such as Bristol which were municipally owned. Once again advocates of Independent Labour representation faced no earlier Lib-Lab tradition.

The impact of these considerations can be seen in successive union conference decisions. The second conference in September 1891 was visited by a Bradford delegation keen to recruit Tillett as an independent candidate. This proposition was debated by the delegates and accepted by 22 votes to 3. Proponents were not always motivated by socialist sentiments. One speaker believed that the union would benefit from its General Secretary 'having the magic letters MP at the end of his name'.[38] Two years later, under the heading, 'Independent Labour Party' delegates discussed the general question of officials standing for political office, and decided by 14 votes to 2 that 'at all times they shall stand absolutely independent of party politics'.[39] The following year this decision was tightened, this time unanimously. Delegates proclaimed:

the necessity of returning to Parliament, to Municipal Councils and to Parish Councils, labour representatives pledged to a complete collectivist programme and independent of the orthodox political parties.[40]

The union never deviated formally from this position. It, too, was the recipient in 1896 of an ILP request to table a resolution for the TUC and then, in 1900, affiliated rapidly to the LRC.

The depiction of the Dockers' as strong partisans of an Independent Labour policy is true in formal terms, but it must be severely qualified. The 1894 decision was taken at a conference including only the union officers plus fourteen delegates; the greatly reduced membership made the union's political pronouncements of restricted significance. Moreover, Tillett was the leading figure in the union, and his political activities reflected his more general instability. On the one side, there stood the Tillett of the West Bradford campaigns of 1892 and 1895, the first time as the candidate of the Bradford Labour Union, the second time as an ILP nominee. Phillip Snowden later painted a positive portrait of his Bradford activities: 'I was living in the district at the time, and it was a thrilling experience. Workers thronged to his meetings in their thousands, and they came away, having seen the vision of a new Earth'.[41] Tillett also served on the NAC for the first two years and was identified generally with advanced positions inside the TUC; he defended the party against the hostility of his old colleague, John Burns — 'you positively have no grounds for saying that the *deadbeats* have the least hold of any useful man in the ILP movement'.[42] But there were always other Tilletts. There was the erratic figure presented by one critical observer as 'a demagogue with the taste of a sybarite; a voluptuary with the hide of a agitator; a hypochondriac and dreamer of dreams that never materialise'.[43] More specifically, there was the chauvinistic outburst at the ILP's foundation conference, which provoked a sharp response from Edward Bernstein.[44] At the same time as he was a leading member of the ILP, he was serving as a Progressive alderman in alliance with the Liberals on the London County Council. By the time of the 1895 TUC and the reform of the Congress's Standing Orders he appeared to be drifting away from the ILP. Although opposing the changes, he was ready to see Hardie excluded from the Congress:

he agreed ... that personalities such as those of Burns and Keir Hardie did not contribute to their doing practical trade union work and he would suggest that they be left outside.[45]

His subsequent causes were to include compulsory arbitration and sympathy towards syndicalism; scathing contempt for pre-war Labour MPs and vociferous support for the 1914—18 war. His connections with the ILP provided just one episode in a confusing kaleidescope of pronouncements and postures.[46] Tillett's brittle attachments inevitably affected the impact of his union as an advocate of Independent Labour politics, but there was another side to this story. The full-time Dockers' organiser Tom McCarthy became the central figure in the one ILP electoral contest in which New Unionist strategy and objectives became a major issue — the West Hull contest of 1895.

Two and a half years earlier, Hull had been a stronghold of Tillett's union, in part because a major shipowner, Charles Wilson, the Liberal member for West Hull had taken a sympathetic attitude.[47] During 1890, Tillett's union increased its Hull membership from 4,000 to 12,000, and achieved complete unionisation on the docks.[48] The port also became a stronghold of Havelock Wilson's Sailors' Union. Wages were raised, foremen and shipping clerks were allowed to join the Dockers' Union and the firm collaborated in the collection of dues. The union became an institutionalised part of the port's life, conflicts were reduced and productivity rose. Wilson attended a meeting of the dockers to congratulate them on the improvements. But this union-induced harmony was increasingly out of tune with developments elsewhere. The Shipping Federation from September 1890 had been involved in aggressive actions to clear the union out of British ports and had attempted with some success to provide preferential employment for non-union labour organised through the British Labour Exchange. 'T. Wilson Sons and Co.' had left the Federation soon after its formation, but early in 1892, they rejoined, apparently after substantial pressure from ship owners and marine insurance companies. This provided the opportunity for a Federation attempt to break the unions in Hull, and from February 1892 industrial relations in the port deteriorated. The union position weakened as organisation in other ports crumbled, and was eroded further by Hull's declining trade during 1892.[49] The Dockers' officials showed some awareness of the need for caution, but Havelock Wilson continued to make belligerent statements.[50] After preliminary irritants, Wilsons' decided unilaterally that their foremen and shipping clerks must leave the union, followed by a more general attempt to give preference to 'Free Labour'. Resistance by most Hull dockers to the proposal that they should register as non-union men led to the importation of 'Free Labour' to work on ships belonging to Wilsons' and two other firms. Union members were withdrawn from all work at these firms and after further negotiations failed, a general strike was called in the Hull docks, effective from 10 August 1893. By now the previously conciliatory Wilson seemed fully in accord with Federation policy, informing a deputation that 'the men must come back on his terms which would not be abated one jot'.[51] In fact, he probably would have been prepared to accept an early settlement, covering union and non-union labour working together, a separate union for foremen and clerks, and no preference for or imposition of 'Free Labour'. But the Shipping Federation, seemingly concerned to break the union, refused to allow Hull employers to accept this. The consequence was a seven-week dispute which grew increasingly violent. Thousands of non-union workers were brought into Hull, protected by police and military; gunboats in the Humber symbolised the tensions in the community; violence, some arson and a polarisation of the classes resulted. Eventually the union was defeated; opponents of 'New Unionism' were jubilant, the liberal reputation of C. H. Wilson lay seemingly in tatters.

Industrial struggle and defeat provided appropriate insights into the bias of Hull Liberalism; local government was dominated by the shipping interest, a factor which trade unionists felt had conditioned the responses of the magistracy, Watch Committee and Guardians.[52] A local branch of the ILP grew rapidly. The Hull Trades Council rejected a resolution for Independent Labour Representation by the narrow margin of 64 votes to 52, and in the autumn of 1893, two ILPers won seats in the municipal elections.[53] Tom McCarthy, who had not been directly involved in the dispute, was adopted as ILP candidate in November 1893 to fight Wilson in his West Hull stronghold. It seemed like a straight contest between Labour and Capital and supporting resolutions appeard readily from branches of the Dockers', the ASRS and the Carpenters and Joiners'.[54]

McCarthy's prospects were hampered however by two fundamental considerations. West Hull was perhaps the least working-class of the three Hull constituencies, it was a Wilson fiefdom and trade union strength, weakened by the strike, could hardly serve as an adequate countervailing force.[55] But more significantly, the Hull labour movement was divided over McCarthy's candidature and support from the trades council was unlikely. This was acknowledged by one local ILPer who informed Hardie that: 'the attitude of that conglomeration of respectabilities, the Executive of the Trades Council is, I believe, either openly, or underneath hostile'.[56] In part this was because the council, despite a recent quadrupling of membership to 20,000, was still dominated by representatives of the craft unions. Their views were epitomised by the Lib-Labism of the President, Millington, a Shipwrights' official. They had resented the aggressive sectionalism of the 'parvenu' Dockers' and Seamen's delegation, a concern perhaps shared by other New Unionists who might have more sympathy with the port workers.[58] The situation was complicated by the role of Hull's most prominent Lib-Lab, Fred Maddison, the Editor of the *Railway Review*. He had fought Central Hull in 1892, backed by both the trades council and the local Liberals. This had disillusioned some local Labour activists who denounced the contest as 'a sham and a fraud'.[59] Maddison was anxious to fight Central Hull again, and having attempted to play a conciliatory role in the strike, he was anxious not to forfeit Liberal support. The possibility of McCarthy securing Trades Council support was a clear threat to his position, and he set out to organise Hull's Old Unionists against the interloper. McCarthy explained to Hardie that:

Maddison has written the Trades Council a strong letter advising them (almost commanding them) to have nothing to do with my candidature because it will, so he says, prejudice his chance as a Liberal-Labour man in Central Hull.[60]

The trades council met in December 1893 and resolved by 77 votes to 44 that it was 'inexpedient' to support the ILP. The public justification was that the Council should be the sole channel for labour representation.[61] But Maddison's interests were clearly significant. One ILP member stigmatised him as 'a paltry mean miserable party hack', relating how 'our Liberal-Labour specimen was at the Trades Council Meeting which our dep. attended. I cannot express my disgust at his dirty tactics'.[62] Another observer was more pointed: 'I have no doubt that Wilson's carriage and personal influence will ... be again at the service of the Labour candidate for Central Hull. No wonder Tom McCarthy is not wanted.'[63]

He was not wanted even by the Hull branch of the Irish National League, despite having been approachd to stand as a Nationalist only eighteen months earlier. Maddison, tailoring his statements to his audience, had informed the Irish voters that he but not McCarthy would make Home Rule a test question[64]

McCarthy's resources in the 1895 contest were thus few, and finance was an ever-present problem. No Conservative stood and Wilson subsequently thanked the Tory Party for standing aside, and its members for voting for him.[65] McCarthy's platform was strongly socialist — he attacked Wilson as 'a typical representative of the system which they believed was the cause of poverty',[66] and emphasised that public ownership was a necessary condition for the abolition of poverty. Wilson initially was reluctant to comment in detail on the strike, but was drawn into more detailed explanations by hecklers. He attacked the alleged dictatorship of union officials:

when they found it was impossible to carry on their business except under the tyrannical dictation of a limited number of men who had been placed in a position which in his opinion they did not make good use of, he was obliged to make a stand.[67]

He appealed to labour to stand together with capital against the threat of foreign competition.[68] The paternalism of the rich capitalist was evident at his meetings; individual employees with grievances were invited to call at the office the following day. The success of Wilsons was identified with that of the community; he appealed to his 'fellow townsmen' and placed union organisers beyond the Pale; 'there came to Hull gentlemen who had not been brought up here ... did not know the difficulties of the situation and caused discord and trouble'.[69] The easy Liberal victory in the context of a divided local labour movement was a foregone conclusion. In the long run, West Hull 1895 highlighted the contradictions of old-style Lib-Labism. Maddison's style was already somewhat passé; his position in Central Hull weakened in 1895. But it also showed the limitations of 'New Unionism' as a political force, even in a community where dock workers were numerous and retained memories of bitter industrial conflict and defeat. Certainly the strike had alienated a nucleus of the work force from Liberal politics, but the virtual collapse of the union meant that Independent Labour politics was only a shadowy presence for the next decade.[70]

Limitations are apparent also in the cse of the second dockers' organisation, the National Union of Dock Labourers. Its founders, McGhee and McHugh, were followers of Henry George, not socialists, but in 1893 the General Secretaryship was taken over by the ILPer James Sexton. The revival of the union's fortunes went along with political work for the ILP. He stood as the party's candidate for Ashton Under Lyne in 1895, and claimed to have propagandised extensively for the party.[71] His views percolated into the union's publications; by 1895, he was advocating to his members 'a perfect combination of Trades Unionists inside and outside the House of Commons where laws are made to perpetuate the present condition of things'.[72] But the NUDL, although clearly committed to independent representation, had severe limitations from the standpoint of the ILP. One concerned the changing position of Sexton. After 1895, he moved away from the official party position of hostility to Lib-Lab trade unionism, and in August 1897, he criticised the party's condemnation of Maddison, then a candidate in the Brightside by-election. This contest resurrected some of the passions of West Hull, and Sexton, as a dockers' leader, might have been expected to hold strong views about McCarthy's treatment. But union solidarity mattered more to him than the enunciation of any political position:

there may be minor political differences between us, but as trade unionists, there is, or ought to be, no difference in opinion amongst honest Labour men in preferring a pronounced trade unionist, ... instead of the nephew of a duke.[74]

The party were acting in a way 'detrimental to the best interests of the labour movement',[75] perhaps because, in many branches, there were party members who were not trade unionists.[76] As a result, he was called before the NAC and reprimanded — Tom Mann condemning his action as 'sheer rebellion'.[77] Sexton's commitment to Independent Labour politics remained: he seconded the ASRS resolution at the 1899 TUC and served on early LRC Executives. But he did not exemplify a distinctively ILP position; his essential view was that 'no one should ram their principles down the throats of the other side'.[78] Indeed, by 1905, he was attacking the ILP for precisely this vice. They were becoming 'the most intolerant section, representing some of the worst features of narrow Sectarianism'.[79] A weakening ILP attachment at the top was matched by a lack of solidarity on independent labour — let alone socialist — politics amongst the membership. NUDL strongholds were dominated by sectarian politics. Sexton, a prominent Home Ruler and a Catholic, met with difficulties when he stood as a Liverpool candidate in 1906 and in 1910. The bases of the union's support might make Labour politics attractive on economic grounds, but cultural divisions frequently worked against this.

These three organisations provide the major cases where some sort of relationship between New Unionism and the growth of the ILP can be indicated. Elsewhere claims are much weaker. The National Amalgamated Union of Labour retained significant membership and had a succession of socialist General Secretaries, but their political role was slight, and the union followed a largely uneventful industrial existence. Other organisations might espouse political independence, but had few resources. The General Railway Workers' Union might proclaim the need for the collective ownership of the means of production, pursued through Independent Labour politics,[80] but there was little that the union could do about this. The Lancashire and Adjacent Counties Labour Amalgamation had an impressive title, and the volatile ILPer, Leonard

Hall, as its leader but by 1895 its membership was down to four hundred.[81] Elsewhere, New Unionism did not always mean even a formal attachment to political independence. John Ward's Navvies' Union was small and reflected the increasingly Lib-Lab propensities of its principal figure, and Havelock Wilson's revived Sailors' Union was identified with the strong anti-socialism of its founder.

If we return to the three central cases, the verdict must be a complex one. On the one side, there are the positive contributions. These organisations were all committed to political independence, and in varying degrees to socialism from the early years. There were no battles within the unions between Socialists and Lib-Labs. The authority of leading figures, themselves often active socialists, extended typically to the making of political policy. Thus these unions gave considerable sustenance to the ILP in its early political campaigns, providing some candidates, local activists and moral support. Moreover, the commitments to independence provided a durable basis for the ILP's strategy of seeking a 'Labour Alliance'.

These contributions are important, but must be balanced by other considerations. The increasing emphases by these organisations on political action was in part a response to growing problems in the industrial field. Yet, in turn, the need to accommodate to a less advantageous economic system could produce its own consequences for political activities. Most simply, the defeat and near-destruction of union organisation, as in Hull, did not provide an effective springboard for political activity. The sense of grievance could be accompanied easily by a feeling of impotence — few New Unionists were likely to participate readily in the voluntary associations that could occupy the time of some artisans. Thus the destruction of the union could be the destruction of any basis for political initiatives. Even where New Union branches survived through difficult years, the heterogeneity of employment often meant that political mobilisation around specific demands was impracticable.

Problems of mobilisation at the base were typically matched by changes in attitude at the top. New Union leaders generally became much more conservative over time. Their organisation's survival and growth became the principal objectives; industrial conflict became something to be avoided. Equally in the political field, New Unionist ILPers tended to loosen their links with the party; they dropped out of its national decision-making bodies, and typically took a broader trade union view of their political role. Their period of political creativity ended effectively with the formation of the LRC. From one view point this represented a significant political development; from another it indicated the limits of the New Unionist's willingness to innovate. The LRC could serve as a channel for their demands within a society to which they had already accommodated in the industrial sphere.

Conclusion: Diversity, ambiguity, clarity

The examination of ILP influence in individual unions shows a daunting diversity — diversity of industrial and political traditions, diversity of union structures, diversity of economic challenges. The alignments within each organisation varied, so did the currency in which debates were transacted, and so did the outcomes. The variety was fundamental, and yet it was contained within a wider unifying theme — the rise of Independent Labour politics, and the creation of the Labour Alliance. Repeatedly throughout the analysis, a focus on purely trade union activities has been shown to be insufficient. Individual trade unionists appear with their political loyalties, anchored perhaps in cultural or communitarian considerations based outside their industrial preoccupations. Unions in their quests for political representation had to come to terms with existing political configurations. Explorations of this dimension will occupy subsequent chapters and will provide an essential complement to the analysis of union influences.

The industrial circumstances of the nineties offered a range of possibilities for ILP activists. Pressures on craft-workers could be effective agents of radicalisation, as could the authoritarian and cost-cutting propensities of railway managements. Faced with such challenges, Lib-Lab leadership could seem simply inadequate. The explosive growth of New Unionism could provide abundant opportunities for socialists to offer leadership to workers lacking any tradition of Lib-Lab dominance. Despite the subsequent recession in New Unionism, this left a permanent mark on the balance of trade union opinion. Even in the coalfields, where Lib-Lab traditions remained deeply rooted, organisations shifted, at different speeds and by a variety of routes, to political independence. Only in the cotton trade where unionism was sectionalised, economistic and relatively effective did the ILP seem marginal — and even there a significant shift occurred. The early impact of ILP propaganda could be expressed in a formal attachment to a socialist objective of the type adopted by the National Union of Boot and Shoe Operatives. More often, the dominant emphasis was on a pragmatic drive towards independent political representation, the path taken by activists in both the Engineers' and the Railway Servants'. Sometimes ILP proposals could produce a belligerent response of the Pickard variety; on other occasions, the Party's activists could barely obtain a foothold in union debates. Yet Pickardian hostility was gradually eroded, and even the political strategy of the cotton workers had to be amended. The ILP strategists played some part in the shift of unions towards involvement in the LRC but clearly other elements were propelling in the same direction several who felt less persuaded by the specifically ILP case.

The shift in the centre of gravity of trade union opinion can be seen in the developing views of the Trade Union Congress and of its Parliamentary Committee.[1] In the late eighties, these had still been bastions of narrow Lib-Labism. Hardie had stood out at the TUC for his attacks in 1887 and 1888 upon the Parliamentary Committee's Secretary, Henry Broadhurst.[2] But the depression of 1884—7 had radicalised many trade union activists, and this and the growth of New Unionism left their imprints on subsequent Congresses, changing the balance of representation, and influencing the tempo and content of debates. The 1890 Congress brought the narrow success of an eight hours' resolution, the arrival, albeit by default, of John Burns on the Parliamentary Committee, and the resignation of Broadhurst. Each of these events was deceptive. Several Lib-Labs were coming to support the type of state intervention involved in eight hours legislation, Burns's socialism was soon to be diluted by a variety of influences, and Broadhurst's successor. Fenwick of the Northumberland Miners, was another dedicated opponent of any eight hours bill.[3] But during the next few years, more Congress decisions hinted at socialist advances. Hardie successfully moved a resolution in 1892, instructing the Parliamentary Committee to prepare a scheme for the financing of Independent Labour candidates.[4] A year later, when a scheme was brought before delegates, James Macdonald of the London Tailors and Pete Curran successfully amended it so that candidates had to pledge themselves to support 'the principle of collective ownership and control of all the means of production and distribution'.[5] By 1894, Hardie and Macdonald could secure the passing of an amendment advocating the nationalisation of the means of production, distribution and exchange.[6] Tom Mann claimed that out of the 370 delegates at this Norwich Congress, over 80 were members of the ILP.[7]

Although these decisions marked significant advances, they should not be exaggerated. The scheme for Labour representation was voluntary, and died when affiliated organisations showed little interest in contributing.[8] Collectivist declarations could encourage socialists, but could also be digested by Liberals who saw them as ritualistic sentiments that committed the Parliamentary Committee to no substantive policies. This important body remained under strong Liberal influence. The supposed representatives of new ideas included Havelock Wilson and Burns, both moving at different rates towards Liberalism, and the politically volatile Tillett. When ILP partisans made formal challenges for the Secretaryship, they were beaten decisively. Hardie lost easily to Fenwick in 1893 despite the latter's opposition to Eight Hours legislation;[9] twelve months later Sam Woods defeated Fenwick, with Mann placed third on the first ballot.[10] The contest between Woods and Fenwick indicated that the immediate division over some acceptance of collectivism ran through Liberalism rather than between Liberalism and political independence. Such Liberal adaptation could perhaps limit a socialist appeal based on policy. More significantly, the socialist current within the TUC was being weakened by the decline of New Unionism. Falling membership readjusted Congress membership in favour of more cautious groups, whilst New Union officials themselves tended to become more circumspect. With such underlying trends, socialist strength depended increasingly on the trades council delegates. This situation, plus the evidence of socialist influence at Norwich, helped to produce the celebrated Old Guard coup of 1894—5.

Socialist influence could be counteracted by increasing the weight of the big battalions of coal and cotton. As early as 1890, the Miners' Federation had successfully moved a resolution that voting at Congress should be in proportion to affiliation fees, but the ready response of the Parliamentary Committee produced criticism and confusion, and in 1892 a compromise was reached — voting by show of hands, and delegates in proportion to fees paid. But after the 1894 Congress, a faction within the Parliamentary Committee decided to take matters further. Under the dubious legitimacy of an 1894 resolution, the Parliamentary Committee set up a Sub-Committee to reconstruct the Standing Orders.[11] This produced proposals that would clearly shift power away from the socialists and the strong partisans of Independent Labour. The representation of trades councils was to be terminated, removing one source of such influence; voting was to be in accordance with affiliation fees, introducing the bloc vote and strengthening the power of coal and cotton; all delegates must be either employed at their trade or be permanent and paid union officials, thus excluding some individual socialists, most notably Hardie. Victory for the proposals was virtually guaranteed when the Parliamentary Committee decided that the vote on whether to use the new Standing Orders would employ the new system.

The changes were supported by a nucleus of officials whose opposition to socialism has been demonstrated in the analyses of individual unions: the two Cotton Union leaders, Mawdsley and Holmes; Pickard's henchman Ned Cowey; and two Lib-Labs fighting against ILPers in their own unions, Inskip and Harford. Opposition was more varied: the socialists Tillett and Thorne, the Lib-Lab New Unionist Havelock Wilson, J. M. Jack of the Scottish Iron Founders and Sheldon, the representative of the Irish unions. Each group also had one unexpected yet leading protagonist. The exclusion proposal would also remove Broadhurst from the Congress, and this veteran Lib-Lab joined with his former critics to oppose the proposals. His position was balanced by that of Burns. His motivation was more obscure as he too would be excluded by the changes. Beatrice Webb suggested that his vanity had been manipulated by Mawdsley. Once the decision had been made in an acrimonious debate at the 1895 TUC she claimed that the Spinners' leader was

the Hero of the Coup d'Etat. Poor Burns has allowed himself to be used as the tool — his egregious vanity, virulent hatred of Keir Hardie and Tom Mann, suspicion of everyone else, prompting him to destroy the representative character of the Congress.[12]

Traditionalists aided by Burns were still strong enough to blunt the challenge of socialists. Outside the Committee there was little agitation. Hardie wrote critically of the proposals in the *Labour Leader*[13] and then abandoned the struggle.

The coup was important in that its amendments left a lasting mark on TUC practice, but it did not have any significant impact on the prospects for Independent Labour politics. Indeed in Scotland the changes arguably improved them. Scottish trades councils were perhaps more significant bodies than their English counterparts, because of the relative weakness of much Scottish trade unionism. This opposition to the exclusion of trades councils was supplemented by a widespread feeling that Scottish questions did not receive adequate discussion in the British Congress. The result was the inauguration of the Scottish TUC, incorporating both unions and trade councils, in March 1897.[14] From the start, the new organisation's political pronouncements were to the left of the British meetings. Several Scottish union activists, finding organisation difficult and Liberalism unsympathetic, had taken readily to socialist or Independent Labour politics. From the start, Hardie was closely involved, speaking to the inaugural Congress, and the Scottish TUC participated with apparently little dissension in the negotiations that led to the formation of the Scottish Workers' Parliamentary Elections Committee in January 1900.[15]

In England, developments were more complex. ILP leaders had to abandon hope of directly converting the TUC to a socialist policy and worked instead for an understanding between unions and party. Electoral collisions between Lib-Labs and ILP members reached a climax at Barnsley, and hardly increased the prospects of harmony. But some forces worked in the opposite direction. We have seen how socialist and Independent Labour sentiments were becoming more entrenched in several unions. Sometimes, the shift was captured in a personality, the election of Barnes, the removal of Harford, the growing prominence of Smillie and Curran. Even when the new officials were Liberals such as Richard Bell, they were typically not so wedded to individualism as their predecessors. Interventionist Liberals and flexible socialists could find a basis for a compromise. Thus the opposition to socialists was uncertain and divided. Pickard might continue to fulminate in Barnsley but elsewhere other Liberals did not see the argument in dichotomous terms.

This shift was in part a product of ILP skill within individual unions, but it was also a response by many Liberals to an increasingly uncertain environment. Some unions such as John Hodge's Steel Smelters developed pragmatic attachments to political independence without a significant socialist agitation. Employers were attacking industrially and legally, and Liberal failures and obduracy held out little hope of increasing Lib-Lab representation. Trade unionists from a wide range of positions believed that old strategies were increasingly sterile and that new ways forward must be found. One response was to develop closer industrial co-operation through a General Federation of Trade Unions. Another response was political — the passing of the resolution at the 1899 TUC that produced the inaugural conference of the LRC.[16]

This meeting, with ILP delegates and members steering a delicate course between what they saw as the Scylla of ill-defined Lib-Labism and the Charybdis of dogmatic socialism, provided one more opportunity for ILPers to demonstrate their readiness to compromise with what they saw as progressive trade union opinion. It is important to emphasise that creative adaptive face of ILP work in the union; it was an opportunity that could have been readily missed or wasted. Yet alongside their creativity, ILPers were often constrained powerfully by circumstances that they could do little to shape. As yet they had made little impact on the ranks of coal and cotton. The fact that these sectors were barely represented at the formation of the LRC widened the possibilities open to ILPers. Equally, although other unions were more receptive, this openness rarely extended beyond some attachment to political independence and some support of collectivist proposals. ILPers could be involved in ambiguous and sometimes far-reaching compromises both within individual unions and at the level of the LRC.

ILP influence as a product of economic pressures, political disappointments and activists' inspiration and toil can be grasped through the complexities of the individual unions where each element was moulded into its distinctive shape, and on the broader plateau of general trade union sentiments where brittle generalisation is at least plausible. Yet having said that ILP unionists capitalised on and moulded important developments, the limitations of their impact must be appreciated. The critical changes concerned the election of officials, formal changes in union policy often centring around the position of putative candidates, or the amendment of rules. Often the election of officers occurred in contests with few members voting, and it is rarely apparent that political priorities were critical determinants. Policy decisions were made characteristically in delegate meetings whose members were chosen usually on even smaller polls. When the wider membership was consulted on an explicitly political question, such as LRC affiliation, or the principle or selection of a parliamentary candidate, then the limited response suggested that most members cared little about their union's position on such questions.

This gap between the concerns of activists and those of many other members could raise problems for the strategy of utilising union attachments to help produce a shift in favour of Independent Labour or socialist candidates. If the arguments and victories occurred largely in the closed community of officials and activists, it would require considerable skill to mobilise union members *en masse* behind a candidate or policy, let alone the often vast numbers of non-unionised workers. The problem was exacerbated by the fact that the political attachments of members were often produced primarily by factors far removed from industrial experiences. Union and socialist spokesmen could attempt to change the priorities on which loyalties were based, but the appeal of communal and cultural loyalties typically lay far beyond their influence. If such ties weakened, union solidarity could perhaps replace them, but even then, there were major problems. Loyalties tended to be sectional; a candidate from the voter's own union could tap emotions which one from another organisation could not arouse. Few unions had geographical concentrations of members. New Unionists and railwaymen could rarely base an appeal on overwhelming electoral strength. It was the later converts to Independent Labour Politics — most notably miners, but perhaps to some degree, cotton workers, who could hope to mobilise communal solidarity and sheer electoral strength behind a union nominee.

The ILP hope of winning the unions for socialism might gain some successes, but this was a long way from securing a strong commitment from many union members, let alone the wider working class. This more extensive task encountered many pitfalls and was a long haul. Within such a timescale, ILP and union members were subject to conservative influences. Young activists who had led the drive for socialism and independence became increasingly cautious officials. Barnes and Wardle both stayed with Lloyd-George in 1918, Clynes was sorely tempted to do so. T. F. Richards and Herbert Smith both became hammers of later left-wing dissent. They were subject to all the oligarchic and insulating influences that Michels subsequently portrayed. The grind of administration eroded whatever radicalism they had once possessed; they found respectability and prized consensus. Yet the legacy of their earlier struggles remained, and sometimes arose to destroy their careers. Their unions were committed to political independence and often to a socialist objective. The limits of what was politically feasible for union officials and activists had shifted so that all but the most recalcitrant had to conform.

There might be continuity of style and policy between several trade union leaders and Radicals, but the establishment of these parameters helped to limit the impact of an organisation such as the National Democratic League with its hope of bringing together Radicals, trade unionists and socialists within a uncertain framework, on a limited political programme.[17] Labour had developed beyond this organisationally if not always programatically. In so many ways, ILP accommodations with prevailing trade union sentiments left ambiguous legacies, but in this direction the consequence was clear. Formal declarations of political position and purpose once made within such rule-governed organisations were most unlikely to be reversed. From the daunting diversity of the ILP's union involvements came one unequivocal message, in favour of independence. How that could be realised in practice necessitates an exploration of the complexities of political alignments and spaces within communities.

Part 2

POLITICAL SPACES

Constraints and hopes

The ILP emerged into a political system in which the legitimacy and the credibility of electoral and parliamentary politics were securely established. The way to secure influence appeared relatively clear cut, and indeed a fundamental justification for the party was the need for labour to secure membership of representative bodies. This objective co-habited with the educational goal of 'making socialists'. Formally these were seen as complementary, but in practice they appeared often as rivals. Over time the pursuit of electoral success squeezed out much of the vitality from the educational emphasis. This development will be discussed later. Now the emphasis must be on the forces promoting or retarding the growth of the party as an electoral force and representative presence. The analysis of industrial and trade union experiences has allowed some appreciation of the economic factors likely to generate or to inhibit support for the ILP. But the political realm has intruded throughout the enquiry. Sometimes, union factions employed and were moulded by accepted political labels. More significantly, there arose the recurrent problem of cashing industrial experiences or trade union loyalties within the established political patterns of a community. Political loyalties might be secured on the basis of district, nation or religion. Such sentiments might offer little scope for labour initiatives, and typically inhibited the forging of links between trade union experiences and political attachments. Alternatively, pre-existing positions might offer the hope of labour influence through an accommodation with congenial traditional sentiments. Here, typically through the appeal of Radical Liberalism, there lay a threat to the political independence of labour. More dramatically, conventional loyalties might be crumbling, leaving a political space into which a new political organisation might move. Assessment of such options requires examination of the potential for growth within a range of communities, but before detailed investigation can begin, some general constraints must be noted.

The formal rules governing electoral competition provided serious handicaps. The first-past-the-post electoral system raised obvious problems for a third party, unable to rely on the strong geographically limited support that had helped to make the Irish Nationalists such a significant force. ILP candidates were frequently vulnerable to Liberal accusations that votes for them were wasted votes, and would damage the chances of the only Radical candidate with any hope of winning. The obvious moral was to try and arrange straight fights. The harsh logic of the electoral system pointed towards a strategy that could erode independence, but a much more serious handicap was referred to only rarely by Labour leaders.

A wide belief persisted that from 1885, the British electoral system was basically an adult male representative democracy. In so far as there were exclusions, these were of individuals and did not constitute a significant social bias. But the effect of the labyrinth of qualifications, residence requirements, registration procedures, and revision court decisions was to exclude almost 4.8 million adult males from the register in 1910.[1] The proportion had remained much the same since 1885. The cumulative significance was that the electoral system was distinguished not just by its exclusion on the basis of sex; it also discriminated against the poor, the illiterate, the mobile and the young. Essentially possession of the vote was linked to property — its ownership, its occupation, or to an economic relationship with a property owner. Calculations of the quantitative significance vary, but all accounts agree that the extent of enfranchisement showed major variations between constituencies. One analysis claims that industrial areas, particularly in cities, did not have high levels of enfranchisement.[2] These included some places such as Dundee (48.1 per cent), Glasgow (52.4 per cent), Manchester (53.1 per cent) and Merthyr (55.7 per cent) where the ILP was of significance. In contrast, a few industrial towns had much higher levels, and again these included places with a sizeable ILP presence. The most notable ones were the West Riding strongholds of Bradford (67.9 per cent), Halifax (70.6 per cent) and Colne Valley (75.5 per cent). These figures were paralleled by Rochdale (71.1 per cent) which development a distinctive socialist tradition.

It would be misleading to claim that high rates of enfranchisement aided the ILP. Many of the most 'democratic' constituencies were in rural or residential regions, and had no ILP presence, and it would be naive to claim that the typically unregistered, unskilled labourers of the city slums represented a potentially mass ILP support. But the limited franchise meant that electorally many constituencies were much less working class than superficial appearances might suggest, and this inevitably affected the performance of a party appealing on a labour platform. ILP candidates often had encouraging meetings, but the ballot boxes presented a very different picture. Perhaps the discrepancy reflected in part the low level of enfranchisement amongst young working-class males. ILP propaganda could appeal effectively to them, it was a young person's party, but young men living with their parents could not claim a vote.

The registration system with its revision courts required a high level of party organisation and finance in order to protect the claims of known supporters, and to torpedo those of opponents. Any new party was clearly at a disadvantage in that respect, but above all it was the mobilisation of bias inherent in the franchise arrangements that presented overwhelming difficulties for a party claiming to represent working-class interests. There were compensations. Some constituencies returned two members, and with each elector able to cast two votes the wasted vote argument was less effective. Sometimes such seats had allowed Liberals to resolve their internal tensions by a ticket balancing Radical against Whig, and ILPers could appear as legitimate heirs to that tradition. Once again though, the logical destination of this strategy was a deal between ILPers and Liberals. It remained questionable how far such an arrangement would be backed by voters. Many committed Labour and Liberal voters might split their two votes in the appropriate manner, but some partisans might plump for their first preference and leave their second vote unused. Affluent Liberals might give their second vote to a Conservative; working-class Tories might decide to split their votes between a Conservative and the Labour candidate. Much would depend on the political traditions of the particular community.

Some compensation for the difficulties of parliamentary elections could be found in municipal politics. The gradual democratisation of local government had generated a glut of political contests for City and Town Councils, County Councils, Urban and Rural Districts, School Boards and Boards of Guardians, and Parish Councils. Sometimes, the franchise was more generous at the municipal level, whilst the system of cumulative voting for School Boards deliberately encouraged the representation of minorities.[3] The most significant feature was that the extensive number of contests meant that the established parties could not hope to compete across the board, and left room for new groups to develop some local credibility. Sometimes the political significance of such successes was limited. ILP candidates could secure municipal victories because of their personal standing rather than as adherents to a political position. Yet such municipal growth could help to give the party a credibility which it could then hope to extend to parliamentary contests. Moreover, the party often co-operated municipally with the local Trades Council, a prefiguration of wider national developments.

If the municipal dimension offered some small compensation for the obstacles posed by the electoral system, it could do nothing to alleviate the other disadvantages suffered by the ILP. One difficulty was the limited funds available for electoral activities. In July 1895, only three of the party's twenty-eight parliamentary candidates spent more than £300, and in seven cases expenditure was less than £150.[4] Such poverty contrasted vividly with the largesse often doled out by opponents. The formation of the LRC helped to reduce the discrepancy, as trade union money was thrown behind ILP candidates. Yet this did not eliminate the underlying problem. The ILP's opponents were often men who were backed not just by wealth, but also by all the inducements and sanctions that went along with established leadership of a community. The growth of a local ILP could be frustrated by the non-availability of rooms for meetings, and the belief — whether justified or not — that economic and social discrimination could result from open involvement. The scope for overt interference in the actual electoral process had declined since the introduction of the secret ballot in 1872 and the Corrupt Practices Act of 1883, but there is evidence that the landlord's 'screw' persisted in some areas until 1910, quite apart from a common belief that the ballot was perhaps not as secret as official claims suggested. Given the much smaller electorates and more stable, knowable communities of small town and rural Britain, beliefs in landlord and employer power could significantly affect political behaviour.[5] The obstacles faced by the ILP went beyond those posed by unsympathetic individuals or groups. Party propagandists also had to counter a web of assumptions and prejudices about what was reasonable, proper and possible. It was a web that included threads from a variety of sources: pulpit, local press, the educational system, and images integral to the local culture. It posed a major challenge for a party supposedly challenging the existing order and yet seeking to work through the existing political system.

Once again, there were some compensating factors. In some places, a unionised section of the working class could act as a counterweight to traditional blandishments and pressures. Perhaps dominant values could contain strands which might legitimise the ILP. The infinite ambiguities of Radicalism could be exploited effectively in such a cause. Sometimes the behaviour of established local leaders could be contrasted harshly with the claims that they utilised to protect their position. The laissez-faire industrial practices of Liberal employers might be set against their protestations of sympathy for labour.

Most crucially, fundamental shifts could provide the ILP with footholds in some communities. It has been shown earlier how, for all its ambiguities, the increased assertiveness of many trade unionists could have political consequences. Deteriorating industrial relations could have implications for the status of employers who served also as community leaders. Indeed, the idea of employers acting as spokesmen for communities was becoming less feasible, as family firms give way to limited liability companies. Beyond economic and social changes, local Liberalism, once an expression of a concordat between capital and labour, was in crisis in several places by the nineties. Liberal Associations had often lost wealthy backers in 1886. Home Rule was not simply a cause, but also an occasion for expressing a wider conservatism. While many working-class voters remained loyal to a Gladstonianism often dominated in the constituencies by the professional classes and tradesmen, others defected. Electorally, some were attracted by Unionist hints about social reform or appeals to imperial sentiments. On the left, some activists were increasingly impatient with Gladstonian attitudes on labour questions and direct representation. These political developments offered hopes and obstacles to the new party. At this point generalisation must end, and attention shift to the complexities of local politics; it was there that ILP activists had to confront and to solve the diverse problems of political space.

7

Scotland

A Liberal inheritance

The rich complexities of the Scottish ILP can be approached through an initial emphasis on its leading figures. Hardie's career and style conjure up some central themes.[1] The early faith in Scottish Radicalism points to the tortuous relationship between Liberalism and Labour, the struggle to develop miners' organisations highlights the weakness of much Scottish trade unionism, the Mid Lanark contest and the founding of the Scottish Labour Party spotlight a precocious political development. The complexities of the Radical inheritance were expressed also in the careers of two other ILP leaders Ramsay MacDonald and Bruce Glasier.[2] Stylistically, all three drew inspiration from a broad demoncratic tradition. They readily 'claimed' the Covenanters and Burns as anticipators of socialism. Other Scottish institutions left their mark. In later life, MacDonald was always keen to pay tribute to the education provided by his village schoolmaster.[3] All three were touched by the earnestness of the kirk. They were strong on self-improvement, and their images of moral behaviour for socialists owed much to conventional Presbyterian stereotypes of 'decency'. They reacted harshly against the hedonism of much working-class life. In the perpetual conflict between two images of Scottishness, they stood severely on the side of abstinence.

Scottish influence within the early ILP did not end with three out of the Party's 'Big Four'. Robert Smillie symbolised the growing influence of the ILP within the Miners' Federation of Great Britain, and Shaw Maxwell provided the Party's first Secretary. Robert Cunninghame Graham, the 'Laird of Gartmore' could make a plausible claim to be Britain's first socialist MP. Elected as Radical Member for North-West Lanarkshire in 1886, he moved rapidly to a socialist position, and achieved fame for his arrest in the Trafalgar Square riots of 1887. For a few years, his romantic style glowed on the British Left, but then he passed politically into a relative obscurity.[4] Prominence was not just a question of individuals. Scottish Labour could claim to be organisationally in advance of its English counterpart. The Scottish TUC from its foundation in 1897 was committed to Independent Labour politics. The creation of the Scottish Workers' Parliamentary Elections Committee pre-dated the formation of the LRC and did not involve the studious blurring of differences needed further south. Individual prominence and organisational precocity neither indicated nor produced massive support. It is a contrast which will recur throughout the analysis.

A second dichotomy must be noted. In Edinburgh in the early nineties, a young unskilled council worker engaged in socialist propaganda; although born in the city, his cultural background differed radically from the ILPers noted above. This was James Connolly, Irish Catholic in background, revolu-tionary socialist and nationalist of the future.[5] Other Irish recruits to the Scottish Labour politics did not evolve in the same fashion. Pete Curran moved from an apprenticeship in Glaswegian land and Irish agitations to become a prominent ILP 'New Unionist'. But the basic distinction is important. Within the Scottish working class, there existed a sizeable section who were distinguishable by nationality and religion. Such a division could be an obstacle to Labour propagandists who claimed to bridge the sectarian divide, but were themselves typically the products of a distinctively Scottish culture.

The characterisation of Scottish distinctiveness is a problematic exercise. Here was a society which remained significantly separate after the Union, a separation symbolised by the twin pillars of Law and Church. Beneath these, there lay an economic and social structure which helped to promote a distinc-tively Scottish politics. One problem is to explain why nineteenth-century Scotland, retaining so many of the preconditions for a separate nation-state, failed to follow the dominant European trend.[6] But already, the native bourgeoisie was participating in the massive trail-blazing growth of British capitalism. What need was there for that class to assert nationalist claims as a springboard for an industrial take-off? Explosive growth created the industries of the Lowlands, fed by migrants from the Highlands and from Ireland. It produced nineteenth-century Glasgow with its packed tenements, prosperous engineering industry and self-confident bourgeoisie.[7] It gave rise to a rash of bleak mining villages, and spawned industrial outposts in the East, such as Dundee with its ill-paid jute workers. The expanding modern Lowlands contrasted with the undeveloped, impoverished Highlands where a social order which might have provided a basis for a nationalist challenge had been too thoroughly pulverised.

The title 'North Britain' indicated an acceptance of incorporation, but such acceptance had to come to terms with the continuing existence of a clearly distinctive society. Accommodation involved a politically neutral celebration of Scottishness. One variation involved the 'Kailyard' school of writing, evok-ing a 'quaint' universe of small communities peopled by dry, wise 'characters', the road to Tannochbrae.[8] An alternative road led, with less sentimentality, to Hampden. The more sentimental response was one in which the ILP pioneers characteristically shared. In part this reflected the situation of the articulate lower-middle or respectable working-class Scot; in part it showed an awareness of an image of Scotland that was marketable not just within its own territory.

The political expression of the Scottish predicament was the traditional strength of Liberalism.[9] This was apparent in the 1885 election, when Liberals dominated the Scottish constituencies in a ratio of six to one. This hegemony reflected in part the absence within Scotland of some of the bases that guaranteed Conservative strength in England. Since the Church of Scotland was Presbyterian, the characteristic English cleavage between Tory Anglicans and Liberals Nonconformists was absent and the style of the Established Church was highly compatible with Liberalism. Yet there were distinctions that had political significance. The breakaway of the Free Church in 1843 had involved many Radical ministers and laity. In some areas, the religious split came close to being one of class, although still containable within the dominant Liberalism.[10] The transfer of government institutions and many accompanying paraphenalia to London had led to many Scottish aristocrats ceasing to be concerned with specifically Scottish matters. This provided a space for a confident Scottish bourgeoisie to exploit in the interests of Liberalism.

The strength of Scottish Liberalism did not depend simply on lacunae. It also appealed positively to divergent groups. Not surprisingly, self-made employers tended to have Liberal sympathies, and they were shared by many of their workers. In part this Liberal community across class lines was one that could be found in many industrial ares of Britain, but Scottish cultural traditions tended to strengthen the links. The ostensibly 'democratic' ethos of the kirk and the educational system could be found more precisely in the Covenanter tradition and the sentiments of Burns. But there was a sense in which by the eighties the strength of Scottish Liberalism was in many ways a conservative force. The sentiments that it expressed could still carry Radical associations, but they could be used to manipulate and disguise the real locus of power.

Any understanding of the character of Scottish Liberalism in the final years of its virtually undisputed dominance must involve a judicious balance. On the one side, Radical potential was far from exhausted; on the other there was some hardening of Liberal arteries. The Radical aspect could be seen most readily on the issue that more than any other gave a distinctive content to Scottish politics — the land question. This mattered almost everywhere. Agricultural tenants in the North-East and in the Lothians had strongly Radical propensities, the royalties question was inevitably important in mining areas — but it was the question of Highland Land Reform that provided the most significant element, not only in Liberalism, but also in the emergence of Scottish Independent Labour. The departure of many chiefs from the Highlands, the facilitation of massive land holdings by the Scottish legal system, the administration of such holdings by middlemen; the introduction of sheep (the first instalment in 'The Cheviot, the Stag and the Black, Black Oil'), rack-renting and evictions. All had contributed to a potent radical brew.

An immediate reaction with the advent of the Third Reform Act was a flowering of agrarian radicalism in the 1885 election, with five Crofters' candidates being elected independent of the official Liberals. These successes offer an admirable insight into the successful utilisation of a 'political space'. In most Highland seats, the electorate had been very small; Whig oligarchies had ruled, and in some seats, contested elections were rare. In 1885, under the new franchise, Crofters' candidates could occupy the vacant space, ventilating disaffection that had had no electoral outlet under the old dispensation. The advance was facilitated in the Highlands by the relative weakness of the professional classes who provided much of the infantry of Scottish Liberalism in other areas. Such 'space' was not normally available to the advocates of Independent Labour.[11]

The Radical consequences of the land question went further than the Highland contests of 1885. Memories of eviction and rack-renting had been exported to industrial areas as the population shifted en masse. Similar experiences had been the lot of many Irish immigrants. However divided the industrial working-class might be on religious matters, they often shared a similar agrarian background, one that was very different from that of their English counterparts. Arguably, a background of agrarian radicalism could spill over into urban political life, and several early Scottish ILPers received their political baptism in land reform agitations. The influence of Henry George was significant. His visit to Glasgow in 1882 led to the emergence of a land nationalisation movement in the West, whilst his return two years later saw the foundation of the Scottish Land Restoration League. Several of its activists, including Glasier and Shaw Maxwell, went from there into the SLP and then the ILP; but the League's founders also included stalwart Gladstonians. The distinctively socialist element was much more apparent in the smaller Scottish Land and Labour League.[12]

The inheritance was complex. Most Highland Radicals demanded nothing so 'advanced' as land nationalisation, nor did they usually press for the peasant proprietorship, characteristic of their Irish contemporaries. Rather their concern was with reforming the legal and economic aspects of their tenancies. Changes of this kind were achievable without too much upheaval. The deliberations of the Crofting Commission led to sizeable reductions in both rents and arrears and most Crofters' MPs became orthodox Gladstonians. Breakaway candidatures had not been restricted to the Highlands. In 1885, six Land Reformers stood independently in the West of Scotland, but here, where official Liberalism was well-established, they generally polled badly.[13] This process of separation from official Liberalism and then reunion was a common one. The land question proved to be something to which Scottish Liberalism could offer some response, although for some dissidents, their route now lay from Land Reform through to the SLP. For this minority the land agitation was the occasion for a farewell to official Liberalism.

Liberalism often left a lasting mark on those who moved to Independent

Labour. Smillie reversed Gladstone as the greatest man he had met, while Hardie produced a lengthy obituary of the Grand Old Man for the *Labour Leader*.[14] No doubt the moral Gladstone of the Midlothian campaigns struck a particularly responsive chord amongst Scotsmen raised on Presbyterianism. But although the mark of Liberalism remained, there were powerful forces tended to alienate advocates of Labour interests. The democratic ethos of Scottish Liberalism must not be taken for the whole story. The same ethos enshrouded both the educational and the religious institutions of nineteenth-century Scotland. But it is important to disentangle myth and reality and to understand a situation in which a widespread belief in educational and religious equality clouded an essentially hierarchical society, in which the mobility offered by the educational system was limited to the few and the laity's involvement in the kirk was restricted often to the relatively affluent.

A similar point can be made about Scottish Liberalism where Radical rhetoric cohabited with respect for established families and a rooted distrust of working-class candidates. Scottish Liberal candidates tended to be men of local standing rather than iconoclastic critics. It was typical that the very safe seat of Aberdeen North should pass in 1896 from a Radical educationalist who had originally won the seat against some official opposition to an ex-military man with local family and industrial connections. The rhetoric was a shroud over a Liberal exclusiveness. The form of this varied. In the burghs, associations tended to be dominated by a local elite knitted together through involvement in distinctively Scottish institutions — the law, religion and universities. In rural divisions, organisation tended to be less complete and dominated even more by wealth.[15] Some industrial areas witnessed the growth of separate Radical or Junior Liberal Associations, often catering at least in principle for working-class Liberals. The young aspiring Hardie helped to form a Junior Liberal Association. in Cumnock in 1884.[16]

Such bodies could take a relatively independent line. In 1885 the Aberdeen Radical Association successfully promoted W. Hunter for the new North Aberdeen seat, whilst in Perth, the Radical Association had a lengthy battle with the Liberal member, culminating in an independent candidature in 1892.[17] Sometimes Radical Associations could shift further away: some became supporters of Independent Labour; the Dundee Radical Association affiliated to the SLP.[18] Scottish Liberalism had its fissiparous tendencies; the traditions of Radical Associations and the tendency for Liberals to fight out their differences at the polls meant that the significance of early Labour candidates was unclear.

Despite these Radical outbreaks, Liberal politics tended to remain socially restricted. Certainly local associations sometimes had a very limited membership. In July 1892, it was claimed — and not denied — that the Tradeston Liberal Association had less than 100 members,[19] a critic of Glasgow Liberalism wrote of it in the same election as involving 'clergymen, Liberal candidates, exploiters of labour, middlemen, douce town councillors, smug faced elders in the kirk and subservient working-men'.[20] One Labour candidate who claimed also to be a 'true Liberal' suggested that 55 former members of Tradeston Liberal Association were now working for him.[21] But the Labour hope of mass secessions from a moribund Liberalism remained often just a dream. In some ways, the cosy, exclusive world of Scottish Liberalism was not a political dinosaur. It adjusted to some degree to the challenges posed by religious, ethnic and land issues. But demands for Labour representation were a very different matter. Any significant change here involved some undermining of an elite's near-monopoly. It was, moreover, a demand which many Liberals believed they could ignore, since Gladstonianism remained popular with the working-class electorate and the policies accepted by Scottish Liberal assemblies were more Radical than those adopted by their English counterpart.[22] Scottish Liberals were not normally confronted with one channel sometimes used by the advocates of Labour representation south of the border. Trade unions were typically weak and therefore could not serve plausibly as a channel for negotiating limited Lib-Lab representation. Only the Scottish miners could make claims for political representation and then not through, but against, the Liberal machine, and until 1914 with very limited success.

In the 1880s Scottish Liberalism like all political organisations contained a potential for decay but its tendencies towards division could be sources of strength — the promise of better things under the Liberal label — or of weaknesses, if breakaways went too far. Its exclusiveness when important decisions were involved obviously frustrated both middle-class and working-class Radicals, but its hold over working-class opinion seemed strong. Over the next decade the situation altered significantly. By 1895 Liberals held only 39 out of 72 Scottish seats compared with 62 a decade earlier.

During this decade the dominance of Scottish Liberalism was challenged on a number of fronts. One, the land question has been noted. Here the challenge came basically from the Liberal left, and the demands could be accommodated relatively easily. The principal and limited negative consequence for the Liberals was the shift of a few Radicals through to Independent Labour. A second challenge sprang from the growing pressures for Church disestablishment within Scottish Liberalism. Despite the lack of enthusiasm of Liberal leaders, many candidates were strongly committed and this provoked the development of some political cleavage along religious lines. Although the issue's importance was clearly exaggerated by contemporaries, it did produce some growth of Conservative strength, as Church of Scotland Ministers and usually affluent devotees left Liberal ranks.[23] This controversy reduced the Liberal presence near the top of the social pyramid, but its impact pales into insignificance besides that of Irish Home Rule. It was this above all that changed the agenda of and alignments within Scottish politics — at precisely the period when pressures for Independent Labour initiatives were increasing.

The impact on the electoral politics of Scotland was dramatic. In 1886, the number of Conservative MPs stood at only twelve, compared with the ten of 1885 — but there were no fewer than seventeen Liberal Unionists.[24] The reasons for the issue's massive impact are clear: geographical proximity to Ireland, close kinship ties between many Scots and Ulster Protestants, the existence of a sizeable Irish Catholic minority largely in the West, with their own educational system and social networks, close stylistic affinities between Scottish and Irish Protestantism and a belief by many Glasgow industrialists that the consequences of Home Rule would be economically disastrous. The collapse of the Irish economy was predicted as likely — the result would be mass immigration into Western Scotland, threatening Scottish living standards. Home Rule could also mean tariffs and a major threat to markets for Scottish industries. So opposition to Home Rule could appear as an issue linking classes with a blend of appeals to economic self-interest, ethnic superiority and religious bigotry. In the long run although not so obviously in 1886, the impact of this question was much greater in the West: when the Labour challenge is discussed in depth it will be necessary to make a basic distinction between Eastern and Western Scotland.[25]

One clear consequence of the Home Rule issue was to shift some of the more affluent Liberals over into the Unionist camp. When that dedicated Gladstonian John Morley spoke in Glasgow his platform 'was marked by the absence ... of the men of property and wealth in the city' while Haldane noted in East Lothian the defection of 'a good many of our most prominent Liberal supporters'.[26] Such shifts were occurring in many parts of Britain in the eighties and it is difficult to separate out the roles of Home Rule as cause and Home Rule as occasion for defection. Clearly men of property did see the issue as a threat both in real and in symbolic terms — the Edinburgh opposition was said to be infused with 'the Bondholder spirit of the Banks and Insurance Companies with property in Ireland'.[27] In the Scottish context, the distinctive factors produced an unusually traumatic split, exemplified by the reluctance of some Liberal Associations to pronounce on the issue. Moreover, it was certainly not just the Whigs who defected — some of the Liberal Unionists were thoroughly Radical on other issues and this injected a further complexity into the Scottish political argument.[28]

Early reaction amongst Liberal partisans seemed to suggest that defections were primarily at the top of the Scottish Liberal pyramid. Haldane drew consolation from his belief that in East Lothian 'the great bulk of the working class are with us'.[29] Rather more critically, Campbell-Bannerman's agent noted working-class support not because of any understanding of the policy but simply as a consequence of faith in Gladstone.[30] When the police fired upon a crowd at Mitchelstown, County Tipperary, in September 1887, causing three deaths, the Gladstonian Aberdeen Trades Council strongly condemned the action of the authorities. Such indications might lead to the suggestion that one consequence of the 1886 imbroglio was to reduce the influence of the affluent minority in local Liberal politics, and to make the Associations more responsive to loyal industrial workers. If this were the case, it would raise a clear problem of political 'space' for Independent Labour partisans.

Such a conclusion would be rash however; there is some suggestion that in Scotland as elsewhere, Liberals clung onto their remaining grandees with an affection enhanced by their scarcity value. Moreover, when Liberals wrote of working-class loyalty, and trades councils opposed British policy in Ireland, such information only illuminates the position of the Lib-Lab activists not that of the mass of working-class electors. But most crucially, these examples indicate nothing about the industrial heartland of the West, where Labour prospects perhaps should have been brightest, but where the Irish issue had most resonance. Here there is evidence of a significant growth in working-class Unionism after 1885. The economic card was a crucial element in this appeal — the Unionist candidates argued that the interests of workers in the West of Scotland required the Irish link and a firm foreign policy. The Conservative candidate in St Rollox emphasised in 1895 that 'There was no city in the United Kingdom more dependent for its prosperity on a good and strong foreign policy than Glasgow ... New markets were wanted ... and it was well known that when shipbuilding prospered, every other industry prospered'.[32] It was the Liberals, allegedly, who neglected the material well-being of the workers by pursuing constitutional and temperance fads. Some Liberals found it difficult to respond to such appeals: self-help and thrift appeared less and less as a viable response. The effectiveness of such Unionist claims in Glasgow can be gauged by their successes in 1900 — they won all seven seats, a complete reversal of the situation fifteen years earlier.[33]

The growth of popular Unionism in the West provides a significant amendment to the generally plausible claims about the dominance of Scottish Liberalism, a growth whose significance should be remembered if the environment for Independent Labour initiatives is to be understood properly. In some ways, it was similar to the Lancastrian case, although in Scotland it was perhaps working-class *Unionism* rather than working-class *Conservatism*, and it developed in a society with strongly Liberal antecedents.

One more complexity remains — that of the political contribution of the Irish population, a crucial element for Independent Labour partisans hoping to appeal to workers across ethnic and religious divisions. The Irish population in Scotland was concentrated heavily in the Western industrial areas, in the early nineties one informed observer calculated that more than half lived in Lanarkshire and about a quarter in Renfrew.[34] There was a massive concentration of Irish-born in Glasgow, and high proportions in Greenock, Govan and in many of the smaller coal and iron settlements. Elsewhere, the Irish formed significant communities in Edinburgh and particularly in Dundee,[35] but in Aberdeen the Irish element was slight. The Irish community was of course strongly working-class, employed above all in coal and iron, but — and this was perhaps significant for political allegiances — its leaders tended to have non-factory occupations. Electorally the Irish were a significant force in many western industrial seats, although it appears that they were enfranchised more thoroughly in the small communities of Lanarkshire than in Glasgow.[36]

The leading role in the organisation of the Irish vote in the West was taken by John Ferguson, an Ulster protestant and part-owner of a successful publishing business. As early as 1871, he had helped form a political organisation in Glasgow, and when the Irish National League was created in 1882, the old organisation became the influential Home Government Branch of the INL. The number of Scottish branches eventually reached more than one hundred. Most of these were in the West, more particularly in Glasgow where the Home Government Branch provided a basis for Ferguson, and the *Glasgow Observer* acted as a single-minded advocate of the Irish cause.[37]

The League's activists faced some formidable obstacles in their attempts to mobilise a large united Irish vote. The franchise system with its network of qualifications created difficulties for a largely poor and often mobile community. The relatively high level of illiteracy also posed problems. Organisers claimed that some Irish electors spoiled their ballots rather than run the risk of victimisation by revealing their preference to a polling clerk.

The nature of the INL organisation also generated friction. The search for a disciplined electoral presence led to attempts by the London-based Executive to make the branches no more than the obedient servants of the Irish Parliamentary Party. Inevitably, there were arguments with powerful branches such as the Home Government, partly out of general resentment at central dictation, but also on specific political issues. Thus in the 1885 election, Ferguson had not accepted the directive that support should be given to Conservative candidates, and along with Michael Davitt, had backed Shaw Maxwell, then standing for the Scottish Land Restoration League. The arguments about local autonomy were a vital element in the readiness of many activists to back the anti-Parnellite line in 1890—91, yet afterwards the relationship between the League and the anti-Parnellite MPs remained essentially the same, and continued when the warring factions were reunited eventually within the United Irish League.[38] The structure of the Irish organisation provided scope for misunderstandings with Labour politicians, as local Irish sympathisers responded to pressures from their national leaders.

The Irish strategy from 1886 clearly implied that in normal circumstances local leaders should advocate a Liberal vote. Irish voters should vote as Irishmen, and not as workers until Home Rule was settled. How far this solidarity was attained in practice is unclear. Connolly acknowledged that a majority would follow the guidance of the League but that 'a solid Irish vote on any subject has never yet been realised, even in the palmiest days of Parnell'.[39] Some League activists followed Davitt in advocating the common interests of British and Irish workers,[40] but after 1886 pressure for universal support for the Gladstonians increased inexorably. The debates over Parnell's future raised the question and resolved it in favour of a continuing alliance. The circumstances of the 1892 election, the introduction and defeat of the Home Rule Bill, the precarious state of the Government's majority, all pointed in the same direction.

In Western Scotland, the situation was even more antipathetic to any Labour—Irish deals because of growing Unionist strength. Irish links with the Scottish Labour Party had already been largely broken, the Irish press vehemently attached Labour interventions in the 1892 election and continued its condemnation when these interventions apparently led to Unionist victories. Within the League's demonology, Labour candidates could appear as the equivalent of Parnellites, damaging the Home Rule cause out of personal ambition and vanity.[41] Inevitably tensions over political strategy continued within the Irish organisation. Activists were predominantly working class and susceptible to Labour appeals, whilst Irish support was taken very much for granted by some Scottish Liberals. As Liberal enthusiasm for Home Rule notably declined after 1895, both Davitt and Ferguson shifted back to a more positive relationship with Labour. Yet the bait of Home Rule remained. Only a Liberal Government could credibly provide this.

Scottish ILPers were generally unequivocal supporters of Home Rule, and hoped for an Irish—Labour alliance. Yet the cultural traditions of Scottish and Irish communities provided abundant scope for mutual misunderstanding. The more devout Catholics amongst the Irish were opposed to the apparent irreligion of many socialists and Radicals. When the United Irish League recommended a vote for Smillie in a 1901 by-election, the *Glasgow Observer* argued tortuously that such a vote would be in no sense an approval of 'socialism'.[42] ILPers had their own religious prejudices. Failure to secure Irish support could be attributed to the malignant influence of priests, although the history of the Irish Nationalist Party was a clear demonstration that it was anything but a straightforward clerical organisation. Glasier, in the privacy of his diary, was prepared to go further. When the Protestant Truth Society leader, John Kensit, was killed at a Birkenhead meeting in 1902, his response was unambiguous: 'I esteem him a martyr. He had real enthusiasm and courage as an agitator and was I think a good man. I feel honest sympathy with his anti-Romanist crusade.'[43] Sometimes prejudices were not specifically religious but indicated some acceptance of stereotypes of Irish inferiority. Concern about the threat to the wages of Scottish workers resulting allegedly from difficulties in unionising the Irish could lead to criticisms that drew on racial stereotypes.[44] Hardie claimed that attempts by miners in the early eighties to maintain prices by output restriction were blighted by Irish immigrants. They had 'a big shovel, a strong back and a weak brain', came straight from 'a peat bog or a tattie field', and produced 'coal enough for a man and a half'.[45]

Leading Scottish ILPers clearly accepted some images that were shared widely within popular Scottish culture. One exaggerated organisational manifestation of the appeal of Protestantism could be found in the strength of the Orange Order. This could cohabit with a populism that some ILPers could find attractive. When a shipyard worker, T. H. Sloan, won a by-election victory in South Belfast in 1902, the *Labour Leader* acknowledged Sloan's extreme Protestantism but queried 'Is Belfast Awakening?'.[46] A Protestant trade unionist had characterised Sloan's programme, to Hardie, as 'extreme sectarianism ... (he was) a bigot strongly in favour of Progressive legislation'.[47] But Labour support for Home Rule automatically ruled out the chance of organisational support which remained committed strongly to the Unionists.[48] As long as the Home Rule question survived, Scottish Labour's hopes could be crushed between Green and Orange millstones, and the Liberal—Unionist split could retain some vitality. Labour's leadership commented ruefully in 1911 on how Scottish prospects were marred by 'an unfortunate sectarian bitterness'.[49]

Discussion of the political universe within which Independent Labour politics emerged in Scotland has concentrated necessarily on the politics of Scottish Radicalism and Irish Nationalism. As will emerge, the Scottish Labour Party, and then the ILP, carried forward many Radical policies and offered a variant on established Radical styles. Yet the break also involved commitments to socialist principles. During the eighties, the SDF and the Socialist League established branches in Glasgow and Edinburgh, and more fleetingly in some other places. These groups provided formative experiences for influential figures such as Glasier, and bequethed a nucleus of committed socialists to later organisations.[50] They could have a significant influence in a situation where some working class activists were becoming increasingly disillusioned with official Liberalism. A principled justification of socialism could fuse with a pragmatic desire for an independent labour organisation.[51] Some socialist pioneers believed that their propaganda must link directly with dominant Scottish concerns. One Edinburgh propagandist recollected that the city's first socialists felt obliged in 1884 to make concessions to Scottish Radicalism:

there were a considerable number of Henry Georges in the land, and it is likely ... that the canny Scot had even more of a narrow patriotism about him then, than he has today. It was a consciousness of such facts, doubtless which prompted certain spirits ... to think it advisable to hit on a name for a Scottish Society more homely, concrete, alluring, less abstract and foreign looking than the one which had been adopted'.[52]

So the title chosen was the Scottish Land and Labour League. Similarly in Aberdeen, a young activist James Leatham came to socialism, following enthusiasm for a host of Radical causes.[53]

The crisis of Scottish Liberalism beset by defections to left and to right formed the setting for the emergence of Scottish Labour politics. Yet the tactics and style of many Labour activists demonstrated that despite their labour demands and their socialism, they retained an awareness of and some attachment to Radical sentiments. The prospects for Scottish Labour were bound up inexorably with those of Liberalism.

The Scottish Labour Party

The West of Scotland provided the location for a significant initiative in Labour politics — the creation of the Scottish Labour Party in the summer of 1888. This organisation has been neglected in many studies, and on one level, the lack of attention is understandable. The SLP made little electoral impact until it was absorbed into the ILP at the beginning of 1895. The character of the party was ambiguous, with its members expressing a variety of responses to the dominant problem of relationships with Liberalism. But the SLP was the earliest constituent of what later became the ILP[54] and Hardie's involvement in the party could be seen as an early enunciation of the strategy that later secured expression in the Labour Alliance. The SLP expressed a commitment to independence but not to isolation, it aspired to become a broadly based alliance of reformers and trade unionists, it spoke often in a Radical idiom but hoped to attract socialists. It has importance as an early contribution to what later became a dominant position, but its development must be placed within a distinctively Scottish setting.

The new party grew immediately out of the celebrated Mid Lanark by-election of April 1888, a contest that has been discussed often but whose significance remains a matter of some controversy. Some subscribers to a traditional Labour historiography found little difficulty:

the election had cleared the air, and had settled one thing for ever, the impossibility of a Labour party *within* the Liberal Party ... From that day onwards the coming of the Independent Labour Party was a certainty ... A new chapter in Labour politics was opened.[55]

The early interpretation of Mid Lanark as a crucial break has been challenged by those who emphasise a major element of continuity, locating Hardie's initiative firmly within the sentiments of Scottish Radicalism, and the fissiparous organisational tendencies of Scottish Liberalism.[56] A counter-claim involves an emphasis on Hardie's trade union experiences. Attempts to develop a miners' organisation and to obtain a hearing for their demands could heighten an awareness of the need for labour representation, and prepare the way for a challenge to the Liberal caucus. They could also generate scepticism about Liberal economic principles and lead Hardie towards an acceptance of socialist arguments.[57]

Assessment of Hardie's relationship with Liberalism must distinguish between organisational and ideological aspects. Discussion of organisational relationships is complicated by the involvement of individuals who imported their own strategic emphases. The 1887 TUC had decided to form a Labour Electoral Association, hopefully to increase Labour representation, but operating typically under Lib-Lab auspices. Its Secretary, T. R. Threlfall, was active on Hardie's behalf, but more significance should be given to the involvement of H. H. Champion, nominally attached to the LEA, but antipathetic to Liberalism. He urged Hardie to work with him to pressurise the Liberals into making concessions to Labour:

I now have some *power* and I am prepared to go to Schnadhorst (the Liberal organiser) at once on hearing from you, and swear to lose the seat for Liberals in South West Ham, Deptford, Battersea, Central Finsbury and Bristol North unless you are allowed a walkover.

If you are not given fair play, stand and split them. It will give you enormous power at General Election. If you have the required determination they *must* bow to you and yours.[58]

Such a tactic implies some degree of organisational independence but leaves open the question of ideological differences. Champion was opposed to many Liberal icons, but Hardie proclaimed himself sympathetic to Radical aspirations.

Hardie's own public position on the organisational question paralleled Champion's, although his sympathy towards Liberalism peeped from beneath his urging of an independent candidate:

Much depends on the position taken up by the Liberal Association. It may or may not select a Labour candidate. In either case my advice would be that the Labour candidate should be put forward. Better split the party now, if there is to be a split, than at a general election; and if the Labour Party only make their power felt now, terms will not be wanting when the general election comes.[59]

When Hardie tested the attitude of the Mid Lanark Liberals by forwarding his own name, he could describe himself as a candidate 'in the Radical interest'.[60] The Liberals, whatever their democratic claims, preferred a well-heeled Radical and eventually selected a Welsh barrister, Wynford Philipps.[61] The lack of strong trade unions meant that Scottish Labour lacked a crucial resource. At least in public, Hardie claimed that Liberal leaders in Scotland and London were ready to reach an accommodation; the fault lay locally with 'those kid-gloved fellows of the shop-keeping and middle-class' who controlled the Associations.[62]

Hardie's Radical credentials meant that he was favoured by some whose commitment to Liberalism was clear. John Wilson of the Durham Miners acknowledged that 'his programme declares him a Liberal',[63] and C. A. V. Conybeare, the Radical Member for Camborne, spoke from Hardie's platform.[64] Yet the organisational question had a corrosive effect on such Radical support. Champion's involvement lent credence to allegations about the source of Hardie's funds,[65] and Radical concern about this was exacerbated when Schnadhorst travelled to Glasgow in an unsuccessful attempt to secure Hardie's withdrawal. Promises of a seat at the next general election, payment of expenses, and a parliamentary salary left untouched the problem of local Liberal obduracy. The rejection led to the departure of Radicals, Conybeare insisting to Hardie that 'we have gained our point'.[66] Hardie had no principled objection to arrangements with Liberals as later SLP and ILP developments would indicate. Yet he argued later that labour could only hope to secure a worthwhile bargain if it had its own separate organisation. A last-minute withdrawal in response to a vague promise would damage the prospects for this. Whatever the continuities of principle and rhetoric, Hardie's intervention clearly implied a commitment to this strategy.

Separation was not simply a means of securing a bargaining position. Whatever Hardie's sympathy towards many traditional Radical nostrums, his industrial experiences had produced a deep scepticism towards Liberal attitudes on specifically labour questions. In the previous July, he had submitted Gladstonian claims to critical examination:

among Radicals and Gladstonian Liberals, what is there in their programme likely to be of benefit, say to the miners of the country? Some vague talk about allotment schemes, and among the extreme men, Disestablishment and free education, with a graduated income tax and perhaps a revision of the death duties are spoken of ... with bated breath.

The miners could hope for little from the Liberal Party. 'Party be hanged; we are miners first and partisans next.'[67] Miners' demands formed a central element in a programme developed by Hardie and Chisholm Robertson in 1887,[68] and provided a major plank in his Mid-Lanark platform. When he urged his candidacy on the Mid-Lanark Liberals, he emphasised the need for Scottish miners to have their own MP.[69] His programme advocated a range of collectivist demands — a legal eight-hour day, insurance and superannuation, compulsory arbitration involving minimum wages, and the nationalisation of mining royalties and minerals.[70] Even his arguments about his rejection by the Liberal Association struck a class-conscious note. He called for the Liberal nominee to be selected by a ballot to allow working-class Radicals a say; Labour representation was essential to end exploitation:

How was it possible for wages to rise or for working-men to get a fair share of the wealth, they created so long as the idle class were absorbing £2 sterling for every 20s that came to the working-men? How was the system to be changed? It was by sending working-men to Parliament, not lawyers or baronets, or the nominees of baronets.[71]

Such appeals could provide a backbone for a distinctive Labour organisation. It remained open how far the collectivist proposals could be assimilated into a revised Liberalism or alternatively whether they would lead inexorably to a socialist commitment. Yet in the circumstances of the late eighties, they imparted a distinctive character to Hardie's campaign. The labour emphasis produced trade union backing. The Glasgow Trades Council decided to support Hardie[72] as did the Steel Smelters' Executive.[73] The limited local miners' organisations predictably favoured him. But trade unionism was generally weak, a situation which spurred activists to develop political organisation as an alternative. Yet in turn such organisation could not rely on trade unions for a steady base of support. This was to be a major problem for the SLP.

If the Labour appeal could secure only limited trade union backing, Hardie had one further resource. He could claim support on grounds of nationality, both Scottish and Irish. The demand for a Scottish miners' MP was based in part upon the distinctive requirements of the Scottish miner and his attacks on the Liberal candidate included a claim that a Welsh barrister could not hope to understand distinctively Scottish issues.[74] These emphases were echoed by Ramsay MacDonald, secretary of the London-based Scottish Home Rule Association.[75] Such support might be an interesting anticipation of the future, but it could offer little concrete benefit. Liberalism, irrespective of a particular candidate's background could still make a potent appeal to feelings of Scottishness.

An appeal to the Irish was another matter. The Nationalist vote was thought to be well organised and sizeable.[76] Hardie appealed to the Home Government Branch of the INL for support, claiming that he would vote with the Irish Party on all Irish issues even if this involved voting against the Liberals.[77] He secured the support of some local Irish leaders, most notably John Ferguson,[78] but the National League's organisation was generally hostile. Threlfall noted gloomily 'you will find the Irish Party difficult to deal with unless you have the support of the caucus'.[79] A local Irish journal proclaimed the justification for voting Liberal: 'We cannot afford much as we would like to serve the interests of the workmen ... We want to settle Home Rule first'.[80] This view reflected those of national Irish leaders. Davitt was distinctive in supporting Hardie;[81] Parnell, despite characteristic Champion threats of a Labour—Unionist alliance threw his influence behind the Liberal.[82]

The problems posed by the continuing appeal of radicalism, by weak trade unionism and by the vagaries of the Irish vote combined to limit Hardie's appeal and offered a foretaste of long-term Labour difficulties in Western Scotland. His vote of 617 was well below the early optimistic prognostications, and Labour activists did not even have the satisfaction of disturbing Liberal security. But the contest led readily to the creation of a Scottish Labour Party. Hardie had been considering such a strategy for some time, and during the campaign he had acknowledged privately the need for an electoral organisation.[83] After his defeat, he attempted to convert the coalition that had supported him into a more durable organisation. His suggestion was modest, a Glasgow conference:

to consider the best methods for securing the return of Labour Members to the House of Commons, and also for carrying on active propaganda work in the Constituencies with a view to the education of the Electors.

At least, a conference could co-ordinate the efforts of discontented Radicals: 'there are a number of active earnest men in every town and village, and if these could be got to work in concert much good would result'.[84] A preliminary meeting was held in Glasgow on 19 May 1888, and a formal conference inaugurated the new organisation there on 25 August.[85] This foundation meeting could be seen as a symptom of the crisis of Scottish Liberalism, bringing together a range of dissenters from the official organisation. Cunninghame Graham took the chair. Irish nationalism was represented by John Ferguson, the land reformers included Dr G. B. Clark, the Crofter's MP for Caithness, John Murdoch the crofters' leader and Shaw Maxwell on his road from Glasgow Liberalism through the land agitation to the ILP Secretaryship. Some represented the miners' organisations and communities of the West, most notably Robert Smillie, whilst Hardie straddled the worlds of radicalism and trade unionism. The few established socialist elements of Scotland remained aloof and no delegates appeared from Scottish branches of either the SDF or the Socialist League.

Those who did come held divergent views of the appropriate strategy. Hardie clearly hoped at least to develop an independent organisation that could bargain effectively with the Liberals. Graham's attitude to official Liberalism remained ambiguous, Ferguson saw the new organisation as a limited tactical device. He maintained a basic faith in Radical politics, and felt that separation should not be pushed too far:

I am delighted to know the Labour Party is for action. My opinion is still it sh^d enter the Liberal Association and work through it. There is certainly an element of danger in two political organisations holding the same principles, coming into collision.[86]

The SLP's officers reflected these disparate origins. Hardie was elected Secretary, the socialist George Mitchell became Treasurer, and Graham took the Presidency, but the numerous Vice-Presidents incluced Clark and Ferguson and — later — Conybeare, whilst Shaw Maxwell was Chairman of the Executive.

The inaugural conference produced a programme apparently on the basis of a draft from Hardie. Its kernel reflected his proposals of the previous year.[87] The labour reforms were carried over almost unaltered. Significantly the additions were more conventionally Radical. Temperance and parliamentary reforms were common to both statements. The SLP platform added commitments to Home Rule all round, no wars without Commons' consent and disestablishment. Hardie's initial proposal for a land tax was amended by the Scottish Land Restoration League element to one for land nationalisation. Essentially, the programme blended Radical and Labour demands without any commitment to a socialist objective. Two delegates did propose the nationalisation of all capital used in production, but Hardie secured this amendment's withdrawal by suggesting that this item could appear in a later statement. This inclusion did not materialise for some time. The SLP moved only tentatively towards a socialist commitment but by 1893, having shed some of its Radicals, its objective was proclaimed as 'the co-operative ownership by the workers of land and the means of production'.[88]

Catholicity of programme was matched by an attempted elasticity of organisation. Initially there was no restriction on the activities of members of other parties within the SLP. It was only after the difficulties encountered in the 1892 election that SLP officials were prohibited from being members of any other party. An attempt to extend the ban to the rank and file was defeated; it would damage hopes of winning Radical recruits.[89] The SLP hoped to establish a network of branches, but it also threw its net wider. The Constitution provided for two different annual meetings. One, known as the Annual Business Meeting, was in effect a party conference at which the Executive could be held to account for its stewardship. There was also a 'Conference' which had a much broader composition. Its basis, as set out in the Constitution was significant:

A Conference of Members residing in localities where no branch exists, and who subscribe not less than Five Shillings yearly to the funds, of Representatives from branches and affiliated associations, and of such kindred organisations as the Executive may see fit to invite, shall be held yearly, at which all questions relating to the policy or programme of the Labour Party may be discussed.[90]

This conception of a broadly-based gathering of labour spokesmen under the auspices of a distinctive party left its mark on the early ILP hope for a federal structure that would incorporate trade unions. More crucially, it can be seen as a significant contribution to the emergence of the Labour Representation Committee. When Hardie argued for such a broad assembly in the late nineties, his SLP experiences could serve as a plausible exemplar.

These gatherings brought a wide variety of Scottish labour activists together. The Party claimed that 170 delegates attended its 1891 Conference.[91] Yet the Party's specific presence was limited. Prior to the creation of the ILP in 1893, it boasted only 23 branches.[92] The most active centres were Glasgow and Edinburgh. In June 1893, the five SLP branches in Edinburgh and Leith claimed 346 members.[93] Elsewhere, although the party claimed to have propagandised from Carlisle to Aberdeen, branches were few, the most significant strength being in Dundee and in some communities in the industrial West.[94]

Two fundamental problems bedevilled the SLP's attempts to develop a strong and distinctive presence. One was the weakness of much Scottish trade unionism, the other involved the equivocal relationship between several of the party's leading spokesmen and Radical Liberalism. Trade union weakness had helped to produce some awareness of the need for an independent political initiative, but then deprived the party of much hope of mobilising sentiments of industrial solidarity for its own purposes. Most crucially perhaps, 'New Unionism' achieved only a limited success in Scotland, and when Hardie and Graham intervened in the 1889 Scottish seamen's strike, only recriminations resulted.[95] We have seen the weakness of much Scottish mining trade unionism in the late eighties. The SLP secured the support of activists such as Smillie and William Small, but they could point to only very limited memberships, and prospects were damaged further when Hardie and Chisholm

Robertson quarrelled at a Miners' Conference in June 1889, with Robertson denouncing Hardie for allegedly neglecting miners' interests in his support of the seamen.[96] The Lib-Labism of the well-organised Fife Miners served only to underline the SLP's problems.

A further attempt for the SLP to secure trade union support seemed to arrive with the bitter Scottish railway strike of 1890—91. The SLP Executive attempted to highlight a political moral. The use of the military to evict strikers' families at Motherwell was presented as an argument for labour representation. More specifically those MPs who were directors of the Caledonian and North British Railways were listed, the SLP pledging itself to try 'to hound these men from public life and secure their defeat at the polls'.[97] But such hopes produced little immediate benefits. The strike collapsed, the secretary of the Scottish Railway Servants opposed independent labour politics. Weak organisation combined with Lib-Lab officialdom to offer a discouraging prospect.

These features of Scottish trade unionism help to explain the early SLP failure to secure the affiliation of trades councils.[98] The Glasgow Trades Council, although backing Hardie at Mid Lanark, had not been represented at the SLP's foundation conference. But in June 1889, the council met a SLP deputation, Hardie, Maxwell and Mitchell.[99] The affiliation question became intertwined with the animosity between Hardie and Robertson, whilst the Scottish Railway Servants also strongly opposed any alliance.[100] The council did not affiliate, and neither did its Edinburgh counterpart. In this case, the council had been represented at the August 1888 conference, but it was subsequently claimed that the SLP's role was already covered by a Labour Electoral Association.[101] Elsewhere opposition was more firmly partisan. The Dundee council was staunchly Gladstonian, whilst a SLP member alleged that in Greenock, the council was 'a good Tory preserve'.[102]

This unpropitious situation was complicated further during 1891 when Champion's distinctive views began to make themselves felt amongst Scottish trades councils. He had considerable influence amongst Aberdonian labour activists and early in 1891 a joint committee representing both the Aberdeen Trades Council and a local labour committee suggested the convening of a Scottish conference of trades council delegates.[103] At this stage, there was no suggestion of a rival to the SLP. Hardie was sympathetic, and an initial meeting at Edinburgh in August 1891 seemed promising. Sixty-seven delegates attended, and an executive was formed to prepare a report on political organisation. The SLP viewed developments with equanimity, characterising relationships with the new group as 'of the most harmonious kind'.[104] But a second meeting in Glasgow in March 1892 set out to develop a new party, the Scottish United Trades Councils Labour Party, having trades councils as the basic local unit. Most major councils affiliated, and the programme was a mixture of labour and political reforms. The new organisation paralleled the SLP but perhaps could become complementary if it could establish a solid trades council attachment. The Secretary, however, was Chisholm Robertson, which hinted at old rivalries, whilst the Championite presence gave a distinctive flavour to the party's Aberdeen stronghold. The SUTCLP disappeared during 1893, and an attempt to revive it in the autumn as part of Champion's feud with Hardie was a disastrous failure.

The confusing state of Scottish Labour politics in 1892—3 was attributable in part to the weakness of the SLP. Failure had led to this second project securing some credibility, with the inevitable overlapping complicated further by personal acerbities. Yet the success of the SUTCLP in cultivating links with trades councils indicated some shift in Scottish trade union opinion which could produce subsequent benefits for the SLP. Over time, like many of their counterparts in the south, the Scottish trade unions reacted to industrial pressures and political frustration by becoming more receptive to the independence argument. Thus in Edinburgh the trades council delegates and local socialists were brought into a closer relationship by the rail strike agitation:

Then they stood on and spoke from the same platforms; *then* the Trades Councillors heard more Socialism preached in an hour than they possibly had heard in all their life before.[105]

A broad alliance of activists came together to back John Wilson the Broxburn Miners' Agent in his Edinburgh Central candidature of 1892. This chemistry led easily to the formation of several SLP branches in the city which were able to work in general harmony with the trades council. Throughout Scotland, trades councils moved to support independent labour. As one SLP member proclaimed in January 1893 a vital change had occurred in Glasgow:

During the last election the Labour Party could hardly force the fighting against the Liberals of the Trades Council ... Since then all this had changed, and the Socialist vote, pure and simple, on the principle of Socialism, had been carried by 44 votes to 3 ... The Council was theirs and they would keep it.[106]

It was an advance, yet one whose significance must not be exaggerated. Union organisation remained limited. Scottish trades councils were important as compensations for individual union shortcomings, but the representational significance on political questions of councils, and of the small unions that often dominated them, was limited. This shift was an important one for the SLP but it was one on which mass support had still to be built.

The SLP slowly developed its position within Scottish trade unionism, removing or neutralising much of the initial hostility and scepticism. The clarification of a political strategy was if anything even more tortuous. The idea of developing an independent organisation capable of achieving deals with the Liberals inevitably encountered difficulties. Some within the SLP clearly regarded a separate organisation as a short-term tactical measure; others had more ambitious, if ill-defined expectations. All shared continuities of idiom with Radical Liberals that could erode independence.

The bargaining strategy was attempted before the formal inauguration of the SLP. Champion's influence was apparent in the appearance of Tom Mann at a by-election in the Ayr Burghs. Hardie also spoke at a meeting in the Irvine Orange Hall, criticising the LEA's Secretary Threlfall for advising an unconditional Liberal vote. Instead Hardie led a deputation to the candidates which quizzed them on labour matters, and then agreed to back the Liberal.[107] Labour optimism grew further when Hardie exposed the anti-trade union sentiments of a prospective Liberal candidate in Greenock. Radical hostility was aroused, and the Greenock Liberals abandoned the idea of inviting him to stand.[108]

Although such developments could be regarded as promising, they also precipitated a problem. Success in persuading Liberal Associations to be more receptive to Labour and Radical sentiments could make the SLP redundant, especially for those who regarded a Liberalism purged of Whiggish prejudices as an attractive option. The appeal of Radicalism remained.[109] It has been shown earlier how the West Fife Miners stood aside for Birrell in June 1889, and later that year there was an abortive attempt to run John Burns at Dundee. This ended with Burns's withdrawal when some Liberals made noises about allowing him a free run in Battersea. Such flexibility could deflect Labour activists. One recalled that 'our committee and enthusiasm collapsed like a cask without hoops'.[110]

The SLP's tactics nevertheless produced a Liberal response early in 1890. Liberal hopes of a by-election gain in Partick led to a meeting between Edward Marjoribanks, the Scottish Liberal Whip, and Graham, Maxwell and possibly Hardie.[111] An arrangement was reached that in return for SLP support in Partick, Labour candidates would be given free runs in three Scottish seats. For Marjoribanks, at least, such candidates should be supporters of Liberal policies on non-labour questions, and the relationship between such putative candidates and the official Liberal organisation remained obscure.[112] Nevertheless, this arrangement soon collapsed. Greenock was specifically mentioned as one of the likely constituencies and local Liberals reacted angrily to any suggestion that their freedom to select a candidate should be circumscribed.[113] Rejection also came from the Liberals in Glasgow Blackfriars, generally reckoned to be another likely venue. Local Liberal antagonism was not the only problem.[114] The SLP side of the bargain seemed worthless, when the Unionists retained Partick. Such a suburban seat was perhaps not the best testing ground for the party's capacity to deliver a significant vote.[115] Indeed, SLP leaders claimed no more than 700 supporters.[116] Liberals argued that concern about the compact had inhibited middle-class electors from abandoning Unionism.[117] The SLP could serve as a convenient scapegoat for Gladstonian failure, but more seriously the credibility of the bargaining strategy had been damaged severely.

The collapse of a formal concordat was accompanied by increasing hostility between the SLP and the Irish, as the latter placed even more hope in a Liberal Home Rule initiative. Yet hopes of accommodations in specific constituencies remained and helped to produce confusion in the 1892 election. Cunninghame Graham, having left North West Lanark, was accepted at one stage by the Camlachie Liberal Association, but then repudiated after he had attacked the Liberal Party.[118] The sitting Liberal Member had already been repudiated by local activists because of his opposition to disestablishment, and they then adopted a third man to beat off challenges from left and right. Graham also forfeited Irish support, despite his strong advocacy of Home Rule.[119]

Throughout his campaign, Graham claimed that he represented the best elements in the Liberal tradition. He was 'the Liberal, Labour and Trades Council Candidate'.[120] Although he supported Home Rule and proclaimed his Republicanism,[121] collectivist reforms were at the centre of his campaign. The Scottish Liberal Association might proclaim its support for eight hours legislation, but Graham claimed that Glaswegian Liberal candidates did not do so.[122] He saw the achievement of Irish Home Rule as the beginning, not the end. The labour problem would remain in a free Ireland.

The contest reached a climax with Marjoribanks's visit to Glasgow. He claimed that he and the Camlachie Liberal candidate had favoured arbitration but that Graham had refused. Marjoribanks summed up the ambiguities of the SLP's strategy:

He did not want to drum Mr. Graham from the Liberal Party, but Mr. Graham's idea was that he should dictate to the Liberal Party that two, three, four, or five candidates should be withdrawn and that his nominees should be allowed to step in.[123]

The situation was, if anything, even more confused in a second Glasgow seat, Tradeston. The Liberal Unionist Member, Cameron Corbet, was a radical and a temperance enthusiast, the adopted Liberal candidate, Caldwell, had been elected as a Liberal Unionist for St Rollox in 1886, and the SLP aspirant, Burleigh, presented himself as a 'true Liberal'.[124] Surrounded by such exotic political pedigrees, Burleigh's was not an outlandish claim. He had attempted to secure the Liberal nomination, and during the campaign scouted the possibility of both Caldwell and himself standing aside for another Liberal candidate.[125] The complex links between Gladstonianism and the SLP emerged in a different form in Perth, where the SLP appears to have supported the nominee of the Perth Radical Association, fighting largely on the disestablishment issue against a Liberal incumbent.[126]

A third SLP candidate stood further down the Tay in Dundee, where James Macdonald, born locally but now based in London, was adopted.[127] The dominant political tone in Dundee was Radical,[128] and Macdonald stood essentially against just one of the Liberal members, Edmund Robertson. He was supported not simply by the SLP branch, but also by the Radical Association.[129] His campaign made little impact. The trades council's Liberalism proved resistant to appeals that Macdonald should be preferred to Robertson as the second candidate.[130]

The complexities of the SLP's 1892 position highlighted the blend of elements that had produced the party. Macdonald's platform was strongly class-conscious;[131] elsewhere the continuities with Gladstonianism were greater. The circumstances of the election, with the Liberals making no concessions, helped to push the party towards a stronger emphasis on the class aspect. The Executive met early in the 1892 campaign, and declared against any negotiation or compromise with other parties. It urged supporters 'to abstain from voting for Liberal candidates, if the opposition to Cunninghame Graham and Bennet Burleigh be not unconditionally withdrawn.[132] The hope of concessions lingered, but the lines were hardening. They hardened still further after the disastrous election results (see table 11). The election also had

Table 11. *SLP Results 1892*

	Unionist	Liberal	SLP	Other
Camlachie (Graham)	3,455	3,084	906	179
Tradeston (Burleigh)	3,366	3,197	783	—
Dundee (2)	5,659	8,484	354	—
(Macdonald)	5,066	8,191		

a purgative effect, with Radicals having to decide on their primary loyalty; some decided that it did not lie with the SLP.[133]

The formation of the national ILP in January 1893 inevitably raised the question of the SLP's absorption into the wider organisation. Although the party was well represented at Bradford, it had decided not to surrender its independence immediately. In part, this reflected doubt about the durability of the new initiative, but it also highlighted awareness that the SLP was a specifically Scottish body, and that this dimension would be lost within a British party.[134] Possibly, Hardie preferred to have a reliable base in the SLP until the ILP prospects had become clearer. Certainly, events during 1893 demonstrated how far the SLP had become a loyal supporter of Hardie and his views. When Champion attempted to resurrect the SUTCLP with a conference at Dundee in October 1893, he met with resolute opposition from the SLP.[135] Independent Labour, with the exception of Aberdeen, was now largely committed to Hardie, and when he took the ILP Presidency in February 1894, the SLP's distinctive career was virtually over. At the end of the year, the ILP absorbed the older organisation.[136]

The extent and the limitations of the SLP's achievements were revealed sharply in April 1894 when a second by-election occurred in Mid Lanark. The local Miners' Association had decided some months before to put forward a candidate, and had chosen their leader, Bob Smillie. Even now, there were lingering hopes of an understanding. The Miners' had attempted to secure a free run from the Liberal Association, but they responded by adopting the ex-Liberal Unionist, James Caldwell, who had fought Tradeston in 1892.[137]

Smillie was committed unequivocally to the standard Radical demands and to Home Rule but his central appeal was a labour one.[138] He drew attention to the constant experience of trade union defeats as a justification for a political intervention. Here was one motif of the SLP experience. Industrial weakness generated an attachment to political initiatives, but the impact of these was damaged by that same lack of industrial organisation. Although local Miners had backed Smillie, union membership remained limited. It exemplified a crucial problem that had bedevilled the SLP since its inception.

An attempt by Hardie to secure some organised backing for Smillie led directly to a second perpetual problem. He wrote to Michael Davitt who had supported him in 1888, asking him to help Smillie. Davitt refused and appeared in Mid Lanark to support the ex-Unionist. He explained to both Hardie and to John Ferguson,[139] that 1888 had shown that the Liberals had the bulk of the anti-Unionist vote, a Labour candidate could only help the Unionists, and less plausibly that the Rosebery Government deserved to have the support of all Progressives.

The campaign grew steadily more acrimonious. Exaggeration, innuendo and misrepresentation became the staple diet of argument on both sides. Davitt referred to Hardie 'and his friends of the Tory Party' and derided Hardie's parliamentary record.[140] How far Davitt's rhetoric was with tongue in cheek is unclear. Smillie claimed during the campaign that Davitt had conceded that he was by the far the better Home Ruler, but had been discounted since he could not win.[141] Press propagandists were even less inhibited. The Radical *North British Daily Mail* alleged that Tories 'and the handful of windbags who call themselves the Independent Labour Party are working hand in hand'.[142] The Irish *Glasgow Observer* turned its fury on the SLP. It was:

a set of the most venomous enemies that Ireland and the Irish people have ... this bogus Labour Party ... aims at injuring Ireland. It is a dishonest party. Every man with Irish blood in its veins should shun it, as he would the bitterest enemy of his race.[143]

Labour Propagandists were quite capable of responding in kind, and did not flinch from raising the ethnic issue. One of Smillie's chairmen claimed the fight was becoming one 'between the Irish working-man and the Scotch working-man'.[144] Hardie wrote of the Irish Party carrying out 'the dirty scavenging work of the Liberal Party'. Home Rule was 'an excuse for defeating Labour candidates'.[145]

The efforts of the previous six years made relatively little impact on the Liberal hegemony in Mid Lanark. Smillie, despite his local eminence and in particular his trade union work, just failed to double Hardie's 1888 vote on a higher poll (see Table 12). The Mid Lanark figures highlight the SLP's limited impact. Labour candidates and propagandists faced a discouraging prospect in appealing to a working class divided on ethnic and religious lines. The lack of any compensatory strong trade unionism was in part a further reflection of this fundamental problem. Yet the SLP's pioneering work was important. It indicated potential for leftward secessions from Scottish Liberalism, it

Table 12. *Mid Lanark 1888 and 1894*

	April 1888	April 1894
Liberal	3,847	3,965
Unionist	2,917	3,635
Labour	617	1,221

brought to prominance talented individuals who could form the nucleus of a labour presence within Scottish politics. Perhaps most significantly, the distinctive Scottish environment produced strategies which were to be applied subsequently in a wider context.

Champion and Aberdeen

The Scottish Labour Party did not monopolise the Labour banner in the 1892 election. Three candidates also stood on behalf of the Scottish United Trades Councils Labour Party: Hardie's old antagonist, Chisholm Robertson in Stirlingshire; Brodie in Glasgow College; and, most importantly, H. H. Champion in Aberdeen South.[146] This separate development reflected to some degree tensions at the national level. Concern over Champion's role in Labour politics, and in particular, criticism of the sources of his funds meant that his involvement inevitably generated controversy and division. This tendency was deepened by his strong antagonism towards Liberalism, a style and strategy far removed from the ambiguous relationship of the SLP and the Liberal Party. To some degree, these splits within Scottish Labour were a consequence of national developments. However, it is important to examine more closely the economic and political situation in Champion's Aberdeen base.

This was in many ways a very different world from Clydeside.[147] Heavy industry was lacking, and the industrial base was heterogeneous. This helped to reduce the impact of depression, a cushion supported by the near monopoly of the dominant granite industry. Even in the relatively weak shipbuilding sector, conditions improved in the nineties with the expansion of steam trawling. Here then was an industrial working class, living often in massive poverty, but nevertheless protected to some degree from the insecurities that could affect communities where one or few industries dominated. One exception to the general expansion was the wide range of textile producers, susceptible like their counterparts elsewhere in the nineties to growing overseas protection.

The Aberdonian working class was also much more ethnically homogeneous than its Glaswegian counterpart. Irish immigration was minimal, one source claiming only 715 Irish-born citizens in the early nineties.[148] The bulk of Aberdeen's expansion was generated by the depopulation of the surrounding countryside. As a result, Aberdeen Liberalism did not suffer the ravages of the Home Rule split to any significant degree, and the Liberals retained a firm hold on both city seats between 1885 and 1910. Here then was a distinctive prospect for Labour. In the eighties links between Aberdeen trade unionists and local Liberals remained close, although inevitably with grounds for discord over candidate selection and the eight-hours question.[149] Such grounds for disagreement could lead to a more permanent political rift if other circumstances were appropriate, including of course the existence of a socialist alternative.

Socialism had 'arrived' in Aberdeen in the autumn of 1887, brought by the ex-Socialist Leaguer J. L. Mahon who had had earlier discussions about strategy with Champion. His visit acquired extra publicity due to Mahon's arrest and acquittal for holding a political meeting on a Sunday, and his ideas found a ready response amongst some of the Aberdeen Radicals.[150] The resulting organisation, the Aberdeen Socialist Society, acquired more importance with increasing unionisation, and was aided by the eight hours agitation and the continual concern with labour representation. Here then we see a socialist movement growing to the left of a dominant Liberalism, a growth helping to generate a wider interest in labour independence amongst trade union leaders.

It was at this stage that Champion made his entry into Aberdeen Labour politics. Backed by the traditional prestige of a local landed family, he established close links with some working-class Radicals in the late eighties, a connection which produced the Aberdeen Labour Committee leading to the Aberdeen ILP. It was this body that was one of the prime instigations in the deliberations that eventually produced the SUTCLP.[151]

It was amidst the complexities following the new party's formation that Champion and his two or three colleagues fought the 1892 election.[152] The strength of Independent Labour sentiment amongst Aberdeen's trade union leaders meant that he secured the trades council's support although he was opposed by the council's Liberal faction.[153] Although he had the support of the majority of union leaders, there were clear doubts about his ability to secure mass trade unionist support in the more working-class North constituency. Here the Radical member was believed to have the support of the bulk of the working-class electorate, and so Champion fought the less promising South seat against James Bryce.[154]

The centre of the Labour campaign was inevitably the eight hours question and the need for Labour MPs to pressurise governments along the lines of the Irish Nationalist model.[155] But Champion's own idiosyncracies soon became central to the argument. Although a Labour candidate, he certainly had a strong sense of his own capacity to lead. One Aberdeen Labour stalwart recollected that 'he was handsome, and clever and well intentioned, but he came among us with the air of making a sacrifice and doing a great favour'.[156] His judgement on the London dock strike of 1889 reflected his assessment of his own indispensability — it would have failed, had it not been that the workers' leaders were backed by one 'able to bring to the conduct of negotiations ... greater facts, better temper and greater education than those men had'.[157] Liberal attacks also made much of his criticisms of the Australian shearers' strike the previous year, with Champion maintaining that his 'lions led by asses' claim had been borne out by the result.[158]

There was more than Champion's personal style to cause socialists to hesitate, there were also his attitudes on political questions. His unwillingness to back disestablishment until the Scottish electorate showed itself clearly in favour provoked cries of 'Tory, Tory' at one meeting.[159] But there were other more important ways in which Champion appeared to be opposing the Radical sentiments that fuelled much of Scottish Labour's enthusiasm. He claimed to have abandoned his army career because 'he came to the conclusion that collecting the bondholders' money in Egypt was no work for a gentleman', but he 'believed in the Imperial mission of his country'. However, it was on the issued most sensitive of all to many Radical enthusiasts — free trade — that Champion raised the strongest passions.

His presentation of his views on the campaign began with a response to a question on the contemporary preoccupation with foreign labour. He expressed himself opposed to the immigration of foreign workers who sought to 'seize the advantages which had been brought about by the skill and by the political intelligence ... of the British workmen'. If such views are placed in context they were a fair reflection of the concern felt by many trade union spokesmen in the early nineties. In this respect, Champion did not seem heterodox and could claim to be merely extending his argument for protecting working-class living standards. It was his development of the case beyond immigration to imported goods that marked a clear distinction — in terms of contemporary views, if not of consistency. He accepted that it was 'necessary in some cases to protect certain industries to prevent foreign goods coming in and taking away trade from our people'. This could be a particularly acute problem, given the enactment of eight-hours legislation and the inevitable consequence — as Champion saw it — of increased wage rates. It was all, he affirmed, a matter of 'quite fair deductions from the trade unionist principle' — a matter of keeping up 'the price of labour of the native workmen'. He even grasped the nettle of food taxes: he was ready to tax corn from countries where wage levels were low, this 'would give to the corn produced in our country and in the colonies a great advantage'.[160]

There were other elements in Champion's appeal that showed greater sympathy for Radical sensibilities. He agreed to support temperance measures, although adding characteristically that he would not work for them, since all his time would be given to labour questions, and in general agreed to vote for the standard Radical measures. Basically Champion's programme involved the protection and emancipation of labour through a programme of national self-sufficiency. It should be seen as an alternative strategy for Labour, one that was prevented from acquiring wider support, possibly in part owing to

Champion's idiosyncracies, but also owing to the almost unanimous view amongst Labour leaders that Labour politics and socialism should be seen as building upon the legacy of Radicalism.[161]

The Labour case in Aberdeen was given a distinctive content by Champion, but it was certainly not a simple case of one individual with considerable local influence attempting to foist his views on working-class leaders and electors. Indeed Champion's Protectionist views evoked a positive response amongst some working-class sections in Aberdeen. As early as 1887, the trades council had raised the question of Polish immigration into Ayrshire — an example where Aberdeen reflected sentiments held much more widely amongst Scottish workers. Aberdeen trade unionists also expressed concern for 'Fair Trade' especially over sugar bounties, again a relatively common position. But after the 1892 campaign sections of labour opinion went further. The trades council backed the exclusion of 'alien paupers' by legislation and more remarkably by 1895 a sizeable minority of the council were backing moves to protect home industries threatened by cheap imports 'made under unfair conditions'.[162]

Such developments are distinctive, but not easy to explain. Should it be claimed that the Aberdonian economy was particularly vulnerable to overseas competition and therefore protectionist doctrines found a ready reception? The evidence on this is unconvincing, although clearly local textile industries were affected by the McKinley and other tariff barriers. Such a comment would be true also of other textile areas where the local economy was much more dependent on disappearing markets, and yet, for example, the West Riding response does not seem to involve a strong protectionist element on the part of Labour organisations. More reasonably, the presence of Champion with his local reputation provided a respectable outlet for protectionist sentiments that are arguably endemic to Labour politics, but which in Radical Aberdeen could find little outlet in working-class Conservatism.

The impact of Champion on the fortunes of Independent Labour politics in Aberdeen was damaging. His defeat in 1892 was followed by a period of hectic activity: the local ILP not only distributed leaflet propaganda, but began publishing from January 1893 a weekly newspaper.[163] As the dispute intensified over the direction of the national ILP the Aberdeen party was drawn into the argument as one of Champion's few supporters. In October 1893, Champion attempted to revive the now defunct SUTCLP at a Dundee Conference. This was a pathetic affair with only 23 delegates (and only five trades councils) represented. Even some of the delegates — representing the Dundee SLP — were hostile. As one witness recollected:

the promoters did their cause no good by devoting the first hour to the discussion and comparison of leaders. Falkirk and Dundee delegates did their utmost to keep the discussion to the question of promoting unity in Labour ranks, whereas the Aberdeen delegates concentrated on the laudation of Champion who occupied the chair.[164]

It all came to nothing; with Champion's final departure to Australia, the Aberdeen ILP decayed. Its strongest sentiments were isolationist and anti-Hardie, and it was now competing with a SDF branch. A crucial episode in this decline was its anti-Liberal, or perhaps pro-Conservative, stand in 1895, when the party backed Bryce's Conservative opponent, and ran J. L. Mahon against the popular Radical, W. Hunter.[165] The resulting fiasco helped to ensure that the SDF became the predominant influence in Aberdeen Labour politics for the next decade.[166]

The early development of Scottish Labour was distinguished therefore by strong personal elements. Disputes about national policy left their imprint on local developments. But it was not just a question of such cleavages being imposed on local activists. Clearly the Championite approach was able to tap sentiments that could find no place in majority Labour developments. With the collapse of Champion's initiatives, the mainstream Radical—Labour link was left almost unquestioned, with all the obstacles that this implied in Scottish circumstances. By 1895, Scottish Labour initiatives were largely contained within the ILP, which now had to deal not only with the peculiar difficulties of the Scottish situation but also with a legacy of organisational and personal divisions.

The Scottish ILP from 1895

The final absorption of the SLP into the main British party, together with the disappearance of Champion's organisation, meant that Scottish Labour developments now conformed more to the standard British pattern on a superficial organisational level. Yet even in structure there continued to be distinctive developments. The creation of the separate Scottish TUC in 1897, and the emergence of the Scottish Workers Parliamentary Elections Committee in January 1900 hinted in organisational terms at the continuation of important differences. From one viewpoint, such developments could suggest that Scottish Labour was more committed to political independence that its English counterpart, but the complexities and obstacles examined were still important.

The presence of the ILP remained limited. The number of Scottish delegates at party conferences was relatively small. Even in 1900, when the conference was held in Glasgow, Scotland provided only 13 delegates out of 75. In other years, the proportion was lower; by 1905, when the total had expanded to 153, the Scottish contribution had fallen back to 11.[167] The nucleus of this presence was provided by Glasgow, with some support from other industrial districts in the West. Edinburgh had a continuous representation, but Aberdeen was absent after 1896, and Dundee provided only an occasional delegate. In 1900, the number of branches claimed was only 29, with a preponderance from the industrial West.[168] The ILP's impact upon the Highlands was minimal;[169] in considering the development of the party, it is possible, therefore, to concentrate on the distinction within the Lowlands between East and West.

The ILP's Scottish election effort in 1895 was focused almost exclusively on Glasgow. The party ran five candidates within the city, and one in adjacent

Govan.[170] Amongst the standard-bearers, the industrial working class was represented by Smillie and by Haddow, the latter presiding over Govan meetings 'straight from the forge in his working clothes, with a muffler round his neck';[171] Shaw Maxwell represented the significant trajectory from Radicalism through the land agitation to the ILP; Woolacott and Hardie's confidant Frank Smith, were both London imports and journalists with Radical backgrounds. The sixth was Watson, a Professor of Chemistry whose polling day literature cited Froude, Carlyle and Burns in his cause.[172] Such allusions cut little ice with the Bridgeton electorate. 'Anything but an ideal candidate' was one activist's subsequent verdict.[173]

The line of demarcation between Liberal and Labour had hardened, and there were few of the ambiguities of 1892. Hopes of any rapport with the Liberals were no longer plausible, and ILP spokesmen criticised Liberals and their policies almost as vehemently as they did the Unionists. Shaw Maxwell related how in 1880 he had quit the Liberal Party over its policy of coercion in Ireland and recalled that 'the Liberal Party in Glasgow was strongly antagonistic to the Irish demands'.[174] Similarly, he attempted to employ the Nationalist demand of an amnesty for political prisoners as a basis for Irish support, contrasting his sympathy with the hostility of his Liberal opponent.[175] These attempts met a stony response from the local Irish press:

Every vote given to Mr. Maxwell is a vote given for Balfour and Coercion for confessedly the policy of the Labourites is a policy of wreck. 'Spoil Home Rule' is how we read it.[176]

Maxwell might attempt to court the Irish vote, but Smillie claimed that social reform and the unemployed were the key issues. Labour was what mattered; disestablishment and Home Rule were 'a thousand degrees behind'.[177] Such were the pitfalls in pushing a Labour appeal before a working class divided on ethnic and religious lines.

This motley army polled disastrously. Even the *Labour Leader* abandoned its characteristically brave face to acknowledge the 'disgracefully small' Glasgow polls.[178] The impoverished party spent over £1,100 on the six contests, raising a loan from a wine and spirit merchant.[179] This inevitably created dismay, allowed dark accusations of 'Tory Gold', and left an albatross for the future. The best result of 696 votes, or almost eleven per cent of the total poll, was achieved by Smillie in Camlachie and as few as 405 and 368 votes were gathered in St Rollox and Tradeston. Turnout was clearly affected by the holding of all but the Govan contest in Glasgow Fair Week, and by the time of the Govan poll any initial credibility enjoyed by the ILP had been destroyed. *Prima facie*, this circumstance might be thought to have had a particularly damaging effect on the level of ILP support, since this would be the one week when industrial workers had some hope of escaping from the city.

Yet this disaster obviously had more fundamental causes. Organisation was minimal, and most of the candidates entered the field late. Liberals played strongly on the belief that ILP candidates could not win, and could only let in the Unionists. This belief was supported by the comments of one Unionist speaker who felt that the ILP 'were going to do the Unionists a good turn ... in the scrimmages, probably four or five Unionists might be returned.[180] Beyond the fears and suspicions, there lay a basic dilemma. The party had achieved a presence in the context of an apparently disintegrating Radicalism, yet this was not based on much durable industrial organisation. The weakness of trade unionism meant that Labour lacked a basis for offsetting the pull of traditional loyalties.

The failure generated a predictable reaction. ILP activities in the city seem to have declined over the next few years. Early in 1897, Glasier was moved to admit that 'all the enthusiasm and glamour seems to have gone out of the movement here'.[181] A local activists painted a gloomy picture: 'a wave of despondency seems to have settled on the ILP in Glasgow ... The average worker looks with suspicion on our party and would be afraid his boss would get to know'.[182] This member blamed the animosities generated by the Party Bazaar of January 1896, itself an attempt to pay off election debts; but more crucially, awareness of marginality led to the dispelling of earlier illusions. Early attempts at Labour politics had been buoyed up by the activists' enthusiasm and optimism. The failures of 1892, and more significantly, given the Liberal Government's record, of 1895, had come as severe shocks. They had revealed the sizeable gulf between the preoccupations of activists and the concerns of the bulk of the Glasgow working class. There were other salutary signs. Early in 1895, Glasier attended an unemployment demonstration in George Square. It was 'a dreadful failure'. Only 1500 attended. There was 'a counter-attraction in the feat of a man walking on the water of the river — 50,000 looked on'.[183]

The late nineties brought one compensation. The Glasgow Trades Council had been moving towards a more independent position in municipal politics, and in June 1895, a Workers' Municipal Election Committee had been established. This brought together not just ILP and trade union branches, but also local Co-operative Societies and branches of the United Irish League.[184] Inevitably, the effectiveness of this broad Progressive front was hindered by its involvement in the sectarian conflict, but on occasions there were striking successes. In November 1897, in Springburn, then a district with a strong Orange presence, Irish and ILP candidates had won in tandem, despite a kirk condemnation of an alliance of 'Papist with atheist'.[185]

Despite such advances, the Glasgow ILP's parliamentary ambitions typically faced two related obstacles, a lack of sympathy from official Liberalism, and Irish hostility. Yet this dominant pattern involved counter-currents. Lib-Lab hostilities concealed continuities of principle and style. Elsewhere we shall find that this led to tacit or open Progressive alliances. In Western Scotland, this option was almost absent. The exception was the 1900 contest in Camlachie.

The circumstances were unusual. The candidate, A. E. Fletcher, had an impeccably Radical pedigree as a journalist, as the Greenock Liberal candidate in 1895, and as a victim of the conservative preferences of Liberal Associations. The context of his Glasgow campaign involved growing harmony between ILPers, Radicals and Irish Nationalists over the Boer War. When a 'Stop the War' meeting in Glasgow was threatened with disruption by students, David Lowe informed Hardie that 'an Irish MP came specially down from London to put the Irishmen on their mettle to combat the disturbing element'.[186] This union of hearts was important, yet the original impetus behind Fletcher's candidature had just pre-dated the war. Fletcher's nomination was complemented by an abortive trade-union candidature in St Rollox by John Hodge of the Steel Smelters. The sponsorship of one by the ILP and the support of the other by local ILPers generated concern amongst some party members, since 'neither ... can by any stretch of imagination be called extreme'.[187] The official Glasgow ILP position seems to have one of readiness to court an understanding with the Liberals. An application from Bridgeton that a candidate should be run there was turned down 'so long as the Liberals in Camlachie refrain from nominating'.[188] Yet Liberal intentions remained unclear. Fletcher claimed that they made repeated attempts to find someone, although they were under Irish pressure to support the ILP nominee. Eventually, shortly before the poll, they decided to back him.[189].

The result was that Fletcher was backed by an impressive range of Progressive bodies, not just the ILP and the Liberals, but also the Trades Council, the SWPEC, the United Irish League, the SDF and the Clarion Scouts.[190] He was unequivocal on the election's principal issue. In a Glasgow campaign where Unionists beat the patriotic drum for all it was worth, he attacked Chamberlain, claimed that the war was being waged in the interest of capitalists, and condemned Unionists for their militarism and neglect of promised reforms.[191] Such comments inevitably generated the response that a vote for Fletcher was 'a vote for President Kruger and the Boer Government'.[192] But he was less bold about his own political affiliation. He proclaimed his agreement with Gladstonian Liberalism and acknowledged that he would go into the Liberal lobby on 99 occasions out of 100. He eulogised the campaign as a demonstration of progressive unity and cited Copenhagen municipal politics as an example of the benefits that could flow from 'a good understanding ... between the Collectivist and Radical parties'.[193]

This Progressive strategy failed in the circumstances of 1900, yet it hinted at the possibility of growth for the Scottish ILP. Liberalism was divided over the war and imperialism, and along with this went increasing doubts about Liberal intentions on Home Rule. These could corrode the Liberal—Irish link, and offer Labour its chance. But in the West, opportunities and pitfalls went together as political developments in North-East Lanarkshire soon revealed. This constituency had Motherwell as its centre, and had sizeable concentrations of miners and steelworkers. Green and Orange elements, particularly the former, had some significance, and predictably it was a Liberal seat. The presence of organised labour was slight. John Hodge's Steel Smelters had some members, but the Lanarkshire Miners, although expanding in the late nineties, still faced severe difficulties, and the ILP had made little impact.[194]

When the seat became vacant in August 1901, national rivalries fused with local factors. The Labour forces moved rapidly to nominate Bob Smillie, despite some trade union leaders' doubts about the danger of opposing a Liberal.[195] The Liberals had serious policy differences. The eventual selection of Alfred Harmsworth, a Liberal Imperialist who strongly supported the war and enjoyed the scurrilous support of his local family concern, the *Daily Record*, angered many Radicals. Smillie naturally emphasised his own Radical attachments, claiming that he was the better Liberal of the two.[196] The tactic worked in so far as he gained the support of several influential Liberals, plus the benevolent neutrality of Campbell-Bannerman.[197]

More importantly, Harmsworth's lack of enthusiasm for Home Rule provoked Irish opposition. For one spokesman, the issue extended far beyond the particular contest to the struggle within the Liberal Party:

if Harmsworth be returned then it is a plain intimation to the Liberal Imperialists that they can run anti-Home Rule Jingoes under a Liberal flag in every constituency in Great Britain. Such a result would be a fatal blow to Home Rule. It would make men such as Asquith and Grey again dominant in the Liberal Party; it would declare to Campbell-Bannerman and the Home Rule section of the Liberal Party that the Irish vote is of no account, and that they were fools for adhering to Home Rule.[198]

Such a view dictated Irish support for Smillie, and the United Irish League Executive decided readily on this course.[199] This seemed a significant breakthrough. Hardie rejoiced that 'for the first time, they had the representatives of Ireland in the House of Commons, supporting and endorsing a trade union candidate'.[200] But implementation in North-East Lanark was more problematic. At both Motherwell and Bellshill, local Irish organisations expressed some opposition. In part, this was a resurrection of the old argument about the propriety of leaders dictating to branches, but beneath this, there lay some suspicion of Labour candidates.[201] This could reflect a legacy of earlier Irish condemnations of such candidates as tools of Toryism, but it also indicated the problems raised for some Catholics by any hint of association with 'socialism'.[202] This combination of 'a small section of the priesthood and Whig Catholics'[203] raised a more serious difficulty than the *Daily Record's* ludicrous claim that Smillie had once been an Orangeman.[204] One Irish response to the anti-socialist argument was to ignore or accept the condemnation of socialism, and to insist on the need to maintain 'the unity of the Irish race, the discipline of the Irish organisation and the potency of the Irish vote'.[205] The pursuit of solidarity went beyond argument and counter-argument amongst the local Irish. Three Nationalist MPs were sent north to quell the rebellion, and hopes of Irish solidarity increased.[206] Smillie did his best to foster this, declaring that 'the cause of the Irish peasantry was the cause of labour'.[207] Yet the doubt remained as to whether formal declarations would produce solidarity at the polling booths. Glasier felt that in the end, the alliance failed. At both Airdrie and Bellshill, he found a lack of Irish support and surmised that they were 'afraid to show their colours, afraid of priests'.[208] He was never reluctant to detect such baleful influences; in fact, the result permitted various diagnoses (see Table 13).

Table 13. *North-East Lanarkshire September 1901*

Rattigan Unionist	5,673
Harmsworth Liberal	4,679
Smillie Labour	2,900

The local Irish press could revel in the defeat of Harmsworth claiming that the Irish vote had been transferred 'practically unbroken' to Smillie. Since the same source had suggested previously that this vote totalled three thousand, a figure disputed elsewhere, this verdict was hardly plausible.[209] The ILP verdict was that the Labour vote was mixed, coming 'in equal proportions from the Irish, the Radicals and the Conservative working-men'[210] and that beneath the Radical rhetoric of Smillie's campaign, his vote was a specifically Labour one that crossed sectarian divisions.

The cultivation of such a vote encountered obstacles not simply on account of sectarian tensions, but also perhaps because of the limited Labour organisation. Glasier and Hardie encountered considerable opposition from a Motherwell audience, whilst Glasier at Newarthill sensed a 'conscious reserve' on the part of his listeners.[211] The difficulties encountered by the Lanarkshire Miners also brought problems for Smillie, especially at Bellshill, where membership of a breakaway organisation was significant.[212]

Labour spokesmen might welcome the formal support of the Irish machine, yet this had been given pragmatically within the broader currents of Liberal factionalism. Indeed, Irish satisfaction at Harmsworth's defeat made precisely this point: 'the result secures the position of Home Rule in the Liberal programme'.[213] This was naive, yet the gradual strengthening of Campbell-Bannerman's position, together with clear signs of a Liberal electoral recovery, meant that Irish support for Scottish Labour candidates was likely to be anything but automatic. This demonstrated decisively when the North-East Lanark seat fell vacant once again in July 1904.[214] Now the alignments were different from three years earlier. The Labour organisations adopted another Miners' official, John Robertson, who gained support not just from local union branches and the ILP but also from the MFGB and the TUC.[215] Yet two elements that had backed Smillie were absent. The Liberals chose Alexander Findlay, Provost of Motherwell and a local employer with none of Harmsworth's Imperialist views.[216] Labour spokesmen might advance the claims of the trade unionist against an employer but Radicals who had backed Smillie now shifted back to the official Liberal platform.[217] So did the Irish organisation, with pragmatic arguments paralleling those that had backed the 1901 decision:

Mr. Robertson can give us good wishes; Mr. Findlay can give us Home Rule ... They are making a party. We must deal with the established firm.[218]

Against this appeal, Labour advanced an argument that would hopefully surmount religious differences. 'Sectarian animosities and old racial hatreds' could be superseded by 'the new consciousness of Labour solidarity'. So:

it may be expected that the Catholic miner and the Protestant miner, who a few weeks hence, will have to fight side by side in defence of their minimum wage will also agree to fight side by side politically in defence of their common interests.[219]

Advocates of both positions could take some comfort from the result. The Liberals regained the seat lost in an abnormal wartime contest, and now contested with Free Trade as a central issue. The Irish could claim that their support was crucial yet had to admit that a significant proportion of the Irish vote had stayed with Labour.[220] For some commentators, it was the growth of Labour support on a platform lacking sectarian support that was the most significant feature.[221] (See Table 14.)

Table 14. *North East Lanark August 1904*

Findlay Liberal	5,619
Touche Unionist	4,677
Robertson Labour	3,984

There was a temptation to see the growth of a distinctive Labour vote in Western Scotland transcending traditional divisions and based on ILP enthusiasm, and increasing unionisation. Yet Labour performances in the West remained disappointing until 1914. It proved possible in several places to develop a core of support, but this failed, nevertheless, to prevent the general revival of Scottish Liberalism.

A class appeal could carry significant weight, but it encountered powerful sectarian constraints which would remain so long as the Irish issue remained alive. Only in three Western constituencies in 1906 did the UIL advocate a Labour vote. The Catholic miner, J. Sullivan, was supported in North-West Lanarkshire rather than a luke-warm Liberal Home Ruler. The result was controversy in Irish circles and a Unionist victory.[222] Similarly, in Camlachie, where the ILP had borne the anti-Unionist banner in 1900, Irish support went to Joseph Burgess, rather than to the last-minute Radical candidate. Once again there was acrimony and with the same result.[223] Only in Blackfriars, where the Irish backed the Engineers' leader and ILP member George Barnes, did the

Irish—Labour link meet with success. Irish sentiment was far more alienated from the Liberals here. They had opposed the Liberal, A. D. Provand in 1900, because of his antipathy to Home Rule, and had argued a vote for the Unionist Bonar Law. In 1906, with Provand standing again, Irish support went to Barnes. Once again, the conflicting currents of Irish politics were apparent. Some urged support for Law because of Labour views on education policy, but in the end, Irish votes were a major element in Barnes's success.[224]

This case hints that in the West, Irish support was probably essential for a Labour breakthrough, but as other contests showed, it was not sufficient. What made Blackfriars different was the weakness of the Liberal challenge. It would be very difficult for any Irish voter to back Provand; that had been demonstrated in 1900. His credibility was damaged by this, and undermined further by his isolation from many Radical sentiments. He stood firmly on the traditional wing of Liberalism, taking a laissez faire line on unemployment, and attacking the socialist's 'robber creed'.[225] Barnes could appear readily as the more fitting representative of progressive Liberalism.[226] In contrast, the Camlachie Liberal candidate, W. R. Pringle, could make an effective appeal on behalf of Scottish Radicalism. The constraints that prevented Scots and Irish from casting Labour votes in Western Scotland were that much weaker in Blackfriars, permitting the core Labour vote to be strengthened by Radical and Nationalist elements. As yet this was not the harbinger of a breakthrough, but an indication of some Labour strength in an environment where traditional tensions still generated complex problems.

These pressures did not apply, at least to the same extent, in the East, although the continuing dominance of Liberalism indicated the prevalence of other obstacles. As indicated earlier, the Fife coalfield remained strongly Liberal well into the new century; other Labour hopes were focused on the East Coast urban centres of Edinburgh, Dundee and Aberdeen. A continual ILP presence in the capital did not yield many rewards. An activist concluded a chronicle of 25 years work in pessimistic vein:

Edinburgh is a very difficult place to work, in the interests of Socialism ... The curse of 'superior personism' is rampant — not only among those classes, very considerable in number in Edinburgh, who are living on dividends and whose interests in this respect are diametrically opposed to the class who *produce* dividends, but even among certain of the workers themselves. They seem to catch something of the tone of their economic superior's exclusiveness — be it commercial, theological, academic or social — hardening into something almost as unbending as caste.[227]

Further north, there were other difficulties. In Dundee and Aberdeen, Independent Labour stalwarts were somewhat isolated. There was no industrial hinterland equivalent to the western coalfields; instead rural Angus and Aberdeenshire offered little scope for Labour agitators. Even in the Montrose Burghs where the ILP considered running a candidate at John Morley's electoral debut in 1896, there were difficulties. Glasier had attentive audiences there that year, but also found a prevalent fear of victimisation.[228]

Despite isolation and the legacy of the Championite involvement, the ILP had some grounds for optimism in both Dundee and Aberdeen. Uniquely for Scotland, James Macdonald's Dundee poll in 1895 showed an improvement over his 1892 performance. It was a relatively small increase, from 354 votes to 1,313, but the contrast with the declining Glasgow votes is noticeable. Its composition suggested the continuing relevance of the religious conflict in an East Coast centre with a large Irish population (see Table 15):

Table 15. *Dundee ILP Vote 1895*

Plumpers	244
Splits with the two Liberals	299
Splits with the Liberal Unionist	554
Splits with the Conservative	16

The most significant feature however was the shift in trades council allegiance. At the 1892 election Gladstonianism had reigned supreme and attempts to secure council support for Macdonald had failed, despite his readiness to support the whole of its programme. Three years later, there seemed initially to be little change. The Dundee ILP asked the council to back their candidate, but the majority view was hostile.[229] However, the council's Liberal delegates encountered a problem with their questionnaire to candidates. Macdonald's responses were favourable but the Liberals equivocated. Even the Council President, himself a Liberal, acknowledged that the Liberals had retreated on the eight hours question, while other delegates emphasised the inadequate Liberal positions on payment of MPs and temperance. The debate was prolonged; the result was decisive. The ILP candidate was supported by 24 votes to 10, in contrast with his 17—6 rejection in 1892.[230] The change was of marginal significance in immediate electoral terms. No doubt the council's decision influenced a few Dundee electors in 1895, but more crucially it began a permanent separation between the Dundee labour movement and official Liberalism.

The ILP proved unable to gain much benefit from this situation. There were hopes of Macdonald standing again but these foundered in July 1900 when he declined since he was now out of sympathy with the party.[231] In 1901, the search began again initially with a view to adopting George Barnes, but this possibility was abandoned after he had become involved in abortive discussions with one of the Liberal members. Hopes that the Liberals would be happy with just one candidate were shown to be misplaced. An ILP member, W. F. Black, acknowledged that 'the Liberals are rather contemptuous over the power of the Labour vote in Dundee ... It will have to be a fight'.[232] Shortly afterwards, Black was endorsed by the NAC as an ILP candidate, but this did not last, and he was withdrawn in May 1904.[233] His explanation suggested that the party were frequently at cross-purposes with Dundee trade union leaders.

Some of the latter claimed that Black's candidature had been 'thrust upon them by Keir Hardie', although the candidate claimed that the real problem was trade unionists' desire for a self-financing candidate. Unfortunately the local ILP were too weak and could not withstand this pressure.[234] Local trade unionists had their wish; the Dundee LRC adopted Alexander Wilkie of the Shipwrights early in 1905. The choice of this highly traditional craft unionist produced a strong response from the local ILP. One anguished member wrote to Hardie:

The most influential and hard-working members of the ILP are in a state of incipient revolt since hearing Wilkie, as he seems to be a man very much less advanced than either of the candidates already before the constituency … You can understand … how we feel in this matter after the hard work some of us has (*sic*) put in here for … 15 or 20 years past.

Now the ILPers had to support someone 'who seems to understand nothing of the causes of poverty, and whose sympathy is only for the trades unionist'.[235]

This was a little harsh. Wilkie's programme in 1906 was conventionally Radical.[236] Yet the Dundee Liberals adopted a London stockbroker to replace a retiring Member, and the local Liberal press attacked him for his socialist allies.[237] Wilkie complained that he had received incompatible criticisms: 'his Socialist friends complained that he was not a Socialist and now his Liberal friends complained that he was one'.[238] In fact, his position and his relationship with the local ILP was similar to that of LRC trade union candidates in England. The difference lay in the continuing claim by Dundee Liberals to possess a monopoly of Radicalism. The poll revealed that the claim was mistaken. Dundee electors favoured a Scottish trade unionist rather than an English stockbroker Liberal. Perhaps predictably, by January 1910 Wilkie was returned in tandem with Winston Churchill, now the city's Liberal MP. The Dundee situation had thrown up the Progressive arrangement characteristic of several double-member English constituencies.

In Dundee the ILP and its SLP forerunner had led the early working-class opposition to Liberalism, but it had not inherited the conseqences of increasing trade union estrangement from Liberal politics. Yet the mere fact of that estrangement suggests that where sectarian tensions were less strong, the Scottish Liberals might find it difficult to contain Labour demands within a once-powerful coalition. It would be expected that a similar case can be mounted for Aberdeen, where the Irish question was even less important and trade union leaders had backed independent political initiatives at an earlier date. Against this promising beginning, there must be placed the Champion legacy, culminating in Mahon's disastrous 1895 campaign and the decline of the local ILP. Yet less than twelve months later, Aberdeen North was the venue for perhaps the most successful of the ILP's Scottish campaigns, Tom Mann's straight fight with the Liberal, Captain Pirie, in a Radical stronghold. Mann's defeat by just 430 in a poll of almost 5,400 was a moral victory. As the local Unionist press reported, perhaps with some satisfaction, 'it was a stunning blow to the Gladstonian enthusiasts'.[239] Yet it had all begun unpropitiously. The eventual selection of a candidate was carried through by a joint meeting of the Aberdeen Trades Council, ILP and SDF,[240] but the choice of Mann did not finalise the matter. The prospective candidate took a pessimistic view of his chances, and preferred not to stand, if the likely Labour vote was only going to be 1,200. However, feeling on the NAC for a contest was strong,[241] and he arrived in Aberdeen to find a more promising situation than he had perhaps anticipated.

Trades council support had been given by a vote of 44 to 2, while the Liberal selection procedure was proving protracted. This enabled Mann to establish an initiative in the campaign which he never really yielded. Moreover, the Liberals were faced with the need to replace a Radical member who had enjoyed wide trade union support, but Radical applicants (including A. E. Fletcher) were unsuccessful, and the choice of a military man with local connections provided a chance for Mann to bid for Radical votes.[242] In fact, this was never a principal emphasis of his campaign, which was developed around the motifs of labour and collectivism. His objective was stated unequivocally as 'the common ownership of the means of production and distribution': his views would not be 'modified to please the electorate'. He stood 'as a workman' advocating the restriction of workers' hours, municipalisation measures, pensions and the nationalisation of selected industries and land.[243] On local matters, he emphasised dock municipalisation and championed the grievances of the line fishermen against the relatively new incursions of the steam trawlers.[244] Aberdeen had been, by Scottish standards, a stronghold of New Unionism and much of Mann's keenest support seems to have come from the dock areas.[245] Inevitably the terms of the contest mean that collectivism. and socialism became central elements of the argument. Pirie appealed for Liberal-Conservative unity against 'Socialistic and Republican ideas' but he refused to make concessions in the time-honoured fashion on the eight-hour day.[246] In his view, it would mean 'famine and poverty'. This plus accusations of anti-union policies at Pirie's local paper-mill must have gained Mann the bulk of the trade union votes.[247]

In Aberdeen North, as in Camlachie 1900, the Scottish ILP achieved a straight fight. But the alignment was very different. In Aberdeen it was not a question of Radicals and Labour uniting against Tories, but of Labour and Collectivism versus Liberalism represented by a soldier with allegedly anti-trade union views.[248] Non-economic issues were hardly mentioned: Ireland was barely raised and, rather strangely, Mann secured the support of the normally pro-Unionist Church Defence Association because he favoured a referendum on disestablishment.[249] More crucially, however, the Aberdeen contest demonstrated the potential for Labour growth where the Irish issue was marginal and Liberalism was elitist and complacent, and as a result failed to cater for Labour demands. There was a potential but in Aberdeen it was not realised. Mann's post-poll euphoric meeting ended with the singing of 'Will ye no come back again?'.[250] It was not just that the mercurial Mann never stood there again: no further ILP candidate stood in the city down to 1914. Indeed, in one sense Mann's candidature was not so much an ILP one as a broad Labour one. Some took the moral to be the need for links with the unions in launching candidates: others saw the implication as lying principally in the role of the SDF.[251] It was a good advertisement for the idea of One Socialist Party. Either way, the Aberdeen ILP continued to descend into oblivion, although the latter stages were as a constituent element in the national party.[252]

So much propaganda, so many hopes — and yet so little achieved. Why was the Scottish ILP's growth so limited?

To St Enoch Station?

The precocious quality of Independent Labour politics in Scotland was still evident in the late nineties. We have seen how the Scottish TUC was dominated from the beginning by advocates of political independence and collectivism. On 4 March 1899, representatives of the ILP, SDF and the STUC Parliamentary Committee met to consider the question of labour representation.[253] The eventual result in January 1900 was the first meeting under Bob Smillie's chairmanship of the Scottish Workers' Parliamentary Elections Committee.[254] Hardie did not hold out the same hopes for its projected London counterpart.[255] There had been little controversy amongst Scottish trade unionists about such collaboration. One resolution carried at the 1899 STUC showed a sharp contrast with the ambiguous phraseology of the labour representation decision reached at that year's British Congress. The Scottish declaration, after referring to the break-up of the Liberal Party, advocated 'the formation of a working class political party, whose ultimate object would be the nationalisation of the land and the means of production, distribution and exchange'.[256] The frontiers of debate amongst Scottish Labour activists were more advanced than amongst their English counterparts.

Yet the SWPEC made little impact. In part this reflected the success of the London based LRC, which refused to allow British unions to divide their affiliation fees on the proportional basis of Scottish/other members, but as we have repeatedly found, the 'advanced' quality of Labour politics was essentially a matter of formal organisations and activists. The Scottish record in terms of both membership of the ILP and Labour electoral successes was disappointing.

There was a formidable collection of obstacles: the continuing and after 1900, reviving strength of Scottish Liberalism, with its capacity to reflect significant Scottish concerns and qualities; the way in which, particularly in the West, the Home Rule issue provided openings for Unionism; and the normal attachment of the Irish vote to the Liberal Party, with sectarianism providing support for Unionism as well. These barriers were confronted by Labour initiatives which lacked the solid base that strong trade unionism would have provided. Indeed in Scotland, as we shall find in the Yorkshire woollen towns, industrial weakness was a spur to political innovation.

There is a temptation to see the climax of the developments that began at Mid-Lanark in the celebrated departure of the Clydeside ILP MPs from St Enoch Station in 1922. And yet the Glasgow that produced such support for Maxton, Wheatley and Buchanan was in some ways far removed from the polity that has been examined here. Some of the changes would fit into a picture of predictable Labour growth without too much difficulty. It is reasonable to argue that the weakness of Scottish trade unionism would have been remedied, independent of other developments. The growing problems of Scottish industry after 1900, and the increasing tendency for unions to seek members throughout Britain would inevitably boost union membership. It then remained for growing industrial solidarity to be translated into a political attachment; a common expectation, but one which earlier chapters demonstrate to be subject to serious qualifications.

Two critical problems in Scotland had been the appeal of Liberalism and the centrality of the Irish question. One needed to be broken and the other apparently settled before Labour made a significant advance. The crucial conjunction was that both occurred at almost the same time. Some tentative solution of the Irish controversy was predictable, although its deposition from the centre of Scottish politics did not entail the destruction of the political loyalties that went along with it. Yet there are reasons for claiming that Irish support for the Liberals was artificial and would decline once the immediate link had been broken. Unionism was not an acceptable option and class ties suggested that much of the Irish vote would go to Labour. Thus, from one viewpoint, Labour weakness was the product of a situation which would have a predictable end.

The destruction of Liberalism raises much more problematic issues. In 1906, Scottish Liberalism recovered much of the ground lost during the previous twenty years, and did so without making any bargains with Labour. Clearly the alliance of ILP and unions would have meant some long-term erosion of the Liberal position, but until 1914, the progress was slight. Apart from commanding Irish support, Liberalism could still make a strong appeal to Scottish electors. That great historical 'Whodunnit', the decline of Liberalism, staged in all industrial areas within Britain had particular relevance for Scotland where Liberal sentiments expressed much that was central to the distinctiveness of Scottish society.

Independent Labour, despite its class base and its socialist claims, expressed many of the same sentiments. As such it could have a legitimate niche within Scotland but whether it was bound to replace Liberalism as a major expression of Scottish identity depended on factors beyond its control. As so often in

Scottish affairs, the critical links ran not only southwards but also across the Irish Sea.

The leaders that characterised these Scottish themes also traced these links. MacDonald, Glasier and Hardie all made their political reputations in the south and shared the anguish of Radicals at the events of 1914. MacDonald survived to attempt a transplant of Radical principles into a refurbished Labour Party. In contrast, Connolly travelled by the United States to the Dublin Post Office. Both trajectories played their part in the destruction of the obstacles that had blocked Labour growth in Scotland. The richness and complexities of their inspirations must be grasped if the origins and the difficulties of the Scottish ILP are to be appreciated.

8

The Yorkshire woollen district

Radical ambiguities

The frail figure, the grave firm features, the thin sensitive lips, the piercing eye, the somewhat ascetic kind of face — all go to make up a personality which may not have been rare in Puritan or Covenanting days, but which is all too seldom met with in our time.[1]

Here was a readily identifiable portrait of Phillip Snowden as the incarnation of the more austere socialist virtues. If Hardie, MacDonald and Glasier brought abundant evidence of their Scottish radical pedigree into the upper echelons of the party, Snowden represented another important early tributary, the radical culture of the woollen towns and villages of the West Riding.[2] Such a specific designation is important. It would be erroneous to portray the ILP as generally strong in the West Riding. The contrast between early growth in the woollen communities, and almost total failure for several years in the adjacent coalfield was acute. Even Leeds, on the periphery of the woollen district, was of only marginal importance for the party once an initial flourish had died, and within the woollen centres, the party did not exhibit a uniform strength. In 1895, it was claimed that the Bradford ILP provided one-thirteenth of the NAC's income, and no less than one-sixth of the affiliation fees.[3] Halifax was a second major source of contributions, and the party also had a significant presence in Huddersfield, Dewsbury, Keighley, and in some of the villages in the Colne and Holme Valleys such as Slaithwaite and Honley.[4] Elsewhere developments were stolid rather than spectacular. One local activist claimed few illusions about the Brighouse branch:

Numerically we are not so strong. Financially not more so but have won a fair share of public confidence ... by a persistent plodding, and by a rigid adherence to a policy of strictly independent action.[5]

Yet most woollen constituencies maintained some ILP presence even in the difficult years after 1895, and this residual vitality helped to sustain the party as a national organisation. Indeed electoral performances at both municipal and parliamentary levels in both Bradford and Halifax played a particularly important role in helping to maintain credibility. A further indication of continuing strength is provided by a summary of the party's parliamentary contests in woollen seats (Table 16).

Table 16. *ILP Parliamentary Interventions 1892—1906*

	1892	1895	1900	1906	By-Elections
Bradford West	√	√	√	√	
Bradford East	–	–	–	–	November 1896
Halifax	–	√	√	√	February 1893 & March 1897
Colne Valley	–	√	–	–	
Dewsbury	–	√	–	*	SDF candidate in February 1902 backed by several ILP branches
Huddersfield	–	√	–	+	

* Contested by an ILP member sponsored by his trade union.
+ Contested by an ILP member sponsored by Huddersfield Trades Council.

Bradford West and Halifax proved to be the most promising seats, both producing victories in 1906. Elsewhere, results were less encouraging, although by then Independent Labour had secured a solid base in Huddersfield, and Grayson's success in the Colne Valley was just over eighteen months away. Such inroads must be balanced by the failure of any ILP challenge to materialise in several woollen seats. Even in Keighley, where an independent organisation existed from 1892, hopes of a candidate were dashed in 1895, through a lack of funds, and no parliamentary candidate stood until October 1911.[6] With the exception of Colne Valley, early ILP contests were restricted to the boroughs where financial inadequacies were less of a handicap; even in the party's Bradford stronghold, efforts were almost completely limited to one seat out of the three. Nevertheless, with all these caveats, the party's record was a comparatively strong one in terms of membership, municipal representation and parliamentary contests.[7]

The search for an explanation of such strength encounters immediately one salient political feature of the woollen towns, the continuing strength of Liberalism. In 1892, as in 1885, all the fourteen woollen seats had been won by Liberals. In the generally bad Liberal year of 1886, they had retained their holdings almost intact, and even in the best Unionist years of 1895 and 1900, Liberals still held a majority of the seats.[8]

This relative Liberal success afforded a sharp contrast with the situation in the ILP's early Lancashire strongholds. In the woollen towns, factors which were propelling voters of all classes elsewhere into the Unionist camp from 1886 were less effective. The Home Rule issue had relatively little resonance. Only Bradford showed striking evidence of working-class Unionism. There was a sizeable Irish population there, and this seemed to provoke the stock Conservative responses on the part of some other voters.[9] But generally the ethnic and religious elements that divided the working class elsewhere were largely absent. Religious Dissent had a powerful support particularly in the industrial villages.[10] Protectionist sentiments seem to have secured little support except in the early nineties, when the woollen trade had been damaged by the recent imposition of the McKinley Tariff.

There are clear parallels here with the continuing influence of Scottish Liberalism, although in the West Riding the lack of impact made by the Irish issue provides one important divergence. There was a second one. We have seen how Scottish Liberalism through its tribulations combined a lack of sympathy towards labour candidates with a continuing Radical commitment. Indeed the flight of many wealthy Scottish Liberals in 1886 could make Radical claims seem even more plausible. In contrast, leading Liberals in many woollen towns were not just unsympathetic to labour candidates, they were also unreceptive to many of the demands put forward by labour organisations. Home Rule had not produced the same defections here, and characteristic spokesmen in the nineties included Alfred Illingworth, millowner, nonconformist and Member for West Bradford, and Sir James Kitson, Colne Valley's MP, and the largest engineering employer in Leeds.[11] They combined wealth, adherence to 'laissez faire' and disregard for labour demands. They seemed able to afford such a cavalier approach, since in the early nineties there appeared to be no electoral grounds for special tenderness towards labour demands. The absence of strong trade unions in the woollen industry deprived working-class electors of one channel through which demands could have been ventilated and pressure imposed. On the one side, the presence of an Illingworth or a Kitson could reassure middle-class voters that here at least Liberalism remained attached to the values that they had grown up with. But, as a bonus, there remained strong ties of sentiment between official Liberalism and many working-class Radicals.[12]

These ties pointed to a dualism that was of fundamental importance for the emergence of Independent Labour. The strong Chartist traditions of the area had become transmuted into a Radicalism that seemed to be assimilated within the Liberal army. This process could produce the vignette presented by E. P. Thompson — old Chartist leaders meeting in Halifax to toast Gladstone in lemonade.[13] Yet if old Chartists had become men of standing, old Radical and Chartist principles cohabited most uncomfortably with Liberal doctrine as understood by Kitson and Illingworth. Principles and memories could serve to integrate working-class leaders into Liberalism, but equally they could provide a standard by which Liberal practices could be judged and found wanting. Absorption was only part of the process, there also existed a vibrant, radical working-class tradition that lacked independent political organisation but could readily justify such a departure.

An understanding of the potential for such a development necessitates some assessment of the district's dominant trade. As with cotton, we are dealing with a complex industry and generalisation can be a hazardous business. Trade conditions could vary radically as between the carpet manufacturers of Halifax, the 'shoddy' mills of Batley and Dewsbury, and the fine worsted producers of Bradford. Three fundamental points can be made however. This was an industry in which mechanisation came relatively late, with handworking continuing into the 1870s in some of the Pennine valleys.[14] The vanishing world of the hand-loom weaver is captured in the reminiscences of Ben Turner — the village entertainments, dialect songs and Chartist hymns.[15] So is the route from this world not just to the factory and union organisation, but also to socialist agitations. Late mechanisation helped to preserve Chartist sentiments; those who made Turner's journey could apply them to a new situation.

The factory-based woollen workers faced a crisis by the eighties.[16] The singular boom of the early seventies had produced inflated entrepreneurial expectations, and as international competition became tighter, profit margins were largely maintained, and production expanded through squeezing the operatives' standards. Wages were cut, mechanisation extended and speed-ups intensified, women workers substituted for men. Such a squeeze could be successful because of the parlous state of union organisation. Small sectors of specifically skilled workers maintained stable unions, but the vast majority of weavers remained outside the Weavers' Union. After a decade of effort, and with the advantage of the New Unionist upsurge, enrolment remained small. In 1891, union officials claimed 2,000 out of 9,000 weavers in the Huddersfield District and 1,000 out of 13,000 in the Heavy Woollen District of Dewsbury and Batley. The Bradford organiser responsible for an area stretching from Halifax to Skipton, containing an estimated 32,000 weavers, claimed only 2,000 members.[17] Some districts were particularly barren soil for trade unionism. One calculation for Colne Valley suggests no more than a thousand union members in this far-flung constituency, and the majority of these were cotton workers on the Lancashire border.[18] Frustrated organisers tended to explain such weakness by reference to the power of intimidation and the 'thoughtlessness' of the weavers.[19] A more thorough explanation would emphasise the novelty of the factory system, the divisive impact of a harshly competitive industry and in such a situation the problems posed for organis-ation by female and half-time labour.[20] The impact on wages was all that cost-conscious employers could desire; for the workers, the problem was com-pounded by the irregularity of the work. An average figure for weavers' wages suggested by the union in 1892 was only eleven shillings.[21] The previous year, the union's Bradford organiser had suggested that in this area, the average was two shillings below this.[22] A further, very different, consequence was to turn Weavers' organisers, who often encountered the hostility of Liberal employers, into staunch supporters of political independence. The two most prominent spokesmen, Ben Turner and Allan Gee were both delegates at the ILP's foundation conference, whilst W. H. Drew, the Bradford organiser was one of the moving spirits behind the whole affair.

West Riding textile workers did not acquiesce readily in their impoverishment; problems of organisation bedevilled attempts to resist wage reductions. Nevertheless, there was potential within the working class Radical tradition for a specifically political response to industrial pressures. By 1889, the *Yorkshire Factory Times* was combining dialect writings, reports of trade union activities and political prescriptions. The catalyst was provided by the Manningham Mills strike, a protracted struggle lasting from December 1890 to April 1891.[23] This confrontation was of crucial importance, indicating and widening the gulf between an articulate section of Bradford working-class opinion, and some at least, of the leaders of Bradford Liberalism. Yet although this confrontation lends itself easily to a dichotomous analysis, over-simplification should be avoided. It would be easy to present 'Manningham Mills' as a penetrating exposé of the hypocrisies of a complacent narrow Liberalism, as a cockpit in which workers acquired political wisdom through industrial struggle. Certainly, powerful sections of Bradford Liberalism ranged themselves with the employer, Samuel Lister, and municipal resources were mobilised to prevent the strikers holding outdoor meetings.[24] But there were other aspects. Some middle-class Radicals did not support Lister, a position reflected in the line taken by W. P. Byles's *Bradford Observer*. Samuel Lister, moreover did not belong to Bradford Liberalism; his Fair Trade beliefs and Conservative connections complicated the reality if not the lesson of the struggle.

These reservations apart, the moral seemed obvious. When Tillett came to Bradford to oppose Illingworth in the 1892 election, he rubbed home the lesson. One reason for his candidature was:

the official local organisation, official Liberals joined hands with Tories to bring soldiers and police to Bradford, to intimidate the work people of Manningham and cause riots.[25]

Industrialists and their municipal henchmen had demonstrated a readiness to use their resources, to manipulate the conditions under which industrial battles were fought. Now old Radical traditions and principles could be applied critically to contemporary controversies.

If 'Manningham Mills' provided a dramatic centrepiece, this was bordered by other incidents that suggested the same conclusion. In Halifax, two labour propagandists were sacked by a Liberal employer with the Liberal Association and Trades Council already having differences over labour representation.[26] In Colne Valley, working-class Radicals could have little confidence in a Liberal Association that adopted Kitson as its candidate.[27] Everywhere

Liberal Associations seemed to cater for the needs of employers and ignore the demands of Radical workers.

This perception helped to precipitate the formation of Labour Unions in several centres, initially in Bradford as a rapid response to 'Manningham Mills' but subsequently in the Colne Valley, Halifax, Huddersfield and Keighley. These represented an attempt at organisational separation with an immediate view to municipal representation. The founding resolution of the Bradford and District Labour Union struck a pragmatic, yet firm, note:

its objects should be to advance the interests of working men in whatever way, it might from time to time be thought advisable ... its operation should be carried on irrespective of the convenience of any political party.[28]

The venture was founded on a belief that working-class demands would achieve proper attention only if some direct representation was secured. Given the attitude of many local Liberal leaders, this necessitated separate organisation. The demand was essentially for a fair crack of the whip, a political equivalent of the traditional 'fair day's pay for a fair day's work' demand. The emergence of Labour Unions was presented in some cases as an extension of trades council work.[29] Apart from Bradford, most woollen town trades councils were very recent creations. This meant that there was typically no Liberal legacy with which Independent Labour partisans had to contend, but it also meant that the councils were typically weak, and a Labour Union could serve as a valuable second string. Indeed in the Colne Valley where trade union organisation was particularly limited, the Labour Union could serve as a substitute for industrial initiatives.

The initial title of 'Labour Union' is revealing. They were bodies for the protection and advancement of labour interests. There was a sense in which they could claim to rise above partisanship, being concerned not with the advancing of a distinctive set of principles but with the safeguarding of a hitherto neglected section. At the start, programmes were largely eschewed, but it is revealing that the only specific planks in the platform of the Keighley Labour Union could be accommodated within a progressive Liberalism — the restoration of the land through the taxation of ground values, the municipalisation of monopolies, and the extension of municipal powers.[30] Here were cases of the district's radicalism adapting to contemporary problems and fashions. The centrality of this radicalism to the emergence of the Labour Unions was apparent in 1892 when George Garside a Radical blacksmith standing for the Colne Valley Labour Union, captured the Slaithwaite seat on the West Riding County Council.[31] This tradition was central to the initial appeal of the Labour Unions, but it could have aided a reabsorption into a chastened Liberalism.

This did not happen, in part because of the unbending quality of much official Liberalism, but also because the Labour Unions imbibed other influences. The leaven of the Leeds and Bradford Socialist Leagues, expressed initially in the activities of pioneers such as Tom Maguire and Fred Jowett, worked through into the Labour Unions. The socialist attachment of trade union officials such as Turner and Gee also left its mark. It was not long before the independence of labour involved more than an organisational separation; it embodied also a socialist commitment. Such a shift was reinforced by national connections. The logic of political independence led to invitations to prominent advocates of an independent position. Thus Tom Mann had a close association with Colne Valley until the 1895 election and Katherine Conway held early propaganda meetings there.[32] Their message was a socialist one, readily acceptable to audiences whose faith in Radical Liberalism had faltered. The communal solidarity of textile villages could bring about decisive shifts in political allegiance. Such a phenomenon was most marked perhaps in some of the Colne Valley villages, where branches of the Labour Union became accepted as a legitimate part of local life.

Basically, there existed political space in the woollen district to the left of official Liberalism. A combination of economic pressures and trade union weakness, Liberal conservatism and complacency, a vital radical tradition and socialist creativity produced a crucial breakthrough of broadly based labour organisations, to which socialists added a distinctive ingredient. As a consequence the nineties were marked by bitter hostilities between Liberal and Labour. But hostility was only one aspect. Labour and Radical Liberalism retained much in common on the levels of ethos, and specific policy positions. Repulsion and attraction competed with one another over time, within individuals and in the various communities. The complexities can be approached through an analysis of the two principal ILP centres.

Bradford and Halifax

Confused beginnings
The expansion of Bradford had been one of the most dramatic features of the woollen trade's nineteenth-century growth. In a district where industrial villages and small towns predominated, Bradford showed many traits characteristic of other northern cities.[33] Compared with most neighbouring towns it had a wider variety of occupations, and this had generated some craft unionism and provided scope for 'New Unionism' to take root. But, as noted earlier, union organisation amongst the woollen workers was slight. If this weakness was an incentive to political action, it also meant that the solidarities of industrial activity could not be used easily as a basis for political support. Moreover, the distribution of the working-class electorate in Bradford exacerbated this problem. Sources agree that until around 1900, Bradford was distinctive in that socially segregated housing had developed only a little compared with other cities; a corollary of this was that there were few municipal wards that could be regarded as solidly working class. Indeed, West Bradford, the central concern of the ILP parliamentary effort over the next two decades,

contained both Manningham Mills and the city's most select residential area.[34] The party's best performances were to be in the more affluent working-class districts, where the appeal of a Jowett could make a ready impact; in the poorer districts, with a sizeable Irish vote, support was less.[35]

If such social heterogeneity reduced the scope for working-class solidarity, it also reduced the incentive for Liberal flexibility. In most wards, Liberal organisations could be controlled by middle-class residents and therefore both the willingness and the need to make concessions were absent.

This situation was strengthened by the respect accruing to the leading lights of Bradford Liberalism. Such families as the Forsters and the Illingworths were identified with the expansion and eminence of Bradford; their spokesmen could reach an accord with trade union leaders through the shared idiom of radical nonconformity.[36] Yet in the late eighties, this settlement came under pressure. The Trades Council experienced rebuffs from official Liberalism in its attempts to promote Labour representation, and both the council and the recently formed Bradford Labour Electoral Association became battle-grounds between Gladstonians and advocates of a more independent strategy. Demands for working-class representation were given much more urgency with the Town Council's partiality over the Manningham Mills affair. The credibility of such demands was enhanced by the growth in Bradford trade unionism; there the size of the community was an asset to the Independent Labour cause, since whatever the weaknesses in the woollen trade, the Trades Council's deliberations were transformed both by the growth of New Unionism, and by the radicalisation of some craft groups faced with the threat of technical change.[37]

The combination of union growth, industrial defeat, and political frustration led pragmatically to the formation of the Bradford Labour Union in May 1891. This was a step beyond even a vigorous LEA, but the superseding of the older body was certainly not a straightforward affair. When the Bradford Labour Union fought its first municipal campaign in the autumn of 1891 it enjoyed no success. The only 'Labour' victory was that of Sam Shaftoe, leader of the Lib-Labs who emphasised to the voters that the only Labour body he belonged to was the Trades Council.[38] The first Independent Labour entry to the Town Council came soon afterwards, but success in an unopposed by-election in Manningham was hardly a dramatic victory. However, the shift of opinion on the Bradford Trades Council showed the impact of the recent events at least on a section of trade union leaders, and the growing rift between Labour and Liberalism was symbolised in the contest between Tillett and Illingworth in the Bradford West election of 1892.

This celebrated confrontation only occurred after some false starts. Originally the Labour Union had considered a contest in East Bradford but the chosen champion, Robert Blatchford, withdrew abruptly and characteristically after a few months to concentrate on the *Clarion*.[39] By then Tillett, after initial hesitation, had agreed to oppose Illingworth. He refused to accept an arrangement with the Liberals whereby he could have a straight fight against the Conservative member in the East Division, if there was no Labour candidate in Bradford West.

This refusal indicates one central element of Tillett's campaign. Whatever his later political gyrations, Tillett was seen in 1892 as one of the key figures in New Unionism, and it was on the industrial division between himself and Illingworth that he concentrated. The Liberal member was presented as an unsatisfactory employer[40] — and he was not the only unacceptable Liberal. Gladstone's position on eight-hours legislation was also criticised.[41] Beyond this, there lay the lessons of Manningham Mills, the use in Bradford of troops and the unwillingness of established politicians to assist labour representation. But regularly, the issue came back to Illingworth: as Jowett expressed it, 'Their ideas and Mr. Illingworth's were totally antagonistic. Mr. Illingworth was a supporter of royalty rents, was also against the eight hour day ... out of accord with the new progressive movement.'[42]

The rift seemed complete — and yet the term 'new movement' was ambiguous. There were, after all, several Radicals who did not demonstrate Illingworth's rooted objections to any amendments to a laissez-faire system. Was the campaign against Liberalism as such, or against the reactionary Illingworth variety? The answer is unclear. Certainly, some Labour activists attempted to gain support from traditional Radical sources. Jowett's intervention in the deliberations of the Bradford Nonconformist Association is the most celebrated. At a stormy meeting, with Illingworth's supporters filling the platform, Jowett moved an amendment to a pro-Liberal motion. This claimed Tillett to be 'at least as good a Nonconformist as Mr. Illingworth ... and as faithful a follower of Jesus Christ' and expressed

its strong disapproval of the attempt of the committee of the Bradford Nonconformist Association to put the Labour candidate ... at a disadvantage in the eyes of the Nonconformist electors.[43]

An attempt was also made to remove the firmly pro-Illingworth commitment of the Bradford Temperance Confederation. Both efforts failed, leaving conclusive proof in Labour circles that these bodies 'were Liberals first and Nonconformist or teetotaller afterwards'.[44] The Irish vote was also directed to Illingworth: only the Trades Council of the traditional Gladstonian pressure groups was under the control of Labour supporters, and even here the vote for Tillett was only 47 to 33.[45]

Supposedly 'independent' pressure groups apart, there was one more manifestation of a bid for Radical rather than Labour votes. Sidney Webb travelled to Bradford to paint a picture of the contrast between London Liberal leaders 'some of whom were anxious to have Labour candidates' and the local wirepullers. He claimed that his visit had the backing of 'men high up in the Liberal party'; he was there 'in the best interests, not merely of Labour, but also of Liberalism', to help defeat Illingworth, a candidate 'not even abreast with the Liberalism of today'.[46]

Such an intervention from the leading advocate of permeation, a man well acquainted with Alderman Tillett's activities on the LCC, suggests amendments to the image of the contest as the occasion for a great rift. Tillett stood as a Labour man, as a progressive, but socialism as such was not an issue. That is not to deny that the Labour Union at this time was linked with socialist agitation. Many of the activists were strongly committed to socialism, and during his visits to East Bradford Blatchford had attacked the existing political economy as 'a thing barbarous in itself and barbarous in its results'.[47] But such sentiments rarely surfaced in June and July 1892. The acrimony of the campaign produced both growing hostility and a growth of Labour enthusiasm. Tillett launched a strong post-declaration attack on the Bradford Liberals and their pulpit allies,[48] but the size of his poll was impressive (Table 17). During the next few months Independent Labour experienced a boom in

Table 17. *The West Bradford election, 1892*

A. Illingworth, Liberal	3,306
E. F. S. Flower, Conservative	3,053
Ben Tillett, Independent Labour	2,749

Bradford. Union disenchantment with Liberalism had been intensified and widened by the contest, and the Labour Union—Trades Council link became more secure. Labour clubs sprang up. In mid 1892 there were just two, but by the end of the year, their number had grown to sixteen. This was the Labour explosion that helped to fix Bradford as the venue for the foundation of the national party.[49] Organisational growth was matched by a significant municipal success in November 1892 when Jowett entered the Town Council. Within a few months of Tillett's campaign, Bradford Labour had established itself as a vital independent force; although what this independence amounted to was not wholly clear. There was now a legacy of hostility to official Liberalism, based on past confrontations and social differences, but there still existed continuities of idiom.

These developments were epitomised in the political style of Fred Jowett. He had moved from Radicalism and nonconformity into the socialist movement of the late eighties, through the LEA to become a leading figure within the Labour Union. In 1892, he was also President of the Bradford Labour Church, a Director of the Bradford Provident Industrial Society, a Trades Council delegate for the Power Loom Overlookers, a Fabian and a member of the Bradford Board of Conciliation. A contemporary portrayed him as a symbol of Independent Labour's earnestness and competence:

He holds no opinion which he is not prepared to argue out clearly and logically, and he never, however great the provocation, loses his self-possession or gives way to violence of expression.[50]

The career of 'Jowett of Bradford' was to become a respected rallying point for later critics of the Labour establishment; he stood somewhat apart from the dominant national figures, and his socialist commitment was seemingly unblemished by the responsibilities of office.[51]

The immediate aftermath of Tillett's campaign was the honeymoon of the Bradford ILP. Certainly, major steps such as Jowett's municipal success laid a basis for future eminence, but by the time of Tillett's second contest three years later, some of the earlier euphoria had faded. The 1894 municipal results had been disappointing. Six contests, five of them three-cornered had yielded no victories, and in the three-cornered fights, the ILP had finished last in every case but one.[52] Nevertheless, municipal voting patterns suggested the existence of a significant and durable Labour vote. Foundations had been laid: Labour was a presence in Bradford politics although its growth was as yet limited. This assessment is borne out by the result of the second Tillett campaign in 1895. Illingworth was no longer a candidate, being replaced at the last minute by a millowner from Cross Hills near Keighley.[53] The campaign was enlivened by a visit from a Keighley ILPer attacking the wages payed to the Liberal candidate's workers.[54] The Labour campaign was now of course integrated into the national ILP effort. Integrated is perhaps an inappropriate word since attempts to use the ILP's leading speakers to help each other ended in a shambles. Tillett departed to Ashton to speak for Sexton, ignorant of the latter's inability to come to Bradford. The result was a mass meeting with only Glasier turning up out of the advertised speakers. As the Liberal press smugly remarked — 'the chief Independent Labour speakers are finding it extremely hard work to fill up the platforms for about thirty candidates'.[55]

Despite such contretemps, enthusiasm seems to have remained high, with Tillett's position more clearly anti-Liberal than in 1892. He saw no essential difference between his two rich opponents who would resist all practical reforms.[56] His supporting speakers were more clearly socialist than three years earlier and the Trades Council now gave him unanimous backing.[57] This provides the clear image of a definite Labour/socialist strategy: as Jowett argued after the poll had been declared, they had lost the support of those who did not understand their position fully 'but there were more Socialists today in Western Bradford than there had been in 1892'.[58] The result of the election is given in Table 18.

This is important; it was part of the sharpening of Liberal—ILP relationships in many places by 1895. But once again another element was present.

Table 18. *The West Bradford election, 1895*

E. F. S. Flower, Conservative	3,936
J. Horsfall, Liberal	3,471
Ben Tillett, ILP	2,264

Tillett's long connection with the seat, and Illingworth's retirement, had produced expectations in Labour circles that there would be no Liberal candidate. Tillett reflected early in the campaign that 'from the moment of Mr. Illingworth's resignation, at any rate, he had the best right to appear as a candidate because the division was a working class constituency and he was directly a working man's representative'.[59] This phraseology certainly suggests at least some sort of common Radical paternity. After the declaration, Tillett was more explicit, accusing the Liberals of a breach of faith, otherwise 'they might have had their two seats and Labour would have got their one seat'.[60]

What, if any, arrangement had been scouted and between whom is obscure. But now the Liberals had lost all three Bradford seats. In such a situation, the attractions of such a deal were obvious, but in the immediate future chastened Liberals and still-optimistic Labour dug in for intensified hostilities.

The Bradford pattern of development over the first four years is therefore one of Labour expansion and Liberal defeat accompanied by a considerable clarification of Labour's political position, a clarification in which both local and national factors played their parts. The significance of the local element is very clear, if we travel the few miles from Bradford to Halifax, and examine contemporary development in the ILP's second major West Riding centre. In this smaller community, woollen textiles were naturally of major importance, but considerable employment was provided by the engineering industry, which was beginning of course, to experience major technical innovations.[61] One Halifax Trades Council spokesman was ready to accept a portrait of Halifax as a town with a relatively prosperous working class, participating in an abundance of voluntary institutions.[62] But working-class standards of living depended frequently on a family income that incorporated ill-paid workers of both sexes, and a local bye-law allowed children to begin as half-timers at the amazingly low level of Standard Two.[63] Politically, there were two crucial features: Halifax was the only two-member constituency in the West Riding, so the scope for both conflict and alliances was increased. And it was a town with a vivid Radical past. Long Liberal dominance had included a tradition of disputes within the Liberal 'family', with these sometimes aired in rival candidatures. Halifax had been contested by Ernest Jones in 1847 and 1852 in opposition to the Whig Sir Charles Wood.[64] Marx had described Jones's denunciation of the Whig and his appeal to the 'Men of Halifax' to 'Turn him out in the name of humanity and of God'.[65] The conflict was awakened once again in 1868 by Jones's oratory and by the candidature of the Co-operator, E. O. Greening. Here were striking reminders of the partial incorporation of working-class Radicalism within mid and late Victorian Liberalism.

This was the context for Halifax's Labour development. The immediate events included the formation of a local Fabian Society in 1891, and growing trades council dissatisfaction with local Liberal leaders. By early 1892, Halifax Trades Council spokesmen were claiming seats on the School Board and Town Council and also one of the parliamentary seats, at the same time insisting that there should be no official connection with the Liberals. Two events then precipitated the formation in August of a Labour Union. The 'Liberal 400' adopted its two sitting members as candidates, a decision accepted with misgivings by the trades council, since no Labour candidate was ready. At this stage, some trades council activists clearly saw their objective as the securing of greater influence within the broad Liberal coalition. They had had an interview with the Liberal Members, and that at least was an advance.[66] Hopes of a concordat were damaged by the sackings of two Labour activists by a Liberal employer. The formation of the Labour Union was presented as a simple extension of trades council work — it was to be the instrument for poltical aspects of the council's business. Yet, one distinctive ingredient was provided by Hardie's presence at a subsequent meeting, moving a resolution for a National ILP. Already, the shift to a more distinctive political position was beginning, aided by the conflict with local Liberalism which was endemic in the Labour Union's inauguration.

The early development of Halifax Labour politics can be understood only if one further element is included: the personality and politics of John Lister of Shibden Hall, the ILP's first Treasurer. If the standing image of an early ILPer is of a self-respecting, self-educated artisan probably with a nonconformist background, then Lister was about as far away from this as possible. A member of a family which had lived at Shibden since 1613, he had been educated at Winchester and Oxford. To this unlikely background, he added a conversion to Roman Catholicism after having been influenced by the Tractarians. But his politics were always Radical and in the early nineties having read *Capital* he moved into the Fabian orbit, and was a central figure at the foundation of the Labour Union. His idiosyncratic involvement inevitably lent a unique dimension to local politics.[67]

Halifax acquired national significance in February 1893 when a by-election vacancy prompted the first campaign of the national ILP, an event complicated both by the town's Radical traditions and by Lister's selection as the Labour candidate. The campaign began with declarations of firm independence — 'no consideration would be given to any other candidate as the Union intended to fight on independent lines'. However, at the same meeting the candidate considerably diluted the effect of this by claiming there was 'no reason why the Liberal party should not adopt him as he was a Home Ruler and thus avoid a contest'.[68] Much more so than in Tillett's first contest, the lines of battle were blurred.

This complexity revealed itself in varied ways. An attempt was made to promote Lister's cause at the Liberal adoption meeting. One Liberal councillor expressed regret at the failure to reach agreement with the Labour organisation and an amendment was moved suggesting that no candidate be run against Lister.[69] This limited concern in Liberal ranks was no doubt a product of fear of electoral consequences, deference towards Lister and concern at the views of the adopted Liberal, Rawson Shaw, son of the deceased member.

He was certainly no Radical, opposing as he did eight-hours legislation and payment of MPs and having only a dubious attachment to Home Rule;[70] this last feature of his policies led Davitt to refuse to speak for him, and produced a split amongst Irish voters despite the INL's policy of voting for the Libeal.[71] Such suspicions of his Radical credentials obtained their final demonstration four years later when he resigned his seat following Rosebery's departure from the leadership.

The facility with which this first ILP contest became one between Radical and Whig rather than one between Labour and Liberal, let alone one between socialist and Liberal, was abetted by Lister's campaign statements. He accused his Liberal opponent of 'endangering a Gladstonian seat', adding that 'if Mr. Gladstone wants a vote, I am the man to give him that vote'.[72] He was the better Liberal, more loyal to the Newcastle Programme and to Home Rule.

Certainly, Lister covered the staple elements of direct Labour politics but his presentation of the Labour commitment was related closely to Halifax's Radical traditions. He aimed for an alliance of Labour and Radicals, and in seeking support drew inspiration from Halifax's past — 'In the Chartist days, the fight of the workers was waged against just the same class of men who rule over the Liberal Association today. Even as John Lister does battle against them now, so Ernest Jones fought them'.[73] He thanked God 'his opinions were too advanced for the Whigs of Halifax, but were not too advanced for the good old Radicals who had always found in these Whigs, their most bitter enemies'. The battle was one of 'money-bags against workers — of democratic Radicals, friends of Labour against capitalistic Whigs'.[74]

Such a campaign inevitably generated a response from Radicals outside Halifax. The *Daily Chronicle* backed Lister, arguing that there was a need in by-elections to balance Whig recruits with 'advanced' men.[75] Within the Labour Movement, John Burns made a unique appearance to support an ILP candidate, and followed up Lister's eve-of-poll rally by addressing a crowd from a lamp-post opposite the Liberal Association offices.[76] Such uncertainties about political divisions were not just a product of Lister's campaign nor of Halifax peculiarities. The local aspects were important, but the tensions within the Liberal coalition and uncertainties about Labour's political development made their contributions.

There was, however, one element in the Lister appeal which rested not on complex Liberal/Labour relations but on his position as a community leader. It seems far removed from the ILP to find an election address that proclaims

Having been myself a considerable employer of Labour and engaged in an industry upon which the other industries of our town largely depend, I claim to be able to understand, in a great measure, the commercial needs of the community. Moreover, being a resident in the district, I should be readily accessible to traders and businessmen generally, in the event of any of their special interests coming within the scope of government action.[77]

So the paternalistic weapon used against the ILP by a Wilson in Hull was on this occasion turned to its advantage. The appeal 'to my fellow-townsmen of all classes' the recall of 'the way he has in past years sacrificed himself for his poorer fellows',[78] no doubt boosted Lister's poll, giving early encouragement to the ILP but also generating illusions about the party's strength.

The peculiar features of independent Labour development in Halifax no doubt help to account for a lack of solidarity during its early years. The lines between the Labour Union and the other parties were not drawn clearly and the result was a tendency for individuals to reach compromises with other bodies. The first such incident occurred as early as the aldermanic elections following the November 1892 municipal results. The two Labour men sacked by their employer had been elected to the Town Council. Both were approached, one, Beever by the Liberals, the other, Tattersall, by the Conservatives, with regard to support for aldermanic places. Lister recalled subsequently that 'a rather unseemly wrangle occurred between Tattersall and Beever ... but Tattersall with the support of the Tories gained the day and was made Alderman'.[79] A more serious split occurred two years later involving the NAC. This time Beever was expelled from the Union for his Liberal proclivities and Lister, refusing to stand for Council again owing to what he saw as restrictions on his freedom, was disowned as candidate.[80] The circumstances of the Union's formation and its early strategy had led to the inclusion of several Liberals and some Conservatives who continued to find links with their earlier parties attractive. Unlike Bradford, there was not the necessary demarcation.

Inevitably, the development of a national party meant that Halifax ambiguities were gradually removed. However, the return of Lister as candidate meant that this had only occurred partially at the time of the 1895 election. The Labour campaign was directed against a new Liberal candidate James Booth and his record as an employer and a councillor. His opposition to Fair Contract clauses and the continuation of Shaw's candidature made it easy for Lister to present the Liberal wirepullers as a reactionary anti-Labour group.[81] Much more contentious was a letter from Tattersall urging, with some apparent success, that Labour voters should give their second vote to the Conservative candidate or, as Tattersall put it, against the nominees of 'an association the wire-pullers of which are the greatest enemies of Labour in our midst'. Tattersall's own defection to the Conservatives was imminent but he was still at this time a significant figure in the ILP — he was the Preston candidate and a member of the NAC.[82] Certainly, Booth's defeat and a rare Tory success were welcomed by Halifax Labour leaders (Table 19).

James Parker, later to work closely with the Liberals, argued that 'they had shown those men who had bossed the show a little further up the street that they could not put any sort of candidate up and carry them'.[83] Once again the ambiguity is present — Liberals have been punished for disregarding the opinions of Labour men. Hopefully they will learn.

Table 19. *Halifax 1895*

	Totals		Lister's Vote	
Arnold Conservative	5,475		Plumpers	1,731
Shaw Liberal		5,085	Splits with Arnold	1,351
Booth Liberal	4,283		Splits with Shaw	638
Lister ILP		3,818	Splits with Booth	98

In Halifax as in Bradford, by very different routes, Labour and Liberal had hostile relations by 1895. In both places Liberals had lost seats: in both places Labour could be held responsible: Liberal Associations still contained many who wished for no deal with Labour, and Labour for its part had shaken off many ideological equivocations. In Halifax, in 1895, the Labour post-poll meeting closed with three cheers for Socialism.[84] The stage was set for a period of Lib-Lab confrontation.

Lib-Lab Hostilities: Two By-elections

This polarisation took place in the context of ILP retrenchment. The party's decline after 1895 still left its West Riding heartlands largely intact, although membership and enthusiasm diminished. In Bradford, the municipal bridgehead remained, although as yet it did not grow. The Bradford ILP fought fewer municipal contests — six in 1895, but only three in 1896 and five in each of the two following years. Victories were few, and municipally the party did no more than hold its own.[85]

It was in this context that the death of the Unionist member led in October—November 1896 to a by-election in East Bradford. This was by Bradford standards not an ILP stronghold: the working-class districts included slum areas where the Labour strength was low. Hardie was to reflect how 'the party feeling is strongest where poverty is greatest. In the poorest part of East Bradford, men, women, and children wear the blue and yellow'.[86] The constituency also contained the Bowling Iron Works, a firm strongly identified with Conservatism.[87] Nevertheless, Hardie was the first candidate to be adopted and seems at first to have been optimistic. The early campaign exchanges were marked by the Liberal Association's feverish search for a candidate. 'Who the dickens is the Liberal to be?' mused Mann.[88] It was only seventeen days after Hardie's entry and after several refusals that the Bradford Liberals secured the acceptance of Alfred Billson, a Merseyside lawyer.[89]

This hiatus inevitably generated expectation that no Liberal candidate would be forthcoming, and it was claimed by some on the Labour side that a section of Liberal opinion felt that a free run for Hardie would be advantageous.[90] A variant on this theme was suggested by the Radical *Bradford Observer* which floated the idea of Hardie's replacement by an ILPer such as Lister, Pankhurst or Brocklehurst (Sydney Webb was also mentioned!) who would be more acceptable to the Radical wing of Bradford Liberalism.[91] But continued Liberal searches for a standard bearer indicated that control of the Liberal organisation still lay with those who believed 'there is more genuine Liberalism in a Tory than there is in State Socialism'.[92]

Hardie's initial reaction to this situation was characteristically complex, a complexity increased by continued signs of discord amongst Liberal leaders at Westminster. He appealed therefore to 'the rank and file of progressive movements throughout the country to consider seriously whether there could not be a fusion of advanced forces'.[93] Nevertheless, even in this flexible phase, he saw the ILP as the core of any Progressive realignment. They had selected him but although

> he had no objection to meeting with the progressive parties in the constituency — the land people, the temperance people, or working-mens' clubs ... he respectfully declined to meet the official Liberal party.[94]

At this stage Radical elements were dominant in Hardie's appeal, but these were backed, of course, by Labour concerns.

The hope of some concession to Hardie was always a false one. Even the Radical press accepted that no such idea had been discussed by the Liberal executive, nor by the Selection Committee — nor was there any chance of such an idea being accepted.[95] Once Billson had been adopted, the style of the Labour campaign changed abruptly. Aggressive attacks were made on a candidate stigmatised by Tom Mann as 'a fat, plutocratic lawyer',[96] and Hardie now argued for the near identity of official Liberalism and Toryism.[97]

This was placed by Hardie in a specifically Bradford context; here Liberalism was as socially exclusive as Toryism — both his opponents 'would have the support of a long row of rich men who were well-dressed, who apparently dined well, who lived in big houses, who were employers of labour, landlords and big merchants in Bradford';[98] and Mann pointed out the moral of the contest for trade unionists. As for Bradford Liberalism, 'there was not a place in the whole country, where there was such a determined body of opponents of even ordinary trade unionism ... West Riding Liberalism (was) especially representative of the capitalistic fraternity'.[99]

As battle lines became clearer, both Liberal and Labour sought to rally the traditional Progressive interest groups. Billson secured the backing of the Irish National League, a significant support in Bradford politics. Despite Hardie's strong advocacy of the Home Rule cause, the Irish leaders refused to consider his claims, arguing that he had broken pledges given to the West Ham Irish in 1892.[100] The temperance lobby refused to make any recommendation, despite Billson's supposed lack of commitment to the local veto and Hardie's strong temperance views. But the most interesting development for Labour's future prospects concerned trade union opinion. By now Trades Council support for a Bradford ILP candidate was a matter of form: it was after all the generally close relationship between the two that gave the local party much of its durability. More interest lay in a meeting held by the Bradford and Laisterdyke branches of the ASRS including speeches by all three candidates. The meeting overwhelmingly backed Hardie and the Bradford branch also condemned the Society's General Secretary Edwin Harford for recommending members to vote Liberal.[101] As yet, it was not clear that advice by union leaders would be followed by rank and file at the ballot box — but clearly the trade union activists of Bradford were now largely estranged from Liberalism. The basis offered a continued incentive for Labour to continue there on an independent path.

Such reassurance was certainly needed in November 1896. Hardie's campaign evoked massive enthusiasm within Labour ranks: a mass rally packed the St George's Hall and Glasier believed that 'no better speaking for Socialism has ever been done'.[102] But local finance was limited, and the local party was attempting to fight three municipal seats as well.[103] Hardie optimistically claimed that he would achieve 3,750 votes, but in fact his poll was disappointing to the activists — just 1,953. The campaign seemed to have made little impact on 'the people of the poorest and most miserable homes who had piled up the majority for the Conservative's candidate'.[104] Even in Bradford, the ILP ran third to a Conservative soldier and a Liberal lawyer.

The complexities of the situation were not limited to the Liberal—Labour relationship. In this West Riding seat, at least, working-class Conservatism was a significant force encouraged by the candidate with vague references to social reform and attacks on his Liberal opponent's views as 'England for the Irish, London for the Polish Jews, cold water for the working-man'.[105] Such a style could appeal perhaps with particular force where Liberalism was identified with the austerity of an Illingworth, and where the Irish vote was significant.

The eventual disappointment after hopes of a clear run served only to widen the gap between Liberal and Labour: equally, a further Liberal humiliation seemed to make their partisans more unbending than ever. This was the setting for a second by-election four months later, this time in Halifax. The Halifax election was precipitated by the resignation of 'the Whig', Shaw. As a replacement the Halifax Liberals selected Billson, fresh from his Bradford defeat.[106] The local ILP had participated in the general decline of 1895—6, but claimed to have shown signs of recovery. In 1896, membership had climbed from 520 to 602; although party officials admitted that the party had not been so much in evidence as earlier, they claimed that much quiet spade work had been done.[107] Nevertheless, in early 1897, the ILP laboured under a dual handicap: Lister was away in Marseilles and unable to stand as candidate, and the contest was rushed by the Liberals. But Mann was adopted quickly and endorsed with only one dissenting vote by the Trades Council, and by a variety of union branches.[108]

What followed was a campaign very different from those held earlier in

Halifax. Initially there had been some attempt at a Progressive compromise; the Scottish Radical G. B. Clark and W. P. Byles both asked the ILP Executive to consider an agreed candidate.[109] But for the locals this was unacceptable, and the resulting campaign showed little attempt by the ILP to appease or attract Liberals. Mann's programme reflected his industrial interests,[110] the Liberal response was a blend of appeals to Radicalism, and accusations of ILP—Tory links.[111] A new dimension was added to the argument by the involvement of leading trade unionists in the campaign. The contest occurred at a time when relations between the ILP and Lib-Lab leaders were bad. Both Broadhurst and Fenwick visited Halifax to speak for Billson, and Pickard sent a letter of support.[112] This was balanced, to some degree, by Mann securing telegraphed support from the newly elected ASE Secretary, George Barnes.[113]

Despite Mann's fighting speeches, there were problems. The ex-ILPer Beever wrote from Barnsley urging a Liberal vote,[114] whilst Hardie sensed a lack of impact: 'The battle here progressing well; but the divine aflatus of white enthusiasm is lacking. Fine meeting last night in point of numbers and quality of audience, but it went flat.' He concluded that 'the Liberals are decidedly in fear of the result' and hoped 'their fears are well-grounded'.[115] They were not; the result was a blow to the ILP. The contrast with the 1893 by-election was only too apparent (see Table 20).

Table 20. *Two Halifax By-Elections*

9 February 1893			3 March 1897		
		%			%
Lib	4,620	38.9	Lib	5,664	43.8
Cons	4,252	35.7	Lib Unionist	5,252	40.7
J Lister ILP	3,028	25.4	T Mann ILP	2,000	15.5

No doubt the ILP's late start had been a handicap; but the crucial factor was Lister's absence. One press report suggested that in the North Ward — a Labour stronghold — Lister voters had gone Liberal;[116] on a logistical level, Lister's candidature had been backed by more resources, including polling-day vehicles; but crucially the difference was one of principle. Mann reflecting on the result, payed respect to Lister's personal qualities and his support for collectivism, but went on to claim that Lister's poll had been increased by 'his particular appreciation of Socialism ... his speaking of it as advanced Liberalism'. Even in 1895 — let alone 1893 — Mann argued that debate in Halifax had not developed to 'that particular stage when the issues were sufficiently clearly defined ... to have a real fight on definite principles'. He maintained that 'there were more Socialists in Halifax today' and that the future lay with both independence and 'a clear definition of the Socialistic policy'. The final broadside was reserved for the Liberal Party 'the obstacle in front of the realisation of their principles, the canting hypocrites, the pretended friends of Labour'.[117] National and local developments had combined to produce an apparently indefinite prospect of three-cornered contests.

Appearances, however, could be deceptive. The two defeats were expensive and such failures in ILP strongholds held little promise for the future. By 1900, ILP electoral strategy had shifted. There were some parallel indications locally. Even in the heat of the 1897 campaign some Halifax Radicals thought along the same line as one of their Bradford colleagues had done. One prominent local Radical, J. H. Whitley, later to become the town's Liberal MP and Speaker of the Commons, had attempted to develop some Lib-Lab understanding. As yet he met with no encouragement.[118] But eighteen months later there was evidence of some shift in Halifax Labour attitudes. Perhaps significantly, the catalyst was not a parliamentary failure, but the frustrations of municipal politics. A Halifax correspondent informed the *Labour Leader* 'All our people are not prepared to continually face defeat, they deserve success at the polls. According to the strength of our vote in the borough, we are entitled to six seats on the Council. The party must make up its mind, not only in Halifax but elsewhere, whether it is going to fight for propaganda, or for winning elections'.[119] A dominant figure in the Halifax ILP of the late nineties was its full time Secretary—Organiser, James Parker, elected to the Town Council in 1897. He was a cautious pragmatist, whose flexibility took him first to the Commons and then into the supporters of the Lloyd-George Coalition.[120]

The continued involvement in municipal affairs was producing a similar pragmatism in sections of the Bradford ILP. In 1898, ILPers were prepared to back progressive Liberals in some municipal contests.[121] But here there were inevitable complexities in any reciprocal relationship owing to the continuing Illingworthite influence. Basically, however, the 1896—7 confrontations mark the height of Lib-Lab hostilities in Halifax and Bradford, the main movement thereafter at the parliamentary level was towards some sort of Progressive arrangement, a development which was protracted due to earlier differences, but which was the dominant movement over the next decade.

Progressive understanding

The claim that the dominant element from 1897 onwards was in favour of a Progressive understanding is an important one to make, since there is a tendency to see Progessivism as a Lancastrian development, with West Riding politics being marked by continuing Lib-Lab hostility. We are referring here of course only to Bradford and Halifax: the hostile manifestation was more frequent in other parts of West Yorkshire, but the focus is on the two principal ILP centres and therefore must affect the overall West Riding assessment. It must be acknowledged also that there was no simple shift to Progressivism in both towns. Each followed its own path, and there is evidence, especially in Bradford, of continuing residual hostility on both sides.

It was in the larger centre that a Progressive understanding first developed. In the context of the khakhi election there were, of course, forces working for Labour—Liberal understandings because of the weakness of both parties and a high level of agreement, at any rate between ILPers and Radicals, over the war. But in Bradford there were obstacles. There had been a reaction within the ILP to the municipal tactic of supporting some Liberals and in November 1899, attempts had been made to organise the Labour vote against the Liberals in retaliation for Liberal intervention against a sitting Labour councillor.[122] In West Bradford the ILP's standard bearer, who now had the endorsement of the LRC, was the highly respected Jowett, a Bradford Alderman and Chairman of the Council's Health Committee. He had been active in the constituency for almost a year at the dissolution,[123] whilst the Liberals had failed to produce a candidate. Nevertheless, the Liberal Old Guard did not yield without a struggle. The Liberal ranks were divided. Some wished to support Jowett and to ask for Labour support in the other two Bradford divisions, but other influential Liberals continued to search for a candidate. Illingworth remained firm in his hostility. He informed Herbert Gladstone that the Bradford Liberal Association 'find it impossible to work with, or even place confidence in the leaders of the "ILP" party'. He claimed that he spoke for the Association in his antipathy to deals, 'we will not be bartered and disposed of in attempting to square circles elsewhere'.[124] Eventually the Liberals made a choice, but met with a refusal. The decision to proceed had been by only 13 votes to 8 and the intended candidate argued that he could not accept on such a basis. This was the end of the road for the Old Guard; the West Bradford Liberals resolved not to fight, and Alfred Illingworth responded by resigning the Presidencies of the Bradford Liberal Association and the Bradford Liberal Club! One claim made was that the Liberal Executive in the other two Bradford seats had asked that no candidate be put forward, not as part of a compromise, 'simply as a proposition that Bradford Liberals should do a friendly action and that Independent Labour might reciprocate or not'.[125]

The Progressive alliance emerged more clearly as the campaign went on. Jowett, attacked by the Conservative Press as a pro-Boer,[126] spoke only briefly on the South African issue,[127] and concentrated on social reforms, using his municipal experience and record as a basis for a wide appeal to Progressive opinion. His programme included a wide range of standard Radical and welfare proposals. There was little indication of any socialist commitment. Even his advocacy of the public ownership of monopolies and the nationalisation of land and railways barely impinged on Radical sensibilities.[128] The question of an understanding with the Liberals inevitably arose; Jowett's response was clear, there was no agreement but:

We are fighting the common enemy which at the present juncture is Toryism. I shall fight it as keenly as the two Liberal candidates, and I have no doubt that our votes in the other two divisions will also fight the common enemy. Is it too much to expect that those who are adherents of the Liberal Party in this division will not refuse, because the instrument happens to be me for the time being, to fight the common enemy?[129]

The itinerant Glasier, visiting Bradford, went on to one of Jowett's meetings, but kept in the background: 'They don't want me just now. Quite right perhaps. They expect Liberal support'.[130]

This Progessive position secured considerable support. Some Independent Labour Clubs in other parts of the city decided to support the Liberals — hopefully as part of a deal. Individual Liberals and also the Great Horton Liberal Club came out in Jowett's favour.[131] Such a shift was relatively easy. Jowett was a well-respected figure in Bradford civic life who had 'long -lived down the reputation of being a local Robespierre'.[132] Progressive unity was obvious on polling day. Labour leaders outside Jowett's division went early to vote against the Conservatives, whilst Jowett's resources were enhanced by the loan of a motor-car by the Keighley Liberal candidate and of a carriage by his Shipley counterpart.[133] However, there were always doubts about Jowett's ability to secure the full Liberal vote. The influence of Illingworth-type Liberalism died hard and was kept alive hopefully by Conservative press emphases on Jowett's socialism.[134] In the immediate context of 1900, the Progressive alliance failed to unseat any of Bradford's Conservative members but Jowett came agonisingly close. In the end his failure to secure adequate Liberal support was decisive (see Table 21).

Table 21. *Bradford West 1900 compard with 1895*

1895		%	1900		%
Cons	3,936	40.7	Cons	4,990	50.2
Lib	3,471	35.9	Jowett ILP	4,949	49.8
Tillett ILP	2,264	23.4			

The ILP press move diplomatically through complexities of the Bradford contest. It was presented as an application of tactics developed in local municipal campaigns: clearly Jowett had secured a considerable number of Liberal votes, but only those 'who definitely preferred Socialism to Toryism'.[135] This was very much a case of packaging for the ILP rank and file. The choice offered to the West Bradford electorate had been basically one between Toryism and Progressive Radicalism with an ILP standard-bearer.

Such a contest and result appeared to make West Bradford a suitable case for inclusion within the Gladstone—MacDonald pact. This did not happen, and West Bradford provided the only ILP — or indeed LRC — victory in England in 1906, against full Conservative and Liberal opposition. By then, Labour support in municipal contests in Bradford had grown. More seats were being fought, more votes were being secured and the number of victories was beginning to increase.[136] In West Bradford, Labour candidates had polled well at the 1905 local elections, and trade union assistance had become much more substantial, following the development of the LRC.[137] Jowett thus had increased his credibility compared with 1900. It was the Liberal employer Claridge who appeared as the interloper, forced to deny claims that he would not go to the poll.

In this three-cornered contest Jowett faced the tactical problem of differentiating himself from the Liberal position without alienating Radical supporters. His response involved three elements: an emphasis on his municipal record, trading on his established place in Bradford politics; an appeal to working-class interests — 'Capitalists in Parliament, irrespective of politics were banded together in opposition to legislative measures desired by wage earners;[138] and, finally, a claim that the new Liberal Government contained both progressive and conservative elements. The crucial task was 'to strengthen the Progressive side'; if so, then 'they could not do better than strengthen the Labour Group'.[139]

Claridge's response was a traditional Liberal one; he suggested to a deputation of the unemployed that excessive drinking was a major cause of loss of work, and he saw land reform as a vital means of social improvement.[140] His concern with standard Liberal causes brought a retort from Jowett that he 'had much to say about Chinese labour and the education question, but not much of real present-day Labour politics'.[141] Moreover, Claridge's credentials as an anti-militarist were dented by claims that his attitude on the South African War had been equivocal.[142] He laboured under the accusation of being Illingworth's nominee,[143] and above all he never shed the 'last minute candidate' label. His credibility remained a problem, and this led to a decision of at least symbolic importance — the local Irish decided to back Jowett. For the Nationalists, 'the first consideration that activated them was to keep the Tory out, and they voted for Mr Jowett because they thought he had a better chance of winning than had the Liberal candidate'.[144] This inevitably had an impact on the closing days of the campaign — Michael Davitt spoke from Jowett's platform,[145] and on polling day, Jowett and his wife toured the constituency with their red badges decorated with emerald green ribbon[146] — a far cry from Hardie's problems with the Irish in 1896.

The reasons for Bradford's distinctiveness in 1906 are complex. The Liberal—Labour antipathies of the preceding 15 years had produced a distinctive Labour—socialist vote in Bradford. This can be demonstrated by noting the performance of the ex-ILPer, E. R. Hartley, standing in 1906 for the SDF in East Bradford. He lacked LRC and Irish support but was backed by local Labour organisations and by Jowett personally. Hartley poured scorn on Liberal and Tory alike, dismissed the fiscal controversy as a sham and emphasised socialist remedies for economic problems.[147] Such an aggressive independent campaign produced a significant electoral response, especially in the light of the SDF refusal to engage in formal canvassing (see Table 22). This performance was better than Hardie's 1896 result, but it was less of a land-mark than Jowett's breakthrough in Bradford West (see Table 23). Here the

Table 22. *Bradford East 1906*

Lib	6,185	45.6%
Cons	4,277	31.6
SDF	3,090	22.8

Table 23. *Bradford West 1906*

Lab	4,957	39.1%
Cons	4,147	32.7
Lib	3,580	28.2

basic Labour vote was probably higher — after all the seat was being contested for the fourth time; but victory also depended in part on Jowett's capacity to achieve some credibility as the most effective anti-Tory candidate. 1906 tends to be remembered as evidence of continuing Liberal—Labour antipathies in Bradford politics, but such an assessment is partial. Jowett's position depended on his ability to capture part of the Liberal vote — he was a better Radical than several leaders of Bradford Liberalism. Moreover, 1906 was an exception. Jowett had enjoyed a straight fight in 1900, and was to have two more in 1910. On both the later occasions there were very decisive victories.

The existence of a Progressive unity in Bradford was obscured to some ex-tent by the 1906 contest, but clearly it was a key development; in Halifax, the change was more straightforward. In the khakhi election little seemed to have altered compared with 1895 and 1897. Two Liberal candidates, Billson and Whitley, were opposed by the Liberal Unionist, Sir Saville Crossley, whose Suffolk residence plus the shift from the traditional family Liberalism spoke volumes about the political and geographical mobility of at least one section of the Halifax bourgeoisie; and by James Parker as the ILP/LRC candidate. But there were differences. No longer was the ILP campaign backed by either the social prestige and political ambiguity of Lister, or the tough independence of Tom Mann. The Labour campaign was based very much on the local record of the candidate, by now with three years' council service. He campaigned on a blend of Radical and municipal proposals, using Halifax speakers and raising most of his funds locally.[148] The organiser-turned-candidate carried out a campaign distinguished in Labour eyes for its 'system, thoroughness and self-reliance'.[149] It was very much a parochial affair; in such a contest, the style of the candidate was clearly important; even in the circumstances of 1900 some

Radicals found Parker politically tolerable. One press writer commented that 'he has managed to refrain from certain causes of offence which other members of his party have appeared to be anxious to give at all opportunities'.[150] Such a sentiment was reflected in the style of the campaign; there was little of the raised temperature characteristic of several early ILP contests. At the count 'members of all the parties discussed the prospects with each other with the openest amiability'.[151] The leadership of the Halifax ILP now seemed well integrated into the local community.

Such acceptability did not imply strong support, especially in the circumstances of 1900 with Liberals under siege. Yet Parker's vote, despite lack of resources on polling day,[152] was well above Mann's total, although short of Lister's 1895 figure. Clearly, in Halifax at any rate, status in the community had an impact on support. Once again Labour intervention had led to divided representation with a parallel result to 1895 (see Table 24).

Table 24. *Halifax 1900*

	Total	Plumpers	Some Splits	
Crossley Liberal Unionist	5,931	4,212		
Whitley Liberal	5,543	42	Crossley/Parker	1,290
Billson Liberal	5,325	77	Parker/Whitley or Billson	582
Parker Labour	3,276	1,404		

The size of the Unionist/Labour combination is interesting, a linkage also evident in 1895,[153] and which gave rise to Liberal accusations of Conservative—Labour plotting. The principal impact of this result was to increase the pressures for a Liberal—Labour understanding. The local Liberal journal totted up the 'Progressive' vote and blamed the 'deplorable' outcome on Labour intransigence;[154] local Labour feeling after the poll could be gauged from a *Labour Leader* report. This hoped that Liberals were realising at last that 'their best policy is to allow the ILP to fight with the Tories for one seat, well knowing that with their help we could win it'. Such a statement shows clearly that Progressive assumptions were now well rooted in the Halifax Party, and Labour 'Progressives' looked to their putative allies with optimism. There seemed to be a Radical backlash with 'disaffection at the policy pursued by the official wirepullers of the Liberal Party: and after the bitterness of political defeat has passed, it is hoped that better counsels will prevail'.[155]

This was a reasonable prognostication, whose fulfilment was aided by the fact that the Liberal member, J. H. Whitley, had argued for an arrangement even in 1897. Thus in the 1906 election the Progressive alliance appeared at Halifax in an unambiguous form.

Parker was certainly the ILP candidate closest to the Liberals, and there were few, even amongst the LRC trade union candidates, who exceeded him in his willingness to express support for the new government. He talked on the platform of 'the mellowing experience of working from the inside'; he spoke of the interests of all classes (he had, after all, been a Trades Council representative on the Chamber of Commerce); the Chinese labour question led him to criticise the introduction of Polish labour into Scotland; he spoke positively of 'the Empire' and suggested that a plebiscite for a British President would result in the election of Edward VII![156]

It was hardly a winning of Halifax for socialism and the Progressive message was hammered home by successive Labour speakers. Parker appealed to electors to use both votes 'so that they will get in the same lobby as often as possible'.[157] The rhetoric of Progressive politics became a staple element in the Labour campaign. Liberals reciprocated accordingly — Whitley appealed for support for Parker and was echoed by the Irish Nationalists.[158] Perhaps the Liberal press with its doggerel echoed the firmness of the link most clearly:

> Liberal! Labour! Smite the foe!
> Use that Second Vote — Ho Ho!
> Then to Parliament — into Parliament
> Whitley, Parker both shall go.[159]

The result (Table 25) showed how effective the strategy had been. It was hardly surprising that Parker 'heartily thanked the Liberal party for the splendid support which they had rendered'.

Table 25. *Halifax 1906*

		Plumpers	Splits	
Whitley	9,354	424	Crossley/Parker	154
Parker	8,937	211	Crossley/Whitley	358
Crossley	5,042	4,529	Whitley/Parker	8,572

This was one of the most thorough Progressive arrangements in 1906. Few Liberals baulked at voting for the ultra-respectable Parker; few Labour men were irreconcilable plumpers, and the Labour—Unionist splits of earlier days had almost vanished. Labour's new incorporation into Progressivism is seen sometimes as a Lancastrian phenomenon. Yet here in Halifax and to a lesser degree in Bradford, it is possible to find ample evidence of a synthesis of ILP sentiments with a chastened and modernised Liberalism. In Halifax and in Bradford, the ILP grew as a response to Liberal inflexibility, but early growth was only cashed into municipal and parliamentary victories through progressivism.

Striking the balance

Consideration of this region of early ILP strength is inevitably a complicated matter. On the one hand, we have seen the dominant trend towards Progressivism in Halifax and Bradford. The pursuit of electoral success led both Liberal and ILP into some sort of rapprochement despite continuing opposition on both sides. The development from early promise through the successes of 1906 and 1910 can be understood only within the framework of Progressivism.

This needs balancing by a reminder of the context within which the ILP emereged. Local Liberalism was successful and complacent, dominated by the millocracy; as such it ignored the representational and policy claims of Labour. This denial was facilitated by the lack of strong trade unions, whereby bargains could have been obtained. There is the ever-pertinent contrast between the politics of wool and the politics of coal in the West Riding. Both had a Liberal dominance; in the mining seats, this was underpinned by trade union solidarity and commitment. In the woollen towns, integration was not disciplined by trade unions, and Liberalism presented a soft underbelly. ILP challenges to the Liberals were not limited to the key centres of Bradford and Halifax, and elsewhere the denouements were different.

In Dewsbury, the emerging ILP faced a Liberal Member, Mark Oldroyd, who almost parodied the Woollen Towns Liberal leadership — coalowner, millowner, supporter of the Salisbury government on South Africa, opponent of the eight hour day for miners, a temperance enthusiast whose Tory opponents made much of a sizeable wine and beer delivery to his house during the 1892 election.[160] The ILP, from its base amongst the bottlemakers at Thornhill, ran Edward Hartley in a very brief campaign in 1895. He struck a strongly class-conscious note, and emphasised the deleterious effect of mechanisation on the woollen workers' standard of life.[161] This first campaign was promising — 1,080 votes; but after 1895, the local party decayed, partly because of rivalry between ILP and SDF stalwarts.

The presence of local branches of both parties, plus a Trades Council, some of whose delegates still inclined to Liberalism, produced a split in the autumn of 1901. A tripartite attempt to produce an agreed candidate collapsed, and the SDF unilaterally announced the candidature of Harry Quelch.[162] The contretemps was given added importance when Oldroyd resigned, and the local Liberals selected a Newcastle shipowner, Walter Runciman, to succeed him. ILPers still saw Hartley as the proper candidate, and local suspicions and national rivalries reinforced one another. Leading local ILPers such as Ben Turner and Tom Myers were anxious to retain the link with the Trades Council, even at the cost of waiving an ILP claim to the seat, and mollifying Lib-Labs:

we could have carried Hartley by a show of hands in the Council at any time. But to have done it, would have cut the Council clear in two, whilst the Miners had visions of Woods.[163]

Others took a different view dismissing the Trades Council as 'wishy-washy'.[164] Most significantly, Hartley reacted to the abandonment of his own candidature by supporting Quelch and condemning the compromises of the ILP leadership. Their objective seemed 'not so much to push Socialism as to try and intrigue some half-a-dozen persons into Parliament'.[165]

National preoccupations led to other pronouncements. Blatchford and the *Clarion* predictably backed Quelch, whilst the opposing view was taken in official pronouncements by the ILP and the LRC. Glasier played a leading role in stiffening the resolve of Dewsbury ILPers against the attractions of a socialist candidate. He drafted an appropriate resolution for the Trades Council and helped to co-ordinate the Council and ILP shift towards the sidelines.[166] For him, this incident was a battle in a much more protracted campaign. SDF isolation would hopefully produce a derisory poll and blunt ILP enthusiasm for joint socialist action. This hope was dashed. Quelch's poll of 1,597 was three times Glasier's private estimate.[167] This error reflected in part the myopia with which he and other ILP leaders viewed all things SDF, but it also indicated that in Dewsbury, Liberal—Labour antagonisms were now sufficient to produce a reputable poll for any candidate who claimed to be fighting in the labour interest. There were other relevant factors. Runciman's support for the war, although apparently acceptable to the Dewsbury Liberal Association provoked some slight Radical opposition,[170] and more significantly, Michael Davitt appealed to the sizeable Irish vote to back Quelch.[171] But clearly the Labour—Liberal rift was well developed, and in 1906, the well-known local trade unionist Ben Turner added more than a thousand votes to Quelch's total.

This classic Radical—Labour opposition was replicated in Huddersfield, where the first ILP candidature in 1895 was in turn ignored, ridiculed and condemned by a hostile Liberal press.[170] Already, Labour—Liberal relations were at a low ebb there. Early in 1893, the local ILP had called for abstention in a by-election and the Liberals had temporarily lost the seat. Now ILP election propaganda attacked local Liberal employers as 'sweaters', condemned Liberal municipal representatives for failing to support 'Fair Contracts' and adversely compared Huddersfield Liberals with their Progressive London counterparts. The ILP campaign raised sensitive issues for woollen workers. Liberal and Tory millowners would introduce a two-loom system and cause widespread unemployment; they would encourage the employment of married women and throw men out of work.[171] The ILP's performance in 1895 caused the Liberals some concern, their newspaper wondering how 'nearly sixteen hundred Huddersfield men could cast their votes for a man who lightly talked about hanging capitalists and landlords to the street lamps'.[172] After 1895, the ILP declined there — 'Clubs were closed, the membership dwindled, and for several years, the party was only kept alive by the devotion of a dozen men and women'.[173] But after 1900, there was a major revival and by 1906, the Labour challenge was significant (see Table 26).

Table 26. *Huddersfield*

January 1906		%	November 1906		%
Liberal	6,302	38.2	Liberal	5,762	36.0
Labour	5,813	35.2	Labour	5,422	33.8
Conservative	4,391	26.6	Conservative	4,844	30.2

The second 1906 campaign was an occasion for massive Labour enthusiasm, with Hardie at the peak of his form, and the Liberals rushing the contest.[174] Inevitably, the content of such a confrontation was very different from the Progressivism of nearby Halifax — Glasier, presented it to *Labour Leader* readers as 'the most distinctively Socialist contest fought in this country'.[175] Here the Liberal—Labour hostility proved extraordinarily durable, with a Conservative—Liberal electoral agreement throughout the 1950s.

Next door to Huddersfield there was Colne Valley, identified of course with Grayson and with a similar political pattern to Huddersfield — conservative, hostile Liberalism, a candidate in 1895, subsequent decline and then revival.[176] There was an extra dimension because of the ILP's strength in some of the small Valley communities. Even in the least promising years, there was a minimum of support, and the Party achieved social as well as political expression. The independence of the Colne Valley party was shown in its adoption of Tom Mann as candidate in 1895. His was a very different presentation of the Labour case from that of Lister. He attributed poverty to private landlordism and capitalism and attacked his Liberal opponent as a reactionary — indeed the Conservative, who supported Female Suffrage, Pensions and better Industrial Compensation, appeared more advanced than Kitson.[177] But the latter triumphed on the basis of tradition and resources. As Mann reflected, in Colne Valley there had been a long domination by 'the Manchester School of Politicians', and more materially late on the eve of the poll, 'a special train came in ... crammed from one end to the other with horses and special conveyances for conveying voters to the polls'.[178]

It was to be twelve more years before Grayson overcame such forces. Mann's campaign helped set the style of the Colne Valley ILP; a performance conjured up by Glasier — Mann campaigning 'with his hair matted upon his forehead, peering out of the gloom, revealed by the flickering light of a farthing candle which a supporter held under the shelter of his jacket' — sending 'a torrent of impassioned argument down upon his hearers, hammering and riveting his statements with hands and fists'.[179]

This was the face of the Yorkshire movement that has become widely known, a picture of pioneers struggling manfully against massive obstacles. It was a crucial part of the truth — the ILP did emerge in part as a response to the Kitsons, Illingworths and Oldroyds of West Riding Liberalism. Yet there is the other face: of Parker and, to a lesser degree, Jowett bidding for support on the basis of 'Progressive' assumptions and rhetoric. Recognition of the dualism is important, although the explanation of why Colne Valley, Huddersfield and Dewsbury came to differ from Bradford and Halifax is debateable. Attempts to demonstrate economic divergences seem unpromising. Perhaps part of the explanation should be that Progressivism was more viable in Bradford and Halifax. In part this was because the ILP had established itself there, had succeeded in blocking Liberal candidates and therefore appeared to have demonstrated that it had something to offer. But more crucially, institutional factors were conducive. Halifax, as the only two-member borough in the West Riding, clearly permitted an understanding, and similar possibilities existed in Bradford, the only divided woollen borough. Elsewhere, such accommodations were neither necessary nor possible — any deal involved Liberal Associations relinquishing their hold over normally safe seats, and this, given their social composition and the lack of strong trade unions, was unlikely. If the West Riding ILP gained its initial footholds in opposition to a reactionary Liberalism, it expanded most readily by drawing on the affinities with Radical and Progressive idioms in communities where institutional rules and political strengths appeared to justify such a narrowing of the rift.

9

*The Lancastrian party**

Popular Conservatism — a barrier or an opportunity?

The journey from Bradford or Halifax to Blackburn or Preston in the late nineties was a relatively short one, through the Pennines, on the tracks of that most provincial of railway companies, The Lancashire and Yorkshire. It was a route taken frequently by the ILP's propagandists as they moved from the party's woollen centres to their cotton-town equivalents. Yet such speakers did much more than cross a county boundary; they also moved into a different political universe. The Yorkshire ILP attempted to expand in a milieu where Liberalism remained electorally powerful, a coalition that, despite strains, still spanned the gulf between textile capitalist and textile worker. But in much of Lancashire by the late nineties, Liberalism seemed a moribund force. Nowhere else did the hope or fear of a Tory working class seem more of a reality. Liverpool had been a Liberal 'lost cause' for many years, and in both 1895 and 1900 the Liberals held only one seat in Manchester and Salford. Blackburn and Preston were bastions of popular Toryism, and the Wigan miners were happy to return a Conservative rather than one of their own officials. In 1895, many previously Liberal cotton towns shifted sharply to Conservatism, including John Bright's Rochdale. Liberal outposts tended to be closer to the Yorkshire border and were very much in a minority.

The Liberal collapse occurred in a period of ILP growth. Lancastria was represented by the delegates of thirty-one organisations at the inaugural Conference. In the Spring of 1894, Tom Mann had seen Lancashire and Yorkshire as the party's two principal strongholds;[1] although Lancastrian strength declined in the aftermath of the 1895 disappointments, these branches remained of major importance, not least because of their place inside the party as a source of opposition to the policies of the national leadership. Even in such a generally unpromising period as 1899—1900, the party still claimed

* By Lancastrian, I mean the counties of Lancashire and Cheshire, plus the economically similar High Peak Division of Derbyshire. This is the same as Fawcett's region used in Pelling, *Social Geography of British Elections*, except that I have ommitted the highly distinctive Potteries.

38 branches in the region. Many were small, but some had significant and durable memberships.[2] Once again, however, it is necessary to insert a cautionary note, parallel to that contained in the West Riding analysis. All parts of the North West did not demonstrate an early attachment to the party.

Merseyside was an extremely weak area — religious and ethnic conflicts combined with the existence of a large, unskilled, and often casual, workforce to provide barren soil for Independent Labour politics.[3] Party standard-bearers made optimistic forays into Liverpudlian municipal politics with disastrous results.[4] An almost equal lack of impact could be found in the coal and heavy industry area around St Helens and Wigan. The growth-points of the Lancashire ILP were essentially limited to Manchester and Salford and to some textile towns, Blackburn and Preston, and to a lesser degree, Rochdale, Oldham, Hyde, Ashton and Stockport. Even in the textile belt, the party made a minimal penetration in some places. This was particularly true in the smaller textile villages. An activist was dubious about the prospects of an ILP by-election contest in the extensive Middleton Division in the autumn of 1897:

> Even in Middleton and Littleboro' where there are branches, not too much has been done, while the other districts might as well be in Ireland for any knowledge of either ILPism or in some cases, Trades Unionism.[5]

In the small communities of the Rossendale Valley, perhaps idealistically portrayed in the young Beatrice Potter's account of Bacup, traditional Radicalism remained powerful. Snowden, who knew his nonconformist Radicals well, was appropriately pessimistic: 'We have no organisation in the district worth taking into consideration. There is strong political spirit, but it is of that type of Radicalism which is most opposed to us.'[6] The unevenness of development was hardly surprising. Here was a complex wealth of work experiences: the lack of heavy industrial employment on Merseyside, the contrast of coal and cotton, and, within the textile industry, not just the traditional distinction between spinning and weaving centres, but also the finely-graded hierarchies embracing spinners and piecers, mule and ring spinners, tape sizers and cardroom operatives and, perhaps most fundamental of all, men and women.

The industrial organisation of these workers was distinctive in that the usual identification of official trade unionist opinion with Liberalism was frequently lacking. We have seen how both coal and cotton unions encountered political difficulties because of the deep-rooted Toryism of many of their members. In the case of the Lancashire Miners, the consequential immobilism engendered an early and heavily pragmatic espousal of political independence. Most elements in the heavily decentralised cotton unions kept aloof from party politics until virtually pushed into the LRC in 1902—3. Such divided political loyalties were an embarrassing 'given' for trade union officials rather than something they had helped to create.

Their explanation requires a more thorough consideration of the basis for working-class Conservatism. This lay primarily in the ethnic and religious divisions within the working class. Liverpool, where the Green of Scotland Road confronted the Orange of Netherfield, was an extreme, more specifically Irish variant on a general theme.[7] Heavy Irish immigration generated a xenophobic response within much of the indigenous working class. In part, this reflected anxiety about employment prospects and wage levels, but it also evinced a distaste for a minority group herded into the most impoverished districts. In the cotton towns, the Irish immigrants were 'regarded with supreme contempt, as utterly beyond the pale, and submerged beneath notice'.[8] Such distaste was fuelled by the fear of the respectable artisan lest he fall into the same morass, and by gratitude that he was not at the bottom of the social ladder. Inevitably the ethnic question was expressed frequently in religious terms. Protestantism' could serve as a shorthand for social superiority. Denominational education meant segregated education, a situation that suited zealots of all persuasions. And, inevitably, Home Rule meant much more in Lancastria than it did over the Pennines. It was the issue above all others that both symbolised and strengthened this division.

Liverpool expressed these tensions not just at the ballot box, but in intermittent rioting and sectarian unionisation. Labour faced a daunting prospect squeezed between the Protestant Working Men's Association of the Tory 'boss', Archibald Salvidge, and the Nationalist machine. In a 1907 by-election initial Labour optimism was doused by the mobilisation of Protestant prejudices. A chastened Macdonald admitted his astonishment to Salvidge: 'whatever the issue appears to be at the start, you always manage to mobilise the full force of Orangeism'.[9] More concretely, there was Macdonald's post-mortem in the *Labour Leader*: 'We had no organisation; the opposition had a perfect machine: they could command the votes of the dead; we had to content ourselves with those of the living.'[10] Liverpool politics were often extensions of Ulster passions — elsewhere the split tended to take less exotic political forms. Separate communal identities were maintained in part through the educational system — a fact that had a significant impact on political attachments. Although nonconformity was significant in several Lancashire towns, it has nothing like the strength of its West Riding counterpart. The championing of Protestant claims was thus largely the preserve of the Established Church. In the mid nineteenth century, Lancashire Anglicanism had reacted to the challenge of a new industrial population by a vigorous policy of church building. Along with the churches came denominational schools. This Anglican growth, together with Catholic support for denominational education, helped to ensure that in several towns — most significantly Preston, but also Warrington, Hyde, Bury, Leigh, Stockport and Accrington — there was no School Board. In this context, Radical campaigns against Voluntary Schools and ILP advocacy of nonsectarian education were unlikely to evoke much sympathy.[11]

Anglican Schools could act as valuable socialisation agents, creating and mobilising support for a complex of values that helped to produce Tory loyalties. Much of this involved the creation of a culture conducive to a particular political attachment, but sometimes the connection was more deliberate. Successive leaders of the Manchester and Liverpool dioceses tended to be firm Conservatives. They were emulated by many of their representatives.

The complex ties between Lancastrian Conservatism and evangelical Anglicanism were a vital element in the cultural fortifications faced by the ILP. But these earthworks were staffed by many besides the consciously devout. The appeal went beyond overt appeals to ethnic and religious identities. This popular Toryism, at its strongest in Preston and Blackburn, was based also on appeals to communal solidarity, although no doubt it was assumed that English Anglicans were particularly well-qualified for membership. Unity across class lines in pursuit of a town's interests was particularly persuasive when the parliamentary representative happened to be a 'fellow townsman' like 't'owd Gam' Cock', Sir Harry Hornby of Blackburn. Such men were not supported for their explicitly political views — Hornby never spoke during his twenty-four years in the Commons — but as symbols of perceived common interests. Such communal representation did not have to be Conservative — rich Liberals could achieve similar eminence — but given the influences dominant in many Lancashire towns, Conservatism was the more likely form.[12]

Such domination was not just the result of appeals to principle, sentiment and prejudice. Hornby combined in Blackburn, a continuing personal involvement in the family mill, with a social prominence notable for conspicuous consumption. This last trait was not restricted to private life: Hornby was a noted local philanthropist. Attachment to doctrines of self-help was softened by the matey, straight-talking accents of Tory paternalism. This network of deference and handouts was a discouraging prospect for ILP candidates. Snowden rhetorically asked the Blackburn voters: 'were their votes to be bought by a man who happened to have the means to subscribe to a boy's football club or a church bazaar?'[13] The long-standing answer of many Blackburn electors was clearly in the affirmative.

Perhaps one insight into the popular appeal of Lancashire Toryism is provided by a response by Blackburn Conservatives to the ILP's growing municipal influence. In 1904, they nominated for a municipal contest, J. H. Forrest, a local publican. That link was of course common where Liberal and ILP members were often temperance enthusiasts. But Forrest's appeal rested on more than his involvement in 'The Trade'. He had been a star of Blackburn Rovers in their most successful years, the possessor of five FA Cup Winners' medals and eleven international caps.[14] It was in Lancashire that professional soccer first became powerful in England; it had been Blackburn men who had broken the grip of the public school old boys' teams on the FA Cup, it was 'Proud Preston' whose feats in the late eighties had earned them the title of the 'Invincibles'.[15] Perhaps it is not without significance that Blackburn's one

Liberal MP in the late nineteenth century was a local sporting personality who included in his qualifications a victory for his dog in the Waterloo Cup![16]

Here was a culture that could integrate a sizeable proportion of a sophisticated working class through a Toryism that characteristically combined support for Free Trade with robust defences of Church, community, working-class pleasures and general 'Englishness'. This evocation of a Lancastrian *panem et circenses* — Thwaites and Ewood Park — could provide easy pickings for Tory politicians. Tory advocates could speak in robust man-to-man tones and the evangelical political style — whether Radical or ILP — could have only limited appeal. Industrial workers typically possessed a sense of their own identity as workers — many textile employees after all were unionised, but this was not expressed readily through political perceptions and attachments. This negative interpretation might be challenged by some Disraelian Tories who viewed Toryism as an appropriate response by class-conscious workers to the sternly laissez-faire Liberalism of many millowners. Distaste for such Liberalism was significant; the millowner responsible for the celebrated Blackburn Weavers' picketing case in 1901 was a Liberal[17] — but such an emphasis fails to do justice to one crucial element. The standard-bearers of Lancastrian Toryism were often employers with the same economic beliefs as their Liberal counterparts. Support for them was attributable more to the absence of class politics than to its expression in terms beneficial to Conservatism.

This provided a distinctive challenge for the early ILP. How could the party gain entry to Lancastrian politics? Inevitably, the hold of Conservatism could be eroded by the sandpaper of changing experiences. Old paternalism could give way to more remote limited liability companies, entrepreneurs who remained as wealthy 'fellow-townsmen' were followed by sons whose regional identity was laundered away through Public School and University. Most crucially, the economic world of cotton was subject to vicissitudes. The trade expanded in absolute terms until 1913, but there were periods of intense depression. Profits were being squeezed by the 1890s and foreign markets were lost or at risk. The living standards of the workers were eroded by rising food and rent costs. Cotton trade union officials might attempt to concentrate on non-political economistic activities, millowners might cling to the forms of paternalism, but economic realities stretched relationships and could subvert a shared culture.[18]

Such erosion occurred, but pre-existing loyalties died hard. The central themes of working-class Conservatism offered little purchase for socialists; but Liberal incapacity did offer some opportunities, a chance to acquire a title to the Radical mantle. Such a prospect also had its dangers, since in many towns, the Liberals seemed to be a clear minority. ILP growth depended on winning Tory support as well as Liberal. This imperative sheds a significant light on central features of the early Lancastrian ILP. The influence of Blatchford, the style of 'Merrie England', his distaste for the puritanism of

Hardie, and other ILP leaders, all struck a particular note in the context of a strong popular Toryism. Blatchford's style offered the prospect of access to the cakes and ale culture of urban Lancashire, an access that could rival the appeal of earthy Tory paternalists.

Many Lancastrian ILPers were attracted by the Fourth Clause Policy, so called from its espousal in the Fourth Clause of the Manchester and Salford ILP's original constitution. This prescribed even-handed hostility to the traditional parties, and was regarded typically as a sign of socialist rectitude. But it could be seen also as opposed particularly to the willingness of some party members to seek deals with Radical Liberals. In Lancastria such a tendency could be condemned as offensive to the Tory voters who must be attracted for an ILP breakthrough. These were the political traditions confronting the early ILP — but the party's preoccupations were not limited to the legacies of the past. Lancastrian politics were distinctive because unlike in other provincial centres, the ILP also faced a viable socialist alternative.

The Social Democratic Federation — a rival or a comrade?

The Social Democratic Federation took root as a significant force in several Lancashire towns: in Salford, Blackburn, Rochdale, and above all, Burnley. It was the only provincial presence of the party that came near to rivalling its London strength. Its most visible signs were the durability of several Lancastrian branches, some municipal successes and Hyndman's sizeable parliamentary polls in Burnley.[19]

Assessment of this situation arouses peculiar problems because of the distorting prism through which ILP—SDF relationships have been typically viewed. It is a prism compounded of the tendentious claims of some ILP leaders and the assessments of later writers who seem keen to present — and dismiss — the SDF as some kind of foreign incursion. Here the idiosyncracies of particular leaders such as Hyndmann and Quelch are taken as sufficient characterisation of the entire SDF. If this were valid, then we would have an unenviable portrait of the Lancashire ILP sandwiched between a popular Toryism and an intractable, dogmatic, hostile SDF. How could a body of such inflexible sectarianism take root within the Lancashire working class? Possibly there is something inadequate about this characterisation — and dismissal — of the SDF.

One way in which this traditional stereotype can be assessed is by considering the evidence of one contemporary witness, Bruce Glasier, the propagandist with probably the most detailed knowledge of ILP branch life. He was no friend of the SDF leadership — he was a leading crusader against the Fusion Policy of the late nineties; he relished attacking 'class conscious' SDF speakers at international gatherings; he privately stigmatised the Federation as distinguished by 'bigotry, brutality, conceit';[20] he argued that 'it would have been better had there never been an SDF in Britain at all'.[21] Yet his

Lancashire experiences hardly fit in with this dismissive tone. He spoke on occasions to SDF branches and was favourably impressed. At Padiham he noted how 'several of members confided to me their dislike of *Justice* and disapproval of its attitude towards the ILP. Seems as if branch really more in sympathy with ILP',[22] and at Charlestown he found a branch composed of 'rather a good set of working chaps'.[23]

Indeed, in Darwen, the conventional stereotypes were turned on their heads. The growth of 'drinking habits' in the ILP Club resulted in some ILP enthusiasts joining the SDF.[24] Even Glasier with his sensitive nose for malignant SDF influences found complexities in Lancashire that would not fit the conventional portrait.

Appreciation of such complexities is strengthened by the discovery that in towns where SDF and ILP both had some following, their relationship, in the nineties at any rate, was typically harmonious. In Blackburn the SDF had roots going back to a weavers' strike in 1883; the ILP emerged a decade later from a local Fabian Society.[25] Thereafter, they co-operated in an attempt to challenge dominant Toryism and decaying Liberalism. Together they produced the *Blackburn Labour Journal* which dealt evenhandedly with the activities of both older parties. In the late nineties what mattered were the successes and failures of the 'Blackburn Socialist Party'.[26] There was a pooling of electoral efforts; the closeness of the relationship is captured in the description of an early attempt to capture one of the town's Elective Auditorships:

the Independent Labour Party communicated with the Social Democratic Federation, suggesting that a joint candidate be run. This was agreed to and Mr. Tom Hurley accepted the invitation to be the joint ILP and SDF Candidate.[27]

And this concordat continued through the election of 1900 with Philip Snowden standing as a 'Labour and Socialist' candidate to meet the wishes of the local SDF. The eventual change of alignments in Blackburn politics was largely a product of forces external to the local ILP—SDF relationship. The national departure of the SDF from the LRC and the affiliation of the cotton unions to the latter body led to the creation of a Labour Representation Committee in Blackburn. This became the primary focus of local ILP endeavours and the SDF gradually became the outsider. By 1906 its leaders were pouring scorn on David Shackleton's suggestion that local labour voters should give their second vote to the Liberal.[28] But even then old loyalties died hard. In January 1910 Blackburn Social Democrats participated in a mass trades council demonstration against the House of Lords, sharing the stage not just with other Labour organisations, but also with Liberal, Free Church, Band of Hope and Irish representatives.[29] Here was no socialist sectarianism but a willingness to participate at a critical moment, in a broadly-based anti-Tory demonstration. A similar pattern can be found in the nineties in Rochdale, where local ILP and SDF groups again ran joint election slates, and produced the *Rochdale Labour News*. Here with a stronger less Radical,

Liberalism than in Blackburn, future developments were different. After 1900, ILP and SDF branches did not move apart, but formed a Socialist Election Committee, without direct support from local unions. This commitment to one Socialist Party, rather than a Labour Alliance culminated in 1906 in the Socialist candidacy of Sam Hobson. This tradition of co-operation died hard in Lancashire. ILP dissatisfaction with Labour parliamentary and electoral performance after 1906 was to produce local Socialist Representation Committees — a prefiguration of the later move towards the British Socialist Party.

The tradition of harmony also left its mark on the national debates of both organisations. Lancashire ILP branches, such as Blackburn, Preston and Ashton, were prominent in urging the creation of One Socialist Party;[30] similarly Lancashire SDF branches campaigned for reaffiliation to the LRC after the 1901 split.[31] Such proposals made sense in terms of the daily experiences of Lancastrian activists. In the late nineties a United Socialist Party virtually existed in Blackburn, Social Democrats later bore the negative consequences of the 1901 disaffiliation as local relationships were strained or broken.

Pressures for fusion within Lancashire ILP branches should not be taken as simple evidence that these branches stood, in some sense, to the left of the party leadership. Certainly many were strong advocates of the Fourth Clause, but the significance of this in Lancastrian terms was ambiguous. No doubt some became more critical of national leaders because of the harsh response to their overtures for fusion. But it is difficult to see the Lancashire SDF branches as being in any sense more 'advanced' in the nineties than their ILP counterparts. A search through local Socialist literature for indications of SDF dogmatism and isolation from the main currents of working-class life would be an unrewarding experience. Blackburn Socialists campaigned essentially on local issues, in a style that included an element of muck-raking. By 1899, Socialist councillors could go before the electors with a record of agitation. They had:

opposed the raising of the salaries of highly-paid officials ... persistently agitated in the Town Council for an improvement in the condition of the scavengers ... repeatedly advocated a reduction in the price of our excessively dear gas ... opposed the waste of the ratepayers' money on picnics and other pleasure excursions ... refused to accompany these pleasure parties ... opposed the making of our policeman's clothing in London and tried to have the orders placed with local firms.[32]

It was a long way from claims of sectarian dogmatism and of isolation from everyday concerns.

The picture emerges of two organisations stylistically and ideologically very similar, and able to work together easily unless the relationship was disrupted by external forces. Why then were there two organisations in the first place? One common diagnosis relates the split to basic features of Lancashire politics:

the SDF most characteristically represented an appeal to Tory working men on socialist terms (as in London), and the ILP to Liberal working men on Nonconformist terms (as in Yorkshire), therefore:

it is not surprising to find Lancashire socialism reflecting the region's socio-religious divisions.[33]

This juxtaposition neatly relates the political division to wider Lancastrian traits — but although initially appealing, there are problems. An evidential one is provided by the case of Burnley, location of the SDF's strongest branch, and with a very slight ILP presence. This explanation would lead us to expect Burnley to be a town with a strongly Tory working class. In fact, it was a Liberal stronghold, and one of the more nonconformist of the cotton towns.[34] More widely, we may ask why it should be thought that working-class Conservatives, often reared in an aggressive Anglicanism, should be ready recruits to secularist socialism. Indeed, it is difficult to make a distinction in Lancashire between a secular SDF and an evangelical ILP. The symmetrical explanation collapses because a characterisation in dichotomous terms is inappropriate.

The question of why there were two organisations remains. Some have explained the Burnley strength of the SDF in terms of the assiduous organising capacities of Dan Irving.[35] Whilst this may account for Burnley's uniquely large membership, it does not explain what was a much broader phenomenon. Clearly, it is question-begging to assume that it is SDF strength that requires special explanation. Perhaps one significant emphasis is on the early development of Lancashire industry. By the eighties, some elements within the working class were relatively available for socialist and Labour politics. The SDF seemed then the only viable option, and it took root in some towns, adapting itself with varying degrees of success to local conditions. It could then spread to neighbouring communities. The Burnley development began in the early nineties, facilitated by the difficulties faced by local miners in their disputes with strongly anti-union coal-owners.[36] So, by the time local ILPs developed, some space on the left was occupied not by a rival but by — in local terms — a fraternal organisation. Rigid demarcations have been largely the preserve of national leaders and historians. Locally the keynotes were harmony and flexibility. Individuals moved easily between organisations — and why not since they all said much the same thing in similar accents?

The party in Tory strongholds

The ILP fought the 1895 election in Lancashire on a wide front. The results were largely disappointing, although the number of candidates shows how far the ILP had formed keen local groups. Where the Liberal—Conservative contest was keen, as in Ashton or Hyde, the ILP was squeezed dramatically. Very different developments occurred in Preston, a two-member Tory stronghold. Here the ILP had sizeable support in 1895 and attracted Hardie as a candidate five years later. How far and by what methods did the party establish a base there?

The town's Conservatism was, to a large extent, a reflection of its religious composition. A sizeable Irish immigration had produced a characteristic response by a significant section of the Protestant population. Indigenous Catholicism was also strong, and was a further bonus to the Conservatives so long as voluntary education remained an issue.[37] The Liberal presence was traditionally weak, and a decisive defeat in 1892 had depressed what forces they had. There was little expectation of any Liberal intervention in a subsequent contest, an absence that could lead ILP members to hope for the capture of Radical votes. But any decisive impact required inroads into the Tory working-class. Here traditional loyalties seemed massive; as one ILP speaker reflected ruefully: 'if a broomstick was put up in Preston under the wing of Conservatism, it would be returned'.[38] Working-class Toryism was expressed and fostered organisationally by a network of Conservative Working-men's Clubs.

Preston ILP was considering the adoption of a candidate by the autumn of 1893. A membership of three hundred was claimed — probably an exaggeration.[39] Its members were inexperienced in electioneering and faced an effective machine that went beyond the purely political to include church organisations. Labour hopes turned towards the Trades Council. This had previously been

simply a piece of the Conservative organisation of the town. It was worked by the wire pullers of that Party on the principle of allowing them to believe they were independent, while the individual members were kept in control by the attractions of a luxurious Working-Men's Club, kept up in large measure by the donations of the two Tory members.[40]

But now the desire for independent municipal representation began to affect this relationship. The Tory faction on the council was challenged by advocates of Independent Labour. One leading Tory and Orange trade unionist joined the ILP and sympathetic council delegates came from a wide range of unions including apparently the Spinners and Weavers.[41]

Hopes of Trades Council support for an ILP candidate were unfulfilled. In January 1894, the Preston Trades Council agreed after a sharp debate and by sixteen votes to seven to meet an ILP deputation about a putative candidacy — but attempts to secure united Council support failed,[42] and in 1895 Preston trade unionists divided between Conservative and Independent Labour.

The ILP candidate, James Tattersall of Halifax, had already had dealings with Conservatives. He had arrived on the Halifax Aldermanic bench through an arrangement with the Conservative Group on the Town Council. His behaviour had provoked considerable argument inside the Halifax Labour Union, and he added fuel to these flames in 1895, with an appeal to Halifax electors to use their second vote against the wire-pullers of the Liberal Association.[43] Tattersall subsequently left the ILP and became a Conservative Agent. His involvement as a candidate in a Conservative stronghold helped to give the ILP campaign some distinctive features.

Whatever his own predilections, Tattersall was inevitably led to bid for the Liberal vote. The local Liberal press might be neutral, but he found traditional Liberals a fruitful source of support. As the *Preston Guardian* accepted:

it is quite possible that a considerable number of Liberal voters would prefer to give him their vote rather than vote for a reactionary like Mr. Tomlinson or a clever obstructionist like Mr. Hanbury.[44]

The ILP also secured significant Irish support. But this backing was inevitably double-edged, as one activist had foreseen:

the greatest obstacle we shall have to fight is the Home Rule question. If the candidate does not promise to vote for it, he will lose the Nationalist vote, which is rather strong. If he does, the Conservative working-man will look upon it as a Radical dodge and require very delicate handling.[45]

One natural delicate response for the ILP was to emphasise labour questions in a bid to persuade Tory working men to at least split their votes. This tactic was facilitated by a belief that one Conservative candidate, Tomlinson, was resolutely anti-labour, a subscriber to the Free Labour Association and a parliamentary apologist for coalowners.[46] In Tory Preston, it was both wise and plausible to depict Tomlinson as:

a man who did not understand the historical position of his own party ... (since) ... if there was one point on which the Conservative Party had a good record, it was in factory legislation.[47]

This appeal by a party propagandist was overshadowed by the verdict of James Mawdsley, the Conservative Spinners' official: 'the best service the workers of Preston could do themselves would be to gracefully kick him out of the representation of the old borough'.[48] ILP gambits in this direction were no more than an espousal of Labour Independence with Tory trimmings — but in Tattersall's case, the Tory courtship went much further than labour issues. He made a series of concessions to conventional Conservative views on non-economic matters. He promised to back rate aid to Voluntary Schools, to oppose Welsh Disestablishment and to support compensation for displaced publicans.[49] His platform was, as one observer noted, 'a somewhat strange mixture of advanced Radicalism and old-fashioned Toryism'. Criticism came from some of Tattersall's supporters. He was accused of: 'giving the party away ... trimming all through the contest ... from first to last, he was inconsistent and pandered to every interest that he feared'.[50] How far Tattersall's concessions represented an exercise in vote maximisation in a Tory seat with no Liberal candidate, and how far they were symptomatic of his own underlying Tory sympathies, is unclear. What is apparent is that he obtained sizeable Liberal support and that a significant number of Conservatives were persuaded to split their votes (see Table 27).

The sizeable ILP vote was no measure of the advance of socialist sympathies; it was intelligible only within the context of traditional Lancashire political alignments.

Table 27. *Preston*

1892		1895	
Hanbury	8070	Hanbury	8928
Tomlinson	7764	Tomlinson	7622
Liberal	6182	Tattersall	4781
		Tattersall had 3224 plumpers and 1397 splits with Hanbury.	

Five years later, Hardie stood against the same Tory opponents. The position of the party seems to have deteriorated in the intervening years. In 1896, an activist acknowledged that 'propaganda has not been all we could desire this summer'[51] and weaknesses remained in the summer of 1900. There appear to have been about sixty paying members and a large number of sympathisers. Emissaries from the NAC found that the branch was weak, had little public importance and, inevitably, lacked funds. Support for joint action in municipal contests gained support from some unions such as the Engineers and the Railway Servants, but the major cotton unions seem to have kept their distance. However, there was one strong consideration in favour of a contest. A failure to fight would damage the ILP's claim to be the second party in the town.[52]

Hardie entered the field late, and no doubt suffered from his nomination for two constituencies.[53] More seriously, the party had few committee rooms, no personating agents and did no canvassing. John Penny — once a Preston activist, now the Party's National Secretary — claimed that:

the only shadow of organisation that we had throughout, was created when I cut up a map of the town with a pair of scissors, and gave a piece to each of the literature-distributors to prevent them overlapping.[54]

Hardie too commented on the discrepancy in organisational resources; the ILP: 'had tried to win by rousing public enthusiasm; the other side won, without a shred of enthusiasm by the sheer weight of the party machine'.[55] The war question was also a disadvantage. War fever was supposedly strong in Preston, and an apprehensive Glasier warned Hardie to avoid stressing his position on the controversy early in the campaign.[56] But although the candidate stressed social reform questions, he made his position on the war clear.[57] This helped to produce a hostile response from a local Liberal newspaper which advised its readers to poll two Conservative votes.[58] In fact the ILP claimed much active support from Temperance workers and other Liberals, and the Liberal vote seems to have gone very much as in 1895. A slight improvement in the ILP's performance had been achieved without Tattersall-type concessions to Conservatism, and at a time when some Irish voters might have been more committed to the education question than to Home Rule (see Table 28).

Table 28. *Preston 1900*

Hanbury	8,944	Hardie had 3,454 plumpers and 1,120
Tomlinson	8,067	splits with Hanbury.
Hardie	4,834	

Such a performance might suggest that the ILP could look on Preston as a future stronghold, but it was not to be. The party had not established itself in municipal affairs. It had secured support essentially in a context of Liberal incapacity. The emergence of the Labour Alliance created a very different format in Preston labour politics, especially with the cotton unions moving towards the LRC. A local Labour Representation Committee was formed in 1902 and readily secured the affiliation of twenty-five trade union branches as well as the local ILP. The party had only three members on the executive of twelve, although perhaps as many more were sympathetic. However, the local ILP played a central role in bringing the unions together for political action,[59] but having helped to create the Preston LRC, the party now became more marginal. When a by-election occurred in May 1903, once again there was no Liberal candidate, but the Labour cause was represented not by an ILP member but by John Hodge of the Steel Smelters. Hardie was discouraged from participating; Hodge telegraphed him: 'think it unwise to overload platform from one side — you will see the position'.[60] The object was to attract Tory trade unionists, an aim that seemed credible when Billington, leader of the Preston Spinners, resigned from the Conservative Club, in order to support Hodge.[61] As yet, such a shift seemed to have only limited support amongst the union rank and file. Hodge lost decisively, and Arthur Henderson, who had worked as Hodge's Agent, reflected on the lack of trade union solidarity and on organisational weakness. Preston's religious divisions struck this North-Eastern Methodist forcibly:

it is estimated that the Catholics form a third of the population, and they and the established Church are the predominant forces in Religious Life. This, needless to say, made the Education Act to play no part in the contest from our standpoint. Deputations from the National Protestant League, the Orange Society and the Catholic Society came and interviewed our Candidate, only to leave with a determination to vote against him ... The position taken up at the last moment by the leading Catholics in issuing a manifesto in favour of the Tory Candidate did most to bring about such an adverse result.[62]

And when in 1906, Labour eventually won one of the Preston seats in tandem with a very laissez-faire Liberal, it was represented by another Steel Smelters' official J. T. Macpherson. The candidate emphasised the need to preserve Free Trade, whilst Billington assured any waverers that the Labour campaign 'was in no way connected with the Socialist movement'.[63] Early ILP endeavours had little long-term significance. The breakthrough resulted not from a distinctively socialist presence, but from the increased political involvement of the Textile Unions, and some Liberal revival on the Free Trade issue. The place of Preston in the ILP's development was a transitory one occasioned by the political topography of a Tory cotton town.

Developments in equally Tory Blackburn were different. The 1895 contest was fought on Liberal/Tory lines,[64] but as we have noted, the ILP and SDF together, had developed by the late nineties, a presence in municipal politics. Bridgeheads were established on the Town Council, the School Board and the Board of Guardians. Contests were portrayed by the Socialists as Landlords and Capitalists versus the Workers. The latter detachment embraced representatives of the Trades Council, although the dominant Textile Unions as yet kept them aloof from the Socialists.[65] Despite their dichotomous presentation of the political struggle, the Blackburn Socialists had an ambivalent attitude towards local Liberals. They mocked them for lacking backbone, and attacked Liberal leaders for favouring Conservatives against Labour candidates; but they distinguished between the capitalist leadership of the local caucus and the radicalism of many of the rank and file. It was anticipated that as Liberalism declined, so many Radicals would shift to the Blackburn Socialists.[66] Such a claim led to considerable controversy early in 1897, when it was widely believed that a by-election was imminent in the town. The local ILP and SDF invited Joseph Burgess to contest any vacancy. He had earlier adopted a positive stand towards Henry Broadhurst in two Leicester contests, and he hoped to attract Lib-Lab support in Blackburn. Such a strategy, of dubious electoral validity anyway, brought widespread criticism.[67] Nevertheless, there was amongst the Blackburn Socialists an emphasis on the continuities between Radicalism and socialism — a somewhat uneasy bedfellow for claims that Labour politics provided a basis for uniting Tory and Radical workers.[68] Yet this chemistry of potentially divergent elements was to provide a basis for ILP growth in Blackburn.

Against the insurgents, there was massed the whole weight of 'Clog Toryism' — the deference and sentimentality, the stereotypes of manliness and Englishness, the appeals to community interests and religious bigotry. By 1900, it was hardly surprising that the Blackburn Liberals had become too disheartened to contest the seat. The Socialists, committed strongly to opposing the war, brought in Philip Snowden reared in Radical nonconformity and backed financially by George Cadbury. The choice, as presented by Conservatives, lay between 'men who have known you a lifetime', and 'a youth of the romancing Socialist type'.[69] Such men had 'a greater claim upon the town, than any foreigner that came here'.[70] On polling day, Conservatives employed the slogan, 'Down with Atheism, Socialism and Anarchy'.[71]

Despite the power of such traditional appeals, Snowden could not be dismissed lightly. Socialist organisation was supplemented by the resources of Blackburn Radicalism. The 1895 Liberal candidate, a local newspaper proprietor, praised Snowden's support for the Newcastle Programme, and hoped to see him amongst the 'Progressive' members.[72] The Radical, A. G. Gardiner, then a local reporter, likened Snowden's campaign to 'one of the great spiritual revivals that periodically sweep over the country'.[73] The orations in the 'Come to Jesus' style, and emphases on land, monopolies and drink, awakened Radical and nonconformist enthusiasm. Snowden emphasised his own background: 'I was cradled and nurtured in Liberalism'. But this appeal was linked to a distinctively labour element that could perhaps attract Tory workers:

The object of Socialists was to weld the whole of the working classes ... into one political power, and by the Independent Labour Party — they formed a neutral meeting ground where Liberal and Tory might meet together and leave behind him his old party prejudices.[74]

The demands of labour at a time of depression in the cotton trade were voiced insistently. this was one attempt at an antidote to the Imperial enthusiasm of the Tories; Snowden asking: 'what had a Blackburn weaver with £1 a week on short time got to do with an Empire or glory?'[75] The enthusiasm was infectious, but beneath popular demonstrations and rhetoric, it was in part a question of organising blocs of voters — the Irish and Temperance votes for Snowden, the Orangemen and Low Church men against him.[76] The Liberals were divided, as in Preston; Snowden obtained a sizeable proportion and had the active help of some Radicals, but other Liberals either went Conservative or abstained. In part compensation, Snowden clearly attracted some traditional Tory voters (see Table 29). Snowden's vote might be presented as the biggest

Table 29. *Blackburn 1900*

Hornby, Conservative	11,247
Coddington, Conservative	9,415
Snowden	7,096
Snowden's plumpers	5,335
Splits with Hornby	1,700

vote yet given to British socialism, but its size must be grasped within the specific context of traditional attachments.

The world of Blackburn politics changed dramatically over the next few years. The LRC became a local reality with the affiliation of the Cotton Unions. A Trades Council that had 'relied on Trade Union effort only' came together with the Blackburn ILP to form a local LRC. The event marked no ideological conversion, but a recognition — heightened locally by the Blackburn Weavers' case — that the legal standing of trade unions had deteriorated.[77] Beneath this lay long-term changes in the position of the cotton industry, as more workers felt their always-precarious standards to be increasingly under threat. Now the primary attachment for the Blackburn ILP became local union branches rather than the SDF. But the consequence was not the same as in Preston. The party counted for far more in Blackburn affairs. Snowden was still available as candidate, and so ILP efforts were not harvested by a trade union nominee.

The ILP's position was affected also by changes in the older parties. Liberal hopes revived now that Free Trade had become a controversial subject. Past Liberal failures and its two-member status made Blackburn an obvious case for inclusion in the Gladstone—MacDonald pact. There were changes on the Conservative side too. Coddington's retirement and the consequential search for a successor involved a decisive shift away from the 'Fellow Townsmen' appeal. A paternalist world was dying both in the mill and on the political platform. The Conservative choice fell eventually on Geoffrey Drage, a carpet-bagging lawyer and devout apostle of economic individualism. This outsider teamed up with Hornby, still an unrepentant Free Trader, despite Protectionist leanings on the part of some activists.[78]

The Liberal-Labour 'understanding' was one-sided, a sharp contrast with the situation in some two-member seats. The Liberal candidate, Hamer, spoke of the two parties as natural allies, but Snowden was more ambiguous. He attacked the Tory record on social reform and more specifically and un-precedently attacked Hornby's record on trade unionism. The labour emphasis also appeared in regular references to the 'Chinese Slavery' controversy, tying together labour and humanitarian concerns with a dash of anti-semitism:

everyone who gave a vote for men who belonged to a party that was responsible for the introduction in South Africa of Chinese forced labour in effect said, 'I don't want South Africa for the British, let the Jews have it'.[79]

These appeals were basically anti-Tory; they contained no suggestion as to what Snowden's supporters should do with their second vote. When the local SDF issued a leaflet advocating plumping for Snowden, he offered no refutation, simply stating that the Federation had no official connection with him.[80] This contrasted with David Shackleton's advice that all Blackburn trade unionists should support 'both Progressive candidates'.[81]

Even in the general Tory debacle of 1906, Snowden found that the traditional elements of Blackburn politics retained much of their power. The continuing appeal of the Hornby style can be gauged from an incident at one of Snowden's meetings:

Mr. Snowden proceeded to argue against Protection. The big audience listened atten-tively until Mr. Snowden made an allusion to Sir Harry Hornby. Sir Harry had, he said, stated that he was a Free Trader and he quite believed he was. (Cries of 'he is' and applause.)

A lady in the body of the meeting: 'He is a gentleman.'

Another voice: 'Hornby for ever.'

The lady: 'He is a gentleman, every inch of him.' (Applause and uproar.)

A voice: 'Fair play sir. Fair play sir.'[82]

In this situation (Tory paternalist and a carpet-bagging Tory lawyer, no Protectionist candidates, and an assymetrical Liberal-Labour arrangement,) a singular outcome was perhaps predictable. The return of Hornby and Snowden symbolised the complexities of Blackburn politics at a moment of transition. Traditional Toryism was decaying, but Hornby stood out against the general collapse in Lancastria, his appeal still powerful enough to offset a limited Progressive understanding (see Table 30).

Table 30. *Blackburn 1906*

Hornby	10,291	Hornby Plumpers	94	Snowden-Hornby	822
Snowden	10,282	Snowden Plumpers	1,504	Snowden-Hamer	7,871
Drage	8,932	Drage Plumpers	10	Drage-Hornby	8,751
Hamer	8,892	Hamer Plumpers	311	Hamer-Hornby	624
				Drage-Hamer	86
				Drage-Snowden	85

The embryonic Progressive understanding matured four years later, with Hornby's retirement and the end of Tory paternalism. Snowden and his Liberal counterpart urged voters to support the two Progressives, and Blackburn followed most other two-member seats.[83] From a very different starting-point, Blackburn politics ended up in January 1910 in much the same shape as its Halifax counterpart. The ILP remained an important element but ultimately it was as a participant in a Progressive alliance, not as a constituent of the Socialist Party that had looked feasible in the late nineties.

An examination of the early ILP in these two Tory strongholds suggests the isolation of three characteristics. Firstly, in both cases, the ILP initially moved into a vacuum resulting from the plight of local Liberalism. As such, it could be a persuasive supplicant for Radical sympathy, although in both towns we find ILP campaigners trying to appeal not just to Liberals, but also to the more numerous Conservatives. The latter could be on a straightforward 'Labour' plank, but it could involve the idiosyncracies of a Tattersall. In both places, the strategy attracted chiefly homeless Radical voters, but it was successful in loosening the allegiance of some Tories. The second feature concerns the changing relationship between the ILP and local trade unionism, which meant principally the local cotton workers' organisations. We have seen how the Blackburn Textile officials played a leading role in keeping Trades Council and socialists apart in the nineties — a similar distance can be found in Preston where some union officials were active Tories. But the adhesion of their unions to the LRC changed matters radically in these cotton towns. The ILP on the positive side found itself linked through local LRCs to powerful organisations having sizeable resources, including perhaps an ability to deliver the votes of many members. But this growth of the Labour Alliance raised problems for the ILP. Preston now became a trade union seat and the ILP's position was much more marginal. In Blackburn, where the party's pre-LRC impact had been greater, the party retained the candidacy but there was a significant shift in the centre of gravity of Labour politics.

And finally, the analysis of developments in these towns raises the crucial question of the Liberal revival. From 1902, the resurgence of Lancastrian Liberalism and the expectation in some quarters of a Progressive understanding raised basic issues for the ILP. We have seen how in Blackburn, despite its singular features, Snowden had by 1910 reached the same position as James Parker in Halifax. The world of the Lancashire ILP was changing radically. Once the challenge had been that of a predominantly Tory working class; now it was emerging as that of a revitalised — and arguably transformed — Liberalism.

Towards Progressivism?

The bare statement that in Lancashire, Liberal—ILP relationships were complex tells us little; the same was true of the West Riding, where Liberal support was much greater. In any region, the continuities of rhetoric and principle as between Radical and ILP inevitably produced harmonious sentiments which had to be balanced against socialist opposition to capitalism, and working-class alienation from bourgeois-dominated caucuses. Lancastrian variations on this theme were in part a product of Tory strength. Ideological qualms about understandings with Radicals were fortified by prudential considerations. But this was counterbalanced to some extent by the unusual flexibility of some Liberals over the question of Labour representation. In part, this reflected Liberal awareness of its own weakness; in part it indicated the survival of strong progressive sentiments on the part of some elements within the bourgeoisie. This fusion of pragmatism and principle had aided Snowden in his first Blackburn contest, but it had wider implications.

The divergent Liberal responses did not fall neatly into the traditional categories of 'Whig' and 'Radical'. Already in the nineties, there is some evidence of a drive towards a Progressive synthesis that could not be accommodated within this dichotomy. This synthesis was not just a question of Liberalism developing as a more interventionist, more welfare-focused creed. It could be found also in a more flexible view of strategy. A concordat with labour was essential, but it seemed less imperative that its organisational form be contained wholly within an official Liberal framework. These developments were central to the politics of C. P. Scott, not just in his championing of Radical causes old and new in the columns of the *Manchester Guardian* but also in his practical attempts to meet the demands of Independent Labour.

In the Spring of 1894, Scott withdrew from the Liberal candidacy in North East Manchester, leaving Leonard Hall of the ILP, hopefully, in a straight fight with the sitting member. His action attracted some support. Richard Pankhurst, then in the process of shifting from Radicalism to the ILP, praised it as 'a signal act of magnanimity'.[84] But Hall was less gracious:

> it is only the plain truth to say that that gentleman has not taken this course from spontaneous inspiration nor philanthropic motives, nor until the proofs of the perfect hopelessness of his opposition to the Labour candidate have become overwhelming. It is very much a case of 'Thank ye for nothing, sir'.[85]

As one Manchester Liberal informed Scott: 'The ILP are hopeless enemies to Liberal principles and we should fight them'.[86] Many Lancastrian Liberals in 1894—5 feared a forthcoming disaster at the polls, and this was amplified by a belief that the tactics of the ILP would make matters even worse. Such a belief, intelligible only on the assumption that ILP candidates attracted more Liberal voters than Tory, indicated both affinities and rivalry.

The complexities of the situation were revealed in the 1895 campaign, no more so than in Gorton. This was an industrially mixed constituency with its locomotive works, coal mines and hat manufacturers. It included not only some industrial suburbs of Manchester, but also some separate industrial villages. Politically, the division had been Liberal since its first contest in 1885. Its member, the industrialist Sir William Mather, had been elected in 1892 despite his opposition to the legislative eight-hour day. He subsequently reversed his view on this question, but decided not to contest the next election in order to avoid accusations of lack of principle.[87] Gorton Liberals faced the problem of finding a new candidate, a difficulty compounded by the fact that, as one Liberal acknowledged, 'the Labour element is militant there'.[88] This temper had already been revealed in the Gorton ILP's unsuccessful attempt to secure George Barnes as candidate, but their subsequent adoption of the Manchester barrister, Richard Pankhurst, posed acute problems for local Liberals.

His well-known sympathy with Radical causes meant that he stood every chance of securing sizeable Liberal support.[89] Although Pankhurst emphasised the place of public ownership in his programme, he stressed that 'on their four principal planks', Home Rule, Welsh Disestablishment, Abolition of the Lords and Local Veto, 'he was with the Liberal party'.[90] Nevertheless, the Gorton Liberals, after much discussion, adopted their own President as candidate. He obtained Irish support, but was withdrawn quickly in the interests, as the Liberals put it, of 'the party of progress'.[91] Some leading Liberals publicly supported Pankhurst. Mather contributed publicly towards his expenses, making a distinction between Pankhurst's ultimate objective and his immediate support for: 'all the measures now within the sphere of practical politics to which the Liberal party is devoted'. He presented the choice as between: 'the lifelong friend and advocate of the labouring classes, and the Tory candidate ... an eminent London wine and spirit merchant'.[92] The juxtaposition no doubt appealed to Liberal sympathies and prejudices. But there was one crucial complicating factor. Pankhurst had angled for a Liberal withdrawal, advising Hardie that: 'this withdrawal should be promoted by our party, if this can be done consistently with the dignity of the party. I think it can'.[93] But local Liberals saw such a move as part of a package deal. A Gorton Liberal withdrawal should be reciprocated by the ILP in North East Manchester, where Hall had been replaced by James Johnston. The NAC met in Manchester during the campaign and found representatives in both constituencies, opposed to any deal.[94] Both ILP candidates went forward, therefore, and the Gorton Liberal withdrawal came the following day.

The lack of a response clearly upset the Gorton Liberals, and dissatisfaction grew when the Liberals failed to take North East Manchester by a margin of less than half the vote given to the ILP candidate. It was hardly surprising that the Gorton Liberals split. The Liberal Council held a lengthy meeting, but failed to issue any recommendation.[95] It was anticipated locally that although committed Radicals would go with the ILP, a sizeable number of Liberals would abstain.

Failure to secure united Liberal support was not Pankhurst's only problem. Even in hitherto Liberal Gorton he encountered something of the strength of Lancashire Toryism. One observer claimed that 'never before in Gorton and Openshaw had such a predominance of blue been seen'. One of the candidate's daughters later recalled her disillusion at canvassing the Gorton working class. Interest in issues was often minimal; rather it was 'a sort of game in which it was important to be on the winning side'. Tactics in the game included the familiar claim that the ILP candidate was an atheist. The rash of blue posters, the union jack streamers across the streets, the carriages taking Tory voters to the polls, a grand Primrose League picnic — all contrasted with ILP workers chalking the flags and attempting to attract attention through a cyclists' parade.[96]

This embryonic Progressive politics failed to develop in 1895 for diverse reasons. Liberal support did not emerge in official form. Gorton Liberals clearly divided between Radicals and those whom Pankhurst castigated in his post-declaration speech as 'disguised Tories'.[97] Liberal schizophrenia was complemented by that of the ILP. Desire for Liberal votes cohabited especially after Hardie's West Ham defeat with resentment towards Liberal activists. Hardie's own sentiments in this direction were placarded around the constituency by grateful Conservatives. Despite these ambiguities, Pankhurst clearly attracted support from the great majority of normally Liberal voters(Table 31). Given his emphasis on his Radical pedigree, he is unlikely

Table 31. *Liberal and ILP candidates in Gorton, 1892 and 1895*

1892 Turnout 87.3%		
W. Mather, Liberal	5,255	51.1%
E. F. G. Hatch, Conservative	5,033	48.9%
1895 Turnout 78.1%		
E. F. G. Hatch, Conservative	5,865	57.9%
R. Pankhurst, ILP	4,261	42.1%

to have won over many Conservative workers in the Preston fashion. Such a contingency was guarded against by the Tory claim that Pankhurst had become 'a fully-fledged Liberal candidate'.[98] But Gorton idiosyncracies and antipathies apart, any Progessive case faced a bleak prospect in 1895, perhaps the hour of Lancashire Toryism's greatest triumph.

The forces making for some sort of rapprochement remained, however. From the side of Independent Labour, John Trevor hoped for some synthesis of Progressives:

I have regarded the policy of 'smashing the Liberal Party' as a foolish one, and have said that a policy of destruction was a policy of weakness ... The present is an opportunity for a more just and generous attitude to be urged upon all the progressive parties. The forces that have built up the Independent Labour Party must be recognised ... so far as the Labour Party is concerned, I hope it may be possible to arouse it to a sense of the realities of the situation and relegate to the SDF those who cannot understand that generosity and honesty are not weaknesses.[99]

Such sentiments have to be balanced against Trevor's contention that Hardie 'will grow more embittered and dogmatic', a carricature in itself, although indicative of the doubts surrounding the chastened party's post-1895 development. In particular, elements within Lancashire parties favoured socialist unity, and by implication, rejected more flexible arrangements with non-socialist organisations. By 1900, they had lost the argument, and already signs of a Progressive understanding could be found in several Lancashire seats. Such combinations were not simply the product of continuities of principle and idiom. They also reflected the weaknesses of Liberals and ILP and also the fashion in which even some laissez-faire Liberals could be brought to agree with socialists on the South African War. This was reflected not just in the surrogate Radical candidacies of Hardie and Snowden. It also surfaced in two different forms in Scott's Manchester base.

Fred Brocklehurst, despite ILP and Radical misgivings about his position on the war,[100] was backed strenuously in South West Manchester by the *Manchester Guardian*. The choice, in the absence of a Liberal, was presented as between a Tory and a 'Progressive'. Brocklehurst's programme was essentially a Radical one.[101] But official Liberal support did not appear. The divisional Liberal Association would only back someone who was willing to put himself before their own organisation.[102] As yet, Progressive understanding could easily run foul of organisational protocol and the proprietorial views of some Liberals.

A much more harmonious situation emerged in Gorton in 1900. Once again the Liberals failed to find a candidate, and the only challenge to the Conservatives came from W. Ward, the nominee of the Gorton United Trades and Labour Council. This organisation had been formed in 1898, and included representatives from most local trade union branches plus two delegates from the local ILP.[103] Ward personified the Progressive alliance in rather different terms. He was a member of West Ham Council where an alliance of ILP, SDF and Trades Council representatives had taken control in 1898. The status of his candidature within the ILP is obscure. He never received LRC endorsement but he was apparently endorsed by the ILP's National Election Conference, although previously the NAC had taken Gorton off their list, leaving responsibility to the Trades Council.[104] Ward sought to galvanise the Progressive coalition: 'Socialists were with him almost to a man; the Irishmen were with him solidly; the nonconformists were joining their forces'.[105] Most significantly, the Liberal Council came out in support of Ward.[106] The consequence of the Progressive rally was a substantial cut in the Conservative majority compared with Pankhurst's effort in 1895.[107]

Events over the next few years served to foster Progressive alliances in Lancashire. The changing diet of controversy — Free Trade, Taff Vale, Chinese Labour, and to some degree, social reform, focused attention on issues that united Liberal and Labour. Such sentiments were boosted further by the involvement of cotton unions in the LRC. Now some Lib-Lab officials could stand under LRC auspices and enjoy local ILP support. The unopposed return of David Shackleton for Clitheroe in July 1902 symbolised the new arrangements, with the strong Nelson ILP backing the Lib-Lab Weavers' official rather than its preferred choice — Philip Snowden. Equally significant was the consequential rift between the Nelson ILP and the local SDF.[108]

Inevitably, Lancastria with its wealth of two-member seats and a history of Liberal failure, was bound to loom large within the MacDonald—Gladstone understanding. And so it proved. Almost half of the successful LRC candidates in 1906 came from the region. None of the victors had a Liberal opponent. The breakthrough carried few benefits specifically for the ILP. Apart from Snowden, only Clynes in North East Manchester was sponsored by the party, and his involvement in ILP affairs was always very limited. A few others, such as George Wardle, carried ILP cards; but others, such as Shackleton and G. D. Kelley, explicitly denied that they were socialists. Some trade union successes, those at Preston and Bolton for example, followed earlier ILP attempts, but some, in the coalfields, owed almost nothing to local ILP initiatives.

If the breakthrough was Labour and trade unionist rather than socialist and ILP, it was also underpinned by strong Liberal sympathy. It was hardly surprising that Liberals could support Brocklehurst's successor in South West Manchester. Kelley after all, had led the Lib-Lab rearguard action on the Trades Council in the nineties. But they also gave strong backing to Clynes, emphasising that this ILP-financed trade union official was 'the only Free Trade and Progressive candidate'.[109] Such a fusion of sentiments swept away much of Tory Lancashire. It was easy to argue that socialist enthusiasm had been harnessed to a new Progressive juggernaut which was remaking Lancastrian politics and given time could have done the same on a wider national canvas.

The emphasis is very important; so too is a realisation that several leading ILPers consented readily to such developments. Clynes could acknowledge readily that in Oldham: 'our progress from the Socialist point of view has been slow, but we have reached the stage where the separate action of the ILP ... would do much harm'.[110] But many activists chafed under the weight of alliances and accommodations. Several within the Manchester ILP pushed, prior to 1906, for a candidate against Arthur Balfour and felt that trade union caution was ruining their chances.[111] Similar dismay could be found in Oldham where some felt, contra Clynes, that the way forward lay not in permeating trade union circles but in an unequivocal stand for socialism.[112] Such sentiments would feed off memories of the early years of the ILP, and the legacy of close SDF—ILP co-operation in many Lancashire centres. The denunciations of compromise in the columns of the *Clarion* also acted as a stimulant; feeling for One Socialist Party remained strong.

Its strength was sufficient to raise the question of whether movement towards the Progressive synthesis was as inevitable as some suggested. Was it a natural progression for the Lancastrian ILP in the context of Labour Alliance and New Liberal revival? Were the dissidents merely kicking against the pricks, or was the One Socialist Party a suppressed alternative, defeated as much by the logic of national agreements as by the inherent inhospitality of Lancastrian conditions? Some signposts towards the solution of this problem can be found through examining a case where the ILP did not follow the dominant Progressive trajectory — Rochdale.

Developments there during the nineties had followed a characteristic Lancastrian pattern. A local ILP had been formed late in 1892; it had fought the 1895 election with George Barnes as candidate. His campaign emphasised socialist principles,[113] he enjoyed SDF support and polled 1,251 votes in a contest which ended the Liberal dominance of the town's representation. Rochdale Liberalism retained perhaps something of Bright's legacy in its somewhat austere unbending bourgeois style, and relationships with the ILP were now predictably bad. The Rochdale Socialists worked together closely in the late nineties; they produced a joint newspaper and electoral slates. Possibly their position was aided by the occupational composition of the local working class. Rochdale was not quite so dominated by cotton workers as many textile centres. The construction of textile machinery was a significant source of employment, and events in the engineering trade, especially the lockout, might have boosted sympathy for socialism.[114]

The local socialists felt strong enough to run a joint SDF/ILP candidate under LRC auspices in 1900. The whimsical campaign of the dialect writer Allen Clarke produced a notably worse result than in 1895. 'The biggest blunder ever made' was one member's retrospective verdict.[115] Cash was very limited, a close contest between Liberal and Tory was rightly anticipated. Once again, however, the socialist candidate held the balance between the two older parties — a Liberal defeat by nineteen votes hardly eased Liberal-Socialist relationships. Here in a single-member seat where Liberalism had every hope of a comeback, accommodation to Labour's advantage was never a possibility. Moreover, despite the national disaffiliation of the SDF, local links remained strong and in 1902, the two local socialist groups selected Sam Hobson, by now a prominent critic of the ILP leaders, as their candidate and formed a Socialist Election Committee to promote his case. Such a development was facilitated by the lack of a LRC in the town, itself a testimony to the lack of enthusiasm of the large textile unions.

Several of the more prominent figures on the Rochdale Trades Council saw socialist politics as simply one more form of partisanship which should be kept out of trade union affairs.[116] Moreover, the four permanent officials of the major textile unions were all Liberals[117] and would not support any candidate who could threaten Liberal prospects of regaining the seat. Local socialists reciprocated such sentiments by attacking union activists who did not belong to either socialist group.[118] The estrangement was significant, but equally a sizeable section of the Rochdale working class seems to have found Hobson's candidature attractive. An observer who hoped for a more orthodox Labour candidate admitted that Hobson would poll well.[119]

Hobson's views were reflected in the Rochdale ILP branch position over the Dewsbury debacle,[120] and ILP national figures were inclined to take a bleak view of the prospects; Glasier dismissed the branch as 'not very brilliant'.[121] Twelve months later, in December 1903, he found a surprisingly cordial reception: 'the bulk of members appear to be quite loyal to the NAC. Indeed, I find a fighting spirit among them against the *Clarion* and SDF intrigue that I did not observe before'.[122] Such observations perhaps reflect leaders' myopia concerning the appropriateness of a United Socialist candidate in certain Lancastrian situations. Supporters of the option did not need to be perennial critics of the party leadership. Hobson suggested in retrospect that the opposition of the Party Establishment essentially reflected their embarrassment in the context of other deals — a claim that no doubt has some validity, although it fails to indicate the way in which such a candidature flew against the logic of the Labour Alliance.[123] Local activists continually attempted to secure the LRC's endorsement of the candidature, but MacDonald was clearly opposed.[124]

The 'Rochdale Socialist Party' as it liked to call itself, campaigned vigorously throughout the remainder of the 1900 parliament. But the lack of a local LRC made some ILP members sceptical. One reflected to Hardie on the attraction of the Alliance strategy even there:

it would have been better for Hobson to have stood as an ILP candidate, and thus secured the endorsement of the LRC. This was advocated by a good many of our members, but unfortunately the element in the branch which I call the 'Clarion' element was too strong and carried the day in favour of working jointly with the SDF.

Whilst progress had been made, relationships with unions remained a major difficulty, especially in the town's major industry:

The Amalgamated Engineers, the Carpenters and Joiners, Gasworkers, Shop Assistants and a good many of the smaller unions are very promising, the only backward lot being the Textile Operatives — Spinners and Cardroom hands especially. The Weavers are not so bad.[125]

In Rochdale, there was little chance of voters making a smooth transition from Liberalism; the prediction was of 'considerable support' from ex-Tories but not so many converts from the Liberals.

Hobson's campaign made few concessions to Progressive sentiments — the education squabbles of the nonconformists were pilloried for delaying social reforms.[126] Asquith was attacked as the man responsible for Featherstone and for despatching gunboats to Hull.[127] Liberal and Tory capitalists were really the same. Workers' salvation 'lay in neither capitalist red nor capitalist blue'. The distinctions in the end mattered little: 'they differed on Home Rule, Tariff Reform and the administration of the Education Act, but they were entirely agreed on the subjection of Labour to Capital'. The class war was 'open and palpable' — the need was 'to smash the present system and put in its place a co-operative commonwealth'.[128] Hobson even scorned one staple point in most Labour and Socialist platforms in 1906 — it was 'not his intention to waste his breath discussing Chinese Labour'.[129] Such claims clearly provoked difficulties. Redfern, a Spinners' official used the excuse of Hobson's unofficial status to speak from the Liberal platform.[130] More dramatically, socialist attacks on Liberal hypocrisy led to pained nonconformist responses and to less high-minded claims that Hobson had been involved in dubious speculations in the cotton trade. This last claim led to a post-poll libel action by Hobson.[131] This welter of recrimination and counter-recrimination lent a somewhat squalid end to Hobson's campaign — but the most crucial fact lay in the result. Despite the lack of interest or hostility of local textile union officials, despite the strength of traditional nonconformist sentiments, despite the handicap of his unofficial status, standing on a platform making few concessions, in a contest where Liberals expected quite rightly that they could defeat the incumbent, Hobson still polled almost one-fifth of the total votes cast. This compared favourably with LRC polls in three-cornered contests. At least in Rochdale, the socialist option was not a utopian dream.

Emphasis on the factors facilitating a Progressive synthesis must be balanced by an awareness of elements suggesting very different possibilities. The starting-point was the cracking of the old Tory supremacy. Changing economic conditions especially in cotton, the growth of limited liability companies and the disappearance of dynasties, the weakening of close ties between workplace, home and recreation — all these factors affected political outlooks only slowly, but their inevitable effect was to erode the bases of Tory influence. But what would take its place? One influential school of thought has seen the dominant motif as the advent of Progressivism. Its key elements were a Liberal revival based on opposition to Protectionism, but fuelled in the longer run by Liberal justifications of the interventionist state, and by the disintegration of many communal bases for political allegiance. The new criterion, especially in Lancastria, was increasingly that of 'class' so a moderate LRC, including cotton textile unions, became an important partner, for a revitalised Liberalism. In such an arrangement the ILP might supply enthusiastic activists and the occasional candidate but it was a marginal element in this new coalition.

Such an interpretation fits many aspects of Lancastrian politics from 1902, and preliminary signs can be read from much earlier. Although a revisionist view in that it emphasises the advent of Progressive rather than Labour politics, it is snugly conventional in seeing a transition to class politics in Lancastria — and perhaps in Britain — as an essentially moderate affair. The emphasis is significant in that it does capture significant developments. But there is another face. Many Liberal Associations in Lancastria did not exhibit a New Liberal smile and welcome the advent of independent, albeit perhaps sympathetic, Labour organisations. Often older ideas and prejudices remained. Equally the Lancastrian ILP retained many who saw the Liberals as capitalist enemies. The attractions of Blatchford and the movement for One Socialist Party remained powerful. Certainly there were good local reasons for Progessivism, but equally there were forces — including the problem of a Tory working class — working in other directions. In the end, these other possibilities were aborted, in part by the weight of priorities decided at national level. The Lancastrian situation contained a range of options. Some were perhaps more likely than others, but in no way can we talk of an inevitable or even of a highly probable outcome. The problem raised is that of the complex inter-relationship of regional and national decisions. Yet within the national party, Lancastria loomed large, and the plasticity of possibilities there had clear implications for developments on a wider canvass.

10

ILP islands

The colliers and ironworkers of Merthyr and Aberdare, and the boot and shoe workers of Leicester in most respects, seemed to occupy different worlds. The turbulent, vibrant political tradition of Merthyr, its heavily industrial and elemental landscape, the distinctive mix of native Welsh and a bewildering spectrum of immigrants seemed an ideal basis for an ILP appeal. Yet Leicester had its own Radical reputation, built on Dissent; Chartism had had its heroes in both communities. The world of 'Dic Penderyn' has to be balanced by that of George Elliot. So too in ILP terms, the Merthyr of Keir Hardie had to be set against the Leicester of Ramsay MacDonald. These crucial successes capitalised on industrial grievances; we have seen how South Wales colliers and Midlands bootworkers could be radicalised through industrial experiences. Both in Merthyr and in Leicester powerful Liberalism underwent crises, allowing space for a nascent ILP but then posing complex dilemmas of attraction and repulsion. These provide obvious bases for ILP growth, starting points for further investigation, yet they must be balanced by an awareness that these successes were for several years little more than islands in surrounding seas of Liberal dominance.

Leicester: 'The unity of the Progressive Party?'*

The early strength of the ILP in England was limited largely to Yorkshire and Lancashire. Nevertheless, beyond these two counties, there were occasional ILP strongholds, surrounded by indifference or hostility. The most significant of these was Leicester — the scene of sizeable ILP parliamentary votes in the 1890s, later the constituency of Ramsay MacDonald and by 1912 exceeded only by Bradford in its ILP membership. But why Leicester? The East Midlands as a whole were in no way an ILP stronghold. Brocklehurst in 1897 could admit that socialism 'scarcely had any foothold in the Midlands. Radical towns like

---

* The phrase, but not the question mark, in *Leicester Daily Post*, 27 June 1903.

Leicester were hard to reach owing to their childlike confidence in the great Liberal Party, and it seemed as though their faith never would be shaken'.[1]

The region's politics bore abundant testimony to that claim. Its other urban centres showed little ILP influence. No ILP candidate — indeed no Labour candidate at all — stood in any Nottingham seat before 1914. Here the local ILP in the late nineties was in a weak state — even before the 1895 election Glasier found the Nottingham party, although reasonably harmonious, was 'without any great enterprise or push'.[2] In nearby Derby the ILP was stronger, but backed the Railwaymen's nominees; firstly the politically ambiguous Richard Bell and then J. H. Thomas. As a result, the local ILPers tended to lose their distinctive identity within a trade union-dominated Labour alliance.[3] Moreover, it was a Labour alliance whose relationship with official Liberalism remained extremely close. It was not just in the larger centres that Liberalism remained strong — it also remained the faith of many miners and hosiery workers in industrial villages. Indeed, the numerous miners in the region remained amongst the most Liberal and the most industrially quiescent in the whole country.

The explanation of Leicester's distinctiveness must begin with an emphasis on its industrial base. In 1903, no less than 13,000 of the 19,500 affiliated members of the Trade Council were members of the Boot and Shoe Operatives — a union whose members had encountered major technological changes in the 1890s and whose activists had been strongly attracted by independent politics and socialist proposals.[4] The factional division within the union between Radical Liberals and socialists was intense amongst Leicester union activists where the socialists had strong support amongst the relatively highly paid piece-workers. But opposed to them, there loomed the figure of Alderman William Inskip, the Union's chief official and a dedicated opponent of separation from organised Liberalism. Despite technical changes and embittered industrial relations, culminating in the great lockout of 1895, Radical Liberalism remained a significant, albeit minority, tendency amongst the Leicester union activists. However, even a small socialist advantage amongst the Boot and Shoe workers affected Trades Council deliberations dramatically because the union was so numerically dominant. In part, this reflected the low level of unionisation in Leicester's other major industry, hosiery. Only 1,600 members of the Amalgamated Hosiery Union were affiliated to the Trades Council by 1903.[5]

If Leicester's industrial base provided some explanation for the development of ILP sympathies, the borough's political record was also important. It was one of the safest Liberal seats in the East Midlands and, moreover, a two-member borough. These factors were important — the Leicester situation contrasted with that in Nottingham with its three single-member seats. There, the Liberals could count on only one seat as reasonably safe, and Tariff Reform perhaps had some appeal to the lace workers. Even in dual-member Derby, the normal Liberal ascendancy had been broken with the defeats of 1895. The need to recapture the seat provided space for Bell's LRC candidature in 1900. But in Leicester, the Liberal control seemed less threatened. In 1885 and 1886 a single Conservative opponent had made no impression and in 1892 the Liberals had been returned unopposed.[6]

This picture of Liberal dominance suggests parallels with the woollen towns of the West Riding, especially perhaps with two-member Halifax and its complacent, bourgeois-controlled Liberal Association persistently ignoring the demands of Labour. The apparent security of Liberalism provides a parallel, but there were some significant differences. Leicester Liberals were prepared to make a few concessions to the Trades Council on municipal representation — one Town Councillor and two School Board representatives in 1889, three more Councillors and one magistrate two years later.[7] Leicester Liberalism lacked an Alfred Illingworth — a deficiency — or advantage — attributable to the absence in Leicester of any equivalent to the millocracy. Boot and Shoe production tended to be concentrated in smaller units and helped to produce a local Liberalism lacking the opulent inflexibility of its West Riding counterpart.[8]

Leicester Liberalism was proud of its Radical pedigree. The influence of the dissenting sects amongst several of the town's leading families left its political legacy. Inevitably by the late nineteenth century, some of the vitality of this Radicalism was lessening. Successful Radical families moved out into County Society, they shifted allegiance to Anglicanism and sent their sons to public schools. One political consequence of this process was the shift of some Leicester Liberals into Liberal Unionism after 1886; but several remained within Gladstonian ranks, proud of their Radical past, but perhaps increasingly satisfied with the world as it was.[9] Such changes, added to the increasing assertiveness of labour, made the previously cosy relationship with the Trades Council seem more problematic.

This relationship had been deteriorating for some time. By the early nineties, some of the delegates reflected the increased sympathy for socialism and Independent Labour representation within the trade union world. In Leicester such changes were given a cutting edge by the threat of technical innovations in the boot and shoe trade. In 1893, there occurred one of those symbolic changes that mark so often the shift from Radical Liberalism to Independent Labour. The Presidency of the Trades Council was assumed by a young cabinet-maker, George Banton — an advocate of Labour independence, subsequently a leading figure in the Leicester ILP and eventually in the early twenties, a Leicester Labour MP.[10]

The Liberal Association responded to the increased demand for labour municipal representation by holding discussions with the Trades Council. The consequence was hardly satisfying for labour partisans. Although Liberal leaders were sympathetic, they refused to interfere with the nominating procedures of the Ward Committees.[11] The continuing hold of Liberalism amongst the Leicester middle class meant that the prospects for labour municipal expansion would be limited.

Such a situation reflected a characteristic Liberal view of politics in which the labour interest was just one important element in the Radical coalition. Yet Leicester Liberals were clearly not opposed to the selection of respectable Lib-Lab candidates. This was demonstrated in March 1894, when one of the sitting members announced that he would retire at the next election. The Liberal choice was Henry Broadhurst, a leading exponent of Lib-Labism, who had frequently been involved in clashes with socialist trade union spokesmen.[12] The immediate grievance of the Trades Council was not an ideological one: it was simply that it had not been involved in the selection process. Yet the fact of Broadhurst's selection was in sharp contrast to the contemporary responses of Bradford and Halifax Liberals.

The underlying tensions were revealed sharply, however, when Leicester's second Liberal Member resigned in August 1894 and it was decided to have a dual by-election. The Association's choice, as running mate for Broadhurst, was W. Hazell, a London printing employer selected very narrowly in preference to Leicester's mayor, Sir Israel Hart.[13] Inevitably, class differences and local partriotism became entwined in criticism of the Liberal selection. Some Trades Council members seemed prepared to accept the Liberal choice, and it was only after Tom Mann had addressed the Council that a majority, 21 to 17, of the delegates decided to support Joseph Burgess as an Independent Labour candidate.[14]

The significance of this narrow decision, and of Burgess's votes — 4,402 in August 1894, 4,009 in 1895 — is complex. At the time of the first contest, there was no ILP branch in Leicester; the town contained a small number of Anarchists, SDFers and Christian Socialists, but the principal initiatives came from an essentially social Labour Club and from union activists in the boot and shoe trade.[15] One of the leading figures was T. F. Richards, a leading militant in the union's factional struggles, who viewed Leicester local politics as inextricably linked to the conflicts within his own union. He was in communication with Hardie more than a month before the second vacancy arose, urging the provision of a suitable candidate to oppose Broadhurst, and emphasising that 'only a very strong man can bring about B's defeat'. The feasibility of such an attack on Lib-Labism was emphasised since already the Boot and Shoe delegates to the Trades Council were pledged to support only independent action.[16] It was hardly surprising that it was Richards who introduced Mann to the Trades Council following the selection of Hazell.

One element, then, in the emergence of Burgess was a firm commitment to independent action, including opposition to Lib-Labism. Such a position acquired credibility not just from the intensive struggles of the Boot and Shoe men, but also from the past animosity between Broadhurst and Hardie.[17] Broadhurst had been rejected by the Nottingham miners over the eight hour question in 1892 and was subsequently attacked by Hardie on his Grimsby candidature in March 1893. At one level Broadhurst symbolised all the features of Lib-Labism that Independent Labour supporters claimed to despise.

As Mann sharply informed the Trades Council 'Mr. Broadhurst was not a Labour candidate, but a Liberal candidate and nothing else'. However, Mann's advocacy of independent action reflected his trade union audience. Although he argued for the collectivisation of industry, the legitimacy of such an appeal was claimed essentially through references to the decisions of individual unions and of the TUC.[18]

This basis for Burgess's candidature was not the whole story. The dispute over Hazell's selection meant that the meeting of Liberal electors convened to endorse his candidature promised to be an acrimonious affair. But the principal source of friction proved to be not the supporters of Leicester's mayor but the advocates of Independent Labour. George Banton — who had been pessimistic at the start of the Trades Council meeting about the feasibility of running a Labour candidate — attended and condemned Hazell for his alleged anti-trade-unionism. More significantly, he attempted to move Burgess's adoption as 'a purely independent Labour man'.[19] Here was a near parallel with the situation in Halifax eighteen months earlier — an attempt to portray an Independent Labour candidature as essentially a quarrel within the Radical family. Once again, as in Halifax, Leicester had a tradition of independent Radical candidates with the wings of Liberalism fighting out their disputes at the poll.

Burgess's own position added a further complexity. He maintained that 'he was not there to oppose Mr. Broadhurst'.[20] This was not just a public flexibility to disarm some members of the Trades Council and, hopefully, to attract votes. He had raised precisely the same position in correspondence with Hardie when the possibility of his contesting Leicester was first raised. He saw Broadhurst as 'coming round a bit, and felt that to oppose him 'would ... do us more harm than good', ... 'but if the Trades Council and ILP could agree to run a second candidate I would be glad to submit my name, not in opposition to him, mind you, but in opposition to a capitalist Liberal or Tory candidate'.[21] This line was taken by several Leicester trade unionists, by the Trade Council as a body and by local ILP workers.[22] It was not what Richards and some of the other Boot and Shoe militants had envisaged when they had first mooted the idea of an Independent Labour candidate. Nevertheless, local Liberal Boot and Shoe officials were isolated in Labour circles in their support for Broadhurst and Hazell.[23] In contrast, Burgess emphasised the range of labour issues on which he and Broadhurst could co-operate: 'the eight hours question, the payment of members, and of candidates' election expenses and other advanced subjects'. He further stressed his harmony with the Radicals on such staples as Home Rule, temperance, Lords' abolition, and universal suffrage.[24] Within the context of Radical Leicester, Burgess was attempting to establish his credentials as a better custodian of its traditions than a Liberal employer.

The Radical tradition to which Leicester ILPers appealed was a complex one. When a propagandist referred to the tradition in July 1895, in order to discredit Hazell, two names were emphasised. One was Thomas Cooper the Leicester Chartist, the other was Peter Alfred Taylor, one of the town's earlier Radical MPs — a supporter of John Stuart Mill and Mazzini.[25] Leicester, like Halifax, had its Radical icons from whom the ILP claimed legitimacy, a pantheon that revealed the complexities within working-class attachments to Radicalism.

Local presentations of the ILP as one more episode in the debates that had enlivened Radical Leicester since the 1830s were viewed with a jaundiced eye by some within the ILP's national leadership — especially Hall, Christie and Curran.[26] After the by-election, there was considerable discussion within the NAC of Burgess's attitude towards Broadhurst, and endorsement of his position for the general election seems to have been far from a formality.[27] Yet this did not affect his tactics in his second contest. Once again the gap between the image of the ILP purveyed by national leaders and the situation in a particular community, was significant.

Burgess's first poll encouraged ILP propagandists, despite reservations about his strategy — the *Labour Leader* saw the performance as the party's best yet, and attached particular significance to the level of trade union support.[28] But the position of the Leicester ILP in 1894-5 revealed the complexities of its links with other tendencies (see Table 32).

Table 32. *The composition of the ILP Vote in Leicester, 1894 and 1895*

	August 1894	July 1895
Burgess plumpers	1,547	1,517
Burgess/Broadhurst	2,072	1,932
Burgess/Rolleston (Cons)	707	453
Burgess/Hazell (Lib)	76	107
Total	*4,402*	*4,009*

Certainly, much of the ILP vote was split with Broadhurst, but the extent of this pales into insignificance besides the numbers prepared to vote the straight Liberal ticket: 6,913 in 1894 and 7,333 in 1895. Trades Council support for Broadhurst and Burgess was outweighed inevitably by the simple fact that Broadhurst and Hazell campaigned together. Clearly, there already existed a significant number of purely Labour electors in Leicester who were not even prepared to back a Liberal trade unionist; these votes presumably shared the position of the Left amongst the Boot and Shoe activists, a position based in part on internal union wrangles and one likely to be strengthened by the creation of an ILP branch. Finally, there seems to have been a smaller section of Tory working men able to express a Labour preference in the absence of a second Tory candidate.

The complex assemblage of support declined in 1895 despite the candidate's optimistic claim that 'we are painting the town red' and 'are certain to win'.[29]

The decline was no doubt due in part to the added pull of traditional party ties at a general election. The aftermath of the boot and shoe lockout was an uncertain influence — in general defeat led to less aggressive union policies, but these received only limited backing from the Leicester activists. Nevertheless, one post-mortem on the 1895 contest noted that 'the shoe hands did not prove revengeful and the Trades Council manifesto in favour of Broadhurst and Burgess was not heeded to any great extent'. Above all, despite Trades Council support, the Labour organisation remained weak, 'lacking money, organisation, committee rooms, vehicles and ability to trace removals'.[30] 'Painting the town red' could not compensate for such deficiences.

Despite failure at the polls, Independent Labour had established itself in Leicester, weaning the Trades Council away from Liberalism and containing a solid nucleus of trade union activists committed to Labour politics. Moreover, the ILP became a perennial feature of the local political scene, with membership rising against the national trend, The euphoria of 1894 had produced only 54 members, but four years later the figure stood at 225.[31]

Such growth was accompanied with problems. The ILP! gained a handful of seats on the town council, but never more than three at any one time. This does not seem to have been a straightforward matter of limited support. The party entered its contests with enthusiasm.[32] Rather, it was a question of finding candidates able to take time off work to attend town council meetings and, above all, it was a matter of finance. Some promising wards were left uncontested; the money raised just about kept the party afloat with a consequential need to raise election funds through special appeals. The major readjustments in the boot trade helped to ensure that although local workers may have been often ready to back the ILP, the aftermath of a major industrial defeat was hardly the best basis for a buoyant organisation.[33]

One positive gain in the late nineties was the strengthening of Labour control of the Trades Council, although individual Lib-Labs still remained significant.[34] But as 1895 had shown, there was a significant difference between the shift of activist opinion and an equivalent shift in the views of the rank and file. Moreover, by the time of the next general election in 1900, with Ramsay MacDonald as the ILP candidate, the situation had been complicated by the Boer War.[35] 'Radical Leicester' certainly contained many enthusiastic supporters of the war, and early in 1900, a 'Stop the War' meeting was broken up after forged tickets had been issued.[36] The Labour press saw the 'khakhi craze'[37] as still important, during the election, although MacDonald argued that the war was 'too sacred a matter' for the platform.[38] The Trades Council was more strongly committed to Independent Labour than in 1895, and only agreed also to support Broadhurst after an angry debate.[39] Attempts to switch the campaign to domestic concerns were a poor second to Conservative posters depicting 'our boys' under fire in South Africa.[40] And the Liberals, now sensing that their own position was precarious, turned their fire on the Labour interloper. The Liberal press alternatively ignored MacDonald's candidature and argued that an ILP vote would let in the Tory. Although MacDonald attempted to legitimise his intervention by presenting himself as the custodian of Gladstonian principles, he was forced rapidly into arguing that Liberals in office had been poor advocates of these ideas. The ILP had grown because of the 'decadence of democratic force in the Liberal Party'.[41]

The result demonstrated a situation parallel to that in Halifax in 1895 and 1900 with Hazell out and the ILP a plausible candidate for the role of Tory catspaw.(See Table 33.)

Table 33. *The Leicester Poll 1900*

Aggregate Result		Some Permutations	
Broadhurst	10,385	ILP plumpers	1,436
Rolleston	9,066	Straight Liberal	8,120
Hazell	8,528	Broadhurst/MacDonald	1,708
MacDonald	4,164	Rolleston/MacDonald	923

This presents basically the same structure from the ILP viewpoint as the two earlier campaigns, although the number of Conservative/ILP splits had increased. Whether this showed an increased propensity for Tory working men to use their second vote, or a spiting of the Liberals by dedicated socialists is obscure. Certainly it was enough to provoke Hazell into proclaiming the existence of an unlikely alliance between the 'ILP, the Tories and the Publicans' - a claim that inevitably sparked off a round of mutual recrimination.[42] But there was always another moral waiting to be drawn. *The Labour Leader* 'sincerely hoped that official Liberalism will take to heart the salutary lesson of Derby',[43] while a Leicester Liberal newspaper linked the defeat to an earlier episode in Leicester Radicalism. The previous Conservative victory had resulted also from a split in Radical ranks, but the consequences had been positive, with defeat generating a more complete unity of the Radical forces.[44]

The past history of Leicester Liberalism, the circumstances in which the local ILP emerged, the continuing presence of some Lib-Labs on the Trades Council and the personal preferences of MacDonald all helped to ease the birth of a Progressive understanding. The Liberals took two steps in the early months of 1901 which could possibly assist the development of a Liberal—Labour understanding. The old-style Liberal, Sir Israel Hart, was eased out of the Association Presidency, following claims that his views on such issues as municipalisation were out of step with those of most members.[46] Then Hazell, no doubt with local encouragement, announced his abandonment of any attempt to seek re-election.[47] Soon afterwards, the Trades Council invited the Liberals to join with Council and ILP delegates to discuss the parliamentary situation.[48] As yet, the possibility of agreement foundered on the Liberal claim that Broadhurst was an adequate labour representative, and that he should be balanced by 'someone who would represent the commercial interests of the borough, with the general body of the Free Churchmen and moderate Liberals'.[49] Although Liberals accepted that the choice of any successor to Broadhurst should involve co-operation between themselves and Labour organisations, they could not accept the prospect of just one Liberal candidate, presumably Broadhurst, plus a Labour man run independently. After the second meeting, it was decided to adjourn indefinitely to allow the local LRC to, discuss the problem. But this organisation responded on 8 March 1902 by readopting MacDonald. The complexities of Liberal—Labour relations in Leicester could be gauged from the consequential letter to the Liberal Association:

sincerely trusting that the Liberal Association will see their way to adopt Mr. J. R. MacDonald, or co-operate in securing his return, or at least that they will not place a second Liberal candidate in the field, as we are convinced that the majority of the workers are anxious that two Progressives should be returned at the next election.[50]

The Liberal Executive responded critically to the nomination of 'a Socialist candidate' and began the search for a second Liberal.[51]

The search proved to be an unrewarding one. Several prominent figures were approached, including Asquith, but all refused, some because of the number of candidates already in the field.[52] By June 1903, these included the former Liberal President, Sir Israel Hart, who had come out as an independent, but hoped to obtain the Liberal nomination. Yet the drift of opinion amongst leading Leicester Liberals favoured some sort of deal, a sentiment expressed particularly by the new President, Alderman Wood. He was ready to push MacDonald's case, and the latter, now concerned in wider negotiations with Herbert Gladstone, was only too keen to reciprocate.[53] It was Wood who laid down three alternative courses of action to the Liberal Executive: to nominate only Broadhurst; to nominate only Broadhurst and 'to make arrangements with the Labour Party so that we could support their candidate in return for their support to Mr. Broadhurst'; to nominate Broadhurst and Hart.[54]

The path was smoothed for an understanding through a powerful campaign in the local Liberal press. Progressives should unite in the face of Chamberlain's fiscal proposals and MacDonald would be more likely than Hart to facilitate this.[55] Similar advice also came from Herbert Gladstone,[56] perhaps, most significantly, Hart destroyed his own chances by his seigneurial style. He would not abide by the Liberal Association's decision on his candidature. In the past, Associations had invited him, and had left him with the final choice.[57] By late July, Hart had effectively disqualified himself, and eventually on 4 September the Liberal General Committee decided to nominate only Broadhurst, and to co-operate with the LRC to return two Progressives. A pro-Hart amendment secured only twenty-six votes.[58] Leicester was a model Progressive understanding for parliamentary purposes, and it was appropriate that the wider Gladstone — MacDonald arrangement should be developed through a meeting at Leicester just two days after the Liberal decision to run only Broadhurst. Jesse Herbert reported to Gladstone, 'MacDonald is immensely pleased with the satisfactory arrangements made here, and says that it will do great good elsewhere; that his own people are delighted and they will give Broadhurst their second vote'.[59]

This understanding was achieved in a situation where the local ILP remained a prominent force, and was not absorbed readily into a trade-union-dominated coalition. The local LRC served mainly as a channel for trade union political expenditure and the burden of local campaigning was left very much to the ILP.[60] Some of the party's leaders had mellowed, most notably the Boot and Shoe Operatives' leader, T. F. Richards, now embarking on his own deal with the West Wolverhampton Liberals. Underneath such a change, there lay the combination of formal socialist commitment and increasingly moderate practice that marked the politics of his union. Yet there was another face to the Leicester ILP. Several of the rank and file who had lived in a state of cold war with the Liberals for a decade found the new harmony irksome. Municipal campaigns provided an opportunity for a very different political alignment to emerge, and the availability of trade union funds following the creation of the local LRC made it possible to fight many more seats. In November 1904, the *Labour Leader* proclaimed: 'there is no town in the country where the ILP and LRC fight with less thought for Liberal feelings'.[61] Such sentiments provoked some concern in Liberal circles. As early as the Spring of 1904, one Ward Committee had attempted to reopen the question of the parliamentary arrangement because of Labour's policy in the Guardians' elections.[62] Concern did not produce any clear response. By 1909, Labour held fifteen seats on both Council and Board of Guardians, and some Liberals began to look favourably towards a municipal arrangement with the Conservatives.[63]

The 1906 election appeared however as a massive vindication of the Progressive platform. Liberal propaganda urged support for Broadhurst and MacDonald as did the LRC's *Leicester Pioneer*;[64] Alderman Wood appeared on the platform at MacDonald's first meeting; the Labour candidate emphasised the centrality of the Free Trade issue.[65] The campaign reached a triumphant conclusion when five to six thousand gathered to hear both candidates, plus Michael Davitt at a Trades Council rally.[66] This harmony was revealed in the result (see Table 34). But some tensions remained. Richards informed MacDonald that:

some of the fools in Leicester have already boasted they shall plump MacDonald, and others in my own Union have decided to plump Broadhurst. I have our EC to ask the members to publish a special leaflet asking all our men and friends to vote MacDonald and Broadhurst.[67]

Table 34. *Leicester 1906*

Broadhurst	14,745	MacDonald/Broadhurst splits	13,999
MacDonald	14,685	MacDonald plumpers	426
Rolleston	7,504	MacDonald/Rolleston splits	260

Differences were revealed sharply within the Trades Council, when the proposal for a joint rally was discussed. Critics felt that such a meeting 'damned the plan of the LRC'. Others took a pragmatic attitude, reflecting the complexities of local Liberal—Labour connections:

Of course if they were going on the question of Socialism they would not vote for Mr. Broadhurst ... (but) ... Socialism would not come in the time of the present generation, it must be built up step by step, and he believed that Mr. Broadhurst had shown a willingness to work for the Labour Party.[68]

The argument prevailed by 43 votes to 11. Although the Trades Council could had an ILP majority, most of them sought political success through a pragmatic deal that enjoyed impressive electoral support. Yet the minority position enjoyed some legitimacy within both the ILP and the trades council, and this could gain support, should relationships with the Liberals deteriorate once again.

Inevitably, the Leicester ILP appears somewhat schizophrenic: on the one hand there was the domination of MacDonald, and in 1910 if anything, a closer relationship with the Liberals, than had been the case four years earlier;[69] but there was also the growth of Labour as an independent municipal force, and considerable rank and file disillusion with Progressivism. The tension changed into public acrimony in June 1913, when MacDonald led a successful attempt to prevent Labour nominating a candidate for a vacancy in Leicester's other (Liberal) seat. But it was a pyrrhic vicotry: Edward Hartley stood for the BSP and was backed by five ILP councillors at his inaugural meeting. For the future, Leicester Labour seemed committed to an independent policy in parliamentary as well as municipal contests.[70]

This ILP outpost owed its strength to a complex skein of developments. Economic and technical changes in a dominant trade were a crucial factor promoting independent political initiatives, whilst local Radical traditions and successes increased the plausibility of such initiatives. But their character was ambiguous. Propagandists emphasised continuities with the Radicalism of the past — such connections were certainly there, and help to encourage the belief that in many ways, there was not that much divergence between the early Leicester ILP and the Radical Liberalism of much of the East Midlands. The organisation was new, but the style and doctrine were not. It was this tendency that reached its consummation in the MacDonald campaigns of 1906 and 1910. But the formation of a distinct organisation inevitably generated a unique identity. From the beginning in 1894, the Leicester ILP pledged itself to 'the nationalisation of the whole of the means of production, distribution and exchange'.[71] So the ILP propagandised on a basis which drew a line between themselves and both Liberal and Tory, — and, with the formation of the local LRC, engaged in an aggressive municipal policy that could undercut Progressivism. It was possible, of course, to be aggressively independent without being in any sense on the left of Labour politics. Many more Leicester activists were probably concerned that MacDonald would compromise Labour's independence, than differed from him on the substance of policy. Radical Leicester witnessed the evolution of a strong local ILP out of the ambiguities of Labour—Liberal relationships; it presented a microcosm of many of the opportunities, pitfalls and ambiguities encountered by the early ILP.

Radical Merthyr: The Red Dragon and the Red Flag*

Bruce Glasier was very active in the 1900 election, both in advising on candidatures and finance, and in speaking for the party's standard bearers. His diary chronicles his campaigning through Northern England, but then on 3 October there is a new triumphant note:

A great day. Hardie returned for Merthyr. I could hardly speak for joy. It is a great event: the turning point in the poor ILP's career. My heart too is glad for Hardie: he has suffered and toiled so much.[72]

The response was justified. Now a party dedicated to parliamentarianism had a new credibility. More specifically, Hardie's presence in Parliament helped to maintain the independence of the LRC. Its future must have been dubious, if its sole parliamentarian had been Richard Bell. Yet Hardie's success at Merthyr, returned along with a Liberal industrialist, was somewhat surprising. Years later, Glasier acknowledged the unexpectedness of Hardie's success; its advent was one of those 'providential occurrences lying outside the region of ordinary political probability'.[73] The singularity of this success is particularly marked when it is viewed in the context of South Wales politics as a whole. No other ILP candidates stood in South Wales down to, and including, the 1906 election. It was not just that the region remained a Liberal citadel; it was also a question of the distinctive features underpinning this hegemony.[74] Some elements had their parallels elsewhere — the dominance of Dissent, and the commitment of such trade union leaders as there were to Liberalism. But Liberal supremacy in Wales as a whole had a unique quality because of the fashion in which Liberalism fused with nonconformity as a means of national identity. Here was a distinctive society in which Liberal politics supported religion, culture and language as manifestations of nationality. Thus Liberalism could embrace most elements within the society — employer and worker alike — and omitted only relatively small groups such as the Anglicanised elements in large centres, or members of the Established Church. Such

* The title of a pamphlet written by Hardie in 1912.

sentiments held sway in a society which had changed dramatically with the industrialisation of south-east Wales. In 1871, the total Welsh population was just less than one and a half million; over the next forty years it grew by a further million. In 1871, one third lived in Glamorgan and Monmouthshire; by 1911, two-thirds lived in these counties plus the industrial districts of Carmarthenshire. In those years, industrial South Wales provided a success story for a faltering British capitalism. The explosive growth moved populations, generated new experiences and transformed expectations. Appropriate notions of 'Welshness' could serve amongst such turmoil as a social cement.[75] The consequences included not only a Liberal near-monopoly of Welsh seats, but also the emergence after 1885 of a distinctively Welsh Party at Westminster. Only in the economic and political depression of 1895 could Conservatism make any inroads; and then it resulted in the capture of only nine seats out of the Welsh total of thirty-four. By the Liberal high tide of 1906, Conservatism had been obliterated from the Welsh electoral map.

Events during the first few years of the new century seemingly conspired to maintain this dominance. The Education Act of 1902 was tailor-made to revitalise the flagging energies of Welsh nonconformity. Politically, such revitalisation was expressed in the ballot box in 1906; in less profane terms, it was expressed in the last great religious revival of 1904—5 which refilled, albeit temporarily, many chapels. Yet this phenomenon could be interpreted also as a response by a population pitchforked dramatically from a vanishing rural world to a sophisticated industrial network.[76] Indeed, Welsh Liberalism seemed to remain strong until 1914, and did so without making many concessions to new doctrines of economic and social interventionism.[77]

Such continuing strength in South Wales was an unattractive prospect for the early ILP. Here was a growing industrial population which seemed largely uninterested in the party's claims.[78] Attempts to establish branches in the region prior to the coal stoppage of 1898 had only limited success. Certainly, only chance prevented Sam Hobson from appearing at the Bradford Conference as a Cardiff delegate,[79] and a South Wales ILP Federation was formed in 1894.[80] But in 1897, there were only four ILP branches in the whole of Wales.[81]

Yet, the successes of Liberalism hid certain weaknesses. Electoral strength did not always entail vigorous local activities. Success could generate complacency, whilst the comparative failure of 1895 provoked complaints about the unrepresentative quality of many local Liberal cliques, and alarm about organisational decay. Such stagnation could heighten the attractions of a rich patron, able to solve an ailing Association's financial problems, but probably not keen to stimulate vigorous rank and file activities.[82] These circumstances could provoke protests from working-class Liberals and also inducements and scope for a Labour initiative.

The possibility of such initiatives was increased by the erosion of those cultural values that had helped to maintain Liberal dominance. The supremacy of nonconformity in Welsh industrial areas was coming under challenge; by the 1890s membership was expanding more slowly and in 1900 actually fell in most denominations. The Revival of 1904—5 was essentially a brief interlude in a long decline.[83] Such a weakening hold represented in part the maturing of an industrial society in which there were now more varied ways of utilising leisure time. But it also indicated a fundamental demographic change. The continuing expansion of the coal industry drew in many English workers, particularly from the depressed rural areas of the South and South-West. They came to the Eldorado of South Wales, particularly to the Valleys of East Glamorgan and Monmouth, contributing over time to a distinctively South Walian culture. The influx meant that responses to the traditional symbols of Welsh identity were less forthcoming; inevitably the proportion of Welsh-speakers declined in many mining communities. The sense and expression of a traditional Welsh identity, that provided Liberalism with a distinctive element in its appeal, were coming under pressure.

This erosion could provide a place for the emergence of class politics, a possibility heightened, as we have noted earlier, by the changing economic prospects within the coalfield. But the scope and timing of this development should not be exaggerated. New Unionism had only a limited impact, and membership in this sector fell drastically in the nineties. Miners remained entangled in the inhibitions and complexities of the sliding scale until the great lockout of 1898. In one sense this was a watershed in the coal communities — the prestige of the Lib-Lab patriarchs such as Mabon never returned to its old eminence. South Wales was drawn into the wider world of the MFGB and coalfield unionisation grew rapidly. But the battle within the SWMF between older Lib-Labs and younger advocates of Independent Labour was a protracted one.[84] The prospects of a political change were there but the tempo in the region as a whole was slow, the Merthyr Boroughs thus stand out as an early enthusiast for the Independent Labour cause.

This political divergence reflected in part a distinctive economic inheritance.[85] Merthyr had been the first industrial Welsh town, growing in the early nineteenth century around the vast ironworks of the Guests and the Crawshays. An early start led to an early decline, as overseas competition began to bite. Some ironworks closed late in the nineteenth century; in 1891 most of the Dowlais Works was shifted to Cardiff; the number of ironworkers showed a marked fall. This depression was balanced by the expansion of the coal industry, especially in the Aberdare Valley. By 1906, one calculation suggested that more than 43 per cent of the electorate were miners.[86] These successive phases of growth, latterly intertwined with the decline of iron, brought successive tides of immigrants; by the 1880s, the Irish were a significant element in Merthyr's population, along with detachments from Spain.

This industrial experience, earlier and more complex than in much of South Wales, brought its political counterparts. The early weight of industrialisation was tied with the Rising of 1831, the martyrdom of Dic Penderyn — a potent if ambiguous symbol for successive generations of the Merthyr working class[87] — and then with Chartist activities. The stabilities of the fifties and sixties brought the 1867 Reform Act and a consequential expansion of a thousand per cent in the Merthyr electorate. This increase helped to produce the 1868 electoral victory of Henry Richard, nonconformist radical and internationalist. As in Leicester and Halifax, early radical or revolutionary sentiments had been accommodated more or less within a politically successful Liberalism. Beneath the important Welsh specificities, it is possible to discern general similarities as working-class protest was incorporated into the Liberal family, a process aided and abetted by ritual obeisance to the heroes of the past, and typically lubricated by nonconformist rhetoric.

The institutionalisation of Merthyr Labour within this Liberal coalition always preserved some notion of Labour separateness; in such working-class communities with the memory of an insurrectionary past, this was perhaps inevitably.[88] Even in 1874, an unpromising time generally for supporters of labour representation, Thomas Halliday of the Amalgamated Miners could poll nearly 5,000 voters in Merthyr. This general economic and political inheritance offered some basis for Independent Labour initiatives, but the possibilities were increased by two developments during 1888. In that year, both Richard and his Radical running-mate died. In Merthyr, there was no possibility of a Conservative victory — all would be decided within Liberalism. The first vacancy was filled unopposed by D. A. Thomas, a colliery owner, later involved in the creation of the Cambrian Combine and thereby a participant in the troubles of 1910 and 1911. Even in working-class Merthyr, an industrialist who was sound on the central Liberal tenets was secure. His links were not so much with the local bourgeoisie as with the merchants of Cardiff; he was the harbinger of a more interventionist form of capitalism, backing cartelisation, along with minimum wage levels and other reform measures. In many ways, he was set apart amongst Welsh Liberals, showing only a limited enthusiasm for many of its cherished icons. He symbolised the integration of South Wales into the international capitalist order, recognisably Welsh but seeking to express this nationality on a world stage.[89] The second successful candidate in 1888 was more exotic — W. Pritchard Morgan, who became better-known for his world-wide gold-prospecting activities. Although nominally a Liberal, he was opposed at his first contest by a more orthodox exponent of that creed, but elected with the help of considerable expenditure, plus some Conservative and, more importantly, some Labour support.[90] Pritchard Morgan claimed to be a Labour candidate, a view welcomed, ironically, by Hardie who suggested that he had been elected 'on a good labour programme'.[91] This response should be assessed in the context of Hardie's Mid-Lanark experiences. In 1912, he recollected that:

great was my joy when I read that a Radical-Labour candidate who had himself been a miner was in the field ... I knew nothing about the man; but he was fighting the official Liberal and that, in those days, was good enough for me, and so in the name of the newly-formed Scottish Labour Party, I sent him a telegram wishing him success and regretted that the distance prevented me from coming to speak for him.[92]

Most critically, Pritchard Morgan was opposed by the newly-elected Thomas; from then on the two 'Liberal members' never ran a joint campaign. This was not just a question of ideological disparities. Thomas's style — the businessman in politics — led him to develop his own organisation and his successes were based on 'Thomas' rather than Liberal machinery. Official Merthyr Liberalism languished. This decay and the continuing labour tradition gave the ILP some hopes. By 1897, a branch had been established in Merthyr; in nearby Aberdare, there already existed a Socialist Society affiliated to the SDF.[93] That summer a local activist could react hopefully to rumours that Pritchard Morgan might retire — 'of course, our ILP membership are not strong, but a deal of propaganda work had been done hereabouts'. Already that summer, the Merthyr and Dowlais Party had held about twelve meetings and the Aberdare Socialists had had the assistance of a SDF organiser for three days.[94] Yet it was the coal lockout of the following year which dramatically increased the ILP's presence. Hardie secured massive publicity with huge revivalist style meetings, his passionate denunciations of coalowners, civil authorities, and Lib-Lab leaders.[95] He viewed these new listeners with enthusiasm, and prophesied that the ILP's hold would not be shaken easily — 'a very few years would revolutionise the whole situation'.[96] He wrote euphorically to David Lowe: 'we are having a kind of royal procession here — I am certain some good is being done'.[97] Propaganda was fortified by more material benefits. A fund opened in the *Labour Leader* to aid strikers and their dependents raised £345, and Hardie successfully solicited cocoa from Cadbury's, tea from Liptons and soup from G. Foster Clark.[98] Support was provided by the ILP organiser Willie Wright, himself an ex-miner. His reports to Head Office indicate a rapid proliferation of branches in South Wales, especially around Merthyr and in the Rhondda.[99] The already existing Merthyr branch claimed 278 members by August 1898; when South Wales branches met the following month, thirty-one were represented. But this growth was just a bubble. Within fifteen months, all but nine branches had vanished.[100] This was hardly surprising. The miners' defeat put an end to the intense agitation and Wright was eventually withdrawn from the area, a victim of the ILP's chronic cash problems. New recruits had been excused membership fees whilst the lockout continued; a reversal of this would have an obvious impact. Perhaps, most crucially with the end of the confrontation, old Liberal sentiments could regain much of their hold. Yet in some places, the ILP presence had been clearly strengthened by the year's events, and nowhere more so than in Merthyr with its distinct economic and political configurations.[101]

Yet it is important to avoid exaggerating ILP strength. By August 1899, Llew Francis, a Penydarren barber could only apologise to Penny about affiliation fees: 'I am sorry that I cannot send any at present. The Financial Position of the Branches generally is very bad'.[102] The poverty of the ILP branches did not prohibit moves being made towards some sort of Labour candidature. Such thoughts had occurred to Hardie during the lockout: 'Merthyr, it seems to me is a seat to be won'. It would need someone who reflected the cultural distinctiveness of South Wales: 'I think I know ... a Welsh-speaking Welshman who could win it'. But the attempt should not be a strictly ILP enterprise:

I would like to see a Conference called not only of the delegates from the ILP branches, but from all the big collieries in the Merthyr Division to discuss the advisability of running a candidate.[103]

Through 1899 and into 1900, local ILP members attempted to interest trade unionists in a Labour candidate. There was always a fear that initiatives would be embraced and then suffocated by Liberalism,[104] yet the hope of developing trades councils afforded a valuable objective for ILP pressure. One was formed in Aberdare during 1899 with ILP members amongst its most prominent members; a second was resurrected for Merthyr and Dowlais.[105] There were other straws in the wind. A contest for miners' agent in Aberdare was won by Charles Butt Stanton of the ILP; the party was establishing a credible presence in the affairs of the recently formed South Wales Miners' Federation.[106] Although the Miners' were numerically dominant, the continuing grip of Lib-Labism meant that other smaller unions tended to take the initiative. Craft union representatives took forward positions in the early days of the Aberdare Council,[107] while a further significant element was the presence of the newly formed Workers' Union at the Dowlais and Cyfartha ironworks. Here employers were fervently anti-union and low wages were prevalent, but a boom had brought 1300 men into the union by the end of 1899. In January 1900, a local ILPer and Irishman Joe Cauhlin was appointed as the union's organiser;[108] he was to play a significant role in the negotiations that brought Hardie to Merthyr.[109]

Such events, although harbingers of later Labour strength, indicated little about the immediate prospects. When the NAC considered the situation in a range of constituencies at the end of May 1900, they characterised the reports from Merthyr as 'vague and unsatisfactory', and Hardie was asked to clarify the situation on a forthcoming visit to South Wales.[110]

Two months later, Merthyr clearly counted as a major hope of returning Hardie. Glasier, now Party Chairman, was anxious to find Hardie a winnable seat:

We all feel that Hardie has a claim to the best constituency that we can offer him and ... that it is the utmost importance to the Party that he should be returned.

He asked Francis about the situation in Merthyr especially the attitude of 'the Trade Unions and miners' leaders'.[111] Three days later, Hardie elaborated on the situation to the rest of the NAC, emphasising that local ILPers were working through the Trades Council in pursuit of a Labour candidate. His own name had been mentioned, and he preferred it to the other possibility, Preston. The NAC, now encouraged, instructed Penny to urge the Party activists to push a candidature in such a way that if the Trades Council withdrew from direct sponsorship, the party could run its own man and still secure backing from a sympathetic Trades Council.[112] Both Glasier and Penny wrote in these terms to Francis,[113] with Glasier keeping Hardie in touch with the manoeuvres.[114]

But Hardie's emergence as a Merthyr Labour candidate was far from a straightforward matter. Some Party leaders, despite their advocacy of his claims, and their tactical dealings with Merthyr activists had some doubts about its wisdom. Only a few days after advocating Hardie's claims to Merthyr, Glasier sounded a note of caution to the prospective candidate, uring the preferability of Preston 'since the war has apparently brought great prosperity to the South Wales Miners'.[115] The principal difficulties lay not in the doubts of the ILP leaders, but in the complexities of local labour organisations. Matters moved very slowly; by September 21, with the election already called, Hardie seemed to inform Francis that he had abandoned hope of Merthyr:

I have decided to accept Preston. It is not likely now that Merthyr will succeed in putting forward a Labour candidate, in which case your wisest policy would be to defeat Pritchard Morgan, and thus leave the way open for a good Labour man at the next election. He is one of the most dangerous types the House of Commons contains.[116]

But now ILPers in Merthyr staged their coup. The day after Hardie's disclaimer, a critical and singular conference was held bringing together members of both Trades Councils and also representatives of groups of un-affiliated workers. Some groundwork had been done; Stanton had urged Francis to attend the meeting;[117] Penny had attempted to persuade him to take a bold line: 'It is now honestly Preston or Merthyr. My advice is to go in and win. Saturday's conference must invite Hardie and so leave the onus of decision with him'.[118] Enthusiasm was backed by some degree of socialist organ-isation. An earlier meeting of thirty ILPers and sympathisers had fully dis-cussed the candidature problem — and in Penny's cryptic phrase, 'a course of action agreed upon'.[119] But many participants in this Abernant Conference seemed to be committed to other candidates. At least some members of the Aberdare Trades Council favoured Tom Mann; this sentiment was allegedly not reciprocated by some of their counterparts in Merthyr and Dowlais who advocated the Welsh Miners' leader, Tom Richards. Others from Penrhiwceiber backed his colleague, William Brace and were committed to supporting a SWMF member. The ILPer, Stanton, had his backers on the Merthyr Trades Council. Some one hundred miners from Mountain Ash met prior to the Abernant Conference and decided to back Brace's claims over those of Richards and Stanton.[120] In such a situation, where the claims of nationality and of miners' representation complicated political divisions, it seemed unlikely that the Conference would reach any clear decision, let alone decide to nominate Hardie, an outsider already apparently committed to another constituency.

The Conference's discussions, under the chairmanship of an ILPer, Enoch Archer, were complex.[121] An earlier meeting had decided that a labour candidate should be run and that constituent organisations should decide on nominations. Archer refused to re-open the question of principle, despite claims by some delegates that they lacked authorisation for either nominating or voting. Most critically, however, a dispute arose about the method of voting. John Powell, a Mountain Ash representative who would support Brace, argued in favour of a card vote.[122] This provoked heated arguments, with Cauhlin prominent in pushing for an independent candidate, and one colliery delegate hinting darkly at the manipulatory intentions of the ILP: 'there were a few present representing only a dozen or so who wanted to rule the meeting'. An observer emphasised the critical importance of this dispute:

this proved the crux of the whole question, the representatives of small lodges of tradesmen on both sides of the mountain being apparently determined to carry their nominee, while the representatives of the colliers especially those from Mountain Ash and Penrhiwceiber who have not joined the Trades Council insisted on the voting being in proportion to representation.

It was decided, on a show of hands, that the selection of a candidate should be by the same method, and several delegates, allegedly representing 12,000 colliers, left the conference.[123] Attempts to prevent further discussion were declared out of order by the Chairman; his own views were made clear: 'it would be far better to lose at the poll than not to contest the seat'. ILP activists then pushed their case, Stanton quoting a telegram from Penny that a near-unanimous vote for Hardie would be likely to produce financial support from the NAC. Not without further recrimination, the remaining delegates voted on a range of possible candidates.[124] Several abstained; one voted for J. W. Evans, a Hirwaun solicitor, the earlier departure of many colliers' delegates was reflected in the votes for Brace and Richards — none and three respectively; twelve voted for Hardie. An attempt was then made to squash the candidature because of the small number in favour, but the remaining delegates came together to defeat this by thirty-two votes to seven.

While these complex manoeuvres were taking place, Hardie, Glasier and Penny were attempting to co-ordinate the ILP campaign in London. At first, the news from Merthyr made Hardie reluctant to accept the invitation; he was concerned about the number of abstentions and about the low support from miners' delegates.[125] He left with Penny to speak in Preston and wired Glasier that he had accepted the invitation to fight in Lancashire. It looked like the end for Merthyr: 'We wire poor Merthyr. What a disappointment to our chaps there. They have worked for him so splendidly.'[126] But then on 26 September, there came the news from Preston that Hardie had agreed to be nominated also for Merthyr.[127]

Although he had been attracted earlier by the prospect of contesting Merthyr, his involvement now seemed very much of an afterthought. He visited Merthyr on 28 September, dashed back to Preston and then returned on the eve of the poll, October 1, following his Preston defeat. It was hardly the court-ship of an enthusiastic candidate, and underlined his position as an outsider in a Welsh constituency.[128] Yet his position was far from hopeless; we have already noted the complexities of Merthyr politics. These gave Hardie oppor-tunities as well as presenting difficulties. National party officials provided some resources; the enthusiasm of the local activists was supplemented by the ser-vices of two NAC members, Joseph Burgess and S. D. Shallard. The singular relationship between the two sitting members allowed some support to be generated. Thomas's initial response was to remain neutral; he claimed that the Abernant selection was unrepresentative; if Hardie's backing had been more broadly based, he would have supported him.[129] Hardie's initial visit to Merthyr produced a claim that Thomas was 'the better of two bad ones'.[130] As the campaign went on, the latter became more positive about Hardie. He was: 'an absolutely sincere and honest man who had only the interests of the country at heart'.[131] Other participants suggested the viability of a Thomas —Hardie alliance. Enoch Archer who had been so crucial in ensuring Har-die's nomination seconded a resolution of support for Thomas;[132] Richard Bell and James Holmes, of the Railway Servants, backed Thomas, following his attitude to the recently ended Taff Vale stoppage;[133] John Davies the Dowlais Miners' Agent, a strong opponent of Hardie at Abernant eventually supported him:

Now that they had had such a clear expression from Mr. Hardie of his democratic prin-ciples, no Labour Leader and no Liberal could fail to agree with every plank in Mr. Hardie's platform.[134]

The development of such rapport was paralleled by a deteriorating relation-ship between the two former members.[135] No doubt this was facilitated by the absence of any Conservative candidate. Thomas and Pritchard Morgan argued over the issue of the war[136] and over the latter's frequent foreign travels; the latter pictured his 'opponents' as: 'a combination of the Cambrian Collieries and Cadbury's Cocoa'.[137] The complete breakdown of relationships between the two Liberals and their dependence on their own private organisations cer-tainly gave an Independent Labour candidate opportunities, but there remain-ed, beyond the personal antipathies, the question of sensitive issues.

The emergence of Hardie's nomination was a symptom of a desire for labour representation; the candidate after victory claimed that one crucial fac-tor was: 'the genuine desire which the great strike left for direct labour representation'.[138] From one viewpoint, the aftermath of the strike damaged Hardie's chances. According to one estimate, 3,500 miners had been disfranchised because of their receipt of relief. But the events of 1898 certainly played their part, and although some trade unionists had opposed Hardie's original selection, no Labour leaders seem to have opposed him once he was in the field. More recent developments helped to emphasise the need for labour representation. Some local railwaymen had been involved a month earlier in the Taff Vale stoppage, the creation of the SWMF, whatever the national and sectional prejudices, was a massive step in the progress of Welsh Labour; more vague but also more immediately, Pritchard Morgan's business interests seemed to threaten local labour interests. His claim that he would invest in Chinese coal could be seen as threatening a Welsh export market; his activities seemed designed to subvert Merthyr living standards by backing the competitiveness of cheap foreign labour. He migh proclaim the claims of Welsh nationality but this hardly seemed an adequate response to the emerging trade-union consciousness of Merthyr workers.[140]

This emphasis was significant but it was far from the whole of Hardie's appeal. He might inform the Merthyr electorate that 'he was a Socialist and rather proud of the fact'.[141] Much of his attraction, however, was a traditional Radical one. In particular, Hardie retrospectively emphasised the attractions of an anti-war position for a sizeable proportion of the Merthyr electorate; the implications of the district's tradition were apparently clear:

Henry Richards of fragrant memory who represented Merthyr ... and who was known as the Apostle of Peace ... had so impregnated his followers with his principles that they hated and abhorred the war from start to finish. The moment Mr Pritchard Morgan declared himself a supporter of the war, and an Imperialist, his doom was sealed.[142]

This diagnosis was backed by other ILP participants. It was claimed that 'the fight turned mainly upon the War';[143] Pritchard Morgan allegedly doomed his cause by issuing a poster — 'Vote for Keir Hardie and D. A. Thomas, both pro-Boers', and 'three days later a majority of the electorate took his advice'.[144]

This explanation fits in with the traditional view of a pacific Wales, contrasting with a jingoistic England; it hardly squares with Glasier's earlier reservations about the popularity of the war in the valleys. Jingoism was certainly not absent from Merthyr — earlier in the year, the ILP rooms in the town had had their windows broken.[145] Yet Hardie was able to draw on a body of opinion, what he described as 'the healthy anti-war sentiment which animated all the better-class Liberals'.[146] The internationalist tradition of Richards was important, but Hardie's appeal to traditional Radical emotions went far beyond the war issue. His eve-of-poll meeting proclaimed his support for disestablishment and the local veto and his opposition to capital punishment.[147] Such appeals were bound to rally Radical support, especially as Pritchard Morgan had acquired the unsolicited support of some licensees.[148]

Hardie was able to secure support from a combination of trade unionists and Radicals. The former might support him regardless of his position on the war, the latter would be attracted by his fidelity to Radical principles. Essentially the contest centred around the theme of who was the more fitting partner of Thomas as a representative of Merthyr. Pritchard Morgan's claims were increasingly incongruous, and although an outsider, Hardie seemed in many ways to conform more to the town's traditions. Once again within this distinctively Welsh setting, there were parallels with other early ILP campaigns, as a divided Liberalism laid itself open to ILP attempts to seize the Radical mantle. From this viewpoint, at least, the ILP position in Merthyr was stronger than in some other centres, not just because of the idiosyncracies of local Liberalism, but because of the abject weakness of Conservatism. The absence of any Tory challenge meant that no Liberal could hope to deflect an ILP candidate by claiming that a vote for him would let in the old enemy. Disgruntled Radicals were free to consider ILP claims on their merits. The result of such considerations was apparent in the pattern of voting (see Table 35).

Table 35. *Merthyr 1900*

	Total	Plumpers	Splits	
Thomas	8,598	2,070	Thomas/Hardie	4,437
Hardie	5,745	867	Thomas/Morgan	2,091
Pritchard Morgan	4,004	1,412	Hardie/Morgan	441

Many of the factors that aided Hardie — the lack of official Liberal machinery, the personality clash between the old members, the continuities between Merthyr traditions and Hardie's own Radicalism — did not carry implications for the replacment of Liberalism by Independent Labour in South Wales as a whole. Even the fact that Hardie's success was based on an independent organisation scarcely seemed unusual in Merthyr. But if Hardie's success was secured by his Radical sentiments, the heart of the initiative that brought him to Merthyr lay with trade unionists and socialists. The future prospects of the ILP and of the Labour Alliance in Merthyr and in South Wales as a whole depended on this complex interplay between the sentiments of Radicalism and the claims of Labour which could sometimes transmute into an abrasive socialism.

In the years after 1900, Hardie identified himself with dominant aspects of Welsh Radicalism, joining the Welsh Party in the Commons, working with Welsh Liberals as the Government inflamed nonconformist passions, backing the key causes of Disestablishment and Disendowment and praising Welsh culture and traditions.[149] His desire to retain independence led to his refusing an invitation from a group of Merthyr Liberals to attend a dinner with D. A. Thomas, but his refusal was couched in friendly and apologetic terms.[150]

This attempt to strengthen the links with Merthyr Radicals, founded in 1900 was important as a guarantor of Hardie's position there, but the ILP was also being strengthened by other developments which could eventually cut across an assiduous courting of Radical opinion.

The number of branches grew dramatically after 1900; in part this reflected developments within the SWMF as Lib-Lab traditions crumbled in the face of economic changes and the impatient challenge of a new generation. ILP branches and Trades Councils collaborated to mount an impressive challenge in municipal politics.[151] In Merthyr, a LRC was formed in 1903 to strengthen Hardie's position and to fight local government elections. In November 1905, all twelve Labour candidates were returned there. Even some nonconformist Ministers came to ally with the ILP, a few forfeiting their positions as a result.[152] Sometimes the distinctively ILP vote was lost in the wider rise of Labour politics — at Merthyr in 1905, there were problems because specifically ILP work was coming second to activities for other organisations.[153] But the long-term callenge to Liberalism by a Labour Alliance was unmistakable. The new men by 1906 were well on the way to control of the SWMF; they were making impressive local government gains; eventually this would lead to Liberalism being pressed on the parliamentary front. The signs in 1906 were that much of South Wales Liberalism would stand and fight Labour rather than make graceful concessions. Only in Merthyr did a dual-member seat permit a ready compromise, and the Liberal ethic in the region, with its emphasis on the shared interests of the community, denied the importance of the class claims that the Labour Alliance ventilated.

These tensions affected the Merthyr contest of 1906.[154] Although Hardie had never shrunk from attacking reactionary Liberals, he had hoped for an unopposed return along with D. A. Thomas. Certainly, during the campaign the two retiring members gave evidence of their mutual regard for one another. But at the last minute, a wealthy Cardiff shipowner, Henry Radcliffe, came forward as an unofficial Liberal. As a leading Methodist, he had abundant nonconformist support, although this was not unanimously in his favour. A few local Ministers spoke for Hardie,[155] and the Dowlais Free Church Council came out for the retiring members.[156] But Radcliffe made a strong appeal to the prejudices of Welsh Dissent.[157] One of his supporters urging Hardie to 'go back among the Scotchman'.[158] The onslaught worried Hardie. He persuaded his old minister from Cumnock to visit Merthyr and testify that charges of atheism were unfounded.[159] If Hardie could still capitalise on Radical enthusiasms, he could also attack on a more specifically Labour platform. Radcliffe's record as an employer was subject to continual attack. He was alleged to employ foreign seamen at the lowest wages in the trade and was heckled by members of the Sailors' Union. One of his meetings was abandoned in disorder.[160]

Hardie's margin as the junior member was secure enough; his campaign blended Radical and Labour appeals in different proportions from 1900, but was equally effective. Yet the contest suggested that the Radical/Labour mix would be increasingly difficult to utilise in the future as events in the industrial and political arenas conspired to drive Welsh Radicals and Welsh Labour further apart. There was a sense obviously in which Hardie's Merthyr success was a 'providential occurrence' — the peculiar nature of Merthyr Liberalism and the tortuous nomination process ensured that this was so. But at another level, he was an appropriately symbolic figure for Welsh — and more specifically Merthyr — Labour at a time of transition. He combined two bodies of sentiment which as yet in South Wales had not drifted irredeemably apart. Soon they would do so, and Hardie the Radical/Labour Member for Merthyr would be left not so much as a portent but as a memento from a dream of Radical—Labour co-operation.[161]

Dogs that did not bark

An appreciation of the factors that might have facilitated the development of strong local ILPs is heightened by an investigation of areas of weakness. Such an exercise must confront the problem of which absences indicate something significant; we need criteria for indicating which non-events might be important. A dog that fails to bark because no-one disturbs it is of little interest; one that does not bark when disturbed should provoke our interest.

The ILP failed to put down strong roots in most places during its first decade. Its weakness in country areas and small towns formed part of a much more persistent failure on the part of British Labour to develop strong rural bases. The sharp contrast in this respect with some other European societies is attributable perhaps to the relatively small agrarian sector in this first industrial society. Here, with some Celtic exceptions, there was no peasantry squeezed by the intruding market and able to generate a significant agrarian radicalism. Equally, the early and extensive industrial development meant that the surplus rural population could be sucked into the cities, avoiding the growth of a vast reservoir of landless rural labourers.

When attention shifts to the ILP's urban failures, the cases become more significant. Here the focus is on communities which Labour came eventually to dominate, and yet the early penetration of the ILP was very uneven. The contrasts between Leicester and Nottingham, or Merthyr and most of South Wales have been noted. But the problem of London loomed largest. The sheer size of the conurbation made a significant dent in the party's credibility as the natural representative of labour, and failure in the metropolis underlined the organisation's provincial ethos.

Although London was a special case, it is tempting perhaps to develop an argument that the ILP's urban failures anticipated the much more recent discrepancy in Labour's urban strength between North and South. This interpretation would be dubious. The party was generally weak in the relatively rural and small-town South, but it also counted for little in some industrial areas. We have seen how miners' unions with strong Lib-Lab traditions could deflect an ILP challenge. These were far from unique. The pottery workers of North Staffordshire remained largely committed to Liberalism until 1914. Elsewhere ILP weakness was attributable to other sentiments. Small-scale manufacturing and Chamberlainite dominance combined to make Birmingham a barren place for the ILP; here the party seemed unable to profit from Liberal weakness. Perhaps the most illuminating and best-documented case of provincial marginality is Sheffield where, for a brief period, a rapid breakthrough seemed possible, but this was not realised, and in some senses the development of Labour politics in Sheffield lagged behind events in most industrial cities.

'Godless' London

Early ILP propagandists continually contrasted the party's strength in some provincial towns with its failure to make headway in London. Attempts were made to remedy this. A London campaign was launched in the summer of 1894, with propaganda aimed at the self-respecting artisan, those 'found in churches and temperance societies' who would 'form the backbone of the Labour movement'.[1] But early hopes soon faded. The ILP intervened, with disastrous results, in the LCC elections of March 1895. The *Labour Leader* reflected ruefully that 'each branch selected its candidate in haphazard fashion, and in most cases the election campaign was badly organised, and loosely conducted'.[2]

   This lack of impact was underlined by the events of that year's general election. The ILP fought only one seat in the LCC area — Fulham, where it obtained its lowest vote. This choice implies perhaps a certain lack of organisation and perception. It was a safe Conservative seat dominated by clerks and artisans, hardly the likely location of a socialist upsurge.[3] There was almost a second ILP candidate in Limehouse, but here the party withdrew in the face of financial difficulties and local hostility.[4] Just across the LCC boundary, however, there was Keir Hardie's West Ham South, in many ways simply a continuation of London. But its contrasting ILP strength was more apparent than real. In the second half of the decade, the general weakness of the party was even more acute. The LCC elections of March 1898 produced an official verdict even more damning than three years earlier — the party's spokesman could not 'pretend to discover in the results ... any indication of the growth of public sympathy towards avowed Socialism in London ... Had a number of candidates been put forward with a programme in favour of devastating London with cholera, they would probably have received no less support'.[5] By 1899, it appears that the party had barely 500 financial members in the capital.[6] Individual branches were small — in 1898, only St Pancras, Fulham and Woolwich were presented in the party press as being within reach of 100 members[7] — and it was only in 1905 that the ILP achieved 20 branches again,[8] a level of organisation that it had claimed a decade earlier. From then on, it was a different story with the London ILP beginning to benefit, although somewhat uncertainly, from the party's national expansion.

Analysis of this initial failure can begin with an assessment of London's industrial base. This possessed some distinctive features. Traditional trades were pursued in small units of production, well-established in the inner areas and often with small, but economically effective unions. Tailors, cigar makers and barge builders might produce occasionally a significant individual, but they could not form the nucleus of a class-conscious, let alone a socialist, movement. At the other end of the industrial spectrum, there were the massive numbers of unskilled, often casual labourers with whom the task of organisation, often in the face of employer hostility, presented major difficulties. Unemployment in the years before 1914 was a malaise which affected London workers more deeply and more persistently. However, the organisation of the dockers and gasworkers of East London provides some central motifs of the New Unionism, although many of the organisational gains made at this period were subsequently lost. Indeed, it is debatable how far London dockers and gasworkers went along with New Unionism, *despite* the socialist claims made by several of their leaders.[9] Overall, there was a lack of large-scale manufacturing industry of the type that could provide a basis for unionisation and class consciousness. This was one respect in which West Ham tended to diverge from the general London pattern. The borough had more permissive pollution regulations than in the LCC area and included not only docks and gasworks but also chemical works and the Stratford Locomotive Works of the Great Eastern Railway.[10]

The peculiarities of the industrial structure were not the only distinctive features. Undoubtedly, working-class London was primarily an areligious world in the late nineteenth century. Certainly, care must be taken not to exaggerate the difference in this respect between London workers and some of their provincial counterparts, but two features should be noted. There was a lack in most working-class London districts of the established Dissenting artisanate that provided a leadership for trade unionism, Radicalism, and then Labour politics, in some other industrial centres. Even when such a leadership no longer adhered formally to religious Dissent, it could be affected profoundly in its idiom, London had no such tradition — in so far as a working class leadership evinced a style, it was that of secularism. The lack of involvement in community institutions epitomised by the epithet 'Godless London' was symptomatic of a more fundamental feature — the comparative lack of settled working-class communities which the ILP had been able to penetrate elsewhere. London workers tended to move house relatively frequently in search of jobs — or if they continued to live in one place, then to travel considerable distances to work. Both situations militated against regular involvement in political and other institutions. This situation was highlighted by the comment of one disillusioned ILPer:

London is not a town, it is a nation. The people within it are stranger and more indifferent to each other than if they had been parted to the farthest ends of the land. No common spirit or sense of civic cohesion, such as we find in Bradford, Manchester, Glasgow or Aberdeen quickens their interest in the common well-being. The unceasing stir, the vastness, the apparently infinite unwieldiness of the place, seems to appal and stupefy the inhabitants.[12]

If these were some of the distinctive characteristics of the economic and social structure, did these provide, or deny political 'space' into which a new party might move? The sheer size of the capital produced from 1885 a significant number of working-class constituencies — a contrast with many other cities where electoral boundaries tended to produce less homogeneous units.[13] The geographical mobility of many London workers, allied to the registration labyrinth, meant that electorates in several working-class seats were small.[14] Nevertheless, the class homogeneity of what electorate there was, meant that traditional parties faced the task of meeting demands without being able to rely on local bourgeois leaderships.

Undoubtedly, class was in one sense a crucial factor in London politics from 1885. How could it be otherwise with the stark contrast between East End and West enshrined in respectable literature and musical hall favourites alike? Such appreciation of social differences did not necessitate of course a solidaristic class consciousness of the type that socialists hoped for, but it was a stark contrast that had to be absorbed into political strategies. Under the new boundaries the affluent London seats were overwhelmingly Conservative, and Liberal strength was confined to working-class neighbourhoods. But London politics did not divide dichotomously into Conservative affluent and Liberal working-class supporters. The first half of the distinction was essentially valid, but the second was not.[15] Many working-class electors were ready to vote Conservative, especially in 1895 and 1900, and Liberal difficulties were compounded by a fundamental tension within their own ranks, between bourgeois moderate Liberals — frequently absentees — and local working-class Radicals.

The continuing strength of working-class Conservatism was significant. It rested to some degree on the demands made by traditional trades for protection of their privileges, whilst the small size of many electorates meant that the benefits offered by local employer-candidates could loom particularly large. Most important of all, there was the anti-alien, or to be more precise anti-Jewish, agitation in the East End, where Conservative spokesmen allied themselves with the protectionist sentiments of many trade unionists, and helped to develop a tradition of xenophobia in local politics. Nevertheless, the impact of working-class Conservatism in London was limited. It was not fuelled by the religious animosities of Lancashire and the West of Scotland, it failed to spawn a mass organisation and it did not attract influential working class-leaders. It subsisted on the largesse offered to voters by Conservative candidates, the hostility of sections of the indigenous population towards immigrants and on Liberal deficiencies.[16] Was there then a political space to the left of the Conservatives that could increase over time with Liberal defeats?

Liberalism's survival in London, and the blunting of any Independent Labour challenge depended on a Liberal capacity to satisfy the demands of working-class electors. As in other regions, evidence about their success in achieving this was mixed.[17] The Liberals made major advances in London in 1892 and 1906, although the earlier one was eradicated three years later. The existence of considerable trade union support for Liberalism is undoubted. Lib-Labs represented London seats and trade union branches provided funds for Liberal candidates. The style of politics on the LCC also aided the containment of Labour within a broad Liberal framework, since what mattered here was the Progressive label, a proposition admitted by the ILP with its shift towards compromise in the LCC elections of 1901.[18] The attractions of Progressivism were apparent in the political trajectory of John Burns. His experiences as a Progressive on the LCC provided a crucial element in his hostility to Independent Labour initiatives. His tendency to interpret all situations in terms of the categories and options that he was familiar with, helped to produce a gradual estrangement from the mainstream of Labour politics. It could be argued plausibly that Liberalism was successfully containing any threat from Labour, and also capturing seats from the Conservatives.

This would be a one-sided analysis. There were forces that could subvert over time the Liberal position. Certainly Liberals held their position well in Bethnal Green where traditional trades were strong,[19] and also in Battersea where John Burns's rapprochement with Liberalism left a distinctive mark on local politics.[20] But in many places the foundations of the Liberal position were weak. Much local organisation was limited. In some places, by 1900, Liberalism no longer existed as an organised force and local parties were resurrected only with the help of money brought from outside the area. Such investments were likely to continue only so long as success obtained or was likely; when funds stopped, the organisation was likely to fold. The Radical Clubs, so often the principal local standard-bearers could be in a state of warfare with the central Liberal machine, a warfare that could lead to outright independence. Here then was an opportunity for advocates of Independent Labour.

The ILP however was not an automatic heir to this opportunity. When George Lansbury finally quit official Liberalism after the 1892 election, he moved, not to the embryonic ILP but to the already well-established SDF. This latter party expanded significantly in London during the 1890s. Its strength in London has been noted frequently, and explanations have tended to stress the continuity with London's Secular/Radical tradition, and to complement this by noting the virtual absence of working-class religious dissent. This emphasis has its place, but any understanding of SDF strength should appreciate two other points. The rift between bourgeois Liberalism and working-class Radicalism came early in London, precipitated no doubt by the growth of homogenous working-class seats. The SDF was available as an alternative and had no real rival. Similarly, in London, as in Lancashire, the stereotype of the inflexible, dogmatic SDF was not an accurate representation of the reality. The London SDF did not begin and end with Hyndman. Activists like Will Thorne and Lansbury were spokesmen for working-class communities of a type that would have joined the ILP in many cases.[21] But in East London they joined the SDF because it was an available instrument, and because on the ground it could fulfil the same role. ILP official propaganda about its London prospects claimed that many 'do not sympathise with much that is taught in the name of Socialism from the SDF platforms' — but this was to present the whole party through the distorting prism of Hyndman's idiosyncrasies. Who, after all, could have been more like the conventional ILPer than George Lansbury?

In London, however, the ILP found itself marginal to the development of independent political action. The attempt of Burgess to form a London ILP in the summer of 1892[22] left little positive legacy and the organisation tended to be identified with disreputable or distrusted figures such as Aveling and Mahon.[23] Aveling's reputation was by then widely known, while Mahon inevitably raised the spectre of Champion. Few significant spokesmen for London Labour felt attracted to the ILP in preference to Lib-Labism or the SDF.

Yet, it was West Ham that provided the ILP with its first parliamentary spokesman and in doing so gave the Labour movement a celebrated symbol — Hardie's arrival at the Commons in a two-horse brake, complete with cornet player, tweed suit, and in some accounts, cloth cap.[24] It was a sharp contrast with the sartorial conformity of Lib-Lab MPs. West Ham South was not a specifically ILP victory, since it occurred six months before the national party was formed, and without the support of any local ILP. But it was an achievement, as significant as the failure at Mid-Lanark, although like Mid-Lanark the nature of the significance remains a matter of debate.

West Ham South was an unequivocally working-class seat — the less salubrious part of a borough described by an Edwardian commentator as 'that great city of the poor, lying like a flat, unlovely wilderness of mean streets'.[25] There was, by London standards, a heavy industrial presence, and the Gasworkers remained relatively strong even in the depressed mid-nineties. The seat had followed a common London pattern — Liberal in 1885, but a Conservative gain the following year.[26] The Liberals' search for a candidate highlighted the tensions within the Radical-Liberal coalition. The West Ham Liberals were divided. One section provided a characteristic response to the problem of Liberal representation in a working-class London seat in the shape of J. Hume Webster, a City financier. His wealth funded registration work and was displayed in the expeditions to Radical Clubs. He expressed sympathy with local New Unionist initiatives. But other West Ham Liberals opposed him.

Not only were some suspicious of an affluent outsider, they also were unhappy about his sympathy with strikes, or his lack of enthusiasm for temperance. The critics supported a second Liberal aspirant — J. Spencer Curwen, but he abandoned the struggle in January 1890. His resignation letter to the press highlighted the forces opposed to Webster who had 'won not the support of a single Nonconformist minister. He has given serious offence to the temperance party ... The Irish National League and the Labour Electoral Association refuse to have anything to do with him'. Furthermore, Curwen believed that 'the cry for a direct representation of Labour which was strong in 1885 will be revived in 1892'.[27] There were local trade unionists, of course, who agreed strongly with Curwen's last comment, and Will Thorne and his Canning Town SDF branch were becoming a significant force. Thorne could hardly hope to unite these disparate elements however, although local Labour was beginning to make its mark municipally[28] and the ambition and flexibility nurtured in such success could help in securing an alternative candidate.

Hardie appeared as someone who could bring these disparate elements together. His continuing Radical style, his intervention at Mid-Lanark, and his challenge to the TUC Old Guard were all relevant to the West Ham situation with its fissiparous Liberalism and the growing self-assertiveness of Labour. In March 1890, he entered the field. His early statements demonstrated his Radical pedigree. He referred to Gladstone as 'their Grand Old Leader', and emphasised his commitments to Home Rule and temperance reform; these claims were complemented by advocacy of the eight hour day and a stress on the need for direct Labour representation in parliament.[29]

Such planks were firmly within the Radical-Liberal tradition, although some of Hardie's early remarks were ambiguous. He used Gladstone as authority to claim that 'only one who was a bona-fide labourer could effectively deal with the Labour problem',[30] and argued for the necessity of a new party. This would be composed of 'Liberal representatives of Labour'.[31] Such planks brought Hardie the support of West Ham Radicals and a clash seemed likely at the polls between the Liberal financier and the Radical Labour man, when the situation was altered dramatically by Webster's suicide in January 1892. In some respects this simplified Hardie's position. He was no longer vulnerable to the charge that he would let the Tory in but it increased the complexity of his relationship with official Liberalism. Local Liberal critics attempted to run the defeated 1886 candidate, Joseph Leicester, a Lib-Lab whilst Hardie's position on his relationship with the Liberals remained unclear. At a conference of Radical and Labour organisations soon after Webster's death Hardie suggested some sort of independence. When asked 'Would he join the Liberal and Radical party?', he replied that 'he expected to form an independent labour party'. The exemplar was clear — 'he would endeavour to follow and copy the tactics of the late Mr. Parnell and Mr. Biggar to push labour questions to the front'.[32]

When the campaign proper began, Hardie described himself as the 'Labour,

Radical and Home Rule candidate'. This strategy involved courting the various blocs of Radicals; the Temperance lobby whose newspaper backed Hardie strongly, the Irish, and the Labour interest. It also involved finally disposing of Joseph Leicester. Hardie hinted that his own candidature, was regarded more favourably in the upper echelons of the Liberal Party[34] but his success in securing local support was perhaps more crucial. One local Radical journal urged Leicester to withdraw, claiming that 'all those whose support is worth having are backing up Keir Hardie, and it is mainly the riff-raff, the rag-tag and bobtail that are supporting you'.[35] Leicester subsequently withdrew after consultation with Francis Schnadhorst, leaving Hardie to fight the sitting Conservative member, a local employer.[36]

Hardie's campaign was energetic, with a rash of meetings and a trade union procession.[37] He secured the backing of the local Nonconformist Council, who recommended him as 'most admirably suited both in character and principle to represent the cause of national righteousness', and also the support of the Irish National League.[38] How could it be otherwise when he backed the Newcastle Programme with special emphases on Home Rule, the Direct Veto and Sunday Closing? In the field of labour reforms, especially in the emphasis on unemployment, he introduced more distinctive notes, advocating the eight hour day, Home Colonies for the Unemployed and the public ownership of major utilities.[39] This labour emphasis generated strong support from local trade union branches, and from the flexible Thorne and other West Ham SDFers. In the poorer wards dominated by dockers and gasworkers, especially in Canning Town, enthusiasm on polling day was intense. A sympathetic observer noted:

Straight from their work, these men came — dockers from the quays and coalies from everywhere. There was no stopping to spruce up or wash faces, or anything else — the first business in the minds of these men was evidently to poll for Keir Hardie.[40]

Here, in this contemporary account, there is perhaps a hint of labour on the march: a body of organised workers, voting for a Labour standardbearer with local socialists doing much of the active work. That was the future significance of Hardie's victory, but much of the groundwork had been carried out in the world of tradition Radical causes — a well-tried tune for which Hardie could provide a convenient score. It was a success that was intelligible also within the constraints and opportunities provided by London politics — the difficulties faced by Liberals in working-class areas, the filling of political space by a flexible SDF and Hardie's ability at this juncture to fuse the various Radical and Labour tendencies.

Three years later, his ability to achieve this synthesis had declined. The formation of a national ILP, its electoral opposition to Liberal candidates, and Hardie's dominant role in the new party all helped to separate him from official Liberalism, a gulf that was widened by his attacks on the Liberal Government's attitude towards unemployment and other labour questions.

This situation created difficulties in West Ham: Curwen wrote informing Hardie of the situation, and emphasised that moderate Liberals were 'much pained at your failure to support the government in the many good things they are unquestionably doing'.[41] It was hardly surprising that there were rumours of a Liberal candidate, but none emerged.[42] Yet many Liberals were reluctant to support him — one journal commented that whereas in 1892 'he was ... regarded as an extreme Radical with perhaps a little hankering after Socialism', now he was seen as 'a Socialist who sometimes votes with the Radicals in the House and sometimes splits the Liberal vote'.[43]

Local temperance and nonconformist groups were now often reluctant to support him because he saw Disestablishment as less crucial than unemployment and poverty[44] and his one local press supporter stigmatised the head of the local Temperance Union as 'a determined foe of trade unionism'.[45] More seriously perhaps, Hardie had abandoned advocacy of the local veto and now favoured municipalisation of the drink trade — a concession perhaps to SDF sentiment.[46]

Difficulties were also experienced with the Irish. Again Hardie strongly urged the priority of the Labour interest: 'Do you say that it is a cause of Home Rule first? I can understand an Irishman in Connemara saying that, but here in West Ham, it is Labour first'.[47] Local priests held a meeting of Irish voters at which Hardie was attacked for opposing Morley at Newcastle, for his general hostility to the Liberal Party, and because of his socialism.[48] Land nationalisation would destroy the security of Catholic schools and churches. Eventually one of the priests claimed that Hardie 'was a bigger enemy to Ireland' than his Unionist opponent, 'they were bound to put him out'.[49] Hardie claimed subsequently that the Home Rule furore was not the central issue, and that the crucial factor had been the readiness of local priests to support Conservative proposals on voluntary schools.[50] Yet although the clerical directive was seen by contemporaries as important, its contribution is debatable. It is unclear how many Irishmen had backed Hardie in 1892; the Irish vote in London was notoriously difficult to organise, and Hardie still had Parnellite support in 1895.[51]

There remained the Labour element in Hardie's 1892 support, but even here there were difficulties. The tide of New Unionism had ebbed, and Labour's municipal representation in West Ham had suffered a setback.[52] Hardie's espousal of the cause of the unemployment had won him sympathy, but it was the sympathy of a group who would not have much electoral significance. The solidarity of labour seemed less than in 1892. Sugar workers promised support for the Conservative on the sugar bounties' question.[53] Havelock Wilson of the Sailors' had backed Hardie in 1892 but now telegraphed his opposition. Hardie believed that this intervention had led members of Wilson's union to vote Tory.[54] In this situation, Hardie's independence was clearer than in 1892. He informed one meeting that 'he saw no solution for the great social and labour problem short of Socalism';[55] and he depicted the

Commons as composed of rich Liberals and rich Tories — 'both alike in their attitude towards the claims of Labour'.[56]

The electoral register also worked against Hardie. Webster had provided funds for registration. Since 1892 all this had ceased.[57] The old strongholds remained, but they were an inadequate basis. Hardie lost decisively against a popular local employer who held no public meeting, but conveyed a vague impression that he was in favour of social measures of a not too precise kind[58] (see Table 36). Whether the low polls represented Liberal or Catholic

Table 36. *West Ham South 1892 and 1895*

1892 (turnout 59.8 per cent)		*1895* (turnout 55.4 per cent)	
Hardie	5,268	Banes	4,750
Banes Cons	4,036	Hardie	3,975

abstentions, or the problem of workers with lengthy journeys to work finding time to vote, is unclear.[59]

Hardie's West Ham success had little to do specifically with the ILP. Indeed it illustrated rather the centrality of these elements that provided little scope for the ILP in London politics. The key aspects were a splintering but still powerful Radicalism, the weakness of middle-class Liberalism and a strong local SDF. In West Ham by the late nineties, Radicalism had declined sufficiently for a Labour Group composed of SDF, ILP and Trade Union representatives to take control of the West Ham Council.[60] This was the first Labour-controlled council anywhere, and when they were ousted three years later it was through a municipal realignment with profound implications for the future. Increased rates and public expenditure had led to the formation of a Conservative—Liberal coalition — or as a contemporary viewed it, Labour was ousted by 'a curious amalgamation of publicans and sinners, Liberals and Tories, pot-house politicians and tee-totallers'.[61] A political realignment had occurred in which the ILP were highly marginal. Hardie's links with West Ham had disappeared gradually in the late nineties as the local SDF boosted Thorne's claims — a natural choice despite ILP criticism. Thorne failed in 1900, but scored a decisive victory in 1906. He did so not as a sectarian SDFer but as a Gasworkers' and Trades Council nominee. In West Ham, the politics of the Labour Alliance dominated, but the socialist ingredient owed little to the ILP. Developments here count against the claim that somehow the ILP was the 'natural' vehicle for British socialism.

London provided one other example of an early, significant socialist development. Woolwich was a community whose very distinctiveness incorporated many of the traits that provided a basis for a strong ILP in some provincial centres. It was traditionally separate from London, with a stable and relatively skilled and unionised workforce, employed predominantly at the Arsenal. This artisanate, reflected in a high ASE membership, could provide a basis for a range of voluntary working-class institutions, most notably a high successful Co-operative Society of the type typically found in some ILP northern strongholds. Moreover, a significant proportion of Woolwich's skilled workers were immigrants from the North or Scotland, and by London standards nonconformity was strong. These factors seemed to suggest a basis for a strong Liberalism, but this was not the case. The dominance of the Arsenal in local employment produced a strong working-class Tory vote. This combination of communal elements but relatively weak Liberalism could be viewed as a promising basis for socialist growth.[62]

In 1899, the local ILP was playing a part along with the Trades Council and Co-operators in promoting local Labour candidacies — a predictable development given the moribund nature of Woolwich Liberalism. Again, it was perhaps to be expected that the Trades Council was the first one in London to affiliate to the LRC. Here then was a broadly based movement for Labour representation incorporating not only committed socialists but trades unionists, and Progressives deprived of any other instrument. It was the Trades Council that was to become the main focus of Woolwich Labour initiatives, some of which did not please ILPers.[63] There was criticism by the national ILP of the selection of Will Crooks as Labour candidate in November 1902 and there was more dissatisfaction with the nature of his successful by-election campaign, the following March. A local member of the ILP wrote to Hardie informing him that Crooks had not mentioned ILP support in his election address, although some of his backers had emphasised support from Radical and temperance bodies.[64] Local ILPers found themselves in an impasse: they decided not to issue socialist literature during the campaign: they felt that it could damage Crooks's chances 'and the work of the party so far as Woolwich was concerned would be rendered more difficult in the future, should Crooks be defeated'.[65]

In fact, Woolwich soon developed a strong local Labour party with individual members, but the bias was strongly towards the trade union side of the alliance, and the growth of individual membership made the local ILP branch increasingly marginal. Eventually the Woolwich ILP with a membership of 500 became a stronghold for the critical left, and joined the British Socialist Party.[66] The Woolwich development was in some ways much more like that in provincial centres, but the ILP did not play the crucial role. This can be attributed to the prior existence of strong trade union branches, the need for activists who would have been Lib-Labs elsewhere to compensate for Liberal weakness, and also because crucial decisions were taken at a time when the Labour Alliance was becoming an attractive option and moreover one which in Woolwich conditions would lead to the unions playing a key part.

The ILP's London weakness was a product in part of a normally unpropitious economic environment with generally weak trade unionism, and more widely the frequent absence of these community structures that would generate a range of voluntary institutions and a solidarity able to provide a basis for working-class political initiatives. Even when, as in West Ham and Woolwich, the situation seemed more promising, there were significant difficulties of timing. In West Ham, the Labour option had been taken up by a flexible and deeply rooted SDF leaving little scope for ILP intervention: in Woolwich a relatively strong ILP did develop, but at a crucial period with strong local union branches, a union-centred Labour Alliance seemed the most attractive option. Even when the characteristic London constraints were less apparent, these experiences suggest that the timing of Labour initiatives was significant for ILP prospects.

Sheffield: 'This Benighted City of Liberal-Labourism'*

This city of steel in its smoke-filled valley could serve as a symbol of the power of late Victorian capitalism. Yet here in this heavily working-class city, the ILP developed much less readily than in the woollen communities to the north. Beneath the grime, economic developments and political legacies provided powerful constraints. Sheffield paralleled both Birmingham and Liverpool in that Conservatism remained a relatively strong force; even in 1906 the Liberals held only two of the city's five constituencies.[67] Yet, in Sheffield, Liberalism remained a significant presence, with a normally secure hold on the city's two most industrialised constituencies. The leading lights of Sheffield Liberalism included A. J. Mundella, one of the city's MPs from 1868 until 1897,[68] and Henry Wilson, a Radical, nonconformist industrialist representing nearby Holmfirth. Both expressed sympathy towards demands for labour representation. The strength of local nonconformity was important; this could give a crusading zeal to local Liberalism, but it could also help to produce a stern self-help variant on the broad Liberal theme. The broad ethos could attract respectable working-class activists; it could also retain the allegiance of austere employers.

The city's politics involved a combination of popular Toryism, and a significant, if rather old-fashioned Liberalism. Both creeds seemed to retain their attractions in the early nineties, presenting the infant ILP with a problem of political space. To understand the seedbeds of political change, it is essential to examine the unique nature of Sheffield's industrial base.[69] Until the mid 1860s, this was dominated by the continuing growth of the highly labour-intensive light metal trades. Expansion was based on a near monopoly in overseas markets and on the development of domestic demand. Problems began to arise with the emergence of foreign competitors and the consequential imposition of tariffs, most damaging in the case of the United States. Yet overall employment in the light trades continued to grow until the 1890s. Production units remained largely small scale and mechanisation advanced only

* A Sheffield Labour activist, LPLF 14/332.

slowly, due in part to determined opposition by trade unions. Many workers were semi-independent and worked irregular hours. Trade union organisation reflected the traditionalism and the complexities of the light trade industrial structure. It was distinguished by localism, sectionalism and instability. Memberships were small, since each specialised trade developed its organisation, but participation rates tended to be high. By the nineties, such groups were, in many ways, anachronisms. Their capacity to regulate control over the labour market had been largely undermined by the introduction of new machinery. They continued to wrap themselves in complex rules which supposedly governed entry to their trades, a policy that was now often little more than a pious hope. The status of the skilled worker was threatened by new techniques; the prosperity of the Sheffield 'Light Trades' by overseas competitors.[70]

The declining security was paralleled by the emergence of the heavy steel and engineering works of the city's 'East End'. Here employment increased by over 300 per cent between 1851 and 1891; by contrast the equivalent rate in the 'Light Trades' was 50 per cent. The differential growth was reflected in the changing proportions of employment; in 1851 the heavy sector employed less than a quarter of the numbers in the 'Light Trades' but forty years later, the proportion was two-thirds. The growth of heavy industry was based on technical innovations in steel making, and on the seemingly insatiable demands of the railway, shipping and armaments industries. In these large-scale production units, factory discipline was essential, with continuous processes necessitating regular hours of work, often on a shift basis. Early recruits into large-scale industry were drawn in frequently from outside the city; a tendency to move again if trade conditions worsened made trade union organisation difficult. Only the ASE established an early and secure foothold in the East End industries, but when organisation developed amongst steelworkers in the nineties, it took the form of national unions — a sharp contrast with the old-style local craft unions in the 'Light Trades'.[71]

Inevitably, the leaders of the old craft organisations dominated the affairs of the Federated Trades Council from its formal inception in 1872.[72] Even when the basis of recruitment widened in the late eighties, its deliberations continued to be led by delegates from the 'Light Trades' sector. These respectable craftsmen were naturally keen to secure representation on municipal bodies, and from the late eighties, they had some success in elections to the City Council, School Board and the Guardians with campaigns organised through a branch of the Labour Electoral Association. Officials such as Stuart Uttley of the Filecutters worked closely with Liberal leaders within the City Council, and in broader political campaigns. The aspirations of these respectable craftsmen fitted easily into the style of Sheffield Liberalism, and local Liberal employers were prepared to give some consideration to the municipal representation claims of sound trade unionists.

These connections need to be discussed further along two dimensions.

The first involves an emphasis on something that did not happen. We have seen how engineers, bootmakers and even ill-organised wool-workers responded to the pressures of technical change and foreign competition by moving to Independent Labour or socialist positions. The spokesmen for the Sheffield craftsmen did not move in this direction; they remained attached to Liberalism, a loyalty that reflected, perhaps, the localised sectionalised quality of their unionism, and also perhaps, optimistic expectations about the flexibility of Sheffield Liberalism. Moreover, as in Birmingham, the small scale of production meant that class differences were not central to work experiences and many craftsmen cherished the hope of achieving some degree of independence in their own workshops.

The marginal status of such producers meant that the problem of market fluctuations ever intensified by foreign competition was always present, and produced a tendency to share in the Birmingham desire for Protection. If Sheffield's traditional craftsmen left Liberalism, it need not be for Independent Labour let alone socialism. Their leaders might speak in impeccable Liberal accents, but many were attracted by Fair Trade doctrines. Sir Howard Vincent, early advocate of Protection, Alien Restriction and Imperialism, a frequent speaker to Trades Councils in the nineties, represented Sheffield Central, the seat where many traditional craftsmen lived, from 1885 to his death in 1908.[73] What seemed in many places to be an eccentric, out-dated, reactionary doctrine did not appear so there.

The Liberalism of the craft union officials was not always an accurate barometer of their members' views, and somewhat ironically, it was the newer industrial areas that provided the strongholds of Liberalism. Brightside was represented by Mundella; the second, Attercliffe, became vacant in June 1894, and provided a flashpoint for Liberal—Labour relations.[74] By now, many on the Federated Trades Council, with its municipal successes and an affiliated membership of 10,000 felt ready to push for parliamentary representation. Although the dominant tone there remained Liberal, some delegates now belonged to the ILP, and were reluctant to support an orthodox Lib-Lab. All sections of trade union opinion seemed able to agree on the nomination of Charles Hobson of the Britannia Metal Smiths, President of the Trades Council and also of the national Labour Electoral Association. He was already a member of the City Council, the School Board and the Guardians, and although sometimes claiming that for him the interests of labour came first, he seems to have been a relatively orthodox Liberal. Nevertheless, he seemed sufficiently radical for Trades Council ILPers to support him, although no doubt there was a fine tactical element in such support.[75] The ILP could not hope to control Trades Council policy. Hobson was at least preferable to some of the more staid Lib-Labs, and if the Liberals refused to support him, then such a lesson in Liberal intractability could benefit the ILP.

Sheffield Liberal leaders were divided. Some were sympathetic to the pressure for Labour representation, but hoped to deflect it by importing a

Labour candidate from elsewhere, or failing this, an advanced Radical. Such a solution would be less divisive than the backing of a local trade unionist. Mundella wrote to Henry Wilson, advancing the claims of Fred Maddison, and also less enthusiastically of Harford of the Railway Servants.[76] For some, the attachment to Labour representation, albeit under Liberal auspices, seemed sincere: 'the working men are not unreasonable in thinking they should have one such for the City. I think Attercliffe is the likeliest for their purpose'.[77] But the attachment of others to Labour representation was a superficial and manipualtive affair. Local Liberal leaders, whilst discussing possible candidates outlined a method of neutralising labour discontent:

it was thought that we should try to concilliate the Labour Party by first of all approaching them and saying have you a man of your own, one who you like and who will support the Newcastle Programme and who you see your way to *return* and *keep*. If you have, we will submit him to our Council. It is thought the financial difficulty will probably prevent their being able to do this, and then we hope their opposition wd. be disarmed.[78]

This devious position was taken by Batty Langley, a self-made timber merchant, a leading Congregationalist and recently the city's Lord Mayor.[79] Others seemed unprepared even to apply a cosmetic. Sir Frederick Mappin, MP for Hallamshire, President of the Sheffield United Liberal Association and a wealthy industrialist, threw his massive influence against Labour representation. He came to Sheffield to clarify the position for Liberal activists. He was:

very strong indeed against a labour candidate of any sort. *We* have only got two seats out of five in Sheffield, and to give up one of these is to efface ourselves ... we cannot carry the seat with a working man ... we are almost as much giving up the seat if a working man is elected as if a Tory was.[80]

This intervention destroyed the hope of even an outside Labour candidate and the Attercliffe Liberal Council nominated Langley with 160 votes against 2 for Hobson, and 2 for a third nominee.[81] Subsequent claims that this nominating body had a working-class majority were disingenuous; the crucial decisions had been made in a far smaller and much more socially select grouping.

The rejection of Hobson was bound to produce a row. A subsidiary element involved Hobson accusing Langley of a breach of faith regarding his attitude to a labour nomination,[82] but centrally, the Trades Council had to react to the rejection of their nominee. On the night following Langley's selection, 23 June, 1894, the Council met for five hours. Committed Liberals argued that Hobson should withdraw to prevent a split in the anti-Tory vote; ILPers urged him to stay in and fight. Eventually, Hobson's own Liberal sympathies ensured his withdrawal, although the tone of the Council's resolution hardly indicated any mending of fences. After expressing 'surprise' and disgust, it informed the Liberals 'that by their mean action, they have alienated the Labour Party from them'.[83] Now the ILP stepped into the breach. Local members contacted Hardie, who travelled to Sheffield, discussed the local situation, and took the first steps towards launching Frank Smith as the ILP candidate.[84] Even before Hobson withdrew, some Lib-Labs had feared this possibility. Uttley had warned Henry Wilson that 'the Keir Hardyites are certain to run a candidate unless Hobson stands'.[85] Yet the ILP faced severe handicaps. It had some adherents amongst Trades Council delegates, in particular Tom Shaw, the Vice-President, but its presence amongst the Sheffield working class was both recent and limited. A local organiser might paint an optimistic portrait for the party's national leadership,[86] but Blatchford's post-poll judgement seems more accurate:

Attercliffe had not been educated by a long and patient series of Socialist lectures. The ILP was a small body and of recent formation. The SDF is but weak ... Our candidate was a stranger and a Londoner. Nearly all our speakers were strangers.[87]

Credibility depended on the establishment of a positive relationship with the Trades Council.

The major stumbling block was that some prominent Lib-Labs were prepared to let their Liberalism override any anger that they might have felt at Hobson's rejection, but they also had to avoid accusations that they were subordinating the Trades Council's interests to party considerations. Three of them, Hobson, Uttley and Wardley, met some prominent Liberals on 28 June; one of the latter summarised the Lib-Labs' dilemma:

they have all enough sympathy with the Liberal Party to be most anxious not to sink the seat by endorsing Frank Smith's candidature, but fear they will lose the confidence of the Trades Council, if they refuse.[88]

Staunch Liberalism was not the monopoly of the 'light trades' delegates; the Miners' representatives almost all reflected the position of Ben Pickard and refused to have anything to do with the ILP.[89]

The Lib-Lab's dilemma was an immediate one, as the Trades Council met the next day. Attempts by Liberal emissaries to produce a compromise involving unity behind Langley now, but consultations before the general election, served only to produce more Radical/ILP recriminations. Eventually a resolution was carried, probably by 43 votes to 38, supporting but not adopting Smith.[90] The reasoning was narrowly pragmatic; Labour had a justifiable claim to the Attercliffe vacancy. Even this consensual justification did not sway many Liberals; the size of the minority is notable. Hobson apparently abstained but almost all the YMA delegates and many from the 'light trades' refused to support Smith.[91] Such a small majority was of limited value and a divided Trades Council could play only a marginal role in the campaign. Lib-Lab trade unionists outside Sheffield failed to translate their enthusiasm for Hobson into support for the ILP's nominee. The LEA had naturally reacted with pleasure to the news that its President might be standing,[92] but after Langley's selection, Threlfall, the LEA Secretary travelled to Sheffield to persuade Hobson to withdraw. He should not do anything which might aid the ILP: 'they are wrong and their policy will be injurious to the best interests of Labour'.[93] Indeed, some Lib-Labs praised Hobson in part because he avoided the ILP's 'excesses' — William Bailey of the Nottinghamshire Miners characterised him as 'a splendid type of the working man, not a Keir Hardie who ran all about the country'.[94] Such supporters were hardly likely to react to Hobson's rejection and withdrawal by supporting Frank Smith.

More pressure on the Liberal caucus came from dissatisfied Radicals outside the city. Langley's selection was criticised by the *Manchester Guardian* and the *Daily Chronicle*,[95] and Robert Hudson, Secretary of the National Liberal Federation indicated that the selection would not generate much enthusiasm amongst Liberal speakers: 'under the peculiar circumstances of your contest, it will be very difficult to get people to come down'.[96] In contrast, the ailing Francis Schnadhorst sought to strengthen the resolve of the Sheffield Liberals against the ILP: 'the crew who have come down from London ought to be faced at all costs, if we cannot settle them, then there will be no Liberal Party'.[97] Some Radicals, perhaps hoping for a realignment on the Left, or at least the discomfiture of narrow Liberal employers, cashed their sentiments; Dilke and Labouchere contributed to Smith's election fund.[98] Other Radicals attempted to mediate. Two representatives of the National Reform Union, Phillip Stanhope and the member for Newcastle under Lyme, William Allan, appeared in Sheffield the weekend before polling. They attempted to reconcile Liberal and Trades Council interests with an eye to future contests; but the exercise failed, basically because the Trades Council spokesmen wished for a commitment to the adoption of a Labour candidate for the general election, but Liberals would agree only generally on the need for future consultations. The initiative degenerated into a fiasco when Trades Council and Liberal leaders found themselves invited to discussions at which Hardie and Smith happened to be present. Whether an accident or a Radical conspiracy, it gave the ILP leaders ample opportunity to accuse the Liberals of devious tactics.[99] Somewhat austerely they dismissed Henry Wilson's apologies: 'we regard the whole proceeding as a deliberate attempt on the part of Messrs Stanhope and Allen to inveigle us into a false and compromising position'.[100]

The campaign was vigorous with the ILP attempting to counteract Liberal organisational strength, with a flood of street-corner meetings.[101] Langley's appeal was a traditional Liberal one, emphasising Home Rule and the obstructiveness of the Lords. The centrality of such issues was heightened by the strongly Orange sympathies of the Unionist candidate. In contrast, the Labour campaign attempted to build on Radical criticisms of the Sheffield caucus. Smith emphasised his agreement with Langley's programme, but expressed doubt about Liberal leaders' capacity and willingness to carry it out;[102] Mrs Pankhurst claimed that the ILP was 'not fighting the rank and file of the

Liberal party, but simply the money bags that governed it'.[103] In response, the local Liberal press took a bitterly hostile line. Smith was 'a political fraud ... doing Tory work'.[104] It would be better for the Tory to win than the ILP.[105] The close ties between respectable craft unionism and Liberalism were appealed to:

Are the manufacturers, the 'little masters', the owners of their own houses and little plots of land, and the depositors in savings banks, prepared to hand over all the provision they have made against a rainy day that it may be shared up with the ne'er do wells, who were always out at the elbows, because they were born tired and have never rested? ... if, as we believe, the working men of Attercliffe represent the thrifty and thoughtful who have exercised prudence in their own affairs, they will support Mr. Langley, who has risen from a position like their own.[106]

Perhaps more significantly, Ben Pickard threw his own authority, although constitutionally not that of the Yorkshire Miners' Association, behind Langley's campaign. The ILP had hoped for considerable support from the mining section of the electorate. But Pickard telegraphed to a Liberal YMA member who was also a member of the Trades Council, and his message was reproduced on a Liberal handbill 'Vote Straight for Langley who is pledged to the Miners' Eight Hour Bill, and who also did so well for our Sheffield Miners during the stoppage of 1893'.[107]

In the end, the combination of Liberal organisational strength, Lib-Lab hostility and local trade union lukewarmness was too much for the hastily improvised ILP campaign. Smith's vote of 1,249 in such circumstances indicated the extent of dissatisfaction at the machinations of the local caucus, but more significantly, Langley's easy victory suggested the existence of obstacles to the establishment of a major ILP presence.

Episodes such as Attercliffe could precipitate the final shift of discontented Radicals into the ILP. One famous consequence of this contest was the formal adherence to the party of Ramsay MacDonald. He had 'stuck to the Liberals up to now', but Attercliffe was 'a rude awakening' — 'Liberalism, and more particularly local Liberal Associations, have definitely declared against Labour, and so I must accept the facts of the situation and candidly admit that the prophecies of the ILP, relating to Liberalism, have been amply justified.'[108] This consequence of Attercliffe is plausible, but within Sheffield it did not occur to any great extent. Optimistic prognostications about ILP development were not fulfilled, the party languished for more than a decade, and much of the ill-feeling between Liberal leaders and major Trades Council figures seems to have vanished.

This reflected in part the staunch Liberalism of many Sheffield trade unionists, most obviously in the 'light trades', supplemented by the support of local Miners' officials. The shadow of Pickard brooded over any attempt by Sheffield ILPers to achieve a breakthrough; they could not turn for support or example to the surrounding coalfield, here the ILP was even weaker than it was in the city. The stultifying of the ILP also owed something to the energy with which some Sheffield Liberals attempted to mend fences. At first, the auguries seemed unpromising, as Liberals attempted to revive the unsuccessful discussions begun during the campaign.

Stuart Uttley felt that the interests of the Liberal Party would be served best by a tripartite meeting between Liberal Party, Sheffield Trades Council, and LEA.[109] This view was reciprocated by some within the Liberal caucus, although Mappin characteristically urged delay.[110] In September 1894, the Trades Council agreed by 38 votes to 35 to meet the Liberals. This represented a significant defeat for the ILP faction — they had failed to capitalise on the events of the summer.[111] But as yet the rift was too recent to permit an easy reconciliation. The Trades Council Report summarised the stalemate:

Shortly after the Attercliffe Election, the council was approached by the Liberal Party with a view of obtaining a more correct understanding of each other's views and attitudes on Liberal and Labour questions. A deputation was appointed and several meetings were held; a programme proposed of leading Labour questions which the representatives of the Liberal party were prepared to recommend to their Association, and which they suggested might form the basis of a working agreement.

The question was submitted to, and fully discussed by the Council, and it was decided in the interests of the Council not to proceed further in the matter.[112]

The ILPers could block a deal between Trades Council and Liberals, but that was the limit of their power. Moreover, the formula in which this impasse was expressed could be turned against the supporters of Independent Labour at a later date: 'Considering the constitution and work of the Council is purely trade union and labour, and its members belong to all shades of politics, co-operation or a working agreement with any political party is absolutely impossible.'[113] Even with this formal deadlock, the close links remained between some Trades Council spokesmen, and some leaders of Sheffield Liberalism.[114]

Further developments of these complex relationships occurred in July 1897, when Mundella's death produced a vacancy in the Brightside constituency. Several local Liberals were anxious to avoid another rupture with the Trades Council, especially since there was once again some expectation that Hobson would go forward as a Labour nominee with Liberal support. But some Liberals had other ideas, inspired by a desire to appear sympathetic to labour claims whilst avoiding divisive local commitments. Tom Ellis, the Liberal Chief Whip, expressed the tactical perception of many Liberal MPs: 'the feeling in the House among a good many level-headed Liberals is very strongly for a Labour candidate, and that if you do decide for a Labour candidate, go for him at once, not under seeming necessity or pressure'.[115] But his suggested nominees did not include local trade unionists. Ellis recommended Harford or Maddison, and felt that possible objections from Hobson should be dealt with through prior consultation. In the end, it was Maddison who was invited up to Sheffield, and adopted rapidly by the Brightside Liberals. The choice of a dedicated opponent of the ILP provoked a hostile response from Hardie, and then from the Sheffield ILP. Maddison symbolised Lib-Labism, and evoked memories of the Hull controversies of 1893—5. His record there could be used to portray him as a Liberal Party hack, ready to court employers and attack trade unionists in pursuit of party and personal advantage.[116]

Maddison certainly seemed ready to tailor his Radicalism in his quest for a nomination. He satisfied the potentially hostile Sir Frederick Mappin that he was sound:

I had a long talk with Sir F. Mappin today, and I think we understood each other fairly well ... it goes without saying that Sir Frederick and myself do not see eye to eye on all points, but I am satisfied that without sacrificing any of my Trade Union principles, my political views would be acceptable to any body of Liberals and Radicals who mean business.[117]

His adoption was carried out without consulting the Trades Council who received formal notification after the selection.[118] The response of Liberal trade union officials was mixed — annoyance at the lack of consultation, disappointment at the importing of a labour candidate and the neglect of local aspirants, but sympathy for Maddison's politics.[119] The leaders of Sheffield Liberalism had moved just far enough to defuse large-scale opposition, and had kept the nominating process in their own hands. But those committed to the ILP remained unreconciled. In part this reflected the factionalism of Sheffield trade union politics, but it also reflected national divisions. This contest occurred near the peak of the hostilities between ILP leaders and some Lib-Labs. Charles Fenwick and John Wilson had strongly urged Maddison's claims. From this viewpoint, Brightside could be seen as one more battle in a war that had included already the Halifax by-election in March 1897, which two months later was to take an even more embittered form at Barnsley. Maddison's position as editor of the ASRS's *Railway Review* was already under fire from union activists, and during the campaign, publicity was given to a resolution passed by the Newton Heath No. 2 branch of the Railway Servants, attacking Maddison's Liberalism: 'he binds himself hand and foot to a Party composed of capitalists, and enemies to the advancement and well-being of the workers generally'.[120] Such a condemnation acquired a particular edge, since railwaymen were thought to be important amongst the Brightside electorate and the Sheffield ASRS had been notable for its opposition to Trades Council deals with the Liberals.[121]

Hardie travelled to Sheffield to discuss the situation with the local ILP, a meeting where a national leader's hostility to Lib-Labs could fuse with local enmity to Liberal wirepulling. Inevitably discussion centered around the desirability and feasibility of repeating the 1894 move. Party members felt that the position of the Trades Council was uncertain. There was resentment over the lack of consultation, and the Council had agreed to take no collective action over Maddison's candidature. But whilst many trade union activists seemed discontented with official Liberalism, they remained 'bitter opponents' of the ILP. The advent of an ILP candidate could provoke such unionists into active support for Maddison. The predicted ILP vote was only five hundred. Even local activists were divided over the desirability of a candidature — the vote in favour was only 31 to 27. Hardie's intervention, opposing a candidate was then accepted with only eight against.[122] Here was abundant evidence of the underlying weakness of the Sheffield ILP and of the additional difficulties posed by the importation of a Lib-Lab.

The ILP decided to issue a manifesto over the signatures of Hardie, Mann and two local leaders. This castigated Maddison as 'the nominee of manufacturers and employers', emphasised the lack of consultation with the Trades Council, and suggested that he was seen by Liberals as more pliable than Hobson. He had 'no present standing as a representative of Labour'. The saga of Maddison's Hull bargainings was presented once again.[123]

This attempt to mobilise trade union opinion against Maddison, and by implication in favour of the Conservative candidate had little success. Whatever his limitations, Maddison carried more plausibility as a Labour spokesman than did his opponent, the nephew of a duke. Hobson sank, whatever regrets he might have felt, and backed Maddison: 'his record as a Trade Unionist is unblemished'.[124] The candidate dismised ILP claims about his Hull activities as 'the fabrications of disordered brains'.[125] The ILP manifesto was circulated by the Conservatives, with the additional injunction to 'Vote for Lord John Hope'.[126] Such a development lent plausibility to Liberal claims that the ILP were 'all Tories at heart'.

After this intervention, and with Maddison's victory indicating the continuing strength of Lib-Labism in Sheffield, the ILP decayed. Within a year, a disillusioned party member wrote of: 'too much Liberal Labourism ... Our Central Council is absolutely defunct. The same with Brightside Branch, and what of Attercliffe, well not much better ... the position has disheartened even some of the brighter spirits'.[127]

This decline was paralleled in 1898, when the Trades Council decided to take no further part in electoral activities.[128] This could be regarded as a means of sterilising much of the political factionalism that threatened its effectiveness; it could also be seen as a method of protecting the position of trade unionist councillors who enjoyed Liberal support, but were not formally Trades Council nominees. Feeling that political activities were likely to produce few benefits for much expense and recrimination was heightened two years later when Maddison was defeated in Brightside. His criticisms of the government's South African policy provoked hostility in a constituency where war contracts provided a sizeable amount of employment. Once again the Tory preferences of sections of the Sheffield working class appeared more significant than activist arguments over the merits of Lib-Lab or Independent Labour politics.

Yet the Sheffield Labour Movement became involved inevitably in the post-1900 discussions about Labour Representation. Whatever the local peculiarities, Sheffield trade union leaders were bound to be concerned about the implications of Taff Vale, and to be influenced by the attempts of the national LRC to establish local organisations. But the weakness of the local ILP together with the traditionalism of the 'light trade' societies meant that developments followed a distinctive and tortuous path. A Sheffield LRC was formed during 1903 following a local conference addressed by MacDonald, and appropriately, by George Barnes of the ASE.[129] The lack of enthusiasm of many local unions was shown by their non-participation. The involvement of the 'light trades' was slight, and tensions soon developed. Lib-Labs such as Charles Hobson attempted to minimise the significance of the new organisation. One of his critics made plain his feelings: 'some of the members are not satisfied with Hobson's idea of the scope and meaning of the LRC; they are of the opinion that they might as well stay in the Liberal Party if he is correct'.[130] But some activists soon attempted to secure Charles Duncan as an ASE-backed candidate in Attercliffe,[131] and differences became more acute as the Trades Council refused to surrender its authority on electoral matters to the LRC. The council seats of Liberal trade unionists would clearly be at risk, if a LRC pledged to independence controlled all electoral matters. A temporary accommodation was reached with the creation of a joint 'Trades Council and Labour Representation Committee' incorporating equal representation from both bodies,[132] but this did not end Liberal anxieties, and in March 1905 the Trades Council voted 45 to 11 to remove reference to itself from the title of the joint body. Attempts to arrive at a compromise had also annoyed committed ILPers. MacDonald reflected ruefully on the barren years:

there seems to be some places where the Labour Movement is cursed, and one is almost incline (*sic*) to say that Sheffield is one of them, considering the very fine work that has been put in your city during the last fifteen years and the very little result that has been reaped from it.[133]

But now the tide began to turn. Conflict between protagonists of the Independent Labour and Lib-Lab positions was becoming endemic. They fought each other in municipal elections and argued vehemently on the Trades Council. Everywhere the Lib-Lab bastions seemed to be crumbling; the growth of Independent Labour in parts of the Yorkshire coalfield threatened to remove a significant prop from Sheffield Liberalism. At last the Sheffield ILP showed signs of revival. The response of the Lib-Labs in December 1906, was to move resolutely against the national tide, disaffiliating from the national LRC and framing new rules omitting all mention of politics.

This was a last stand by the old guard in the 'light trades' and provoked a response from supporters of Independent Labour. Their growth was not just a matter of an ILP revival; unions in the heavy trade sector were now much more stable and were committed nationally to political independence. They had dominated the local LRC from its inception; now some branches of the

Ironfounders and the ASE quit the old Federated Trades Council and in June 1908 formed a revived Trades and Labour Council which would act as an advocate of Independent Labour politics. It was an appropriate, if fortuitous, prelude to the election of Sheffield's first Labour MP, when Joseph Pointer, a leading local ILPer won Attercliffe in a four-cornered contest in May 1909.[134]

Conclusion: the mosaic of ILP politics

The complexities of ILP politics within particular communities seem even more daunting than the legacies of ILP activity within the unions. There, at least, trade conditions and organisational loyalties could generate some unifying themes. In contrast, the variety and vagaries of local political traditions and conditions have necessitated highly detailed explorations. Respect for such specificities should not prohibit however the search for some broader features. Perhaps the mosaic will yield some patterns.

Industrial experiences continue to appear in various guises as a critical element. Possibly, the purest example is the contribution of Leicester's Boot and Shoe activists to the growth of the local ILP. The confrontations of the nineties, and subsequently the more cautious industrial strategy, both left their imprints on political attitudes and relationships. A less clear-cut case is provided by the contribution of the 1898 coal lock-out to the Merthyr victory of Keir Hardie. Thus, one traceable, albeit variable, development was that of organised workers reacting to their industrial difficulties by taking initiatives that affected local political alignments. An alternative development involved the absence of significant industrial organisation. In the Yorkshire woollen towns, and in several centres in the West of Scotland, unions were weak, and workers sought to advance their claims through political action — Labour Unions in the West Riding; the SLP and some politically active trades councils in Scotland. Workers could see political organisation as an indispensable complement to a weak trade unionism, or in extreme cases, as an alternative to the absence of union organisation. In contrast, some union experiences could serve as insulators against the appeal of independent political action. Such barriers can be found in the continuing dominance of Sheffield trade unionism by spokesmen for the light trades, and in the nature of much London unionism with its prominent representatives of small societies.

Such reflections are valid as far as they go, but they provoke further enquiry. Why did the Merthyr and Aberdare miners move only slowly from Liberalism after 1898, yet still more rapidly than many of their colleagues elsewhere in the coalfield? Why did trade union weakness amongst Lanarkshire miners and Yorkshire woollen workers produce political initiatives, but fail to do so amongst the unorganised workers of large cities? Why did the Lancashire cotton towns, where dominant unions clearly insulated member against a radical questioning of the economic system, nevertheless contain so many socialist groups?

Now the quest for answers stretches far beyond the industrial realm. Some contrasts were embedded in divergent types of community. The ILP found little support in the slums of large cities, nor usually in small towns and villages where the dominance of a few employers could be secured readily. Often the Party's most secure bases were in communities large enough to avoid such control, yet not so vast as to produce the transitoriness and atomisation of many city areas. In such stable settings, with a degree of social space, the more self-confident members of the working-class might already have considerable participation in voluntary organisations. The ILP could be one more addition to a record of self-reliance, expressed also through trade unionism, friendly societies and religious dissent. Yet the ILP was essentially a political organisation; another earlier expression of working-class self-reliance had been Radical politics, and it is upon political opportunities and constraints that the primary focus should fall.

A vital element, apparent throughout the specific accounts, was the strength and quality of local Liberalism. The years of the ILP's emergence were years of deep crisis for the Liberal Party. Damaged by both Unionist defections and the threat and sometimes reality of secessions to the left, it was confused over policy and uncertain about the leadership. The Liberal inability to satisfy Labour demands was just one aspect of the crisis, but arguably the one that had the deepest implications. Sometimes the Liberal failure had an ideological element, with laissez-faire industrialists refusing to countenance Labour demands for state intervention. Such a characterisation applies particularly to the stern unbending creed of some Woollen Town spokesmen in the 1890s; then, the dichotomy between Liberal and Labour could appear simple and harsh. More frequently however, the rift had a strongly organisational base, which nevertheless reflected a belief that the labour interest was just one important constituent of the Liberal army. Local Liberals often claimed to accept the legitimacy of Labour candidates, but insisted that they should be run under Liberal auspices, an insistence which effectively blighted prospects of a significant Labour expansion. Sometimes such an outcome was cynically anticipated; on other occasions, Liberal protestations seemed sincere, but the social composition of caucus leaderships meant that the outcome was disappointing from a Labour viewpoint. The sticking-point varied, but in industrial Scotland, in Leicester, Sheffield and elsewhere, Liberal offers were regarded by at least some Labour partisans as inadequate.

One consequence might be a Labour protest followed by reintegration into the Liberal coalition; an alternative might be some breakaway at first of uncertain direction and durability, but eventually acquiring a clear organisational and political character. The first response was exemplified by Sheffield, the second occurred in varying fashions in many of those communities where the earliest significant ILP developments occurred. Breakaways clearly contributed to, and were influenced by national developments. The emergence of a national ILP owed much to the credibility of local initiatives, and they in turn were strengthened and moulded by the national organisation. Local parties were marked also by features of local Liberalism. Often this incorporated a complex variety of principles. Liberal politics in much of Scotland, in the Woollen Towns, in Leicester and in Merthyr had embraced and domesticated traditional Radical sentiments which could be turned against Liberal failures to meet expectations. Such sentiments could legitimise Labour criticisms and even sanction separate candidates, but they could hold out also the hope of a Radical revival within the Liberal framework, thus hinting that separation need not be total nor permanent. Liberal—Labour relationships were a complex force-field of attractions and repulsions, reaching an apogée perhaps in Merthyr, where the idiosyncrasies of the Liberal Members permitted flexible interpretations of Radical pedigrees.

Within these complexities, one predominant movement from the late nineties involved the emergence of electoral understandings between Labour and a chastened, and perhaps more interventionist Liberalism. This was most prevalent in parts of Lancashire where the ILP had not faced a dominant Liberalism and had been able to make a bid for Radical support, in a context of Liberal incapacity. The tendency emerged in distinct and local forms in Leicester and Merthyr; even where Liberalism was traditionally less yielding, there was a classic example of such an understanding in Halifax, and considerable evidence of Progressive sentiment in Bradford. The Scottish experience is typically interpreted as one of Liberal/Labour antipathies, yet even here there was often an expectation of some kind of arrangement. Such tendencies could utilise a common idiom, and were backed by the gradual shift of Liberal opinion away from Gladstonian preoccupations to a greater emphasis on economic and social issues. ILP activists could come to perceive an understanding as increasingly worthwhile, as they were domesticated through their experience of municipal political bargaining. Within such a Progressive synthesis, Labour had an assured, albeit junior, place; if the ILP had not been reabsorbed, at least it had reached a viable understanding.

The emphasis is significant yet it must be complemented by others. We have seen how the activities of ILPers within specific unions established commitments which constrained the political strategies and attachments of union spokesmen. This created a potential for ILP influence which could have a variable influence on Liberal—Labour relationships. Most significantly, within a specific communtiy, connections could be made through the activities of the local trades council.[1] These were regular forums for ILP manoeuvres as party members tried to increase their influence, through converting, or making deals with, other delegates. There were obvious limitations on the extent to which trades councils represented or gave an effective lead to local workers on political questions. Many working-class voters were outside unions altogether, and council delegates might not reflect the political views of their more passive members. Yet the winning over of trades councils as with advances in specific unions, laid down parameters for the expression of official working-class opinion.

Such developments were not attributable simply to the activities of ILP delegates. The broad direction of municipal preoccupations meant that trades councils had to concern themselves increasingly with questions of housing, health and local initiatives to combat unemployment. Such questions, although not the monopoly of socialists, provided an appropriate meeting ground for ILPers and trade union activists. Such collaborations could be initiated or strengthened by experiences of local disputes and of the stern responses of existing municipal leaderships. Sometimes a link between trades council and ILP could be made easily. In particular, this could happen when a council was of very recent foundation, and had not acquired a political position identified with an established leadership. In such plastic circumstances, ILP influence could quickly mould the council into a co-operative body. Thus in many West Riding Woollen Towns where trade unionism was weak, trades council and Labour Union arose almost simultaneously as complementary weapons in the same struggle; in Merthyr and Aberdare, the creation of trades councils was an important contribution in the movement towards an Independent Labour candidate.

Often the change if not devoid of acrimony, was relatively straightforward. The Bradford Trades Council, once staunchly Liberal, moved towards ILP control, as the consequence of craft-union radicalisation, New Unionism and the political implications of Manningham Mills. More simply, its Leicester counterpart was influenced by the dominant Boot and Shoe section, and was attached to Independent Labour from 1894. The Manchester and Salford Trades Council had shifted from Liberalism to political independence by the mid-nineties, as younger delegates capitalised on the continual haggling between Council and Liberals about municipal representation.[2] Major trades councils in Scotland had abandoned the older parties by 1895.

Elsewhere the ILP found trades councils less receptive. In several cotton towns, domination of councils by textile unions produced rebuffs of ILP overtures on the grounds that a trade union body should not become embroiled in partisan controversies. This mood ended when these unions affiliated to the national LRC; now the ambiguities within the term 'labour' could be employed to claim that such an attachment was not partisan, but simply the pursuit of trade union objectives by another method. This shift did not entail much influence for local ILPs, as their distinctive contribution could be absorbed readily within a sectional trade-union-dominated appeal. Only when the Party had previously attained considerable eminence, as in Blackburn, was there much hope of maintaining a strong specifically ILP contribution.

More serious difficulties were encountered when a local trades council remained committed to Liberalism. Sometimes the ILP attempted to secure support by agitating about Liberal neglect of Labour's representational claims, as at Sheffield in 1894. This tactic could be counteracted by a flexible Liberal Association. Ramsay MacDonald's hopes of securing Trades Council support for his Southampton candidacy were ruined when Liberals adopted a local trade unionist as their second candidate.[3] At a more fundamental level than such tactical gambits, Lib-Lab influence could be protected by specific economic factors. Once the Sheffield Light Trades delegates had provided the leadership of the Trades Council, they proved difficult to dislodge. They were not radicalised by economic pressures, and as they secured some municipal representation, self-interest fused with sentiment to oppose Independent Labour attacks. Ultimately, their position was eroded by the changing balance within the local economy and by the weight of national alignments.

The growing roll-call of ILP—trades council understandings provided a basis for local LRCs and for Labour's municipal expansion. Such arrangements could mean compromises for local ILPs, as support was given to non-socialist trade union candidates. The strategic implications were ambiguous. Understandings with local Liberals could be facilitated as pragmatists were attracted by the promise of easy electoral profits, alternatively a more independent strategy could be sustained, especially in municipal politics, as union money permitted Labour to attack on a broader front. Here was a political translation in a variety of local accents, of the increasing union commitment to political independence, suggesting the feasibility of a class-based alternative to the public high-mindedness of Liberal politicians.

The sentiments surrounding this independent option could connect with others indicating the desirability of a united socialist opposition to capitalist parties. This theme had become popular in the mid and late nineties as ILP groups clarified their position, before declining again in favour of trade union alliances and Progressive understandings. Yet it was always present. It could flare up again if local Liberals proved unbending and was expressed in embryonic form perhaps in municipal co-operation with the SDF, or in candidatures of the type engaged by Sam Hobson at Rochdale in 1906. This subordinate tradition continued to enjoy significant support, not just within the party but also on specific occasions within the wider electorate.

These strategic options and their implications — Progressive understanding, trade union alliance, socialist unity — dominated ILP debates from the late nineties until 1914. The focus on the politics of particular communities demonstrates how these alternatives could be explored within distinctive situations. The national posture of the ILP was anticipated in a variety of local initiatives. So were critical alternatives and responses. Their credibilities depended on local circumstances, such as the style of local Liberalism and industrial and trade union experiences. But they were influenced also by the logic of national events. As the ILP and subsequently the LRC became durable organisations, so the choices made at that level left their mark. Later ILP growths occurred not just within local constraints, but also within those laid down by national organisations. It is time to complement the fundamental emphasis on local initiatives by examining the emergence of the party as a national presence.

Part 3

A NATIONAL PARTY

12

Formation

The ILP's foundation conference in January 1893 was the culmination of several months of discussion and organisation. Significant decisions were taken by a relatively small number of people, but they were responding to local initiatives. The ILP grew from the bottom upwards, with independent parties emerging in several places well before the national meeting. Such groups reflected local circumstances. Attitudes towards political rivals varied with the character of local Liberalism, or conditions in dominant local industries. The preferences of individual personalities also had their impacts. Some local groups blazened forth their socialist commitment; others emphasised their primary concern as 'Labour representation'. The strength of their political independence might vary but they could usually unite in a defence of local autonomy.

Thus, the Labour Unions of the West Riding woollen towns, reacting against a Liberal millocracy and born out of industrial difficulties claimed a staunch attachment to political independence, and contained many activists who had passed beyond Labour Representation to socialism. The style west of the Pennines characteristically differed. Here the influence of both Clarion and SDF was greater; so was the need to secure Tory working-class support. Such factors helped to produce a sharper view of political independence, enshrined in the celebrated Fourth Clause of the Manchester and Salford ILP:

All members of this party pledge themselves to abstain from voting for any candidate for election to any representative body who is in any way a nominee of the Liberal, Liberal Unionist or Conservative Party.[1]

Further north, the Scottish Labour Party pursued its complex gyrations between independence and negotiations with Gladstonians. Here matters were confused further by the emergence of the Scottish United Trades Council Labour Party, and the particular strength of Champion and his supporters in Aberdeen. The West Riding, Lancashire and Scotland were to contribute most towards the inaugural conference, although inevitably the special position of London affected the negotiations. It was here that many Labour journalists and trade union officials could meet to discuss common problems, and such a facility could serve as a counterweight against provincial initiatives. Behind such considerations, there lay the debris of successive failures to develop a genuinely Independent Labour organisation. Why should it work out differently this time?

Those who were willing to make the attempt had to come to terms with a decade of frequently unsuccessful socialist agitation. British socialism was frequently identified with the Social Democratic Federation, an organisation which has rarely received a favourable press from historians. Its membership remained small in the early nineties, although it had relative strongholds in London and parts of Lancashire. At the top, it reflected the idiosyncracies of its founder and dominant personality H. M. Hyndman, including the adoption of a somewhat phariseeical attitude towards involvement in trade union activities. Such deficiencies could culminate in a sectarianism expressed in interminable theological debates and subsequent secessions. The official ILP view of the SDF was all this and something more — the Federation was presented as the vehicle of a dry, dogmatic, irrelevant Marxism, wholly out of touch with working-class experiences. This depiction was a caricature. Such elements were there — but they could be found amongst SDF leaders rather than the rank and file. Amongst the latter, there were many who worked actively in trade union branches or with other socialists or advocates of Independent Labour representation in the political sphere. Such a split between leadership and activist experiences could generate future tensions. But inevitably the negative portrait gained credibility, in part because it contained elements of truth. It could serve as a warning and a justification for those who wished to create a new organisation.[2]

If those seeking an ILP often hoped to distinguish themselves from the dogmatic narrow SDF stereotype, they also hoped to separate themselves from the London Fabians and their tactic of permeating the Liberal Party.[3] Experiences of provincial Liberal caucuses were sufficient to exorcise any belief that Liberal Associations could be utilised for labour — let alone — socialist purposes. Here, then, were two alternatives between which the ILP could hopefully situate itself. Yet, a claim that the ILP hoped to be notable for a blend of undogmatic independence and socialist idealism was to say very little. The picture had to be filled in with a vision of strategy. If the ILP were to seek to organise the labour vote in pursuit of, at first ameliorative and later, perhaps socialist objectives, how should this be done?

Late Victorian politics afforded abundant experience of organised interests seeking to influence governments. Indeed the Liberal Party itself sometimes appeared to be little more than a collection of enthusiasms — temperance reform, nonconformity, land reform and, of course, labour. Lib-Labism involved, amongst its beliefs, a claim that the best way for labour to acquire influence was as a member of the great Gladstonian coalition. In extremis, this might involve the use of threats — abstention or the running of independent candidates — as a means of securing either the adoption of an acceptable Liberal, or the adoption by the Liberal candidate of appropriate positions on sensitive issues. Organisations such as the Labour Electoral Association might attempt to promote Labour candidates and proposals, either within the Liberal Party or with Liberal blessing. They met with very little success.

An initial independent response could be that of the individual wrecking candidate, but beyond that loomed more sophisticated arrangements. An independent party could use its position to try and secure the election of enough MPs possibly to hold the balance in the Commons, and therefore reach a bargain with one of the main parties on selected issues. It could also attempt to organise voters in seats that it did not contest, so that deals could be struck with amenable candidates. Such an organisation would not advance a general programme, or attempt to run for office. It would achieve a position by sticking to its special concern. This prospect had been exemplified for many strategists by the Irish Nationalist Party — in particularly during the mid eighties before Nationalist fortunes were hitched to Gladstonianism.[4] But although the Irish example was discussed in the debates leading up to the formation of the ILP, there were problems in seeking to apply it. Labour had no electoral equivalent of the Irish constituencies that could provide a durable parliamentary base. Labour voters were less identifiable than were Irish voters in British seats. Whether contemporary and retrospective accounts have exaggerated the homogeneity of the Irish vote is debatable;[5] what seems clear is that it was at least more united than the 'labour' equivalent. Indeed what did the latter indicate? Any slick identification with a working-class or trade unionist electorate begs a massive range of questions about how far and under what conditions prospective labour voters would come to see themselves in such terms. Irish voters might make Irish issues their priority — it was less likely that labour voters would do the same. This did not just reflect the concern of labour voters with other issues. It also indicated an inadequacy of the exemplar on the question of objectives. Nationalists could agree readily on what they viewed as an advancement of Irish interests — what would qualify as an equivalent promotion of labour interests was much more debatable. Indeed, Parnellite politics had worked with such effectiveness because the objective was a highly specific state of affairs; with its attainment the independent bloc would presumably disappear. What equivalent could there be in labour politics? Pursuit of a series of distinctively labour reforms did not seem to have any obvious point of fulfilment. 'Socialism' as an objective raised much more fundamental problems of strategy. Now such pressure politics did not always seem appropriate. Blatchford, with his perspective of 'making socialists' looked forward to a fundamental realignment of the parties:

The object of the Labour Party ... should be to drive all the Whigs and Tories into one camp, and win all the others over to our side, and the best means to that end is education.[6]

For Blatchford, 'our side' was unambiguously socialist. Differences over objectives could lead to tactical arguments about organisation and strategy.

Many protagonists of Independent Labour also hoped to avoid the risk of sectarianism through working closely with sympathetic trade unionists. We have looked at the quests for influence within individual unions: there was some hope that an independent party would be some sort of alliance of political and industrial groupings. Such optimism failed to weigh properly the obstacles to socialist advance within many individual organisations, but it was a significant product of the increased tempo and raised expectations of much union activity in the late eighties and early nineties. In these years, the alliance of socialists, advocates of political independence and trade unionists seemed feasible. But by 1892, the peak of union mobilisation had passed, the employers' offensive was beginning and although the dream of such an alliance continued to inspire, the reality was increasingly recalcitrant.

Here was a world of attractive exemplars, stereotypes to be avoided, local creativity and optimism that sometimes collapsed into naivete. There were those who aspired to the leadership of a Labour Party — Champion, Burns and Hardie, all made their claims. Each had his vanity — once again the Parnellite parallel, the leader who could mobilise a united army, cast its shadow.[7] Against such claims there were those typified by Blatchford who poured scorn on the necessity for and desirability of leaders. In the end, the processes generating a foundation conference, although obviously influenced by the deeds of potential Parnells, owed much to local and journalistic initiatives.

Joseph Burgess, like many Lancashire children in the 1850s had gone to work in a cotton mill at an early age. In the early eighties, he entered journalism in Oldham, and then worked for the *Cotton Factory Times*. Crossing the Pennines, he edited an equivalent labour paper — the *Yorkshire Factory Times*, and then moved to London to edit the *Workman's Times*.[8] This journal blended political comment, short stories and reports from local labour correspondents. Although the columns were open to all of broadly progressive sympathies, Burgess's own position was reasonably clear. He had been a supporter of Independent Labour representation for several years: his West Riding experiences gave him an appreciation of the significance of developments there, and from his London base, Burgess was by the autumn of 1891, publishing socialist articles by Blatchford, and advocating the formation of Labour Unions on the Bradford model. At the end of April 1892, Burgess took the first step in what proved to be a decisive process. He inserted a leading article on the need for an Independent Labour Party. But he went further than a simple expression of opinion, and asked sympathetic readers to forward their names.[9] Eventually, 2,843 names were published, and

Burgess later claimed to have written 5,000 words a week on the need for a national ILP from then until January 1893.[10] Thus, a clearing house was created as a step towards some sort of national organisation.

Throughout the summer of 1892, the *Workman's Times* carried details of local initiatives, sometimes reproducing the programmes of the new groups.[11] Some parties — like the Manchester and Salford ILP — were to prove durable. Others were to have only a brief existence. No doubt, in those months political interest was heightened by the prospect, and then the actuality of a general election. Once again Liberals showed only minimal interest in Labour candidacies, and the performance of some independents suggested that the time for a national initiative had come.[12] Tillett polled well in West Bradford — but more dramatically, three candidates with claims to Independent Labour status were elected. Havelock Wilson of the Seamen, successful in Middlesborough and the only one of the three to face Liberal opposition, soon became an orthodox Lib-Lab, but others were more significant. John Burns, eventually to move in the same direction, was returned in Battersea. For some time afterwards, he was regarded as the most eligible Leader of Independent Labour. One facet of the emergence of the ILP and more particularly of Hardie, was the gradual destruction of this eligibility. A symbolic episode in this process concerned Burns's differences with Hardie over where to sit in the Commons. The latter's declaration that he would sit in Opposition provoked a critical response from his putative colleague.[13] In part this indicated an irritation that Hardie had gone it alone, but it also highlighted Burns's perception of the tactical possibilities:

it was our duty to support the 14 or 15 men who come most our way ... We can do much better for the present by sitting with the Radicals — with whom Hardie has expressed political agreement to a needless extent — and let them give us reasons to compel us to sit in opposition if they ignore our social demands, a much stronger position than that assumed by Hardie ... On the LCC the wobbling Progressives have been kept to their work by candid and independent friends.[14]

Most fundamentally, July 1892 was a crucial step for Hardie. As Independent Labour member for West Ham South, he emerged more and more as the parliamentary spokesman for independent labour, and therefore as a crucial focus of any new organisation.

If there was now some promise of a breakthrough, there remained a problem of ensuring that such expectations were not dissipated. There was also a fear of being 'nobbled'. Earlier initiatives had been absorbed by the Liberals, and there was concern in some quarters about Champion's activities. Any new organisation should not become the tool of an ambitious clique. Such control would dash the hope of a broadly based movement. Moreover any organisation would have to deal with Champion, even if he were prevented from obtaining a dominant position. He had the reputation of being a political free-booter, and such individualists could be highly damaging. They could appear at by-elections, using allegedly dubious financial blandishments to influence local parties, and thereby torpedoing any attempt at a coherent strategy. If local initiatives were not to be damaged by such manoeuvres, it was important that some form of central organisation, not least of finance, should be instituted.

An attempt to take the drive towards a national organisation a stage farther came from a meeting of what was labelled — rather prematurely — 'the London Executive of the National ILP'.[15] This proposed that an Executive should be created to organise a national conference. Individuals - all London residents - were suggested as representing various interests:

Cunninghame Graham	Scottish Labour Party
H. H. Champion	Scottish United Trades Council Labour Party
Tom Mann	London ILP
H. Quelch	London SDF
Ben Tillett	Yorkshire ILP
Stephen Fay	Manchester and Salford ILP
Joseph Burgess	

In addition:

the Midlands and the North of England could nominate some Midlander or Northerner, residing in London to act on their behalf.

This proposal had two striking features. One was its optimistic catholicity, covering not just both Scottish organisations, but also the London SDF. Indeed, it was hoped that the Labour Electoral Association — widely dismissed by then as a Liberal front organisation — would also be involved.[16] More significantly, the proposal could appear easily as an attempt to dominate the developing movement by metropolitan wire pullers. This, if successful, would impose an organisational form from above and marginalise the contributions of lively provincial centres. This feature provoked a sharp response from W. H. Drew, President of the Bradford Labour Union:

Depend upon it, no executive will suit the provincials that they have had no part in forming. What you should set your face toward is a conference of provincial men and Londoners, and you cockneys ought to unbend, and come say to Bradford, a central town, where you will find plenty of food for reflection.[17]

This view was reflected in other provincial branches, and a consensus began to develop that such a conference would be a crucial next step. Further evidence of the need for some uniformity of policy was supplied by the Newcastle by-election in August. Here the local ILP — influenced by Champion — decided to support the Tory against John Morley, and Hardie eventually acquiesced with some reluctance.[18]

The difficulties were demonstrated even more harshly when a vacancy arose in the Liberal seat of South Leeds. Eventually Mahon stood, backed by

Championite money and anti-Gladstonian polemic. Leeds Liberals and Irish were provoked into retaliation and one of Mahon's meetings ended in a riot. The fiasco terminated when Mahon's candidature was disqualified because of an error in his nomination papers.[19] Yet once again Hardie had given his support,[20] a response that was bound to damage his relationships with Gladstonian Radicals. Such incidents awoke old fears of Tory Gold. They could be dispersed perhaps through the establishment of a central electoral fund, controlled by a democratically elected national body. The fact of locally formed bodies interacted with fear of electoral machiavellianism and confusion to produce a pragmatic quest for electoral effectiveness.

The 1892 TUC held in Glasgow provided an occasion for those interested to take matters further. About fifty delegates and ILP representatives met and formed an Arrangements Committee to organise a national conference. Hardie's significance was suggested by the fact that he chaired the meeting. The resulting committee was perhaps rather more representative of rank and file interests than the one suggested a few weeks earlier:

W. H. Drew	Bradford Labour Party
W. Johnson	Manchester ILP
Miss K. St John Conway	Bristol ILP
James Macdonald ⎫	
Pete Curran ⎬	London District NILP
George Carson ⎭	Scottish ILP

One decision of the Glasgow meeting concerned the basis of representation at the forthcoming conference. The resulting circular limited eligibility to 'authorised delegates from the Independent Labour Party'.[21] This provoked criticism, not least from Hardie himself. He noted how some objected to Fabians because they backed permeation, and others to the SDF, because they were 'impracticable theorists'. Similarly the representation of trade union branches and trades councils was regarded sceptically because there was no means of enforcing Conference decisions on members. But he, nevertheless, resisted the restriction of representation to those labelled formally as ILP delegates. He saw the common stereotypes of other elements as often misleading:

Provincial Fabians are, as a rule, as good stalwarts in the Independent cause as are to be found anywhere, while the bulk of the rank and file of the SDF and the best of the leaders are favourable to the Labour policy for present purposes.

Hardie preferred a much wider invitation:

making the one condition of admission, the signing of a declaration on the part of societies taking part in favour of independent political action on the lines to be agreed by the Conference.[22]

This broader criterion secured wide support and was accepted by the Arrangements Committee.[23]

The complement of liberality on the issue of representation was a desire to avoid too tight a structure for the national organisation. Hardie opposed any attempt by the Conference to formulate and impose a constitution: 'The pathway of the past fifteen years is strewn with the skeletons of Labour organisations strangled by their constitutions'. Instead, he stressed three fundamentals on which he thought that there was agreement:

organisations and members of the Labour Party should not be in membership with any party organisation, or in any way connected with Liberal or Tory parties ... Labour candidates, when run, should be put forward as Independent Labour men, and not under the auspices of either Liberal or Tory ... the Labour programme and policy of such candidate should be Socialistic'.

This was to be the starting point. Other disputes should be seen as differences over application where distinctive tactics reflected variations in local conditions. Such a minimal basis harmonised with the desire to retain as much local autonomy as possible. Hence, Hardie — and the Bradford Labour Union — opposed the adoption of the Manchester Fourth Clause as a national organisation could develop around the basic principle of independence, but it would be preferable if 'each locality ... be left to apply the Independence principle in its own way'.[24] This general position was not held by everyone. The Championite SUTCLP were prepared to accept members of other parties provided they held that labour interests took priority.[25] More significantly for the future, Blatchford, the *Clarion* and many sympathisers, especially perhaps in Lancashire, held to a different conception of the ILP. Arguments over the Fourth Clause raised more fundamental issues.[26] Rather than attempting to construct an essentially electoral organisation, pursuing perhaps the Parnellite path of independent pressure politics, Blatchford saw the central role of the ILP as the making of socialists, with electoral agitation and perhaps parliamentary and municipal representation as means to this end. Anything less than a clear commitment to the Fourth Clause meant the risk of entanglements with other parties, and the erosion of the educative potential of an Independent Socialist Party. Such differences were expressed also in the pre-Conference suggestions about the party's name. A *Workman's Times* correspondent acknowledged that many would prefer the title 'Socialist Labour Party', 'But if the name independent will bring more to our standard, then let us adopt it'.[27] These competing conceptions were to produce various arguments over the years. In January 1893, the crucial question was whether the delegates — meeting in Bradford, rather than the other suggested places, Manchester and Carlisle — could secure enough agreement to launch some sort of national party.

The representation at Bradford was biased overwhelmingly towards the North of England and Scotland. This is so, even allowing for the location of the conference. Indeed, the choice of Bradford reflected to a considerable degree the distribution of active and interested organisations[28] (see Table 37).

Table 37. *Location of organisations represented at the Bradford Conference*

Bradford	22	compared with London	14
Manchester & Salford	11	Midlands	6
Leeds	8	South & South-West	3
Huddersfield	5		
Halifax	3		
Rest of Yorkshire	8		
Rest of Lancashire	18		
Other Northern Groups	11		
Scotland	11		

Even this comparison exaggerates the London representation as an indication of local strength. Several London delegates were nationally significant people, with little standing in the politics of the localities they claimed to represent.

The representation can be considered also from the standpoint of the type of organisation represented. The bulk of the representation from the largest centres were ILPs, ILP Ward organisations and Independent Labour Clubs. Clearly these differed as to their importance and, in the case of some Clubs, their politicisation, but it seems most appropriate to bracket these together with the ILPs from other towns, giving a total of 81 Independent Labour groups. The remainder of the representation came from:

Social Democratic Federation
 6 branches, all from Lancashire
Scottish Labour Party
 8 branches, plus Hardie representing the Executive.
Scottish United Trades Council Labour Party
 1 delegate — originally Champion was chosen but, because of illness, Chisholm Robertson came instead.[29]
Fabians
 2 London and 11 provincial branches
Trade Union and Trades Council[30]
 Cumberland and North Lancashire Workmens' Federation
 Chemical and Copper Workers (St Helens)
 Gas workers and General Labourers (Lancaster)
 Carlisle Trades Council
 Medway District Trades Council
 London Trades Council Labour Representation League
Miscellaneous
 Manchester Labour Church
 Glasgow Labour Army
 Southport Socialist Society
 Bloomsbury Socialist Society
 Legal Eight Hours and International Labour League

It would be easy to view this gathering as one of young idealists, to picture it through Hardie's retrospective portrait of a meeting of enthusiasts:

in the hey-day of life for whom 'difficulties' and 'doubts' had not been born. There was a cause to be fought for, a battle to be won, and that was all they knew and cared. Not an office to be plotted for, nor a job to be intrigued for.[32]

Certainly an emphasis on youth was important. Lister and Aveling stood out amongst the delegates, having been born before 1850. The others were largely in their thirties — and sometimes in their twenties. Yet enthusiasm was in many cases tempered by a pragmatic concern for representation and influence. For some it was the beginning of a long connection with the ILP. This was true not only of Hardie but also of Jowett who was to remain within the party after the 1932 disaffiliation. Seven delegates would sit as Labour MPs,[33] others would become national trade union leaders. Many would become leading political or union figures in their own districts. Blatchford, who represented Manchester and Salford ILP, was perhaps the leading socialist journalist of his generation, and Shaw, representing the Fabian Society, was just beginning the production of plays that would display dramatic genius, and idiosyncratic politics. In contrast, Aveling still a significant figure was soon to be engulfed by the ignominy that would distort assessments of his earlier position. So, many delegates carried parliamentary or trade union batons in their knapsacks — in a crucial sense Bradford January 1893 was a rally of a coming generation. Awareness of who was there must be balanced, however, by an appreciation of the gaps. The London SDF leadership kept aloof, holding that the proper place for socialists was in their organisation. So too did Tom Mann, for reasons that were less clear.[34] He was soon to move to the ILP; a third absentee, John Burns, never did. These spaces served to underline the metropolitan weakness of the movement for an Independent Labour Party. But to bring the representatives of so many organisations together to discuss a new political departure represented a formidable achievement. They now had to resolve fundamental problems of structure, identity and strategy.

The published agenda provided a framework for discussion. It bore the imprint of the views of the largest groups — Bradford, Manchester and the SLP; whilst the London leaders also submitted a series of resolutions.[35] Prior to the central debates, three events of some importance occurred. The delegates elected a Standing Orders Committee, which amongst its tasks, helped to produce an order of debate involving, on occasions, the division of tabled resolutions.[36] Secondly, the credentials of three delegates were questioned: Aveling, representing both the Bloomsbury Socialist Society and the Legal Eight Hours and International Labour League; and Shaw and de Mattos, representing the London Fabian Society. The Standing Orders Committee agreed unanimously that Aveling's credentials should be accepted, and by a majority favoured the seating of the two London Fabians. The latter recommendation provoked a discussion on whether the Fabian policy of permeation would prevent any affiliation of the Society to an ILP, and the Committee's proposal was accepted by the narrow margin of 49 votes to 47.[37] Finally, there arose the question of chairing the conference. Early formalities had been dealt with under the chairmanship of the local leader, W. H. Drew, but some felt that he was lacking in the qualities needed to chair a potentially fissiparous meeting. So when the delegates elected the meeting's officials, Hardie yielded to pressures, stood for the chairmanship, and defeated Drew by 55 votes to 27.[38] This choice foreshadowed the long-lasting identification of man and party. It also perhaps facilitated the decision-making of Bradford. Blatchford, a far from sycophantic observer, acknowledged that:

his good humour, his firmness, his ready wit, his large grasp of the question under debate, as well as his knowledge of procedure saved endless waste of time, and averted many a burst of anger.[39]

These qualities were brought to bear initially on the question of the party's name. The alternatives were presented sharply. Two SLP delegates — George Carson and Robert Smillie — went further than the SLP's ambiguous past practice in urging the adoption of the title 'Socialist Labour Party'. Carson argued, perhaps rather surprisingly given his party's flirtations with Gladstonianism, that: 'in Scotland the Labour Party had come to the conclusion that it was best to call a spade a spade'.[40] The alternative, 'the Independent Labour Party', although moved by the Londoner, H. A. Barker, and seconded by the Mancunian, Alf Settle, had its basis in a proposal by the powerful Bradford group.[41] Defenders of the Socialist option sought justification from continental practice; perhaps predictably, it was a SDF delegate who argued that elsewhere Labour parties had been ready to take the title of Social Democrat. Supporters of the Labour alternative argued on a pragmatic electoral basis: 'the new party had to appeal to an electorate which had as yet no full understanding of Socialism'. In the case of Tillett, the advocacy took the form of an agressively chauvinistic defence of English methods:

he would sooner have the solid, progressive, matter of fact, fighting Trades' Unionism of England than all the hare-brained chatterers and magpies of Continental revolutionists.[42]

Pragmatism and, perhaps, patriotism, combined to give near-unanimous backing to the Labour option.

Several speakers who had backed the majority position had acknowledged their attachment to 'socialism' as an objective. They could be sympathetic, therefore, to the next resolution moved by the delegate from Heywood SDF:

that the object of the Independent Labour Party shall be to secure the collective and communal ownership of the means of production, distribution and exchange.[43]

Here, the alternative was pressed by a supporter of Champion, J. L. Mahon, the former Socialist Leaguer, present as a Leeds delegate. This was simply 'to secure the separate representation and protection of Labour interests on public bodies'. This alternative could be justified on grounds of practicality, but the socialist objective could be backed by two arguments, other than that of conviction. One was the fear of absorption by larger groups: 'a path would be opened by which more men such as Mr. Fenwick and Mr. Broadhurst would creep into the same offices and damn the Labour Party to all eternity'. Moreover, many local ILPs had included socialist objectives in their own constitutions. How could the national party be less advanced? An amended version of the socialist objective was adopted overwhelmingly after the Leeds alternative had been rejected by 91 votes to 16.[44] So, in their first two substantive decisions, delegates developed a classic compromise — a Labour title and a socialist objective. It foreshadowed by a quarter of a century the Labour Party formula of 1918.

Delegates turned next to the complexities of party structure, beginning with a consideration of the organisational basis for a national party. The starting point was a Bradford proposal that the Conference of delegates, agreed on the principle of Independent Labour Representation, 'agrees to federate for the speedier accomplishment of their own common object.' Once again, an alternative was provided, rejecting the proposal for federation and urging the amalgamation of the organisations represented into a national ILP.[45] And once again, delegates found themselves discussing fundamental principles. The federation proposal represented an awareness that delegates represented a variety of groups which might not wish to sacrifice their identities, plus a more general attachment to local autonomy, but even the federal proposal seemed too much for some. Shaw claimed that the Fabian Society could not federate, a claim denied by provincial Fabian delegates.[46] Similarly, a SDF delegate claimed that his organisation could not be pledged in this fashion. For some, such reservations clearly constituted a Rubicon, and they were unwilling to participate in any federating process. There seems to have been optimism that the federal basis would attract a wider variety of organisations, and the amalgamation option secured only two votes. But federalism proved to have little relevance. Provincial Fabian Societies dissolved themselves into ILP branches. Otherwise foreign bodies kept aloof. Only the two organisations represented at Bradford by Aveling applied to join on a federal basis and both were dubious quantities. The federal basis was clearly redundant: by 1894 only ILP branches could be represented at Conference.

Some delegates envisaged federation as a chrysalis stage from which a more homogenous party would, hopefully, emerge. Perhaps this helps to account for the next Bradford decision on party structure, an easily reached agreement: 'that the supreme and governing authority of the Independent Labour Party shall be the Conference of Branch delegates'.[49] The final phrase implied a structure somewhat different from that indicated by the acceptance of a federal basis, although discussion continued to be influenced strongly by a desire to defend local powers. Thus, delegates should elect a Secretary who should work under the control of the Executive. This body was to have very limited authority. Here the key proposals had been tabled by the Manchester and Salford ILP, a body influenced by Blatchford's deep-rooted suspicion of leaders. The Manchester and Salford proposals referred not to an Executive, but to a National Administrative Council, a significant variation, and a title which was to become part of ILP vocabulary. The NAC:

should not have the power to initiate the policy of the Party, but shall confine itself to the instructions given to it at the annual or special Conference of delegates.

In Manchester and Salford's view, leaders should be avoided: 'the Conference do not elect a President or permanent Chairman of the Party'. This was not a universal view. Some felt that the party required its Parnell: Bradford had proposed the creation of a Presidency. But at this stage in the party's development, such roles were viewed with suspicion.[50]

The composition and method of election of the Executive/National Administrative Council was influenced by a concern that the various parts of the country should be represented fairly. Several proposals had been submitted. The London ILP advocated eight provinces, each electing one member, a suggestion clearly weighted against the stronger centres. In contrast, Manchester and Salford had suggested a Council of fifteen with four from the North, and from London and the South, three from Scotland, and two from the Midlands and the East, and from Wales and the West. There were also schemes from Bradford and from Scotland.[51] Once the principle of geographical representation had been accepted,[52] there remained the question of the precise weighting. Its solution was remitted to a committee composed of delegates from each of the heavily represented centres: Ben Tillett (Bradford), Shaw Maxwell (London), George Carson (Scotland), J. L. Mahon (Leeds) and William Johnson (Manchester),[53] who prounced in favour of a scheme similar to the Manchester proposal.[54] The Council would have fifteen members:

Scotland	3
Midland and Eastern	3
Six Northern Counties	5
London and South	4

Despite the regional basis of the selections, it was envisaged by the proposers that the whole Conference would retain the final word in the approving of nominations. An attempt to give each provincial division absolute supremacy was defeated by 44 votes to 32.[55] More significantly, objections were made on grounds of expense, but were ignored.[56] At that stage, the only alternative seemed to be a London-based Executive, which the provincial strongholds were reluctant to accept. Twelve months' experience would reveal the urgency of the financial problem; the party's failure to develop readily in London and the South would lead to a tension between the representation of regions and the representation of centres of strength.

Once this geographical basis had been approved, delegates divided into four sections in order to make nominations. The surviving evidence suggests that SDF delegates did not participate in the Northern selection, and the same appears to be true of several trade union delegates. But Chisholm Robertson of the SUTCLP participated as that party's delegate and was nominated.[57] Similarly, Shaw apparently tried unsuccessfully to influence the London choices but found himself hampered by the predominance of star names amongst the delegates:

The moment I got to my table ... I saw that London was practically out of the Conference. By far the most representative men there were Joseph Rogers of Battersea, and F. V. Connolly of Clapham; and de Mattos and I did our best to get them nominated but without success. It ended in the selection on grounds of general popularity and celebrity of Burgess, Pete Curran, Katherine Conway, and Aveling. Now neither Curran nor Miss Conway establish any real link between the ILP and London. Even Burgess who was at the top of the poll represents the circulation (of the *Workman's Times*), the centre of which is certainly further north than London. Aveling, alone, was emphatically a London delegate; but Aveling's peculiar Marxism has isolated him so completely that he is more out of the movement in London, than any other equally well-know Socialist.[58]

The full composition of this first NAC was:[59]

London	*Northern Counties*
Joseph Burgess	Alf Settle (Manchester)
Pete Curran	W. H. Drew (Bradford)
Katherine St J. Conway	J. C. Kennedy (Carlisle)
Edward Aveling	W. Johnson (Manchester)
	John Lister (Halifax)

Midland Counties	*Scotland*
Geordie Christie (Nottingham)	William Small (Blantyre)
Arthur Field (Leicester)	George Carson (Glasgow)
A. W. Buttery (Stafford)	R. Chisholm Robertson (Glasgow)

Northern and Scottish representatives had strong local bases, but in the Midlands the situation was perhaps more fragile. Indeed, Field's connection with Leicester seems to have been little more than nominal. He was also the Bromley delegate and returned to Kent immediately after tne Conference.[60]

The Secretaryship stood out as a possibly significant position within the party's self-consciously democratic structure. Some prominent figures — Burgess, Hardie and Drew — were nominated but declined to stand.[61] The contest became a two-horse race between the Scottish London delegate, Shaw Maxwell, and William Johnson; Maxwell succeeded with 66 votes to 28. Shaw regarded this as the better of two inadequate options. Johnson, he saw, as:

a brilliant fellow with a combination of dash and determination, with unaffected pleasantness in social intercourse. If the secretaryship had involved the command of a cavalry regiment, Johnson would have been just the man for it. But like most of the 'fourth clause' men, he is a thorough Tory by temperament, and would never consent to permeate a Liberal with anything more soothing than a sabre.

But Shaw also suggested limitations in Maxwell:

he is hot-headed and has occasioned one or two quarrels — most notably one with John Burns ... He is also subject to fits of impossibilities and is too little in touch with the old trade union interest.[62]

Yet, Glasier who knew Maxwell from his Glasgow days believed he had 'a thorough capacity for business details'[63] and competence, disguised perhaps for some by his resembling 'a Parisian Bohemian'.[64]

Whatever the competences or inadequacies of the Secretary and individual Council members, they included few of the leading figures in Labour circles. In part, this might indicate a rank and file distrust of 'leaders', but also perhaps reservations in some quarters as to the politics and likely permanence of the new party.

Some indications as to the first question could be gleaned from conference decisions on policy and strategy. The original agenda had included a variety of resolutions on policy, some advocating familiar labour demands such as the legislative eight-hour day, and others Radical proposals on land and political questions. At the close of the first day's business, a committee of six was elected to draft a programme: Blatchford, Curran, Maxwell, Russell Smart, Aveling and Drew.[65]

Aveling presented the draft programme on the following morning, arguing that in the light of the party's socialist objective, there should be a preponderance of social rather than political reforms within the programme. In fact, the suggested political reforms — a standard list of Radical objectives, including abolition of both Monarchy and Lords — were dropped in favour of a general formula backing: 'every proposal for extending electoral rights and democratising the system of Government'.[66] The social proposals occasioned much more discussion. The first plank, the abolition of overtime, piecework and child labour, produced some opposition on the piecework element, but a proposal for its deletion secured the support of only twelve delegates.[67] Presumably one was Shaw, who dismissed aboliton as:

a curious remnant of the old unionism in unnatural alliance with what I may call for want of a better name, British Museum Socialism ... it will certainly repel members of highly organised trades in which the workers prefer to work by the piece, and can fight the masters to the greatest advantage on that system.[68]

In fact, ILP members within such unions as the Boot and Shoe Operatives were quite prepared to accept the piece-rate principle when this seemed likely to increase their influence.

The social programme had as its centrepiece the advocacy of a legislatively restricted working day, a proposal sharpened up during debate from a limitation of a forty-eight hour week to a specifically eight-hour day. This was supplemented by a broad proposal for provision for the sick, disabled, aged, widows and orphans (the funds would be raised through a tax upon unearned increment) and the social section ended with a statement of the party's socialist objective.[69] Delegates added two new elements to this section. One covered 'free unsectarian education, right up to the universities', avoiding any divisive reference to secular education. The other concerned policy towards the unemployed. At first opinion seemed to favour the provision of home colonies, a nostrum of Hardie and the SLP, but Shaw attacked such a scheme as:

only temporary amelioration of a problem, the solution of which was the ultimate goal, and the declared main objective of the Independent Labour Party.

— a view supported by Aveling. The criticism was enough to produce a broader proposal for 'properly remunerated work for the unemployed'.[70]

The programme's third section covered two points of fiscal reform. The first — to abolish indirect taxation — was extended on Shaw's suggestion to include 'taxation to extinction of unearned incomes': the second, for a graduated income tax, passed apparently without discussion.[71] Here was a programme which was concise and based on a socialist objective. Its range of specific proposals could be justified as steps towards the achievement of that ultimate goal. Ironically, two of the principal figures in the development of this programme, Aveling and Shaw, were to have few subsequent dealings with the party.

There remained the difficult question of protecting the party's independence against would-be proprietorial influences emanating either from the older parties, or perhaps from Champion and his associates. This problem arose on the issue of restrictions on membership. Jowett argued on the basis of the Bradford experience that no one having links with established parties, or indeed any party opposed to ILP principles should be allowed to join. some felt that this was too restrictive. Shaw argued that it would undermine the advancing of labour interests through — in his case — a Liberal Association. Eventually delegates accepted a loose formulation by Aveling that 'no person opposed to the principles of the party shall be eligible for membership', although local parties could retain a more exclusive criterion, if they wished.[72]

The independence question was raised again immediately from another standpoint, with a Manchester attempt to commit the national party to the Fourth Clause. Bradford argued for local autonomy, a position backed by Shaw with a misleading account of Hardie's West Ham contest, and by Aveling arguing that the SPD had increased its representation through playing rival parties off against one another. Blatchford agreed that the Manchester resolution should be seen as an expression of opinion, not a binding declaration, but it was still defeated by 62 votes to 37.[73] This decision was significant, not so much because of the fine print within the competing proposals but because of the competing conceptions of the party that lay behind them. Buoyed up by the prevalent belief in local initiative, it indicated the pragmatic bent of many delegates, and also the continuing connections between some delegates and some manifestations of Radicalism.

The party had to defend its independence through financial viability. The delegates accepted a Bradford proposal that the national affiliation fee be 3*d* a year. A Hull proposal favouring 1/ – , the amount as from April 1895, was defeated overwhelmingly.[74] Finance raised once again the spectre of independence, since there remained a fear of gifts with electoral strings attached. Once again, the decision was a compromise. Burgess moved a resolution for the establishment of a Central Election Fund, to be administered by the Executive. Any contribution would be declined, regardless of the amount, if it were hedged with conditions, whether these covered a limitation on the contribution's use to a specific candidate, or any other stipulation that constrained the Executive.[75] This was accepted in preference to two other suggestions. One went beyond the inadmissibility of conditions to exclude gifts from Liberal and Tory politicians. This tighter version secured only 18 votes[76] — most delegates seemed willing to accept such gifts, provided that there were no strings attached. The other option, also rejected, was the Championite position moved by Mahon, and involving no restrictions.[77] Independence was to be protected, but hopefully not at the expense of beneficial contacts with other elements.

The desire to protect independence and the integrity of the party also came out in the discussion of candidacies. The previous fragmentation of Labour political efforts meant that the delegates had to pay some attention to the question of candidacies that were unmistakably labour, but were not approved by the party. This once again provoked suspicions of Championite manoeuvres, and aid in such circumstances was only approved by a margin of two votes. Financial support was specifically excluded.[78] Such decisions indicated a desire to have a disciplined party — a wish expressed further in the conditions laid down for approval as an ILP candidate. The aspirant must agree in writing:

1st that he subscribe to the objects and programme of the ILP.

2nd that if returned to Parliament, he will form one of the ILP there, and sit in opposition no matter which party is in power.

3rd that he will act with the majority of the ILP in Parliament in advancing the interests of Labour, irrespective of the convenience of any political party.[79]

The first requirement hopefully ensured a socialist commitment, the second and third offered the basis for a united independent force.

And so the conference ended with 'Auld Lang Syne', and the hope that this time the independent initiative would not be smothered in its cradle. Not all the delegates were to remain involved in the ILP; the federal basis, the NAC structure and the financial provision were to prove respectively, redundant, impracticable and inadequate. The official SDF view was supercilious: the Bradford delegates were no doubt well meaning but their pragmatism would lead to failure.[80] The uncertain quantity that Champion represented was still an important element in many calculations.[81] Even Hardie seems to have had his doubts; the SLP remained as a distinct organisation for two more years.

These were the scepticisms, the reservations and the dangers. But the Conference had set up the skeleton of a party. The keen young delegates from the North represented a significant new political force. Their absorption into Liberalism was unlikely, and became more remote as the government's stability became more obvious. Even the sceptical Shaw felt that the results were on balance worthwhile: 'although we did not succeed in making much of a party, we might have done worse. The Conference was well worth holding.'[82] From Regent's Park Road, Engels gave his blessing:

the *masses* of the members make good decisions ... the weight lies in the provinces and not in London, the centre of cliques ... the programme in its main points is ours.[83]

And yet the development was only a tentative one. The party 'must be content', thought Shaw, 'to offer itself to the people on approval'.[84] Much about structure and strategy would be resolved as dilemmas arose. The Bradford decisions were at least testimony to a broad desire for independence. Much diversity had been brought into a platform for unity and growth on the basis of Hardie's dictum, proclaimed from the chair — we 'maun gang oor ain gait'.[85]

13

The National Administrative Council: from servant to oligarch

Settling down

The creation of at least the hope of a national party through the decisions of the Bradford Conference implied the formation of a stable group to administer the party between conferences. Yet the fact that Bradford had been the product of a host of local initiatives meant that local autonomy would be guarded jealously and that the powers of any potential elite would be limited sharply. Such intent was indicated by the name of the party's permanent national representative. Discussions at Bradford had referred sometimes to the formation of an Executive, but the body eventually created was labelled, revealingly, the National *Administrative* Council (NAC). Its duties, as prescribed by the initial constitution, were:

1st To carry out to the best of their power the resolutions passed by the Annual Conference.

2nd To raise funds for carrying on an active propaganda work by means of distributing suitable literature and holding public meetings.

3rd To raise a Special Election Fund to aid districts financially when running Independent Labour Candidates for Parliament.

4th To take such action as circumstances may justify in constituencies when an election is pending, and in which no Independent Labour organisation exists.[1]

These were yoked with a robust defence of local independence. Thus:

each section of the party shall have local autonomy giving full control over policy and finance within the constitution ... The Administrative Council shall not interfere with the rules, constitution or internal affairs of any local organisation.[2]

Indeed, the Bradford Conference seemed clear in its prescription regarding NAC—Conference relationships:

the Executive should not have the power to initiate the policy of the party, but should confine itself to the instructions given it at the Annual or Special Conference.[3]

But the NAC 'may report to the Annual Conference any breach of principle on the part of any organisation seeking representation at such conference'.[4] This last possibility, whilst reflecting the ultimate authority of Conference could be a potential basis for some degree of NAC control, as over time, adroit leaders could be expected to develop techniques that would secure majority Conference support. Likewise, the obligation to raise money for electoral and other purposes could be viewed as a springboard for control. If successful in raising money, leaders would control a scarce resource which branches wished to utilise. Equally, the initiative reserved for the NAC in election contests where no local ILP existed showed how leaders could find themselves making decisions that went beyond Conference declarations. Even these national duties enshrined a potential for some erosion of local autonomy.

Whether the inaugural NAC was a suitable instrument for exploiting such possibilities was debatable. The regional basis for its election had meant that the NAC was an unwieldy body of fifteen members, many of whom were barely known outside their own localities.

Not only was it very much an ILP Second Eleven — no Hardie, no Blatchford and no Tillett — but it also embraced a variety of political priorities. Aveling, already regarded widely with scepticism or dislike, had an ambivalent attitude to the ILP.[5] Chisholm Robertson was a close associate of Champion, and neither he, nor the other Scottish members, nor Field signed a Council circular denouncing Champion and his close associate, Maltman Barry.[6]

The lack of any Chairman meant that the potential linchpin was the Secretary, Shaw Maxwell, whilst John Lister, the Halifax Squire, was to confront the perplexing task of managing party finances. Lack of money was a principal constraint on the operations of the first NAC. The cost of convening such a sizeable body was considerable, and helps to explain why, after an inaugural Bradford meeting, the NAC managed only two gatherings over the next year: in Manchester in March, and in Halifax in November.[7] Even these cost more than £48 in a year, when total income was only £130, and affiliation fees brought in just £56.[8] Financial stringency was not the sole reason for the lengthy hiatus from March to November: several Council members showed little enthusiasm. A meeting had been programmed for May, but as Maxwell informed Lister: 'Some time ago, I wrote all the members of the N.A.C. reminding them of meeting proposed for the 20th and inviting notices for the Agenda. I have received practically nothing.' Shaw Maxwell welcomed delay on political grounds, since he also believed that: 'the Champion—Barry business shd be allowed to simmer down, and if we meet this month, the time may be consumed in unseemly wrangling'.[9] By mid July, Maxwell's line had shifted: 'The time is at hand when by hook or by crook, we must have a meeting of the N.A.C.'[10] Even then, there was little sign of life for several months. Burgess commented ruefully to Hardie that: 'When the next meeting is likely to take place, you know as little as I do.'[11] Criticism began to be directed at Maxwell. In particular, Johnson attacked him for neglecting his duties,[12] a verdict with which Burgess reluctantly concurred: 'I cannot say Maxwell is entirely blameless ... I wish somebody would put a little energy and method into Maxwell.'[13] The principal pressures for a NAC meeting came from a few of the larger branches, most notably Bradford, who wanted to see some sort of response for their affiliation fees.[14]

Even a council member who saw danger in an energetic NAC found deficiencies. By October, the Council had taken few steps to meet the Bradford instruction to issue a manifesto:

At the last Council meeting (i.e. in March) a sub-committee of three, *viz* the secretary, treasurer and Dr. Aveling, were appointed to draw this up. It has not yet arrived, nor have the members of the Council received any official explanation of the delay.

Indeed, this member complained that the officials rarely supplied others on the NAC with information, even on such questions as expenses and affiliation fees. Such minimal co-ordination required little, perhaps 'the aid of a half guinea gelatine duplicator, and the expenditure of a few dozen stamps in less than a day each month'.[15] But the ILP nationally remained an itinerant body with no central office. Co-ordination was therefore difficult. Yet the picture was not entirely gloomy. The NAC in its two meetings did make some important decisions.

Some of the earliest concerned Champion, and were engendered by a fear that he and his followers were keen to take over the ILP. The March NAC meeting spent considerable time on the issue, a discussion complicated by pro-Champion sympathies amongst some Council members. By November, the NAC was repudiating any action of Champion involving Independent Labour politics.[16] NAC decisions in this area were protective of the party's identity and independence, and were to be backed strongly by the 1894 Conference. Such decisions carried wider implications. One of the first NAC responses to the threat of Championite candidacies has been a refusal of responsibility for any Labour candidate not endorsed by either Council or Conference.[17] Here was a first step towards a regularising of branch electoral activity.

The party's electoral commitment meant that early NAC meetings began to discuss possible candidacies. The November meeting endorsed seven candidates, and discussed prospects in several other constituencies. Attempts were made also to provide a lead for branches on the development of an unemployed agitation. In both cases the NAC was reacting to events at the local level. New branches were enthusiastic about promoting candidates, while growing unemployment gave local ILPs a powerful cause which could not only recruit members, but also provide a focus for branch activities.

Despite this activity, NAC involvement in by-elections was restricted. The adoption of the only party candidate — Lister at Halifax — was not just a highly individualistic affair; it also occurred before the Council's March meeting.[18] Party officers did intervene at Grimsby to condemn Broadhurst,[19] whilst involvement at Accrington carried rather more consequences for

NAC—branch relationships. Here the local party, acting with what the NAC later termed 'impulsive zeal', wished to run a candidate, but Maxwell, after discovering local organisational weaknesses, persuaded local activists not to contest, and urged a policy of abstention.[20] Central control proved effective on a crucial issue; moreover it was a control based not on a decision of the full NAC, but rather on the decisions and knowledge of a few.

The relationship between Council and branches was changed in a more formal fashion through the replacement of the original federal structure of the party by a unified one. This recognised the irrelevance of the federalist basis, since provincial Fabian Societies had largely transformed themselves into ILP branches, and the SDF had decided to remain independent. The question of affiliation by bodies other than ILP branches thus became marginal, and in November the NAC resolved that only ILP branches would be invited to the second conference.[21] Even this weak, ungainly NAC found itself engaged in other activities that were typical of central bodies, and strengthened its position vis-à-vis the branches. A draft Constitution was prepared by the Council as was the long-awaited National Manifesto.[22] Perhaps of more significance for the development of Council—branch relationships was the Secretary's action in producing an agenda for the 1894 Conference. This was discussed by a pre-conference NAC and then remitted to a sub-committee.[23] Such a development was very much the shape of things to come, and could lay the basis for future Council domination at Conference. But in 1894, a weak NAC still acknowledged that they were very much the servants of the membership. That year's conference began with Maxwell reading the NAC minutes to the delegates,[24] a much more radical interpretation of accountability than was acknowledged in future years.

Such a tight view of accountability did not just reflect adherence to rank and file democracy. It also flowed from awareness of the less than dynamic performance of the Council. This was widely shared amongst the delegates. It surfaced in extreme terms through one participant's depiction of the 'mass of concentrated stupidity relieved with a touch of knavery that we elected at Bradford ... a corporate dunderhead'. The explanation of this failure prefigured proposals for reform:

it was a first congress composed of men, the majority of whom were unknown to each other. Some of the branches represented were mere bogus organisations, or composed of a few ranting wasters, and pot-house politicians, and as the Congress instead of electing its Council by a general vote, divided itself up into territorial sections, one or two of these bogus delegates coming from localities where there was practically no organisation were enabled to foist their men upon the administrative body, while the districts where the movement was strong were under-represented. This was a very serious error which arose from a democratic wish that the minorities should not be swamped.[25]

Such a diagnosis was reflected in the range of reform resolutions tabled for the 1894 Conference. These included proposals for the reweighting of the

NAC's geographical basis, so that the party's northern strongholds would be more thoroughly represented, and, more radically, for abolishing the geographical basis and reducing the membership to nine including Secretary, Treasurer and the new post of Chairman.[26]

Decisions on NAC reform at this Manchester Conference reflected not just general criticisms but also an even more acute geographical concentration of delegates than the previous year. London sent only seven delegates out of the total of 94 — two more came from the south, in contrast, there were 31 Yorkshire delegates and 28 Lancastrians. It was not surprising therefore that when the delegates elected a Standing Orders Committee, they chose five northern delegates.[27] This group considered the future composition of the NAC and recommended reduction to nine members including the three officers, but left open the means of composition and election. When the reduction had been carried unanimously, two Yorkshire delegates proposed that NAC members 'be elected at and from the Conference, irrespective of geographical area'. This vital change was carried by a margin of only two votes,[28] but when the election of the new Council took place, the full significance of the reform became apparent. Only three survived from the old NAC. The new body was not only more streamlined; it had a more prestigious membership:

NAC February 1894
President: Keir Hardie
Secretary: Tom Mann   unopposed
Treasurer: John Lister*

Other members:

Pete Curran*	Georgie Christie*
Ben Tillett	Fred Brocklehurst
J. Tattersall	Leonard Hall

(* Member of old NAC)

Trade union voices within the NAC were to be momentarily strong. Mann, Tillett, Curran and Hall had links with New Unions, whilst Hardie had achieved national prominence initially as an opponent of the TUC 'Old Guard'. The industrial element was balanced to some degree by Lister the Wykehamist and by Brocklehurst, a Cambridge graduate and secretary of the Labour Church Union. But, above all, this was to be Hardie's party. As he acknowledged:

he had always preferred to act as a free-lance, and to be unconnected with any organisation, but the time had come when it was imperative that men should show without doubt on whose side they were. He was on the side of the I.L.P.[29]

The identity of man and movement was to endure to the end of Hardie's life.
The reforms were welcomed, even by some who had forfeited their

Council places, although Joseph Burgess reflected that a desirable development owed something to devious practices:

We have seen introduced into the Conference the very worst features of the Trade Union Congress — namely, the lobbying for seats which distinguishes the process of elections to the Parliamentary Committee ... Lists are prepared and bargains made.[30]

Russell Smart claimed fourteen years later that he:

called a meeting of the Lancashire and Yorkshire delegates ... previous to the Conference. We arrived at a common agreement, the result of which was that the whole of the first NAC was ejected from office, the Party was reconstituted and Tom Mann was elected secretary.[31]

This claims too much. Not only did some Council members retain their seats, but the forces favouring constitutional change and Mann's election were broader than this. However, factional organisation did matter. Bruce Glasier's 1908 recollection, tinged with hostility to both Smart and Mann acknowledged this:

The Party at that time, was in a wholly disorganised state, and the name of Mr. Mann had not been before the branches for nomination ... a cabal ... had taken steps to ensure his nomination before the Conference met.[32]

Whatever the background to the changes, the tempo of the NAC's activities now changed. A constitutional amendment underpinned this, ensuring that the Council would meet at least quarterly.[33] Mann claimed following the initial meeting under the new regime that the reforms 'had made it possible to get to work more smoothly and with less expense'.[34] Attempts were made to keep in closer contact with the branches. Mann produced monthly circulars urging greater effort and conveying information on NAC decisions, and attempted to make his post into a linchpin of party organisation. It was decided that he should devote three days a week to work in various districts where his organisational experience and oratorical skills could be turned to good use.[35] This quest for more efficiency made the question of finance more urgent. Clearly it was hoped that a more active NAC could generate a better financial response from the branches. This was fulfilled to some degree. In 1894—5, income from affiliation fees rose to £134,[36] but this improvement was overshadowed by demands generated through expanding party activities.

The Council's drive for greater effectiveness inevitably began to produce sub-committees as various activities were hived off. Some sub-committees were created to deal with specific problems — for example, to negotiate with the SDF in order to reach a more harmonious relationship. But more significantly, in May 1894, an Election Sub-Committee was formed, composed initially of the three officers. Its purpose was to represent the NAC at all by-elections, and to decide questions relating to ILP candidates. Moreover, 'no person (would) be supported as a Parliamentary Candidate by any member of the NAC whose candidature has not been endorsed by the sub-Committee *or* the

NAC' (emphasis added).[37] Thus the Sub-Committee was to be an independent source of authority, and did not need to have its decisions approved by the full Council.

It is a revealing insight into the NAC's order of priorities that whilst its meetings were continually preoccupied with electoral matters, the formulation of policy was a much less structured affair. A sub-committee was formed to produce a policy statement, but with a membership less weighty than that of its electoral counterpart.[38] Nevertheless, its proposals were accepted, most without amendment, by the full NAC, and then by the 1895 Conference.[39]

The NAC's principal task in 1895 was the conduct of the general election. Here was the first major test of party support and effectiveness. That year's Conference tightened provisions for candidatures on the initiative of the NAC. Now no branch could announce its choice of candidate officially until its selection had been approved by the Council, and the candidate should be run only when the branch was able to satisfy the NAC that it could meet the election expenses.[40]

When the election was called, the party's immediate response was determined by a constitutional provision that: 'On the near approach of a General Election, a Special Conference shall be convened by the NAC to decide the policy of the I.L.P. for such election.'[41] Here, once again, was evidence of a belief that the rank and file should control potential leaders. But how did it work out in practice amidst the excitement of an election campaign? This Special Conference was held privately in London on 4 July.[42] Sixty-one delegates attended, fewer than at Bradford or Manchester, although the voting figures suggest that some of them were empowered to cast proxy votes.[43] Hardie ruled from the chair that any decisions must be binding, and delegates went on to decide that party members should vote only for ILP and SDF candidates. A significant minority seems to have favoured the making of particular exceptions, but essentially the outcome was in harmony with the Fourth Clause position of no support for non-socialist candidates. This was the one collective incursion by the rank and file into decision-making on the election. Otherwise the NAC met repeatedly in the early days of July. The day before the Special Conference Mann informed Lister: 'we carefully went into the financial possibilities and it looks as though at least 20 candidates will be run under our auspices, probably 25'.[44] Financial questions dominated subsequent Council meetings. On the day of the Conference the NAC met deputations from hopeful branches and eventually decisions were made as to assistance, and advice proffered on the desirability of contesting. Council members found the transactions difficult.[45] Six of them were candidates, including the Chairman, Treasurer and Secretary, and could involve themselves in Council discussions only to a limited degree. Branches tended to give wildly optimistic estimates of their financial resources, and naive under-estimates of the amount of money needed. The sizeable overlap between Council members and candidates together with the centrality of the financial question meant that more work was taken on by a Parliamentary Finance Committee, formed earlier in the year, to look after election finances. It was composed of relatively well-heeled party members and began its work by circularising party sympathisers. But under the exigencies of the campaign, this appointed body took a more central role. Acting, so it was said, under NAC instructions, it circularised branches contesting the election, informing them of the principle on which central funds would be allocated.[46] How far the circularisers were acting under NAC instructions as executors of a decision arrived at by an elected body is debatable. Certainly one subsequent meeting, nominally of the Council, was dominated, at least in terms of numbers, by the Financial Committee members who attended supposedly to give advice. They considered and approved a manifesto embodying the decisions of the Special Conference and drafted by the absent Hardie.[47]

The decision-making during this campaign demonstrated two aspects of the NAC's powers which were of general significance. One was that, election conference apart, key decisions were taken at the apex of the party. The pressure of events saw to that. Often they were not even taken by the full NAC but by a few, abetted perhaps by financial experts. This tendency towards elitism is important as is a proper diagnosis of its causes. These lay not in the desire of Council members to accumulate power, nor in their adoption of priorities and a style emanating from exposure to the seductions of parliamentary life. Rather they seemed to be occasioned to a considerable degree by requirements following from a commitment to electoral competition.

But this tendency towards hierarchical control must be balanced by countervailing factors. Council members were taking important decisions that affected the party's fundamental direction, but the quality of those decisions and the capacity to impose them were subject to significant limitations. NAC members depended heavily on information from branches about electoral prospects, and this was frequently unreliable. Moreover, financial weakness limited the extent to which the NAC could affect branch behaviour. The Finance Committee's efforts had given the Council a source of income, independent of branch fees, but the amounts that coult be disbursed were small. They provided only a limited inducement to conform to central decisions.

This weakness was an instance of a more basic countervailing tendency. Election funds apart, a principal prop of NAC authority had to be its ability to provide or withold financial benefits. These were not only limited, but to a considerable degree were themselves the products of branch affiliation fees. The NAC's ability to coerce recalcitrant or laggard branches was dependent on a prior ability to secure a regular flow of funds from members. This capacity was restricted by a combination of members' poverty, their tendency to give first place to local efforts and their suspicion of central power and initiatives. In the last five years of the century, the tension between the centralisation of decisions and lack of resources to carry them forward was to become increasingly obvious.

The arrival of the Big Four

The 1895 general election was a watershed in the party's development. It was the death of easy optimism. The next five years were to be a period of retrenchment during which the party developed a more thorough commitment to the idea of a Labour Alliance. This transition period left an important imprint on the style, membership and influence of the NAC.

Council membership had been unstable in the early years, but by 1898, a nucleus of four dominated the NAC and remained there taking turns as Party Chairman until 1909. The remaining New Unionists dropped out from any deep involvement in party affairs. Tillett did not stand for re-election to the Council in 1895; Curran resigned from the NAC in 1898, claiming that his union work was making increasing demands on his time.[48] Tom Mann resigned from the Secretaryship during the same year,[49] and was replaced by the Preston ILP member John Penny. The new man was much less well known and took a less activist stance as Secretary. The post was now on the way to becoming a more strictly administrative one, and duly became so with the selection of Francis Johnson to succeed Penny in 1903. Much the same was true of the Treasurership, with Lister giving way to the Honley mill-owner, France Littlewood.

The principal continuity at the head of the ILP lay in Hardie's involvement. His links with the trade union world were now relatively slight. He appeared much more as the archetypal socialist propagandist with a penchant for passionate rhetoric and polemical journalism. This image of the party was bolstered in the late nineties by the arrival on the NAC of three men who were to become strongly identified with the party — Ramsay MacDonald in 1896, Bruce Glasier in 1897 and Phillip Snowden in 1898. None of the three had direct experience of industrial working class life, and in several respects Hardie's style seemed closer to them than to his own origins. It was now that the image of the ILP as a party of lower-middle-class socialists became established. These practised orators brought a formidable armoury of skills to bear in their running of the party.

Crystallisation of a leadership group developed along with further clarification of party organisation. This grew in part out of decisions taken in 1893—4 for uniformity of structure; it also reflected a recurrent political tension. Some uniformity had been generated by the decision that representation at the 1894 Conference should be limited to ILP branches,[50] but this left two fundamental problems. One was the definition of a branch; this was settled, for the moment, at the 1895 Conference where the primary organisational unit, the branch, was established as being congruent with a parliamentary constituency.[51] Where the party was strong, the branch would presumably spawn sections and clubs. But this solution left a major gulf between NAC and membership. One obvious response was to develop intermediary tiers to co-operate action on a local or regional basis. The ideal, as enunciated at the time of the 1894 Conference, involved two intermediary levels. District Councils should be elected by local branches:

to endorse and carry out a common policy for the District, instead of leaving the work to be done by Branches acting independently of each other which would be certain to result in confusion.

Secondly, County Federations should be developed:

to enable the educational and organising work to be taken in hand, and to distribute the work in connection with this more equitably than could be the case if no such body existed.[52]

Examples of both types of co-ordination already existed. In both Bradford and Manchester and Salford, city-wide organisations attempted to co-ordinate more local initiatives, whilst a Lancashire Federation had emerged in the second half of 1893.[53] It was hoped that the party structure would develop pyramidically, with each level electing representatives to the next tier.[54] It is not clear whether this occurred in practice, or whether branches elected directly to the Federations.

It appears that the NAC initially envisaged its ideal structure as a method of encouraging united action, short-circuiting the difficulty of trying to control numerous remote branches. For example, it was anticipated that the federations would play a significant role in the endorsement of candidates. The formation of federations was encouraged: four were represented at the 1895 Conference and according to one study they ultimately numbered 16.[55] But at the 1896 Conference, the NAC succeeded in having the federations removed from the authorised party structure. This about-turn occurred for two related reasons. The first was political: several of the federations were viewed by many NAC membes as foci of discontent. The federations were identified with Blatchford's criticisms of the ILP leadership and with advocacy of a United Socialist Party.[56] Instead of providing a mechanism for propelling branches closer to the centre, they tended to mobilise branches against the centre. The second reason was financial. It had been anticipated that the middle tiers would act as a means of channelling funds to the centre. It appears, however, that some ILP branches paid dues only to their federations, and that some federations allowed direct membership by individuals who did not belong to any ILP branch.[57]

Once the NAC had decided to act against the federations, it did so with efficiency. In January 1896, the Council settled the basis of representation for that year's conference. It was to be based on membership certificates purchased by branches from the NAC rather than on affiliation to a federation. Furthermore, the qualification was to be applied as of the previous month, December 1895, thereby loading the scales in favour of branches that had retained a primary loyalty to the NAC, and also disfranchising some branches in arrears with payments because of heavy election expenditure.[58] Activists evinced considerable opposition to this ruling, and also to the manner in which the NAC promoted the change within the conference. It did not appear on the agenda, but was introduced within the NAC report. Under these favourable conditions, the Council's bid succeeded.[59] The failure of branches to pay fees punctually could be used paradoxically to weight the decision making process, whilst the NAC's inevitable advantages in the field of conference procedures was a vital resource. The concern of critics was not supported by much organisational response: indeed the NAC was aided by the suspicion with which some critics viewed systematic organisation. This was a milestone in the party's development, the Council moving swiftly to destroy a perceived threat to its authority.

The 1896 Conference was significant also for a confused debate on the Party Presidency. Following the creation of this post, two years earlier, Blatchford's *Clarion* had campaigned against it, as a denial of democratic principles. This position was accepted by several branches, and in 1896, ten resolutions were submitted for the abolition of the Presidential office. The Conference accepted abolition by 51 votes to 38, but then Hardie — not the most disinterested participant — ruled that a further vote must be taken on a NAC amendment to substitute the word 'Chairman' for that of 'President' in the Constitution. This raised difficulties for some abolitionists who advocated the substitution of a Chairman provided that the incumbent was not elected by the whole conference, but simply chosen by the NAC. But the NAC proposal was restricted to the substitution of one word for another, and in this confused situation 55 backed the change to Chairman compared with 22 who wished to stick to President; then after yet more tortuous arguments, retention of the chairmanship was backed by 46 votes to 36.[60] All remained the same except for a name. An initial success in removing a leadership role had been aborted by a combination of general confusion, divisions amongst critics and the rulings of the President/Chairman.

The stabilisation of the late nineties witnessed some organisational growth that strengthened the centre. The party began to develop more specialised structures. The establishment of a central office was followed in 1896 by the formation of a publications department, and the following year by the inauguration of the monthly *ILP News*.[61] Attempts were made to develop systematic organisational work, with a paid organiser hired on a short-term contract, to conduct propaganda, initially in mining areas where the NAC had hopes of a break-through. Here shortages of money imposed limitations, and some Council members claimed that the result hardly justified the outlay.[62] Even in public, the NAC were coy, claiming that the value of the innovation 'cannot be judged by the number of members gained or new branches opened'.[63]

Despite the financial constraints, such ambitions generated an elaboration of the Council's committee structure, and a further concentration. In the late nineties there were typically sub-committees on Publications, Organisation and

Parliamentary issues, with other committees making brief appearances.[64] These small bodies took some vital decisions; in particular the Parliamentary (formerly Elections) Committee played a pivotal role in several by-elections. Such expansion of committee initiatives provoked criticism within the NAC, but marginal modifications did little to offset the underlying trend.[65]

Now the party had at its apex a small group, who, whatever the tensions on a personal level, had a reasonably cogent and agreed view on what the party could achieve. In particular, the Big Four wished to keep the party away from fusion with the SDF and were anxious to court trade union, and to some extent Radical—Liberal, opinion. There were major constraints on their ambitions. Branches were often reluctant to pay fees to the centre, and the relatively infrequent Council meetings found it difficult to cope with all the outstanding business. Glasier commented regretfully on a two-day Council meeting in January 1898: 'A long day of much anxious discussion. There is so little time, and so much work that we ought to give more care to.'[66] It was not just a problem of overloaded agendas. Some Council members felt, perhaps unfairly, that Penny's activities as Secretary were not always as vigorous as they might be. As early as August 1898, Hardie was complaining that Penny was: 'too languid to do anything ... It looks as if a mistake has been made in making him Sec',[67] and almost two years later he felt that the situation had not improved:

A note from JRM this morning says that the work at 53 (Fleet Street) is getting further into arrears ... In the parlous state of our Movement this may easily be fatal ... There is lethargy where there shd be energy and a spirit of heaviness where an inspiration is needed.[68]

But it was the efficiency-conscious MacDonald who seems to have been Penny's most astringent critic. In April 1899, the latter hit back at what he believed to be unfair claims, and in so doing painted a graphic picture of the burdens under which an impoverished NAC operated.[69] Penny claimed to have worked initially more than twelve hours each day, and still spent more than sixty hours a week trying to meet the party's requirements. Some of his time was spent attempting to compensate for inefficiencies within the NAC's committee system:

Committees meet sometimes with, and sometimes without my knowledge. When I know about the meeting it may be several days or even weeks before I get the minutes, and when the minutes do arrive I cannot carry them out so well as I could, if I knew the spirit as well as the actual wording of the resolution. In some cases I have not heard of the meetings at all.

He was reluctant to take decisions on his own initiative, and tried to consult Council members before dealing with important correspondence:

I have tried to subordinate myself entirely. I have endeavoured to keep out of sight. That, I think, is the right attitude for a secretary but with a committee scattered all over the country it means delay.

The preparation of the NAC Report for the 1899 Conference had been a complicated affair:

I received reports from Hardie, Glasier and Smart dealing with elections, fusion, organising and publishing. When I went through these, I found that they did not make anything like a complete report. I had to write an introduction and conclusion, bring in a number of other matters, and string the whole lot together.

Similarly Penny found himself weaving between the broadsides of individual NAC members. On the complex exchange of letters with the SDF over fusion, for example:

The most important ... was drafted by Hardie, that letter you cut to pieces. Then Hardie came along and did not approve at all of your suggestions. That left me between two stools and I had to re-write the whole letter on my own responsibility.

ILP leaders might have had considerable elbow-room in their dealings with the rank and file, but they faced problems both in taking collective decisions, and then in rendering them effective. Nevertheless, the NAC made considerable headway in two crucial and related areas — those of electoral policy and relationships with other organisations.

Electoral optimism had been damaged severely by the setback of 1895. Frequently thereafter, the NAC discussed by-election vacancies, but seldom discovered any justification for entering a candidate. When seats were contested, the results were often disappointing and financially damaging. One legacy, emanating in particular from the Barnsley failure of October 1897, was to strengthen NAC insistence on its own control of such contests. Barnsley had been expensive and had provoked claims of organisational deficiencies, both hardly surprising given the length of the campaign, and the party's weakness in the Yorkshire coalfield.[70] The NAC responded by proposing that one of its representatives take sole charge of financial matters during any by-election, that if the original financial grant had to be supplemented then authorisation by the Parliamentary Committee was required, and that any by-election agents should be appointed by the same committee.[71] It was not just a question of increasing the central control of campaigns; the locus of control was to be effectively a small sub-committee of the NAC.

Election matters also occupied the NAC in a more fundamental fashion. The party faced the perennial problem of any small group aspiring to national status. Should an electoral campaign be waged on as broad a front as possible in order to maximise the party's total vote, or should a limited number of winnable seats be selected, and resources concentrated in those? The Parliamentary Committee in July 1897 advocated the first alternative:

running as many candidates as there is legitimate demand for, and thus polling the largest vote possible for socialism ... it is of the first importance that the vote at the polls ... bear some proportion to the relative strength of the movement in the country.[72]

This position was reiterated broadly in the NAC's Report to the 1898 Conference, and was then struck out after a Conference debate. Superficially, this appears to be a case of the NAC's position being over-turned by a rank and file vote. But it is not quite that simple. The party's financial position seemed even worse after Barnsley, and this no doubt affected the views of some Council members. Hardie, responding to a challenge from one Conference delegate, admitted his reservations about the published policy:

He was on the Parliamentary Committee last year, and was responsible in part for the policy proposed. If the matter were being considered now however, he would certainly give the matter fuller consideration before deciding in the way they had.[73]

This was hardly a stirring defence of Council policy — and the deletion of the relevant paragraphs from the Report was carried apparently without any significant opposition.

This decision handed a considerable initiative to the Council, as it would play the principal role in deciding which seats should be fought. This became clear within a few months when the NAC was faced with a request from the Manchester and Salford ILP that they should be allowed to contest three seats. The Council strongly urged that one of these be dropped and Glasier attended a meeting of Manchester members to successfully promote this reduction.[74] By July 1898, the commitment to limited candidacies had developed a more concrete form. The Parliamentary Committee proposed that candidacies should be restricted to twenty-five and began to develop a list of possibilities. The full Council accepted the numerical restriction the following day,[75] and this was to be the framework within which the NAC considered candidacies over the next two years. The number of likely contests gradually declined, and from February 1900, Council decisions on candidates were affected radically by the party's affiliation to the Labour Representation Committee.

This last development was to affect fundamentally the temper of ILP politics. It represented a triumph for those within the party who advocated a close attachment with the unions rather than Socialist Unity. It also involved a triumph for the views of the great majority of NAC members over a critical element within the rank and file. Many ILP members had always been attracted by the hope of Socialist Unity, at the heart of which lay the goal of some sort of link with the SDF. Early NAC attempts to promote joint action had produced little result; Tom Mann, an advocate of a closer relationship had raised the matter with the SDF late in 1895, but with no success.[76] However, the ILP's 1896 Conference had resolved that the objective of a socialist conference to discuss united action be pursued.[77] Eventually in April 1897, a joint conference of ILP, SDF and Fabian representatives was held, whilst a second meeting three months later did not include Fabians. Later that July, an informal meeting of five NAC members and five from the SDF Executive discussed the feasibility of fusion. They concluded that:

in the opinion of those present expressing their opinion as individuals, it is desirable in the interests of the Socialist movement that the S.D.F. and I.L.P. be united in one organisation, provided it be found that there is no question of principle to keep them apart.[78]

Members of both bodies were ballotted on this somewhat imprecise formulation, a move sufficient to provoke criticism from some opponents of the SDF, especially Glasier.[79] Moreover, the informal status of the July 1897 meeting meant that the position of the NAC remained unclear. Hardie acknowledged subsequently that an error had been made in holding this discussion without a prior NAC meeting. When the five reported back to the NAC they found hostility to the decisions on the part of 'a very strong minority'.[80]

The NAC's next intervention came in January 1898 when it considered the results of the ballot: 5,158 votes favouring the July resolution and 886 against. The Council's response was cold:

on the grounds (1) that only a very small proportion of the members had voted (2) that some members had declined to vote until the question had been discussed at the Annual Conference, (3) that as the Conference was near, it was decided that nothing further should be done, beyond ascertaining opinion on the question of a name, until the matter had been brought before the Conference.[81]

Now those opposed to fusion leaned on the principle of Conference sovereignty to justify their inaction. No previous conference had declared specifically for fusion with the SDF, and therefore it was claimed the NAC had no mandate for a policy.

By the eve of the Conference, the Council had abandoned neutrality. In a Supplementary Note on Fusion, delegates were presented with a hostile portrait of the SDF with its 'rigid, propagandist phrases', cut off from trade unionism, co-operation and 'the advanced elements in the humanitarian movements'. Dissolution of the ILP would be a loss to the Socialist Cause, immediate fusion would import existing tensions into a supposedly united party; federation was, at present, the only judicious step. The portrait was supplemented by recommendations that ensured a complex debate: Conference should settle

upon one or other of the following courses of action: — (1) Instruct the NAC to proceed with arrangements for federating with the S.D.F., and other independent Socialist bodies; or as an alternative (2) Refer the matter to the Branches, and that the members be asked to vote whether they are in favour of a federation, or dissolution of the I.L.P., and fusion with the S.D.F. In the event of the second course being adopted, we recommend that the rule of the trade unions be followed, which insists on two-thirds of the members voting 'Yes' before the organisation can be dissolved.[82]

These complex proposals were decided on by the NAC immediately before the Conference.[83] Hardie read the declaration to delegates, noting that: 'as it was holiday time, there had been no chance of getting it printed'.[84] Whereas Conference could decide on federation, the NAC was proposing no such possibility for the fusion option; rather, despite the earlier ballot, a second vote was proposed. Moreover, the fusion alternative was now equated steadfastly with the dissolution of the party, an association calculated to provoke defensive reflexes.

The NAC set the tone of the Conference debate further, by starting it with a paper read by Glasier, the most dedicated opponent of all things SDF. Such a move involved ambiguity about Glasier's status — was he speaking for the NAC or giving his own position? His views were hardly the neutral ones that the NAC had claimed earlier that year:

the ways of the S.D.F. are not our ways ... the ways of the S.D.F. are more doctrinaire, more Calvinistic, more aggressively sectarian than the I.L.P. The S.D.F. had failed to touch the heart of the people.[85]

The debate was predictably confused. Some speakers attacked the Council either for refusing to accept the earlier membership vote, or for confusing the issue.[86] Equally, some speakers blamed the NAC for failing to give a lead, a far cry from the 1893 prescription of limited NAC powers. Thus Brocklehurst accused the NAC of timidity: 'He was quite convinced that they of the rank and file would have been content to follow the lead of the N.A.C.'[87] NAC members even demonstrated disagreement on the detail of the federation alternative. Curran, speaking allegedly on behalf of the Council, provided a very restricted definition of federation — electoral alliance, plus a court of appeal to deal with any problems. But this interpretation was disavowed by Hardie.[88] When the vote was taken on the NAC's alternatives, that of the branch vote was favoured by 80 to 48.[89] Presumably this majority was composed of fusionists, opponents of any arrangement with the SDF and the confused. The only change to the NAC's proposal was to strengthen the qualification for the dissolution of the ILP from two-thirds to three-quarters of the total membership[90] — a major hurdle given the discrepancy between active and paper membership. It was only after the vote that official definitions of the fusion/federation alternatives were produced.

The results of the ballot were made known at the end of July. 2,397 members favoured federation, and 1,695 fusion. Now there was no suggestion that the verdict should not be accepted on account of the small poll. Instead the NAC approached the SDF to pursue the federation option. The response was a dusty one. H. W. Lee, the SDF Secretary, claimed that earlier discussions had taken fusion as the objective, and that this had been accepted overwhelmingly on the first ballot. The SDF Executive had no mandate to consider federation. Here the matter rested.[91] Sympathy for a united Socialist Party continued to smoulder in some branches, but the NAC had killed off the topic for several years, as a central argument at national conferences.

The decline of interest in this conception of Socialist Unity was paralleled by an increased willingness to invest ILP energies in the idea of a Labour Alliance. Here the NAC could secure legitimacy initially from the 1896

Conference. The Council were empowered: 'to act as convenors in conjunction with other Socialist and Trade Union bodies for a British Socialist Congress'.[92] Their authority did not come from any resolution but from a paragraph in the Council's Report accepted in the debate on a United Socialist Party. The NAC then contacted the Secretaries of the SDF and Fabian Society, and Sam Woods, the Lib-Lab Secretary to the TUC's Parliamentary Committee. Socialist responses were favourable, but Woods insisted on the need for TUC approval, and suggested the submission of an appropriate resolution to that year's Congress.[93] The July 1896 NAC therefore authorised the drafting of such a resolution to be forwarded to three, hopefully sympathetic, unions: Tillett's Dockers, the Gasworkers and the Tailors. Unfortunately, these unions received the resolution too late for submission to that year's Congress.[94] Matters then hung fire, but following the fusion imbroglio, the 1899 Conference accepted as uncontroversial a resolution:

That the NAC use every means at its command, consistent with the Constitution, to bring about joint action with the Trade Union Co-operative and Socialist Societies in both Municipal and Parliamentary elections.[95]

The decision, taken separately from arguments about socialist federation,[96] said nothing about organisational form, but was the springboard from which the NAC moved into involvement with the Edinburgh and London Conferences on Labour Representation. It also provided the basis for opposition to SDF attempts to commit these bodies to specifically socialist objectives. ILP delegates employed the 1899 resolution to deny that socialism was a suitable reference point for the new organisations, since such a commitment had been extraneous to the resolution taken by the Council as guidance for their involvement.[97] Once again, ILP leaders were able to use Conference decisions as a cloak for subsequent flexibility.

The emergence of the Labour Alliance obviously had radical long-term implications for the distribution of power within the ILP. But the previous five years had themselves seen major changes against a backdrop of stagnant membership, financial stringency and reduced expectations. Despite limited resources, the NAC had increased its control over the party, with a more elaborate committee system, the beginning of an attempt at professional organisation, and victories for the leadership on the key issues of Fusion and the Labour Alliance. The Big Four who now dominated the party were able to hold sway over the activists, or most of them, through their popularity, rhetorical skills and procedural expertise. Grumbles came from those suspicious of elitism, or enthusiastic about socialist unity, but rarely took a clear organisational form. Indeed many activists accepted, or even welcomed, the dominance of leaders. Party membership was now fairly stable; the ILP was a distinct community with strong sentimental ties between leaders and led, ties that could operate strongly to the advantage of the former.

As yet, the financial constraint led Council members to portray their powers as limited:

A close, detailed, business-like following out of work is impossible. We meet four times a year — quite often enough, if we are to be a strictly administrative body. If we are to be an executive body, we must meet at least six times as often. Were there no other difficulties in the way of this, there is the financial one, and that settles the matter.[98]

A close, detailed scrutiny was clearly not possible, but the NAC did wield considerable independent power. The official position was a myth:

Every year at its Annual Conference, the branches have power to depose any or every-one of their office-bearers, and to determine absolutely what their National Council shall do in their behaviour.[99]

Even in the small poor ILP of the late nineties, this was an illusion. The new century brought the complexities of the Labour Alliance, renewed hopes of electoral success, and growing financial optimism — all factors suggesting a strengthening of the Big Four's position.

The impact of the LRC

The formation of the Labour Alliance had major consequences for the internal politics of the ILP. It injected further complexities into decision-making, especially on the question of candidacies: it associated the party with LRC victories both in by-elections and then, most crucially, in January 1906; such advances, together with the prospect of more, helped to recruit members and expand party finances. Growth permitted more elaborate party organisation, and made the decisions of the party leadership more significant. This expansion of leaders' resources was heightened from January 1904 when the party acquired Hardie's *Labour Leader* as an official paper. Glasier, as editor, set out to utilise it as a powerful instrument for the views of the Big Four.

Such a strengthening of the Party elite bred its own countervailing tendencies. The critical notes of the nineties continued, although at reduced volume. Relationships between ILP branches and their SDF counterparts could become matters of controversy after the SDF's early secession from the LRC. The sometimes tortuous negotiations to produce united support for a cautious trade union candidate could produce tensions within the party, as local branches felt sacrificed to the requirements of Labour Alliance 'realpolitik'. The increase in party membership produced difficulties for the leadership, as new members lacked a ready respect for established leaders. The party could become less manageable.

Such implications of the inaugural LRC conference, were barely visible when the ILP was confronted with the September 1900 election. The LRC was in no shape to contest a wide range of seats and the ILP had no hope of contesting the twenty-five constituencies, projected two years earlier. The decline of the late nineties plus the impact of the war had blunted the enthusiasm of branches.

A feeling that it was hopeless to resist the militarist and reactionary spirit raging in the Press and in the streets prevailed not only in the ranks of the ILP but amidst all sections of the community who were opposed to the war, and who were interested in social reform.[100]

Unlike 1895, the NAC found itself under little pressure to undertake new contests. Indeed the Council took the initiative, attempting to generate activity in places where members seemed apathetic, but a candidate seemed worthwhile. Thus in May the NAC attempted to galvanise the Preston branch into action and later attempted to force the pace in Merthyr.[101] Clearly, Council members felt credibility depended on electoral participation. 'It was imperative for the ILP to participate in the struggle if the Party was to continue as a national political movement.'[102]

Even with its limited number of candidates, the ILP sponsored nine plus one joint with the SDF, there were major problems. Inevitably money was a worry. An Election Finance Committee was formed once again. This issued a circular asking for £1,000, but the response was almost twice as much.[103] Even if the party could not achieve a consistently stable financial position, it could transmute electoral enthusiasm into cash. As in 1895, decisions during the campaign tended to be taken by a very few people — most notably Glasier — as others were occupied in their constituencies. It was this small group that dealt with the complexities of Hardie's two attempts at Preston and Merthyr, and which dispensed 'money like millionaires' to the candidates.[104]

The rank and file could make its presence felt only at the Special Election Conference prescribed by the constitution and held at Bradford on 29 September. The principal controversy was a result of the war. Already there had been attempts at local ILP—Radical collaboration on an anti-war basis. An abortive attempt to promote a Peace Candidate at York in January[105] had been followed by local ILP support for Leif Jones's South-West Manchester candidacy in May.[106] Some of the party's general election finances came from sympathetic Liberals such as George Cadbury.[107] He clearly saw the ILP as part of the Radical family and hoped that he could reduce antagonisms. He reassured Herbert Gladstone, 'any influence I may have acquired will be used to prevent the ILP opposing Liberals; if this is not the case, they will get no more from me'.[108] Agreement on the war led to the suggestion that perhaps the ILP could support specific anti-war Liberals. The possibility of a 'white list' was scouted by Hardie as early as August:

Are there any circumstances in the present political situation which would justify a departure from what may with reason be regarded as the traditional policy of the party? ... The whole question is one of expediency in which no question of principle is involved ... The question which is agitating the minds of many members of the ILP is whether these men should not have the support of Socialists at the polls.

Such an electoral tactic could harmonise with the ILP's position on the war; it could be used also to counteract claims about the party's isolationaism. Anti-war Liberals will be assailed by all the forces of reaction and will have the official heads of their own party against them ... It would prove that on occasion we can discriminate, and are not driven by an unreasoning hostility to oppose everything which is not branded with our own special brand.[109]

This kite produced a mixed response, some opponents arguing that it was an error to use the war as a sole criterion when some anti-war Liberals were antipathetic to social reform.[110] Campaign demands meant that only two NAC members, Littlewood and Glasier, came to the Election Conference, along with ninety delegates.[111] Two of the NAC recommendations — support for Socialist and LRC candidates, and local autonomy in other cases — were carried. The third was a strong recommendation to support candidates with good anti-Imperialist and Labour credentials. This clearly represented an attempt to meet the critics' case about social reformers, but it was defeated by 42 votes to 39. Glasier felt that defeat resulted in part from the proposal's apparent contradition of the local autonomy decision, but there were surely more significant factors. Such a recommendation was bound to divide the party, raising as it did the spectre of political independence; and the absence of many of the NAC perhaps helped to ensure a majority for the critics.

Although the 1900 election was fought under LRC auspices, it was in many ways, the last act in the politics of the nineties. Financial difficulties still hampered the NAC, and decision-making in the campaign was as unco-ordinated as in 1895. The ILP still dominated Independent Labour politics with as yet few trade union candidates. From October 1900, the situation began to change. Hardie's Merthyr victory, together with Bell's at Derby, seemed justifications for the LRC and helped to guarantee its continued existence. The Taff Vale judgement was to provide a harsher justification and a firmer guarantee.

The ILP leaders were committed firmly to the Alliance, perhaps even more so after the early secession of the SDF. Individual ILPers held key positions within the new organisation. MacDonald as Secretary was its linchpin, and Hardie, one of its first two MPs. They accepted that the balance of influence within the LRC would change, as trade unions became more committed to the organisation. In some districts, this would mean that the spadework carried out by ILP enthusiasts would be cashed in terms of trade union candidates.

Such transactions were sometimes reasonably smooth. It appears that local ILPers accepted David Shackleton's Clitheroe candidacy in July 1902 with good grace.[112] But by the following year, even some ILP leaders were having reservations about the operation of the Alliance. Crook's Woolwich campaign produced considerable ILP criticism,[113] but it was with the Preston by-election of May 1903 that strong doubts emerged at the top of the party. Preston had produced sizeable ILP votes in the absence of a Liberal, in 1895 and 1900, but now John Hodge of the Steel Smelters stood as LRC candidate. He discouraged Hardie from coming to Preston, since such an appearance could stir memories of 1900, and deter Tory trade unionists from voting Labour. Glasier after a conversation with Hodge, poured out his concern to Hardie:

We are all — those of us who teach the faith — held to be a bit disqualified in these days, not only with the trade unionists, but with some of our own men, for the final election call. But what does it matter if we sow and they reap — the harvest is ours, or rather our cause's, just the same ... yet the wisdom of keeping Socialism and Socialists in the background, at the last moment, or at any time, is not true wisdom, nor is it successful electioneering policy.[114]

The excluded Hardie replied that 'momentarily at least, it is apt to stir strangely rebellious thoughts'.[115] Such doubts were deepened by that summer's Barnard Castle contest. Henderson, with his Liberal past, had long been an object of suspicion for ILP enthusiasts, and now he wished to avoid alienating the Liberal vote. Gowland of the Crook ILP was unambiguous in his explanation: 'we think it would not be prudent for any of the prominent ment of the ILP to share in the fun. *It might spoil the game.*'[116]

Such incidents did not undermine the attachment of ILP leaders to the principle of the Alliance. Possibly Snowden and MacDonald, both of whom went to Barnard Castle, were less worried about such tensions; all four continued to regard the strategy as the best available option. Moreover, the ILP was integrated into the Labour Representation Committee in a way that made it difficult for party critics to make any impact on particular LRC decisions. ILP involvement was at two levels: locally, where branches affiliated to local LRCs could seek to influence policy, and were involved in candidate selection; and nationally, through ILP representation at LRC Conferences and on the LRC Executive. Decisions at the national level laid down terms for local relationships, and discussions at this level were very much restricted to the party hierarchy.

This style was foreshadowed in the preparations for the inaugural Conference, when the NAC determined the composition of the ILP delegation, and then the delegation nominated Parker and Hardie as the ILP representatives on the LRC Executive.[117] This control was maintained the following year, with the Council not only appointing delegates, but also nominating for the two reserved Executive places, and approving five resolutions for the LRC Conference agenda.[118] The NAC had to consider also the consequences of the LRC decisions and arguments. Hardie and Parker reported back on the Executive's first meeting, especially the lengthy debate on whether to approach the Whips of various parties to ascertain their attitudes to Labour candidates. The early threat to independence had been defeated on the casting vote of the Executive's Chairman, but Hardie and Parker suspected that the issue would emerge again, and asked the NAC for guidance. The Council's verdict was predictably one of opposition to such approaches.[119] Such issues were never referred back to the ILP membership.

The cosy relationship between the NAC and the LRC Executive was facilitated by the important roles of MacDonald and Hardie in both organisations. It was also aided by the degree to which it was insulated from the critical attentions of the ILP rank and file who had little awareness of what was happening until long after the event, and then found that they lacked the necessary resources to check their leaders anyway. By now, accountability to the rank and file had become a very attenuated affair. The NAC were involved very deeply in consultations with the LRC over candidates, but members found great difficulty in obtaining a clear picture. At the 1903 Conference, a Salford delegate moved a resolution instructing the NAC to publish fuller reports of its proceedings. The Chairman's response yielded nothing:

much of the business of the NAC was of a consultative kind that could not be satisfactorily summarised in a brief report. Nor was it advisable to give too much publicity to the private business of the party.[120]

It was a far cry from the 1894 Conference, when Shaw Maxwell had read the previous year's NAC Minutes to the assembled delegates. The opacity of many dealings with the LRC was one factor behind a Conference decision the following year, that in future all party delegates to LRC Conferences, except for NAC members, should be elected by the branches.[121] This could be employed as a means of providing some leverage for those within the party who were unhappy about some aspects of the Alliance. But the Council simply did not act on this resolution, pleading cost as a justification, and proposing successfully to the 1905 Conference that that body should elect the additional delegates.[122] It was a very limited opening up of the relationship.

Suspicions about the implications of the LRC connection would have been much greater, if party members had been aware of the development of the Gladstone—MacDonald arrangement on candidacies.[123] Neither the NAC nor the LRC Executive were involved as institutions, but several members, apart from MacDonald, were clearly aware that something was afoot. Hardie, for example, was informed of MacDonald's inclinations by the sympathetic Cadbury who

thought Mr. MacDonald's suggestion at the little conference last Friday week was a wise one, that the fifty constituencies to be fought by Labour should be definitely decided upon, and submitted to the Liberal whip. He would then see whether it was possible to effect some compromise.[124]

Within little more than a decade after the ILP's formation, its leaders could be involved in, or know about, decisions that would have a dramatic effect on the party's future, which were kept from the membership, and which would have provoked massive protests, had they been more widely known. The autonomy of leaders increased, as they moved out of their previous political marginality. Now the stakes seemed higher, and they acted with the confidence that flowed from current success and the hope of more to come.

One symptom of the party's improved prospects lay in its growing financial strength, and in the more sophisticated organisation that resulted from this. After the 1900 election, some NAC members met, and decided to establish a Propaganda Fund, separate from the often unreliable flow of affiliation fees.[125] The object was to concentrate the party's efforts on winnable constituencies. Although the response did not reach the projected £1,000 a year, early missionary efforts were made in Preston and Bradford. Then, at the end of 1901, it was decided that the money could be more effectively used to finance lecture tours, and to make grants to districts for the maintenance of organisers.[126]

The scheme was buoyed up by the general revival of the party. As the financial condition of the party strengthened so paid organisers became a practical possibility. Even affiliation fees had risen, £257 in 1900/01 to £482 five years later. Enthusiastic districts made demands for organisational assistance.[127] Such requests to a relatively well endowed Council increased the possibility of more central control.[128] There was a growing tendency for regional conferences to be held, where NAC members delivered the official message.[129] Organisers could be employed not just to propagandise, but also in attempts to canalise branch enthusiasm into 'respectable' channels. By 1905, a number of organisers were hard at work, and the NAC had formed an Organisation Committee to supervise their activities.[130]

Leaders also benefitted from other developments. The publication of pamphlets under NAC control was expanded and, more crucially, after much wrangling, the party acquired the *Labour Leader*, as from January 1904.[131] The *ILP News* had not been a success. Its monthly publication meant that its impact was limited; circulation was always disappointing, and its finances were weak.[132] The *Leader* was a journal with a sizeable readership. Under Glasier's editorship it became unashamedly partisan, defending the established leadership, and attacking its critics.

There were those within the party who reacted to this centralisation of resources with acceptance, or even pride. Such changes could be viewed as indices of the party's progress, foreshadowing the long-awaited electoral breakthrough. By now, many within the party who had been members from the early days had acquired their own niches in local politics, and were reluctant to have their careers upset by what they saw as excessive iconoclasm. Yet traditions of rank and file democracy had deep roots within the party, and especially when these fused with concern about features of the Labour Alliance, and a preference for socialist unity, then there was clear potential for a critical response. The NAC were always aware of the possibility of dissent, the furore surrounding Quelch's candidacy at Dewsbury in 1902, was evidence of the ease with which a cry of 'socialism' could attract ILP enthusiasts from the rigours of LRC politics.[133]

Sporadic — if embarrassing — dissent was one thing. Influencing policy was quite another. The inequality of resources did not just lie in their concentration at the apex; even the Conference, the traditional locus of rank and file endeavours at control, was less effective than previously. In part, this reflected the developing expertise and ascendancy of the Big Four, in part it showed how acceptance of the principle of the Labour Alliance carried many other acceptances in its wake. It perhaps also suggested that many who had been unhappy about the direction of ILP policy after 1895 had drifted out of the party. Moreover the remaining critics often lacked organisation and failed to think through the implications of their actions. It was Sam Hobson, a long-standing advocate of socialist unity who put a powerful weapon into the hands of the NAC at the 1903 Conference. He moved a successful motion that three months before the next conference:

the NAC should be empowered to appoint a committee ... to revise and classify the resolutions sent in by branches, and to place resolutions dealing with important matters on the agenda.[134]

Motivated presumably by a wish to rationalise and accelerate Conference business, the resolution enabled an Agenda Committee, appointed by the NAC, not only to combine and presumably modify the sense of resolutions submitted by branches, but also to concoct resolutions of its own.[135] In future years the Agenda Committee was to become the object of dark suspicions on the part of critics who saw it as a means of aborting or loading discussion.[136] Yet it came, not as the result of a NAC initiative, but from a delegate whose own actions frequently challenged the politics of the Labour Alliance.

Those who were unhappy about the dominance of the Council suggested a variety of reforms for increasing the influence of the rank and file. The office of Chairman — now occupied in turn by Glasier, Snowden and MacDonald — was a frequent candidate for abolition. More significantly, proposals were made that continuous membership of the NAC should not be permitted beyond a two- or three-year stint, a change aimed clearly at the lengthy tenures of the Big Four. Another tack involved the employment of referenda, either to elect officials, or to decide significant questions of policy.[137] These reforms were all defeated — itself perhaps a testimony to NAC power as well as to the intrinsic merits of the arguments.

There was only one significant exception to this record of failure. The 1905 Conference accepted, by 55 votes to 33, a Darlington resolution that:

it be an instruction to the NAC to devise a scheme whereby the country may be divided up into suitable districts for the purposes of divisional representation on the NAC. The same to be elected by a vote of the members of the Branches previous to the annual conference. The result of such voting to be declared at the conference.[138]

This was to produce the first significant change in the composition and method of election of the NAC since February 1894. Hardie and MacDonald drew up a scheme, dividing the country into six, subsequently seven, Divisions and allowing for six national representatives as well. The scheme which included other suggestions was accepted by the Council and commended to the 1906 Conference.[139] The only item rejected by the delegates, ironically in view of earlier arguments, was that the Chairmanship should be abolished.[140]

The old Council saw the Divisional reform as one which would facilitate the co-ordination of efforts between centre and branches, with Divisional representatives serving as transmission in both directions.[141] Such expectations were fulfilled to some degree. Several Divisional representatives agreed politically with the Big Four. But as with the Federations of the mid nineties, some Divisions eventually elected representatives critical of the leadership. Whilst these were always in a minority on the NAC they were symptomatic of the growth of criticism within the party.

The electoral successes of 1906 crowned a period of success for the ILP leaders. Hardie, Snowden and MacDonald all won, Jowett, Parker, Clynes and Summerbell were further ILP-sponsored successes, and many party members were elected under trade union sponsorship. The Big Four dominated their party; they had pursued the strategy of the Labour Alliance with some success. Some of them knew of the illicit, yet effective, deal with the Liberals. Their resources were extensive and showed every hope of further growth. Yet within the ILP 1906 was in some ways their high noon. The centralisation of resources had already provoked concern in a party where sentiments of rank and file democracy remained strong. The politics of the Labour Alliance were now very much on trial. ILP involvements with trade unionists who were suspicious of socialists, and Labour acquiescence in Liberal policies, could produce angry socialist reactions. The explosions centring around Victor Grayson were symptomatic of these tensions. The Big Four tended to react in turn in a hypersensitive and high-handed fashion. This was perhaps not just the response of a complacent elite. For MacDonald, and perhaps Snowden, 1906 and the clear arrival of the Labour Party tended to make the ILP and its arguments less crucial.

Yet much of the gunpowder for later explosions had been manufactured before 1906, when leaders had accumulated power and led members in a direction to which many had never consented. One disillusioned ex-member of the NAC looked in 1908 at what he saw as an oligarchic party — it was:

a mere machine for registering the decrees of the three or four able men who for so many years, have formed the inner circle of the NAC ... all the wires are in their hands, the newspaper is theirs, one of them always occupies the chair at the annual Conference, one of them is on the Agenda Committee, and the power that they have acquired enables them to impose their will upon the Conference and the Party, even when the general sentiment of the Party is in opposition to them ...

The NAC is an organised body, knowing what it wants, and how to get it, while the Conference is an amorphous mass of well-intentioned inexperienced men with no common understanding, and no opportunity of consultation prior to the Conference. Under such circumstances, a strict adherence to the rules of debate unduly favours the Executive.[142]

This Michelsian portrait is exaggerated. A dichotomous classification of leadership and rank and file carried its own dangers. Leaders differed on occasions, either on personal or political grounds. Rank and file could fall into various gradations from perpetual critic to super-loyalist. Yet the portrait does present a significant aspect of relationships within the party. Any understanding must distinguish between the contributions made by various factors. Some departure from the original democratic conception of the ILP was occasioned by the fundamental dynamics of party life. A search for coherence as a national organisation produced some decisions taken by the few and sanctioned, retrospectively, by the many. The pursuit of electoral success inevitably added its own weight to this centralisation process. Then came a series of substantively political choices centering around the idea of a Labour Alliance, and producing yet more centralisation. Electoral and parliamentary prestige were the icing on the oligarchic cake. Leadership resources resulting from party activity *per se* must be distinguished from those stemming from political choices that must be seen in a specific context.

Similarly, rank and file responses require similar distinctions. The umbilical chord of finance clearly connected leaders and led. Branches, by witholding funds could limit leaders' power; once the central exchequer became larger this gave leaders the scope to cajole or coerce recalcitrant branches. Yet whilst the financial power of the centre was by its nature a co-ordinated force, that of the branches was atomised. Individual groups could withold funds on specific points, but the likelihood of a co-ordinated witholding of fees was remote. Equally the success of the party in expanding membership after 1900 produced problems for the leaders, in that the membership became that much less of a knowable community. The charms of an established elite were that much less effective. But equally such expansion made the chances of a co-ordinated critical response less, at the very time that it helped to increase the likelihood of dissatisfaction. There were basic reasons why the rank and file might appear as 'an amorphous mass'. Yet there were also contingent political reasons. Many of the critics shared many of the opinions of Robert Blatchford, including a distaste for organisation as such. If so, then it is perhaps hardly surprising that the critics rarely organised themselves against established leaders, relying instead on propaganda and spontaneous combustion. The control of the Big Four was aided not just by the internal dynamics of the party and the implications of the key political choices, but also by the style and preferences of potential critics.

14

Pragmatic visionaries: a portrait of branch life

The activities of leading ILP members help us to understand how the party gradually acquired a national identity. Yet it must be remembered that the party grew upwards from the localities and that, despite increasing NAC influence, branch activities remained of crucial importance. Success or its absence in particular communities provided a basis for national decisions. The varying styles and achievements of local branches show how far the ILP reflected 'fin de siècle' politics, with its mosaic of regional attitudes and loyalties. A view of local party life shows that the party amounted to much more than the machinations of a few. It depended also on the creativity, ingenuity and stamina of local activists. Local party life was marked also by a shift in pre-occupations. Activists continued to talk of the need to 'make socialists' but, at least in the larger branches, a growing preoccupation with electoral success tended to push earlier preoccupations with the 'Religion of socialism' to the margin.

The terrain can be hinted at in these general terms, but difficulties begin when attempts are made to be more specific. The problem of sources is acute. Branch records are few, and cannot be taken as representative. Reports by local activists to Labour newspapers were often wildly optimistic — for example, predictions of electoral victories. Branch decline was seldom publicised, the most frequent symptom being the disappearance of references from the press. Some insights can be gleaned from the private writings of national figures, although often these are affected by political sympathies or antipathies, as between writer and branch.

Problems arise not just in the sphere of qualitative judgements. It is even difficult to develop a reliable picture of the extent of party membership. Some early impressionistic statements were over-optimistic. At the 1894 Conference, Hardie claimed 'close upon 400 branches'.[1] The following year he was talking of 35,000 members, and went so far as 50,000 in an article directed at a non-Labour audience.[2] Such estimates reflect the burgeoning optimism of a new organisation. They also indicate perhaps the ambiguity attached to the status of 'party member'. Early growth often rested heavily on Independent Labour Clubs. Clubs could provide a relatively firm base within a community, but involvement in club activities could carry minimal political commitment. Moreover it is clear that not all 'members' regularly paid dues. Contemporary reports tended to distinguish between financial and other members.[3] As might be expected, there existed a sizeable penumbra of people who might pay dues occasionally, and could drift in or out of involvement, depending on the general political climate or their own priorities.

A shift from impressionistic optimism brings us to the much harder criterion of national affiliation fees as a basis for calculating membership. Perhaps this may be viewed as an excessively stringent measure, or as a surrender to the law of the instrument — that, these, at least, are quantifiable, even if partial, representatives. Certainly Party spokesmen believed that affiliation fees furnished an underestimate of the membership, as payments tended to arrive unevenly, sometimes reflecting the fluctuating economic fortunes of members. Yet from one year to the next, the returns (Table 38) do reveal a striking

Table 38. *Membership as Based on Affiliation Fees 1893—1906*[5]

Year	Affiliation Fees	Method	Financial Membership
	£　s　d		
1893—94	56– 6– 0	3*d.* per year	4,504
1894—95	133 – 19 – 11½	3*d.* per year	10,720
1895—96	315 – 1– 8	1*s.* national certificate	6,301
1896—97	431 – 11 – 8	1*s.* paid in monthly or quarterly instalments	8,631
1897—98	449 – 0– 0	,,	8,980
1898—99	354 – 12 – 1	,,	7,092
1899—1900	304 – 4– 0½	,,	6,084
1900—01	257 – 5– 0	,,	5,145
1901—02	281 – 9– 3	,,	5,629
1902—03	291 – 4– 8	,,	5,824
1903—04	332 – 15 – 10	,,	6,655
1904—05	356 – 10 – 5	,,	7,130
1905—06	477 – 16 – 4	,,	9,556

(Figures as *Given to National Conferences*; February in 1894, thereafter Easter.)

degree of consistency, and it was on this stable core of paying members that the party's national survival depended in the difficult years around 1900. Indeed, distortion was not just in one direction; some branches probably over-affiliated.[4]

These figures suggest some reflections about national fluctuations in financial membership. Clearly there was a high tide in financial membership before the 1895 election, as well as in optimistic expectations. The sizeable decline by April 1896 is probably the resultant of a number of factors. Electoral disappointment and consequential apathy and indebtedness were noted widely by contemporaries. A four hundred per cent increase in the fee may well have been significant, although the method of affiliation, the purchase of a 1s. certificate, was perhaps more of an obstacle since it required a single outlay. Purchase of the certificates did not always reflect a branchs' active membership. The Keighley branch took up twenty-five certificates which it disposed of amongst its most committed members, but the active membership, as measured by attendance at monthly meetings, was considerably more than this.[6]

Some general support is given to this last claim, method rather than amount, by the recovery in financial membership during the next year, despite the party's continuing political difficulties. It is striking that it is 1897—8, the year of the Barnsley financial extravaganza, that saw a peak of members under the one shilling system. Only after 1898 did a decline set in. Official comment tended to blame the unpropitious political environment, particularly after the start of the South African War. Certainly in some places, propagandising became a risky activity, and the party's prospects seemed less favourable. Yet decline also begins with the defeat of the move for fusion with the SDF. Some branches certainly felt disillusioned and broke with the national party. It is less clear how many disappointed individuals drifted away from the party over this issue.

The decline did not end with the formation of the LRC. A slow recovery began only in the last year of the war, and the 1898—9 figure was not surpassed until 1904—5. The twelve months ending at Easter 1906 saw the most significant expansion for more than a decade, establishing a new high under the 1s. system. Clearly ILP revival was not an instantaneous consequence of affiliation to the LRC. The new organisation had to prove itself in terms of its own cohesion and in electoral competition — developments that depended in part upon the declining popularity of the Unionist Government. No doubt, ILP expansion did indicate the heightened interest of some trade unionists in Labour politics, but it also involved a renewed interest in the principles of socialism, an enthusiasm that would lead later to arguments in the branches.

These national affiliation figures masked major disparities in the size of branches. Throughout the nineties Bradford remained a major source of financial contributions, whilst some other parties such as Halifax, Leicester and Manchester also had sizeable memberships. In 1898—9, Bradford and Halifax provided over one-eighth of the total affiliation fees.[7] The relatively small financial membership at the end of the decade was concentrated mostly in a few well-established branches. Elsewhere the party's presence was much weaker and sometimes intermittent. Centres such as Newcastle and Nottingham, which had been active at the start, now languished. In many towns, periods of activity, perhaps with visiting propagandists as catalysts, were interspersed with periods of lethargy. The expansion after 1902 tended to reduce these imbalances. Old branches revived, and new ones were created on a wide scale as the ILP, often with trade union support, put down roots in previously weak areas.

The extent and distribution of the committed membership is reasonably clear — but what sort of people were these activists? There is a tendency to view the ILP as a party in which the middle-class element was always strong and generated a style at odds with that of many trade unionists. Certainly in the post-1900 revival, the party did attract perhaps a significant white collar support, although the influx of younger trade unionists should also be emphasised. More crucially, its Great War pacifism did isolate it from a vast majority of the organised working class. Yet it would be dangerous to read such images and divisions back into the early years, without further investigation.

The occupations and styles of the emerging ILP leadership tend to support the white collar stereotype. Amongst the Big Four, Hardie had the deepest roots in the industrial working class, but his days at the coalface were long past, and he now had all the idiosyncratic style of the self-taught Radical journalist. He had much in common with the other leading figures — Snowden the ex-Civil Service Clerk, Glasier the ex-architect and MacDonald the ex-political secretary who had aspired to a scientific career. None had the background of a professional middle class family; MacDonald and Glasier, like Hardie, were illegitimate. Yet each of them had achieved some sort of niche in the later Victorian middle class. MacDonald and Glasier both married women whose middle-class credentials were much stronger than their own and who shared their political interests. The same is true to a lesser extent of Snowden.[8]

ILP leaders demonstrated Scottish and Yorkshire variants on the social ethos depicted by Wells. They were effective, literate propagandists, having tenuous links at bést with the industrial working class, but lacking the assured status given by accepted qualifications. Lesser lights sometimes revealed similar backgrounds. Russell Smart moved from the stage to commercial travelling for a firm of sanitary engineers.[9] Sam Hobson was also able to conveniently combine selling and propagandising.[10] Parker, once a warehouseman, achieved some kind of white collar status as the full-time secretary of the Halifax ILP and after election to parliament, allegedly did well out of investment tips from wealthy MPs.[11] Brocklehurst, a theology graduate of Queens' College, Cambridge, later qualified for the bar and left the ILP to become a Tory candidate in December 1910.[12] Journalists such as Joseph Burgess and Frank Smith were common amongst the upper echelons of the party.[13] Yet if some ILP luminaries aspired to varying degrees of social status, others had no need. This assured status could be found in Richard Pankhurst, the Manchester barrister, and in the successive Treasurers, Lister, the Halifax Squire, Littlewood, the millowner and Benson, the estate agent.[14]

This portrait of early ILP spokesmen tends to suggest that it was a party that was strongly middle class from the start. This view can be elaborated by noting that the early women propagandists who achieved considerable prominence within the party — Katharine St John Conway, Enid Stacy, Carrie Martyn[15] — were all from securely middle-class families. So were later members of the NAC such as Emmeline Pankhurst and Isabella Ford. Yet this profile of women propagandists should inject an element of caution. It was almost inevitable that women prominent in the early ILP should be from such backgrounds. Any emancipation was difficult, and such a life was virtually inconceivable for the wife or daughter of an industrial worker. A parallel comment can be made in a more minor key about male propagandists. It was always likely that they would be either aspiring or arrived white-collar workers. Such a status afforded advantages of technique, confidence and often free time. But the social origins and current status of leaders and propagandists need not be representative of the party members as a whole.

Indeed, the image of the petit-bourgeois propagandist was something that only evolved over time. At the beginning, trade union spokesmen were prominent in the party. The Bradford Conference included several delegates who were to hold significant trade union posts — Tillett and Sexton amongst the Dockers, Curran amongst the Gasworkers, Allan Gee amongst the Woolen Workers, Ben Turner in the same trade, and also in the upper echelons of the TUC, Robert Smillie in the Miners' Federation. Other delegates including Drew, Pickles and Cowgill of Bradford, and William Small of Blantyre were important in local trade union activities. This connection was not just a brief, Bradford affair. In the 1895 election, several leading trade unionists stood as ILP candidates. These included not only Tillett, Sexton, Smillie and Curran from the 1893 delegates, but also Tom Mann and George Barnes, both identified with the socialist faction in the ASE, whilst Tom McCarthy of the Dockers fought West Hull against a local shipowner.

This was the peak of trade-unionist involvement in the upper echelons of the party. By 1898, there were no significant trade unionists on the NAC. In part, this reflects the complex relationship between the ILP and trade union developments in the nineties. Declining prominence could reflect a diminution of industrial self-confidence. Some ILP trade unionists moved away from the party as party leaders became embroiled in conflicts with Lib-Lab leaders. Sexton, for example, disagreed with ILP opposition to Maddison at the Brightside by-election of 1897.[16] Declining involvement also indicated the increasing preoccupation of some ILP stalwarts with the minutiae of trade union administration.[17] By 1900, Curran, Tillett, Sexton, Barnes and Smillie all held important union positions. Such posts were not just a drain on time and energy: the grind of administration could blunt earlier political enthusiasms. Moreover, the creation of the LRC meant that political ambitions could be realised more readily through trade-union sponsored candidacies. There were good industrial and political reasons why the trade union presence at the top of the ILP should have declined after 1895. Whether the same can be claimed of the local membership is much less certain.

Attempts to establish the socio-economic composition of local branches encounter serious difficulties. For the most part, evidence is simply unavailable. It is difficult to claim that municipal candidates were reflective of the wider membership, since many of the factors facilitating the prominence of white collar members nationally would operate here. Council meetings were held normally in the afternoon, so that industrial workers had difficulty in attending. Branches seem sometimes to have been pleased to have middle-class standard bearers in municipal contests, as this vouchsafed them a status which would have been lacking. Thus, Brocklehurst became an early ILP councillor in Manchester,[18] Littlewood could turn his position as millowner to good account in Honley,[19] as could Lister in Halifax,[20] and Richard Barrett in Ashton Under Lyne.[21] Trade union officers also had opportunities to engage in municipal politics. Freddie Richards of the Boot and Shoe Operatives was an early ILP recruit to the Leicester Council. Sometimes, ILP candidates were small-businessmen. Charles Higham of Blackburn was a tailor, Bradford had its counterparts, whilst in Halifax both Beever and Tattersall set up in business after their dismissals by a local Liberal employer.[22] Such cases should not be regarded as indicating significant ILP support amongst the petit bourgeoisie. Often, involvement in such commercial activities was a response to victimisation, and provided a reasonably effective basis for propagandising. Local ILP candidates often blended the worlds of trade union solidarity and self-improvement. In Keighley, one ex-secretary of the Trades Council and ASRS member became a newsagent, a second moved from a woollen mill to become a drawing teacher. Others remained in the workplace.[23]

Attempts to grasp the character of that elusive figure 'the average member' must be highly tentative. A detailed study of early party life in the Colne Valley was able to base its claims on a complete set of party records. Here, a small middle-class leadership was significant. Littlewood, the owner of a sizeable mill was backed by a retail tailor, a master cotton-spinner and a commission spinner. One master boot-maker joined — his business folded as the result of a political boycott. Some members combined work in textile mills with farming; but the largest single occupational group at the start of the Colne Valley Labour Union were textile workers, mostly weavers.[24] A similar pattern seemed to apply in 1906. Shareholders in a project aimed at the construction of Socialist Halls could well be a sample of members, skewed away from industrial workers, yet weavers, other textile operatives and labourers account for over half of those listed.[25] It is difficult to resist the conclusion that, although Independent Labour in the Colne Valley might have included a significant bourgeois element amongst its leaders, its rank and file reflected the district's dominant industry.

Colne Valley may be atypical in that its notoriously weak trade unionism induced some workers to organise politically, and given the conservative-bourgeois quality of local Liberalism, such mobilisation was likely in the 1890s to take an independent form. This argument would apply in its essential terms across much of the woollen district. If so, then this suggests something about the rank and file in such strongholds as Bradford and Halifax.

More broadly, it is striking how often the parlous financial position of branches is attributed to the poverty of members. The slump of 1894—5 hit some branches very hard. A Darlington correspondent replied to a request from Tom Mann for money:

owing to the distress that is existing in this town — one third of our members being on the non-payment list, it is impossible for us to pledge the sum of £5 as requested.[26]

Also in the North East, a Gateshead correspondent regretted that it was impossible to send £5, since many of the financial membership of thirty had lost their jobs.[27] Even in Bradford, Jowett felt on the eve of the 1895 election that the local electoral levy might not reach the anticipated amount, because of members' poverty.[28] Similar statements recur in later years. Hopes of a Peace Candidate at York, early in 1900, were dampened by the state of the local branch. One activist informed Hardie that: 'the branch — consisting as it does of men in somewhat poor circumstances who, already levied up to the hilt, can't be relied upon for very much financial support.'[29] In the Merthyr district little more than a year before Hardie's victory, the local Secretary was unable to send any affiliation fees as 'the Financial Position of the Branches generally is very bad'.[30] The conclusion seems inescapable that the membership of many ILP branches was hardly affluent. Such a supposition is strengthened by other evidence. Activists sometimes pointed to threats of victimisation as a reason for low membership. Such accusations were made frequently against the dominant employer in railway towns. A Crewe activist enduring the yoke of the London and North Western claimed:

there are tyranny and toadyism everywhere. Men are in perpetual fear of losing their employment and the officials play upon that fear ... it is considered a bold thing to be an ILP man at Crewe.[31]

But fears were most prevalent in small towns and rural areas. It was claimed in 1898 that in some Gloucestershire villages: 'farmers have threatened to discharge their labourers, if they see them attending Socialist meetings'.[32] Two years earlier, and several hundred miles away, Glasier experienced difficulties on a visit to Forfar: 'Never felt so much an alien in any town. Local chaps almost afraid to be seen with me'.[33] Such fears could be effective only if potential recruits were working class.

Earlier chapters have shown how the party could establish a presence amongst particular occupational groups or in specific districts, where there were distinctive economic and political opportunities. But within the present analysis a further distinction is important. It seems reasonably clear that the poverty of many members was that of the later Victorian tradesman, miner and railwayman, whose precarious solvency could be threatened by technical innovation, recession or dispute. The party struck few chords amongst very poor, unskilled, unorganised workers. The ILP counted for little in the teeming slums of great cities, where trade unionism and Victorian institutions of self-help had little foothold. Some activists almost adopted the conventional stereotype of the undeserving poor in discussing the party's weakness there. Edward Hartley looked back in anger at an municipal defeat in Bradford's South Ward in 1895. Its people were:

bitter, intolerant, unsympathetic and insolent, prone to live on charity rather than on the rights of manhood and womanhood ... not until the death rate, the insanitation and the horrible mode of life are changed, shall we ever see the South Ward of Bradford taking an intelligent interest in the things mostly concerning it.[34]

The ethos of at least some ILP branches was far removed from such deprivations. An outpost in West Birmingham was claimed in 1898 to be composed chiefly of

quiet and intelligent artisans with moderate socialist views ... not particularly aggressive — in fact rather too mild (working) quietly and effectively and as far as possible without giving offence.[35]

Propagandists with their zeal for self-improvement and sobriety eagerly noted such activists. Glasier was pleased to discover how a new branch at Usworth in County Durham had deep trade union roots, he found the Darlington membership to be a 'reasonable fair type of working men', whilst at Felling, ILP supporters were 'the cream of the working class'.[36] This particular batch of comments comes from 1902, and suggests that during the party's growth, in the North East at any rate, the working-class composition was maintained. Certainly in districts and trades such as the Durham coalfield, where independent politics was a cause amongst the younger union activists, this could be expected.

The frequent image of the party also places a significant emphasis on the role of women, captured in the popularity of the early women propagandists. This prominence was relatively short-lived. Carrie Martyn died in 1896; Katherine Conway and Enid Stacy tended to be less active after their marriages; Margaret Macmillan's activities were largely limited to Bradford municipal politics. Other women activists, such as the Pankhursts and Theresa Billington, came to concentrate predominantly on women's issues and to drift away from the ILP.[37] Such estrangement was reciprocated by some ILP male leaders. Glasier, ever touchy about criticism, reflected gloomily on a visit to the Pankhursts:

A weary ordeal of chatter about women's suffrage ... belabouring me as Chairman of the Party for neglect of the question. At last, get roused and speak with something like scorn of their miserable individualist sexism; and virtually tell them that the ILP will not stir a finger more than it has done for all the women suffragettes in creation.[38]

Such tensions were very much at the top of the party. Amongst the less-publicised membership, it is clear that in some places, women played significant roles in local parties, particularly perhaps in some Lancashire towns, where patterns of employment and unionisation in the cotton trade had given women a degree of both economic independence and organisational confidence.[39] But frequently, women were pressed into traditional roles, such as the preparation of teas after ILP demonstrations. Some indication of the limited impact of women can be found perhaps in their slight presence at party conferences. Throughout the first decade, it remained in single figures, before rising with the expansion of the membership to reach thirteen out of a total of one hundred and fifty delegates in 1906. Despite the formal equality accorded to women in both procedures and rhetoric, the party, like the society that surrounded it, was heavily male-dominated.

The age of the party activists was perhaps their last striking feature. At Bradford the vast majority of the delegates were in below forty. The birth dates of the Big Four - Hardie (1856), Glasier (1857), Snowden (1863) and MacDonald (1866) — are revealing and seem on a par with those of many leading activists. This was a generation that frequently sought political influence through the Gladstonian Liberal Party and found themselves rejected by older more socially exclusive groups. They acquired political awareness through the disappointments of successive Liberal Governments in the eighties and nineties, and often encountered the inflexibility of the local Liberal caucus. They saw the first cracks in the dominance of British capitalism, often participated in the trade union struggles of the late eighties and early nineties, and turned to a new political organisation, and often to socialism, as responses. Typically, they shared the optimism of many Radicals. Once the party had been created, the young men and women of the nineties tended to remain in the foreground for several years. At the top this process involved the growing dominance of the Big Four. Locally, the young aspirants could graduate to middle-aged worthies with a stake in existing arrangements.

The image of the party that leaders liked to propagate and which had a considerable basis in reality was one of enthusiastic, respectable, self-improving working men and women, ready to ally with other groups of progressives. But, as leaders tartly observed, the reality sometimes departed from the expectation. Often criticism of branches focussed on the tendency for the social — especially the drinking — side of activities to become dominant. Local members were sometimes unhappy about this. In December 1896, a meeting of Stockport members heard complaints of 'the apathy and indifference which causes members to absent themselves from Business meetings, while regularly frequenting the Club for purposes of amusement'.[40] Hardie with his temperance background, was more specific. Speaking at a new Labour Club in Leicester, he 'warned them against turning the club into a lounge for loafers, as was apt to be the case when liquor was sold'.[41] Glasier's censorious eye looked critically on some branches. He dismissed the Darwen Club: 'Some of men obviously are members merely for 'booze', and have a bad reputation as fathers and husbands.'[42] He attributed the party's weakness in Bolton to the practice of selling drink in clubs.[43] Failure in Barnsley was attributable to the branch being based in a 'stuffy drinking-hole',[44] rather than presumably to the strength of local Lib-Lab trade unionism. Sometimes ILP propagandists seemed to place almost as much emphasis on drink as some of those Liberals whom they attacked for simplifying and distorting the problem of poverty. But for Glasier at least, respectability was crucial. He welcomed the improvement in the 'type' of Rochdale audience; he noted that the party maintained a 'higher tone' on its platform,[45] and he was impressed by a family of colliers in the Erewash Valley. They were 'quite refined and intelligent'![46]

For many within the party, the style was important. This emphasis is important as a basis for understanding party activities, but it must be complemented by an awareness of how this style changed over time. The ILP was created towards the end of a decade of socialist revivalism, in which commitment to a new form of society was expressed in diverse ways, and was wrapped in a buoyant optimism; it was a period of expectation which those involved were to look back on with a moving sense of vanished experiences and lost hope. Fred Jowett could recall how in the late eighties:

Sometimes in summertime the joint forces of Leeds and Bradford Socialism tramped together to spread the gospel by printed and spoken word in neighbouring villages. And at eventide on the way home, as we walked in country lanes, or on river bank, we sang.[47]

This quality of experience with its attempt to prefigure the forthcoming society can be found readily in the early ILP. Local zealots attempted to organise a wide range of activities. It was hoped that the branch would become an expanding island of socialism with its own ethos and relationships. One observer claimed:

Nothing is too hard for the members in their virgin enthusiasm to do. They run their little prints, they sell their stocks of pamphlets, they drop their pennies into the collecting box, they buy their ILP tea and cocoa as though they were members of an idealistic Communist society.[48]

This vision did not last.[49] The trading side of ILP activities declined rapidly. By January 1895, an Ipswich activist admitted that:

Our Trading which was started off in July last year, has turned out such an utter failure, that we are giving it up, and intend going straight for educational work.[50]

All branches claimed to be 'making socialists'. Educational work was the chief preoccupation of the smaller branches. More powerful groups could hope to contest elections, sometimes at the parliamentary level, but more often for municipal bodies. The range of contests — for City, Borough and County Councils, for Urban and Rural Districts, for School Boards, and for Boards of Guardians, for Auditorships and, from 1894, for Parish Councils gave even moderately sized branches the hope of success. As electoral success became a dominant preoccupation, so others shifted to the margin. A desire for electoral support could lead to stylistic changes. The NAC's post mortem on the 1895 election argued that it was important to end

the wholesale denunciation which hitherto has been almost a necessity. To our knowledge tens of thousands are looking towards us, more or less kindly disposed. It must be our aim to enlist these under our banner, not by any sacrifice of principle, but by avoiding unnecessary offence.[51]

Almost three years later, municipal successes had induced some modification of the party's position — at least, in the opinion of Glasier:

if we have altered it (our programme), in any way, it is because — from the very circumstances of our success — laying upon us the charge of directly acting in legislative and administrative affairs — our speaking has become less insurrectionary, less extreme, more opportunist.[52]

But much more was involved in this change than a mere temporising of attitudes. Concentration on electoral politics and acceptance of administrative constraints were based on a narrower, more conventionally political view of socialism and of the means for its achievement. Once wider cultural experiences and aspirations were included within the ILP then all tended to succumb to the electoral imperative. Cultural symbols tended to remain as mobilising devices, with which enthusiasm could be roused, and the party's identity maintained.

Party activites must be seen therefore in terms of the gradual canalisation and dilution of older, wider enthusiasms. That is not to say that such restrictions and subsequent ritualistic references were simply the product of manipulations by electorally conscious leaders. Such elements were present, but electoral ambitions weree also significant locally, as many activists came to taste at least the expectation of municipal success.[53] In addition, there was something cramping about efforts to finance electoral projects. Activities tended to concentrate on removing the last electoral debt, or in attempting to ensure that there would not be one next time. Cultural activities tended to be assessed for their effectiveness in contributing towards such objectives. This withering vision did not flow, of course, just from priorities within the party. By the mid nineties, a decade of socialist enthusiasm had not produced a persuasive answer to the problem of agency. ILP preoccupation with electoral politics was a worldly answer to a baffling question.

Throughout these shifts, propagandising remained a dominant concern. In summer, this was carried on outdoors, often in a traditional spot for oratory such as Tib Street, Manchester. Occasionally such gatherings provoked conflict with local authorities, the most celebrated one being the Boggart Hole Clough meetings in 1896. A Council ban was imposed on ILP Sunday meetings; these continued, attracting much greater audiences and gaol sentences for some leading party figures.[54] Rural propaganda tended to be a risky activity owing to the possibility of violent opposition. Frequently, outdoor meetings were held by local activists, although occasionally there were visits from well-known speakers. Propagandists travelled widely, making long tedious journeys by train. Each must have been a devotee of Bradshaw; Glasier and Snowden were perhaps the the most travelled, although in the early years, Carrie Martyn, Tom Mann and Katherine Conway were equally popular. Visits from Hardie were perhaps the most prestigious of all. Often, the theme was a straightforward advocacy of socialism or of the ILP. Sometimes, topics were of a broader ethical, cultural or religious nature. Perhaps recent events or controversies were used as pegs for more fundamental messages. The styles of leading propagandists were distinctive. Glasier affected an artistic romantic image long after he had abandoned the barricades for the long haul of Labour parliamentarianism. Snowden's 'Christ That Is To Be' was combined with a talent for biting invective. Hardie was unique with a mystique that fed upon legends of the Cloth Cap, and his early life. He embodied many of the emotions that lay at the heart of the ILP's appeal. Glasier, a critical supporter, was moved by one Hardie performance to acknowledge that: 'There is no other man in our party who can speak with such sturdiness, such range of wisdom and such tact as he at his best'.[55] Such outdoor meetings were opportunities to sell literature — *Labour Leaders, Clarions* and often shortlived, party newspapers, and pamphlets. Collections were taken, and, hopefully, new members enrolled. The more established branches held winter meetings, often dignified as 'lectures'. These followed broadly the same format as summer propaganda although more often preaching to the converted. Such meetings also required access to premises, often rented, but occasionally a specifically Labour or Socialist Hall.

Early activities extended beyond conventionally political means of making socialists. The first flush of ILP enthusiasm coincided with the peak of the Labour Church movement, and activities often were combined. Here was a clear attempt to demonstrate that the spread of socialism required a removal of the habitual distinction between political and ethical or religious procedures and objectives. ILP interests could also take recreational forms. Members participated frequently in the range of Clarion activities, with choirs and cycle clubs amongst the most popular. Once again, such involvements expressed the belief that the transition to socialism was a multi-faceted process. But the electoral strategy gradually became primary, and the divide between conventional political activities and the rest became sharper. Singing and cycling became recreational activities rather than anticipations of a wider socialist fellowship.

The central political propagandising could be very successful. Propagandists, especially Hardie, could attract massive audiences. But there was another side to this: Glasier's Diaries convey the shifting fortunes of an ILP propagandist. Sometimes meetings could be held successfully in previously barren areas, but often the response could be very disappointing. When he toured Shropshire in December 1897, Glasier was depressed by a visit to

Oakengates: 'An abominable place, Houses mean, Workmen limp and spiritless. No trade unions. No local public spirit.'[56] The impact of speakers was not blunted just by local apathy but also by the way in which meetings tended to be viewed as part of the public entertainment of the time. Thus, Glasier's underlying prejudice was aroused by a challenge at Blantyre:

A nigger medicine man, children on swings and variety show - all against me. But I beat the dammed nigger! I spoke him down. Twice or thrice, he came over to my crowd ... he shouted, he sang ... but the crowd kept faithful to me.[57]

The value of such activities probably declined over time. In part, this might reflect the growth of mass commercial entertainments — but it also suggested difficulties within the ILP strategy. Rhetorical performances were of limited value beyond the immediate occasion. Even in the optimistic early days, an observer mused on how:

it is easy to get a big audience in Manchester to have their eyes tickled by a first-rate speaker. It is not at all so easy to get even a few members together to transact practical, routine business.[58]

Such rhetorical performances could become repetitive. The tedious journeys from town to town, the growing weight of party administration, the intoxication of an enthusiastic meeting could all inhibit the germination of new ideas. Indeed, repetition was almost inherent in several propagandists' perceptions of the socialist creed — simple, emotional, without the need for complex theoretical elaborations. Such sermonising could have a conservative impact on the branches, By 1899, branch officials were said to be claiming frequently that meetings 'are not so well attended as formerly, and that lecturers fail to win fresh recruits ... there is no doubt a slackening of interest in our routine propaganda'.[59] An activist with wide experience of branch life could lament a year later how 'five or six years ago, all was serious purpose, but now one sees a woeful falling off'.[60] No doubt, this reflected in part wider political fortunes. Indeed, this contrast was exaggerated, since many branches had always been fragile. But it showed also perhaps how the party was preaching more and more to the converted. Audiences were composed often of those who came by custom. They no longer wished to be jolted by novel, iconoclastic thoughts, and heard what they expected and wanted. The enthusiasm of the propagandists did not disappear, although, for some, it was dulled by the treadmill of meetings, but it did become increasingly an activity to be undertaken alongside more pragmatic political concerns.

It would be easy to view the growing pragmatism of many branches in the late nineties, as indicating the collapse of a vibrant strategy. Yet it was only those branches strong enough to have an electoral presence, that enabled the party to survive. Periodic enthusiasms were not enough in those years, unless underpinned by evidence of local influence. In many centres decay or stagnation was the dominant character. Carlisle had been represented at the Bradford Conference, but now the local scene was characterised by 'laziness, indifference and ignorance'. There were occasional lectures, thirty-five names were on the books and 'for a year or two, meetings have been held weekly with an average attendance of about 10'.[61] Even in Colne Valley, activities declined steeply. Activity in many villages folded up after 1895, and by 1900 public and party meetings were infrequent.[62] Rural activities were severely limited and made only a slight impression:

a visit to a village or a district, once in a year or two may keep alive the flame of discontent but can never show the people the practical road towards realising the ideals which the the ... Socialist lecturers preach.[63]

In such a political climate, the preoccupation of more stable branches with municipal politics was some form of ballast. Even so, there is a danger of exaggerating the durability of the larger branches. The years of retrenchment led to a rationalisation of activities in such centres as Bradford, where the wide network of branches and clubs, so evident at the inaugural conference gave way to a more centralised and slimmer organisation. This could inject greater effectiveness into electoral competition, but it could also be symptomatic of diminished enthusiasm. Even in the stronger towns, periods of activity were interspersed with bouts of apathy,[64] and strength tended to be concentrated in particular wards. The larger branches enjoyed some regular income, although nowhere near as extensive as their more affluent rivals. In 1897, Halifax claimed an income of £364. This was relatively high, as was Leicester's £337 in 1898. Blackburn gathered in £222 in the latter year, and York, a rather weaker group, £175 in the same year.[65]

Such incomes at least allowed for contests in selected wards and for Boards of Guardians and School Boards. Early experiences showed that enthusiasm was no basis for success. 'Shouting at street corners does not win elections' was Hardie's verdict after the defeats of 1895.[66] Yet organisation required resources that the party could not command. There was little hope of becoming involved in the expensive machinations of the revision courts: ILP branches could count on few vehicles to carry their supporters to the polls. Attempts to mobilise voters had to require considerable improvisation by party workers. A Leicester activist provided a graphic description of their municipal campaign in 1898:

We paraded the ward with a home-made lantern three foot square, set upon two poles, with mottoes on each side and a naphtha lamp inside, and accompanied by an ILP Brass Band. Others do canvassing ... whilst we are canvassing, we are making Socialists, which is our principal object, and we insist on a good energetic canvass. Whilst one portion are doing this, and addressing circulars, the agitators are holding fifteen to twenty minute meetings, and we make a point of holding a meeting in each street in the ward, and often four or five upon a good, central spot ... On the polling day, we insist that all poll and give them no peace till they do.[67]

This blend of revivalism and electoral practicalities could be highly successful, but even in Leicester, where the party continued to grow in the late nineties, cash still imposed a heavy constraint.[68] Contests were limited to a handful of wards. In Keighley, a relatively small town, the ILP built up its representation by concentrating on one ward. An attempt to spread the batttle led to all-round defeat.[69]

ILP members who were successful in municipal politics sometimes became prestigious figures in their towns. 'Jowett of Bradford' was the most prominent of several. Such individuals helped local branches to become more integrated into their communities, with leading figures, accepted as spokesmen not just for a party, but also in certain circumstances for a community. Local branches sought support from accepted insitutions of their town or village. The small Dalbeattie branch challenged Scottish sabbatarianism by 'having the Town Band out to play music on *Sunday* afternoon',[70] and Colne Valley Labour demonstrations typically involved parades with local bands.[71] Some branches hoped for support, not just from brass bands but also from sympathetic religious leaders,[72] a hope that could raise delicate questions about relationships with Liberalism.

Once the quest for community identification went beyond band and pulpit, and became tied in with the commitment to electoral success, then inevitably the question of relationships with other political groups became critical. ILP councillors rubbed shoulders with councillors of other persuasions. Emnities might soften, the desire to be re-elected would probably grow. Essentially two such relationships mattered for local branches. One was with local trades councils, who had often sponsored a few municipal nominees, typically under Lib-Lab auspices. We have noted how a local alliance sometimes came easily, but on other occasions was achieved only with difficulty. Such alliances were important. Resources were channelled into united efforts; the understandings anticipated the local LRCs that were to follow, and they helped to establish a synthesis between the views of party activists and those of trade union spokesmen.

Association with a trades council, even if it carried negative implications for ILP high-mindedness, was very much in conformity with basic party principles about winning the support of trade unionists. There could be no such justification about alliances with Liberals, although obviously continuities of opinion between ILPers and local Radicals could be significant. Such continuities, together with the intimacies of municipal politicking, could lead to hopes and sometimes the realisation of a specific understanding. As with the union connection, an important national development was foreshadowed by municipal instances. But such connections were always vulnerable to the feverish relationships between local Labour and Liberal organisations, with both often divided over the appropriate reaction.[73]

Ultimately perhaps, it was not connections with particular bodies that were most important, but the way in which concern with municipal success led to a preoccupation with the niceties of tactical alliances. The council elections of 1898 revealed that the Keighley ILP had made such flexibility into a fine art. A victory in their electoral stronghold gave them all three councillors there, and also the balance of power on the council. They employed this to ally with the Conservatives in the aldermanic elections securing the election of one of their own councillors to the Aldermanic Bench. They then defeated a Liberal in the resulting by-election and increased their numbers to four. Such manoeuvrings could be justified as a furthering of socialism, but such an objective was not allowed to interfere with more immediate requirements:

Fight always on the claims of Labour representation. Do not issue programmes and literature of too far-reaching a character but take into consideration local requirements, and when once you have secured a foothold in the Council chamber, by sound, steady work there, you will find that voters come over faster.[74]

By now the indices of socialist advance were limited and in some ways, paradoxical — municipal victories, accessions to the Aldermanic Bench, acceptance within the community. The rhetoric of qualitative social change remained, but for many it had floated free from immediate political choices.

Preoccupation with electoral effectiveness was an important element in the party's accommodation within the Labour Alliance. For many activists, work within a local LRC was a logical extension of what had happened already. Yet the split within party activity — the 'ideal' of the lecture or the propaganda platform, the 'real' of electoral graft and compromise — provided fuel for dissent amongst activists. For many established figures within the party, the 'real' had become the only feasible means to the 'ideal', over time it could become a world in itself. Yet the principled claims of the party remained an essential component of its identity. Leaders wrapped themselves in traditional rhetoric to maintain their influence. In so doing, they trod a tight-rope since too great an emphasis on such principles could lead to arguments about how far pragmatism had undermined the vision.

Part 4
SIGNIFICANCE

15
Proposals and assumptions

Party policy

The party's principal spokemen spent only limited time on policy matters in the early years. Power remained at best a very distant prospect, and the widely accepted image of the ILP as predominantly a pressuriser of other larger blocs meant that policy proposals were restricted to a limited range of immediate concerns. Moreover, any attempt to formulate a comprehensive programme faced the difficultly of relating concrete proposals to progress towards wider socialist vistas. After 1900, interest in specific proposals increased, influenced perhaps by a greater optimism about parliamentary representation, but attributable more to the experiences of party members in municipal affairs. Although the drive for a more detailed elaboration of policies remained relatively weak, it did inevitably raise the problem of what distinctive contribution the party could make to contemporary controversies. Socialist rhetoric served well on ceremonial occasions, but more specific proposals raised the problem of ILP relationships with other sections, especially the Radical Liberals.

The delegates at the party's foundation conference had been more concerned with establishing a structure, and attempting to protect party independence than with spending much time on the construction of a programme which could well have a divisive influence. Nevertheless, the Bradford discussions succeeded, as we have seen, in producing a short programme which was amended at the 1894 Conference to include support for Disarmament and International Arbitration.[1] A more detailed discussion of policy occurred at the Newcastle Conference of April 1895. A sub-committee of the NAC had produced a revised programme which was discussed by the full Council,[2] and then debated by the delegates.[3] This included a lengthy new section on rural reforms — a bid to expand party influence in hitherto neglected territory. This reflected a common Radical belief that the growth of industry had distorted the balance between country and city. Other sections of the draft, industrial, educational and social, and fiscal, embodied and elaborated the proposals of the previous two years.[4]

This lengthy statement was felt by many to be something of an incubus, and the 1896 Conference instructed the NAC to produce a shorter statement.[5] This was developed initially by the Council's Programme Committee, and then adopted unanimously by the full NAC.[6] It began with a firm statement of the ILP's socialist objectives. Both land, 'the storehouse of all the necessities of life', and 'the capital necessary for industrial operations' should be owned collectively. Control should be exercised by the community, and both work and consequential wealth 'should be equitably distributed over the population'. The frame of reference was not that of a class but of the community — a significant trait in the party's self-consciously ethical appeal.[7]

The ideal was to be pursued initially through five types of measure. Four were presented tersely: the eight hour day; state pensions for all over fifty and provision for widows, orphans, the sick and disabled workers; free maintenance for school children; the abolition of indirect taxation together with the gradual shifting of all public burdens on to unearned incomes. There was more elaboration of the plank on employment. The objective was the provision of work to all capable adult applicants at trade union rates with a sixpence an hour minimum. Employment opportunities could be expanded by giving local authorities powers to engage in commercial activities. Once again, as in the initial Bradford document, there was an omnibus commitment to electoral and other democratic reforms.

This draft was subject to some amendment and extension at the 1897 Conference. The educational plank was expanded, and included for the first time, the potentially explosive commitment to secular education.[8] More significantly, two further items were added bringing the total to seven. One, taken from the 1895 programme, demanded 'Municipalisation and popular control of the Drink Traffic'.[9] More contentiously, the delegates debated the question of the half-time system. The 1895 programme had advocated the raising of the minimum age to fifteen; now a move was made to commit the party to complete abolition. This provoked criticism from delegates representing textile centres, with a Bradford member arguing that the half-time system reflected an ecomonic necessity. Snowden, present as the Keighley delegate, advocated a gradual cessation of child labour, but Tom Mann rejected the Yorkshire reservations, advocating trade unionism as the means to render child labour unnecessary. A compromise along the lines suggested by Snowden was adopted — 'the raising of the age of child labour with a view to its ultimate abolition'.[10]

This proposal constituted the core of the ILP programme for many years. A further item, 'the Municipalisation and Public Control' of hospitals, was added in 1903.[11] The following year, growing concern over women's suffrage left its mark on the political programme. The formula accepted adult suffrage as the objective, but also advocated 'the immediate extension of the franchise to women on the same terms as granted to men'. This elaborated statement of political objectives also incorporated commitments to triennial parliaments and the second ballot.[12]

The programme remained essentially an outline, with little attempt made to develop detailed analyses of how specific reforms could be carried through, or of how they could contribute towards more fundmental objectives. When ILP members dealt with details, they often utilised Fabian work. Only in 1904 did the Party decide to develop a network of 'Socialist Constructive Committees' to study and report to party conferences on specific problems. Very little emerged from this suggestion.[13]

Inevitably, the pressure of events drove the party to make declarations on issues other than those contained in the offical programme. The great domestic and international controversies of the period impinged on the party membership. Declarations had to be made about topics where socialist precepts gave scant guidance. In such uncharted territories, the likelihood of joint action with Radicals was increased.

The party's early horizons had been primarily domestic, but the growth of a more aggressive popular imperialism, the risk of war over such incidents as the Fashoda crisis, and increasing tensions in South Africa generated party declarations on foreign and defence policy. Support for 'disarmament and universal peace', as expressed at the 1894 Conference was simply a predictably vague aspiration. The party's position became a little more precise four years later, when delegates expressed opposition to conscription. The justification was a libertarian one, based on distaste for State compulsion in matters of individual conscience.[14] More specifically, socialist idealism was evident a year later when support for any reduction in armaments was yoked with a claim that a durable peace could be secured when 'the workers of all countries recognise their solidarity of interest and unite on a co-operative basis of production and exchange'.[15]

But such ultimate aspirations now had to be measured against the immediate crisis in South Africa. The question had been raised obliquely at the 1896 Conference in the aftermath of the Jameson Raid, when a resolution had contrasted the treatment of both Walsall anarchists and Irish political prisoners with 'the striking leniency shown towards the South African raiders'.[16] The outbreak of war in October 1899 was a major challenge for an already impoverished party. Many leading figures feared the unpopularity of an anti-war stand amongst sizeable sections of the working class, and support for the war from both Blatchford and leading Fabians led to divided socialist counsels. Yet the ILP leadership drew on a fund of socialist and Radical idealism and opposed the war from the beginning. The NAC claimed that the party branches were recognised as 'the backbone of the opposition to the South African capitalists in this country'.[17] This opposition was identified particularly with Hardie. He condemned the attempt to coerce the Boers, a manoeuvre motivated by capitalist greed for profits; he stigmatised the war as a costly drain on the British economy; he expressed concern about the corrosive impact of the war on domestic liberties and civilities. His arguments synthesised apparently Marxist claims about the war as a symptom of capitalist crisis, with

Radical accusations of conspiracy by financiers, politicians and journalists. In reality, the latter ingredient was dominant. The war was attributed far more to the machinations of specific individuals, than to the inexorable operation of an economic system largely independent of the wills of those involved. The conflict was portrayed as 'begotten in lies and fraud, nurtured in corruption and had for its prime motive the enslavement of black labour and the pauperisation of white labour'.[18] Despite evidence of popular support for the war, Hardie remained optimistic about the radical potential of the working class;

With a venal press, a cowardly pulpit, and creature politicians, their hope for wisdom in this matter lay with the working classes who, after all, were freer and less trammelled than any other section of the community.[19]

The party's 1900 conference expressed unanimity on the war, passing a resolution condemning Imperialism as anti-internationalist, anti-democratic, supportive of capitalism and producing neglect of domestic resources.[20]

Such agreement was impressive,, although perhaps it masked some divergences. The party press earlier in 1900 contained a lengthy wrangle over Brocklehurst's alleged pro-war opinions in which the NAC became involved,[21] and party spokesmen differed on the extent to which they favoured British defeats rather than a speedy end to the conflict. Such divergences were slightly more apparent when delegates returned to the issue at the 1901 Conference. Now the war had taken an uglier form. The defeat of the Boer armies, the growth of guerrilla activities, the burning of farmhouses by British forces and the formation of camps for the displaced families — these developments antagonised further, the British left both socialist and Radical. Yet when a resolution was moved on these policies, some delegates objected to the wording. Eventually, a reference to 'British troops ... burning the farms and belongings of helpless and inoffensive people' was amended, with 'military authorities' substituted as the guilty party. After all, delegates should not 'accuse British soldiers of inhuman conduct'. Similarly, a characterisation of this 'capitalist policy of extermination' as 'fiendish' was removed. Perhaps it was prudence that dictated such modifications. Sam Hobson reminded delegates that 'the policy of the war had been endorsed as much by the working men of the country as by the capitalist class'.[22] Possibly such prudence was backed by a form of nationalism. ILP members saw characteristically British liberal virtues as betrayed by the war. Such a sentiment provided a basis for opposition to government policy, but it did not justify attacks on British troops. ILP critics often opposed, not nationalism as such, but what they regarded as a perversion or denial of national virtues.

The complexities of national and racial feeling were demonstrated further by one legacy of the war — the Chinese labour question. The party's 1904 Conference condemned the importation of Chinese labour into South Africa. The conditions of service were 'repugnant to modern ideas of liberty'; such labour was bound to 'lower the standard of living', the compound system was 'tyrannous in its methods'. The resolution claimed that such opposition was based on economic and not on racial grounds, but felt that:

in the present stage of civilisation, a grave responsibility is incurred by forcing prematurely upon us, the difficult problem of civic and industrial co-operation with races widely different in feeling and habit from our own.[23]

Here was an issue that blended together radical-humanitarian sentiments, support for labour interests (since more Chinese workers meant less opportunities for British emigrants), and a genuflection towards ethnic prejudices.

Such a synthesis relfected a much broader development within the party from 1902, as Liberal self-confidence grew, and issues emerged into the centre of political argument that seemed specially designed to revitalise traditional Radical appeals. ILP reactions on such questions, although studiously affirming the inadequacy of Liberal nostrums, tended to blur the distinctions between the party and Radical Liberals, a process alreay facilitated by the war issue. This was taken further by the Unionist Government's Education Act which abolished the School Boards, replacing them with administration through local councils. The Act could be regarded plausibly as an attempt to modernise part of the complex, inadequate structure of local government administration. As a step on the road to 'National Efficiency' the policy had the enthusiastic backing of the Webbs. But Liberal opposition was vehement. The aid given, through the Act, to denominational education provoked non-conformist opposition and held out the hope of attracting back bourgeois non-conformists from the Unionists.

The ILP's broad commitment to free education at every level offered few guidelines on this controversy. The party, aided by the cumulative voting system, had fared reasonably well in its attempt to gain representation on School Boards, and advocacy of 'secular' education could be seen as a reason for opposing government support for Anglican and Catholic schools. ILP members of local School Boards were always much more likely to ally with Radical nonconformist members than with supporters of denominational education. But ILP propagandists had often attacked the sectarian enthusiasms of Radicals, and claimed that their religious views diverted them from paying adequate attention to economic and social injustices. The party anticipated government legislation, declaring at its 1901 conference that the principle of separate administrative bodies for education should be maintained. A year later, Fred Jowett moved a resolution placing the party alongside the Liberals on this question. Abolition of School Boards involved a retreat of public control from the educational sphere. Moreover women could no longer be elected directly to the administrative bodies; their involvement now depended on decisions on co-option taken by wholly male local authorities. Such grounds for opposition could be justified by reference to the ILP's well-established position on political reforms. Finally, the bill should be opposed since it strengthened public funding of denominational education, whilst providing only for the most nominal control.[25] Traditional Radical suspicions of priest power combined with notions of community involvement and accountability. Here was an ILP position which could be legitimised by reference to party principles. Such principles aligned the party closely with the Liberals. For many ILPers they proved a stronger attraction than claims that modernisation required a shift away from sectional shibboleths. Links between ILP and Radical viewpoints had been common on non-economic issues in the nineties. Now the passions stirred by the educational issue threatened to influence votes, and with the development of the MacDonald—Gladstone pact, such links could have had electoral significance for the ILP.

Agreement with the Liberals on education was perhaps predictable, given the Radical antecedents of many prominent party members. Much more crucial was the ILP reaction to Chamberlain's campaign for tariffs which dominated political argument from May 1903 until the 1906 election. There had been those in the nineties, most notably Champion, who had argued for protection as a crucial element within a wider Labour programme. Proposals for the exclusion of 'pauper aliens' had gained wider support within the labour movement. Blatchford's 'Merrie England' had argued for national self-sufficiency and had poured scorn on the trading obsessions of 'Manchesterism'. But many within the ILP — perhaps most significantly its emerging financial expert, Philip Snowden — were committed to free trade. Its rhetoric blended with the rhetoric of internationalism. Trade unions were opposed overwhelmingly to Chamberlain's proposals, with dominant union groups such as coal and cotton regarding a free-trade system as a guarantor of their prosperity. The party reacted strongly against Chamberlain's proposals, with a response that incorporated two elements.

One was negative. Tariffs should be rejected on grounds of both national self-interest and international harmony. Particular emphasis was placed on the impact on working-class living standards of duties on imported foodstuffs. The second element was more positive. The tariff campaign at least demonstrated an awareness that the British economy faced serious difficulties. This gave the ILP a chance to advance its own proposals. Protection would simply safeguard existing inefficiencies. Britain's economic problems could be attributed to the burden of 'exorbitant ... rents, royalties and railway rates'. The parlous condition of industrial workers was common to both free trade and protectionist systems; neither offered remedies for the evils of low income, poor housing and uncertain employment. The ILP responded with a blend of socialist and Radical proposals for social reconstruction:

legislation to nationalise the land, mines, railways, and other industrial monopolies, ... encouragement of scientific, commercial and technical education, the taxation of land values, a cumulative income tax ...[26]

These proposals could be heralded as a distinctively socialist response to the tariff controversy. But this claim involved difficulties. Most immediately, it was tariffs *per se* that dominated contemporary argument, and there ILP arguments supported the Liberal position. The socialist fine print was less important than the agreement over free trade. Such agreement proved to be of a very long-term significance. ILP spokesmen might evince an ethical distaste for the individualism of Manchester School economics: but the casting of such distaste into actions was to be deferred indefinitely. Until the time was ripe, a capitalist economy had to be administered by sound liberal precepts. This separation between immediate prudence and an ultimate replacement of capitalist structures again underlined the lack of coherent connection between immediate measures and any socialist transformation. Whatever justification there was for viewing such proposals as distinctively socialist rested on scepticism about the capacity of capitalism for co-existing with specific cases of state intervention. ILPers remained largely bewitched by an identification of 'capitalism' with 'laissez faire'. They viewed almost any State involvement in economic life as a frequently unpremeditated step towards socialism. Such a view made difficult an awareness of the extent to which some Liberals would argue for redistributive interventions as an alternative to the attractions of protection. Even if the ILP prescriptions are viewed as simply interventionist rather than potentially socialist, the adequacy of the diagnosis remains questionable. The ILP viewed the British economy as potentially adequate but handicapped by the parasitic activities of landlords and monopolists, blunted by inadequate educational facilities, and rendered anaemic by a maldistribution of wealth. There was no hint that the economy might be declining in competitiveness as rivals making later starts with industrialisation reaped significant advantages. At a more fundamental level, there lurked a tacit and unsupported assumption that modernisation could occur without damaging the prospects of industrial workers. Presumably the objective of the ILP proposals was to make British industry into a more effective participant in the international capitalist contest. The British nation and economic 'success' remained key units of reference, merging somewhat uneasily with dreams of a socialist commonwealth.

ILP declarations in favour of specific economic and social interventions increased after 1900. The party attempted to develop a housing policy, characteristically proposing municipal or national ownership as its ultimate objective and advocating expanding local authority powers as a first step.[27] The long-standing support for pensions was reiterated along with other welfare proposals, such as wider provisions for school meals.[28] The widespread anxiety over physical decline and the need for state action to counteract this left a clear mark on the party's proposals. So did its growing involvement in municipal affairs. The party advocated expanding municipal enterprises with the hope that profits could be used to improve housing or other public facilities.[29]

Potentially, the most significant question considered by the party was that of unemployment.[30] Here was an issue forming a central part of the concerns of the labour movement. Socialists could use the recurrence of high levels of unemployment as evidence of capitalism's failure to guarantee adequate levels of income and security. The issue could be employed to persuade pragmatic trade unionists of the relevance of a distinctively socialist perspective. It was hardly surprising, therefore, that the ILP, and especially Hardie, became closely identified with the cause of the unemployed. This association began during Hardie's first parliament, as he attempted to publicise the plight of the unemployed during the depression of the mid nineties. It became prominent once again as the trade boom associated with the war diminished after 1902, and the ILP became active once again, backed now by the wider resources of the LRC.

Despite these advantages, the unemployment question raised difficulties for the party. Its significance depended on the vagaries of the trade cycle. Little was heard of the question between 1896 and 1902; it hardly provided a stable base on which to build a sizeable political organisation. Even when the issue was dominant, the party had difficulties in reaching and mobilising many of the unemployed. As we have seen, the bedrock working-class support of the ILP tended to be drawn from the respectable artisans and from other sectors such as railways where employment was reasonably stable. Penetration into the unskilled masses of the great conurbations was limited, and yet it was there that the great bulk of the unemployed were to be found. Sceptical of long-term political solutions for their plight, the self-consciously respectable style of many ILP speakers was far removed from their preoccupations.

If the ILP faced difficulties in mobilising the unemployed, did they possess, at any rate, a distinctive set of proposals which could hopefully influence policy makers? The ILP's ultimate solution inevitably lay in the formation of a socialist society. Only then would it be possible to remedy the maldistributions of income that depressed demand, and the dominance of market forces that generated instabilities and distortions. Characteristically, however, ILP spokesmen sought immediate remedies. One response — that of eight-hours legislation — had been relinquished as a remedy for unemployment by the mid nineties. Socialist and trade unionist advocates of such a reform found themselves caught between two arguments. On the one hand, they viewed it as a means for employing more workers, but on the other, they wished to claim that a reduction in hours would raise productivity and enhance efficiency. Experience in the early nineties tended to support the latter claim, leading to a relinquishing of eight-hours legislation as a method of increasing employment.[31]

The unemployment agitation of the mid nineties, therefore, centred on the provision of public works for the unemployed. This was a cause, advocated by elements with a variety of standpoints inside and outside the labour movement. Hardie became identified with attempts to involve the central government in the provision of relief works. His case was underpinned by the predicament of many of his constituents. West Ham was a borough which shared the typical London problems of casual work and overcrowding, a blend which produced an appalling situation when the harsh winter of 1894—5 was imposed on an already depressed economy. But the West Ham unemployed, living as they did outside the LCC area, lacked even the very limited relief provided by the metropolitan agencies. The agitation produced the formation of a Commons Select Committee with Hardie as a member. He used this as a forum to advance his ideas on State responsibility for the unemployed; however, the work of the Committee ended with the dissolution of Parliament in June 1895.[32] Little came of the Committee's deliberations, trade revival seemed to make the issue less important, and for five years Hardie lacked a parliamentary pulpit. But the link had been made between the man, the party, and the issue.

When the question re-emerged in the years following the South African War, Hardie once again threw his energies into the controversy. The proposals put forward by the ILP showed a diverse set of influences. The Fabian contribution could be seen in the advocacy of a Ministry of Labour, which would co-ordinate work in suitably decentralised administrative divisions;[33] such a co-operation could serve as a means of implementing specific measures. ILPers still accounted for unemployment in part as a result of a distortion in population distribution as between urban and rural areas: they proposed that central and municipal authorities could combine in forming agricultural schemes to drain off surplus urban population.[34] Here, traditional Radical images of the virtues of a decent rural life hinted at a utopian response to the problem. Public authorities should also engage in counter-cyclical activities, undertaking works at times of depression. Such developments had to be self-financing, paid for by taxes on the land values, higher death duties, and a cumulative tax on unearned income.[35] Advocacy of public projects was viewed principally as a method of relief with each project supported from revenue. Despite the claim that socialism was the only adequate solution, some ILP leaders, notably Hardie, were prepared to welcome any step that seemed to admit some governmental responsibility for the unemployed. Thus Hardie expressed qualified support for the Balfour Government's Unemployed Workmen's Bill in 1905, and led agitation to prevent backsliding from the original modest proposals.[36]

The ILP's central programme was amplified, as the party gained footholds in representative bodies and responded to specific controversies. Although spokesmen still proclaimed the socialist objective, specific proposals led the party more and more into a close relationship with Radical Liberals. Such developments inevitably increased the risk of internal arguments, as various elements within the ILP placed more or less emphasis on socialist objective or immediate measures. Yet the party's politics depended on much more than an official programme of measures plus an objective plus a growing number of declarations on specific controversies. These proposals were based themselves on a series of assumptions about British society and the advent of socialism. Sometimes attempts were made to justify the assumptions explicitly; often they were assumed. But either way, they provided a foundation for the party programme.

The intellectual basis of the ILP

The principal spokesmen for the party were citizens of the uncertain territory where respectable manual workers and aspiring white-collar merged. Their ideas were largely the result of self-education; their reading blended social, economic and literary works characteristic of late Victorian Radicalism. Carlyle and Ruskin were typically formative influences; Dickens and, from a more distant Radical past, Bunyan added their weight. Popularisations of historical and biological works were significant. Scots were attracted to Burns. It was a rich inheritance, much of it falling under the tradition sometimes seen as the Romantic critique of capitalism. The ideas of such propagandists were essentially Victorian and typically insular in their formation.[37]

The spaces are obvious. Passionate rejections of aspects of the existing order or that order *per se* were common as inspirations. These were couched often in a literary or quasi-religious style. There was little attempt at a detailed study by socialists of existing economic or social arrangements; such investigations as were beginning to appear by the end of the century were typically the preserve of interventionist Liberals. Equally, there was no developed critique of conventional economic theories that was accepted by most British socialists. In one sense such gaps marked the lack of a marxist tradition. The range of writings by Marx and Engels available in English remained restricted, and such marxism as was known was frequently identified with the mechanistic views of the SDF leadership.[38] Yet there remained also the writings of William Morris, unmistakably marxist in inspiration, yet stylistically at one with much of the writing that early ILP propagandists felt most at home with. Several of them, most notably Glasier, were at some time close to Morris, and his death in 1896 produced a widespread response. Glasier wrote how 'Socialism seems all quite suddenly to have gone from its summer into its winter time'.[39] Blatchford demonstrated his grief in the *Clarion*:

I cannot help thinking that it does not matter what goes into the *Clarion* this week because William Morris is dead ... He was our best man, and he is dead.[40]

Here was an inheritance in an accessible idiom which was not taken up. The bowdlerisation of Morris went on apace, as his work was domesticated and accommodated within an elastic, gradualist view of socialist potential.[41] So what emerged as the characteristic ILP view of socialist possibilities was not an inevitable product of a theoretically impoverished British radicalism. It involved decisive choices — or perhaps misunderstandings of a recent legacy.

The impact of evolutionary modes of thought furnishes a useful starting point in any examination of basic ILP assumptions. These were associated particularly with MacDonald, but were accepted in their essentials by many propagandists. Doubt remained about whether this was simply a beguiling metaphor or whether the view of society as an organism developing over time as new tasks were set and then accomplished through appropriate adaptions, provided a basis for explaining and predicting the course of social change. The next principal task, presumably, was to render society more efficient through the development of collectivist organisation:

It appears to be the principal task of the twentieth century to discover a means of co-ordinating the various social functions so that the whole community may enjoy robust health and its various organs share adequately in that health. But this is nothing else than the aim of Socialism.[42]

Whatever the epistemological status of the organic image, its widespread acceptance carried with it significant implications, or at any rate, it did so provided that one other assumption was built into the framework. It would be possible to hold the belief that the ultimate and desirable state of a society should be an organic integrated unity, but that the present system was exploitative and contained fundamental divisions of interest. This state of affairs would have to be destroyed before a genuinely organic community could be constructed. Such an argument could clearly license a strategy of revolutionary, indeed violent, change. For the organic image to serve as a basis for gradualism, it would have to be employed not as a representation of what could and should be the case, but as a claim about what existed within the present social order, at least in potential terms. The image could lead on occasions to emphases and arguments that would have gladdened Edmund Burke:

nobody who understands the power of habit and of custom in human conduct ... and ... who understands the delicate and intricate complexity of production and exchange which keeps modern Society going, will dream for a single moment of changing it by any act of violence.[43]

Clearly the existing capitalist order worked inefficiently and immorally. The grind of daily industrial struggles could change the consciousness of workers. Hardie, fortified by such beliefs, could write hopefully of the polarising industrial relations of late 1897:

I feel this week as if great events were going on all around us, the old tumbling down, the new beginning to be upraised — colliers, engineering, railways.[44]

The consciousness of workers and the consciences of bourgeois reformers could be stirred by such developments, but such growing awareness should be turned to constructive uses, not to a revolutionary endeavour to overthrow the capitalist system.

This projection rested on a range of related assumptions and contrasts. Most critically, there was a failure to discuss central features of marxian economics. At its most superficial this could be seen in the characteristic assertion that:

no doubt not every ILP member would pass an examination in 'Das Capital' (*sic*), but at least they knew that 'Liberty, Equality, Fraternity' were the true laws of life.[45]

Here, supposedly narrow economic marxism of the SDF variety was contrasted with the warm-hearted, spontaneous, ethical inspirations of the ILP. Beyond such stereotypes there lay claims about what was wrong with the workers' present situation. ILP writers frequently referred to the exploitation of workers under capitalism. In part, they emphasised poverty, insecurity of employment, high mortality rates, and low standards of health and amenities. Thus Blatchford could write movingly of Manchester slums and Hardie could contrast the fatalities of mining with the frivolous rituals of monarchy and aristocracy. Many propagandists echoed the official party line that a prime defect of capitalism was a lack of purchasing-power continuously exacerbating low living standards and overall instability. On occasions, party leaders could write graphically of the impact of the factory system — the monotony of mass production, the callous impersonality of the wage-relationship, the nomadic insecurity generated by the operation of the trade cycle. Hardie could summarise the results in language which exhibited the influence of the widely-read Victorian critics of industrialism:

The result of all this is to produce demoralisation of the most fatal kind. There is no sense of unity between the man and his work. He can have no pride in it since there is nothing personal to him which will attach to it after it is finished. It will be sold he knows not by whom nor to whom. All day long he works under the eye of a taskmaster set over him to see that he does not shirk his duties. At the end of the week, he is paid so many shillings for what he has done, and naturally enough, his one concern is with the number of shillings he will receive. This is the cash nexus which binds him to his employer.[46]

Such a portrait was a moving presentation of the alienated worker. It placed the roots of the worker's predicament in arbitrary impersonal authority and a deadening system of production, generated at least in part by a complex division of labour and the arbitrariness of market relationships. There was little suggestion that the drive for profit of itself systematically robbed the worker at the point of production. Perhaps more importantly, ILP writers rarely suggested that the economic system might approach some sort of terminal crisis, and never justified such claims by reference to a theory of capitalist breakdown. They faced therefore an economic system against which they had formulated a heavy indictment, but which they did not expect to collapse of its own contradictions. It should evolve, therefore, into a higher form of social organism, as a consequence of harsh experience and careful thought.[47]

The forward-looking tone of such a claim must be set against the heavy emphasis in much ILP writing on 'The World We Have Lost'. ILP writers frequently lamented the loss of a rural arcadia, of independent and staunchly individualistic producers. Hardie looked back to the romanticised world of the independent Scottish colliers,[48] and beyond this to a retrospective vision of the Golden Age:

taking Europe as a whole, it lasted from the beginning of the thirteenth to the middle of the fifteenth century ... there were neither Millionaires nor Paupers in those days, but a rude abundance for all.[49]

Blatchford's 'Merrie England' contrasted the ersatz pleasures of a factory-based civilisation with the idyll of rural life:

does a week at a spoiled and vulgar watering-place repay you for fifty-one weeks' toil and smother in a hideous and stinking town? ... the relative beauty and pleasantness of the factory and country districts do not need demonstration ... You would rather see a squirrel than a sewer rat. You would rather bath in the Avon than in the Irwell. You would prefer the fragrance of a rose-garden to the stench of a sewage-works.[50]

Even the pragmatic MacDonald saw the growth of urban connurbations as a damaging destruction of a natural balance:

the rural districts of every commercial country are emptying their people into the cities, and as the sources of healthy manhood are depleted, the reserve forces of the race are drawn off.[51]

Such claims, although influential, rested clearly on a naive view of rural life. The beguiling image could give a seductive standard for judging the present, but it ignored the exploitative relationships of rural communities along with their attendant miseries. As a guide to action, such images offered little.[52] Their impact can be seen in proposals to ameliorate unemployment by settling surplus urban population on the land. More influentially, the rural retrospect could be used as a justification for supporting the Boers. They had not lost their innocence:

As Socialists, our sympathies are bound to be with the Boers. Their Republican form of Government bespeaks freedom and is hateful to tyrants, while their methods of production for use are much nearer our ideal than any form of exploitation for profit.[53]

But the rural dream could be only a beguiling utopia. Staunchly practical evolutionary socialists faced more immediate problems.

The ILP condemnation of capitalism rested to a large degree on a portrayal of the plight of the worker. Equally, propagandists expected the labour movement representing the interests of the working class to form an indispensable part of the campaign for socialism. Yet although the party's central endeavour was to win over the working class to the idea of socialism, the leadership — and a good many of the rank and file — rejected a distinctively working-class appeal and denied that the class struggle would act as the motive force for the transition to socialism. Glasier, in particular, came to see this rejection as a cardinal point of ILP doctrine. What he termed the 'class-war dogma' constituted a damaging deviation foisted on the socialist movement by Marx. A major justification for the party's existence was 'the rescuing of the cause of Socialism', from the SDF with its preaching of 'the Class War and other inane questions'.[54] Such a mission was not without a dash of national justification. It was necessary to set 'our ILP or British (should I not say our Scottish?) conception above all German formulas'.[55] Not surprisingly, Glasier attacked the notion of 'the class war' at the Amsterdam Congress of the International in August 1904, and received criticism from SDF delegates, but approval from Jaures.[56]

This rejection was echoed by other ILPers with a range of arguments. They centered around the claim that since a socialist society was ethically preferable to capitalism, the agency for producing it must embody its ideals. There was no reason to believe that a worker's revolt would do so. 'A mere class movement ... the peevish and bitter strife of the oppressed'[57] would be unlikely to produce a constructive advance. MacDonald took the argument further. He made clear his assumption that there should exist a basic consensus about progress towards socialism, when he examined what he saw as the empty slogan of the class war:

all that the class war ... means is that an enlightened proletariat, not blinded by its immediate interests but guided by its permanent ones, will be Socialist. But so also will a similarly enlightened bourgeoisie.[58]

Such harmony would facilitate progress towards a more perfectly functional social organism.

As it was, class antagonisms were embodied in existing trade union organisations, but although these were important as defenders of workers' interests under capitalism, they had minimal value as agencies for a transition to socialism. Trade union sectionalism was seen as a destructive quality:

each of the wings of an army for carrying on the class war is bound in the nature of things to fight its battles mainly for its own hand. Trade solidarity rather than proletarian solidarity is the real outcome of a class war in practice, and trade interest is ultimately individual interest.[59]

This view was shared by Blatchford. Although frequently in dispute with MacDonald on strategic issues, he condemned trade unionists for their sectionalism:

If his own wages and hours are affected he will move, but he is languid about the hard conditions of the millions outside his own union.[60]

Alongside his organic view of society, MacDonald steadfastly reduced putative class interests to the interests of individual members of a class. Such interests were seen as short-term and materialistic; they could not provide a basis for a superior form of social organisation.

These arguments raised crucial problems about the viability of trade union organisation and activity as a lever for fundamental changes. MacDonald's belief that trade union involvements could not produce more specifically socialist attachments was not shared by those ILPers who worked within trade union factions, although the diverse problems encountered by them suggested that the translation of industrial struggle into political progress was a far from simple matter. Scepticism about the value of trade unionism as a basis for socialist advance was widely shared in the party. Sometimes it rested principally on a belief that trade union struggles would barely effect the lot of the worker, and that political action was vital. Most ILPers saw the political wing as providing the vital socialist ingredient, whilst trade unions protected immediate interests. But some shared Richard Pankhurst's view that the strike was an out-moded weapon whose use should be deplored.[61] Eventually, the commitment to gradualism produced the Labour Alliance, but concern about trade union activities continued. There were conflicting elements in the ILP position. The evolutionary attachment dictated alliance with other groupings including trade unions; the ethical attachment to socialism led to a sceptical view being taken of union sectionalism and short-term material goals.

If the working class alone could not provide a basis for the socialist transition, and if there was neither practical nor ethical justification for postulating the class struggle as the motive power, then the ILP had to provide an alternative basis. At one level this lay in the claim that the justification for socialism lay in the inefficiencies of capitalism. The social organism would operate in a more healthy fashion when rampant individualism was replaced by collective ownership and responsibility. Some progress towards the objective could be achieved through the patchwork reforms of those who sought to improve the existing order without being convinced socialists. But significant change required the self-conscious application of ideas:

When we think systematically of the scattered fragments of reform promised by the political parties, we see that they are but the foreshadowing of socialistm; when the tendencies begun by scores of experiments — factory laws, public health laws, municipalisation — are followed out, joined together, systematised, Socialism is the result.[62]

Such formulations are as far as the notion of the transition underwent any clarification. Blatchford was even less precise:

how can Socialism be accomplished? I confess that I approach this question with great reluctance. The establishment and organisation of a Socialistic State are the two branches of the work to which I have given least attention.[63]

Typically, the case rested on an optimistic belief that the drift of the evolving organism was in an appropriate direction, that socialists should seek to ease developments and suggest effective methods for facilitating the change. Beneath the rhetoric, the scenario was that of the Fabian Essays.

The ILP diverged from the Fabian position — at least as taught by the latter's London leadership — over the question of mass involvement. For the Webbs, the drive towards a collectivist society did not require the positive involvement of the masses. A system of rational administration was to be created on their behalf, rather than made by them. The ILP propagandists with their ethical arguments for socialism required involvement and consent. Unhappy, and sceptical about the basing of this on a class, they sought an alternative foundation.

Two aspects of this are important. One follows closely from their organic imagery and their rejection of class struggle as a key determinant. Now the crucial reference was to be the notion of community, in all its ambiguity. Sometimes this meant the whole society; on other occasions it could mean a local community, an identification clearly growing in significance as the party extended its representation on local authorities. Such a criterion for policy assumed that there were no intractable conflicts of interest within the given community. Whether an individual qualified as a worthy member, depended not on the class to which one belonged but on what one's priorities and values were.

The crucial step in becoming a socialist was akin to a 'conversion'. The individual turned to socialism just as sinners turned to Christ in revivalist missions — hence the significance of socialist propaganda, the importance of 'making socialists'. It was not the strategy of 'making socialists' as such that distinguished the early ILP, but what was involved in this process. The formally marxist German Social Democrats sought to spread socialist doctrines through a network of party institutions; the SDF had its study circles devoted to the discussion of marxist texts. The ILP process did not involve such detailed doctrinal studies, but rather a change of heart and the evincing of socialist endeavour. The socialist convictions of the ILP blended simple warm enthusiasms with prudent pragmatism — the characteristic blend of the nonconformist chapel in which intention and good works counted for more than doctrinal exactitude.

If socialism was to be brought forward by the activities of a host of individually consenting enthusiasts, rather than by the struggles of a class, if it depended on the moral rectitude of the converted, then deviation from the appropriate standards was an inescapable problem. The party propagandists saw themselves as living for the cause and looked reprovingly on backsliders. When the ex-ILP candidate Fred Hammill became a publican in Thirsk, Glasier's response was sharp: ''Twill be hard on us if Lab Agitators descend to the level of prize fighters and footballers.'[64] The socialist message could easily be lost in the welter of commercial distractions. Disillusioned party activists sometimes felt that sober, thoughtful recruits were scarce:

The uprising of Jingoism, and the huge growth of popular interest in betting, football, and all forms of garish entertainment ... are incidents in the career of the democracy which were not foreseen by the earlier band of political democrats.[65]

The decline in party membership in the late nineties was one source of disillusion, but the response of many urban workers to the South African war was much more corrosive of ILP optimism. Cosy notions of inevitable progress were bruised. Glasier walked Liverpool streets 'seething with men and women shouting like maniacs', and found a 'blatant and brutal war feeling' amongst their Sheffield counterparts.[66] Lister was attacked by a jingo crowd in Brighouse. Glasier admitted he was a pessimist for the first time in his life.[67]

Yet his diagnosis was one that many Radicals could accept. Progress was essentially a product of ethical decisions by individuals. Thus the jingo reaction must be explained in individual terms — the gullibility of potentially decent people in the face of manipulation: 'The people seem to have gone back. The *Daily Mail* and the other great capitalist and Jewish papers have excited madness among them.'[68] The damage was retrievable but these experiences showed the frailty of any socialist strategy based on this type of ethical argument. It served to strengthen ILP leaders' distaste for what they saw as irresponsible mob oratory — whether jingoist or socialist. They had had an anticipation of August 1914.

The potential for disillusion was always there because ILP arguments tended to begin with a broader view of human nature than their Hyndmanite or Webbian counterparts. There was certainly in the marxism of the nineties a tendency to dismiss moral argument as utopian or sentimental. That dismissal is typically associated with Hyndman, but was a much wider phenomenon.[69] It marked for marxists a declension from the achievements of Morris. The possibility of a socialism integrating both elements was lost in the nineties. On the one side, the official SDF viewpoint tended to present marxism as a narrowed scientific system, a firm defence against sentimentality. In contrast the ILP position retained the moral concern but, lacking a rigorous basis for investigating social relationships, this degenerated easily into sermonising verbiage. A parallel split could be found between ILP propagandists and Fabian pamphleteers, with once again the implication being that the Fabian view of human potential was a narrow utilitarian one with the satisfaction of immediate material benefits as the ruling criterion. Yet although the ILP vision with its borrowings from ethical, literary and religious sources could seem more attractive than its rivals, it was also increasingly amorphous. Rhetorical flights could be used to deck out tactical manoeuvres in approved terms. The deliberate relegation of reason — 'Socialism is much more an affair of the heart than of the intellect'[70] — allowed free rein to the manipulative arts of the orator. Such methods suggested a short cut for the arousal of socialist enthusiasm, but its durability and perspicacity were more debatable.

Optimism about social evolution and emphasis on individual commitment fitted in readily with the ILP's optimism about the viability of existing institutions as instruments for the achievement of socialism. Belief about the likelihood of an emerging consensus on collectivist reform implied that no significant section within the society would seek to use existing institutions to obstruct change. Moreover, there were many aspects of existing political practices that served as a springboard for further advance towards socialism. Since the feasibility of socialism depended on individual conviction, well-informed and determined reformers could use the existing machinery to bring about significant changes. Acceptance of the existing political arrangements sometimes involved praise of the constitution in terms that few Conservatives could criticise. The party by 1899 was proclaiming its acceptance of 'the

traditional customs of British political and economic change'.[71] Such conformism was based on a fundamental optimism that in Britain 'there exists
no oppression that the people desire to rid themselves of, which they cannot
overthrow, if resolved upon it'.[72] This produced two crucial conclusions:
Firstly, the parliamentary road must be the way forward:

However heroic an appeal to guns, swords and dynamite — the weapons of imperial
and religious barbarism — may sound, it nevertheless resolves itself eventually into
a prosaic counting of noses; and noses may as well be counted peacefully and accurately
at the ballot box as turbulently and inaccurately amid the dropping of blood and the
splashing of brains.

Secondly, there was an attempt to signpost the reasons for present disappointments:

it is not the force of the landlords and capitalists, nor their armies nor police that keeps
the workers in servitude, or keeps back Socialism, but the ignorance and apathy and
the force of the workers themselves.[73]

It was a view echoed by Blatchford in moments of disillusion:

The greatest obstacles in the way of Social Emancipation are not the greed and power
of the rich, but the ignorance and disunion of the working-classes ... Interest in political
affairs is rare amongst the workers and knowledge rarer.[74]

So the hard way forward remained through education. This was the important dimension.

ILP optimism in this respect was based on a number of elements. The party's
spokesmen had no perception of capitalism as a hostile structural unity. The
spectre conjured up in 1886 by Morris was absent from their fears. ILPers could
be counted amongst those who 'very much underrate the strength of the
tremendous organisation under which we live'. Such expectations, for Morris,
were naively optimistic since 'Nothing but a tremendous force can deal with
this force ... rather than lose anything which it considers of importance, it will
pull the roof of the world down upon its head.' It was far removed from the
ILP hope for gradual peaceful persuasion. The distance was further increased
because of the characteristic ILP view of relationships between party and those
whom it attempted to represent. Morris painted a vision of how a gradualist
government could blunder into a confrontation through arousing expectations
that it was unable to satisfy:

For, indeed, I grant these semi-Socialist Democrats that there is one hope for their
tampering piecemeal with our Society; if by chance they excite people into seriously,
however blindly, claiming one or other of these things in question, and could be successful in Parliament in driving it through, they would certainly draw on a great civil
war, and such a war once let loose would not end but either with the full triumph of
Socialism, or its extinction for the present.[75]

This complex scenario — elaborated further in 'News From Nowhere'[76] —
went far beyond the simplicities of the ILP vision of progress. In the latter,

the 'people' must be educated in the virtues of the long haul. Fear of the masses was not restricted to manifestations of jingoism. ILP spokesmen also evinced an almost neurotic anxiety about disorder on the left.

Some ILP beliefs about the feasibility of reformism rested, therefore, on beliefs about the neutrality of existing institutions, the goodwill of putative opponents and the stability of any transitional process. This transition was also inexorable. ILP leaders might come to accept that 'the road to Socialism is going to be a slow and matter-of-fact one'.[77] But the ultimate arrival was never doubted. MacDonald after two years of parliamentary dealings remained convinced: 'I ... can no more see how the realisation of this idea can be prevented than I can see how any puny device of man can stop the earth pursuing its path in the universe.'[78] Such certainty clearly rested in part on their belief in the availability of a collectivist consensus as a product of both experience and education. But it also depended on a belief that such a collectivist advance could lead to socialism. Such a view was facilitated by the peculiarities of the British situation. The distinctive equating of capitalism and laissez-faire made almost any collectivist development seem a possible move towards socialism. There was no realisation that an essentially capitalist system could live with, and indeed be strengthened by, the rationalising impact of the State. Indeed, the basing of the case for socialism upon the perceived inequities and inefficiencies of a largely free-market capitalism left the door open for precisely such an accommodation.

The myopic view of the relationship between the State and a capitalist economy was one way in which inevitability could be presented persuasively. But ILP optimists faced a further difficulty which grew out of their view of reformers' involvements within the overall society. We have noted how socialist reformers might hope to intervene judiciously to further the transitional process, and also how non-socialist interventions could assist in this process by demonstrating the inadequacy of free-market practices in a particular sector. Crucially, both self-consciously socialist and other piecemeal interventions contributed towards the transformation in a fashion that could be grasped by the perceptive thinker. The process would be facilitated as self-consciously socialist interventions became predominant. So the inevitability of socialism was based also on an optimistic portrait of social engineering. A socialist programme could be implemented and, questions of class opposition apart, the results would be relatively predictable. Socialists would act upon the social organism to bring it to a higher evolutionary level. The relationship between such agents of change, and the apparently passive society of which they also formed a part remained a mystery.

Such obscurity blanketed a fundamental problem — that of agency and the constraints faced by agents, constraints in part generated by earlier interventions, but also the unintended product of a host of individual acts. Inevitability, a belief in inexorable progress appeared far more plausible if the complexities of this problem were by-passed. Once they are raised then the ponderings of the later Engels become important. So too does William Morris:

> I pondered all these things, and how men fight and lose the battle, and the thing that they fought for comes about in spite of their defeat, and when it comes turns out not to be what they meant, and other men have to fight for what they meant under another name.[79]

The difficulties of the transition were compounded by the ever-optimistic and ever-confounded attempts of agents to master the historical process.

The intellectual foundations of the early ILP have been dismissed frequently as superficial, woolly sentimental examples of Ethical Socialism. On one level, such characterisations are legitimate. ILP positions were often formulated very loosely, and were couched in language that appealed more to the emotions than to any process of reasoning. At its best this could appear as a robust defence of the experiences of the self-taught against the theological disputations of socialist schoolmen; at its worst it would appear as a philistine rejection of careful, reasoned discussion. Certainly such a style of argument could be highly functional for a party leadership, granting considerable freedom of manoeuvre, since many shared sentiments could license most likely courses of action.

But beneath the emotional rhetoric there lay a body of assumptions which were relatively clear. The ILP position was fundamentally a hopeful one. It was optimistic about the possibility of a transition to socialism. A collectivist consensus was possible, existing institutions could be used, the impact of certain changes was reasonably predictable. Such assessments and prognostications were based on a critique of capitalism as immoral, inefficient but not tending to an inevitable breakdown. The transition to socialism would build on the achievements of capitalism, not on its collapse. The motive-power for change would not be class struggle, but the moral conviction and informed opinions of 'the people'. Such a movement was possible given fervent propaganda. It was also desirable, given the typical ILP view of human capacities. This rejected utilitarian images as manifest in Fabian and SDF proposals. A change to socialism would satisfy more than immediate material benefits; it could realise social, moral and artistic qualities that other socialist groups tended to ignore. Such an image of human potential added to the vagueness of much ILP argument, but also endowed it with a powerful appeal. The optimism of the activists could be bruised by the socialist recession of the late nineties and by the chastening experiences of the South African War. Yet it remained fundamentally intact. ILP leaders were typical Victorian Radicals in this respect. In the end, the forces of progress were irresistible. It was 'the Springtime of Nations ... a Springtime of Society'.[80] The weight of history was on the side of the ILP.

16

Connections and exclusions

'The divided forces of democracy'*

The ILP as a political newcomer, inevitably had to relate to non-socialist political groupings. Its commitment to gradualism, and its liking for evolutionary images suggested that such relationships need not be completely hostile. The most crucial question was that of the party's relationship with Liberalism. The connections constituted a tangled skein which defies a slick, simplified account. At one level the complexities were captured in the careers and views of many of the party's leading figures. Typically, they served their time as Radical activists, they then broke with Liberal organisations, and engaged in passages of bitter recrimination with their erstwhile allies. But they remained strongly attached to many Liberal policies and typically viewed Liberals as preferable to their Tory counterparts. Thus Glasier stigmatised Herbert Samuel's candidacy at Cleveland in November 1902 as 'discreditable', but welcomed his victory: 'I don't want to see the working-class vote Tory — there is no hope in such folly.'[1] Tradition and immediate concerns could lead ILP leaders to back Liberal candidates. Glasier voted Liberal in the High Peak by-election of July 1909, to support the People's Budget, to back the time-honoured Radical causes of Free Trade and anti-militarism and 'because like my father before me I detest Toryism'.[2] Yet such closeness was balanced by bitter hostilities. The creation and the survival of the ILP was, to some extent, an institutional indictment of Liberalism by disillusioned Radicals.

Appreciation of attachments and tensions must be placed in a wider context. Most ILP leaders were drawn from the politically active sections of the working and lower-middle classes. In the 1880s, the predominant political attachment of these groups was Radical. This reflected the traditional advocacy by Radicals of wider political rights, and also mirrored the widespread belief that little could halt the march of democratic forces. The franchise reform of 1884 was one more milestone in an inexorable process of democratisation. Hardie could recommend Liberalism to the Ayrshire miners in 1885. Gladstone's Party

---

* From a letter written by Hardie To H. W. Massingham, 30 April 1903.

has fought for you, and won for you the right of citizenship. They have given you cheap bread to feed the body, and a cheap Press to feed the mind. They have always stood up for the Rights of Man, no matter what his creed or colour ... They desire the greatest good for the greatest number.[3]

This common brand of rhetoric proved attractive to several old Chartists who found acceptable accommodation in the Gladstonian mansion.[4] Political optimism was buttressed by trade-union experiences under a still dominant capitalism — Lib-Labism seemed a natural creed for industrial leaders in an age of equipoise. Radical Liberalism seemed typically to inspire and guarantee British freedoms, British stability, and perhaps British superiority.

This was only one side of the picture. There were always enthusiasts for labour representation who endorsed Radical principles, but who objected to their efforts being canalised and perhaps perverted by Liberal wire-pullers. The performance of the Liberal Governments often disappointed Radicals, who complained bitterly about the excessive influence of Whig landlords and laissez-faire industrialists. Indeed, this last element in particular raised a wider question of the other faces of Liberalism. Liberal reforms might have gone a considerable way towards guaranteeing formal political rights, but this assault on privilege and restriction had been paralleled by another assault on behalf of economic freedoms. Liberalism might signify the force of free democratic argument, but it also could indicate the harsh individualism of Manchester economics.

Detailed case-studies show that working-class Radicals would experience this conflict in diverse ways. They might find their local Liberal caucus subscribed formally to radical democratic nostrums, but was dominated in fact by local employers and tradesmen; they might discover that Liberal employers could be at least as abrasive in their industrial relations as their Tory counterparts. Such disillusion could be precipitated by national developments. The post-1886 confusions within the Liberal party made party managers more eager to retain the services of their few grandees and their diminishing number of industrialists. They also rendered the party a vehicle for sectional enthusiasms in which the Labour interest was one voice amongst many. Such confusions occurred alongside dramatic development in the trade union world, as hitherto quiescent workers began to make demands and previously secure craftsmen found themselves under technical threat.

It is important to emphasise how far the drift from Liberalism was occasioned in the first instance by organisational frustrations, a feeling that Labour was not given legitimate weight in Liberal counsels, rather than by the emergence of an ideological rift. Thus many spokesmen for Independent Labour abandoned the Liberal Party as an instrument, but did not abandon many of their Radical Liberal principles. Yet these principles were themselves undergoing major reappraisal in the nineties. The erosion of the Gladstonian coalition, the failures of 1892—5, increasing awareness of industrial problems and social inequities, the challenge of a more aggressive imperialism — all these helped to produce widespread intellectual arguments about Liberalism's capacity to cope with immediate problems. Responses often involved attempts to justify extensions of state involvement based on impeccably Liberal principles. Such shifts could be seen by ILP spokesmen as part of the inevitable, semi-conscious drive towards socialism.

Relations with the Liberals were at their nadir in the ILP's early years. The varied causes of this estrangement emerge from earlier discussions. Partly the distance was the result of the ILP attempts to prevent their new organisation from being reabsorbed into the Liberal coalition. It also reflected local experiences. Often ILP branches had emerged with particular strength in areas where Liberalism was relatively secure, complacent and backward-looking. ILP activists were often preoccupied with the unbending self-help creed of local Liberal employers. Equally, trade union experiences contributed to estrangement. Lib-Lab leaders saw the ILP as the instrument of trouble-makers at all levels — in the TUC, on Trades Councils, within individual unions and in specifically political contests. The polarisation was expressed in such confrontations as the Newcastle ILP's repeated attacks on John Morley,[5] and the bitter by-election contests of 1896—7. Estrangement reached a climax at York early in 1898, when the party, first locally and then nationally, resolved to back the Tory, Charles Beresford, against the Liberal employer, Sir Christopher Furness. The latter was seen as one of a group of reactionary north-eastern industrialists who dominated the region's political life. At the height of the Engineers' lockout, the return of Furness would represent 'a great triumph for the enemies of trade unionism'.[6] Similar arguments supported the evocation of Asquith as the 'butcher' of Featherstone, and assertions of Liberal Ministers' belligerence over the Hull Dock Strike.

ILP attitudes to Liberalism in these early years distinguished frequently between instrument and ideas. The instrument was regarded as hopeless. At local level, working-class demands received unsympathetic responses from Liberal caucuses — Smillie wrote of the Mid-Lanark Liberal Association 'contemptuously' setting aside requests for a miners' candidate.[7] Nationally, it was argued that conservative elements would always dominate the Liberal Party. Rosebery's emergence as leader was seen as yet one more example of this control:

The Whigs have prevailed, the Radicals have been dished once more, an operation to which they should be by this time well accustomed.[8]

At the level of ideas, the ILP position was less clear. Sometimes it appeared that the line betwen the two creeds was very sharp. It was the fundamental distinction between 'capitalistic' Liberalism and socialistic Labourism. Yet the continuities were important: the ILPers agreed with Radicals on a wide range of political issues, on temperance, on Home Rule, and on specific economic reforms. The characteristic ILP justification for this agreement owed much to the evolutionary image. Liberal principles and the Liberal Party had

provided valuable bases for reform, but now the principles required support
from collectivist economic precepts, and the party would no longer carry these
through. Such a perspective was implied in Hardie's requiem for Gladstone:
'Gladstone's work has made Socialism possible — nay, has been the necessary,
the indispensable pioneer of the Socialist movement'.[9] The ILP was the
legitimate heir to the Progressive mantle. As such, its leaders frequently bid
for the support of local Radicals, disillusioned with Whiggish sell-outs. Such
bids seemed more attractive amidst the futilities of the Rosebery Government.
After the 1895 debacle, the future of the Liberal Party seemed precarious, and
Hardie could rejoice: 'Liberalism has gone ... the future is ours if we know
how to claim it.'[10] But whatever Liberal disarray, the arrival of a Unionist
Government presented the ILP with a tactical problem. Anti-government
agitation would run the risk of rehabilitating Liberalism.

After the 1895 election, ILP speakers continued to bid for Radical support
but with limited success. Expectations of a breakthrough were foiled by the
continued attachment of most Radicals to the Liberal machine. This was
demonstrated in Hardie's East Bradford campaign in the autumn of 1896,
when W. P. Byles of the *Bradford Observer* emphasised that he differed from
the ILP not on principles, but on the most effective instrument:

> Yes, 'fight on' is, I suppose, all we can do at present for we are in different camps ...
> tho' I am still in the Liberal party, your principles are mine.[11]

But, in the end, 'bad and reactionary as many Liberals are',[12] that party
would be the means of salvation.

Radical reservations were not just the product of affectionate ties to a long-
standing political home. ILP attitudes could swing sharply from courtship to
contempt, as Radical responses failed to meet expectations. Moreover, some
propagandists although hoping for the same realignment as Hardie, might use
more dismissive language about the Liberal record. Blatchford, in his early
involvement with the ILP, saw the future in conventional terms. The ILP
should 'break this party in half, driving the Whigs into the Tory camp, and
bringing the Radicals into the ranks of Labour'.[13] But such an eventuality was
hardly aided by Blatchford's dismissal of Liberalism as the apotheosis of free-
market capitalism. Liberals stood for 'all that we hate', their ideal was 'unfet-
tered competition'. The moral was clear:

> Before we can do anything to ameliorate the lot of Labour in this country, we must
> pull down all the fabric of the Liberal temples and break all the idols of their faith.[14]

Such views were significant, perhaps, especially in Lancashire where the growth
of the ILP reflected the distinctive contribution of a popular, indeed populist,
Toryism.

 Nevertheless, by 1898—9, a series of events had driven ILP leaders and
several Radicals closer together. The defeat of the movement for One Socialist
Party, and the diminished interest of the *Clarion* in ILP affairs left the way

open for other strategic options. By 1897, the policy of contesting Liberal seats had proved expensive in finance, and sterile in precipitating any sort of Radical realignment. The decision to fight a maximum of twenty-five constituencies at the next election carried the hint of some sort of understanding with local Radicals. Although the Liberal by-election record had been encouraging, divisions within the party remained acute, and Campbell-Bannerman's emergence as leader hardly seemed a harbinger of purposeful, imaginative leadership. Intellectual discussions brought some Radicals and some socialists closer together. MacDonald participated in the mid nineties, with Radicals such as J. A. Hobson and Herbert Samuel, in the Rainbow Circle. Eventually in 1896 their discussions produced the *Progressive Review* — ostensibly neutral in politics but sympathetic to 'the more thoughtful and practical advocates of experimental collectivism'. Although the publication had a limited circulation, and survived less than twelve months, the position that it advocated held out the prospect of some sort of ILP—Radical rapprochement.[15]

This possibility was taken further in an important article, essentially by MacDonald but with Hardie's name attached, in *The Nineteenth Century* for January 1899.[16] This began with the standard ILP depiction of Liberal disarray, presenting this not simply as a matter of personalised factional squabbles, but as symptomatic of the fulfilment of Liberalism's historic task. Now the next stage must begin:

The ideas of the early Radicals though far from having been fully realised are yet complete enough to enable the questions peculiar to an enfranchised democracy ... to be raised, and these questions must inevitably refer to the use of political power for the attainment of certain economic ends which working-class communities are sure to attempt to reach. In other words, a democracy in power must raise the abstract question of Socialism, and the practical remedies which the Socialist proposes for the specific evils of his time.[17]

The socialist objective of the party was emphasised, but now the ILP was established sufficiently 'to identify ourselves with those questions of immediate reform upon which Radicals and Socialists are alike agreed'.[18] So an immediate programme was identified — reform of the Lords, the eight hour day, land reform, the public ownership of mining royalties, railways and canals.[19] But there remained the question of co-operation with non-socialist groups. The article attempted to locate the ILP firmly within indigenous traditions: 'The Independent Labour Party is in the true line of the progressive apostolic succession',[20] and as for the party's socialism 'the waste and inefficiency of commercialism, the economy and efficiency of co-operation can be proved without a single reference to Marx'.[21] Already the party had made local arrangements with trade union, co-operative and land-reform movements. The espousal of independence did not entail isolation.[22] The selection of twenty-five likely seats could be used as a guarded invitation to local arrangements:

It is but fair, if we are to ask for independent democratic support, that we should make no secret of our plans for the next general election. If there is any serious intention to let us alone in a certain number of constituencies, an early announcement of what these constituencies are, may lead to that harmony which we are constantly assured some of our opponents desire.[23]

Optimism about some kind of Progressive realignment remained high during 1899. Hardie saw Dilke, J. W. Logan, Atherley Jones and Lloyd George as the potential core of a Radical Party: 'Such a movement having proved itself would prepare the way for that combination of advanced forces that the future holds in store.'[24] Hardie hoped that socialists and socialist-Radicals would work together against the forces epitomised by Chamberlain and Rosebery — 'a common enemy'. The hope of such a rapprochement was increased dramatically by the outbreak of the South African War, yet at the same time the complexities of ILP—Radical relationships were heightened further.

The war produced some divisions in the socialist ranks: Blatchford and some leading Fabians supported the Government, but the ILP and the anti-war Radicals were brought closer together. This closeness was revealed in specific electoral co-operations, and in the abortive proposals for a White List in September 1900. Hardie saw such an arrangement as an instalment in the creation of a new Progressive synthesis. It could be the:

means of adding one more element to the slowly uniting forces of Democracy by bring-ing into line those Radicals who are with us in all but name, but who remain outside the Socialist movement under the mistaken impression that we are mere wreckers and nothing more.

Yet the anti-war Liberals were a heterogeneous collection; as Hardie acknowledged:

these men hold mixed opinions on many matters and include such unbending in-dividualists as John Morley and Leonard Courtney, together with some Socialists like Dr. Clarke (*sic*) and Mr. Lloyd George.[25]

The most striking case of an individualistic Liberal opposing the war was that of Hardie's old antagonist John Morley. In June 1900, in the aftermath of the Mafeking hysteria, Hardie optimistically called on Morley to lead the anti-war forces, fusing Radicals and working-class opposition into one bloc. He did so in terms that were even-handed in their presentation of Liberalism:

Liberal principles in trade and commerce are responsible for ... Imperialism ... Despite the nobility of the conception underlying Liberalism, its practical application was sordid to the last degree. Its glorification of buying and selling lowered the whole tone of our national life ...

Hardie's indictment of laissez-faire cited one of his favourite anti-liberal writers, Thomas Carlyle, but he balanced this attack by suggesting that Morley could legitimately, if improbably, transfer his loyalty to socialism: 'the principles of freedom expounded by Bentham and enlarged and systematised by Mill, lead logically to Socialism'.[26] The appeal failed to stir Morley, but the anti-war position of the ILP did attract support from many Radicals who found themselves out of sympathy with many inside their own party. Glasier, speaking as Ashton Under Lyne, found that several Liberals of the 'old school' were 'much touched by my references to Gladstone and Bright'.[27]

Empathy and sympathy were one thing; firm political co-operation was quite another. The 1900 election saw a number of cases where Liberals stood aside, often out of weakness, and Radicals gave support to ILP candidates. Later, in October 1901, Bob Smillie fought North-East Lanarkshire, and secured support from some Radical MPs against a Liberal Imperialist. One anti-war Radical justified his action in impeccably Liberal terms: 'although Mr. Cecil Harmsworth claims to be the Liberal candidate, in my view, Mr. Smillie occupies that position'.[28]

Although the intensity of the war issue brought critics close together, there were limitations. On the ILP side, there were those who insisted that socialism remain the dominant criterion for action and that this should extend to criticism of the war. Sam Hobson reacted to negotiations for a 'Peace Candidate' at York by sounding a warning:

it is essential that the Socialist position should be made clear. We are not 'Liberal' in our foreign politics — very much the reverse ... we should do well to go nap on the general proposition that the war is an act of unmitigated blackguardism ... On that we all agree, and it would not commit us to any dangerous concessions as to 'rights of property', 'peace and plenty', 'trade' and all the other shibboleths of Manchesterism.[29]

There was always a risk that under pressures of the war issue, the distinctive case of the ILP would be lost.

The dominance of the war controversy led to the ILP acquiring a further ally, both inside the Commons, and also in some by-elections. The Irish Nationalist Party had eventually, in 1900, reunited behind John Redmond, after almost a decade of squabbling following the fall of Parnell. Nationalist members were aggressively pro-Boer, some cheering the news of British military defeat in the Commons.[30] They soon evoked sympathy from Hardie when he took his seat as member for Merthyr, their strong opposition contrasted with the nerveless showing of many Liberals. 'The Irishmen are an inspiration and dominate the entire assembly.'[31] He coached fifteen Nationalist MPs to make contributions to the debates on the Railway Bill of 1901,[32] and hoped for an alliance of Labour, Irish and Radical members over the Civil List.[33]

The alliance could also be found at local level at that year's North-East Lanark contest. The United Irish League backed Smillie, although not without some local dissension.[34] Despite the disappointing result, Hardie visualised in North-East Lanark the prefiguration of 'a union of the fighting elements in politics'.[35] At that moment some saw the Irish as a more reliable component of a Progressive alliance than disenchanted Radicals. They were, after all, 'a democratic party acting for the poor'.[36] This emphasis is important. The widely-discussed possibility of such a broad Radical alliance was an option which has been lost in the complex acerbities of Anglo-Irish relations. Yet it was the Nationalists, rather than Labour, who first eroded in the 1880s, the socially select style of the Commons.

But there was a negative side to this option. Relationships between ILP and Irish had been bad in the nineties as the Nationalist machine regularly backed moderate Liberals against ILP candidates.[37] Home Rule was the sole criterion for allegiance; ILP candidates were presented as analogous to Parnellite splitters. There was a powerful legacy of mistrust which current preoccupations might find it difficult to counterbalance. The earlier estrangement had also revealed how far popular prejudices about the Irish lurked behind the ILPer's progressive visages. The prejudices might be based on a strict Protestant up-bringing, or on allegations of the deflationary impact of Irish immigrants on wage levels; either way, the possibility of mistrust and misunderstanding was present. On many issues, such as temperance and denominational education, cultural and religious differences led to divergences between Nationalists and ILP positions. Finally the possibility of alliance raised the question of how far such co-operation, as in the Radical case, undermined the ILP's socialist claims. Certainly, the party's flirtations with the Nationalists provoked criticism from the old Edinburgh ILPer James Connolly. He repeatedly dismissed Nationalist MPs as bourgeois politicians;

neither the Parnellites nor the McCarthyites were friendly to the Labour Movement. Both of them are essentially middle-class parties, interested in Ireland from a middle-class point of view.

Any radical proposals could be dismissed as manipulative;

Their advanced attitude upon the land question is simply an accident arising out of the exigencies of the political situation and would be dropped tomorrow if they did not realise the necessity of linking the Home Rule agitation to some cause more nearly allied to their daily wants.[38]

Whatever the problems, ILP leaders keenly discussed the possibility of some sort of Radical realignment, in which the party would supplement its involvement in the LRC with appropriate connections elsewhere.[39]

Yet such expectations were never fulfilled. They depended on the Liberal Party splitting into imperialist and anti-imperialist wings, with the former joining the Liberal Unionists and the latter available for a Progressive alliance. Hardie continued to envisage this scenario early in 1903. He considered a likely development to be the formation of a Rosebery—Chamberlain Coalition,[40] and employed this expectation as a means of inveigling Radicals away from official Liberals. Once again he selected a Radical personality as the subject of a public appeal. This time, it was Lloyd George:

By remaining aloof, you would in time become the recognised leader of that force in politics which desires genuine reform, and which is not bound by doctrinaire theories or traditions. Radical candidates would be asked to pledge themselves to support Lloyd George and thus, a distinct line of cleavage would be set up between Whiggism and Radicalism.

Realignment would take place in the Commons where there would be:

eighty-five Irish members, fifty Labour members, and say twenty-five Independent Radicals ... Faced by such a fighting combination, Whig and Tory would be driven to combine, and People versus Privilege would become the battle-cry.[41]

It was a pipe-dream. With the end of the war, a flood of events conspired to minimise the likelihood of Liberal splits. Education and tariffs were the two controversies best suited to heal Liberal differences — and both brought the ILP essentially into agreement with all Liberals, not just the Radicals. Rosebery's eclipse made the favourite scenario of Hardie a non-starter. As Liberal by-election successes accumulated, this prospect was replaced by the question of how many Liberal Imperialists would consent to join the next Liberal Government, probably under the premiership of the arch-conciliator Campbell-Bannerman. The changing political agenda brought many Radicals back to their old allegiance. When the second by-election was held in North East Lanark in the summer of 1904, a Radical Liberal candidate not only had a united party behind him, he also secured Irish support. Labour, lacking Radical appeal, had to rely on trade union and socialist sentiments.[42]

Even in Liberalism's fissiparous years, Hardie and his colleagues over-estimated the readiness of such Radicals as Lloyd George to quit Liberalism. The latter's Radical credentials were not always quite what they seemed; his opposition to the South African War did not make him an anti-Imperialist; his diatribes against the Education Act reflected the theatre of Welsh nonconformist politics rather than any unbreakable attachment to principle. His knowledge of the world of industrial labour was inevitably limited by his rural Radical background; he felt no attraction to socialism. There was much more hope of influence within a majority Liberal administration than in any quixotic attempt at Progressive realignment.[43]

There were also restraining forces in the ILP camp. Most obviously, enthusiasts for One Socialist Party had reservations about such aspirations — but there were also difficulties for the party's leaders. Self-taught men such as Hardie, were easily irritated by what they saw as the bland superior patronising stance of many Radicals. They could respond by reciting cases of Radical maltreatment of the ILP or with practical immobilism. Hardie remonstrated with H. W. Massingham that at least the ILP element had a proposal for uniting 'the divided forces of democracy'.[44] Until such a suggestion was reciprocated, independence must be the first requirement. The necessity for this seemed to be underlined by arguments within the LRC. Hardie was suspicious of attempts by Dilke to bring Radical and Labour members together, and his suspicions were increased by the increasing evidence of Bell's Liberalism. They were compounded by attempts by Radicals to ally with Lib-Lab MPs in a fashion which risked the marginalisation of the LRC.[45] The rift between Lib-Lab and in-dependent trade unionists remained critical, belying hopes of a broad Radical grouping. Once again attachment to instruments, the strength of organisational loyalties was maintaining divisions where significant harmony existed on immediate issues.

This distinction underlaid the MacDonald—Gladstone agreement. Organisational separation was accepted; agreement on a wide range of policy issues was recognised. such a settlement could be regarded as a relatively stable solution to the complex Labour/Liberal gyrations of the previous decade. But the pact involved from the ILP view point a jettisoning of the frequently-held expectation that the Liberal Party was on the point of disintegration. Now the stability of the Liberal Party was accepted, at least for the immediate future.

This stability was to be a fundamental factor in subsequent ILP debates about policy and strategy. The complicated relationship between Liberals and ILPers had been resolved in a way that gave the latter a limited foothold in parliament. But it was a foothold rendered precarious by its dependence on Liberal goodwill. Harmony and discord characterised every aspect of the relationship. The ILP proclaimed an anti-capitalist objective, but grew out of and continued to advocate a range of Radical claims that could cohabit with, and linked intimately with, liberal capitalism. The ultimate aim might be a qualitative economic and social change, but the party was very much of the world that it claimed to reject. It attracted adherents who stigmatised some Liberals as capitalists, but who felt a community of sentiment with the claims of many Radicals. Liberal leaders might be pilloried but, in part, this was because they repeatedly denied the aspirations of decent supporters. Much of Hardie's political and cultural style could be located readily within a Radical pedigree — the same applied to other ILP luminaries — but there could also be friction with the glossy, suave Radicals of the Commons and the Progressive press. Equally, ILP trade unionists could agree with their Lib-Lab adversaries on a wide range of topics, but this had to be balanced by a heavy legacy of suspicion, institutionalised in union factionalism. ILP spokesmen could still look forward with some optimism to the advent of a Liberal government, but such expectations were balanced by memories of past diasppointments.

There was an important sense in which many ILP perceptions of Liberalism had been formed in the context of the Gladstonian Party. These typically in-volved the division of the Liberal Party into a Whig Right and a Radical Left, with the implication that the latter tendency could coalesce eventually with the ILP. But such a view of Liberal politics was of diminishing relevance. The Liberal Right contained very few Whigs in the traditional sense of liberally inclined aristocrats, and also a diminishing number of major capitalists — laissez-faire or otherwise; and the Radicalism which ILPers often supported was somewhat passé. It acquired its credentials on such issues as temperance, land reform, the democratisation of the political system and anti-militarism, but such views were often accompanied by economic individualism and a very limited espousal of state intervention. As interest in social reform developed amongst younger Liberals, the consequences could not be accommodated easily within the traditional perception. Relationships between social reformers and individual ILP members could be close. MacDonald's involvement in the Rainbow Circle has already been noted. The ILP press gave considerable coverage to J. A. Hobson's views on the South African War, whilst the same issue brought L. T. Hobhouse into contact with ILP circles in Manchester.[46] Such developments were noted; they could be accommodated readily into an evolutionary socialist perspective, but they led to little modification of the ILP view of Liberal prospects. Social Radicals did not fit neatly into the Whig—Radical dichotomy.[47] A concern for 'National Efficiency' could blend support of imperialism with advocacy of welfare schemes; the appeal of Lloyd George lay in his apparent support of traditional Radical causes, not in his, as yet, undisclosed taste for state intervention. The ideological bearings which had helped to locate the ILP vis-à-vis Liberalism were shifting. Appearances might remain the same, but beneath these the outline of a reformed, welfare capitalism was beginning to emerge as a possible Liberal cause. The implications of this for the British labour movement, and in particular for socialists would be profound.

The exclusion of Tory socialism

There is more of the true spirit of comradeship in the tap room than in the modern temple. On the one hand you have social chat, freedom from work-a-day cares and restraints, equal footing and fraternal feeling; on the other you have stiff formality, ostentatious respectability, class distinctions carefully maintained, and fraternity accepted in name and repudiated in essence, which latest item is cant and hypocrisy.

I like the cakes and ale. I want more to like them ... The fanatics who would absolutely veto our cakes and ale would mostly hold up their hands in pious horror at a universal Eight Hours Bill.
Harry Lowenson: *In England Now — Vagrom Essays by a Vagrom Man*, pp. 90—91.

The complex tangle of Radical and socialist sentiments that came together in the ILP could appear to emerge readily from decades of dealings between working leaders and official Liberals. It seems to fit readily into broad visions of a working class under a successful and dominant capitalism, accommodating to the existing order, prior to the availability of a socialist perspective. The outlook of the ILP seems to be one important episode in the unfolding of the 'Peculiarities of the English'. But there were other traditions on which an emerging ILP could draw. It is an anachronistic simplification of late nineteenth-century political divisions to view them in terms of Radical and Liberal progressives opposed to Tory reactionaries. Perhaps Toryism embraced popular currents that could have furnished connections to a different brand of socialism. The emergence and consolidation of the ILP as a leading vehicle for socialism marks amongst other things the victory of the Radical variant and the virtual demise of any attempt at 'Tory socialism'.

One basis for the incusion of Tory elements into Labour politics lay in the inherently protectionist nature of trade union activities. Attempts to advance living standards and to improve working conditions, expanding into pressure for legal limitations on the working day, could provoke inquiry into whether this was a logical resting place. Why not extend the safeguards to embrace protection against cheap foreign imports and labour? Indeed, it could be argued that trade union success in improving standards would necessitate protection of domestic industries. Such claims acquired a more immediate relevance for some groups in the eighties; as foreign competition became apparent in sections of the engineering trade and other industries 'Fair Trade' became a slogan for some working-class spokesmen as well as for Tory backbenchers.[48]

If some putative connections between Toryism and socialism were economic and sectional, others could develop out of intellectual criticisms of Victorian capitalism. The tracing of what is often seen as a predominantly Romantic critique of capitalism involved both reactionary and socialist potentials. Such figures as Cobbett, Carlyle and Ruskin were often profoundly ambiguous in their social criticism and their political remedies.[49] The tradition could inspire Disraelian Toryism, with its declension of the literary insights of the forties to the largely manipulative rhetoric of the seventies. It could also help to produce the socialist insights of William Morris.

Aspects of this tradition were absorbed by many ILP figures. They cited their encounters with the writings of its leading proponents as featuring amongst their formative influences.[50] Yet, often, key elements were diluted or lost. Emphases on the underlying organic unity of society, or on 'community' as a yardstick for change, often served within the ILP as alternatives to a militant emphasis on class cleavages. Denunciations of the narrow, materialistic individualism of laissez-faire capitalism continued, but often concentrated on laissez-faire rather than on capitalism as such. ILP propagandists demonstrated awareness of the damaging impact of industrialisation on human relationships, but frequently saw individual conversion as a necessary condition for social improvement.

This tradition had limitations and ambiguities, but its unwillingness to take the narrowly defined rational economic individual as the basic unit for social analysis and ethical judgements at least gave socialists a potential vantage-point from which they could begin to grasp the totality of social relationships. In particular, it might be thought that this style of argument could link closely with, and reflect the felt closeness of, homogeneous working-class communities. But the insights culled from this tradition functioned largely for rhetorical purposes only. They were rarely put to work as tools of critical analysis, and were generally subordinate to other elements in the ILP perspective that were derived from Radical Liberalism.

At a less elevated level, there were traditions associated with popular Toryism that socialists might find attractive, because of their earthy quality, embodied in a matey, if somewhat spurious egalitarianism. The erstwhile Radicals introduced into the ILP a substantial injection of moral earnestness, demonstrated in a general passion for self-improvement, and enthusiasm for puritan causes. Such preoccupations might be shared by a sizeable proportion of working-class activists, but had only a limited impact on the class as a whole. Here appeals based on the popular culture and prejudices of 'pub society' and the sportsman could perhaps make more inroads. Protectionism, Romanticism, Hedonism — each could generate socialist or Labour appeals. Each was available to the ILP but secured little support. In particular, these emphases were associated with two significant individuals — H. H. Champion and Robert Blatchford. The failures of 'Tory socialism' cannot be detached from the failures of their principal exponents.

Champion's distinctively Tory Labour style emerges clearly from his Aberdeen activities and a glimpse of the possibilities for Tory socialism is afforded by the relative strength of Protectionist sentiments in Champion's bailiwick.[51] His views on the Free Trade issue had been expressed widely for some years before 1892. He began from a robustly practical concern to develop a programme that could propel the labour question to the forefront of political argument in the way that the Parnellite agitation had made Ireland the defining factor in determining many political allegiances. His most fundamental demand was for the legislative eight-hour day — but this immediately raised the question of protection. Champion did not shrink from what he regarded as the logical consequence:

I do not deny that it may prove to be necessary, failing international agreements as to a general reduction of hours, to contemplate the protection of our own workmen from the competition of countries where a lower standard of comfort prevails. The necessity would have to be clearly proved, but if that were done, no one who puts the interests of labour first, would object to such a step.[52]

This implication of an immediate proposal was supported by a variety of arguments. One saw it as the logical extension of trade unionism 'for what is trade unionism, but the most direct form of Protection?'.[53] Sometimes the trade-unionist argument was extended to incorporate a hint of xenophobia:

The terms applied by trade-unionists to those workmen who play into the hands of their enemies by working for less than the trade-union rate of wages, or by taking the place of unionists on strike against a reduction, show that they understand that their worst enemies are their fellows who underbid them. Similarly they entertain bitter feelings against foreigners who undersell them in the labour market.[54]

The British workman will vote for the most rigid exclusion of the foreign 'blackleg' or unfair competitor, as surely as his Australian brother votes for the exclusion of Chinese or Kanaka labour.[55]

Workers' attempts to rig the labour market in their favour could be seen as first attempts to erode competition. The growth of workers' political influence would mean an end to Free Trade, since this system meant that goods were

produced where wages were lowest. This assault on Liberalism's most sacred
icon could by itself brand Champion as a Tory sympathiser, but there were
further elements in his policies which distanced him at least from traditional
Radicalism.

His views on the increasingly central question of Imperialism placed him
in a different camp from many Radicals. The Empire contained 'the makings
of an irresistible force on the side of true freedom and progress'. Such a portrait
made a closer-knit Empire seem desirable, a step that would require fiscal
reform:

that Empire contains within its boundaries the variations of soil and climate which would
enable it to supply all its needs within its own borders. The colonies must find in their
alliance with us some material benefit, and that can only come from a revision of our
trade policy.[56]

A hope for self-sufficiency was a common one amongst socialists in the
nineties. Champion's variation was more plausible, foreshadowing the
'Socialism in One Country' prescriptions of Mosley.

Champion's newspaper, the *Labour Elector*, also attacked the Radical
concern with Irish Home Rule. In March 1889, immediately following the
revelation of the Pigott forgeries, Champion grotesquely developed an attack
on Nationalist MPs by emphasising the Irishness of Parnell's traducer:

The character of Mr. Richard Pigott is overflowing with all the characteristics of his
countrymen ... we are more than justified in treating them and their 'grievances' with
all possible contempt ... The Irish people have been so long kicked and cuffed, and
treated as an inferior race by England, that it has developed all the vices of an inferior
race and become one in point of fact.[57]

English pride had to be safeguarded — 'We have their hatred and it does not
hurt us, but their friendship would under present circumstances be a humiliation too great to be borne ... England can't eat dirt and live as England.' When
the Second Home Rule Bill was introduced, the *Labour Elector* took what was
in socialist terms an idiosyncratic line. Home Rule was supported — but
without illusions:

Let us give the Irish justice, for even our enemies are entitled to that, but don't let us
bestow gifts upon them under the delusion or pretence that they are our friends, for
they are nothing of the kind. They are bitter and unappeasable enemies.

But the dictates of justice extended to Ulster, whose 'industry' entitled it 'to
a respectful hearing':

No one ... will venture to say that it would be just to hand over the people of Ulster,
Protestants in religion as they are, and warmly attached to the British connection, to
the tender mercies of the anti-British Roman Catholics of the South and West.[58]

Instead, there should be partition with Ulster either remaining part of the
United Kingdom, or having a Home Rule settlement alone. This, like all
Champion's proposals was sternly unsentimental. On the one side, the

innuendo about the likely fate of Protestants under Home Rule could be labelled plausibly as one more example of a British exacerbation of Irish difficulties. But it could be argued also that this was a difficulty about which most Radicals and ILPers chose to remain oblivious and that they often shared surreptitiously in Champion's lack of enthusiasm about the substantive question.

The overall Championite position was one that reflected the national prejudices of much of the working class. At the level of proposals, his 'Tory socialism' represented a distinct alternative in the early nineties. Yet his attempts to control the ILP failed utterly. Was this because his ideas were less popular than a cursory view might suggest, or because of personal and tactical idiosyncracies?

His views on the instruments to be used for promoting his ideas are difficult to present with precision. He certainly did not believe that the Conservatives or the Liberal Unionists offered a generally effective instrument for promoting a labour programme. Indeed, in several specific contests he urged support for Liberal candidates because of their views on labour questions.[59] But partly because of his own distaste for Liberal principles, and partly because of the long history of Labour failures, he had a deep-rooted fear of any Labour initiative being reabsorbed by the Gladstonians. One of his last interventions in British politics before leaving for Australia was to issue a warning against the ILP losing its independence — 'the Liberal Party has a strong stomach and will swallow anything'.[60] His opposition to Gladstonianism perhaps helped him to take a positive view of the labour programme offered by Joseph Chamberlain in the autumn of 1892:

I agree with Mr. Chamberlain that the Gladstonians have neither the power, capacity nor will to carry anything like so large a number of changes as he has indicated. I am further willing to admit it conceivable that the Unionist Party might endorse and carry such a programme. If they can give evidence that they will do so ... the working classes would be fools indeed not to give them ... power.[61]

Such a view was extremely optimistic. The flight of wealth and property to the Unionist ranks was helping to associate that side of political argument increasingly with economic individualism. But it was not an unintelligible choice. The shift of some Radicals into Unionist ranks in 1886 had produced some divergences of view on social questions which could perhaps be exploited. In contrast, Gladstonian Liberals seemed unlikely to make much headway on social questions. Their leader was generally unsympathetic, and Ireland loomed as a first priority.

Such views did arouse the prejudices both of Lib-Labs and of many Labour enthusiasts who had been weaned on Radicalism. Most critically, the tensions produced by pursuing Champion's strategy emerged in the two electoral confrontations with John Morley at Newcastle in 1892. The attempts of the Championite Newcastle ILP to defeat Morley by voting Unionist led to widespread ructions, with Lib-Labs springing to Morley's defence and Shaw writing of 'a formidable Unionist intrigue with Champion at the wires'.[62] Yet, Morley was not opposed just by Champion's close associates. Hardie, despite his recent dependence on Liberal votes in West Ham, backed the anti-Morley tactic.[63] Indeed, the ploy was not unique. The previous month, no less a trade union personage than Henry Broadhurst had lost his seat in West Nottingham after a campaign in which the eight hours question figured strongly.

It was not so much the specific strategic choices as the style of many of Champion's operations that provoked suspicion. It was one thing to punish a Liberal candidate because he seemed inadequate on a specific crucial issue; it was quite another to do so in a fashion that suggested no weight should be given to hallowed Liberal causes. Champion's homilies on the dangers of absorption by the Gladstonians were answered by claims that he was manipulating Labour politics in the Unionist interest. Particular weight was given to such charges and innuendoes by his close association — not least through the *Labour Elector* — with Maltman Barry, once of the First International but by 1892 the Tory candidate for Banff,[64] This connection provided scope for a mounting campaign of claims that Champion's political funds were channelled from the Conservative machine.[65] Such suggestions touched a sensitive nerve for many Labour partisans. The Social Democratic election fiasco of 1885 had provided a basis for allegations that Labour candidates were often dupes, financed by 'Tory Gold' to divide the Radical vote. Now fresh grist was provided for the mill. The accusations provoked a particularly angry response from those Radicals who had joined the ILP. The basis for opposition to Champion went beyond his 'Tory socialism' extending to his essentially manipulative view of the political process. The creation of the ILP was a protest against the activities of wire-pullers; it could not afford to be associated with one.

Champion proved during 1893 that he could not be accommodated within the party's structure. He subtitled the *Labour Elector* 'The Organ of the Independent Labour Party'; he intervened in the Grimsby by-election against Broadhurst, claiming that he was acting for the ILP.[66] There was no way in which the Bradford decisions about democratic control of the party could be reconciled with his private initiatives. Such activities were a facet of the seigneurial attitude towards Labour activists noted by one of his Aberdeen supporters.[67] Throughout 1893, he chided his contemporaries for their shortcomings. Hardie, after attacking the *Labour Elector* was warned as to his future conduct and advised to stick to practical politics, leaving policy to more elevated minds.[68] Fred Hammill, the candidate of the Newcastle ILP, was advised to remember his limitations:

he cannot be blinded by his own egotism as to suppose that if the Newcastle men had any real hope of winning the seat outright that he would be their man.[22]

And the economics of Blatchford's 'Merrie England' were dismissed as 'sentenious nonsense'.[70] It was not a matter of the validity of individual judgements, but rather that such lordly depreciation did not fit the homely, democratic ethos of the ILP.

Champion's failure resulted both from his principles and his style. His proposals, particularly on the fiscal question, stirred the Radical prejudices of many gravitating towards Independent Labour. Unsentimental presentations of the labour interest could not compensate for the dismissive attitude towards Radical icons. Champion might admire the traditions of British politics, and write of the need for and possibility of peaceful transition,[71] but he showed himself unconcerned or unaware of the role of sentiment in influencing political allegiances. Similarly, his chess-board view of politics with blocs of support, shifting in response to the demands of self-appointed leaders seemed oblivious to a crucial strand in the emergence of the ILP. The creation of the party was a revolt against those who saw the labour interest as something to be manipulated and cajoled. Instead supporters of labour's claims would now determine their own position and involved in that choice, there was a desire that final authority would rest with the membership. As the emergence of the Big Four would show, the way to dominance of the ILP lay not in the overt flouting of such sentiments, but in a formal courtship of them.

In principle, it is possible to distinguish Champion's leadership from his specific proposals. There would be nothing incongruous in holding such 'Tory socialist' views yet taking a far more positive view of rank and file activities. But his manipulative style was very much in accordance with that of contemporary Tory democracy. The vision of Randolph Churchill was of a Toryism making radical bids for working-class support, but such bids would be made by members of the traditional governing elite. The masses would be recipients, not agents, of their own improvement. Radical Liberal views on participation, however threadbare their practice, at least offered a hope of self-determination.

One major problem faced by Champion was that his appeals were directed principally to Labour partisans who were, or who were likely to become, politically active. And these tended to be heavily committed to Radical sentiments. It was the much less active majority often heavily involved in community institutions around the workplace and the 'pub' who were perhaps more available for a more populist, less self-consciously high-minded socialist appeal. But Champion's unsentimental style was of little value here. A much more apposite vehicle was provided by Robert Blatchford's *Clarion*.[72]

Some contrasts with Champion were sharp. Blatchford moved from Radicalism to socialism, and carried a range of values with him, most notably a sharp distrust of leaders and wire-pullers. In contrast to Champion the would-be Labour Parnell, there stood Blatchford, the Radical democrat. He opposed the institutionalisation of formal offices within the ILP, argued that decisions must emerge through rank and file debate, and regularly advocated the referendum as an aid to such involvement.[73] Socialism could be achieved only through educational propaganda, and formal organisation tended to corrode the necessary catholicity and spontaneity of the process.

It was necessary that the rank and file should be able to exert a tight control over their public representatives. Blatchford, therefore, supported the Halifax activists late in 1894, when they reacted against what they saw as the lack of independence shown by their ILP councillors, Beever, Tattersall and John Lister.[74] This robust defence of local control brought a bitter public response from Hardie: 'If branches are to exist only as centres of discord and sordid squabbling, they are hindrances and not helps to the movement.'[75] And a private threat: 'Better far sink the whole business than have it live in this atmosphere of bigotry, suspicion, distrust, and I fear, malice.'[76] Such emphases tended to place Blatchford on the left of socialist argument, beyond the ILP Establishment. Similar characterisations could be made of his continuing support for socialist unity and also his attacks on the Liberal Party. Here no continuities with Radicalism were claimed, but rather an ideological chasm:

It is not a question of gradually driving the Liberal Party forward. The Liberal Party are the champions of all that we hate. They are the avowed upholders of competition and the avowed enemies of Socialism.[77]

This hostility to Liberalism was apparent also in Blatchford's advocacy of the Manchester Fourth Clause. And yet it is here that the ambiguities arise. As the discussion of the Lancastrian ILP in Chapter 9 made clear, the Fourth Clause could be seen not just as a declaration of socialist purity, but also as an appropriate strategy for a party faced by a working class in which Toryism had considerable appeal. In a world where popular Toryism had established strong claims to qualities of manliness, straight-talking and Englishness, attacks on Liberalism could be read also as dismissals of the self-righteous claims of temperance fanatics, and hypocritical employers.

This robust style typified the *Clarion* particularly in its early years. Vigorous support for socialism and denunciations of capitalism rubbed shoulders with columns on football, cricket and the theatre. The contrast with the somewhat narrow earnestness of the *Labour Leader* was obvious. The latter would be read only by committed partisans; Blatchford's style at least offered the hope of penetrating the ranks of the hitherto uninvolved. The evocation of a 'cakes and ale' culture of socialist abundance drew heavily on elements of the Romantic tradition and of popular working-class culture. The utopian best-seller, *Merrie England*, yearned for the recovery of a pre-industrial idyll, and *Clarion* journalism drew steadily on stereotypes of English fair-dealing and sportsmanship. Violent roads to socialism were for foreigners, and even if the need arose in England, socialists would be fastidious about tactics: 'The weapon selected by an English Revolutionary army would not be dynamite. Were they to fight, the English would come out into the open and fight like Englishmen.[78] Blatchford also claimed that he was a reluctant recruit to politics. He would prefer to be a cricketer with the fame of Grace, or the writer of works such as *The Dream of John Ball* or *Tess of the D'Urbervilles*, rather than a Gladstone or a Marx. His self-portrait was of 'a plain easy-going rather idle person'.[79] Periodically he withdrew in disillusion:

I know little and care little about politics ... I love men and women and books. I am happy here in my den with the great authors all about me. And the wrangle, vulgarity, littleness, and blind jealousies of politics sadden and disgust me.[80]

He was certainly no full-time politician; deprecatory about his worth as a speaker, he preferred convivial conversation to politicking. Glasier noted how when invited to a grand ILP bazaar in Glasgow in 1896 he put in only inter-mittent appearances, spending most of his time in neighbouring bars.[81]

Stylistically, he was poles apart from the puritanical dedicated Hardie for whom politics was almost a complete life. Blatchford interpreted Hardie's zeal as a narrow dedication to furtive political fixing which denied the essence of socialism: 'I have tried very hard to believe in that man but I cannot stand him.[82] ... (he is) stealthy, weakly malicious and impudently untruthful.[83] Blatchford liked to see socialism and its advocacy as above all an enjoyable affair, and reacted against the tendency of ILP leaders to present an austere image, backed by manipulative proclivities. In 1931, when he had long retired from political activity, he drew a simplistic dichotomy which contained a significant truth:

The Labour Leader people were Puritans; narrowly bigotted, puffed up with sour cant. We ... disliked them because we were ... Cavaliers. They were nonconformist, self-righteous ascetics, out for the class war and the dictation by the proletariat. We loved the humour and colour of the old English tradition.[84]

Such emphases clearly distinguished Blatchford from many of the earnest puritans who were prominent in the ILP. Such hedonistic appeals clearly deviated from the high-minded style of much Radical argument, but they were not uniquely Tory. Many Liberal voters participated in the activities portrayed by Blatchford and shunned by their Radical contemporaries. Yet these em-phases went along with a nationalism that became increasingly central to Blatchford's position, and served eventually to distinguish him from most of his socialist allies.

Unlike most British socialists in the nineties, Blatchford had had experience of military life. He often portrayed his army experiences in positive terms, and at times he came to employ these memories in defence of nationalist policies. Arguably, his military background left its mark on his view of the socialist society, which was often presented in terms similar to the comradeship of the mess room. This was depicted in self-consciously masculine terms — Blatchford's style readily absorbed conventional stereotypes about the role of women.[85]

For much of the nineties, these preferences revealed themselves in robust imagery, and in arguments for national self-sufficiency. This was the burden of much of his classic *Merrie England*, and later of his revealingly named *Britain For The British*. The South African War shifted Blatchford to a position of unashamed nationalism. Previously he had proclaimed himself a patriot, but not a jingoist. He professed no illusions about the growth of Empire. It had 'been built up of shame and sin. It is founded on murder, on pillage, on perjury, rape and rapine'.[86] Even in 1899 as the likelihood of war increased, he saw the growth of jingoism as an anti-socialist development:

Here float the banners of a swaggering insular Patriotism, of a mean and unmerciful Individualism, of a stealthy insidious Militarism, of an insolent vulgar Mummerism; here stand the serried forces of Whig and Tory, of recreant Liberal and misguided Radical, backed by all the scum and riff-raff.[87]

But when war was declared his position changed. He still distanced himself from the jingoists. He opposed the breakup of anti-war meetings and attacked the pro-war press for raising 'clouds of falsehood, innuendo and ... bluster'. But he also condemned the behaviour of the war's opponents. They had obscured the issues 'in a haze of humanitarian cant'. They painted the Boers as 'saints' and the British as 'devils'.[88]

Blatchford's own diagnosis descended into unconditional support for the government whilst hostilities lasted. He admitted the validity of some of the anti-war claims, but passed them over as failing to get to the root of the issue:

Mr. Chamberlain's conduct of the negotiations may be open to criticism, there has doubtless been some unholy financial intrigue on the Rand and many of the British 'Jingo' papers have uttered a good deal of pernicious folly but ... the real cause of the present war is the ignorance and the bumptiousness of the Boers.[89]

'Generous forbearance' had been tried after 1881. It had failed. War could only have been avoided by a pre-emptive show of strength, the sending of an army to South Africa whilst negotiations were still in progress.

The reasons provided by Blatchford for his own position were basically two — his English nationalism and his military past:

I love England more than any other country ... I am an old soldier and I love Tommy Atkins ... You cannot teach me to cheer my country's enemies nor to pray for the defeat of the British soldiers.[90]

So he ordered his daughter to play 'Rule Britannia' every night, whilst the war lasted, and drank 'the health of the Queen and the success of the British army'.[91]

These views produced other major divergences from the trajectory of the ILP. Whilst Hardie was moving towards a closer relationship with Irish Nationalists, Blatchford was attacking those Irishmen who fought for the Boers — 'they are enemies of England, and England's enemies are my enemies'.[92] He argued that Hardie was guilty of 'Socialist cant' on the war and decried a socialist portrayal of British officers as gilded fops:

these gilded fops are the finest gentlemen I have ever known ... There are some Socialist leaders who are not worthy to carry a British officer's portmanteau.[93]

Early military reverses led him to emphasise the need for the defence of Britain, opposing conscription but suggesting the desirability of military training. His views now included a more positive characterisation of Empire.[94] After the end of the South African War, his thoughts moved towards the risk of invasion 'Can England be invaded?' he asked, 'the Germans think so and say so, and are openly and steadily preparing to make the attempt'.[95] His response was clear, 'a voluntary citizen army would be of immense advantage to the workers'.[96] Such sentiments, allied to his deeply-rooted distaste for a competitive industrial system, produced a distinctive response to Chamberlain's protectionist crusade. It was a 'bold counterblast to Balfour's academic Cobdenism'. He shared in the desire for a closer imperial system, but with one crucial provision:

Were Socialism established as the governing principle of this vast realm — if we might regard the British Empire as really belonging to the British people — we should have no hesitation in agreeing with Mr. Chamberlain that no sacrifice could be too great that gave promise of averting that empire's disintegration'.[97]

But as matters stood, it was likely that the workers would meet most of the cost.

The emergence of Blatchford as a passionate supporter of the South African war put him well outside the mainstream of ILP sentiment and probably hampered his later attempts to develop opposition to the Labour Alliance. His views are significant since they concern the most crucial issue for all socialists between 1890 and 1914 — that of attitudes towards nationalism, imperialism and war. 1914 would reveal many Blatchfords in all social democratic and labour parties. Yet even then ILP leaders and activists were to be relatively free from chauvinistic excuses. Even self-consciously moderate figures such as MacDonald and Glasier were able to rehabilitate their standing with the left because of their position on this question. Both in 1899 and in 1914, ILP opposition to the war owed much more to Radical Liberal traditions than to any socialist analysis. The internationalist connotations of this tradition, as well as its democratic ones, gave the party an identity and distinguished it from Tory socialist tendencies.

Yet the ILP and its members lived within a society in which stereotypes of national differences and superiority were prevalent. The extent to which the party succeeded in developing an alternative value-system based on its Radical Liberal inheritance and its socialist commitment can be gauged from noting ILP attitudes to topics where anti-semitic emotions were readily aroused. The immigration question concerned many trade unionists in the 1890s, especially in trades such as tailoring and boot manufacturing where the pressures of transition to mechanised factory production were already being felt. Restrictionists argued that immigration depressed wages and undermined trade union effectiveness. Such diagnoses led to the TUC passing restrictionist resolutions, most notably in 1895, and Unionist politicians, particularly Chamberlain, made restriction part of their labour programme.[98] Trade union support for restriction included at least one organisation — the Boot and Shoe Operatives — in which socialist influence was significant.[99] Tillett's dislike of foreigners, already revealed at the Bradford Conference, came out once again with his claims that some of the London dockers' problems were attributable to immigration.[100] Leonard Hall, an ILP candidate, active in the Manchester and Salford ILP and in Lancashire 'New Unionism', supported restriction in the *Clarion*. He used Blatchford-style 'bluff commonsense' to develop his case on the reasons for bad industrial conditions: 'If you ask John Smith the tailor why, he will answer, and with undoubted force, "the Jew", the economic basis of Socialism notwithstanding.' He also employed loaded hyperbole in a manner foreshadowing later advocates of restriction: 'there is scarcely a town of any dimensions in the country in which the foreign element has not menaced and injured the position of local workmen.'[101]

Blatchford himself had expressed anxiety earlier in 1892, writing articles under the title 'The Invasion of England', and querying the 'racial results likely to follow on the infusion of so much alien blood into the British stock'.[102] As the Unionist Government moved towards some form of restriction after 1900, the *Clarion* engaged in periodic anti-alien forays, and in 1903 a resolution for legal restriction was debated at the ILP conference. An affirmation of faith in socialist internationalism was sufficient to generate a unanimous rejection.[103]

It is this note of opposition which is the more striking. It was symbolised by Hardie's parliamentary response to the 1905 Aliens Bill, when he condemned attempts to prevent the entry of refugees often from Czarist Russia, and to offer racial answers to the poverty of British workers.[104] Hardie was not alone. James Macdonald, a tailor heavily involved in the London Trades Council and ILP candidate in Dundee in 1895, had spoken strongly against restriction at that year's TUC. Will Parnell of the Cabinet-makers', a trade supposedly threatened by immigrant labour, and also an ILP candidate, similarly opposed restriction. So did Sexton of the National Union of Dock Labourers.[105] On this issue, despite interpretations of the 'labour interest' that suggested restriction, these were more than counterbalanced for almost all prominent ILP figures by appeals to internationalism and to the tradition of Britain being sanctuary for refugees from foreign tyrannies.

The balance of forces regarding recourse to anti-semitic stereotypes changed when the Jews concerned could be stigmatised as rich capitalists. Tillett identified them in 1894, as devoted to 'the commercialistic ideal of clean hands and blood-stained money'.[106] But it was the South African War and its aftermath which demonstrated how Radicals and ILPers could slide easily from condemnations of capitalism, through the blaming of specific capitalists, through the identification of such capitalists as Jewish, to anti-Semitic abuse. The shift from 'capitalism' to 'capitalists' has been noted already as indicating the lack of structural analyses of capitalism in the ILP position; the identification of these capitalists as Jewish could be defended perhaps as a puncturing of the myth that British interests were at stake. But such an identification inevitably summoned up anti-semitic associations. Snowden and other Labour candidates could later claim that Chinese labour imported at Jewish instigation had cheated British workers of employment opportunities in South Africa; Glasier could condemn the allegedly corrupting power of popular newspapers supposedly under Jewish control.[107] Beyond such accusations, there lay claims of a vast plot, engineered by wealthy financiers, lacking roots in Britain, motivated simply by monetary gain and employing British wealth and lives to secure their objectives. The party's official organ painted the scenario:

It is worth noting ... that the most prominent of the Jingo organs are owned and financed largely by stalwart patriots whose names have curiously foreign terminations and whose features seem to indicate they are of the circumcision. In whatever walk of life, the Jew adopts he generally becomes pre-eminent, and the stock-exchange Jew is no exception to the rule. He is the incarnation of the money idea, and it is no exaggeration to say that the Jew financier controls the policy of Europe.[108]

The guileful were leading the gullible: 'Our soldiers are a body of brave ignorant men, excited by blood lust, and engaged by more cunning hands for the perpetration of a brutal crime.'[109] An ILP critique of British imperialism could draw very heavily on racial prejudices.

The relationship between the ILP, and the rival Radical—Liberal and Tory traditions finally must be explained at the level of practice and characterised at the level of sentiment. The need for the party to inspire trust and secure support from Labour activists with Radical sympathies supplemented the similar prejudices of many ILP activists. The strength of the constraints could be seen in the estrangement of Blatchford; the particular power of the courtship factor can be seen on the one occasion when ILP leaders supported a 'Tory socialist', the case of East Bristol in March 1895.[110]

In the mid nineties, the Bristol Labour movement still retained many links with Liberalism. Admittedly New Unionism had had some radicalising effect upon the city's industrial relations, and perhaps more significantly, strikes and accompanying disorders in the winter of 1892—3 had divided local Liberalism, and given local socialists their chance. But many trade union activists still hoped to forward their political claims through enlisting the support of local Radicals. The Bristol Labour Electoral Association was strong, and perhaps less under Liberal control than in several other centres; and whilst there was no ILP branch, socialists were organised in a Socialist Society.[111]

Bristol Liberalism faced a demand for Labour representation in March 1895, when a vacancy arose in East Bristol, a constituency which was heavily working class and securely Liberal. The Liberal caucus rejected the claims of the Radical, later ILPer, A. E. Fletcher, and adopted Sir W. H. Wills who could hope to mobilise his local wealthy connections.[112] Labour spokesmen failed to secure any satisfaction from Liberal officers and set about searching for their own candidate, members of the Trades Council, the Labour Electoral Association and the Socialist Society acting in concert. Unsuccessful suggestions covered a wide range of Labour opinion: Tom Mann, Will Thorne, and two Lib-Labs, Albert Stanley of the Miners and the Weavers' leader, David Holmes.[113]

The unsuccessful search took place despite the existence of an apparently strong local candidate. Hugh Holmes Gore was a solicitor, born in bourgeois Clifton but living in the constituency, in proletarian St Phillips, and engaged in social work. He had served on the Bristol School Board since 1889, coming second then, and topping the poll in 1895.[114] Yet Bristol Labour activists were dubious about Gore, although his name had been suggested by Hardie. They regarded him as 'unreliable', and had not supported him in his second School Board election. When Gore came out against Wills, the Bristol Labour movement divided. Some socialists, including Enid Stacy, supported him; so did Whitefield, the Lib-Lab leader of the Bristol Miners'.[115] His following was swelled by the election taking place during a lockout of boot-workers, and local union activists campaigned for him. Outside speakers included several ILP personalities, amongst them Hardie, Mann, MacDonald and Sam Hobson.[116] Gore's defeat by only 130 votes after a short contest seemed to justify this socialist stand against a Liberal capitalist. But this was far from the whole story. Many local trade union leaders remained at best neutral, and the local ASRS backed Wills.[117] The ILP branch, formed during the campaign, faded away after 1895.[118] It could be argued that local suspicions had been intensified by the intervention, and that ILP influence in Bristol had been substantially retarded.

The root cause of local suspicions of Gore was that he was close to the Tories. His Anglicanism had led to controversy about his role on the School Board, where he had opposed the appointment of a Jewish teacher.[119] Hardie's support for Gore produced a sharp response from local ILP sympathisers:

the contest will not strengthen the hands of those who are striving to plant the banner of the I.L.P. in Bristol ... Who are Gore's supporters and where does the money come from to support him? ... It is already hinted that the High Church Party *subscribes* towards his election expenses.[120]

Another correspondent wrote of Gore's 'Unionist leanings',[121] not surprisingly it was an accusation that Liberal campaigners were only too willing to use.[122] Gore's own election address lent weight to these charges. He opposed Welsh Disestablishment and Irish Home Rule, advocating in place of the latter a more elaborate scheme of local government.[123] His position on the drink question brought him the support of 'The Trade' who welcomed his advocacy of full compensation for terminated licences and his opposition to Sunday closing. They urged electors to 'vote for Gore who will oppose tee-total tyranny and injustice'.[124] Such sentiments went along with a claim that the interests of capital and labour inevitably conflicted, advocacy of a graduated income tax and the urging of the unemployed's claims as the first priority.[125] Gore's campaign was a clear demonstration of the feasibility of a Tory-socialist position.

Faced with the recriminations, Hardie ignored these aspects of Gore's appeal and implicitly ascribed the difficulties to the lack of local ILP organisation which would have facilitated united action. This was disingenuous. What was thoroughly misleading was the accompanying claim that Gore never put himself forward to the ILP as a possible candidate.[126] In fact, he had written to Hardie before the Liberal nomination was settled, and had been explicit about his own position:

> If a capitalist Liberal is run ... a strong I.L.P. or Socialist or Labour candidate may succeed. He would have to get the Conservative vote by some means or another ... *Confidential* The Unionist Party would support me for East Bristol ... I should detach a certain proportion of the Liberal vote, and, with the illiterate, I might oust a Liberal ... If I were to stand, I should stand as a Unionist Socialist. Home Rule is rather played out, and to my mind, merely a Liberal party cry.[127]

Hardie's willingness to back an acknowledged Tory socialist despite his own continuing adherence to Radical principles, resulted from the involvement of the ILP in the unemployed agitation, and the general disappointment felt by both Radicals and Labour activists at the record of the Rosebery Government. But, in the end, the strength of activists' values remained a vital consideration. Their dissatisfaction was not assuaged by the closeness of the result — 'everyone seems to think that Gore, aided by Hardie, Mann and the ILP, has played the Tory game almost to a win'.[128] Gore's record and arguments might attract the support of many working-class electors, but he alienated office holders in labour organisations, and their support was critical for ILP progress.

Support for Gore from leading ILP figures was feasible only in the party's infancy. As its organisation stabilised, individualistic challenges became less credible; as policy, style and strategy became settled, so the Radical inheritance became a central part of the party's identity, welcome on grounds both of principle and of tactical necessity. The strengths of this identity can be found in the generally firm ILP opposition to militarism and imperialism, extending sometimes into a more specifically socialist internationalism. Weaknesses included a familiar Radical tendency to explain social evils in individualistic terms, rather than as a result of systemic distortions. Radical rhetoric could incorporate a naively optimistic view of late-Victorian political institutions, whilst awareness of prejudice and degradation could collapse into smug puritanism. In contrast, the Tory socialist tradition, with its greater tolerance towards the diversions of existing society, might offer more socialist links to contemporary working-class attitudes, but such tolerance could slide easily into racism, xenophobia and support for imperialist expansion.

Both traditions with their divergent messages reflected aspects of long-running British debates over industrialisation, progress, democracy and culture. Neither contained unambiguously socialist implications; both contained aspects that could lead in that direction; both involved regressive components. From one standpoint, concentration on these alternatives serves only to underline the lack of a strong, indigenous, specifically socialist tradition. But the ILP's close identification with one tradition and its virtual exclusion of the other constitutes a fundamental feature of its development.

17

Some thoughts on alternatives

This lengthy investigation began with some questions about the predictability of the ILP's emergence as the primary expression of British socialism. We have examined the varied implications of attempts to expand the party's influence within particular communities with their own cultural features and balances of political forces, or within unions each with its distinctive industrial tradition, and immediate challenges. We have indicated the complex ways in which local predicaments and solutions interacted with the decisions and squabbles of national leaders. On one side there stands a tangled web of local opportunities, constraints and responses; on the other stands an increasingly coherent party with an agreed structure, a characteristic mode of operation, and a broad policy which, if it sometimes provoked internal criticisms, nevertheless developed along reasonably coherent lines. Activists might have developed their own local initiatives, but they defined themselves increasingly as members of a particular national organisation. Although immediate local concerns remained impor- tant, such a definition had a limiting effect on activities. The parameters of debate were affected significantly by dominant understandings of the ILP tradition. The party's establishment meant inevitably that some priorities and symbols became central to debate on the British left, others became marginal.

This emphasis raises the question of 'suppressed alternatives'.[1] Some examples have appeared in earlier chapters. The image of the Social Democratic Federation as a narrow dogmatic sect unsuited to the pragmatic rigours of British politics is a tendentious, partial and misleading one, in which the polemical judgements of some ILP contemporaries have been canonised into firm historical verdicts. Clearly the reality was more complex than this. At least until 1900 and in some cases until later, the two organisations often worked amicably on local issues without any clear sign that the ILP was becoming the naturally predominant body. Similarly, there was the hope of some ILP leaders that a democratic alliance of Labour, Radicals and Irish Nationalists could become a leading element in a political realignment. Today, when the Irish dimension is frequently dismissed as a carbuncle upon the British body politic, it is difficult to recapture the earlier centrality of Irish themes for many on the left. There is an important sense in which Partition and the growth of Labour as a political force conspired to produce a political agenda in which social and economic issues and divisions appeared normal, and questions of nationality declined into marginal irritants. Yet in dealing with the emergence of the ILP we are dealing with events at a time when this norm had not yet been established. In the process of 'becoming', other possible alliances and priorities were perhaps lost. From a very different standpoint, there is the selectivity involved in the continuities between Radicalism and ILP socialism. It was a range of attachments that gave a distinctive stamp to Labour politics, and which also excluded putative connections between 'Tory democracy' and socialism.

Talk of suppression implies that events could have developed in a significantly different way, but that such possibilities have been forgotten. Such losses leave their marks on many historians' accounts, in which what actually happened was virtually what had to happen and the crucial quality of certain key episodes may be lost. The style of many of the previous chapters, focussing on detailed local developments and on individual agents who were baffled, ill-informed and yet creative and resourceful, tends to emphasise the range of opportunities. It helps to promote a provisional verdict along these lines. There was no straight path from the Bradford Conference, by way of the successful search for an alliance with the unions, and the MacDonald—Gladstone Pact, to the 1906 victories. The permanence of the ILP was in no way guaranteed in the early months. Previous initiatives for some form of independent Labour representation had collapsed or had been absorbed back into the Liberal coalition. Rather than assuming that the ILP contained some distinctive ingredient that ensured survival, explanation requires a more judicious estimate of opportunities and choices at both local and national levels. Moreover, once the party had achieved a relatively stable structure, leadership and identity, there remained fundamental strategic questions. The securing of an alliance with the unions was resisted bitterly by sections on both sides. Many party members sought unity with the SDF inside 'One Socialist Party' rather than an arrangement with trade unionists, some of whom they dismissed as reactionary. Such critics were mastered by tactical skill and manipulation, not convinced by arguments. Equally some union officials opposed anything that involved a risk of being taken for a ride by socialists. Some were convinced of the need for a new initiative by the industrial and judicial pressures of the late nineties, but others remained suspicious even hostile. The formation of the LRC owed much to the assiduous cultivation of ambiguities by both sides. The Gladstone—MacDonald pact appears even less as a natural development. This secret deal between the few would have been opposed bitterly by many within the ILP, if it had become widely known. The 1906 victories owed much to this compact, and not a little perhaps to Liberal ignorance. Their generosity might have been less if they had had some inkling of the forthcoming landslide.

These emphases are crucial for their celebration of creativity, guile, and error, an indispensable corrective to images of the political realm as the determined product of inexorable economic forces. And yet clearly political initiatives were not sketched on a blank canvas. The early members of the ILP and those whom they sought to deal with, were constrained by a profusion of elements — some perceived clearly, others vaguely, some not grasped at all. Thus they operated within a society where for half a century industrial workers had accommodated, often with ingenuity, to industrial capitalism. Here was no workforce pitchforked from a traditional peasant world into the typhoon of Turin or St Petersburgh, but a class that had begun to develop countervailing institutions — trade unions, friendly societies, co-ops — not to overthrow capitalism at a stroke, but to make it more tolerable, perhaps to transform it from within. Equally, they had to confront a political system which could claim plausibly to protect certain individual rights, in which working-class and socialist groups enjoyed basic legality. Lack of Bismarckian repression meant there was little need for socialists to erect a State within a State. We have seen the importance of this mid Victorian legacy in many guises — in trade union traditions and the erosion of the distinction between New and Old Unions, in the optimism of ILPers about the electoral process and State power, in the continuities of Radical idiom that facilitated and consolidated the operation of the 1903 pact, above all perhaps in the homely, anti-theoretical tone of not just Radical politics, but also much of the wider culture to which it related. This legacy had to cope with economic difficulties and growing awareness of social tensions. Such emphases lead us to view ILP development not as the consequence of critical choices, but positioned and moulded by a battery of forces.

Repeatedly, we have examined the activities of ILP members working purposefully within a given situation, cramped by the legacy of the past, often bemused or caught unawares by the pressures of the present, with the consequences of earlier choices appearing as constraints. The image suggests a need to survey and to reconcile the fluctuating realms of constraint and agency. Such a suggestion can generate impatient responses, on the one hand from the determinist, overt or covert, who would argue that it is an illusion to talk of a realm of choice, and on the other from pragmatic investigators who abjure all this nonsense and utilise concepts such as 'cause' without a neurotic survey of the metaphysical implications.

Without sinking into the philosophical quicksand, the problem is perhaps too important for either of these rejoinders. In the task of explanation, we characteristically use concepts and images which contrast agency and constraint. The determinist would see this as evidence of naivety, although his counter-prescription hides complex problems behind its simple headline. The contrast is where acute problems of explanation arise; the appropriate response is surely to grapple with the dilemma. More immediately, there is a practical issue in that our subject focusses on the problem. The creation of the ILP represents one attempt to innovate politically as a means to the restructuring of economic relationships in a way that would remove many of the constraints on human development. As a project for expanding the realm of agency the ILPs' contribution was ambiguous, in part perhaps because of the choices made, in part perhaps because of the range of choices available.

Further consideration involves some investigation of the alternatives debated. The proposition that the ILP was the natural predictable development must be grasped at some level of generality. It is not necessary to be pinned on the hook that precisely that organisation headed by those leaders was the predictable outcome. Rather the claim would be that the most likely outcome, given relevant features of the British experience, was a party that followed the ILP's strategy of electoral politics and a pragmatic understanding with the trade unions. The second issue relates to the nature of constraints. Some were physical or technological, and can be readily assessed, but many related to beliefs. We can ask how compelling beliefs were, and whether the compulsion was as great as felt by those involved. This raises the thorny issue of the reasonableness of agents' beliefs and how far creative thought can be accommodated within the analysis. In searching for suppressed alternatives, one indispensable source of evidence is clearly the range of ideas discussed by contemporaries. Yet it is also necessary to ask whether the actual limits were inevitable. Sometimes it seems reasonable to ask why certain ideas failed to appear in contexts where their emergence might have been anticipated.

Bearing in mind this blurred margin, the ILP's developing strategy can be located within a range of apparent alternatives. Initially, attention should be focussed on the commitment to political action defined in more or less conventional terms — electioneering, the pursuit of parliamentary and municipal representation, the quest for influence within established institutions, all underpinned by a belief that this was the most effective method of advancing working-class interests and possibly socialism. This attachment to established definitions can be contrasted with that heterogeneous range of activities sometimes known as the 'Religion of Socialism'. The style of ILP branches shows both the continuing influence of notions of 'Making Socialists' and of 'Living as Socialists', and how they were subordinated increasingly to the worldly business of electioneering. Such ethical sentiments could provide ILP leaders with abundant fig leaves to cover their opportunism. Most fundamentally, the ILP's emergence and survival involved the canalisation and dilution of energies that had ignored the boundaries of conventional politics. Loss lay not just in the rapid subordination of ethical sentiments to electoral imperatives, but in a long-lasting strait-jacketing of thought, not just about means to socialism, but about also the content of any socialist society. One consequence has been the suppression or distortion of a tradition whose recovery and rehabilitation have been a long and costly business.

It is one exercise to perceive and appreciate a loss; another to decide whether it was predictable. Once a political party had been formed with the objective of securing electoral support, then the logic of the situation led readily to the subordination of the ethical elements. The critical point was the formation and initial survival of a group committed to conventional political tasks, a development that can be assessed through a consideration of the alternative's weaknesses. A fundamental problem for groups concerned essentially with propaganda and the prefiguration of the socialist alternative involved their durability. Members could speak on street corners, write propaganda sheets, attend Labour Church services, but lack of progress could dishearten some and drive others into sectarian isolation. Erosions could be counteracted by the development of social activities which could be seen as anticipations of a future society, but these could come to dominate propaganda activities, and to lose their socialist content. Failure could damage the quality of discussion. Distance from political developments could generate abstract or scholastic debate; some members could pine for contact with the masses.

Although such socialist experiences during the decade prior to the formation of the ILP included a wealth of ideas and activities, they barely began to settle the problem of agency. There was no basis for the advance to socialism other than joining and doing likewise, a solution which had obvious difficulties of slowness and limited appeal. It was hardly surprising that, as socialists in the late eighties came increasingly into contact with the broader labour movement, they were drawn into specific trade union struggles and into consideration of pragmatic schemes for Labour representation. At least such preoccupations could guarantee some permanent organisational form for socialist activities, and provide a basis for an expansion of support. Hopefully the socialist ingredient would remain central, and the road to a socialist society would be mercifully short. The pursuit of socialist ideals by available political actions was readily intelligible; the alternative offered a rich suggestiveness but lacked stability.

The selection of conventional political action paralleled choices made by contemporaries in other industrial societies; it was a strategy that had not yet been attempted and which might yield easy benefits. But within this broad attachment there were various possibilities. The ILP emerged as a flexible, formally socialist party, eventually allying with the unions. This development can be seen as involving the defeat of an alternative project for a United Socialist Party, essentially unity with the SDF in preference to a formal link with trade unionists who might or might not be socialists. Clearly, many ILP members considered socialist unity as a significant option to be pursued or avoided. The most prominent evidence comes from the tortuous debate on the question in the late nineties. It is supported by a wealth of other examples — the harmonious relationship between many local ILP and SDF branches, the continuing undercurrent in favour of the option, manifestations of the sentiment such as Hobson's Rochdale campaign and the argument over Quelch's Dewsbury candidature. The feeling was strengthened by the restraints involved in the Labour Alliance. When these tensions grew after 1906, it needed only the advent of Grayson to ignite a new controversy.

The outcome of the fusion controversy came after a long, complex argument in which the manipulations of the leadership played a significant part. This emphasis on the guile of individuals suggests that this critical decision was not a certainty. This verdict can be supported by noting that the tactical weakness of proponents of socialist unity was supported by the vagaries of individuals. It would be possible to conceive a situation similar in all relevant respects except that the advocates of unity did not exhibit a Blatchfordian distaste for organisation of any kind, nor suffer the handicap of his chauvinistic reputation in later years.

On this basis, it would seem reasonable to argue that the ILP might have entered into unity with the SDF, since the crucial decisions owed much to the skill and preferences of key individuals. This emphasis is important but it must be balanced by a further question — what made some people particularly important? Chapter 13 charted the emergence of a leadership group, opposed to socialist unity, showing how beneath the party's formally democratic rhetoric, resources were being concentrated at the party's apex. This process was characteristic of avowedly socialist parties. Elsewhere, no effective antidotes were found, and it is therefore plausible to claim that there were few grounds for anticipating a substantive response within the ILP, and that once the organisation had stabilised, leaders stood an excellent chance of blocking unpalatable proposals. In this case their preference for a trade union alliance rather than socialist unity was supplemented by a proprietorial wish not to relinquish the ILP's identity and their own position within a wider socialist organisation. Such factors suggest that the defeat of the unity option was more likely than appears at first sight. The actors played their singular parts within a framework of rules and a distribution of resources biased towards a leadership victory.

Prospects for the socialist unity option were affected also by developments favouring a rapprochement with the unions. The struggles of ILPers inside specific unions were complex and their achievements were not always clear, but frequently, a shift can be detected, symbolised often in the capture of union posts by ILP members and in the commitment of unions to political independence, and perhaps to a socialist objective. The struggles also tended to affect the outlook of ILP trade unionists, as they reached compromises with other tendencies inside their unions. Moreover, an alliance with the unions solved one problem that socialist unity could not deal with, that of providing enough resources to generate a strong electoral challenge.

If there were compelling arguments in favour of such a Labour Alliance, one ILP fear concerned the safeguarding of the party's independence. At least a United Socialist Party held out the hope that ILPers would remain immune from the temptations of Liberalism. An alliance with trade unionists, several of whom were virtually Lib-Labs, seemed to offer no such guarantee. The characteristic tenderness of ILP leaders towards Radical sentiments, if not Radical organisations, suggested another alternative. The ILP, or at least a substantial part of it, could be assimilated within a modernised Liberalism. Again there is supportive evidence. The 1903 pact was a furtive consummation of a succession of hopes for a Progressive understanding, in which the ILP would look not to the SDF but to Radicals, and perhaps, Irish Nationalists, who had broken their links with the reactionary elements in Liberalism. Hopes for accommodation and realignment varied between and fluctuated within localities. One vital element was the expectations of Liberal politicians. Once electoral revival looked more credible, as free trade emerged as a major issue, then hopes of a substantial realignment died. Yet there remained the possibility that the compact of 1903 and the successes of 1906 could serve as the prelude for a more complete Progressive synthesis extending from style and idiom, through electoral alliance and agreement on burning issues to a closer organisational relationship. Whatever the appeal at the levels of sentiment, electoral success and immediate policies, there was a vital constraint. Both ILP and LRC had established themselves as separate organisations, an achievement proclaimed in the formal commitments of many unions. Whatever the empathy between some Liberals and some ILPers, the legacy of ILP struggles within the unions rendered organisational reabsorption implausible. This was particularly apparent in municipal politics, where ILP—union concordats could be demonstrated initially in the shift of Trades Councils to independent politics, and then in the emergence of local LRCs conducting vigorous municipal campaigns against all comers.

The ILP pursuit of trade union influence rendered socialist unity a still feasible but less likely option. An extremely uncertain and clumsy ILP leadership could have mismanaged their dealings so as to produce this alternative. In contrast, ILP/trade union developments blocked off any organisational reabsorption into Liberalism. A sceptic might argue that such organisational developments made little difference at the level of action and ideology. Such a case can be spelt out easily. In respect of the socialist unity alternative, it could be argued that since the organisation would still have been concerned with electoral success, the quest would have compelled appropriate compromises. These need not involve formal links with unions nor covert pacts with Liberals, but nevertheless an increasing flexibility in the pursuit of votes could produce largely the same outcome. The careers of specifically socialist parties operating in other parliamentary systems at the same period offer little support for a radically different development. Equally, it can be argued that the lack of organisational links with Liberalism was of little significance and that one of the most salient features of Edwardian politics was the emergence and viability of Progressivism.

Emphases on such tendencies are important yet partial. The success of the socialist unity option, whatever the electoral pressures, would have produced a dominant form of British Socialism in which SDF conceptions would have played a more prominent part. Such conceptions had their confusions, their dogmatisms and their omissions. There existed no marxist master-plan for the way ahead. But in critical areas such as the emphasis on class conflict and the scepticism about the neutrality of the British state, the claims were significantly different from their ILP equivalents. The defeat of this option helped to strengthen and to propagate widespread beliefs about what socialism should involve, and equally significantly, what it should not.

This development can be placed in the context of the complex relationship between Liberalism and working-class politics, in a fashion that makes the ILP's involvement in the Labour Alliance appear as a crucial step on the road to Progressivism. But the organisational constraint that prevented assimilation at that level also carried ideological implications. Organisational separation was both the product and the manifestation of working-class distinctiveness and opposition to established policies and modes of thought. The style of the ILP's accommodation with the unions indicated the limitations of what had gone before and of much that was to come afterwards. Separation might be encapsulated frequently within the continuing dominance of sentiments supportive of the capitalist order, but it remained a substantial achievement. It provided the stone at the heart of the Progressive peach.

This tension between a powerful, albeit limited, sense of class and the Radical ethos of several ILP leaders can be found in one of our initial images. It is easy to see how the assumptions and preferences of the early ILP leaders could help to promote the tragedy of 1931. The emphasis on community and the denegration of class conflict, the belief in evolutionary change and the quest for agreement on reforms, distaste for confrontation and the dearth of sceptical appraisals of existing institutions and sentiments — such conceptions could lead all too easily under pressure to a 'National' solution. Yet there was another side to 1931 in the instinctive flinty resistance of the vast majority of Labour activists. Here was another legacy of the early ILP, a revelation of the limitations and strengths of the 1900 settlement. Deep suspicion of 'theoretical' criticism helped to provide considerable room for governmental manoeuvre, but in the end, the basic sense of class asserted itself. Like Lloyd George before him, MacDonald bit on the stone.

The contrast highlights the profoundly ambiguous legacy of the early ILP. The ambiguities have been expressed regularly throughout later Labour political battles. *In Place of Strife* employed new players to demonstrate old values. The continuing strength of this amalgam of Liberal sentiments and class consciousness pull us back to an awareness of the constraints encountered by socialists in late-Victorian Britain. Awareness of continuities and of obstacles emphasises the realm of necessity. Yet the emergence of the ILP and of the Labour Alliance must be seen as a product of political skills exercised within unforgiving limits. Such creativity was not the monopoly of national leaders but was exemplified in a variety of local situations. Lanarkshire miners and Yorkshire woollen workers attempted to come to terms with the challenges of trade union weakness and Liberal inflexibility. Lancastrian socialists faced the problems of working-class Toryism and 'business' trade unionism.

Merthyr ILPers attempted to give a new interpretation to an old Radical tradition. Boot and Shoe, and Engineers' activists encountered the unnerving impact of technical change. Railwaymen fought managerial hostility and pioneered ILP branches in unpromising territory. Socialists tackled the intractable problems in extending unionism to the unskilled. Everywhere there were formidable pressures; often there was a creative response, an attempt to connect socialist principles to immediate concerns and to establish new scales of priorities in unions and communities. The emergence of the ILP with its strengths and ambiguities, was a testament to the creativity of working people. That affirmation furnishes both conclusion and challenge.

Notes

List of abbreviations

ASRS — Amalgamated Society of Railway Servants
ASE — Amalgamated Society of Engineers
BL — British Library
BLPES — British Library of Political and Economic Science
BO — Bradford Observer
DFP — Aberdeen Daily Free Press
DMA — Durham Miners' Association
GH — Glasgow Herald
GO — Glasgow Observer
GRWU — General Railway Workers' Union
HC — Halifax Courier
HG — Halifax Guardian
ILPCR — ILP Conference Report
INL — Irish National League
LCMF — Lancashire and Cheshire Miners' Federation
LDP — Leicester Daily Post
LEA — Labour Electoral Association
LLA — Leicester Liberal Association Minutes
LPLF — Labour Party Letter Files
LRC — Labour Representation Committee
MA — Mattison Collection, University of Leeds
MFGB — Miners' Federation of Great Britain
MG — Manchester Guardian
MFP — Midland Free Press
MR — Monthly Report (of ASE or NUBSO)
MT — Motherwell Times
NAC — National Administrative Council
NBDM — North British Daily Mail
NDT — Northern Daily Telegraph
NLS — National Library of Scotland
NUBSO — National Union of Boot and Shoe Operatives
NUM — National Union of Mineworkers
PG — Preston Guardian
RBC — Report of Biennial Conference (of NUBSO)
RR — Railway Review
SDF — Social Democratic Federation

SLP — Scottish Labour Party
SWPEC — Scottish Workers' Parliamentary Election Committee
WSPU — Womens' Social and Political Union
WT — Workman's Times
YDO — Yorkshire Daily Observer
YMA — Yorkshire Miners' Association

Chapter 1: Images and emphases

1   For Hardie's early career see Fred Reid, *Keir Hardie: The Making of a Socialist* (Croom Helm, London, 1978); K. O. Morgan, *Keir Hardie* (Weidenfeld, London, 1975); I. McLean *Keir Hardie* (Allen Lane, London, 1975).
2   See David Marquand, *Ramsay MacDonald* (Cape, London, 1977).
3   For the LRC, see F. Bealey and H. Pelling, *Labour and Politics 1900—1906* (Macmillan, London, 1958).
4   For an account of, and documentation on, the pact, see F. Bealey, 'Negotiations between the Liberal Party and the Labour Representation Committee before the General Election of 1906', *Bulletin of the Institute of Historical Research*, 1956.
5   See Lord Snowden, *Autobiography*, volume 1 (Nicholson and Watson, London, 1934); Colin Cross, *Phillip Snowden* (Barrie & Rockliff, London, 1966).
6   See L. Thompson, *The Enthusiasts* (Gollancz, London, 1971).
7   On the early years of miners' representation, see R. Gregory *The Miners in British Politics 1906—14* (Clarendon Press, Oxford, 1968).

Part One

Preliminary reflections

1   J. L. Garvin, 'A party with a future', *Fortnightly Review*, 1 September 1895, pp. 338—9.
2   Curran Election Address as cited in *Labour Leader*, 2 October 1897.

Chapter 2: Mining

The Federation ethos

1   On the formation and early years of the MFGB see R. Page Arnot, *The Miners, 1889—1910* (Allen and Unwin, London, 1949), and also the histories of the coalfield unions cited in appropriate sections. Accounts of the careers of many of the miners' leaders discussed here are available in successive volumes of the *Dictionary of Labour Biography*.

The MFGB: The Lib-Lab coalfields

2   On this see R. Gregory, *The Miners and British Politics 1906—14*, and also his 'The miners and politics in England and Wales, 1906—14', unpublished D.Phil. Thesis, University of Oxford, 1963, hereafter referred to as Gregory, *Thesis*.
3   For a discussion of these factors in a Yorkshire context, see David Rubinstein, 'The Independent Labour Party and the Yorkshire miners — the Barnsley by-election of 1897', *International Review of Social History*, 1978, pp. 102—34.

4   Even when, in 1893, locked-out Yorkshire miners were engaged in confrontation with military and police under a Liberal Home Secretary. See R. G. Neville, 'The Yorkshire miners and the 1893 lockout — the Featherstone massacre', *International Review of Social History,* 1976, pp. 337—57.

5   See Gregory, *Thesis,* pp. 181—2.

6   *Labour Leader,* 14 July 1894, for text of telegram.

7   See Rubinstein, 'The Independent Labour Party and the Yorkshire miners', and Page Arnot, *The Miners,* pp. 300—302.

8   *Labour Leader,* 24 October 1897. This paper contains detailed, although over-optimistic, reports on prospects throughout October 1897.

9   *Clarion,* 30 October 1897.

10 *Barnsley Chronicle,* 23 October 1897. Pickard added that miners should sort out the ILP in the YMA as 'farmers had stamped out the rinderpest'.

11 See a series of letters in the ILP Archive, eg. 1897/83, Hardie to Penny, October 19 1897 asking for details on Walton's North-Eastern shareholdings hoping to 'implicate any well known Tories in the management of these concerns'.

12 Curran in *ILP News,* November 1897; see also the verdict in *Labour Leader,* 6 November 1897.

13 Hardie to David Lowe, cited in the latter's *From Pit to Parliament* (Labour Publishing Co. London 1923); see also Tom Mann's post-mortem 'I didn't feel depressed over *Barnsley* but I was expecting about 250 more', Mann to Hardie, 17 November 1897, ILP Archive 1897/93.

14 For material on South Kirkby, see YMA Records for 1897: Executive, 19 August, including the references cited above; Council, 23 August, where the Executive view was carried by 620 to 344; Executive, 13 September; Council, 4 October. Note also the resolution from the ILP-dominated Rothwell lodge, backing the South Kirkby men.

15 *Clarion*, 30 October 1897.

16 For Rothwell in 1896, see a series of items in the *Labour Leader*, 4 April, 22 August, 19 September; also *ibid.*, 17 April 1897; also *Colliery Workman's Times,* 9 December 1893.

17 *Labour Leader*, 2 October 1897, for Rothwell resolution on the Barnsley contest.

18 Glasier Diary, 12 March 1900.

19 *Labour Leader*, 29 August 1896.

20 *Ibid.*, 14 July 1905. Note by John Penny.

21 A claim based on the detailed evidence on lodge voting containing in the YMA Records.

22 For Herbert Smith, see Jack Lawson, *The Man in the Cloth Cap*, (Methuen, London, 1941).

23 Will Lunn to Hardie, 15 May 1898, ILP Archive, 1898/39.

24 See the following items in the ILP Archive: 1898/25, R. Smillie to Hardie, 9 May 1898; 1898/28,34,37, all Lunn to Hardie — 9, 10 and 12 May 1898; 1898/40, James Sinclair to Hardie, 16 May 1898; for the public results see *Labour Leader,* May 1898.

25 Lunn to Hardie, 10 December 1899. ILP Archive, 1899/137.

26 Cited in J. Benson and R. G. Neville (eds.) *Studies in the Yorkshire Coal Industry* (Manchester University Press, 1976), pp. 141—2. Also on the dispute in the same volume at pp. 145—62 'In the wake of Taff Vale: the Denaby and Cadeby miners' strike and conspiracy case, 1902—6'. Also on some factors facilitating or inhibiting militancy Pat Spaven, 'Main gates of protest: contrasts in rank and file activity amongst the South Yorks miners, 1858—94', in R. Harrison (ed.), *The Independent Collier* (Harvester, Hassocks, 1978).

27 For example, neither voted for Herbert Smith in the contest for the Normanton nomination in November 1905 — a selection viewed widely as a test of ILP strength in the Association. See YMA Executive Minutes, 27 November 1905.

28 For *Labour Leader* material on the case see amongst others the issues of 12 May, 30 June, 25 August (John Penny on the Hemsworth evictions), 29 September, 6, 13, 20 and 27 October, 1 December.

29 *Ibid.*, 13 October 1905 — he prophesied 'the avalanche in Yorkshire is beginning to move'.

30 *Ibid.*, 27 October 1905.

31 Letter of 11 January 1906 published in *Sheffield Daily Telegraph*, 16 January 1906 and also in *Labour Leader*, 19 January 1906. Reproduced in YMA Minutes, January 1906.

32 See 'To our members', YMA Circular, January 1906 signed by J. Wadsworth, J. Dixon, F. Hall, J. Hoskin. For early evidence of Lib-Lab animosity see W. O. Bull (Hemsworth) to Hardie, 23 October 1905, ILP Archive, 1905/129.

33 YMA Council Minutes, 26 February 1906 and 12 November 1906. The votes were 616 to 493 and 646 to 447. See also the lengthy debate in Council, 9 October 1906.

34 YMA Records, January 1906.

35 YMA Council Minutes, 15 June 1905 — not entertained by 78 to 22.

36 On the complexities of the YMA Lib-Lab attempts to expand their parliamentary representation see Gregory, *Thesis*, pp. 182—91.

37 YMA Council, 11 February 1904, for the vote to fill the Normanton vacancy.

38 YMA Executive, 7 March 1904, for the recommendation to appoint five more candidates, and 6 June 1904, for selection of candidates.

39 W. Lunn to Ramsay MacDonald, 15 September 1904, Labour Party Letter Files (LPLF), 17/287.

40 YMA Council, 31 October 1904.

41 W. Lunn to MacDonald, 19 December 1904, LPLF, 18/168.

42 For the decision to contest see YMA Council, 31 October 1904.

43 Source as in note 41.

44 On 1904, Lunn to Hardie, ILP Archive, 1904/3, 9 February 1904; he noted then 'There was a number of Socialist delegates who will back me up'. On 1905, *ibid.*, 1905/144, 150 and 180, Lunn to Hardie, 13 and 16 November, 5 December 1905.

45 YMA Records, November 1905.

46 Penny to Hardie, ILP Archive, 1905/140, 9 November 1905.

47 This second circular concentrating on *industrial* solidarity follows the previously noted one in YMA Records, January 1906. It was signed by the Lib-Lab officials plus Smith.

48 On the East Midlands coalfields, see Gregory *Thesis*, chapter 4. J. E. Williams, *The Derbyshire Miners* (Allen and Unwin, London, 1962); A. R. Griffin, *The Miners of Nottinghamshire, 1881—1914* (NUM Notts Area, Mansfield, 1955).

49 Griffin, *The Miners of Nottinghamshire*, pp. 79—80.

50 *Labour Leader,* 12 June 1897.

51 In Chesterfield, September 1897, cited in Williams, *The Derbyshire Miners*, p. 494.

52 Hardie to G. B. Ward (Sheffield), 22 April 1903, ILP Archive, 1903/61.

53 W. E. Harvey at Clowne, January 1903, cited in Williams, *The Derbyshire Miners*, p. 389.

54 Williams, *The Derbyshire Miners*, pp. 487—8. There is a good discussion of

the consequential tortuous Labour politics in these coalfields in McKibbin, *The Evolution of the Labour Party, 1910—1924* (Oxford University Press, London, 1974), pp. 54—62.

55   Or so local activists claimed in correspondence to Joseph Burgess during the *Workman's Times* campaign. See H. Pelling, *Origins of the Labour Party 1880—1900* (2nd Edition, Clarendon Press, Oxford, 1965) p. 110.

56   H. Bristol to MacDonald, 18 and 28 June 1904, LPLF, 15/30 and 189.

57   Gregory, *Thesis*, pp. 352—8.

58   T. A. Pierce to J. R. MacDonald, 31 July 1906 — cited in Gregory *Thesis*, p. 336.

59   See R. Page Arnot, *The South Wales Miners, 1898—1914* (Allen and Unwin, London, 1967), Hywel Francis and David Smith, *The Fed* (Lawrence and Wishart, London, 1980), chapter 1, and K. O. Morgan, *Wales in British Politics 1868—1922* (University of Wales Press, Cardiff, 1963). Also Gregory, *Thesis*, chapter 5. There are no minutes surviving of the South Wales Miners' Federation before 1908.

60   For this vignette see Michael Foot, *Aneurin Bevan 1897—1945* (Paladin, St Albans, 1975), pp. 14—15.

61   A point made particularly in Morgan, *Wales in British Politics*.

62   Robert Smillie, *My Life for Labour* (Mills & Boon, London, 1924).

63   See the series of Reports from the South Wales organiser Willie Wright in the collection of ILP material deposited in BLPES; and the series of articles in *Labour Leader*, 25 June, 2 July, 9 July and 10 September 1898.

64   *Ibid.*, 2 July 1898.

65   Cited in Page Arnot, *The Miners*, p. 48.

66   *Labour Leader*, 9 July 1898.

67   Traceable in monthly reports back page of *ILP News* 1898—9. See also K. O. Fox, 'Labour and Merthyr's Khakhi Election of 1900', *Welsh History Review*, 1964—5, pp. 351—66 and Morgan, *Wales in British Politics*.

68   See Francis and Smith, *The Fed*, chapter 1, on these points.

69   George Barker to Hardie, 31 May 1903, ILP Archive, 1903/118.

70   D. Davies to MacDonald, 28 June 1900 and 6 August 1902, LPLF 2/208 and 5/254.

71   On candidature problems see Gregory, *Thesis*, pp. 392—406.

72   Hardie to MacDonald, 19 October 1904, LPLF, 17/408.

73   Vernon Hartshorn to MacDonald, 10 and 24 April 1904. LPLF, 14/163 and 232.

74   James Winstone to MacDonald, 2 July 1905, LPLF, 24/275.

75   Gregory, *Thesis*, pp. 407—10.

The MFGB: Labour's vanguard

76   See R. Challinor, *The Lancashire and Cheshire Miners* (Frank Graham, Newcastle, 1972); I.Scott, 'The Lancashire and Cheshire Miners' Federation 1900—14', unpublished Ph.D. Thesis, University of York, 1977, hereafter referred to as Scott, *Thesis*.

77   G. Trodd, 'Political change and the working class in Blackburn and Burnley 1880—1914', unpublished Ph.D. Thesis, University of Lancaster, 1978, hereafter referred to as Trodd, *Thesis*.

78   On this area, see *Labour Leader*, 1 December 1894; 17 April 1897. Also, see the files of the *Swinton and Pendlebury Pioneer*.

79   One of whom, Jack Sutton, became a Labour MP in January 1910.

80   See Thomas Ashton, 'Circular to non-unionists', 12 April 1893 in Lancashire and Cheshire Miners' Federation Minutes.

81 The cost of the two 1895 defeats had been £387 15*s* 5*d*. See LCMF monthly balance sheet, 27 July 1895.
82 For the discussion, see LCMF Conference Minutes, 11 November 1899. Greenall and Aspinwall went as delegates.
83 For the initial decision to stay outside, see LCMF Conferences, 31 March, 28 April, 26 May (show of hands) and 16 June 1900 (card vote).
84 LCMF Conferences, 25 April and 23 May 1903.
85 For details on political developments in the interim period see Scott, *Thesis*, pp. 121—31, and for developments 1903—6, pp. 132—47.
86 *Ibid.*, p. 131.
87 *Labour Leader*, 30 June 1905.
88 See Gregory, *Thesis*, pp. 491—505 for discussion of candidates; and LCMF Conference Minutes, 23 May 1903, for selection of candidates.
89 LCMF Conference Minutes, 5 November 1903.
90 *Ibid.*, 3 December 1903.
91 See Report of the Committee, included in LCMF Conference Minutes, 31 December 1903.
92 Clegg, Fox and Thompson, *A History of British Trade Unions Since 1889* (Clarendon Press, Oxford, 1964), vol. 1, p. 300.
93 On Small, see the collections of material in NLS MS Acc 3350 and the discussion in Fred Reid, *Keir Hardie: The Making of a Socialist*, pp. 80—81.
94 For Smillie, see his *My Life for Labour*.
95 For material on Scottish miners unions see Fred Reid, *Keir Hardie*; R. P. Arnot, *A History of the Scottish Miners* (Allen and Unwin, London, 1955); Alan Campbell and Fred Reid, 'The independent collier in Scotland', and Alan Campbell, 'Honourable men and degraded slaves: a comparative study of trade unionism in two Lanarkshire mining communities' both in R. Harrison (ed.), *The Independent Collier*. Gordon M. Wilson, 'The strike policy of the miners of the west of Scotland, 1842—74' in Ian MacDougall (ed.), *Essays in Scottish Labour History* (John Donald, Edinburgh, ND). J. D. Young, 'Working class and radical movements in Scotland and the revolt from Liberalism, 1866—1900', unpublished PhD thesis, University of Stirling, 1974. Hereafter referred to as Young *Thesis*. See also his *The Rousing of the Scottish Working Class* (Croom Helm, London, 1979).
96 The debate over the role of the Irish in Scottish trade unionism can be followed in J. E. Handley, *The Irish in Modern Scotland* (University Press, Cork, 1947) p. 320; cf. Young, *Thesis*, p. 137.
97 For a summary, see Reid, *Keir Hardie*, pp. 88—93.
98 *North British Daily Mail*, 8—10 February 1887.
99 *Ibid.*, 8 February 1887 (Report of meeting at Hamilton).
100 *Ibid.*, 14 February 1887.
101 *The Miner*, July 1887.
102 For the formation of the Federation and the subsequent stoppage, see Page Arnot, *A History of the Scottish Miners*, pp. 71—88. Developments can be traced also in the MFGB Records for 1894; see in particular, the Minutes of the Carlisle Conference, 30 May 1894, and of the Edinburgh Conference 27—28 September 1894.
103 For Robertson, see his comments at p. 60 of the Edinburgh Conference Minutes; for Shaw Maxwell, see the reference by Cowey and Smillie at p. 72 of same. Robertson's actions are also dealt with in MFGB Executive Minutes 22 August 1894. Hardie's views can be found in *Labour Leader*, 20 October 1894.
104 Scottish Miners' Federation Minute Book, Annual Conference, 20 December 1901. N.L.S. Acc. 4312.

105 On the tempo of industrial relations see R. P. Arnot, *A History of the Scottish Miners*, pp. 98 ff.

106 For Brown, see Alexander Gammie, *From Pit to Palace* (James Clarke, London 1931).

107 Scottish Miners' Federation Minute Book, Executive, 5 October 1896.

108 The numerical dominance of the Fife Union within the Scottish Federation was such that at the Annual Conference in December 1897, the Lib-Labs there were able to carry the Scottish vote for MFGB President in favour of Pickard, the socialists' greatest opponent. Pickard received 9,000 votes, the Derbyshire Lib-Lab Haslam, proposed by Smillie, 6,700 — Scottish Miners' Federation Minute Book, Annual Conference, 23 December 1897. For Weir, MFGB Conference Report, January 1897, pp. 52—3.

109 On the land agitations, see in particular James Kellas, 'The Liberal Party in Scotland 1885—1895', unpublished Ph.D. Thesis, University of London, 1962, hereafter referred to as Kellas, *Thesis*.

110 See Campbell and Reid, 'The independent collier in Scotland'.

111 Smillie, *Minutes of Evidence to Royal Commission on Labour*, Group A, Volume 1, 10149, and almost the same claim by W. Small, *ibid.*, 10285.

112 For Lochgelly, see *Labour Leader*, 8 September 1905; for ILP weakness in the West, see the piece by 'Gavroche' (W. Stewart), *ibid.*, 6 January 1905.

113 For details, see Glasier Diaries, August—September 1901, ending on 14 September with the entry 'Conference of Ayrshire delegates a fiasco'.

114 J. W. Robertson to John Penny, 29 August 1899, ILP Archive, 1899/92.

115 *Dundee Courier*, 20 June 1889.

116 On expectations that Weir would stand see Scottish Workers' Parliamentary Elections Committee Executive Minutes, 4 August 1900, with claim that Weir had accepted the SWPEC Manifesto.

117 For these later developments see Henry Pelling, *Social Geography of British Elections 1885—1910* (Macmillan, London, 1967), pp. 394—5.

118 See *Hamilton Advertiser*, 24 and 31 March 1894 for details of pit collections.

119 Scottish Miners' Federation, Minute Book, Executive, 11 January 1902.

120 The political themes are explored in Chapter 7.

121 For Cumbrian developments see Gregory, *Thesis*, pp. 486—90, and 531—41; and on the political background, Pelling, *Social Geography of British Elections*, pp. 330—31 and 340—41.

122 See the material in LPLF, 2nd series, Boxes 4—7. The contest is discussed in *Labour Leader*, 10 July—24 August 1906.

MFGB: politics

123 For a general discussion of the MFGB matters during these years, see R. P. Arnot, *The Miners, 1889—1910*.

124 MFGB Conference Report. January 1894, p. 18. 'I am not a mines nationaliser. I don't think that if the mines were nationalised, the miners would be a penny better off than they are today. The crux of the whole question ... is not as to whom the mines belong, but as to how the coal should be sold.'

125 MFGB Conference, 1897 — for text of resolution, see p. 36 — the debate headed 'Socialism and trade unionism' extends from p. 36 to p. 66.

126 Moved by J. Wilson, pp. 36—9, Smillie was the seconder, pp. 39—41.

127 *Ibid.*, pp. 41—2.

128 *Ibid.*, p. 47 and again at p. 51.

129 *Ibid.*, p. 65.

130 Harvey, p 49; Haslam, p. 56. The nationalisation of mines had been accepted by the 1894 MFGB Conferences by 158—26. See 1894 Conference Report, p. 26.

131 For the votes, see MFGB 1897 Conference Report, p. 66; for the pragmatic Lancashire argument, see Aspinwall's remarks at p. 47.
132 MFGB Conference, October 1900, p. 25.
133 For material on genesis of the scheme, see MFGB Conference Report, October 1901, p. 25, and MFGB Executive Minutes for 25 October, 8 November, and 6 December 1901.
134 See Pickard speech in MFGB Conference Report, October 1900, pp. 9—10.
135 MFGB Conference, September 1904, p. 67.
136 MFGB Conference, October 1903, Resolution 11 from Scotland in the debate on Labour Representation, pp. 13—29. The Scots' attempt was blocked by 285,000 to 55,000.
137 MFGB Conference, October 1904, pp. 39—53, see p. 39—40 for the ruling out of resolutions from the agenda.
138 *Ibid.*, pp. 46—7.
139 MFGB Conference, October 1908, p. 100.
140 MFGB Conference, October 1904, pp. 51—2.

The North-Eastern coalfields

141 For material on these coalfields, see John Wilson, *A History of the Durham Miners' Association 1870—1904* (J. H. Veitch, Durham, 1907); E. Welbourne, *The Miners' Unions of Northumberland and Durham* (Cambridge University Press, Cambridge, 1923); Gregory *Thesis*, chapter 2 and G. H. Metcalfe, 'A history of the Durham Miners' Association 1869—1915', unpublished M.A. Thesis, University of Durham, 1947, hereafter referred to as Metcalfe, *Thesis* (typescript at NUM Offices, Durham). And for one Lib-Lab leader, John Wilson, *Memories of a Labour Leader* (T. Fisher Unwin, London, 1910).
142 See Robert Moore, *Pitmen, Preachers and Politics: the Effects of Methodism in a Durham Mining Community* (Cambridge University Press, Cambridge, 1974), and also the review by E. P. Thompson, 'On history, sociology and historical relevance', *British Journal of Sociology*, 1976, pp. 387—402; also E. J. Hobsbawm, 'The labour sects' in *Primitive Rebels* (Manchester University Press, Manchester, 1959).
143 Wilson, *Memories of a Labour Leader*, p. 245.
144 For a discussion on working hours in Durham, see the evidence given by Paterson and Wilson to the *Royal Commission on Labour*, Group A, Volume 1, 1—383 (Paterson); 384—692 (Wilson).
145 DMA Executive Circular, 21 September 1892 — this argument and variants on it were repeated regularly.
146 On the negotiations of 1885, see Gregory *Thesis*, pp. 71—2; also Wilson, *History of the DMA*, pp. 191—7 and Welbourne, *The Miners' Unions of Northumberland and Durham*, pp. 199—200 for a suggestion of some Conservatism amongst Durham miners based on anti-Irish sentiment.
147 References to the Lloyd Jones campaign in the three sources cited previously in note 146, also Metcalfe, *Thesis*, p. 432, for Crawford's views.
148 For an account, see E. P. Thompson, *William Morris: From Romantic to Revolutionary* (Merlin, London, 1977), pp. 439—45.
149 See Gregory, *Thesis* maps of the North Eastern coalfields for location of ILP branches.
150 Welbourne claims (p. 259), that possibly Paterson's style 'was strictly in accordance with the rules and the democratic ideas of the union'.
151 For material from contrasting positions see MFGB Special Conference, 19 and 20 July 1893; and from Durham, the Executive Circular of 7 December

1892 and Wilson's report on the 'Hen and Chicken' Conference, 21 July 1893. The December Circular noted on levies 'Durham was a very good, prolific and patient milk cow, and there was a large demand for the yield we could give.'

152   See, for example, the Council decision of 6 February 1897 on eight hours, and the accompanying Executive advice in DMA Records.

153   T. Richardson to J. R. MacDonald, 24 June 1903, LPLF, 9/317.

154   See Welbourne, *The Miners' Unions of Northumberland and Durham*, p. 294 and Hardie to David Lowe, 12 May 1899, ILP Archive, 1899/40. For the emergence of the ILP in north-west Durham dated at 1895, see L. Atherley-Jones, *Looking Back* (Witherby, London, 1925), p. 112.

155   Jack Lawson, *A Man's Life* (Hodder, London, 1944), p. 64.

156   Resolutions in DMA Records especially in programmes for Annual Council held each December. On conciliation see the ballots of 15th January and 9 May 1896 — and also the detailed 1899 lodge vote on the same topic.

157   See Wilson's critical response, DMA Records, 24 December 1898; also the Executive Circular of the same date.

158   For Wilson's view see his Monthly Circular, February 1898; also Welbourne; *The Miners' Unions of Northumberland and Durham*, pp. 300, 304, 308, and Metcalfe, *Thesis*, p. 442.

159   For text of resolutions from Victoria Garesfield and Spen Lodges, respectively, see programme for Annual Council meeting 12 December 1896 — also the Official's response is added.

160   See Wilson's Monthly Circular, July 1898.

161   Including Ryhope, Marsden, and Spen.

162   Lodge vote on conciliation 1899, DMA Records.

163   Lawson, *A Man's Life*, p. 37.

164   For comments on economic changes see Welbourne, *The Miners' Unions of Northumberland and Durham*, pp. 305—7.

165   For an early example see the Washington resolution for Council, 3 August 1900. See also the Official's response, 19 July 1900.

166   Wilson's Monthly Circular. March 1900 — he cited approvingly John Burns's remarks at the LRC Conference.

167   See the Circular of August 1903 — vote 30,841 to 12,899 in favour of 'trade union effort' rather than 'state interference'.

168   The move towards MFGB affiliation can be found in Council Minutes and resolutions for ballot 12 October 1907 — followed by details of the individual lodge vote with big pro-affiliation votes at, amongst others, Washington, Ryhope, Boldon, Hebburn, Marsden, Monkwearmouth.

169   *Labour Leader*, 26 March 1904.

170   *Ibid.*, 20 October 1905.

171   *Ibid.*, Sim's reports on both Durham and Northumberland appear in *Labour Leader* during much of 1905.

172   Lawson, *A Man's Life*, p. 75.

173   On Usworth see *Labour Leader*, 18 January 1902, 21 February 1903, 19 February and 12 March 1905. Glasier Diary, 14 June 1902 notes a meeting with 'Richardson (Councillor and Colliers' Check-Weighman, an admirable working man type)'.

174   See Richardson to MacDonald, 12 August 1902, LPLF, 5/347 and 19 January 1903, *loc. cit.*, 6/343.

175   Durham Labour Council Circular, *loc. cit.*, 9/362.

176   See Minutes of the Federation Board 20 February 1903 in DMA Records.

177   *Labour Leader*, 28 March 1903 — letter from ILP which claims, however, that the candidate selection was carried out by the DMA not the four sections meeting together.

178   Wilson *Circular* for March 1903.

179   Developments 1903—5 are outlined in Gregory *Thesis*, pp. 71—2. See also the retrospective account in Durham Federated Board United Council Meeting, October 1905.

180   For text of Hobson Lodge resolutions see Programme for Council 13 February 1904 — Executive response was that Johnson was 'supported by all the progressive forces'.

181   *Labour Leader*, 22 August 1903 for resolutions on theme from Ravensworth and Chopwell Lodges.

182   For a discussion of Taylor's candidature see Gregory *Thesis*, pp. 73—8, and on Taylor's attitudes see also J. Jeffrey to Hardie, 18 September 1904, ILP Archive 1904/34.

183   *Durham Chronicle*, 8 December 1905.

184   *Ibid.*, 22 December 1905.

185   *Ibid.*, 5 January 1906.

186   *Ibid.*; see also Richardson's letters on the contest in LPLF.

187   Account of the discussion in *Durham Chronicle*, 12 January 1906. Also MacDonald to Richardson, 5 January 1906, LPLF 29/382.

188   For the campaign see *Durham Chronicle* and *Labour Leader*, 19 and 26 January 1906.

189   *Durham Chronicle*, 12 January 1906.

190   *Ibid.*, 19 January 1906 — speaker Robert Parker.

191   The emergence of this generation into the leadership of the Durham Miners is traced in W. R. Garside, *The Durham Miners 1919—1960* (Allen and Unwin, London, 1971), pp. 71—81.

192   See his regular reports in *Labour Leader* during 1905.

193   *Labour Leader*, 20 July 1906 — article by Bruce Glasier — 'Northumberland on the march'.

194   For the Northumbrian cases see Gregory, *Thesis*, pp. 139—59.

Chapter 3: Cotton

1   For background on the politics of the cotton towns, see P. Clarke, *Lancashire and the New Liberalism* (Cambridge University Press, Cambridge, 1971); Patrick Joyce, *Work, Society and Politics: the Culture of the Factory in Later Victorian England* (Harvester Press, Hassocks, 1980); J. Hill, 'Working class politics in Lancashire 1885—1906: a regional study in the origins of the Labour Party', unpublished Ph.D. thesis, University of Keele, 1969, hereafter referred to as Hill, *Thesis*; Henry Pelling, *Social Geography of British Elections*, chapter 12; and, more specifically, Trodd, *Thesis*.

2   For a lucid summary of the main production processes, see Jill Liddington and Jill Norris, *One Hand Tied Behind Us: The Rise of the Women's Suffrage Movement* (Virago, London, 1978), pp. 84—95.

3   On cotton unionism see H. A. Turner, *Trade Union Growth Structure and Policy: A Comparative Study of the Cotton Unions* (Allen and Unwin, London, 1962), also Clarke, *Lancashire and New Liberalism*, chapter 4; also for influential images the various comments by the Webbs in their *History of Trade Unionism* (Longmans, London, 1907), and their *Industrial Democracy* (Longmans, London, 1920).

4   See S. J. Chapman, 'Some policies of the cotton spinners' trade unions', *Economic Journal*, 1900, pp. 467—73, esp. p. 470 for a summary of the problems confronting any collective action by piecers.

5   *Ibid.*; also J. R. Clynes, *Autobiography*, vol. 1, pp. 47—9 (Hutchinson, London, 1937).

6   For his campaign there, see *Manchester Guardian*, 26 June—7 July 1899.

7   Quoted in *Labour Leader*, 15 February 1902.

8   *Manchester Guardian*, 4 July 1899.

9   For condemnations see *ibid.*, 3 July, (Oldham Twiners Branch) and 4 July 1899 (Royton Spinners).

10   Trodd, *Thesis*, chapter 4.

11   Turner, *Trade Union Growth Structure and Policy* for the Weavers' structure and style; also Liddington and Norris, *One Hand Tied Behind Us*, pp. 9—99.

12   Trodd, *Thesis*, p. 221.

13   *Lancashire Daily Post*, 29 September 1900.

14   On Burnley, see Trodd, *Thesis*; on Nelson and Colne see various references in Liddington and Norris, and F. Bealey and H. Pelling, *Labour and Politics 1900—1906* chapter 5.

15   This political point is developed in Joyce, *Work, Society and Politics*.

16   See Liddlington and Norris, pp. 92—9 for a discussion of women weavers.

17   On these developments see *ibid.*, pp. 86—9 and Clegg, Fox and Thompson, *A History of British Trade Unions*, pp. 112—16; also Card Room Amalgamation Quarterly Report, December 1892, esp. p. 5, and 1893 Reports for membership decline.

18   On wages, see Joseph L. White, *The Limits of Trade Union Militancy: The Lancashire Textile Workers 1910—1914* (Greewood Press, Westport, Conn., 1978), chapter 3. All following figures from this source.

19   *Ibid.*, p. 35 for working conditions; also Trodd, *Thesis*, p. 232.

20   On family income see White, *The Limits of Trade Union Militancy*, pp. 25—30: on women in the workforce, pp. 41—56, on 'half timers', pp. 56—63.

21   Joyce, *Work, Society and Politics* for a development of these themes.

22   The classical portrait can be found in the Webbs' *Industrial Democracy*, pp. 195—204.

23   The lockout is discussed in Clegg, Fox and Thompson, *A History of British Trade Unions*, pp. 113—17.

24   *Ibid.*, p. 119.

25   On its early activities, see Clarke, *Lancashire and the New Liberalism*, pp. 84 – 99.

26   In *Industrial Democracy*, p. 259.

27   See Clegg Fox and Thompson, *A History of British Trade Unions*, pp. 242—6.

28   *Industrial Democracy*, p. 260.

29   *Cotton Factory Times*, 26 July 1895.

30   *Cotton Factory Times*, 2 November 1894.

31   For Bolton, see P. A. Harris, 'Class conflict, the trades unions and working class politics in Bolton 1875—1896', unpublished M.A. Thesis, University of Lancaster, 1971.

32   For Gill's candidature, see *Bolton Chronicle*, 16 December 1905—20 January 1906 — note especially his defence of the status quo regarding piecers (6 January 1906) and his praise of John Burns (13 January 1906).

33   See the discussion of the Burgess incident in Chapter 9; on the municipal split see Blackburn Trades Council Report, 1897.

34   *Blackburn Labour Journal*, May 1898.

35   Cited in E. Hopwood, *The Lancashire Weavers' Story (Amalgamated Weavers'
      Assoc. Manchester, 1969), p. 41.*
36   *White, The Limits of Trade Union Militancy*, pp. 157—61.
37   Trodd, *Thesis*, p. 324.
38   Nelson Weavers' Association Executive Minutes, 14 August 1890, for decision
      to nominate. Nelson and District Trades Council Minutes, 16 July 1890 for
      resolution backing labour representation, and 13 October 1890 for endorse-
      ment of Weavers' nominees.
39   *Ibid.*, 21 March, 18 and 25 April, 16 May 1893.
40   *Ibid.*, 19 November 1893.
41   *Ibid.*, 19 February 1894.
42   *Cotton Factory Times*, 2 Novembere 1894 — the Nelson Weavers voted in
      favour by 2,227 to 673.
43   Nelson and District Trades Council Minutes, 28 May and 17 September 1895.
44   Nelson Weavers' Association Minutes of Members Meeting, 24 August 1897.
45   Bealey and Pelling, *Labour and Politics*, 102.
46   For decisions not to attend Foundation Conference see Weavers' Amalgamation
      General Council Minutes, 12 January 1900 and Cardroom Amalgamation
      Minutes of Representative Meeting, 27 January 1900.
47   Changes are discussed in White, *The Limits of Trade Union Militancy*, chapter
      2; also from a variety of angles in Trodd, *Thesis*.
48   The significance of this case is discussed in Clarke, *Lancashire and the New
      Liberalism*, pp. 91—2; Clegg, Fox and Thompson, *A History of British Trade
      Unions*, pp. 323—4 and Bealey and Pelling, *Labour and Politics*, pp. 78—80.
49   See A. B. Newall to J. R. MacDonald, 4 June 1900, Labour Party Letter files
      2/70; and 9 January 1901, *loc. cit.*, 2/326.
50   Nelson Weavers' Association Minutes of Members' Meeting, 19 August 1901.
51   *Manchester Guardian*, 14 January 1902; Weavers' Amalgamtion General
      Council Minutes, 11 January 1902.
52   *Ibid.*, 28 February 1902.
53   In his letter of 4 June 1900, see note 49.
54   *Nelson Chronicle*, 17 January and 7 February 1902.
55   *Ibid.*, 7 March 1902; also 25 July 1902 for report of local ILP Manifesto stating
      what had happened at the March conference.
56   Nelson Weavers' Association Executive Minutes, 31 March 1902; Minutes of
      Members' Meeting, 12 May 1902.
57   *Nelson Chronicle*, 11 July 1902 for the ballot result — the vote for financing
      a candidate was 4,563 to 826. Nelson Weavers' Association Letter Book for
      copy of letter to Ramsay MacDonald formally affiliating.
58   A. B. Newall to J. R. MacDonald, 26 June 1902, LPLF 4/37.
59   *Nelson Chronicle*, 4 July 1902.
60   Glasier Diary, 26 June 1902 and Glasier to John Penny, 26 June 1902, Glasier
      Correspondence, 1902/63.
61   LRC Executive Minutes, 3 July 1902.
62   They met under the guise of the Parliamentary Committee of the NAC. See
      its report in the NAC Minutes, 28 and 29 July 1902.
63   *Nelson Chronicle*, 11 July 1902; *Manchester Guardian*, 7 July 1902.
64   For Shackleton's politics, see the entry on him in *Dictionary of Labour
      Biography*, volume 2.
65   *Nelson Chronicle*, 11 July 1902; see also *ibid.*, 18 July 1902, for Shackleton's
      exchanges with local SDFers and *Manchester Guardian*, 10 July 1902, for
      sceptical assessment of likelihood of SDF intervention.
66   *Nelson Chronicle*, 18 July 1902.

67　*Labour Leader*, 12 July 1902.
68　*Nelson Chronicle*, 15 March 1901; also a series of articles on Local Liberal organisation in the paper during the same year.
69　For Stanhope's attitudes see the discussion in Bealey and Pelling, *Labour and Politics*, chapter 5; also the letters from Stanhope in Herbert Gladstone Papers, BL, Add MSS 46059.
70　*Manchester Guardian*, 3 July 1902.
71　*Ibid.*, 11 July 1902, for reference to a letter received by Shackleton from Jacoby, the Radical Member for Mid Derbyshire promising support from Dilke and other Radicals.
72　*Ibid.*, 15 July 1902.
73　Glasier to Hardie, 13 July 1902, Glasier Correspondence, 1902/35.
74　Ditto, 15 July 1902, *loc. cit.*, 1902/36.
75　Ditto, 17 July 1902, *loc. cit.*, 1902/37.
76　*Ibid.* and Glasier Diaries, 17 July 1902.
77　*Manchester Guardian*, 18 July 1902.
78　*Ibid.*, 19 July 1902; same source for copy of his election address.
79　For accounts of the growth of Nelson ILP, see *Labour Leader*, 24 January 1903, 24 October 1912, 12 March and 28 May 1914.
80　Phillip Stanhope to Herbert Gladstone, no date, Herbert Gladstone Papers, BL Add MSS 46059, f 249.
81　For earlier Weavers' decisions, see Weavers Amalgamation General Council Minutes, 21 June and 9 August 1902; and for the result see *Cotton Factory Times*, 6 February 1903.
82　A. B. Newall to J. R. MacDonald, 5 December 1902, LPLF 6/108.
83　*Cotton Factory Times*, 6 February 1903; *Labour Leader*, 7 February 1903; *Manchester Guardian*, 2 February 1903.
84　Newall to MacDonald, 2 February 1903, LPLF 6/109.
85　On the politics of these two cases, see Hill, *Thesis*, pp. 357—61; for the two comments by Gill, see *Bolton Chronicle*, 16 December 1905 and 6 January 1906.

Chapter 4: Railways

1　For a discussion of the situation as it affected one, perhaps not wholly typical, company, see R. J. Irving, *The North Eastern Railway Company 1870—1914* (Leicester University Press, Leicester, 1976). For railwaymen's interest in state involvement in railway affairs see Clegg, Fox and Thompson, *A History of British Trade Unionism*, pp. 229—39; P. Bagwell, *The Railwaymen* (Allen and Unwin, London, 1963), and P. S. Gupta, 'History of the Amalgamated Society of Railway Servants 1871—1913'. Unpublished D.Phil. thesis, University of Oxford, 1960, hereafter referred to as Gupta, *Thesis*.
2　For fascinating evocations of railway life, see Frank McKenna, 'Victorian railwaymen', *History Workshop* (1) 1976, and his *The Railway Workers, 1840—1970* (Faber, London, 1980).
3　See *Royal Commission on Labour Minutes of Evidence*, Group B, vol. III, para 25, 949.
4　For evidence, see *ibid.*, paras. 24, 327—34, 352 (evidence of Joseph Clifton ex-LNWR employee); also for the London and North Western Railway's purge of 1896, see Bagwell, *The Railwaymen*, pp. 177—80.
5　Comparative membership figures for 1889 and 1895 are ASRS 20,000—38,000, ASLEF 3,000—8,000 and GRWU 14,000—4,000.
6　There is a discussion of this in McKenna, 'Victorian railwayman'. See also for illuminating insights, Raymond Williams, 'The social significance of 1926' in

Llafur 1977, pp. 5—8 and also his recollections of his father in *Politics and Letters* (New Left Books, London, 1979).

7 See Irving, *The North Eastern Railway*, chapter 9, for modernisation on the North Eastern.

8 For a detailed discussion of labour relations on the NER see Irving, chapter 3. Discussions from the ASRS viewpoint can be found in the major works by Bagwell and Gupta. See also the latter's 'Railway trade unionism in Britain *c.* 1880—1900', *Economic History Review*, 1966, pp. 124—53. Note the table on p. 137 showing the distribution of ASRS membership 1887—1903. Hudson is examined in an entry by Bagwell in the *Dictionary of Labour Biography*, volume 2, pp. 197—200.

9 Bagwell, *The Railwaymen*, pp. 129—76.

10 The development and fate of the first All Grades' Campaign is discussed by both Gupta and Bagwell. Note also the analysis in Gupta's 1966 article at pp. 143—9.

11 See Gupta, *Thesis*, pp. 325—30 for developments down to 1892. Harford's career is examined in the *Dictionary of Labour Biography*, volume 5, pp. 104—7.

12 Gupta, *Thesis*, pp. 332—3 examines the Northampton situation made more complex by the Bradlaugh tradition.

13 ASRS Executive Minutes, June 1894. The resolution was moved and seconded by London Area delegates — this being a stronghold of Liberalism within the Society.

14 The critical resolutions are discussed in Gupta, *Thesis*, p. 334 and by Bagwell, *The Railwaymen*, pp. 201—2. See also the resolutions laid out in the Supplementary Agenda for the AGM, October 1894.

15 For a note on Peacock, recently elected to the ASRS Executive, see Gupta, *Thesis*, p. 357.

16 *Ibid.*, p. 335. The appropriate issue of the *Railway Review* is missing from the Unity House file. This account is based on Gupta's analysis at p. 335 and Bagwell's at p. 202.

17 *Labour Leader*, 13 October 1894.

18 See his Report to the October 1895 AGM, p. 8.

19 For a note on the debate see *Railway Review* (*RR*), 11 October 1895.

20 For an account of ASRS structure see Sidney and Beatrice Webb, *Industrial Democracy*, p. 46, fn. 2.

21 For this classification see the reference in Bagwell, p. 203. This in turn is based on Gupta's researches — see his thesis, pp. 340—41 and his list of Independent Labour Executive members and other activists, pp. 353—8. This latter is most useful, although it is not clear how many of those listed were card-carrying ILPers as opposed to being broadly sympathetic to political independence. Moreover the Executive supporters of political independence did not always act in unison. Both Turton and Kirkby were prepared to condemn Steels's Doncaster branch for developing strike organisation in December 1897, rather than seeking a peaceful settlement. See Executive Committee Minutes, December 1897.

22 For the voting figure, see ASRS Executive Minutes 1896, Results of executive elections for 1897. The previous year, Miller had been returned with 837 votes against three opponents. Total poll 1,379.

23 For an account see Gupta, *Thesis*, pp. 339—41. Text of the 1895 resolution is in *RR*, 4 October 1895 and in the Supplementary Agenda for the October 1895 AGM.

24 ASRS Executive Minutes, June 1897. The resolution was proposed by Steels and seconded by Bancroft. For the AGM discussion see *RR* 15 October 1897.

25   *Ibid.* (the speaker was Kelly, a Liverpool delegate).

26   For background, see Bagwell, *The Railwaymen*, pp. 181—4, and Irving, *The North Eastern Railway*, pp. 61—3.

27   For Bell's election see Bagwell, *The Railwaymen*, p. 192. There is an account of Bell's career by David Martin in *Dictionary of Labour Biography*, vol. 2, pp. 34—9.

28   *Labour Leader*, 14 August 1897. The same issue contains the text of a manifesto — 'Why the ILP does not support Mr. Fred Maddison'.

29   ASRS Executive Committee Minutes, June 1897 — originally Bancroft and Turton had attempted, without support, to express disapproval of Maddison for refusing 'to print resolutions coming from branches in support of Trade Union candidates for parliament'. The case presumably referred to was Tom Mann's ILP candidature at Halifax in March 1897.

30   *RR*, 8 October 1897. Resolution was moved by a Miles Platting delegate — the original resolution coming from the Newton Heath No. 2 Branch. This latter branch had opposed Maddison's Brightside candidacy, *Labour Leader*, 7 August 1897.

31   *RR*, 8 October 1897. The resolution was lost by 47 to 3.

32   *Ibid.*, 3 December 1897.

33   ASRS Executive Minutes, December 1897 — Turton and Steels had failed to secure support for an amendment asking Maddison to send in his resignation.

34   For a study of Wardle, see the entry on him in *Dictionary of Labour Biography*, vol. 2, pp. 373—6. Also the biography by Horner of the Keighley ILP in *RR*, 1 April 1898.

35   Thus he allowed a loaded discussion to develop in its columns between, on the one side, the ILPer Steels and, on the other, an opponent of parliamentary representation. The Lib-Lab case was not included. See Gupta, *Thesis*, p. 348.

36   For the initial article, see *RR*, 9 September 1898.

37   *Ibid.*, 7 October 1898. The cited delegate was Hubbard of Colwick Junction.

38   Gupta, *Thesis*, pp. 343—4 and ASRS Executive Minutes, September 1898 for Hudson's involvement at Darlington.

39   See *RR*, 7 October 1898. The ambiguity over the voting arises from this report suggesting 32—31 defeat. But it must have been carried, see Official Report of AGM Decisions and Bagwell, *The Railwaymen*, p. 229, footnote 17. For discussions of this AGM, Bagwell, pp. 204—5 and Gupta, *Thesis*, pp. 344—5.

40   *RR*, 7 October 1898.

41   *Ibid.*

42   See L. Hawcroft to John Penny, 23 October 1898 (ILP Archive, 1898/115).

43   Gupta, *Thesis*, pp. 345—6. See for formal statements, General Secretary's Report, 5 December 1898.

44   ASRS Executive Minutes, December 1898, the opponents on the Executive were Tye (Peckham), Cody (Dublin), Loraine (West Hartlepool).

45   Gupta, *Thesis*, p. 347.

46   *RR*, 23 December 1898.

47   ASRS Executive Committee Minutes, March 1899. Gupta, *Thesis*, pp. 349—50. Bagwell, *The Railwaymen*, p. 206. The opponent was Loraine (West Hartlepool), the mover Benson (Leeds), the seconder Topping (Huddersfield).

48   See Bell's Report to Members, 6 March 1899, p. 10 for complete text with the request that 'the Doncaster Branch desires you to forward the following resolution to the Parliamentary Committee to be placed on the agenda of the next Trades Union Congress'.

49   See Gupta, *Thesis*, pp. 348—9 for developments in the railway world generating scepticism about the Liberals. The debate on the ASRS resolution at the 1899

TUC can be traced in TUC Report 1899, pp. 64—6; also *RR*, 15 September 1899 and 20 October 1899; *Labour Leader*, 16 September 1899. For election of ASRS TUC delegation see General Secretary's Report, 12 June 1899.

50   Gupta, *Thesis*, p. 348.

51   Tom Taylor to John Penny, 25 August 1899, ILP Archive, 1899/89.

52   For debate see *RR*, 6 October 1899. Debate was on an overtly Liberal proposal rather than on a more subtle resolution from New Cross that the AGM should give an opinion on the 'independence' resolution of the previous year's AGM. See Gupta, *Thesis*, p. 350.

53   *RR*, 15 September 1899.

54   LRC Report, 1900 and *RR*, 9 March 1900. Bell was not at the Conference — Wardle and Benson were the leading figures. Gupta, *Thesis*, p. 352.

55   For decision to affiliate, see ASRS Executive Committee Minutes, March 1900.

56   For Bell's victory as depicted by the ASRS see *RR*, 28 September, 5 and 12 October 1900. The last of these emphasised Bell was 'pledged to an independent action on Labour matters' but also 'received and reciprocated the co-operation of all the progressive elements in the town and also that of the Liberal Party'.

57   ASRS Executive Committee Minutes, March 1900, for a parallel sentiment *RR*, 9 March 1900.

58   For discussions of Taff Vale, see Bagwell, *The Railwaymen*, and Bealey and Pelling, *Labour and Politics*, chapter 3.

59   For an analysis of these aspects, see Gupta, *Railway Trade Unionism in Britain*, pp. 149—51.

60   Keir Hardie to Richard Bell, 16 March 1903 (copy), ILP Archive, 1903/38. For earlier background see Hardie to Bell, 9 March 1903 and Bell's replies 9 and 11 March, ILP Archive, 1903/30/31/33.

61   See General Secretary's Report and Minutes of ASRS Executive Committee. March 1903 and the critical resolutions from Bradford and Laisterdyke contained therein. The expression of regret was moved on the Executive by Palin of the Bradford ILP.

62   ASRS Executive Committee Minutes, March 1903. For general account of 1903 developments, see Gupta, *Thesis*, pp. 424—6.

63   *Ibid.*, p. 424.

64   See, for example, the resolution from the Staveley Branch regretting, 'the one-sided decisions of the Newcastle Conference of the Labour Representation Committee considering the 800,000 Trade Unionists represented thereon are men of various political views'. See R. Bell, 'My political action', in ASRS Executive Committee Minutes, March 1903.

65   Gupta, *Thesis*, p. 426.

66   For ILP response see the piece by Glasier in *Labour Leader*, 23 January 1904. Also Glasier to Hardie, 15 January 1904 — contrasting Bell's behaviour with Henderson, Glasier Correspondence 1904/33. For Curran, see P. Curran to MacDonald, 21 January 1904, LPLF, 12/72.

67   For lists of branch resolutions, see ASRS Executive Committee Minutes, March 1904.

68   *Ibid.*, pp. 85—147 for verbatim report.

69   *Ibid.*, pp. 136—7.

70   *Ibid.*, p. 139.

71   Richard Bell to MacDonald, 13 April 1904, LPLF 13/10.

72   *Ibid.*, for resolution to postpone decision to 1904 AGM.

73   Decisions of 1904 AGM for text; Gupta *Thesis*, p. 428 for general description of 1904, AGM.

74   *Ibid.*
75   See Joseph Cross to Ramsay MacDonald, 10 October 1905. LPLF, 28/73. MacDonald to W. Hudson, 13 October 1905, *loc. cit.* 26/226; and including quotation, Hudson to MacDonald, 14 October 1905, *loc. cit.*, 26/227.
76   *Ibid.*, p. 430. See also *Labour Leader*, 7 October 1906.
77   For this instance, see the reference to Howell the signalman in Glasier Diary, 5 August 1901.
78   *Blackburn Labour Journal*, July 1899 for a reference to Fred Sheppard ILP Secretary and ASRS delegate to the Trades Council; *Bolton Evening News*, 12 July 1895 for claim on LNWR's employees' ILP sympathies by John Johnson of the ASRS.
79   A leading figure in the Stockport LRC and on the Trades and Labour Council was A. E. Bellamy, later the Railwaymen's national President. For material on Wardle's selection see *Cheshire County News*, 22 and 29 May 1903.
80   For Crewe see *Labour Leader*, 3 November 1894 and for Derby *ibid.*, 13 and 27 October 1894, 11 June 1898.

Chapter 5: Two craft unions

The Amalgamated Society of Engineers
1   For general discussions of the ASE see James B. Jeffreys, *The Story of the Engineers 1800—1945* (Lawrence and Wishart, London, 1945): the appropriate sections of Clegg, Fox and Thompson, *History of British Trade Unions* and B. C. M. Weekes, 'The Amalgamated Society of Engineers 1880—1914: a study of trade union government, politics and industrial politics', unpublished Ph.D. Thesis, University of Warwick, 1976 — hereafter referred to as Weekes, *Thesis*.
2   For his career, see the entry in J. Bellamy, and J. Saville, *Dictionary of Labour Biography*, volume 4; also his autobiography *From Workshop to War Cabinet* (Herbert Jenkins, London, 1923).
3   On technical change see Jeffreys, *The Story of the Engineers*, pp. 117—33 and also the summary in Clegg, Fox and Thompson, *A History of British Trade Unions*, pp. 139—9.
4   For such responses, see *ibid.*, pp. 139—41.
5   For Burns, see W. Kent, *John Burns, Labour's Lost Leader* (William and Norgate, London, 1950), and Kenneth D. Brown, *John Burns* (Royal Historical Society, London, 1977).
6   For Tom Mann in the eighties, see Dona Torr, *Tom Mann and His Times*, volume 1, 1856—1890 (Lawrence and Wishart, London, 1956). The quotation is at pp. 206—7 — the original source being Tom Mann's *Memoirs* (Labour Publishing Co., London, 1923), pp. 43—4.
7   Proctor's career is summarised in Weekes, *Thesis*, p. 282.
8   See Torr, *Tom Mann*, pp. 251—8; and P. A. Harris, *Thesis*.
9   S. and B. Webb, *Industrial Democracy*, p. 48.
10   For outlines of the contest, see Jeffreys, *The Story of the Engineers*, p. 112, and Clegg, Fox and Thompson, *A History of British Trade Unions*, p. 142.
11   *Workman's Times*, 4 June 1892.
12   See the breakdown of voting by branches contained in ASE Monthly Report, May 1892.
13   Discussed generally in Jeffreys, *The Story of the Engineers*, pp. 136—9. See also the Webb's summary in *Industrial Democracy*, pp. 49—50. For detail, see Minutes of the Seventh Delegate Meeting of the ASE, 1892.
14   Cited in Clegg, Fox and Thompson, *A History of British Trade Unionism*, source given as *Workman's Times*, 20 August 1892.

15 For this decision, see Minutes of the Seventh Delegate Meeting, p. 89.
16 See Jeffreys, *The Story of the Engineers*, pp. 140—41.
17 Minutes of the Eighth Delegate Meeting, 1896, pp. 48—50 for debate and decision.
18 For general summary, see Jeffreys, *The Story of the Engineers,* pp. 137—8.
19 ASE Monthly Report (MR), June 1893, pp. 54—5.
20 MR, July 1893, pp. 50—51; see also MR August 1893, p. 50.
21 MR, October 1893, p. 49 for announcement of this Executive decision.
22 MR, November 1893, cited Jeffreys, *The Story of the Engineers,* p. 138.
23 ASE Quarterly Report, December 1894. Anderson on 'Using the Society's name for political purposes'; see also the clarifications in response to a request by the Burton-on-Trent Branch of the ASE, regarding involvement in an unemployed demonstration initiated by the local ILP, Quarterly Report, March 1895, p. 28.
24 See Weekes, *Thesis*, pp. 44—5. The reference to Barnes is in the context of a request by Gorton ILP that Barnes be their candidate — but Weekes suggests wrongly that a by-election occurred there in July 1894.
25 For this candidature, see the files of *Rochdale Observer* and *Rochdale Times* both for July 1895.
26 References to this campaign are in *Colne Valley Guardian* and *Huddersfield Examiner,* July 1895.
27 For this clash see Weekes, *Thesis*, pp. 50—55. Both speeches were in Sunderland. The original source for Burns is given as *Sunderland Echo*, 13 March 1895.
28 From Barnes's Election address contained in volume of ASE Reports 1895.
29 MR, May 1895.
30 See Jeffreys, *The Story of the Engineers*, p. 141. MR, August 1896, pp. 17—19 refers to 'dereliction of duty of so serious a character that left the Council no alternative' and claims discrepancies in the accounts. See also Executive Council defence of the position, MR, September 1896, p. 19.
31 See the Election Addresses of the candidates bound in ASE Reports 1896, the cited emphasis comes from a group of Sheffield supporters and is characteristic of many more.
32 James Firth to MacDonald, 26 August 1903, LPLF 10/349.
33 See in the ASE Reports a testimonial from the author of the *History of Trade Unionism*. Webb drew a parallel between Barnes, young, enthusiastic, competent, and William Allan , the Society's Lib-Lab founder.
34 For a lucid discussion of the problems facing exponents of any distinctive political line, see Weekes, *Thesis*, pp. 275—6.
35 For an analysis of the lockout see Jeffreys, *The Story of the Engineers*, pp. 143—9; Clegg, Fox and Thompson, *A History of British Trade Unions*, pp. 161—8; R. O. Clarke, 'The dispute in the British engineering industry 1897—8: an evaluation', *Economica*, May 1957, pp. 127—37. For contemporary discussion, the second one very anti-ASE see Ernest Aves, 'The dispute in the engineering trades', *Economic Journal*, March 1898, pp. 116—24; and F. W. Hirst, 'The policy of the engineers', *ibid.*, pp. 124—7.
36 *ASE Journal*, August 1897, p. 49.
37 *Ibid.*, November 1897, p. 49.
38 Clarke, 'The dispute in the British engineering industry', p. 135.
39 Brown, *John Burns*, p. 88.
40 Jeffreys, *The Story of the Engineers, p. 147.*
41 *Ibid.*, pp. 147—8.
42 Cited Clegg, Fox and Thompson, *A History of British Trade Unions,* p. 164.

43   *The Times*, 13 August 1897, cited Clarke, 'The dispute in the British engineering industry', p. 134.
44   Claims in Hirst, 'The policy of the engineers', pp. 124—6.
45   For example, report of meeting organised by South West Manchester ILP, *Labour Leader*, 24 July 1897; letter of support from Paul Campbell, Secretary of London and Home Counties Federation of the ILP to Barnes, printed in *ASE Journal*, September 1897, p. 55. See also the NAC Circular of 20 July 1897 in *Labour Leader*, 24 July 1897.
46   For example, the case of Leicester Trades Council reported in *Labour Leader*, 18 November 1897.
47   *Ibid.*, 4 December 1897.
48   For York, where the ILP finished by backing the Conservative Lord Charles Beresford, see *Labour Leader* throughout January 1898.
49   *Ibid.*, 11 September 1898.
50   See, for example, the reports of the delegates to the 1896 TUC, MR, December 1896, where one claimed the ASE vote had been a 'steady, progressive' one.
51   See letter from Proctor in *ASE Journal*, December 1897, pp. 11—12. Note also the letter in the *Journal*, December 1898 from a Plaistow member on the successful consequences of Trade Union—ILP—SDF collaboration in West Ham municipal politics.
52   Weekes, *Thesis*, p. 278.
53   Brown, *John Burns*, p. 89. Burnes's attitude is typified at p. 11 of the Foundation Conference Report.
54   Barnes to MacDonald, 7 November 1900, LPLF 1/32.
55   See Bealey and Pelling, p. 88.
56   Weekes, *Thesis*, p. 280, for this move to affiliation. Also Barnes to MacDonald, 5 March 1902, LPLF, 3/132.
57   Executive Council Minutes, 9 February 1900, cited in Weekes *Thesis*, p. 280. These Minutes are not normally open to researchers, all citations are from Weekes's work.
58   H. Holyland, to MacDonald, 15 February 1906, LPLF, 31/147.
59   See, for example, material in LPLF, Box 11, 158—163.
60   On these developments see Weekes, *Thesis*, pp. 285—6 — a crucial phase in the North-Eastern constituencies being the decisions of the Executive in April 1903. See also Weekes's use, p. 287, of minutes of Meeting of Adopted Candidates with an EC Sub-Committee, 24 September 1903, at which question of political independence was discussed. Weekes also notes, p. 290, that Mitchell late in 1903 addressed Darlington Liberals against EC advice (EC Minutes, 9 October 1903). For a discussion of Barnes's attempts to reach an arrangement with local Liberals, see Weekes's *Thesis*, pp. 291—6.
61   *Ibid.*, p. 291.
62   Burns's Diary 27 January 1904, cited in Brown, *John Burns*, p. 99.
63   For these cases, see Weekes's *Thesis*, p. 284, for Glasgow, pp. 286—7 for Barrow.

The National Union of Boot and Shoe Operatives — a socialist union?

64   Alderman Lennard of Leicester in *Leicester Post*, 30 March 1895.
65   J. Griffin Ward, *ibid.*
66   NUBSO Report of Biennial Conference, 1894 (RBC), p. 16.
67   RBC, 1904, p. 39.
68   See the speeches of James Gribble, LPCR, 1907, p. 52 and 1908, pp. 58—9.
69   For Leicester see Chapter 10 of this work: for Norwich Alan Fox, *A History of the National Union of Boot and Shoe Operatives 1874—1957* (Blackwell,

Oxford, 1958), p. 327; for Northampton and Gribble, *ibid.*, pp. 286—7. He stood there as SDF candidate in 1906 and in January 1910; for Frank Sheppard of Bristol see Alan Bullock, *The Life and Times of Ernest Bevin*, volume 1 (Heinemann, London, 1960), pp. 14—15 and 57, and the entry on him in *Dictionary of Labour Biography*, volume 3.

70   For Richards, see the entry in *Dictionary of Labour Biography*, volume 3 and also the discussion in Fox, *Boot and Shoe Operatives*, pp. 333—9.

71   By far the best source is the official history by Fox, although this has a significant bias against left-wing critics.

72   Cited in *ibid.*, p. 131. Fox discusses the impact of technical changes, especially in chapters 14—25.

73   For Inskip's political and social views, see *ibid.*, pp. 120—22.

74   For union structure see Sidney and Beatrice Webb, *Industrial Democracy*, p. 47.

75   On centre-branch tensions see Fox, *Boot and shoe Operatives*, pp. 46—7; on early collective bargaining developments, *ibid.*, chapter 7 and subsequently chapter 16.

76   For a discussion, see *ibid.*, chapter 18.

77   S. and B. Webb, *Industrial Democracy*, p. 186.

78   *Ibid.*, pp. 187—92 for the problems.

79   Report of Special Delegate Meeting, April 1893, p. 40.

80   *Ibid.*, p. 41.

81   *Ibid.*, p. 44 (Stanton of Northampton).

82   *Ibid.*, (Bland of Northampton) arguing that *both* arbitration and strikes had failed.

83   *Ibid.*, p. 46 (Crew of Leeds).

84   *Ibid.*, p. 43 (Bland); also the comments of Richards at pp. 31 and 55—6. Ten delegates opposed a vote of thanks to the employers for their remarks.

85   *Ibid.*, p. 53.

86   On these issues, see Fox, *Boot and Shoe Operatives*, chapter 21.

87   For positions on the hand-team system see *ibid.*, pp. 204—6; on restriction of output pp. 206—9.

88   For discussions of this response to the machine question see *ibid.*, pp. 212—14, and S. and B. Webb, *Industrial Democracy*, pp. 400—404.

89   *Ibid.*, p. 397.

90   For an early occasion on which this issue arose see Fox *ibid.*, p. 18, and for a later comment on East End Jews see Monthly Report (MR) January 1901, p. 3 — 'their slave-masters are co-religionists and ... the main ambition in life of the slave is to become slave owner'.

91   MR, February 1891, p. 3; for a general discussion of parliamentary representation see Fox, *Boot and Shoe Operatives,* chapter 20.

92   MR, April 1891, p. 26 — from Edward Bush, President of Leicester No. 2 Branch.

93   *Ibid.*, May 1891, p. 6, A. R. Burns of Leicester No. 2.

94   For debate see RBC, 1892, pp. 11—17.

95   *Ibid.*, p. 12.

96   *Ibid.*, p. 14. For Inskip's Leicester activities see D. Cox, 'The rise of the Labour Party in Leicester', unpublished M. A. thesis, University of Leicester, 1959.

97   RBC, 1892, p. 15 — Judge of Leeds, insisting on need for political independence.

98   Hornidge at p. 16.

99   For vote, p. 17; for formulation of resolution with vital independence commitment, see p. 15.

100   MR, February 1893, pp. 24—7. 'A Labour candidate for Northampton: selection of Mr. William Inskip J. P.'.
101   *Ibid.*, p. 26.
102   *Ibid.*, p. 27.
103   For developments over the next twelve months see MR February 1894, pp. 6—7, 'Ald Inskip and the Representation of Northampton'. At this meeting organised by the two local union branches, a proposal was made that Inskip should not be supported, but any candidate should be who was pledged to the collective ownership of the means of production. This was lost.
104   RBC 1894, pp. 16—17 — it was seconded by Charles Freak.
105   *Ibid.*, p. 17. Stanton, a Northampton Liberal, 'saw no harm' in passing the resolution.
106   For the debate, *ibid.*, pp. 34—46.
107   For Inskip's position, *ibid.*, pp. 36—7.
108   *Ibid.*, p. 39 for the Leicester Lib-Lab Woolley; p. 40 for Sheppard.
109   *Ibid.*, p. 42.
110   *Ibid.*, p. 43.
111   *Ibid.*, p. 45.
112   For Freak's political position see RBC p. 41. 'Socialism and Radicalism had permeated to a large degree the Liberal party of the country.' Poulton had backed Inskip at his February 1894 meeting in Northampton; for a general assessment of Poulton, see Fox, *Boot and Shoe Operatives*, pp. 331—3. The membership of the committee is given in RBC, 1894, p. 46. There was a fifth member, Bradley.
113   *Ibid.*, p. 98.
114   *Ibid.*, p. 99.
115   Stanton, *ibid.*, pp. 98—9 and Poulton p. 99.
116   *Ibid.*
117   MR, May 1894, for details of Inskip's withdrawal and his own justification of the step.
118   MR, March 1894; for allegations of canvassing and lack of representativeness see Woolley's speech in RBC, 1894, p. 56.
119   For details of voting on second ballot, see MR, August 1893; for first ballot in which Hornidge had polled, 1,078 and Votier 605, see MR, July 1893.
120   RBC, 1894, p. 37 (Steeles of Rushden).
121   For a discussion, see Fox, *Boot and Shoe Operatives*, chapter 22.
122   Letter from Ward on behalf of the Employers' Federation in MR, November 1894.
123   For a discussion of the 'Seven Commandments' see Fox, *Boot and Shoe Operatives*, pp. 220—27.
124   For votes, see MR, March 1895.
125   Both claims, by Lilley of London and Ward of Leicester respectively, appeared in *Shoe and Leather Record*, 5 April 1895 and are cited in Fox, *Boot and Shoe Operatives*, p. 228.
126   'The Boot War', *Labour Leader*, 6 April 1895.
127   'The Boot War' (2), *ibid.*, 13 April 1895.
128   *Ibid.*, 6 April 1895.
129   The terms of the settlement are analysed by Fox, *Boot and Shoe Operatives*, pp. 231—7.
130   See MR, May 1895, a reprint of an extract from *Leicester Daily Post* of 23 April. Richards was attacked by Stanton and Woolley.
131   For an analysis of factors promoting decline see Fox, *Boot and Shoe Operatives,* chapters 23—25; on Norwich see *ibid.*, p. 244 and MR, February 1897 and subsequent reports.

132 For a breakdown of the voting see MR, August 1899, p. 8; for the first ballot with Hornidge 2,922, Richards 2,397, Freak 1,652, Woolley 805 and Cort 473, see MR, July 1899.

133 RBC, 1896, pp. 23—6.

134 *Ibid.*, p. 24 (Votier).

135 *Ibid.*

136 For impact of financial constraint see RBC, 1898, p. 28.

137 The final totals of votes are in MR, December 1898, along with list of dis-qualified branches; for original figures on 1st ballot, *ibid.*, June 1898; and on second ballot Richards 833, Stanton 817, *ibid.*, August 1898. The first list of disqualified branches is in MR, September 1898. This resulted in a win for Stanton by 817 to 684.

138 TUC Report, 1899, p. 66. T. O'Grady of the London Metro Branch. See also the report of the TUC delegates of the union in MR, September 1899.

139 MR, March 1900, report by Freak and Richards.

140 RBC, 1900, pp. 47—8. His speech emphasised independence.

141 *Ibid.*, pp. 48—9.

142 *Ibid.*, p. 49 — McCarthy of Leicester.

143 *Ibid.*, p. 50.

144 Both votes are in MR, July 1900, pp. 14 and 12 respectively.

145 RBC, 1902, p. 39.

146 See Stanton at RBC, p. 39 for a Liberal viewpoint, and Freak's contribution on p. 40. The alternative object, passed by 29 to 8 is also on p. 40.

147 *Ibid.*, p. 42, moved by Parker (Leicester), seconded by Bannister (Leeds).

148 For a pro-Broadhurst anti-MacDonald contribution see that of W. H. Lowe, *ibid.*, pp. 42—3; for the dilemmas of a Leicester 'Progressive', Hornidge at p. 43.

149 *Ibid.*

150 *Ibid.*, p. 44, Hammond of Stafford.

151 *Ibid.*, Robinson of Kettering.

152 Richards at p. 45, claiming that he too had always backed Broadhurst.

153 This recommendatory resolution had also come from Leicester, covering members as well as officials. There were protests from some Leicester delegates at the ruling of the Standing Orders Committee that they be taken as alternatives; *ibid.*, p. 43.

154 RBC, 1904, p. 39.

155 Executive Council Minutes, 23 and 24 September 1900; MR, September 1900.

156 MR, February 1903.

157 *Ibid.*, July 1903.

158 For Free Trade, MR, January 1905; anti-Government stance, MR, March 1905. By then he had found the Liberals 'very friendly indeed', MR, October 1904.

159 Text of resolution in W. Hornidge to MacDonald, 27 October 1903, LPLF 11/528.

160 J. K. Hardie to T. F. Richards, 15 December 1905, ILP Archive, 1905/206. For earlier communications see Hardie to Richards, 5 December 1905 and Richards to Hardie, 9 December, ILP Archive, 1905/178 and 196.

161 Richards to MacDonald, 24 December 1905, LPLF, 31/323. See also the earlier exchanges LPLF 28/28—31.

162 The vote for Gribble had been 930 — the other two successful candidates were Richards (1,022) and Freak (901), MR November 1906. He had been elected to the Executive Council in July 1906.

163 MR, February 1907, p. 99.

164 For the case of East Northamptonshire, see F. A. Channing, *Memories of*

Midland Politics (Constable, London, 1918), Pelling, *Social Geography of British Elections*, p. 114, and Janet Howarth, 'The Liberal revival in Northamptonshire, 1880—1895', *Historical Journal*, 1969, pp. 78—118.

165   On this episode, see Fox, *Boot and Shoe Operatives*, pp. 466—70 and R. Martin, *Communism and the British Trade Unions 1924—33*, (Clarendon Press, Oxford, 1969), pp. 94—5.

Chapter 6: New Unionism

1   For details of membership figures see Clegg, Fox and Thompson, *A History of British Trade Unions*, p. 83; for a more general discussion see chapter 2 of the same work. Also, Eric Hobsbawm, 'General labour unions in Britain 1889—1914', *Economic History Review*, 2nd series 1 (1949), pp. 123—42; J. Saville, 'Trade unions and Free Labour: the background to the Taff Vale decision', in Briggs and Saville (eds.), *Essays in Labour History* (Macmillan, London, 1960); A. E. Duffy, 'New Unionism in Britain, 1889—1890: a re-appraisal', *Economic History Review*, 2nd series 14 (1961), pp. 306—19; Eric Taplin, 'The origins and development of New Unionism 1870—1910' (unpublished M.A. Thesis, University of Liverpool, 1967).

2   The Engels quotations are from his January 1892 Preface to the English Edition of *The Condition of the Working Class in England*, at pp. 34—5 in the edition introduced by Hobsbawm (Panther, St Albans, 1973).

3   Leonard Hall, *The Old and New Unionism* (1894), p. 5.

4   Figures in Clegg, Fox and Thompson, *A History of British Trade Unions*, p. 83.

5   W. Collison, *The Apostle of Free Labour* (Hurst and Blackett, London, 1913), p. 256.

6   Estimate in J. Sexton, *Sir James Sexton: Agitator* (Faber & Faber, London, 1936).

7   See Saville, 'Trade unions and Free Labour'.

8   For a discussion of leadership see Clegg, Fox and Thompson, *A History of British Trade Unions*, p. 89.

9   See Hobsbawm, 'General labour unions', for an examination of specific categories of membership.

10   See De Mattos in *Labour Elector*, 23 November 1889 — the socialists were De Mattos and Champion.

11   On the expansion of fringe benefits, see Clegg, Fox and Thompson, *A History of British Trade Unions*, p. 94; for an argument on this as crucial to trade union survival, see Mancur Olson, *The Logic of Collective Action*, (Schocken, New York, 1971).

12   See Saville, 'Trade unions and Free Labour', pp. 317—22, for the growth of opposition.

13   E. P. Thompson, 'Homage to Tom Maguire', in Brigg and Saville (eds.), *Essays in Labour History*, pp. 299—301 for a description of this episode.

14   For Dipper, see *Labour Leader*, 20 April 1895.

15   E. P. Thompson, 'Homage to Tom Maguire', pp. 295—9.

16   J. Hill, *Thesis*, pp. 89—90.

17   *TUC Report*, 1891, p. 77.

18   On Thorne, see his *My Life's Battles* (Newnes, London, 1925); G. and L. Radice, *Will Thorne: Constructive Militant* (Allen & Unwin, London, 1974).

19   Gasworkers' and General Labourers' Yearly Report, 1890—91, pp. 12—13 for links between Thorne, Engels, Bebel and Liebknecht.

20   Gasworkers' Yearly Report, 1891—2.

21   *Ibid.*, 1893.

22   On the Gasworkers in London politics, see Paul Thompson, *Socialists, Liberals and Labour: The Struggle for London 1885—1914* (Routledge and Kegan Paul, London, 1967), p. 47 and pp. 101—3.
23   Gasworker's Yearly Report, 1894—5.
24   *Ibid.*, 1896—7, cited Paul Thompson, *Socialists, Liberals and Labour*, p. 47.
25   Gasworkers' Yearly Report, 1894—5.
26   Preamble to Gasworkers' Rules 1892, cited E. Hobsbawm, *Labour's Turning Point 1880—1900* (Lawrence and Wishart, London, 1948).
27   NAC Minutes, 3 July and 1 October 1896. The other unions were Tillett's Dockers' and the Tailors'.
28   For the affiliation, see Bealey and Pelling, *Labour and Politics*, p. 36; for willingness to support Thorne as candidate, *ibid.*, p. 22, fn. 1. The decision was by union ballot, the majority 10, 415.
29   Thorne, *My Life's Battles*, pp. 184—5.
30   For Curran's career, see the entry in *Dictionary of Labour Biography*, vol. 4.
31   NAC Minutes, 1 and 2 July 1898.
32   See Chapter 2 for details.
33   LRC Report, 1903, for details.
34   See Hill, *Thesis*, pp. 273—80 for illustrations.
35   F. Potter to Hardie, 6 November 1905, ILP Archive 1905/139; and for Clynes reply to Hardie, 17 November 1905, *loc. cit.*, 1905/154.
36   See Chapter 11 for details.
37   For McCarthy, see *Labour Leader*, 18 May 1895; for Kay, see Paul Thompson, *Socialists, Liberals and Labour*, p. 53.
38   Dock, Wharf, Riverside and General Labourers' Union Report of Conference, 22 September 1891, pp. 25—6.
39   *Ibid.*, September 1893, p. 16.
40   *Ibid.*, September 1894, p. 17.
41   Preface to Ben Tillett, *Memories and Reflections* (Long, London, 1931), p. 9; see also Chapter 8 for a discussion of Tillett's Bradford campaigns.
42   Ben Tillett to John Burns, 6 September 1893. *John Burns Papers*, BL, Add MSS 46285 f 150.
43   Collison, *Apostle of Free Labour*, p. 251.
44   See Chapter 12.
45   *TUC Report 1895*, p. 36. Tillett lost his seat on the Parliamentary Committee at that Congress, *ibid.*, p. 55.
46   See the entry on Tillett in *Dictionary of Labour Biography*, volume 4.
47   For accounts of the Hull strike of 1893, see Clem Edwards, 'The Hull shipping dispute', *Economic Journal*, 1893, pp. 345—51; Saville, 'Trade unions and Free Labour', pp. 328—30; also the columns of the *Hull Daily News*, April and May 1893; more generally Raymond Brown, *Waterfront Organisation in Hull, 1870—1900* (Occasional Papers in Economic and Social History, No. 5, Univeristy of Hull, 1972).
48   Brown, *Waterfront Organisation in Hull*, p. 45.
49   *Ibid.*, p. 59.
50   *Ibid.*, p. 61.
51   Cited Edwards, 'The Hull shipping dispute', p. 349.
52   For figures, see Saville, 'Trade unions and Free Labour', p. 330.
53   Brown, *Waterfront Organisation in Hull*, p. 72.
54   Resolutions published in *Hull Daily News*, in November and December 1893.
55   For discussion of the three Hull seats, see Henry Pelling, *Social Geography of British Elections*, pp. 294—5.
56   J. Northen to Hardie, 28 November 1893, ILP Archive 1893/148.

57   See the letter in *Colliery Workman's Times*, 30 December 1893, from C. H. Reynolds of Hull, listing the prominent Lib-Labs.
58   Brown, *Waterfront Organisation in Hull*, p. 64.
59   *Ibid.*; on Maddison's early career in Hull, see the entry in *Dictionary of Labour Biography*, volume 4.
60   Tom McCarthy to Hardie, 4 December 1893, ILP Archive, 1893/154.
61   *Hull Daily News*, 16 December 1893.
62   J. Northen to Hardie, 22 December 1893, ILP Archive, 1893/166.
63   Reynolds, as in note 57.
64   *Hull Daily News*, 18 December 1893.
65   *Ibid.*, 18 July 1895.
66   *Ibid.*, 12 July 1895.
67   *Ibid.*, 11 July 1895.
68   *Ibid.*, 13 July 1895.
69   *Ibid.*, 12 July 1895.
70   *Labour Leader*, 9 November 1895, acknowledged a poor performance in the municipal elections with only a dozen active workers.
71   For one example, see *Debate on Socialism*, by R. J. Macartney, and James Sexton, held Salford, 3 December 1894, Verbatim Report (Young England Patriotic Association, Salford, 1895).
72   *National Union of Dock Labourers' Report*, 1895, p. 15.
73   See *Sheffield Independent*, 1—5 August 1897, for claims and counter-claims about Maddison's behaviour in Hull.
74   Letter in *Labour Leader*, 14 August 1897.
75   *Ibid.*, 21 August 1897.
76   *Ibid.*, 28 August 1897.
77   NAC Minutes and Glasier Diaries, 9 October 1897.
78   LRC Report, 1901, p. 21.
79   Sexton to MacDonald, 17 June 1905, LPLF. 24/393.
80   See GRWU General Secretary's Report, June 1894.
81   See Hill, *Thesis*, p. 96.

Conclusion: Diversity, ambiguity, clarity

1   On these developments, see generally B. C. Roberts, *The Trades Union Congress 1868—1921* (Allen and Unwin, London, 1958), chapters 3 and 4; and Clegg, Fox and Thompson, *A History of British Trade Unions*, chapter 6.
2   See TUC Reports, 1887, pp. 29—32; and 1888, p. 26.
3   See Fox and Thompson, *A History and British Trade Unions*, pp. 256—7.
4   TUC Report, 1892, p. 43.
5   *Ibid.*, 1893, pp. 44—8.
6   *Ibid.*, 1894, pp. 53—5.
7   *Labour Annual*, 1895, p. 40.
8   TUC Report, 1894, p. 23.
9   *Ibid.*, 1893, p. 257. The vote was 257 for Fenwick, 89 for Hardie.
10   *Ibid.*, 1894, p. 81. Vote on first ballot Woods 140, Fenwick 117, Mann 105.
11   See TUC Parliamentary Committee Minutes, 10 October 1894, 6 February and 25 April 1895. Also the Parliamentary Committee Report in TUC Report, 1895, p. 25. The sub-committee was Holmes, Burns, Mawdsley and Woods.
12   Beatrice Webb Diaries, 9 September 1895.
13   *Labour Leader*, 29 December 1894.
14   See J. M. Craigen, 'The Scottish Trade Union Congress, 1897—1973: a study of a pressure group', unpublished M. Litt. thesis, Heriot Watt University, 1974,

esp., pp. 20—30. Also the MSS Account of the foundation Congress, NLS Acc 4682 (microfilm).

15   See Chapters 2 above and 7 below, for discussions of aspects of the Scottish ILP. The Secretary to the Scottish Parliamentary Committee suggested that some of the larger unions were unhappy about Hardie's manipulation of Congress business for socialist ends. She wrote in May 1899 of a fear that 'our Congress is being nobbled by Keir Hardie and will be run by him and wasted on the desert air', Miss Irwin to J. R. MacDonald, 4 May 1899, MacDonald Papers, 5/9. The successive Congress Reports show little evidence of such concern.

16   TUC Report, 1899, pp. 64—6.

17   On the National Democratic League, see Tom Mann, *Why I Joined the National Democratic League* (April 1901). Also the files of *The Democrat*, June— November 1902.

Part two
Constraints and hopes

1   For analyses of the restrictive nature of the franchise see N. Blewett, 'The franchise in the United Kingdom, 1885—1918', *Past and Present*, December 1965, pp. 27—56; H. C. G. Mathew, R. McKibbin and J. A. Kay, 'The franchise factor in the rise of the Labour Party', *English Historical Review*, 1976, pp. 723—52; Clarke, *Lancashire and the New Liberalism*, chapter 5.

2   See Mathew *et al.*, 'The franchise factor', also for Colne Valley, D. G. Clark, 'The origins and development of the Labour Party in Colne Valley, 1891—1907' (University of Sheffield, Ph.D. thesis, 1978), p. 45.

3   For details on local government franchises, see B. Keith-Lucas, *The English Local Government Franchise: A Short History* (Blackwell, Oxford, 1952).

4   Details of expenditure, ILPCR, 1896, pp. 14—15.

5   For some rural examples see Clarke, *Lancashire and New Liberalism*, pp. 251—2.

Part two
Chapter 7: Scotland

A Liberal inheritance

1   For Hardie, see William Stewart, *J. Keir Hardie* (ILP, London, 1921); David Lowe, *From Pit to Parliament: The Story of the Early Life of Keir Hardie* (Labour Publishing, 1923); K. O. Morgan, *Keir Hardie, Radical and Socialist*; I. McLean, *Keir Hardie*; Fred Reid, *Keir Hardie: The Making of a Socialist*.

2   See David Marquand, *Ramsay MacDonald*; L. Thompson, *The Enthusiasts*.

3   Marquand, *Ramsay MacDonald*, pp. 10—15.

4   See C. Watts and L. Davies, *Cunninghame Graham: A Critical Biography* (Cambridge University Press, Cambridge 1979).

5   See C. Desmond Greaves, *The Life and Times of James Connolly* (Lawrence and Wishart, London, 1976), chapters 3 and 4.

6   See Tom Nairn, 'Old and new Scottish Nationalism', in his *The Break-Up of Britain: Crisis and Neo-Nationalism* (New Left Books, London, 1977).

7   On Glasgow see S. G. Checkland, *The Upas Tree: Glasgow 1875—1975* (Glasgow University Press, Glasgow, 1976), chapters 1 and 2.

8   Nairn, 'Old and new Scottish Nationalism', pp. 156—63.

9   For background to Scottish politics see H. J. Hanham, *Elections and Party Management: Politics in the Age of Gladstone and Disraeli* (Longman,

London, 1959), chapter 8. Pelling, *Social Geography of British Elections*, chapter 16. There is a brief examination of labour developments in W. H. Marwick, *A Short History of Labour In Scotland* (Chambers, Edinburgh, 1967). On Scottish Liberalism see the theses by Kellas and Young cited in Chapter 2.

10   See Pelling, *Social Geography of British Elections*, pp. 373—5 for a discussion of the religious dimension of Scottish politics. Also Ian Carter, 'The changing image of the Scottish peasantry, 1780—1980' in R. Samuel, *People's History and Socialist Theory* (Routledge, London, 1981).

11   See Kellas, *Thesis*, chapter 4, especially p. 230 for the circumstances of the 1885 contest, and also D. W. Crowley, 'The Crofters' Party, 1885—92', *Scottish Historical Review*, 1956, pp. 110—26.

12   On George, see C. A. Barker, *Henry George* (Oxford University Press, New York, 1955), chapters 12 and 13, also John Saville, 'Henry George and the British labour movement', *Bulletin of the Society for the Study of Labour History*, 1962; and on the mixture of individualist and collectivist sentiments, see J. Bruce Glasier, *William Morris and the Early Days of the Socialist Movement* (Longman, London, 1921), p. 26.

13   The most successful was Shaw Maxwell with 1156 votes in Glasgow Blackfriars, see Kellas, *Thesis*, p. 221.

14   For Smillie see his *My Life for Labour*, pp. 262—4. The Hardie piece is in *Labour Leader*, 28 May 1898. For a rather different memory of Gladstone, see David Lowe, *Souvenirs of Scottish Labour* (Holmes, Glasgow, 1919), pp. 84—5.

15   Both Hanham, *Elections and Party Management* and Kellas *Thesis* are useful on the social composition and style of Scottish Liberal Associations.

16   As described in Fred Reid, *Keir Hardie: The Making of a Socialist*, p. 58.

17   For Aberdeen, see K. D. Buckley, *Trade Unionism in Aberdeen 1878—1900* (Oliver and Boyd, Edinburgh, 1955). The successful candidate was asked first by the Trades Council, then by the Radical Association and only belatedly by the Aberdeen Liberal Association. For Perth, see Kellas, *Thesis*, p. 303.

18   *Labour Leader*, January 1892.

19   *Glasgow Herald (GH)*, 20 June and 5 July 1892 — statements by the SLP candidate Bennett Burleigh, who referred also (1 July 1892) to control by 'a few Whiggish members'.

20   *Ibid.*, 5 July 1892 — letter by Peter Anderson.

21   *Ibid.*, (Bennett Burleigh).

22   See the examination of Scottish Liberal policies in Kellas, *Thesis*.

23   See Kellas, *Thesis*, chapter 3 and his 'The Liberal Party and the Scottish Church disestablishment crisis', *English Historical Review*, 1964, pp. 31—46.

24   For an account of this significant year, see D. C. Savage, 'Scottish politics 1885—6', *Scottish Historical Review*, 1961, pp. 118—35. Also John F. McCaffrey, 'The origins of Liberal Unionism in the West of Scotland', *ibid.*, 1971, pp. 47—71.

25   Kellas, *Thesis*, outlines the changes in chapter 7.

26   On Morley, see letter from James Davidson to Gladstone, 11 May 1886: on East Lothian, Haldane to his mother, 14 June 1886: both cited in Kellas, *Thesis*, p. 383.

27   Davidson to Gladstone, as above.

28   For example, A. Cameron Corbet, the Liberal Unionist MP for Tradeston; see Pelling, *Social Geography*, pp. 402—3 and *GH*, 11 July 1895 for his support for votes for women.

29   See note 19, Haldane to his mother.

30   See R. Yellowless to Campbell Bannerman, 27 April 1886, cited in Kellas, *Thesis*, p. 380.

31   Buckley, *Trade Unionism in Aberdeen*, p. 97 — a Conservative failed to find a seconder for the previous question.

32   *GH*, 9 July 1895.

33   For an example of Unionist anti-Irish propaganda in the general election of 1895, see the *Bridgeton and Calton Star* in *1895 Election Literature* (Mitchell Library Local Collection, Glasgow).

34   J. E. Denvir, *The Irish in Britain* (Kegan Paul, London, 1892), pp. 447—56; James Handley, *The Irish in Modern Scotland*; W. Walker, 'Irish immigrants in Scotland: their priests, politics and parochial life', *Historical Journal*, 1972, pp. 649—67.

35   Connolly claimed in 1889 that Dundee had more Irish relative to the population than any other town in Britain, Greaves, *James Connolly*, p. 30.

36   For the political involvement see Ian Wood, 'Irish immigrants and Scottish Radicalism, 1880—1906', in Ian MacDougall (ed.), *Essays in Scottish Labour History*.

37   For Ferguson and early growth of the organisation, see *ibid.*, pp. 69—71; for the ownership and policy of the *Glasgow Observer*, see Handley, *The Irish in Modern Scotland*, pp. 274—5; 284—5.

38   On these aspects see Wood, 'Irish immigrants and Scottish Radicalism', pp. 71—3.

39   James Connolly to Hardie, 12 April 1897, ILP Archive 1897/30.

40   For Davitt, see T. W. Moody, 'Michael Davitt and the British labour movement', *Transactions of the Royal Historical Society* (1953), pp. 57—77; and his 'Michael Davitt', in J. W. Boyle (ed.), *Leaders and Workers* (Mercier Press, Cork, 1978), pp. 47—55.

41   This was Davitt's position. See Moody, 'Michael Davitt and the British labour movement'.

42   *Glasgow Observer*, 28 September 1901.

43   *Glasier Diaries*, 8 October 1902.

44   See L. P. Curtis junior, *Anglo-Saxon and Celt: A Study of Anti-Irish Prejudice in Victorian England* (University of Bridgeport, Conn, 1968).

45   *Ardrossan and Saltcoats Herald*, 8 September 1882 cited Reid, *Keir Hardie*, p. 67.

46   *Labour Leader*, 30 August 1902. For the significance of Sloan's victory see F. S. L. Lyons, *Ireland Since the Famine* (Weidenfeld, London, 1978), pp. 295—7.

47   W. Walker to Hardie, 19 August 1902, ILP Archive 1902/93.

48   For Smillie's experience with an audience of Orange trade unionists see his *Life for Labour*, p. 111.

49   Labour Party Executive Minutes, report on Scottish Conference, 5 August 1911.

50   See the references to Scottish branches of the Socialist League in E. P. Thompson, *William Morris*. Also J. Bruce Glasier, *William Morris and the Early Days of the Socialist Movement*.

51   See the discussion of this in Fred Reid, *Keir Hardie*, pp. 94—5 with special reference to Hardie and William Small.

52   John Gilray, 'Early days of the socialist movement in Edinburgh', NLS Acc 4965. Hereafter Gilray, MS (extended version of a sketch for the 1909 ILP Conference).

53   Bob Duncan, *James Leatham 1865—1945: Portrait of a Socialist Pioneer* (People's Press, Aberdeen, 1978), chapters 1 and 2.

The Scottish Labour Party

54 A claim made by Hardie in 'The pioneers of the ILP', *Socialist Review*, April 1914, pp. 113—17. For studies of the party and of Mid Lanark, see James Kellas, 'The Mid-Lanark by-election (1888) and the Scottish Labour Party', *Parliamentary Affairs*, 1964—5, pp. 318—29. Also material in Kellas *Thesis*, chapter 5.

55 William Stewart, *J. Keir Hardie*, p. 43.

56 See Morgan, *Keir Hardie*, pp. 23—33; McLean, *Keir Hardie*, pp. 25—33.

57 See Fred Reid, 'Keir Hardie's conversion to socialism' in Briggs and Saville (eds.), *Essays in Labour History* (Macmillan, London, 1970), and also his *Keir Hardie*, chapters 4 and 5.

58 Champion to Hardie, 14 March 1888, ILP Archive, 1888/2; also his letter of 16 March *loc. cit.*, 1888/4.

59 *The Miner*, March 1888.

60 Hardie to Baillie Burt, 15 March 1888, NLS, Dep. 176—8, vol. 8.

61 For material on the Liberal selection, see *North British Daily Mail* (*NBDM*) March—April 1888.

62 *Ibid.*, 14 April 1888.

63 John Wilson to Threlfall, 6 April 1888, ILP Archive, 1888/34.

64 See, for example, *NBDM*, 14 April 1888.

65 These are noted in Conybeare to Cunninghame Graham, 20 April 1888, ILP Archive 1888/64. For offers of money see Champion to Hardie, 14 March 1888; Maltman Barry to Hardie, 21 March 1888, ILP Archive 1888/2&11. The sources of all Hardie's funds remain obscure, see Reid *Keir Hardie*, pp. 114—15.

66 C. A. V. Conybeare to Hardie, 24 April 1888, ILP, Archive 1888/74. What actually was promised and by whom remains in doubt. Conybeare referred to the promise of a conference between the Liberal Whips and the Labour Party. See also discussions in Reid, *Keir Hardie*, p. 112; McLean, *Keir Hardie*, pp. 29—30; Morgan, *Keir Hardie*, p. 30 and Hardie's recollections, *Labour Leader*, 12 March 1914.

67 *The Miners*, July 1887.

68 'The Sons of Labour' Programme of the New Labour Party, *ibid*.

69 Hardie to Baillie Burt as in note 7.

70 *The Miner*, April 1888.

71 *NBDM*, 14 April 1888.

72 Glasgow Trades Council Minute Book, 4 April 1888.

73 See ILP Archive, 1888/44&45.

74 For example, *NBDM*, 14 April 1888.

75 Text of letter in McLean, *Keir Hardie*, p. 30.

76 Hardie claimed that the miners and the Irish together accounted for 3,500 electors. Hardie to Champion, 15 March 1888, NLS, Dep. 176/8, vol. 8.

77 Hardie to Secretary of INL, Home Government Branch, 24 March 1888, NLS MS 1809.

78 See Ferguson's letters to *NBDM*, 28 March and 20 April 1888. Also *ibid.*, 16 April for speeches by Hugh Murphy and Ferguson backing Hardie.

79 Threlfall to Hardie 23 March 1888, ILP Archive 1888/16. For a sceptical assessment of the extent of local Irish support for Hardie, see Wood, 'Irish immigrants and Scottish radicalism', p. 78.

80 21st *Glasgow Observer*, April 1888.

81 T. W. Moody, 'Michael Davitt and the British labour movement'.

82 Champion to Hardie, 22 March 1888, ILP Archive 1888/12.

83 Hardie to Cunninghame Graham, 15 March 1888, NLS Dep 176/8, vol. 8.

84 Hardie statement dated 11 May 1888 in NLS MS 1809, f 73.

85 For an account see David Lowe, *Souvenirs of Scottish Labour*, pp. 1—5; also Reid, *Keir Hardie*, pp. 117—18; McLean *Keir Hardie*, pp. 33—4; Morgan, *Keir Hardie*, pp. 33—5. Also account in *The Miner*, September 1888.

86 J. Ferguson to Hardie, 17 May 1888, ILP Archive 1888/85.

87 See Lowe, *Souvenirs of Scottish Labour*, pp. 3—4.

88 *Labour Leader*, February 1893.

89 *Ibid.*

90 *Ibid.* This distinction between 'Conference' and 'Annual Business Meeting' has not always been appreciated in subsequent writings. See Lowe, *Souvenirs of Scottish Labour*, pp. 153—66 where the 1894 Conference is discussed but the status of the trade union delegates is left unclear; cf. Reid, *Keir Hardie*, p. 146 and p. 154 fn 43 where he states that Lowe was wrong to describe this as a SLP 'Conference', and refers as evidence to *Labour Leader*, January 1894 which includes the description 'a Conference of Labour organisations convened by the SLP'. This was what the SLP 'Conference' as opposed to 'Annual Business Meeting' involved.

91 *Labour Leader*, February 1891.

92 *Ibid.*, February 1893.

93 Edinburgh SLP Minutes, 29 June 1893.

94 For branch strengths see George Carson, 'The position of the movement in Glasgow and the West', *Labour Leader*, 15 March 1893; also list of SLP delegates at 1894 Conference in Lowe, *Souvenirs of Scottish Labour*, pp. 164—5.

95 See *NBDM*, 11 June 1889; also Reid, *Keir Hardie*, p. 121.

96 *NBDM*, 11 and 21 June 1889.

97 *Labour Leader*, February 1891. More generally on the stoppage see James Mavor, *The Scottish Railway Strike 1891: A History and Criticism* (William Brown, Edinburgh, 1891).

98 For a discussion of this theme see W. Hamish Fraser, 'Trades councils in the labour movement in nineteenth century Scotland', in MacDougall (ed.), *Essays in Scottish Labour History*, especially pp. 17—19.

99 See Glasgow Trades Council Minutes, 15 May (for request to receive deputation) and 6 June 1889. Also *Glasgow Trades Council Centenary Brochure 1858—1958* (Glasgow, 1958), pp. 15—16.

100 Glasgow Trades Council Minutes, 12 and 19 June 1889 for dispute on whether to take it further, and *Centenary Brochure*, pp. 15—16 for Railwaymen's opposition.

101 Fraser, 'Trades councils in the labour movement', p. 18.

102 For Dundee and Greenock, see *Labour Leader*, January 1892.

103 For an account of these developments, see Fraser, 'Trades councils in the labour movement', pp. 19—21; also Buckley, *Trade Unionism in Aberdeen*, pp. 136—9.

104 *Labour Leader*, January 1892.

105 Gilray MS.

106 At 4th SLP Conference, 3 January 1893, *Labour Leader*, February 1893.

107 *Labour Elector*, July 1888.

108 Reid, *Keir Hardie*, p. 119.

109 Thus in January 1889, the SLP supported the Liberal in the Govan by-election, *NBDM*, 16 January 1889.

110 Lowe, *Souvenirs of Scottish Labour*, p. 37. See *Dundee Courier*, 18 September 1889 for programme of 'the John Burns Committee'.

111 For discussions see Reid, *Keir Hardie*, pp. 119—20. Kellas, *Thesis*, pp. 300 ff.

112 See his statement in *NBDM*, 1 March 1890.

113   See letter from G. W. McNaught of Greenock Radical Association to Marjoribanks dated 5 February 1890 in *ibid.*
114   *NBDM*, 4 March 1890.
115   For a note on Partick, see Pelling, *Social Geography*, p. 408.
116   *Labour Elector*, 8 February 1890.
117   *NBDM*, 3 March 1890.
118   See speech by Marjoribanks in *Glasgow Herald (GH)*, 4 July 1892. Also *Labour Leader*, January 1892.
119   For his friendship with Parnell, see Watts and Davies, *Cunninghame Graham*, p. 95.
120   *GH*, 24 June 1892.
121   *Ibid.*, 8 June 1892 for Home Rule; 28 June for Republicanism.
122   *Ibid.*, 30 June 1892.
123   *Ibid.*, 4 July 1892.
124   *Ibid.*, 15 June 1892.
125   *Ibid.*, 25 June 1892. Also see *Labour Leader*, January 1892.
126   Case noted by Kellas, *Thesis*, p. 303. The dispute seems to have been very much one within Liberalism.
127   On the Dundee search for a candidate see *Labour Leader*, January 1892. On the campaign, see Lowe, *Souvenirs of Scottish Labour*, pp. 83—7.
128   See, for example, speech by the Liberal candidate, Sir John Long, *Dundee Advertiser*, 25 June 1892.
129   For the link between Radical Association and SLP, see *Labour Leader*, January 1892; *Dundee Advertiser*, 21 June 1892.
130   *Ibid.*, 2 July 1892 for Macdonald's meeting with the Trades Council. The vote for the two Liberals was 17—6.
131   See for example *ibid.*, 1 July 1892.
132   *GH*, 17 June 1892.
133   *Labour Leader*, February 1893.
134   *Ibid.*, report of discussion at SLP Conference.
135   *Ibid.*, October 1893, for relevant material.
136   For the last SLP gathering, see Lowe, *Souvernirs of Scottish Labour*, p. 170 and *Labour Leader*, 5 January 1895.
137   See J. Cronin to Hardie, 21 November 1893, ILP Archive 1893/139, and Hardie to John Burns, 22 March 1894, John Burns Papers, BM, Add MSS 46287 f 195. Also *Hamilton Advertiser*, 24 March 1894.
138   *Ibid.*, 31 March 1894.
139   Davitt to Hardie, 25 March 1894, ILP Archive 1894/55; Davitt to Ferguson published in *NBDM*, 30 March 1894. Even at this period Davitt did not invariably back the Liberal. See Moody, 'Michael Davitt and the British labour movement', p. 72.
140   *NBDM*, 2 April (Cambuslang) and 4 April 1894 (Larkhall).
141   *Ibid.*, 5 April 1894.
142   *Ibid.*, 4 April 1894.
143   *Glasgow Observer*, 7 April 1894.
144   *NBDM*, 3 April 1894, J. Adam Anderson at Cambuslang.
145   *Labour Leader*, 7 April 1894.

Champion and Aberdeen

146   For Champion, see Henry Pelling, 'H. H. Champion: pioneer of Labour Representation', *Cambridge Journal*, January 1953, pp. 222—38. His impact on national politics in terms of organisation and of ideas are discussed below, Chapters 12, 13 and 16.

147 The local economy is analysed in Buckley, *Trade Unionism in Aberdeen*, chapter 1.

148 J. Denvir, *The Irish in Britain*, p. 384.

149 Buckley, *Trade Unionism in Aberdeen*, part IV, contains a detailed account of the deteriorating relationship between Liberals and trades council.

150 For accounts see E. P. Thompson, *William Morris* (1977 edition), pp. 473—6; and Bob Duncan, *James Leatham*, chapter 2.

151 See Aberdeen Trades Council Annual Report, 1891, pp. 12—13.

152 Typically, there is doubt about the precise number. Robertson was certainly a Championite, and so it seems was Brodie, see *Glasgow Herald*, 14 June 1892. W. Marwick, *A Short History of Labour in Scotland*, p. 71 ignores Brodie but claims John Wilson (Central Edinburgh). He seems to have run as a Labour candidate with support from the Scottish Socialist Federation, the SUTCLP and temperance groups — the Liberal was a McEwan!

153 The adoption was by 23 votes to 8, *Aberdeen Daily Free Press* (*DFP*), 23 June 1892.

154 The Bryce Papers (Bodleian Library), contain some material on the contest.

155 For Champion's position, see speech reported in *DFP*, 24 June 1892.

156 Comment by James Leatham cited in Buckley, *Trade Unionism in Aberdeen*, p. 139.

157 *DFP*, 24 June 1892.

158 *Ibid.*, 2 July 1892.

159 *Ibid.*, 24 June 1892.

160 *Ibid.*

161 Chisholm Robertson was also accused of 'coquetting with the Tories', *Glasgow Herald*, 1 July 1892, a common Scottish response of Liberals to early Labour candidates that in the Championite case had some credibility. For a development of this theme on a broader canvas see Chapter 16 below.

162 For these developments, see Buckley, *Trade Unionism in Aberdeen*.

163 The *Aberdeen Labour Elector*, later the *Aberdeen Standard*, this was discontinued early in 1894. Champion's distinctive views were exemplified in its columns. Thus on the Featherstone killings, he affirmed 'those who go outside the law must take the consequences', *Aberdeen Standard*, 19 October 1893.

164 Lowe, *Souvenirs of Scottish Labour*, p. 151.

165 For the Aberdeen ILP's anti-Liberalism see *DFP*, 10 July 1895 and also 13 July for the text of an anti-Bryce manifesto.

166 Pelling, *Social Geography*, p. 390 expresses surprise at the size of later SDF polls. Perhaps part of the explanation lies in the potential for Labour growth, combined with the idiosyncratic failure of the local ILP.

The Scottish ILP from 1895

167 Material from ILPCRs 1895—1905.

168 See Directory of Branches in ILPCR 1900.

169 See for example on Inverness, Ramsay MacDonald to John Penny, 17 August 1899, ILP Archive 1899/82.

170 For election propaganda by Watson, Smillie and Smith, see the collection of 1895 Election Literature in Mitchell Library, Local Collection.

171 Smillie, *A Life for Labour*, pp. 112—17 for this and other insights into the atmosphere of the contests.

172 *GH*, 18 July 1895.

173 W. J. McGowan to John Penny, 15 September 1898, ILP Archive 1898/82.

174 *GH*, 9 July 1895.

175 *Ibid.*, 11 July 1895.

176   *GO*, 13 July 1895.
177   *GH*, 12 July 1895.
178   *Labour Leader*, 27 July 1895.
179   For individual expenses see ILPCR 1896, pp. 14—15; for the loan see W. M. Haddow, *My Seventy Years* (Robert Gibson, Glasgow, 1943), pp. 37—9.
180   *GH*, 3 July 1895.
181   Glasier Diaries, 18 March 1897.
182   James Macdonald to John Penny, 18 June 1898, ILP Archive 1898/61.
193   Glasier Diaries, 26 January 1895.
184   See Glasgow Trades Council Annual Report, 1895—6 and 1896—7; also Wood, 'Irish immigrants and Scottish Radicalism', pp. 84—6.
185   *GO*, 6 November 1897.
186   David Lowe to J. K. Hardie, 26 February 1900, ILP Archive 1900/70.
187   *Labour Leader*, 2 September 1899 for background.
188   *Ibid.*, 30 September 1899.
189   *ILP News*, November 1900; *GH* 2 October 1900; and for Irish attitude, *GO*, 15 September 1900.
190   *ILP News*, November 1900.
191   See reports of his speeches in *GH*, 24, 26 and 27 September 1900.
192   *Ibid.*, 2 October 1900.
193   Comments in speeches reported in *GH*, 3 October, 27 September and 4 October 1900 respectively.
194   For a discussion of the contest, see Bealey and Pelling, *Labour and Politics*, pp. 129—32; for a description of North East Lanark, Pelling, *Social Geography*, p. 408.
195   Glasier Diaries, 29 August 1901; *Motherwell Times* (*MT*), 30 August 1901.
196   *MT*, 6 September 1901; *Labour Leader*, 7 September 1901 for a report by Burgess emphasising this point.
197   See *ibid.*, 28 September 1901 for support from Bryn Roberts and J. H. Wilson; Scottish Liberal support came from Murray of Elibank, Captain Sinclair the Scottish Whip, and other MPs. See *MT*, 27 September 1901; also Bealey and Pelling, *Labour and Politics*, p. 130, which also cites evidence on Campbell-Bannerman's position.
198   *GO*, 14 September 1901.
199   *Ibid.*, for interview with John Redmond.
200   *MT*, 13 September 1901.
201   *Ibid.*; also *GO*, 14 September 1901.
202   For a discussion of this point see Wood, 'Irish immigrants and Scottish' Radicalism, pp. 86—7.
203   *Clarion*, 28 September 1901.
204   *Daily Record*, 18 September 1901.
205   *GO*, 21 September 1901.
206   *Ibid.*, for reports of United Irish League Meetings and also *GO*, 14 September 1901 for copy of letter urging Smillie vote from Redmond, Dillon, O'Connor and J. F. X. O'Brien.
207   *MT*, 20 September 1901.
208   Glasier Diaries, 26 September 1901.
209   *GO*, 28 September 1901; *ibid.*, 21 September for claim of 3,000 Irish votes. Also *Labour Leader*, 21 September 1901 for a discussion of its size, suggesting that it could be as low as 2,000.
210   *Ibid.*, 5 October 1901 for a claim based on scrutiny of ballot box contents.
211   Glasier Diaries, 10 and 19 September 1901.
212   *Labour Leader*, 14 September 1901.

213 *GO*, 28 September 1901.
214 For a discussion of the contest see Bealey and Pelling, *Labour and Politics*, pp. 242—4.
215 *Labour Leader*, 15 July 1904.
216 For the selection and the limited sentiment favouring a deal with Labour, *MT*, 15 July 1904.
217 *Ibid.*, 22 July 1904.
218 *GO*, 6 August 1904; see also *ibid.*, 30 July for UIL Executive decision. For cases of Irish speakers backing Findlay whilst preferring Labour, *ibid.*, 13 August (speeches by John Ferguson and Joseph Devlin).
219 *Labour Leader*, 22 July 1904.
220 *GO*, 13 August 1901.
221 See comment of the *Scotsman* cited *MT*, 12 August 1904.
222 For the candidature see *Clarion*, 14 April 1905; the controversy is noted in Wood, 'Irish immigrants and Scottish Radicalism', pp. 83—4.
223 See *GO*, 23 December 1905—13 January 1906.
224 Wood, 'Irish immigrants and Scottish Radicalism', p. 83. *GO*, 13 January 1906; *GH*, 4 and 13 January 1906.
225 *Ibid.*, 9 January 1906.
226 In the campaign he stood for 'Labour and Progress'; after the declaration for 'Labour and Socialism', *GH*, 5 and 19 January 1906.
227 Gilray, MS.
228 Glasier Diaries, 11—16 May 1896, and also Brocklehurst's report in NAC Minutes, 2 January 1896.
229 *Dundee Advertiser*, 4 July 1895.
230 *Ibid.*, 13 July 1895. See also the comments on the campaign in *Labour Leader*, 27 July 1895.
231 NAC Minutes, 28 May and 28 July 1900.
232 W. Black to J. K. Hardie, 10 August 1902, ILP Archive 1902/88. It seems that the Engineers' had been ready to finance Barnes only if one Liberal stood. See James Reid to Hardie, 26 March 1902, *loc. cit.*, 1902/27. Also Glasier Diaries, 9 November 1901 for note on Barnes' amicable interview with one of the Liberal members.
233 NAC Minutes, 1 and 2 December 1902; 13 and 14 May 1904.
234 W. Black to Francis Johnson (?), 9 May 1904, ILP Archive 1904/16.
235 John Carnegie to Hardie, 12 March 1905, ILP Archive 1905/23.
236 See *Dundee Elector*, January 1906, 1st Issue (Lamb Collection 18[13]) for his election address.
237 For example, *Dundee Advertiser*, 27 December 1905.
238 *Ibid.*, 5 January 1906.
239 *Aberdeen Daily Free Press* (*DFP*), 2 May 1896. See also Buckley, *Trade Unionism in Aberdeen*, pp. 175—7, for an account of the contest.
240 *DFP*, 23 April 1896.
241 NAC Minutes, 22 and 23 April 1896 and also the letters from Hardie and Mann on arrangements, *DFP*, 23 April 1896.
242 Fletcher claimed that he was not prepared to oppose Mann. See his letter to Mann, 22 April 1896, ILP Archive 1896/42.
243 The principal emphases of Mann's campaign are set out in an interview in *DFP*, 25 April and in a speech reported in *ibid.*, 27 April.
244 For docks, *ibid.*, 28 April 1896; for line fishermen, *ibid.*, 28 April and 1 May. The background to the line fishermen's case is in Buckley, *Trades Unionism in Aberdeen*, pp. 5—6.
245 *DFP*, 1 May 1896 for this support. Buckley, *Trades Unionism in Aberdeen*,

pp. 38—41 for evidence on local New Unionism. *DFP*, 2 May for an analysis of Mann's support.

246   *Ibid.*, 29 April 1896 for Pririe's appeal and 30 April for his comments on the eight-hour day.

247   The accusations centered around a dispute in 1889, and were raised, for example, by Dr Beveridge of the local ILP, *DFP*, 1 May 1896.

248   A combination that was inevitably the subject of *Labour Leader* attacks for example in issue of 16 May 1896.

249   *DFP*, 29 April and 1 May 1896.

250   *Ibid.*, 2 May 1896.

251   See for instance comments in *Labour Leader*, 9 May 1896.

252   For information on the dispersal of Aberdeen ILP members see J. Duncan to Hardie 25 May and 12 June 1905, ILP Archive, 1905/77 and 94.

To St Enoch Station?
253   Scottish TUC, Minutes of Joint Meeting of Representatives from the ILP, SDF and Parliamentary Committee of the STUC, 14 March 1899; NAC Minutes, 14 March 1899.

254   SWPEC, 'Minutes of workers' conference on parliamentary and local representation', January 1900.

255   *Labour Leader*, 13 January 1900.

256   *Scottish TUC Report* 1899, pp. 49—50. See also pp. 15—17 and 30—31 for material and resolution on proposed conference.

Chapter 8: The Yorkshire woollen district

Radical ambiguities
1   *The ILPer. The Monthly Record of the Liverpool Branch of the Independent Labour Party*, No. 2, February 1904.

2   For his early life, see volume 1 of his *Autobiography* (Nicholson and Watson, London, 1934).

3   The claim was made by Paul Bland of the Bradford ILP. See J. Reynolds and K. Laybourn, 'The emeregence of the Independent Labour Party in Bradford', *International Review of Social History*, 1975, p. 315.

4   For details at a time of relative strength, see *ILP Directory of Branches*, 1895.

5   J. Tattersall to John Penny, 12 June 1898, ILP Archive 1898/55.

6   See Keighley Independent Labour Party Minutes, June—July 1895, especially meetings of 11 and 12 July.

7   For the early West Riding ILP, see E. P. Thompson, 'Homage to Tom Maguire', in Briggs and Saville (eds.), *Essays in Labour History* (Macmillan, London, 1960); for specific places, see Reynolds and Laybourn, 'The emergence of the Independent Labour Party in Bradford'; Clark, 'The origins and development of the Labour Party in Colne Valley', hereafter, Clark *Thesis*.

8   For details see Pelling, *Social Geography*, pp. 297—305. In 1886, the Unionists won Bradford Central, and in Colne Valley the sitting member was returned unopposed as a Liberal Unionist.

9   See Reynolds and Laybourn for claim that in 1891, one-ninth of the population had Irish Catholic connections.

10   Clark, *Thesis*, p. 68 claims that the strength of nonconformity in the Colne Valley has been exaggerated; for a note of scepticism see also Thompson, 'Homage to Tom Maguire', pp. 289—92.

11   See *ibid.*, pp. 290—91 for Illingworth, and p. 311 for Kitson; see also Clark *Thesis* for various references to the Colne Valley Member.

12   For a discussion of elements promoting such a synthesis, see Joyce, *Work, Society and Politics*, for example at pp. 321—3.

13   In Halifax in 1885, see Thompson, 'Homage to Tom Maguire', p. 288, as part of an argument emphasising the concurrent vitality of the independent Radical tradition.

14   See Joyce, *Work, Society and Politics*, pp. 62—3.

15   Ben Turner, *About Myself* (Toulman, London, 1930), chapters 1 and 2.

16   For a summary of the economic situation see Thompson, 'Homage to Tom Maguire', pp. 283—5.

17   See the evidence of Allan Gee, W. H. Drew and Ben Turner, to the *Royal Commission on Labour, Minutes of Evidence*, Group C, volume 1, especially 4788, 5075, 5383, 5682—3.

18   Clark, *Thesis*, p. 58.

19   See for example in *Royal Commission on Labour, Minutes of Evidence*, Group C, vol. 1, 5536 (Drew), 5735 (Turner).

20   The evidence to the Commission suggests that women formed the majority of the membership.

21   *Yorkshire Factory Times*, 30 September 1892, cited Clark, *Thesis*, p. 62.

22   See Drew's evidence to the *Royal Commission on Labour, Minutes*, Group C, vol. 1, 5389.

23   See Cyril Peace, *The Manningham Mills Strike in Bradford, December 1890—April 1891*, University of Hull, Occasional Papers in Economic and Social History, No. 7, 1975. Also Thompson, 'Homage to Tom Maguire' and A. F. Brockway, *Socialism Over Sixty Years: The Life of Jowett of Bradford 1864—1944* (Allen and Unwin, London, 1946).

24   For a detailed account of the confrontations, see *Yorkshire Factory Times*, 17 April 1891.

25   *Bradford Observer*, (*BO*), 23 June 1892.

26   See John Lister, 'The early history of the ILP movement in Halifax' (MS in Mattison Collection); hereafter Lister MS.

27   In July 1892, the Colne Valley Labour Union found both candidates unsatisfactory, and could not recommend either to Labour voters, Colne Valley Labour Union Minutes, 2 July 1892, also Clark *Thesis*, pp. 83—4 and 93.

28   *Yorkshire Factory Times*, 28 May 1891; for developments elsewhere see Colne Valley Labour Union Minutes, 21 July 1891; *Yorkshire Factory Times*, 25 September 1891, for Huddersfield; Lister MS and *Halifax Courier* (hereafter *HC*) 6 and 13 August 1892, Keighley Labour Union Minutes, 3 and 19 October 1892, *Keighley News*, 8 and 22 October 1892.

29   See the press references in note 28 to Halifax and Keighley.

30   Keighley Labour Union Minutes, 19 October 1892.

31   Clark, *Thesis*, pp. 140—41 and *Yorkshire Factory Times*, 26 February 1904.

32   See Clark, *Thesis*, for details of visiting speakers; Thompson, 'Homage to Tom Maguire' for the strength of local socialism, and the early numbers of *Keighley ILP Journal* for reports on visiting speakers.

Bradford and Halifax Confused beginnings

33   See Fred Jowett, 'Bradford seventy years ago', in Brockway, *Socialism Over Sixty Years*.

34   On the social geography of Bradford, see Reynolds and Laybourn, 'The emergence of the Independent Labour Party in Bradford', and Pelling, *Social Geography*, pp. 298—300.

35   Reynolds and Laybourn cite Hartley, in *Bradford Labour Echo*, 30 November 1895 on the problems of mobilising the slum vote.

36   Joyce, *Work, Society and Politics*, p. 323.
37   On the Bradford Trades Council, see Thompson, 'Homage to Tom Maguire', and Reynolds and Laybourn, 'The emergence of the Independent Labour Party in Bradford'.
38   *BO*, 24 October 1891.
39   On Blatchford's involvement, see *Yorkshire Factory Times*, 12 June 1891, and Joseph Burgess's recollections in *Clarion*, 1, 8 and 15 October 1909.
40   Pete Curran presented him as having 'got rich on the pence of the work people', *BO*, 25 June 1892.
41   *Ibid.*, 18 June 1892.
42   *Ibid.*, 14 June 1892.
43   *Ibid.*
44   *Ibid.*, 22 June 1892. Tillett also earned the opposition of the Methodist Times, *BO*, 20 June 1892.
45   Reynolds and Laybourn, 'The emergence of the Independent Labour Party in Bradford' and *BO* 15 June 1892. Tillett was supported by the delegates of the Dyers, Gasworkers, General Railway Workers' Union and Typographical Association — but not by the Power Loom Overlookers, and the Stuff Pressers. For individual union views, *BO*, 20, 28 and 29 Jne 1892.
46   *Ibid.*, 27 June 1892.
47   See the references to Blatchford's candidacy in note 7. Thompson, 'Homage to Tom Maguire' also notes at pp. 312—13 Blatchford's firm advocacy of a socialist objective.
48   *BO*, 5 July 1892.
49   Figures in Reynolds and Laybourn, 'The emergence of the Independent Labour Party in Bradford'; it was at this time that W. H. Drew wrote to Joseph Burgess inviting the 'cockneys' to Bradford 'where you will find plenty of food for reflection', *Workman's Times*, 13 August 1892.
50   *Bradford Labour Journal*, 30 September 1892.
51   Brockway, *Socialism Over Sixty Years, passim*.
52   Detailed results are in *Labour Leader*, 10 November 1894.
53   *BO*, 6 July 1895.
54   *Ibid.*, 9 and 10 July 1895.
55   *Ibid.*, 13 July 1895. See also Glasier's Journal, 12 July 1895 and his accompanying comment — 'Magnificent meeting electrical enthusiasm — but half of the audience have no votes'.
56   *BO*, 6 July 1895.
57   *Ibid.*, 13 July 1895 — TUC policy was cited as a justification, i.e. the decisions of the 1894 congress.
58   *Ibid.*, 16 July 1895.
59   *Ibid.*, 6 July 1895.
60   *Ibid.*, 16 July 1895.
61   Pelling, *Social Geography of British Elections*, p. 300.
62   J. H. Beever, *Royal Commission on Labour: Minutes of Evidence*, Group C, vol. 1, 9770—3.
63   *Ibid.*, 9784.
64   On the Radical tradition and Chartist links see Thompson, 'Homage to Tom Maguire', pp. 286—9.
65   See Marx's report of Jones's 1852 campaign (10 August 1852 — for the *New York Daily Tribune*, 25 August 1852) in *Survey From Exile* (1973), (Penguin, Harmondsworth), pp. 262—71. The quotation is at p. 271.
66   *HC*, 30 April 1892.
67   For Lister's career see the obituary in *Halifax Courier and Guardian*, 12 October 1933.

68   *Halifax Guardian*, hereafter *HG*, 21 January 1893. For a rumour that Tories would not oppose him if Liberals did not, see Shaw Maxwell to Lister, 18 January 1893, ILP Archive, 1893/3.

69   *HG*, 28 January 1893. Only five voted for the amendment.

70   In Lister's words, he 'was half-a-Tory who had been screwed up to the point of voting for a measure of Home Rule', *ibid.*, 4 February 1893.

71   *BO*, 30 January and 7 February 1893 — also Lister on Davitt, *HC*, 28 January 1893.

72   *HG*, 4 February 1893.

73   See the reprint from *Halifax Free Press*, January 1893 (Halifax Public Library).

74   *HG*, 4 February 1893.

75   Cited in *HG*, 21 January 1893. Lister, three decades later, claimed he had support also from *Reynolds's, Bradford Observer, Leeds Daily News, Western Mail, Echo, Sunday Chronicle, Labour Elector, Clarion* and *Irish News* (Lister MS).

76   *HG*, 11 February 1893.

77   Copy of Lister's Election Address in Mattison Collection.

78   *Halifax Free Press*, January 1893.

79   Lister, MS.

80   See the collection of press cuttings in the Lister Papers and NAC Minutes, 3 December 1894. Also series of pieces in *Labour Leader* and in *Clarion* both from 3 November 1894. The ILP Archive contains several letters on the dispute.

81   *HC* and *HG* both 6 July 1895.

82   Text of the letter is in *HG*, 13 July 1895 — 'An appeal to the working men of Halifax'. On Tattersall's subsequent quarrel with the Halifax ILP, see NAC Minutes, 2 January and 4 April 1896.

83   *HC*, 20 July 1895.

84   *Ibid.*

Lib-Lab hostilities: two by-elections

85   See Reynolds and Laybourn, 'The emergence of the Independent Labour Party in Bradford' for figures — they suggest (p. 313) that 1897 marked a turning point in Bradford Labour fortunes. See also Brockway, *Socialism Over Sixty Years* for Jowett's increasing influence in municipal affairs.

86   *BO*, 5 November 1896.

87   On Bowling, see Reynolds and Laybourn, 'The emergence of the Independent Labour Party in Bradford'; also there is a brief description of East Bradford in Pelling, *Social Geography of British Elections*, pp. 299—300. The campaign is described in the context of Hardie's political development in Morgan's biography, pp. 91—3.

88   Tom Mann to Hardie, 23 October 1896, ILP Archive, 1896/77.

89   The search is described in *BO*, see especially 24—30 October 1896.

90   *BO*, 19 October 1896 and *Labour Leader*, 17 and 24 October 1896.

91   *BO*, 28 October 1896.

92   *Ibid.*, letter 26 October 1896 — the *Observer*'s correspondence columns demonstrated the lack of agreement by Liberals on attitudes towards Labour.

93   *Ibid.*, 17 October 1896.

94   *Ibid.*, 24 October 1896.

95   *Ibid.*, 19 October 1896.

96   *Ibid.*, 5 November 1896.

97   In fact he claimed (*BO*, 2 November 1896) since 'the Liberals made fair promises of friendship which were not however redeemed, they were the more dangerous of the two to the workers' interests'.

98   *Ibid.*, 4 November 1896.
99   *Ibid.*, 29 October and 5 November 1896.
100   *Ibid.*, 29 October and 2 November 1896. On the Irish and temperance votes, see *Hardie's Election Herald and East Bradford Campaigner*, 4 November 1896.
101   See *BO*, 9 November 1896 and Glasier Diaries, 8 November 1896.
102   *Ibid.*, 11 November 1896. Glasier had expected 2,500 votes.
103   *Labour Leader*, 24 October 1896.
104   *BO*, 11 November 1896.
105   *Ibid.*, 30 October 1896. The Conservative candidate was the Honourable Ronald Greville, son of an Irish landlord.
106   For Shaw's letter of resignation, see *HC*, 20 February 1897.
107   *Ibid.*; see also *The Record: The Organ of the Halifax ILP* No. 4, July 1897.
108   *Labour Leader*, 13 March 1897.
109   *Ibid.*, 27 February 1897.
110   *Ibid.*, 13 March 1897. It was very similar to Mann's programme in Aberdeen North.
111   These claims had a long life — see *ibid.*, 25 March 1899.
112   For Fenwick, see *HC*, 27 February 1897.
113   The 'battle' of the telegrams is noted in *HG*, 6 March 1897. The ILP response is in *Labour Leader*, 6 and 13 March 1897.
114   *HC*, 27 February 1897.
115   Hardie to David Lowe, 27 February 1897 in David Lowe, *From Pit to Parliament*, p. 112.
116   *HC*, 6 March 1897.
117   Mann's post declaration speech is in *HG*, 6 March 1897.
118   *HC*, 6 March 1897.
119   *Labour Leader*, 19 November 1898. This account also contains details of the 1898 municipal elections.
120   For his entry into the council, see *ibid.*, 6 November 1897. There is an account of Parker's career in *Dictionary of Labour Biography*, vol. 2.
121   *Labour Leader*, 19 November 1898.

Progressive understanding
122   For an initial hostile reaction, see *Labour Leader*, 8 January 1899. For a Liberal post-mortem on November 1899 see the letter in *BO*, 21 September 1900.
123   Hist first meeting as candidate had been held in the Autumn of 1899. He had been spoken of as candidate more than a year before that. *BO*, 19 September 1900.
124   A. Illingworth to Herbert Gladstone, 27 September 1899, Gladstone Papers, BM Add. MSS 46057 f 200.
125   *BO*, 22 and 24 September 1900.
126   See for example, *Bradford Argus*, 26 September 1900.
127   Jowett accepted the annexation of the Boer Republics, *BO*, 27 September 1900.
128   Details of his programme in *ibid.*, 1 October 1900.
129   *Ibid.*, 25 September 1900.
130   Glasier Diaries, 29 September 1900.
131   *BO*, 1 October 1900.
132   *Ibid.*, 29 September 1900. For Keighley ILPers' willingness to consider support for the Keighley Liberal candidate if Bradford Liberals aided Jowett, see Keighley ILP Minutes, 23 September 1900.
133   *Ibid.*, 3 October 1900.
134   *Bradford Argus*, 26 and 29 September 1900.
135   *ILP News*, October 1900.

136 See figures in Reynold and Laybourn, 'The emergence of the Independent Labour Party in Bradford'.

137 A Workers' Municipal Election Committee had been formed in 1901. See *ibid.*, p. 313. On links between Trades Council and ILP in 1905—6, see *Yorkshire Daily Observer* (*YDO*), 8 December 1905.

138 *Ibid.*, 15 December 1905. He defined his chief concerns as unemployment and poverty, *ibid.*, 12 January 1906.

139 *Ibid.*, 29 December 1905.

140 *Ibid.*, 5 January 1906, and 29 December 1905.

141 *Ibid.*, 13 December 1905.

142 See for example *ibid.*, 6, 8 and 12 January 1906.

143 *Ibid.*, 11 January 1906.

144 *Ibid.*, 9 January 1906.

145 *Ibid.*, 13 January 1906.

146 *Ibid.*, 15 January 1906.

147 See, for example, *ibid.*, 3, 5, 10 and 11 January 1906 — Hartley did not receive Irish support.

148 *HC*, 29 September 1900.

149 *ILP News*, October 1900.

150 *BO*, 27 September 1900.

151 *HG*, 6 October 1900.

152 *HC*, 6 October 1900 — 'Colours of the Labour candidate were met with only here and there'.

153 In 1895 it had been larger — 1351 votes; cf. 736 split betwen the ILP and the two Liberals.

154 *HC*, 6 October 1900.

155 *Labour Leader*, 17 November 1900. Parker had been ready to support discussions between LRC leaders and the Liberal Whips before the election, although not believing there was 'any probability of the Liberal "*local*" leaders opening the door for Labour candidates'. See Parker to J. R. MacDonald, 3 April 1900, LPLF 1/310.

156 See *HC*, 16 December 1905, 6 January 1906.

157 *Ibid.*, 9 December 1905. *Labour Leader*, 15 December 1905 expressed regret at Parker's attitude but also suggested it could be a slip by a 'weary and overstrung speaker'.

158 *HC*, 16 December 1905 and 6 January 1906.

159 *Ibid.*, 6 January 1906.

Striking the balance

160 On Dewsbury, see Christopher James, *MP for Dewsbury* (Published by the author, Brighouse, 1970), especially chapters 6 and 7.

161 See *Dewsbury Chronicle*, 7 July 1895.

162 For an account, see Bealey and Pelling, *Labour and Politics*, pp. 165—6. The official SDF position is in *Clarion*, 27 December 1901; for the position of the ILP leadership, see *ILP News*, November 1901—February 1902, and *Labour Leader* over the same period. Also NAC Minutes, 22 and 23 November 1901 and LRC Executive Minutes, 15 November 1901.

163 T. Myers to Hardie (no date), ILP Archive 1901/68.

164 James Field to Hardie, 10 November 1901, ILP Archive 1901/51.

165 Letter in *Clarion*, 13 December 1901.

166 See in particular, Glasier to Hardie, 26 and 28 November 1901, Glasier Correspondence 1901/23 and 24, and Glasier to Penny, 29 November 1901, *loc. cit.*, 1901/40.

167   Glasier Diaries, 23 November 1901 and 29 January 1902.
168   Henry Labouchere supported Quelch. See James, *MP for Dewsbury*, p. 134. Also W. Beardsley (Dewsbury Liberal Association) to Herbert Gladstone, 1 October 1901, Gladstone Papers, BM, Add MSS 46059 f 64 wating 'a commercial man' who backed the supremacy of the British flag in South Africa.
169   James, *MP for Dewsbury*, pp. 134—5; 138.
170   See the files of the *Huddersfield Examiner*, July 1895. The Conservative *Huddersfield Weekly Chronicle* offered a more objective picture.
171   *The Huddersfield ILP Election Herald*, No. 3, 13 July 1895.
172   *Huddersfield Examiner*, 20 July 1895.
173   J. B. Glasier in *Labour Leader*, 30 November 1906.
174   Glasier Diaries, 21—28 November 1906 for the notes of one participant. He was preoccupied with the involvement of WSPU speakers on a strictly anti-Liberal platform.
175   *Labour Leader*, 30 November 1906. The Labour candidate T. Russell Williams declared 'if the defence of private property was the policy of the Liberal Party, then he was at war with the Liberal Party', *Huddersfield Weekly Chronicle*, 24 November 1906. His Liberal opponent was a social reformer and associate of Rowntree. See *Labour Leader*, 23 November 1906.
176   On the Colne Valley pattern of development, see Clark, *Thesis*, especially chapters 8, 9 and 10.
177   See *ibid.*, chapter 7 — also *Huddersfield Examiner*, 6 and 13 July 1895.
178   *Huddersfield Examiner*, 27 July 1895.
179   The original entry is in Glasier Journal, 19 July 1895. Park of this is reproduced in L. Thompson, *The Enthusiasts*, pp. 98—9.

Chapter 9: The Lancastrian Party

Popular Conservatism — a barrier or an opportunity?

1   Monthly Report, March 1894, in NAC Minutes.
2   See the Directory, ILPCR 1900, pp. 35—43.
3   On Labour weakness in Liverpool, see Sam Davies, 'The Liverpool Labour Party and the Liverpool working class', and Andy Shallice, 'Orange and green and militancy: sectarianism and working class politics in Liverpool, 1900—1914', both in *North West Labour History Society Bulletin*, **6**, 1979—80.
4   See, for example, *Labour Leader*, 7 November 1896.
5   J. W. Scott to John Penny, 8 October 1897, ILP Archive 1897/71.
6   Snowden to Hardie, 6 February 1900, ILP Archive 19800/62.
7   For important discussions, see Patrick Joyce, *Work, Society and Politics*, and his 'The factory politics of Lancashire in the later nineteenth century', *Historical Journal*, 1975, pp. 525—53; Peter Clarke, *Lancashire and New Liberalism*; Geoffrey Trodd, *Thesis*.
8   M. McCarthy, *Generation in Revolt*, p. 22, cited Trodd, *Thesis*, p. 249.
9   Cited in Stanley Salvidge, *Salvidge of Liverpool* (Hodder, London, 1934), the constituency was Liverpool Kirkdale; for a discussion of this and other Liverpool seats in this period see Pelling, *Social Geography*, pp. 247—52.
10   *Labour Leader*, 4 October 1907; other material in issues of 13, 20 and 27 September.
11   See Joyce, *Work, Society and Politics*, chapter 7 and Clarke, *Lancashire and the New Liberalism*, for discussions of this aspect.
12   On Blackburn, see Joyce, Clarke and Trodd, *Thesis*; also Clarke, 'British politics and Blackburn politics, 1900—1910', *Historical Journal* 1969, pp. 302—27.

13   *Blackburn Weekly Telegraph*, 6 January 1906.
14   *Blackburn Labour Journal*, November 1904 — Forrest lost to the ILP incumbent, Charles Higham. For Forrest see Tony Mason *Association Football and English Society 1863—1915* (Harvester, Hassocks, 1980), p. 121.
15   For the significance of such changes, see *ibid.*
16   Clarke, *Lancashire and The New Liberalism.*
17   Trodd, *Thesis*, p. 158.
18   *Ibid.*; for discussion of changing economic situation of the cotton industry, see Joyce, *Work, Society and Politics*, pp. 331—42 for a summary of changes.

The Social Democratic Federation — a rival or a comrade?
19   See Trodd, *Thesis*, for a discussion of Burnley.
20   Glasier Diary, 30 July 1897.
21   *Ibid.*, 26 July 1898.
22   *Ibid.*, 16 November 1896.
23   *Ibid.*, 19 June 1900.
24   *Ibid.*, 3 June 1896.
25   For background, see Clarke, 'British politics and Blackburn politics' and Trodd, *Thesis*.
26   See *Blackburn Labour Journal*, November 1899 for this usage.
27   *Ibid.*, 2 February 1898.
28   *Ibid.*, 2 February 1906; see also *Northern Daily Telegraph (NDT)*, 15 January 1906.
29   *NDT*, 5 January 1910.
30   See material in successive national conference debates on the issue.
31   See Trodd, *Thesis*, for continuing Burnley SDF involvement in local Labour politics.
32   *Blackburn Labour Journal*, October 1899.
33   Clarke, *Lancashire and The New Liberalism*, pp. 40—41.
34   See Trodd, *Thesis*, pp. 167 ff for comparison of religious strengths in Blackburn and Burnley. By 1900, the Burnley Methodists owned twenty-four chapels with 15,000 seats — double that of the Anglicans.
35   Pelling, *Social Geography*, pp. 262—3.
36   Trodd, *Thesis*, pp. 324 and 241 for characterisation of local Miners as a SDF stronghold. Lancashire and Cheshire Miners' Federation Records for the 1890s contain abundant evidence of discontent in the Hargreaves and Towneley Collieries.

The party in Tory strongholds
37   For Preston background, see Pelling, *Social Geography*, pp. 261—2, and various references in Joyce, *Work, Society and Politics*.
38   *Preston Guardian (PG)*, 13 July 1895.
39   John Penny to Hardie, 9 November 1893, ILP Archive 1893/127.
40   Penny to Hardie, 30 December 1893, ILP Archive 1893/180.
41   From both letters — other unions' representatives mentioned in ILP Archive 1893/180 were Boilermakers, Engineers, ASRS and Bakers. The Spinners also showed some opposition. See *PG*, 3 January 1894.
42   Penny to Hardie, 14 January 1894, ILP Archive, 1894/11. See also for account of the ILP deputation and Tattersall's address, *PG*, 10 and 24 February 1894.
43   For a profile, see *Labour Prophet*, October 1894. For his 1895 Halifax intervention, *Halifax Guardian*, 13 July 1895. For an early Preston reaction to him, see Penny to Hardie, 22 December 1893, ILP Archive, 1893/167.
44   *PG*, 29 June 1895.

45 Penny to Hardie, ILP Archive, 1893/127.
46 *Ibid.*, The Preston contest is covered in a book of press cuttings 'How the Preston ILP fought the parliamentary election of 1895', located in the ILP collection in the British Library of Political and Economic Science.
47 *PG*, 13 July 1895 (Enid Stacy).
48 *Lancashire Daily Post*, 11 July 1895.
49 *PG*, 13 July 1895.
50 *Ibid.*
51 *Labour Leader*, 22 August 1896.
52 See Glasier's report on visit dated 10 July 1900 in Glasier Correspondence, 1900/68; also his Diary entry for 8 July. For links with local unions see *ILP News*, July 1899.
53 On his early experiences there, see his letter to David Lowe undated, ILP Archive 1900/70 also cited in David Lowe, *From Pit to Parliament*, pp. 184—5.
54 *Labour Leader*, 20 October 1900.
55 *PG*, 6 October 1900.
56 Glasier to Hardie, 8 August 1900, Glasier Correspondence, 1900/55.
57 See *PG*, 29 September 1900; also the Conservative newspaper *Preston Herald*, same date.
58 *Lancashire Daily Post*, 1 October 1900 — 'Preston's verdict on Mr. Keir Hardie'. George Toulmin, one of the proprietors, dissociated himself from this position in the following day's issue.
59 See in particular John Hodge to MacDonald, 27 November 1902, LPLF 6/197; see also his letter to MacDonald 20 November 1902, *loc. cit.*, 6/194 and W. Marshall to MacDonald, 10 November 1902, *loc. cit.*, 6/224. Also Hodge to Hardie, 27 October, 26 November and 12 December 1902, ILP Archive 1902/112/117/126 respectively, and A. Collis to Hardie, 4 May 1903, ILP Archive 1903/52.
60 Hodge to Hardie, 11 May 1903 (Tel.) ILP Archive 1903/91. See also Snowden to Hardie, 29 April 1903, *loc. cit.*, 1903/72, and also their letter of 1 May — 'The ILP is in most friendly co-operation with the local LRC', *loc. cit.*, 1903/77. For post-mortems, Hodge and Collis to Hardie, 16 and 17 May 1903, *loc. cit.*, 1903/194 and 5. Note also the material on ILP speakers' exclusion in Glasier Correspondence, Glasier to Hardie, 15 May and the reply, 18 May 1903, 1903/37 and 38.
61 For Tory attempts to label Hodge as either a Liberal or an ally of Socialists, see *Preston Herald*, 13 May 1903.
62 See report by Henderson, LPLF, 9/333 and for an earlier emphasis on religious issues, see Hardie's letter to Lowe cited in note 17.
63 For the assurance, see *PG*, 10 January 1906; for Macpherson's Free Trade emphasis, *ibid.*, 3—17 January 1906.
64 Some 300 voters wrote 'ILP' or 'socialist' on their ballot papers — see Clarke, 'British politics and Blackburn politics'.
65 See Blackburn Trades Council Report, 1897, p. 14 for decision to rely on 'Trade Union effort only'.
66 For Socialist views of Liberal division, see *Blackburn Labour Journal*, November 1898 and August 1899.
67 NAC Minutes, 5 January 1897 and 26 February 1897; ILPCR 1897, p. 13; pp. 18—19.
68 See, for example, *Blackburn Labour Journal*, October 1900.
69 *NDT*, 2 October 1900.
70 *Blackburn Weekly Standard and Express*, 29 September 1900.
71 *Ibid.*, 6 October 1900.

72   *NDT*, Leader, 28 September 1900.
73   Cited Colin Cross, *Phillip Snowden*.
74   *NDT*, 1 October 1900.
75   *Ibid.*, 22 September 1900.
76   *Ibid.*, 24 September 1900 for Snowden's speech at United Irish League Club and 28 September for Free Church appeals for Snowden.
77   The inaugural meeting took place on 28 November 1903. See Blackburn Trades Council Report, 1904.
78   For the genesis of the 1906 alignment see Clarke.
79   *Weekly Telegraph*, 6 January 1906.
80   *NDT*, 11 January 1906.
81   *Ibid.*, 15 January 1906. This issue also carried a Liberal advertisement citing Halifax (Parker) and Derby (Bell) as examples for Blackburn to follow.
82   *Weekly Telegraph*, 6 January 1906.
83   See, for example, Snowden's election address cited *Northern Daily Telegraph*, 4 January 1910.

Towards Progressivism?
84   Richard Pankhurst to C. P. Scott, 24 March 1894, Manchester Guardian Archive, C. P. Scott Correspondence 120/15.
85   *Clarion*, April 1894 in Manchester Guardian Archive, Scott Correspondence together with conciliatory Scott reply.
86   Edwin Guthrie to Scott, 25 May 1894, *loc. cit.*, 120/29.
87   For background, see Pelling, *Social Geography*, p. 246.
88   Arthur Symonds to C. P. Scott, 25 March 1894, Manchester Guardian Archive, Scott Correspondence, 120/16.
89   For Pankhurst's earlier career and a description of the Gorton campaign see Sylvia Pankhurst, *The Suffragette Movement* (Virago, London, 1977), Books 1—3.
90   *Gorton Reporter*, 6 July 1895.
91   *Ibid.*, 13 July 1895.
92   *Ibid.*
93   Pankhurst to Hardie, 9 July 1895, ILP Archive, 1895/116.
94   NAC Minutes, 9 July 1895.
95   *Gorton Reporter*, 20 July 1895 — also *Manchester Guardian*, 17 July 1895 for letters exhibiting Gorton Liberal criticism of ILP tactics in other seats.
96   *Gorton Reporter*, 13, 20 and 27 July 1895 for imbalance of resources; Pankhurst, *The Suffragette Movement*, p. 135 for a daughter's experiences.
97   *Gorton Reporter*, 27 July 1895.
98   *Ibid.*, 20 July 1895 — according to the *Manchester Guardian*, 16 July 1895, Pankhurst claimed he was 'the strongest Liberal candidate in the North of England'.
99   John Trevor to C. P. Scott, 14 August 1895, Manchester Guardian Archive, Scott Correspondence, 120/147.
100 For ILP criticisms, see *ILP News*, February—May 1900; *Labour Leader* issues in March and April 1900; for Radical concern see C. P. Scott to L. Hobhouse, 7 March 1900, Manchester Guardian Archive, Hobhouse Correspondence, 132/87.
101 See *Manchester Guardian* throughout campaign — especially on 26 September 1900.
102 The official Liberal attitude was apparent much earlier. See *Labour Leader*, 1 April 1899.
103 See Ward's account of his nominating body, *Gorton Reporter*, 6 October

	1900. See also Glasier's 1899 Report to the NAC in Glasier Correspondence, 1899/63, and printed circular on the Gorton United Trades Council, LPLF 1/149.
104	NAC Minutes, 28 July 1900, for its exclusion; Minutes of Parliamentary Committee, 11th October 1900, for endorsement by Election Conference.
105	*Gorton Reporter*, 6 October 1900.
106	*Ibid.*
107	Although Hatch, the Conservative, received support from the Miners' leader, Thomas Ashton, as 'one of the best friends of labour ... a tried and trusted friend of the Miners' Eight Hours Bill'.
108	See *Labour Leader*, 24 January 1903 for rift.
109	A Liberal statement cited *Manchester Guardian*, 15 January 1906.
110	Clynes to Hardie, 17 November 1905, ILP Archive, 1905/154. For an earlier account by Clynes see his letter to MacDonald, 29 March 1901, LPLF 2/21.
111	For example, Mrs Pankhurst to Hardie, 27 May 1905, ILP Archive, 1905/80.
112	F. Potter to Hardie, 6 November 1905, ILP Archive, 1905/139. For Clynes' responses see the 1905 letter cited in note 110 above; also his letters of 15 and 21 November 1905, LPLF 27/42 and 43.
113	See, for example, his statement cited in *Rochdale Observer*, 3 July 1895 but note also a later claim that Barnes was at least as much 'Independent Labour' as 'Socialist', J. Firth to MacDonald, 28 June 1903, LPLF 10/349.
114	On this point, see Pelling, 'Social Geography', p. 255.
115	M. Ashworth to Hardie, 5 April 1905, ILP Archive, 1905/unclassified. See for Labour campaign, *Rochdale Labour News: Special Election Edition*, 27, 29 September and 1 October 1900; Glasier Diary, 28 September notes a 'quaint' speech by Clarke.
116	For the hostile attitude of some towards links with socialists see J. Firth to MacDonald, 28 December 1902, LPLF 4/149.
117	Firth to MacDonald, 26 August 1903, LPLF, 10/349.
118	Firth's letter of 28 December 1902 as in FN 33.
119	As acknowledged by Firth, 28 December 1902 and 26 August 1903.
120	Glasier Diary, 12 January 1902.
121	*Ibid.*, 30 November 1902.
122	*Ibid.*, 20 December 1903.
123	S. G. Hobson, *Pilgrim to the Left* (Longmans, London, 1938), pp. 111—13.
124	See, for example, responses from headquarters in January, February and December 1905, LPLF 19/396, 20/207, 28/410.
125	Ashworth to Hardie, as in note 115. For Joiners' support see S. Wise to MacDonald, 14 February 1905, LPLF 19/206.
126	*Rochdale Labour News*, November 1905.
127	*Ibid.*, December 1905.
128	*Ibid.*, January 1906.
129	*Rochdale Observer*, 6 January 1906.
130	*Ibid.*, 3 January 1906.
131	*Ibid.*, 10 and 13 January 1906. Also *Clarion*, 2 February 1906.

Chapter 10: ILP islands

Leicester — 'The Unity of the Progressive Party'

| 1 | *Labour Leader*, 9 October 1897, cited in Cox, 'The Rise of the Labour Party in Leicester', hereafter referred to as Cox, *Thesis*, p. 36. |
| 2 | See Glasier Journal, 10 July 1895 — see also *Labour Leader*, 27 June and 11 July 1896; 10 July 1897; 10 September 1898. |

3   On Derby and Bell's emergence as candidate from the ILP viewpoint see Tom
    Taylor to John Penny, 25 August 1899, ILP Archive 1899/89.
4   Figures from *TUC 1903 Official Souvenir* published by Leicester Trades
    Council. For NUBSO developments see Chapter 5 above.
5   *1903 TUC Souvenir*. The Hosiery Workers voted 597 to 356 for affiliation to
    the National LRC, J. Chaplin to MacDonald, 11 November 1902, LPLF 6/206.
6   On the background see Pelling, *Social Geography of British Elections*, chapter
    10.
7   For detail on this see Cox, *Thesis*, pp. 5—8.
8   On the size of Leicester Businesses, see Pelling, *Social Geography*, p. 211.
9   See Malcolm Elliott, *Victorian Leicester* (Phillmore, Chichester, 1979), p. 166.
10 Cox, *Thesis*, p. 6.
11 Leicester Liberal Association Minutes (hereafter LLA) Executive, 4 October
    1893.
12 LLA Executive, 6 and 15 March 1894; General Committee, 21 March 1894.
13 LLA Executive, 13 and 16 August 1894; General Committee, 20 August 1894.
    The vote was Hazell 194, Hart 191; Hazell's candidature did not generate uni-
    versal enthusiasm in national Liberal circles. Francis Schnadhorst's verdict was
    'I shd not have weeped, if Hazell had been beaten. I have my knife into that
    gentleman.' Letter to Henry Broadhurst, 31 August 1894, Broadhurst Papers.
14 For detailed account of the Trades Council Meetings, see *Midland Free Press*,
    (*MFP*), 25 August 1894. Banton had begun the meeting by expressing personal
    satisfaction at Hazell's selection.
15 Cox, *Thesis*, pp. 5, 6, 9.
16 T. F. Richards to Hardie, 18 July 1894, ILP Archive, 1894/161.
17 But by 1894, they seemed on closer terms. See Broadhurst to Hardie, 30
    December 1894, ILP Archive, 1894/220.
18 *MFP*, 25 August 1894.
19 *Ibid.*; support was given by 'very few' according to this report, which claimed
    also that 'the hooting and interruption were very loud and prolonged'.
20 *Ibid.* — this was in the candidate's interview with the Trades Council.
21 Burgess to Hardie, 16 August 1894, ILP Archive, 1894/178.
22 *Clarion*, 1 September 1895, for 'Inskip's manifesto: trade unionists' reply',
    advocating support for Burgess and Broadhurst and signed by Banton,
    Richards, the Trades Council Vice-President, one other NUBSO officer, two
    Hosiery Union officers and twelve boot-workers.
23 *MFP*, 15 September 1894 for the Trades Council resolution condemning Inskip
    and Cort for their opposition to Burgess. It was adopted with 4 against.
24 *Ibid.*, 13 July 1895.
25 *Ibid.*
26 See Burgess to MacDonald, 11 April 1896, MacDonald Papers, 5/6. Burgess
    claimed that Hall and Christie 'went out of their way to visit Leicester and to
    suggest to the comrades there that I should not be run at the General Election
    … Pete Curran is reported to have said he would rather have voted for a Tory
    than for me'.
27 NAC Minutes. 10 September and 4 December 1894; 6 and 7 February and 15
    April 1895.
28 See *Labour Leader*, 25 August; 1 and 8 September 1894.
29 Burgess to Mann, 8 July 1895. ILP Archive, 1895/110.
30 *MFP*, 20 July 1895. *Labour Leader*, 27 July 1895 emphasised registration
    probelms.
31 For an account of the foundation, see *MFP*, 15 September 1894; for member-
    ship statistics see Cox, *Thesis*, p. 11.

32 *Labour Leader*, 3 December 1898.
33 On funds and council contests, see Cox, *Thesis*, pp. 14—15 and 37.
34 *Ibid.*, pp. 16—20.
35 MacDonald had been adopted as candidate in October 1899, see D. Marquand, *Ramsay MacDonald*, p. 64. His earlier dealings had revealed the central role of Boot and Shoe activists behind Independent Labour politics. See, for example, McCarthy to MacDonald, 24 July 1899, MacDonald Papers, 5/9, on the hope that MacDonald would speak to his Boot and Shoe branch.
36 *MFP*, 24 February 1900 — the platform had included ILPers and Liberals, also on the Trades Council attitude, *ibid.*, 3 March 1900. Distaste for the war was strong amongst the Liberals. They decided in October 1899 to explore the possibility of joint action with the ILP and other bodies. LLA General Committee, 6 October 1899; Finance and General Purposes Committee, 9 October 1899.
37 *ILP News*, October 1900.
38 *MFP*, 29 September 1900.
39 *Ibid.* — the vote to back Broadhurst as well was 22 to 16.
40 Marquand, *Ramsay MacDonald*, p. 73.
41 *MFP*, 29 September 1900.
42 Marquand, *Ramsay MacDonald*, pp. 73—4.
43 *Labour Leader*, 20 October 1900.
44 *Leicester Daily Post*, 3 October 1900 cited Marquand, p. 74.
45 For an account of changing Liberal-Labour relations in Leicester see Cox, *Thesis*, Chapter 2; also Marquand, *Ramsay MacDonald*, pp. 81—3.
46 LLA General Purposes Committee, 10 December 1900; General Committee, 18 February 1901 with insertion of printed correspondence.
47 LLA Special Sub-Committee, 23 and 30 April, 17 May 1901, including the view that Hazell was not strong enough, especially with ILP opposition.
48 T. Carter (Trades Council Secretary) to T. W. Smith (Liberal Association Secretary), 5 July 1901, in LLA.
49 Printed Report of Liberal Delegates to the Conference, *loc. cit.*
50 Printed copy of letter from T. Carter, 10 March 1902, *loc. cit.*
51 Printed Liberal reply, *loc. cit.*, see also Executive, 28 January and 21 March 1902; General Committee, 21 April 1902.
52 See material in LLA: Candidate Sub Committee, 6 October, 11 November 1902; 16 June 1903; Finance and General Purposes Committee 8 June 1903; pencilled Note for Candidate Sub-Committee 16 June 1903; letter from Sir William Collins to Tudor Walters, 15 June 1903, declining invitation because of number of declared candidates.
53 See the material in the MacDonald Papers cited in Marquand, *Ramsay MacDonald*, pp. 81—2.
54 LLA Executive, 26 June 1903.
55 See, for example, *Leicester Daily Post*, 27 and 30 June 1903.
56 Marquand, *Ramsay MacDonald*, p. 82; also in LLA telegram from Herbert Gladstone to Wood, dated 16 July 1903, when the question of Hart's candidature was reaching its climax — 'Am unfavourable. Am writing'.
57 LLA Executive, 20 June, 17 and 24 July 1903; Candidate Sub-Committee 17 July 1903. Also printed copies of correspondence, especially Hart's letter of 23 July.
58 LLA Executive, 4 September 1903.
59 Jesse Herbert Memorandum, 7 September 1903, Herbert Gladstone Papers, BM, add. MSS 46106. (Jesse Herbert was private Secretary to Herbert Gladstone.)
60 Cox, *Thesis*, pp. 21—4.

61   *Labour Leader*, 4 and 11 November 1904.
62   LLA Executive, 12 April 1904; also Finance and General Purposes Committee, 8 February and 11 March 1904; Executive, 7 October 1904.
63   Cox, *Thesis*, pp. 56—60.
64   *Leicester Daily Post*, 29 December 1905; *Leicester Pioneer*, 13 January 1906.
65   *Leicester Daily Post*, 6 January 1906.
66   *Ibid.*, 15 January 1906.
67   T. F. Richards to MacDonald, 24 December 1905, LPLF, 31/323. *Leicester Daily Post* (*LDP*), 12 January 1906 for statement by Leicester NUBSO branch.
68   *LDP*, 3 January 1906 — speeches by McCarthy of NUBSO and Chaplin.
69   Cox, *Thesis*, p. 63 cites the *Leicester Pioneer*, 26 February 1910, for a claim that Liberals had paid for and organised help for MacDonald. Also the copy of his election address for January 1910, MacDonald Papers, 7/46.
70   On June 1913, see Marquand, *Ramsay MacDonald*, pp. 152—6. Ross McKibbin, *The Evolution of the Labour Party*, pp. 62—8; also *Labour Leader*, 19 and 27 June; 3 July 1913, and the subsequent correspondence; and the file in MacDonald Papers, 7/48.
71   Cox, *Thesis*, p. 85, for an early hostile Liberal reaction see LLA General Committee, 28 September 1894.

Radical Merthyr: the red dragon and the red flag
72   Glasier Diary, 3 October 1900.
73   J. Bruce Glasier, *Keir Hardie: The Man and His Message* (ILP, London, 1919), pp. 8—9.
74   On the general political development of Wales, see K. O. Morgan, *Wales in British Politics 1868—1922* (University of Wales Press, Cardiff, 2nd edition, 1970); cf. the Welsh chapter in Pelling, *Social Geography of British Elections*. For illuminating themes, see David Smith (ed.), *A People and A Proletariat: Essays in the History of Wales 1780—1980* (Pluto Press, London, 1980).
75   See Smith in *People and Proletariat*, pp. 215—39; also his introduction at pp. 7—15.
76   See Norman Williams, 'Evan Roberts and the 1904—5 revival', *Glamorgan Historian* (3), pp. 28—37; also Smith in *People and Proletariat*, pp. 224—5 for an emphasis on the revival's anti-authoritarianism, and a locating of it within the context of social change.
77   On this point, see K. O. Morgan, 'The New Liberalism and the challenge of Labour; the Welsh experience, 1885—1929' in K. O. Brown, *Essays in Anti-Labour History* (Macmillan, London, 1974), pp. 159—182.
78   On the emergence of Independent Labour in part of South Wales, see K. O. Fox, 'The emergence of the political Labour movement in the eastern section of the South Wales Coalfield' (Unpublished M.A. Thesis, University College Wales, Aberystwyth, 1965), hereafter referred to as Fox, *Thesis*.
79   See Hobson's *Pilgrim to the Left*, p. 35, for details.
80   *Labour Leader*, 28 April 1894.
81   See Fox, 'Labour and Merthyr's Khakhi Election of 1900', *Welsh History Review*, March, 1965, p. 356.
82   See Morgan, *Wales in British Politics*, pp. 166—70.
83   *Ibid.*, pp. 172—3.
84   See Chapter 2: also on the forces making for change in the pre-1914 coalfield, Hywell Francis and David Smith, *The Fed*, chapter 1.
85   On Merthyr, see Glanmor Williams (ed.), *Merthyr Politics: The Making of a Working-Class Tradition* (University of Wales Press, Cardiff, 1966), esp. the chapter by K. O. Morgan, 'The Merthyr of Keir Hardie'. The Merthyr

Boroughs seat covered Merthyr, Aberdare, Mountain Ash, Dowlais and Penydarren, *ibid.*, p. 59.

86   *Ibid.*

87   On 1831, see Gwyn Williams, *The Merthyr Rising* (Croom Helm, London, 1978); and also his 'Dic Penderyn', *Llafur*, 1978, pp. 110—20.

88   For detail, see K. O. Fox, 'Labour and Merthyr's Khakhi Election of 1900', pp. 352—5; and Morgan, 'The Merthyr of Keir Hardie'.

89   See K. O. Morgan, 'D. A. Thomas: industrialist as politician', *Glamorgan Historian* (3), pp. 33—51.

90   For material on all Pritchard Morgan's Merthyr contests, see the J. John Vaughan Papers (D/D Vau) in Glamorgan Record Office.

91   See *The Miner*, April 1888.

92   J. K. Hardie, 'My relations with the Merthyr Boroughs', in *Souvenir of 20th Annual Conference of the ILP at Merthyr Tydfil 1912*.

93   For accounts of the early days in Merthyr, see Hardie 'My relations with the Merthyr Boroughs' and William Laurence 'Political history of Merthyr Tydfil' abo in *Merthyr Conference Souvenir*. For the Aberdare Socialist Society, see Note Book of the Society and later of Aberdare ILP in Glamorgan County Record Office (Dep. D/D Xhj 2), listing officers, members, etc. Also Minute Book, 1901—6 in Aberdare Local Collection, P44/5.

94   Oliver Jenkins to Tom Mann, 18 August 1897, ILP Archive 1897/55.

95   See *Labour Leader*, 25 June, 2 and 9 July 1898.

96   Both quotes from *ibid.*, 9 July 1898.

97   Hardie to David Lowe, June 1898, ILP Archive, 1898/67.

98   For details of assistance, see Fox, *Thesis*, pp. 31—2.

99   Wright's reports to the Head Office are filed with the NAC Minutes in BLPES.

100 Memberships are traced in Fox, *Thesis*, pp. 33—4, and these, together with levels of branch activity, can be traced in successive numbers of *ILP News*.

101 For a mention of the Merthyr nucleus, see William Stewart, *J. Keir Hardie*, pp. 138—9.

102 Llew Francis to John Penny, 3 August 1899, ILP Archive, 1899/64.

103 Hardie to Francis, 1 July 1898, ILP Archive, 1898/68.

104 For an early manifestation, see *Labour Leader*, 10 September 1898.

105 For Merthyr and Dowlais, see Laurence, 'Political history of Merthyr Tydfil'; for Aberdare, see Edmund Stonelake, JP, *Aberdare Trades and Labour Council Jubilee Souvenir* 1900—1950 (Aberdare 1950).

106 On trade union developments see Fox in *Welsh History Review* at pp. 357—8. For a reference to Liberalism amongst Miners' leaders see D. Davies to J. R. MacDonald, 28 June 1900, LPLF 2/208.

107 *Ibid.*, p. 10.

108 R. Hyman, *The Workers' Union* (Clarendon, Oxford, 1971), pp. 24—6. His name is given as Caughlin in *Merthyr Express*, 29 September 1900; and also as 'Collins of the steelworkers', *South Wales Daily News*, 24 September 1900.

109 So also did Charles Duncan of the Workers' Union, see his letter to Llew Francis (n.d.) but clearly prior to the 1900 election, ILP Archive, 1900/117.

110 NAC Minutes, 28 May 1900.

111 Glasier to Llew Francis, 25 July 1900, cited in Stewart, *J. Keir Hardie*, pp. 163—4.

112 NAC Minutes, 28 July 1900.

113 See Glasier to Francis, 2 August 1900, cited in Stewart, *J. Keir Hardie*, pp. 164—5, and Penny to Francis, 4 August 1900, ILP Archive, 1900/86.

114 Glasier to Hardie, 2 August 1900, Glasier Correspondence, 1900/53.

115 Glasier to Hardie, 8 August 1900, *loc. cit.*

116 Hardie to Francis, 21 September 1900, ILP Archive, 1900/96. Also cited in Stewart, *J. Keir Hardie*, p. 166.

117 Stanton to Francis, ILP Archive, 1900/94.

118 Cited in Stewart, *J. Keir Hardie*, p. 165.

119 *ILP News*, September 1900.

120 On the various preferences, see *South Wales Daily News, 21 and 22 September 1900.*

121 The fullest account is in ibid., 24 September 1900; it can be supplemented by *Merthyr Express*, 29 September 1900; the quotes here are from the former source.

122 The normal Trades Council voting system was apparently one vote for up to 100 members and extra votes for each additional 100 up to a maximum of 600, *Merthyr Express*, 29 September 1900.

123 According to the *Merthyr Express* about six delegates from the lower Aberdare Valley left. The same source gives the total attendance as about 70; either many abstained in the final votes or more than six left.

124 Some miners remained; there were also members of the ASRS and the Steel Workers. See *South Wales Daily News* and *Merthyr Express* accounts; also Pelling, *Social Geography*, p. 352.

125 See John Penny to David Davies (telegram), 24 September 1900, ILP Archive, 1900/98; also Glasier Diary, 24 September 1900.

126 *Ibid.*, 25 September 1900. See the three telegrams, Glasier to Francis, 25 September 1900, Glasier Correspondence, 1901/1—3; also *South Wales Daily News*, 26 September 1900.

127 Glasier Diaries, 26 September 1900; note also the telegram from Penny at Preston to Francis, 25 September 1900, ILP Archive, 1900/99 — 'Hardie in honour bound to fight Preston — if nominated also in Merthyr, could give some time'.

128 For the campaign, see the accounts of Fox, *Welsh History Review*, 1965; Morgan, *Keir Hardie*, pp. 116—18; Stewart, *J. Keir Hardie*, pp. 166—9.

129 *South Wales Daily News*, 25 September 1900.

130 *Ibid.*, 29 September 1900.

131 *Merthyr Express*, 2 October 1900.

132 *South Wales Daily News*, 25 September 1900.

133 *Ibid.*, 1 October 1900. Thomas had chaired a mass demonstration in Cardiff on 25 August 1900, expressing sympathy with the Taff Vale strikers, Bealey and Pelling, *Labour and Politics*, p. 62.

134 *Merthyr Express*, 6 October 1900.

135 See, for example, the exchanges in *South Wales Daily News*, 1 October 1900.

136 For the latter's view, see *ibid.*, 21 September 1900.

137 *Ibid.*, 2 October 1900 — the latter being a reference to George Cadbury's donation to the ILP Election Fund.

138 *Labour Leader*, 13 October 1900.

139 *South Wales Daily News*, 20 September 1900.

140 For a discussion of this point and of Thomas's attempts to secure Labour support, see Fox, in *Welsh History Review*, pp. 361—3.

141 *South Wales Daily News*, 29 September 1900.

142 *Labour Leader*, 13 October 1900.

143 *ILP News*, October 1900.

144 *Labour Leader*, 20 October 1900.

145 For an account strongly emphasising the war, see Bealey and Pelling, *Labour and Politics*, especially pp. 48—9. The accounts by Morgan and Fox give weight to the pro-war sentiments as well as the continuing strength of anti-militarist

principles. On the general issue of War and Wales, see the discussion between Pelling and Morgan in *Welsh History Review*, 1969.

146   *Labour Leader*, 13 October 1900; for his views in Merthyr, see *Merthyr Express*, 6 October 1900.

147   *Ibid.*

148   *Ibid.*; also *South Wales Daily News*, 2 October 1900.

149   For an account of these developments, see Morgan's biography, p. 118.

150   See D. A. Thomas to T. J. Rice, Secretary of Brecon Road Liberals, 11 April 1902, enclosing a copy of letter from Hardie to Thomas 10 April 1902 in Correspondence of Brecon Road Liberal Association. Merthyr, Glamorgan Record Office, Dep. D/D Xes 5.

151   For Hardie's encouragement, see his Address to the Aberdare Trades and Labour Council on Labour Representation on Public Bodies 1901. Aberdare local collection, P43/1; also Stonelake, *Aberdare Trades and Labour Council*, pp. 14—17. For an indication of the growth in Aberdare ILP activities, see W. W. Price, letter to Members, 1907, *loc. cit.*, P44/10.

152   These developments are discussed in Fox, *Thesis*, chapter 3, and summarised in Morgan, *Wales in British Politics*, pp. 207—8.

153   See Report of South Wales ILP Federation Conference, 29 October 1905.

154   The campaign is described in Morgan, *Keir Hardie*, pp. 150—51.

155   *Ibid.*, p. 151.

156   *South Wales Daily News*, 8 January 1906.

157   See, for example, his speeches in *Merthyr Express*, 20 January 1906; this tactic led to Labour attacks on religious leaders after the result was declared; see Hardie and the views of the Merthyr District Miners — both in *ibid.*, 27 January 1906.

158   *South Wales Daily News*, 13 January 1906.

159   *Merthyr Express*, 20 January 1906; also letter in *South Wales Daily News*, 18 January 1906.

160   *Merthyr Express*, 20 January 1906. For Hardie's response see *The Merthyr Borough Labour Pioneer*, January 1906, containing his election address; and the handbill 'Yet another Radcliffe lie nailed' both in Aberdare Local Collection, P43/3 and P43/4—1.

161   For an exotic example of the rupture see the material on Pritchard Morgan's Independent Liberal campaign of January 1910 in the Vaughan Papers; also Hardie's response in Election Bulletin in Aberdare Local Collection, P43/2/1—3. For a more central clash, Christopher Howard, 'Reactionary radicalism: the Mid Glamorgan bye-election March 1910', *Glamorgan Historian* (**9**), pp. 29—42; also Peter Stead, 'The language of Edwardian politics' in *A People and A Proletariat*, pp. 148—65.

Chapter 11: Dogs that did not bark

'Godless London'

1   *Labour Leader*, 21 July 1894.

2   *Ibid.*, 9 March 1895.

3   For some details on Fulham see Pelling, *Social Geography*, pp. 40—41.

4   Limehouse was included in the list of endorsed candidatures at the start of the campaign. NAC Minutes, 4 July 1895.

5   *ILP News*, March 1898.

6   Paul Thompson, *Socialists, Liberals and Labour*, p. 165.

7   *ILP News*, February 1898.

8   Thompson, *Socialists, Liberals and Labour*, p. 221.

9   On the industrial base and trade unionism, see Gareth Stedman-Jones, *Outcast London* (Clarendon, Oxford, 1971) and Thompson, *Socialists, Liberals and Labour*, chapter 3.
10   On West Ham, see Pelling, *Social Geography*, pp. 63—4.
11   For religion, see Thompson, *Socialists, Liberals and Labour*, chapter 2.
12   *ILP News*, March 1898. For a discussion of contemporary views of London, see Raymond Williams, *The Country and the City* (Chatto and Windus, London, 1973), chapter 19. For an illuminating discussion see Gareth Stedman-Jones, 'Working-class culture and working-class politics in London, 1870—1900: notes on the remaking of a working class', *Journal of Social History*, 1973—4, pp. 460—508.
13   Thompson, *Socialists, Liberals and Labour*, chapter 4; and Pelling, *Social Geography*, chapter 2.
14   This was particularly the case in the East End — in 1906 Limehouse had 6,234 electors. Mile End 5,419, St George's 3,246, Stepney 5,176 and Whitechapel 4,279.
15   See the discussion in Pelling, *Social Geography*, of the voting records of various types of London seat.
16   For working-class Conservatism see Thompson, *Socialists, Liberals and Labour*, pp. 86—9; Pelling discusses the bases of Conservative support in individual East End seats. For the anti-alien agitation, see J. Garrard, *The English and Immigration 1880—1910* (Cambridge University Press, Cambridge, 1971).
17   For a discussion see Thompson, *Socialists, Liberals and Labour*, chapter 5.
18   *Ibid.*, pp. 222—3. Ramsay MacDonald had stood in harness with a Radical in a by-election at Woolwich in February 1900, see Marquand, *Ramsay MacDonald*, p. 64.
19   The last Liberal MP did not lose his seat there until 1945. See Sir Percy Harris, *Forty Years In and Out of Parliament* (Melrose, London, 1947).
20   On this see the chapter by Chris Wrigley in K. D. Brown (ed.), *Essays in Anti-Labour History* (Macmillan, London, 1974); also K. O. Brown, *John Burns*.
21   For the SDF see Thompson, *Socialists, Liberals and Labour*, chapter 6. For Lansbury, R. Postgate, *The Life of George Lansbury* (Longmans, London, 1951), and for Thorne, G. Radice, *Will Thorne, Constructive Militant*.
22   *Workman's Times*, 18 June 1892.
23   Thompson, *Socialists, Liberals and Labour*, pp. 159—62.
24   For a discussion of what Hardie's headgear was, and what it symbolised, see Morgan, *Keir Hardie*, pp. 54—5.
25   Arthur Copping and Moira Wilson, *Pictures of Poverty: Studies in Distress in West Ham* (Daily News, London, 1905) — cited in Radice, *Will Thorne*, p. 50.
26   There is a detailed account of the background to Hardie's campaign in Fred Reid, *Keir Hardie: The Making of a Socialist*, pp. 127—31; also Morgan, *Keir Hardie*, pp. 44—51 and Thompson, *Socialists, Liberals and Labour*, pp. 130—31.
27   *Stratford Express*, 4 January 1890. Curwen had already been in touch with Hardie about a candidature. See the latter's reply, 5 August 1889, NLS 176.8, vol. 8.
28   By 1892, there were seven councillors described as Labour members, although as yet no organised Labour group. Thompson, *Socialists, Liberals and Labour*, p. 131.
29   *Stratford Express*, 19 and 26 April and 24 May 1890.
30   *Ibid.*, 24 May 1890.
31   *Ibid.*, 19 April 1890.

32   *West Ham Herald*, 20 February 1892; those represented included the Canning Town Co-op, the Gasworkers (Thorne and Curran were there), Glassworkers, Shipwrights, the Land Restoration League, Glassbottle hands, temperance bodies, the Seamen and Firemen, Painters and Bakers, plus some of Webster's former committee.

33   *West Ham and Stratford Express*, 18 June 1892.

34   *Ibid.*, 11 June 1892.

35   *West Ham Herald*, 25 June 1892.

36   *Ibid.*, 2 July 1892.

37   For a description see *West Ham and Stratford Express*, 25 June 1892 and *West Ham Herald* same date. There were union banners from the Coalporters, London Carmen, London Painters, Navies, Bricklayers and General Labourers, and the Seamen and Firemen. Those present included Thorne, Reverend Bruce Wallace, Mann, Havelock Wilson, Shaw Maxwell and Burgess.

38   *West Ham and Stratford Express*, 2 July 1892; and for temperance support, *West Ham Herald*, 18 June 1892.

39   *Ibid.*, 25 June and 2 July 1892. *West Ham Herald*, 2 July 1892. See also Reid, *Keir Hardie, The Making of a Socialist*, p. 131, on his official manifesto.

40   *West Ham and Stratford Express*, 9 July 1892.

41   See J. S. Curwen, to Hardie, 27 April and 1 May 1894, ILP Archive 1894/78 and /81.

42   For rumours, see Morgan, *Keir Hardie*, p. 94.

43   *West Ham and Stratford Express*, 29 June 1895.

44   *West Ham Guardian*, 13 July 1895.

45   *West Ham Herald*, 20 July 1895.

46   See Reid, *Keir Hardie*, p. 173. In fact there was some later bargaining and some temperance support. See *West Ham and Stratford Express*, 20 July 1895.

47   *Ibid.*, 13 July 1895.

48   For descriptions see *ibid.* and *West Ham Guardian* both 20 July 1895.

49   Quoted in account in *West Ham and Stratford Express*. The account in the *West Ham Guardian* suggests that this advice was shouted out as the meeting broke up, and that the motion passed was not to support Hardie. This had four dissentients.

50   *West Ham Herald*, 20 July 1895; also *Glasgow Herald*, 18 July 1895.

51   *West Ham Herald*, 20 July 1895.

52   Thompson, *Socialists, Liberals and Labour*, pp. 131—2.

53   *West Ham and Stratford Express*, 13 July 1895.

54   See *Glasgow Herald*, 18 July 1895, *West Ham Herald*, 20 July 1895, and telegram Hardie to a Middlesborough ILPer 16 July 1895, suggesting retribution against Wilson, ILP Archive, 1895/unclassified.

55   *West Ham Guardian*, 6 July 1895.

56   *West Ham Herald*, 13 July 1895.

57   *West Ham Guardian*, 13 July 1895.

58   *Ibid.*, and, for a sympathetic portrait, *West Ham and Stratford Express*, 29 June 1895.

59   For the claim for Liberal and Catholic abstentions see Pelling, *Social Geography*, p. 64 — but the poll there was the highest in three of the four winter elections when the working day in some trades was shorter.

60   On these developments see Thompson, *Socialists, Liberals and Labour*, pp. 132—5. He suggests (p. 133, fn 2) that although the socialists in the Labour group tended to be divided evenly between the ILP and SDF in 1898, the SDFers were more influential, having strong trade union connections, while the ILPers tended to be more middle class.

61   *Justice*, 26 April 1902.
62   See Thompson, *Socialists, Liberals and Labour*, pp. 250—51.
63   On developments, see *ibid.*, pp. 251—4.
64   For accounts of the Woolwich campaign, see Bealey and Pelling, *Labour and Politics*, pp. 144—6, Poirier, *Advent of the Labour Party*, pp. 168—9. For dissatisfaction with the Crooks campaign see ILP Archive 1903/17 (J. T. Brownlie to Hardie, 24 February 1903); /20 (Hardie to W. Barefoot, 25 February 1903); /21 (R. Banner to Hardie, 25 February 1903); /23 (Barefoot to Hardie, 26 February 1903); /25 (Crooks to Brownlie [copy] 5 March 1903); and /26 (Brownlie to Hardie, 5 March 1903). See also the sources in the Labour Party Archive, cited Thompson, *Socialists, Liberals and Labour*, p. 255, fns 2 and 3.
65   Brownlie to Hardie, ILP Archive, 1903/26, 5 March 1903.
66   For some critical statements see the speeches by the Woolwich delegate at the 1910 ILP Conference, ILPCR 1910, pp. 52 and 69.

Sheffield, 'This Benighted City of Liberal Labourism'

67   The political complexions of the Sheffield constituencies are analysed in Pelling, *Social Geography*, pp. 230—33.
68   For Mundella, see W. H. G. Armytage, *A. J. Mundella, 1825—1897: The Liberal Background to the Labour Movement* (Benn, London, 1951).
69   For Sheffield's industrial development see Sidney Pollard, *A History of Labour in Sheffield* (Liverpool University Press, Liverpool, 1959).
70   On the 'light trades' sector, *ibid.*, chapter 5.
71   *Ibid.*, chapter 6 for the growth of heavy industry.
72   *Ibid.*, pp. 147—8 for early Council developments.
73   The politics of Sheffield Central are discussed in Pelling, *Social Geography*, p. 233; see also Samuel Jeyes and Frederick How, *The Life of Sir Howard Vincent* (Allen, London, 1912).
74   For a detailed discussion of this contest, see Joyce Brown, 'Attercliffe 1894: how one local Liberal Party failed to meet the challenge of Labour', *Journal of British Studies*, May 1975, pp. 48—77.
75   See *Labour Leader*, 23 June 1894, where Hobson is referred to as 'a man of advanced views, though he does not belong to the ILP'.
76   A. J. Mundella to H. J. Wilson, 15 June 1894, H. J. Wilson Papers, MD 5950.
77   J. W. Wilson to H. J. Wilson, 17 June 1894, *loc. cit.*
78   J. W. Wilson to H. J. Wilson reporting on a meeting of local Liberal leaders, 12 June 1894, *loc. cit.*
79   See J. W. Wilson's letter of 17 June 1894.
80   J. W. Wilson to H. J. Wilson, 19 June 1894, *loc. cit.*
81   For the nomination, see *Sheffield and Rotherham Independent*, 23 June 1894.
82   On this question, see J. W. Wilson's letters to H. J. Wilson on 25 and 26 June 1894, Wilson Papers, MD 5950. *Labour Leader*, 30 June 1894.
83   *Ibid.*; *Sheffield and Rotherham Independent*, 25 June 1894.
84   *Ibid.*
85   Fragment to 'H' from H. J. Wilson, 22 June 1894, Wilson Papers, MD 5950.
86   The letters dealing with Attercliffe in the ILP Archive were missing when this collection was examined. Brown, 'Attercliffe 1894' uses two lettes with citations — A. G. Wolfe to Hardie, 15 June 1894 cited pp. 51, 61, 64; F. Sharp to Hardie, 21 June 1894, cited pp. 61, 64. Similar optimism can be found in *Labour Leader*, 9 June 1894.
87   *Clarion*, 14 July 1894.
88   J. W. Wilson to H. J. Wilson, 28 June 1894, Wilson Papers, MD 5950.

89　See, for example, the pro-Liberal letter of J. Shepherd, the Tinsley Park checkweighman, *Sheffield and Rotherham Independent*, 2 July 1894.

90　*Ibid.*, 30 June 1894; *Labour Leader*, 7 July 1894; the figure given here is accepted by Brown 'Attercliffe 1894', p. 66 on the basis of her examination of the Sheffield Press — the *Labour Leader* gives the vote as 45 to 37.

91　For Hobson's abstention, see S. Uttley to H. J. Wilson, 30 June 1894, Wilson Papers, MD 5950. Uttley had voted with the minority.

92　For report of the LEA Bradford Conference, see *Sheffield and Rotherham Independent*, 20 June 1894.

93　Threlfall to H. J. Wilson, 28 June 1894. Wilson Papers, MD 5950.

94　Quoted in *Sheffield and Rotherham Independent*, 25 June 1894.

95　See W. J. Wilson to H. J. Wilson, 26 June 1894, Wilson Papers MD 5950 for Manchester Guardian; and Brown, 'Attercliffe 1894', p. 68 for Daily Chronicle.

96　Telegram, Robert Hudson to H. J. Wilson, 25 June 1894, *Wilson Papers*, MD 5950.

97　F. Schnadhorst to H. J. Wilson, 29 June 1894, *loc. cit.*

98　*Sheffield and Rotherham Independent*, 5 July 1894 — source given as Frank Smith.

99　For material on this see *ibid.*, 2 July 1894; *Labour Leader*, 7 July 1894.

100　Hardie and Smith to H. J. Wilson, 1 July 1894, Wilson Papers, MD 5950. This was in response to apology from Wilson same date, *loc. cit.*

101　The campaign is covered in *Sheffield and Rotherham Independent, Sheffield Daily Telegraph*, 24 June to 5 July; and also in *Labour Leader*, 7 and 14 July 1894.

102　*Sheffield and Rotherham Independent*, 4 July 1894; there is a copy of Smith's address in Wilson Papers, MD 5951.

103　*Sheffield and Rotherham Independent*, 3 July 1894.

104　*Ibid.*

105　*Ibid.*, 2 July 1894.

106　*Ibid.*, 3 July 1894.

107　A copy of the handbill is in Wilson Papers, MD 5951; *Sheffield and Rotherham Independent*, 5 July 1894 has a post-poll claim that its impact was significant, and it is commented on in *Labour Leader*, 14 July 1894.

108　See *Labour Leader*, 28 July 1894; its context is discussed in Marquand, *Ramsay MacDonald*, p. 36 and Brown, 'Attercliffe 1894', p. 75.

109　For Uttley's views see W. S. Clegg to H. J. Wilson, 16 July 1894, Wilson Papers, MD 5954.

110　See the correspondence between Clegg and Wilson, July/August 1894, *loc. cit.*

111　See *Labour Leader*, 22 September 1894; *Clarion*, 29 September 1894.

112　Sheffield Federated Trades Council Annual Report 1894—5, p. 6.

113　See a copy of Trades Council resolution dated 11 January 1895, Wilson Papers, MD 5953.

114　See for example Sheffield Federated Trades Council Annual Report, 1895—6, p. 9 — for the election of a TC delegate from the ASE to the City Council, with Liberal support.

115　Tom Ellis to H. J. Wilson, 21 July 1897, Wilson Papers, MD 5943.

116　For partisan accounts of the contest, see *Sheffield and Rotherham Independent*; and *Sheffield Daily Telegraph*, 20 July to 6 August 1897.

117　F. Maddison to H. J. Wilson, 21 July 1897, Wilson Papers, MD 5943.

118　See the formal notification to the Sheffield Federated Trades Council, 27 July 1897, *loc. cit.*

119　See S. Uttley to F. J. Wilson, 28 July 1897, *loc. cit.*

120   See the handbill 'Railway workers and Mr. Maddison', in *loc. cit.*; also *Labour Leader*, 7 August 1894.
121   For demonstrations of this in 1894, see *Sheffield and Rotherham Independent*, 25 June 1894; *Clarion*, 29 September 1894.
122   For an account of this meeting, see Minutes of the Parliamentary Committee, 29 July 1897, in NAC Minutes.
123   'Why the ILP does not support Mr. Fred Maddison', *Labour Leader*, 14 August 1897, and copy in MacDonald Papers, PRO 5/227.
124   *Sheffield and Rotherham Independent*, 3 August 1897.
125   *Ibid.*, 1 August 1898.
126   Copy in Wilson Papers, MD 5943.
127   Dick (?) to John Penny, 31 May 1898, ILP Archive 1898/51.
128   On these developments, see summary in Pollard, *A History of Labour in Sheffield*, pp. 198—9.
129   See Sheffield Federated Trades Council Annual Report. 1903—4, pp. 10—11; also the correspondence in LPLF 6/358—361.
130   H. Sykes to MacDonald (no date but probably early 1903), LPLF 6/362.
131   Sykes to MacDonald, LPLF 11/462, 11 November 1903.
132   For material on the move to a joint body see C. Hobson to MacDonald, 13 February 1904, LPLF 13/450; also Report of Sheffield Trades Council and Labour Representation Committee, 24 July 1903 to 28 February 1905 in *loc. cit.*, 22/274.
133   MacDonald to Joseph Pointer, 25 September 1905, LPLF, 24/304. See also Pointer's letter of 23 September and also Ward's 19 September *loc. cit.*, 6/307.
134   For an account of Pointer's place in Sheffield politics, see the entry on him in *Dictionary of Labour Biography*, volume 2.

Conclusion: the mosaic of ILP politics

1   For a discussion of the role of trades councils, see Alan Clinton, *The Trade Union Rank and File* (Manchester University Press, Manchester 1977), chapters 1—3.
3   L. Bather, 'A history of the Manchester and Salford Trades Council', unpublished Ph.D. Thesis, University of Manchester, 1956.
4   See *Southampton Times*, 7 July, 4 August, 6 October 1894; 6 and 13 July 1895.

Part three

Chapter 12: Formation

1   *Workman's Times (WT)*, 27 May 1892.
2   For the SDF see Pelling, *Origins of the Labour Party, passim*; Henry Collins, 'The marxism of the Social Democratic Federation' in Briggs and Saville, *Essays in Labour History, 1886—1923*; C. Tsuziki, *H. M. Hyndman and British Socialism* (O.U.P. London, 1961); the later chapters of E. P. Thompson, *William Morris: From Romantic to Revolutionary*; Yvonne Kapp, *Eleanor Marx*, volume 2, *The Crowded Years* (Virago, London, 1979).
3   A. W. McBriar, *Fabian Socialism and English Politics 1884—1918* (Cambridge University Press, Cambridge, 1962) contains a chapter estimating the extent of Fabian influence on the ILP.
4   For analysis of the Irish example, see Conor Cruise O'Brien, *Parnell and His Party 1880—1890* (Clarendon, Oxford, 1957); F. S. L. Lyons, *Charles Stewart Parnell*; for a contemporary comment, see *WT*, 23 July 1892.

5   For a denial of the existence of a solid Irish vote in England, see James Connolly to Hardie, 12 April 1897, ILP Archive 1897/30.

6   *Clarion*, 11 February 1893.

7   See *WT*, 11 June 1892 — 'the Parnell of this party has yet to be found'; Blatchford's *Clarion* article (note 6), lists his objections to the parallel.

8   On his early career see *The Labour Annual* 1895.

9   *WT*, 30 April 1892.

10   As recalled in *Clarion*, 3 December 1909; Burgess's account of 'The Independent Labour Party: its origins and early history' was serialised there from 10 September 1909 to 28 January 1910.

11   E.g. Manchester and Salford ILP, and Swinton and Pendlebury Labour Union — both 27 May 1892; Plymouth, Stonehouse and Devonport ILP, 4 June 1892; London programme of ILP, 18 June 1892.

12   For Engels's optimism after the results, see his Preface to the second German edition of *The Condition of the Working Class in England* cited by Eric Hobsbawm in the Panther edition of the same work, pp. 35—6. 'The spell which the superstitious belief in the "great Liberal Party" cast over the English workers for almost 40 Years is broken.'

13   See J. K. Hardie to John Burns, 22 (27?) July 1892. Burns BM Add MSS 46287 f 184 and Burns to Hardie, July? 1892, *loc. cit.*, f 185.

14   Burns to R. Cunninghame Graham, 29 July 1892 (marked 'copy'), Burns Add MSS 46287 ff 239. Graham clearly thought Burns and Havelock Wilson would emulate Hardie. See his letter to Burns, 17 July 1892, *loc. cit.*, f 227.

15   *WT*, 30 July 1892.

16   Some delegates at Bradford clearly did not reject the LEA entirely see ILPCR 1893, p. 14, reaction to claim that its record was 'one of failure and disasters'.

17   W. H. Drew to Joseph Burgess published in *WT*, 13 August 1892.

18   See Fred Reid, *Keir Hardie*, for a discussion of Newcastle; also *WT*, 20 and 27 August, 3 September 1892.

19   For South Leeds, see E. P. Thompson, 'Notes on the South Leeds election' at the end of his 'Homage to Tom Maguire'. This quotes correspondence from Champion to Mahon. For the latter's account, see *WT*, 1 October 1892.

20   *Ibid.*

21   *WT*, 10 September 1892; for notes on the informal meeting; and 17 September for the text of circular and list of committee members.

22   For Hardie's views and expectations, see *ibid.*, 8 October 1892 — 'The coming conference'.

23   See, for example, London reservations, *ibid.*, 24 September 1892; Bradford, *ibid.*, 22 October — revised basis for representation is in *WT*, 8 October.

24   Comments from 'The coming conference'.

25   *WT*, 1 November 1892.

26   For example, W. Johnson in *WT*, 24 September 1892; and the *Clarion* columns in latter months of the year.

27   Tom Proctor of Devonport, *WT*, 19 November 1892.

28   Material on the Conference is taken from ILPCR 1893; and also from a handwritten account in the Mattison Collection, Brotherton Library, University of Leeds (hereafter MA). This is entitled 'Independent Labour Party, First Conference held at Bradford, January 13th and 14th 1893, Official Record'. It differs from or amplifies in some respects the published account. For difficulties in achieving precision about the number of delegates, see Appendix 2, 'The Bradford Conference', pp. 485—6. In view of these problems I have used 'organisations represented' as the unit of comparison. My geographical boundaries differ slightly from the official divisions.

29   For his selection, see *WT*, 1 November 1892; for his apologies, MA, 1st day, p. 9.

30   Two of the Cumberland and North Lancashire Workmen's Federation delegates were Andrew Sharp, leader of the Cumberland Miners, and Patrick Walls, of the Blastfurnacement'. For London Trades Council Labour Representation League, see Pelling, *Origins*, p. 101.

31   For Bloomsbury Socialist Society and Legal Eight Hours and International Labour League, see Kapp, *Eleanor Marx*, especially pp. 248, 384—5; and pp. 389—95 respectively; Thompson, *William Morris*, pp. 564—5.

32   *Labour Leader*, 9 April 1914.

33   Hardie, Jowett, Smillie, Tillett, Sexton, Turner and Curran.

34   See Leader in *WT*, 23 September 1893, and the reply by Fred Hammill.

35   Copy of agenda at front of MA.

36   ILPCR 1893, p. 2 — the members were Gee (Huddersfield), Johnson (Manchester), Tattersall (Halifax), Robinson (Bradford), Muse (Carlisle).

37   The two principal accounts show some discrepancies. ILPCR 1893 gives the whole discussion, pp. 1—2, without a break. MA more realistically gives raising of the original issue and then a gap before the committee reported (1st day, p. 5). If this ordering is accepted then the Chairman's interventions, ILPCR 1893, p. 2, should be credited to Hardie and not to Drew. The vote to hear the Fabians is given as 43 to 29 in ILPCR and 43 to 39 in MA.

38   See *Labour Leader*, 9 April 1914, for Hardie's recollection; MA gives Hardie's vote at 54 (1st day, p. 2) cf. ILPCR 1893, p. 2.

39   *Clarion*, 21 January 1893. See also John Trevor's praise, *WT*, 21 January 1893.

40   ILPCR 1893, p. 3.

41   Agenda, 'As to title', Resolution 3. See MA, 1st day, p. 3, for Hardie's suggestion that just the last line be moved as an amendment.

42   All in ILPCR 1893, p. 3; for Blatchford's criticism of Tillett, see *Clarion*, 21 January 1893; for Bernstein's see ILPCR 1893, p. 5.

43   All quotations on this issue, *ibid.*, p. 4. Agenda, 'as a programme'. Noted similar resolutions from London ILP, (Central Executive); Nelson SDF; Bradford Labour Union; Glasgow SLP; Camberwell ILP.

44   On Tillett's suggestion, the words 'and communal' were omitted 56 to 23; a compromise to insert 'ultimate' before objective was lost 56 to 36.

45   For the options, see ILPCR 1893, p. 4. MA, 1st day, p. 6, has slightly different wording for the amalgamation option.

46   ILPCR, 1893, p. 6.

47   *Ibid.*, pp. 6—7.

48   Maxwell, *ibid.*, p. 7 — then in MA only, 1st day, p. 7, Mahon moved that as a point of procedure Fabians and those SDF members who would not federate should withdraw from the conference. Hardie said this should go to Standing Orders Committee. It was not raised again.

49   ILPCR 1893, p. 8.

50   The account in MA is much more detailed, see especially 1st day, p. 10, cf. ILPCR 1893, p. 7. The full text of the Manchester resolution is in Agenda, 'As to constitution', Resolution 5.

51   See Agenda for full details of the various schemes.

52   MA, 1st day, p. 9, for geographical principle — a section of a resolution tabled originally by London ILP.

53   *Ibid.*, p. 9, for Drew-Maxwell proposal for committee — and p. 10 for statement that its composition would be determined in this fashion.

54   For committee report, MA, 2nd day, p. 1. ILPCR 1893, p. 8.

55   ILPCR 1893, p. 8, for Conference's last word, and p. 9 for defeat of attempt to give provinces last word.

56   *Ibid.*, p. 8, for A. K. Donald's objection on grounds of cost; see also Shaw's comments on this, *WT*, 28 January 1893.

57   For breakdown of places, not organisations represented in the four groups, see MA, 2nd day, p. 2 — the Doncaster representative went with the Midland group.

58   *WT*, 28 January 1893.

59   MA; pencilled into the agenda are the votes for the Northern representatives — Settle 38, Drew 29, Kennedy 29, Johnson 26, Lister 26.

60   See Burgess's comments on the members who made up the first NAC, *Labour Leader*, 8 March 1912; note also the letters from Buttery and Settle, *ibid.*, 15 March 1912.

61   ILPCR, 1893, p. 7, for mode of election of Secretary; and p. 10 for Secretary's election.

62   *WT*, 28 January 1893. John Trevor claimed Manchester delegates voted for Johnson because he was one of them — but really preferred Maxwell, *WT*, 21 January 1893.

63   *Labour Prophet*, April 1893 — cf. Buttery's comment, *Labour Leader*, 15 March 1912, that there was much dissatisfaction with Shaw Maxwell from the start.

64   Hardie's retrospective comment — *Labour Leader*, 9 April 1914.

65   ILPCR 1893, p. 7, refers briefly to the Committee's formation; MA, 1st day, pp. 12—13, shows that a Keighley policy resolution was moved, but that the previous question was carried 50 to 34. Votes are given for the Committee election in the case of three candidates — Smart 57, Aveling 52, Drew 38.

66   For original list see ILPCR 1893, p. 10; for replacement, *ibid.*, p. 12.

67   *Ibid.*, p. 11.

68   *WT*, 28 January 1893.

69   For discussion, ILPCR 1893, p. 11.

70   Additions are on p. 12 — the home colonies proposal had been backed initially by 57 to 28.

71   Proposals, p. 10; debate pp. 12—13.

72   *Ibid.*, p. 13.

73   *Ibid.*, pp. 13—15. The issue was debated in the *Clarion*: Blatchford, 21 January and 11 February; De Mattos, 18 February; Hamill, 25 February; Aveling, 18 March; W. Johnson, 25 March 1893.

74   MA, 2nd day, p. 16.

75   ILPCR 1893, p. 15.

76   MA, 2nd day, p. 17.

77   ILPCR, 1893, p. 15 — no vote given.

78   Votes were 32 to 30 and 40 to 28, MA, 2nd day, pp. 17—19.

79   Conditions given, ILPCR, 1893, p. 16. MA, 2nd day, p. 20, traces the vicissitudes of the first condition — originally 'A Socialist in Economics and a Democrat in Politics' — amended by 46 to 32 on Shaw's initiative to 'a Socialist and a Democrat' and then by 48 to 37 to final form moved by Smart seconded by Mahon.

80   *Justice*, 21 January 1893.

81   *Labour Elector*, 21 January 1893 for the Championite position.

82   *WT*, 28 January 1893.

83   Engels to Sage, 18 January 1893 — cited, *Labour Monthly* 1934, p. 749f; subsequently in Pelling, *Origins*, p. 123.

84   *WT*, 28 January 1893.

85   ILPCR, 1893, p. 6; see also his view in *WT*, 21 January 1893.

Chapter 13: The National Administrative Council from servant to oligarch

Settling down

1 ILPCR 1893, pp. 15—16.
2 *Ibid.*
3 *Ibid.*, p. 7.
4 *Ibid.*, p. 16.
5 For Aveling's position, see Yvonne Kapp, *Eleanor Marx: The Crowded Years*, pp. 527—32.
6 See *Clarion*, 29 April 1893; although by the November NAC Meeting Robertson was proposing an anti-Champion resolution. NAC Minutes, 18 November 1893, For Field's refusal see *Workman's Times*, 6 May 1893.
7 For a published description of the Manchester meeting, see *Workman's Times*, 25 March 1893.
8 For the financial statement for the first year, see ILPCR 1894.
9 Shaw Maxwell to Lister, 4 May 1893, ILP Archive 1893/28.
10 Shaw Maxwell to Lister, 21 July 1893, ILP Archive 1893/65.
11 Burgess to Hardie, 18 September 1893, ILP Archive 1893/99.
12 For Johnson, see *WT*, 14 October 1893; also Johnson to Maxwell, 28 September 1893, ILP Archive 1893/104.
13 Burgess to Hardie, 29 September 1893, ILP Archive, 1893/105.
14 G. W. Smith (Bradford) to Lister, 13 October 1893, enclosing a resolution demanding a NAC meeting, ILP Archive 1893/112 and also in *WT*, 21 October 1893.
15 Buttery in *WT*, 21 October 1893.
16 NAC Minutes, 18 March and 18 November 1893.
17 *Ibid.*, 18 March 1893.
18 Maxwell wrote to Lister on basis of a press report as to whether he could help. Maxwell to Lister, 18 January 1893, ILP Archive, 1893/3.
19 Hardie informed Maxwell, 'if I did go to the poll, it would be to vote against Henry Broadhurst', Hardie to Maxwell, 2 March 1893, ILP Archive 1893/7.
20 For a retrospective account, see ILPCR 1894, p. 3.
21 NAC Minutes, 18 November 1983.
22 *Ibid.*
23 NAC Minutes, 1 February 1894. The sub-committee was Maxwell, Buttery, Aveling and Lister.
24 ILPCR, 1894, p. 2.
25 Russell Smart, 'Open letter to non-joiners', *WT*, 30 September 1893.
26 Such reforms were proposed by amongst others Bradford, and Manchester and Salford ILPs, and the Lancashire and Chesire Federation. See the provisional agenda in *WT*, 8 January 1894.
27 Leonard Hall, Fred Brocklehurst, Kennedy, Pickles and James Sexton.
28 ILPCR 1894, p. 8. The vote was 35 to 33. The mover was Fred Jowett and the seconder Ben Turner.
29 ILPCR 1894, p. 12.
30 *WT*, 10 February 1894.
31 *Labour Leader*, 15 May 1908. Smart also urged Mann's claims prior to the 1894 Conference, *WT*, 20 January 1894.
32 *Ibid.*
33 ILPCR 1894, p. 11.
34 Secretary's Monthly Report, February 1894, in NAC Minutes. Such reports imply a continuing conception of accountability to the rank and file, but they did not last very long.

35　NAC Minutes, 28 February 1894.
36　ILPCR 1895.
37　NAC Minutes, 28 May 1894; initially members were the three officers.
38　*Ibid.*, Members were Brocklehurst, Tattersall and Hall.
39　*Ibid.*, 3 December 1894; 15 April 1895. ILPCR 1895, pp. 10—12; p. 29.
40　ILPCR 1895, p. 25.
41　ILPCR 1894, Constitution.
42　The near-illegible record of this conference is contained in the NAC Minutes. See also ILPCR 1896, pp. 14—15.
43　Thus, 105 votes were cast in support of the proposal to abstain from supporting any non-socialist candidate, and 10 for alternative courses of action.
44　Mann to Lister, 3 July 1895, ILP Archive 1895/99.
45　For details, see NAC Minutes. 3, 4 and 9 July 1895.
46　See its report to NAC, ILPCR, 1896, pp. 23—5.
47　NAC Minutes, 9 July 1895 — the only NAC members were Brocklehurst (on PFC anyway), Tattersall and Lister.

The arrival of the Big Four
48　NAC Minutes, 1 and 2 July 1898.
49　Mann's resignation was prefaced by strong criticism amongst some NAC members of his private life. See Glasier Diary, 30 August, 11 and 19 September, 6 December 1897.
50　NAC Minutes, 18 November 1893.
51　ILPCR 1895, p. 24.
52　ILPCR 1894, p. 15. Tom Mann, 'The method of organisation'.
53　For the creation of the Lancashire Federation see *Clarion*, 1, 15 July, 18 November 1893; and Judith Fincher, 'The Clarion Movement: a study of a socialist attempt to implement the co-operative commonwealth in England, 1891—1914', unpublished M.A. Thesis, University of Manchester, 1971, pp. 205—6. Hereafter, Fincher, *Thesis*.
54　See Mann, 'The method of organisation', for admission of gap between ideal and reality.
55　The four were Yorkshire, London, Midlands and North-Eastern. For the sixteen, see Fincher, *Thesis*, p. 239. This work offers a clear account of the rise and fall of the Federations.
56　Fincher, *Thesis*, pp. 227—36.
57　Some activists were also sceptical acout the Federations' value. See the note from a Bradford correspondent *Clarion*, 11 January 1896, claiming that the Yorkshire Federation 'has not proved to have the degree of effectiveness which was looked for ... certain of the branch organisations are falling out of it instead of remaining to improve it'.
58　NAC Minutes, 2 January 1896. The 1895 Conference had decided by 52 votes to 17 that branches should purchase a 1s. certificate of membership for each member. ILPCR 1895, pp. 24—5.
59　ILPCR 1896, p. 29. It is very difficult to grasp the significance of the decision from the official report.
60　ILPCR 1896, pp. 7—8. For a critical account see Joseph Burgess, *Clarion*, 11 April 1896.
61　For publications department see NAC Minutes, 22 April 1896. The *ILP News* lasted from 1897 to 1903. The Glasier Papers suggest that he often wrote most of it.
62　For the appointment of Tom Taylor, see NAC Minutes, 3 July 1896; for view that results hardly commensurate with the cost, NAC Minutes, 21 April 1897.

63   ILPCR 1897, p. 7.
64   For summary of committee structure, see NAC Minutes, 9 October 1897.
65   See NAC Minutes, 5 January, 21 April, 3 July 1897.
66   Glasier Diaries, 8 January 1898.
67   Hardie to Glasier, 20 August 1898, Glasier Correspondence, 1898/9.
68   Hardie to Glasier, 27 June 1900, Glasier Correspondence, 1900/51.
69   For the defence, see Penny to MacDonald, 12 April 1899. MacDonald Papers, 5/9.
70   The Stockport ILP reacted by resolving that unless the NAC consulted the whole membership on any putative contest, it would subscribe no more money for electoral purposes, Stockport ILP Minute Book, 31 October 1897. It was disclosed at a subsequent NAC that 5,000 pamphlets had been printed for Barnsley and a large number were still lying there. NAC Minutes, 8 April 1898. The Barnsley contest took over £449 from the Election Fund, ILPCR 1898, p. 11.
71   NAC Minutes, 8 April 1898.
72   Minutes of Parliamentary Committee, 3 July 1897 in NAC Minutes.
73   ILPCR 1898, pp. 44—6 for debate; Hardie's comment at p. 44.
74   NAC Minutes, 1 and 2 July 1898; Glasier Diaries, 23 July 1898 for meeting with Manchester members.
75   Parliamentary Committee Minutes, 22 July 1898 in NAC Minutes, 23 July 1898.
76   See ILPCR 1895, pp. 16—17 and 1896, pp. 16—17; for an early attempt see setting up of the committee, on Hardie's suggestion, to negotiate with SDF 'for harmonious working between the two bodies', NAC Minutes, 26 February 1894.
77   ILPCR, 1896.
78   For an official account, see ILPCR 1898, p. 31.
79   See his diary entry, 30 July 1897, the day after the informal meeting.
80   See ILPCR 1897, p. 30. Glasier noted (Diary, 30 July 1897) that 'Hardie seems greatly pleased that am against union. Evidently so is he, but he has not dared to show it.'
81   *Ibid.*, p. 6.
82   *Ibid.*, p. 8.
83   NAC Minutes, 8 April 1898.
84   ILPCR 1897, p. 29.
85   *Ibid.*, p. 27. See also Glasier Diaries, 9—11 April 1898.
86   Discussion is on pp. 29—36 of ILPCR 1898.
87   *Ibid.*, p. 31.
88   *Ibid.*, p. 33.
89   *Ibid.*, and then passed as substantive motion by 96 votes to 21 (p. 35).
90   By 78 votes to 23 (p. 35).
91   See ILPCR 1899, pp. 6—9 for summary of later developments.
92   See ILPCR 1896, p. 17, for paragraph where NAC ask 'the authorisation of this Conference' for this course of action. For debate, summary, and adoption of this section of report, *ibid.*, pp. 5—6.
93   ILPCR 1897, p. 8.
94   NAC Minutes, 3 July and 1 October 1896.
95   ILPCR 1899, p. 33 — carried in a debate on election policies.
96   For their continuation see *ibid.*, pp. 31—2; 38—41.
97   ILPCR, 1900, pp. 5—7.
98   Letter from MacDonald, *ILP News*, July 1898.
99   *ILP News*, March 1899.

The impact of the LRC

100   ILPCR, 1901, p. 5.
101   See NAC Minutes, 28 May and 28 July 1900 for Preston and for Merthyr. There is further discussion of the two seats after the dissolution — in minutes of meetings of available NAC members, 21—24 September 1900 in NAC Minutes. See also on Preston, Glasier's report of his visit there with John Penny in Glasier Correspondence 10 July 1900, 1900/68.
102   ILPCR, 1901, p. 5.
103   For the Finance Committee's appointment, see NAC Minutes 28 July 1900; for a statement on its work, ILPCR 1901, p. 8.
104   See the minutes of the September meetings noted above (note 101); see also Glasier Diary, 21—26 September 1900. The 'millionaires' reference is in the entry for 26 September.
105   The York negotiations are documented copiously in ILP Archive, 1899 and 1900 (various items), also *Labour Leader*, 20 January—10 February 1900, and NAC Minutes, 8 January 1900.
106   On South-West Manchester, see NAC Minutes, 28 May 1900; also Peter Clarke, *Lancashire and the New Liberalism*, p. 181, fn 2 and p. 311.
107   For Cadbury's financial role see Glasier Diaries, 21 September 1900. W. T. Stead was another contributor, *ibid.*, 22 September 1900. Note also the later letters from Cadbury to Glasier over the latter's Birmingham Bordesley fight in 1906. See Glasier Correspondence, January 1906 1906/1—3. Note also the letters from Cadbury to Herbert Gladstone 13 September, 2 and 8 October 1900, Gladstone Papers, BM Add MSS 46058 ff. 45, 120, 129.
108   Cadbury to Gladstone 8 October 1900.
109   'Should there be a White List?' *Labour Leader*, 11 August 1900.
110   See the following discussions in *Labour Leader*, 11, 18 and 25 August 1900 and the leader advocating a list in the *ILP News*, August 1900. NAC Minutes 28 July 1900 refer to a discussion on electoral policy and to the opinion of several NAC members that anti-war MPs should be supported.
111   For material on this Conference, see *Labour Leader*, 6 October 1900, and Glasier Diary, 29 September 1900. There is a copy of the NAC's circular on the Conference in MacDonald Papers 5/10. Also report in Minutes of the Parliamentary Committee, 11 October 1900 in NAC Minutes.
112   On Clitheroe, see the discussion and references in Chapter 3 above.
113   For ILP concern about Crooks see the references to material in the ILP Archive noted in the earlier section on London politics.
114   Glasier to Hardie, 15 May 1903, Glasier Correspondence, 1903/37. Also Glasier Diaries, 19 May 1903.
115   Hardie to Glasier, 18 May 1903, Glasier Correspondence, 1903/38. This contest is also covered in ILP Archive 1903 — note in particular 1903/91, Hodge to Hardie telegram, 11 May, 'Snowden and MacDonald speaking tonight and tomorrow — think it unwise to overload the platforms from one side' and 1903/94, Hodge to Hardie, 16 May admitting that he had pandered to fears of Tory converts about Hardie.
116   J. Gowland to Glasier, 6 July 1903, Glasier Correspondence 1903/30. Also other material in same collection including Hardie's reactions. ILP suspicion about Henderson is well captured in the comments of a Preston activist after the contest there. A. Collis to Hardie, 17 May 1903, ILP Archive, 1903/95.
117   NAC Minutes, 8 January 1900.
118   NAC Minutes, 30 and 31 January 1901.
119   NAC Minutes, 28 May 1900. Parker in fact could 'see *no* harm in an interview with the *Liberal Whips*'. Parker to MacDonald, 3 April 1900. LPLF 1/310.

120 ILPCR, 1903, p. 33.
121 ILPCR, 1904, p. 39. Carried by 63 votes to 45.
122 ILPCR, 1905, pp. 12—13.
123 For discussions of this see Bealey and Pelling, *Labour and Politics*, chapter 6; Marquand, *Ramsay MacDonald*, pp. 78—80, and Poirier, *The Advent of the Labour Party*, chapter 10; the lengthy correspondence between Jesse Herbert and MacDonald, MacDonald Papers, 5/13 and his account of relations with the Liberals, *ibid.*, 5/81, date probably Winter 1906—7. Correspondence between Herbert and Gladstone in the Gladstone Papers is reproduced by Bealey in 'Negotiations between the Liberal Party and the LRC before the general election of 1906', *Bulletin of the Institute of Historical Research*, 1956.
124 Cadbury to Hardie, 25 March 1903, ILP Archive, 1903/43.
125 Meeting held in Manchester, 26 November 1900. Reported in NAC Minutes, 30 and 31 January 1901. ILPCR, 1901, pp. 14—15 and pp. 44—5 for Hardie's advocacy.
126 ILPCR, 1902, pp. 9—10 and 12.
127 See for example, ILPCR 1903, p. 34.
128 For satisfaction at improved financial situation, see *ibid.*, p. 8.
129 *Ibid.*, for a note on a Lancashire conference held under NAC auspices.
130 The National Organiser was Matt Simm who spent much time in his native North East, ILPCR 1905, p. 14; for his appointment, NAC Minutes, 3 April 1905. The Organising Committee's formation is in NAC Minutes, 25 and 26 April 1905. See also Organisation Committee Minutes, 18 September 1905, NAC Minutes.
131 For the expansion of the Publication Department, see ILPCR, 1906, p. 12. The lengthy discussions over the acquisition of the *Labour Leader* can be traced in NAC Minutes from 26—27 May 1902 through to 25—26 January 1904. There are also comments in Glasier Diaries.
132 See for example, ILPCR 1903, p. 9.
133 For Dewsbury, see the discussion in Chapter 8 above.
134 ILPCR 1903, p. 34 — no debate nor vote given in official report.
135 For its first report, see ILPCR, 1904, p. 26.
136 Its abolition was unsuccessfully proposed in 1905, ILPCR, 1905, p. 51.
137 For a characteristic range of proposals, see ILPCR 1903, pp. 35—6.
138 ILPCR, 1905, p. 53. The proposal had been defeated three years earlier, ILPCR, 1902, p. 34.
139 NAC Minutes, 7 and 8 July and 2 and 3 October, 1905, 8 March 1906.
140 ILPCR, 1906, pp. 36—7.
141 *Ibid.*, pp. 22—3.
142 Russell Smart in *Labour Leader*, 22 May 1908.

Chapter 14: Pragmatic visionaries: a portrait of branch life

1 ILPCR 1894, p. 4. A membership of 38,000 is claimed in *Labour Leader*, 22 September 1894.
2 ILPCR 1895, p. 5 and *The Nineteenth Century*, January 1895, respectively.
3 See, for example, A. T. Sutton to John Penny, 8 October 1897, on the Norwich ILP claiming 108 members of whom 50 to 60 contributed regularly, ILP Archive 1897/70.
4 Thus the Manchester Central ILP affiliated in its early years on more than its actual number of members. See Minute Book of Manchester Central Branch of the ILP, 8 August 1905.
5 Figures from ILPCRs 1894—1906.

6   See Keighley Labour Union Minute Book, Executive 8 November 1895, for decision to purchase 25 certificates; and 28 November 1895 for decision to defer the certificates until January 1896 and then make them out for the following year. The latter meeting also made a decision to pay on 102 members to the Yorkshire Federation. There is a rough list of prominent members to whom certificates were sold in the back of the minute book.

7   ILPCR 1899.

8   For discussions on this point see the biographical works by Thompson, Marquand and Cross.

9   See the profile in *Labour Prophet*, March—April 1894.

10   See his *Pilgrim to the Left*.

11   See the entry in *Dictionary of Labour Biography*, volume 2. For a comment on his style in Parliament far removed from 'the plodding secretary of the Halifax Labour Party at 30/- a week', Glasier Diaries, 11 March 1913.

12   For early profiles, see *Keighley ILP Journal*, February 1894 and *Labour Leader*, 28 July 1894. There are references to his later career in Clarke, *Lancashire and the New Liberalism* and in Sylvia Pankhurst, *The Suffragette Movement*.

13   For Burgess, see his account of the formation of the ILP in *Clarion*, September 1909—January 1910. For Smith, see the references in K. O. Morgan, *Keir Hardie* and the profile in the *Labour Prophet*, September 1894.

14   For Pankhurst, see Sylvia Pankhurst, *The Suffragette Movement*; for Lister, see his obituary in *Halifax Courier and Guardian*, 12 October 1933; Littlewood is discussed in Clark *Thesis*. there are several references to Benson in the Glasier Diaries.

15   For Katharine Conway, see Thompson, *The Enthusiasts*; for Carrie Martyn, see the references in Tom Mann, *Autobiography*.

16   For Sexton's position, see NAC Minutes, 9 October 1897. Glasier's description is in his Diaries, 9 October 1897.

17   Curran resigned from the Council because of trade union duties. NAC Minutes, 1 and 2 July 1898.

18   He defeated Needham the Councillor responsible for the ban on ILP meetings in Boggart Hole Clough in November 1897. *Labour Leader*, 6 November 1897.

19   For Littlewood's council success in Honley, see Clark, *Thesis*, p. 254.

20   Lister's idiosyncracies helped to produce dissent in the Halifax Labour Union and between *Clarion* and *Labour Leader*. See both journals November 1894 to January 1895 and a wealth of correspondence in ILP Archive — in particular perhaps Lister to Hardie, 1 January 1895, *ibid.*, 1895/1.

21   See S. Carter, 'The ILP in Ashton-Under-Lyne, 1893—1900', *North West Group for the Study of Labour History, Bulletin* No. 4, esp. p. 71.

22   Higham advertised his products in the *Blackburn Labour Journal*; for Bradford cases, see Reynolds and Laybourn, 'The Emergence of the Independent Labour Party in Bradford'; for Tattersall, see *Labour Prophet*, October 1894.

23   *Keighley Labour Journal*, 28 October 1901, and 29 March 1902.

24   Clark, *Thesis*, pp. 95—113.

25   *Ibid.*, p. 361.

26   H. Hughes (Darlington) to Tom Mann, 21 January 1895, ILP Archive 1895/13.

27   J. W. Kennedy (Gateshead) to Tom Mann, 23 January 1895, ILP Archive 1895/16.

28   Fred Jowett to Tom Mann, 6 July 1895, ILP Archive 1895/105.

29   Fred Morley to Hardie, 19 December 1899, ILP Archive 1899/146.

30   L. M. Francis to John Penny, 3 August 1899, ILP Archive 1899/64.

31   *Clarion*, 24 February 1894.

32   G. Williams to Parliamentary Committee. No date. ILP Archive, 1898/153.

33 Glasier Diaries, 11 May 1896.
34 *Bradford Labour Echo*, 30 November 1895.
35 E. Spires to John Penny, June 1898, ILP Archive 1898/65.
36 Glasier Diaries, 11 January (Usworth); 11 June (Darlington); 17 June (Felling) all 1902.
37 See for example the arguments over their intervention in the Cockermouth by-election of 1906. *Labour Leader* 10, 17 and 24 August 1906 — and for the branch most concerned, Manchester Central ILP Minute Book, 4 September 1906.
38 Glasier Diaries, 18 October 1902.
39 For a valuable discussion see Jill Liddington and Jill Norris, *One Hand Tied Behind Us*.
40 Stockport ILP Minute Book, 6 December 1896.
41 *Labour Leader*, 3 June 1894.
42 Glasier Diaries, 4 June 1896.
43 *Ibid.*, 7 October 1900.
44 *Ibid.*, 12 July 1905.
45 *Ibid.*, 28 May 1905.
46 *Ibid.*, 10 May 1904.
47 F. Jowett, 'What made me a socialist' (no date) cited in E. P. Thompson, *William Morris* (1977 edition) pp. 667—8.
48 *Seedtime*, July 1894 — the writer, Ramsay MacDonald, was soon to join the ILP.
49 On this general theme, see Stephen Yeo, 'A new life: the religion of socialism in Britain, 1883—1896', *History Workshop* (4), Autumn 1977, pp. 5—56.
50 F. J. Ellis (Ipswich) to Tom Mann, 21 January 1895, ILP Archive 1895/14.
51 NAC Minutes, 13 August 1895.
52 ILPCR, 1898, p. 26.
53 By 1897, the Annual Conference Report was listing ILP membes on public bodies — 34 on Boards of Guardians, 48 on Parish Councils, 52 on School Boards, 45 on City and Town Councils, 24 on Urban District Councils and one on a Rural District Council.
54 For details see *Labour Leader* and *Clarion*, June and July 1896.
55 Glasier Diaries, 10 April 1898; Glasier's accounts often give information on topics, and sizes of crowds and collections.
56 *Ibid.*, 12 December 1897.
57 *Ibid.*, 3 May 1897.
58 *Labour Leader*, 16 June 1894.
59 *ILP News*, March 1899.
60 Matt Simm to Hardie, 29 January 1900, ILP Archive 1900/55.
61 J. Armstrong to John Penny, 4 June 1898, ILP Archive 1898/53.
62 Clark, *Thesis*, and Minutes of Colne Valley Labour Union 1899—1900.
63 *Labour Leader*, 29 June 1901.
64 See *Labour Leader*, 5 September 1896 for Bradford apathy: *Manchester*, September 1899 for apathy there.
65 For figures, see *Labour Leader*, 5 March 1898 (Halifax); 11 February 1899 (Blackburn); 22 April 1899 (York); *ILP News*, February 1899 (Leicester).
66 *Labour Leader*, 27 July 1895.
67 *Labour Leader*, 3 December 1898.
68 See the discussion, D. Cox, 'The rise of the Labour Party in Leicester', pp. 14—16.
69 *Keighley Labour Journal*, 29 November 1901.
70 J. Rae (Dalbeattie) to John Penny, 28 May 1898, ILP Archive 1898/47.

71   See, for example, Colne Valley Labour Union Minutes, Special Council, 9 June 1894.
72   For a Keighley hope, see *Labour Leader*, 4 January 1896.
73   See, for example, attempts by ILPers to court Liberal support in parliamentary contests in Bradford and Manchester 1900.
74   *Labour Leader*, 10 December 1898 and *Keighley Labour Journal*, 5—26 November 1898.

Chapter 13: Proposals and assumptions

Party policy

1   ILPCR, 1894, p. 7.
2   NAC Minutes, 3 December 1894; 15 April 1895.
3   ILPCR, 1895, pp. 11, 12, 21.
4   For the revised statement, see *ibid.*, p. 29.
5   ILPCR, 1896, p. 8.
6   NAC Minutes, 22 April 1896; 5 January and 26 February 1897.
7   ILPCR, 1897, p. 10, for text of NAC proposal.
8   *Ibid.*, pp. 21—2.
9   *Ibid.*, p. 22.
10   *Ibid.*
11   ILPCR, 1903, and programme inside cover.
12   ILPCR, 1904, pp. 37—8, and programme inside cover.
13   *Ibid.*, p. 36 and ILPCR, 1905, p. 51.
14   ILPCR, 1898, pp. 47—8.
15   ILPCR, 1899, p. 44.
16   ILPCR, 1896, p. 25.
17   ILPCR, 1900, p. 4.
18   *Ibid.*, p. 21, for a sample of Hardie's views see also the general discussion in Morgan, *Keir Hardie*, pp. 104—9.
19   ILPCR, 1900, p. 21.
20   *Ibid.*, pp. 27—8.
21   See *ILP News*, February—May 1900; *Labour Leader*, during March and April 1900; NAC Minutes, 1 March 1900; also Brocklehurst in *Clarion*, 21 April 1900.
22   All references in ILPCR, 1901, p. 36, vote on p. 37.
23   ILPCR, 1904, p. 27.
24   ILPCR, 1901, p. 42.
25   ILPCR, 1902, p. 24 and p. 25 for defeat of amendment approving the principle of unification.
26   ILPCR, 1904, p. 27.
27   ILPCR, 1901, p. 39; 1902, p. 31; 1903, p. 28; 1904, pp. 31—33.
28   For pensions, ILPCR, 1902, p. 31; 1903, pp. 25—6; for meals and allied benefits, 1904, pp. 33—5.
29   ILPCR, 1903, pp. 26—7.
30   For general discussions, see José Harris, *Unemployment and Politics 1886—1914* (Clarendon Press, Oxford, 1972); Kenneth D. Brown, *Labour and Unemployment 1900—14* (David and Charles Newton Abbot, 1971); Morgan, *Keir Hardie*, pp. 73—9 and 143—8.
31   See Harris, *Unemployment and Politics*, on this point.
32   See *ibid.* on the specific problems of West Ham.
33   ILPCR, 1904, p. 28; 1905, p. 32.
34   *Ibid.*
35   *Ibid.*

36 See Morgan, *Keir Hardie*, pp. 145—7; Brown, *Labour and Unemployment*, chapter 2.

The intellectual basis of the ILP

37 For a summary of influences, see W. T. Stead, 'The Labour Party and the Books that Helped to Make It', *Review of Reviews*, June 1906, pp. 568—82.

38 For a summary of the availability of texts in English, see Stuart Macintyre, *Proletarian Science: Marxism in Britain 1917—1933* (Cambridge University Press, Cambridge, 1980), pp. 91—2.

39 Glasier Diaries, 4 October 1896.

40 *Clarion*, 10 October 1896.

41 For Glasier's later dilution of Morris's inheritance see his *William Morris and the Early Days of the Socialist Movement*; note also E. P. Thompson's criticism of Glasier's treatment in his *William Morris*, 2nd edition, pp. 741—50.

42 Ramsay MacDonald, 'Socialism and Society', as presented in B. Barker (ed.), *Ramsay MacDonald's Political Writings* (Allen Lane, London 1972), p. 58.

43 ILPCR, 1909, p. 48 (MacDonald's address from the Chair).

44 Hardie to David Lowe, 8 December 1897, ILP Archive 1897/99.

45 *Labour Leader*, 22 September 1894.

46 Keir Hardie, *From Serfdom to Socialism* (George Allen, London 1907), p. 53. Note the discussions of this work in Morgan, *Keir Hardie*, pp. 205—8, and by Dowse in the introduction to the republished edition of this and other works (Harvester, Hassocks 1974).

47 For an analysis of the primary elements in this long-lasting Labour tradition which compares it with marxism, see Macintyre, *Proletarian Science*, chapter 7.

48 See Reid, *Keir Hardie*.

49 Hardie, *From Serfdom to Socialism*, p. 46.

50 Robert Blatchford, *Merrie England* (Clarion, London 1895) pp. 22—3.

51 In 'Socialism and Society' at p. 54 in Barker, *Ramsay MacDonald's Political Writings*.

52 For a valuable analysis of this and related themes, see Raymond Williams, *The Country and the City*.

53 *Labour Leader*, 6 January 1900.

54 Glasier to Hardie, 2 March 1903, Glasier Correspondence 1903/28.

55 Glasier to Hardie, 9 September 1904, Glasier Correspondence 1904/39.

56 See the series of letters to his wife and sister from Amsterdam, August 1904, Glasier Correspondence 1904/115 and 1904/122—28.

57 *ILP News*, April 1899.

58 'Socialism and Society', in B. Barker (ed.), *Ramsay MacDonald's Political Writings*, p. 84.

59 *Ibid.*, pp. 89—90.

60 *Clarion*, 29 July 1899.

61 ILPCR, 1898, pp. 48—9.

62 MacDonald in Barker, *Ramsay MacDonald's Political Writings*, p. 95.

63 In *Merrie England*, p. 104.

64 Glasier Diaries, 10 June 1896.

65 *ILP News*, March 1901.

66 Glasier Diaries, 10 and 14 March 1900.

67 *Ibid.*, 15 March 1900.

68 *Ibid.*, 13 March 1900.

69 For a discussion of this theme, see Macintyre, *Proletarian Science*, chapter 2; also the postscript to E. P. Thompson, *William Morris*, 2nd edition.

70 Hardie in *Labour Leader*, 30 March 1906.

71   *ILP News*, January 1899.
72   *Ibid.*
73   Glasier, *On Strikes*, p. 18.
74   *Clarion*, 29 January 1898. See also *ibid.*, 11 June 1892.
75   These quotes are from *Signs of Change* (Reeves and Turner, London, 1888), p. 46; note the contrasting of this publication with Fabian Essays in Thompson, *William Morris*, pp. 533—49.
76   See the chapter, 'How the Change Came'; note also the discussion of Morris's views on the problem of reformism in Perry Anderson, *Considerations on Western Marxism* (NLB, London, 1980), pp. 176—85.
77   Glasier Diaries, 26 July 1909.
78   ILPCR, 1908, p. 38.
79   'A Dream of John Ball' in *Three Works by William Morris*, edited by A. L. Morton, (Lawrence and Wishart, London, 1977), p. 53.
80   ILPCR, 1908, p. 39 (MacDonald).

Chapter 16: Connections and exclusions

'The divided forces of democracy'

1   Glasier Diaries, 6 November 1902.
2   *Ibid.*, 22 July 1909.
3   *Ardrossan and Saltcoats Herald*, 20 November 1885, cited in Reid, *Keir Hardie*, p. 77.
4   See for example the West Riding cases cited in Thompson, 'Homage to Tom Maguire', pp. 281—2.
5   For the Newcastle by-election of 1892, see *Daily Chronicle*, 16—27 August 1892.
6   *Labour Leader*, 29 January 1898; the campaign can be traced in *ibid.*, 7—29 January 1898; see also NAC Minutes, 7 January 1898; and also Glasier Diaries for the same date. He claims Smart, Curran, Mann — 'and to all our surprises' — MacDonald, advocated a Tory vote.
7   *Labour Leader*, 31 March 1894.
8   *Ibid.*, 14 July 1894 — in the aftermath of the Attercliffe by-election.
9   *Ibid.*, 28 May 1898.
10   *Ibid.*, 27 July 1895.
11   W. P. Byles to Keir Hardie, 16 November 1896, ILP Archive 1896/82.
12   W. P. Byles to Keir Hardie, 21 November 1896, ILP Archive 1896/84.
13   *Clarion*, 11 February 1893.
14   *Ibid.*, 14 May 1892.
15   On the Rainbow Circle and the Progressive Review, see Marquand, *Ramsay MacDonald*, pp. 55—7; and Peter Clarke, *Liberals and Social Democrats* (Cambridge University Press, 1978), pp. 56—61.
16   See Keir Hardie and Ramsay MacDonald, *The Nineteenth Century*, January 1899, pp. 20—38; also *ILP News*, January 1899. For evidence that MacDonald was the principal author see NAC Minutes, 1 October 1898. The piece is discussed in Morgan, *Keir Hardie*, pp. 93—4 and Marquand, *Ramsay Mac-Donald*, pp. 62—4.
17   *Nineteenth Century*, January 1899, p. 23.
18   *Ibid.*, p. 27.
19   *Ibid.*, pp. 29—34.
20   *Ibid.*, p. 25.
21   *Ibid.*, p. 32.
22   *Ibid.*, pp. 35—6.
23   *Ibid.*, p. 37.

24   *Labour Leader*, 20 May 1899.
25   Hardie, 'Should There Be A White List?', *ibid.*, 4 August 1900.
26   'On the Banks of the Rubicon: An Open Letter to John Morley', *ibid.*, 16 June 1900.
27   Glasier Diaries, 20 March 1900.
28   Bryn Roberts cited in *Labour Leader*, 28 September 1901.
29   Sam Hobson to Hardie, 10 January 1900, ILP Archive, 1900/23.
30   On the Nationalists in this period, see F. S. L. Lyons, *The Irish Parliamentary Party 1890—1910* (Faber and Faber, London, 1951).
31   Hardie to David Lowe, 24 February 1901, ILP Archive, 1901/2.
32   Hardie to David Lowe, 13 March 1901, ILP Archive, 1901/6.
33   *Labour Leader*, 16 March 1901.
34   See Chapter 7 above.
35   *Labour Leader*, 5 October 1901.
36   Glasier, *ibid.*, 26 October 1901.
37   Note, for example, Davitt's attitude at Mid Lanark, 1894, discussed in Chapter 7. Compare *Labour Leader* view of him, 14 April 1894, with later portrait, 4 January 1902.
38   James Connolly to Hardie, 3 July 1894, ILP Archive, 1894/140. For a discussion of Connolly's disquiet at Hardie's attitude during the Boer War, see Morgan, *Keir Hardie*, p. 108.
39   For a range of opinion, see *Labour Leader*, 26 October and 2 November 1901.
40   *Ibid.*, 10 January 1903.
41   *Ibid.*, 7 March 1903.
42   See Chapter 7 above.
43   For views on Lloyd George, see John Grigg, *The Young Lloyd George* (Methuen, London, 1973), chapter 10, and *Lloyd George: The People's Champion* (Methuen, London, 1978), chapter 2. Also his involvement with labour questions. Chris Wrigley, *David Lloyd George and the British Labour Movement* (Harvester, Hassocks, 1976).
44   Hardie to H. W. Massingham, 30 April 1903, ILP Archive, 1903/75.
45   For these developments, see Bealey and Pelling, *Labour and Politics*, pp. 133—8, and Chapter 8 above.
46   See also Hobhouse to Hardie, 16 January 1900, ILP Archive, 1900/38, on the abortive discussions for a Peace Candidate at York. The views of both Hobson and Hobhouse are discussed in Clarke, *Liberals and Social Democrats*.
47   On the emergence of the Social Radicals, see Clarke's works as cited previously; also H. V. Emy, *Liberals, Radicals and Social Politics, 1892—1914* (Cambridge University Press, 1973).

The exclusion of Tory socialism

48   For a discussion of these developments, see B. H. Brown, *The Tariff Reform Movement in Britain 1881—1895* (Columbia University Press, 1943), chapter 2.
49   The seminal presentation of this tradition is Raymond Williams, *Culture and Society 1780—1950* (Chatto and Windus, London, 1958); for some later thoughts on the same theme, see his *Politics and Letters*, pp. 97—132.
50   See W. T. Stead, 'The Labour Party and the Books that Helped to Make It'.
51   See the earlier discussion and references in the 'Scottish Dimension' chapter; on Champion see also Stanley Pierson, *Marxism and the Origins of British Socialism*, pp. 175—190 where Champion is considered as a 'realist' along with Engels and Mahon.
52   H. H. Champion, 'The New Labour Party', in *The Nineteenth Century*, July 1888, pp. 87—8.

53   This comment is voiced by 'Blake', the advocate of socialism, in Champion's dialogue, 'The Labour Movement: A Multitude of Counsellors', *ibid.*, April 1890, p. 550.

54   'An Eight Hours Law', *ibid.*, September 1889, p. 515.

55   'Protection as Labour Wants It', *ibid.*, June 1892, p. 1030.

56   *Ibid.*, p. 1031.

57   *Labour Elector*, 2 March 1889; for the Pigott case, see F. S. L. Lyons, *Charles Stewart Parnell*, pp. 308 ff.

58   *Labour Elector*, May 1893.

59   He urged support for the ASRS General Secretary, Harford, a putative opponent of Walter Long at Liverpool, West Derby, *ibid.*, 7 January 1893.

60   See his letter, *MG*, 2 February 1894.

61   See Joseph Chamberlain, 'The Labour Question', *The Nineteenth Century*, November 1892, pp. 677—710; and *ibid.*, December 1892, p. 882 for Champion's comment. This can be compared with the following much critical response of Hardie at pp. 883—90.

62   See George Bernard Shaw to John Burns, 12 August 1892 cited Dan H. Laurence, *The Collected Letters of George Bernard Shaw*, vol. 1, (Max Reinhardt, London, 1965), pp. 355—8. The second Newcastle campaign is described and discussed in detail in *Daily Chronicle*, 16—27 August 1892; note the letter by Champion, 19 August.

63   His views are expressed in *ibid.*, 15 August 1892.

64   For Barry, see Paul Mertinez, 'The "People's Charter" and the Eningmatic Mr. Maltman Barry', *Bulletin of the Society for the Study of Labour History*, Autumn 1980, pp. 34—45.

65   See the series of attacks in *WT* during 1893.

66   *Labour Elector*, 4 and 11 March 1893.

67   See the comment of James Leatham's cited earlier in Chapter 7, note 156, p. 157.

68   *Labour Elector*, 8 and 15 April; July 1893.

69   *Ibid.*, September 1893.

70   *Ibid.*, December 1893.

71   See, e.g.:

> the tolerance for all opinions, the good feelings still existing amongst all classes, the common sense, patience and fairness of rich and poor, that do exist here, give good grounds for the hope that as our race taught the world the lesson of political liberty, so it may set it an example in the rapid and peaceful attainment of economic freedom

'The New Labour Party', *The Nineteenth Century*, July 1888, p. 82.

72   On Blatchford and the *Clarion* movement, see the thesis by Fincher; also Logie Barrow, 'The Socialism of Robert Blatchford and the *Clerion* Newspaper 1889—1918', Unpublished Ph.D. thesis, University of London, 1975; also the brief discussions in Pierson, *Marxism and the Origins of British Socialism*, pp. 149—61 and in Bernard Semmel, *Imperialism and Social Reform* (Allen & Unwin, London, 1960). Note also Robert Blatchford, *My Eighty Years* (Cassell, London, 1931), and Laurence Thompson, *Robert Blatchford: Portrait of an Englishman* (Gollancz, London, 1951).

73   See *Clarion*, 11 February 1893 for an early presentation of some of these themes.

74   On this controversy, see the columns of *Clarion* and *Labour Leader* and also correspondence of the ILP Archive, December 1894 and January 1895.

75   *Labour Leader*, 12 January 1895.

76   Hardie to Lister, 25 December 1894, ILP Archive, 1894/213.

77   *Clarion*, 14 May 1892.
78   *Ibid.*, 16 January 1892.
79   *Ibid.*, 18 August 1894.
80   R. Blatchford to Bruce Glasier, 25 December 1901, Blatchford Correspondence.
81   Glasier Diaries, 1 January 1896.
82   R. Blatchford to Bruce Glasier, 26 February 1897, Blatchford Correspondence.
83   R. Blatchford to Bruce Glasier *circa* December 1901, *loc. cit.*
84   R. Blatchford to A. M. Thompson, 2 November 1931, *loc. cit.*
85   For example, his description of Labour activists who sought promises from Liberals as pursuing 'a policy unworthy of a pack of big lassies', *Clarion*, 16 July 1892.
86   R. Blatchford to Katherine St John Glasier, 8 March 1897, Blatchford Correspondence.
87   *Clarion*, 27 May 1899.
88   *Ibid.*, 21 October 1899.
89   *Ibid.*, 28 October 1899.
90   *Ibid.*, 21 October 1899.
91   *Ibid.*
92   *Ibid.* This was in the context of an earlier piece in the *Clarion*'s 'Julia Dawson' Column, 14 October 1899, presenting Maude Gonne's views on the war.
93   *Ibid.*, 4 November 1899.
94   *Clarion*, 13 July 1901, for a characteristic argument.
95   *Ibid.*, 10 June 1904; see also 16 September 1904 for an attack on TUC attitudes towards defence.
96   *Ibid.*, 16 September 1904.
97   *Clarion*, 22 May 1903.
98   For a discussion of trade union attitudes, see J. A. Garrard, *The English and Immigration 1880—1910*.
99   See Chapter 5 on the NUBSO.
100   See Garrard, *The English and Immigration*.
101   *Clarion*, 12 October 1895.
102   Cited Fincher, *Thesis*, p. 271. The articles are in *Clarion*, 15 and 22 October 1892.
103   ILPCR, 1903, p. 30.
104   For Hardie's views, see Morgan, *Keir Hardie*, pp. 179—80; and for his Commons speech on the bill, *HCDeb*, 4th Series, volume 145, columns 778—82.
105   Summarised in Garrard, *The English and Immigration*.
106   *Labour Leader*, 29 December 1894.
107   See Lancastrian ILP chapter for Snowden's comments during 1906 Blackburn election, and Glasier Diaries, 13 March 1900.
108   *ILP News*, October 1899.
109   *Ibid.*, November 1899.
110   For background and a discussion of the contest, see Brian Atkinson, 'The Bristol Labour Movement 1868—1906'. Unpublished D.Phil. Thesis, University of Oxford, 1969 (hereafter referred to as Atkinson, *Thesis*); the 1895 contest is dealt with specifically at pp. 338—44. See also the description of East Bristol in Pelling, *Social Geography of British Elections*, pp. 145—6.
111   Atkinson, *Thesis*, *passim*, for detail on these developments.
112   *Bristol Times and Mirror*, 16 March 1895; *Western Daily Press*, 12 and 14 March 1895.
113   On Labour efforts to find a candidate, see *Bristol Times and Mirror*, 16 March 1895. Also letter and telegram, W. Oxley to Hardie, 10 and 11 March 1895, ILP Archive, 1895/49 and 50, for efforts to obtain Mann, Thorne and Stanley;

and S. Hobson to Mann/Hardie, 19 March 1895, ILP Archive, 1895/62 for Holmes's final withdrawal.

114   For detail on Gore, see Atkinson, *Thesis*, pp. 319 and 338. Also p. 326 for his support of the Conservative in the 1890 Contest in East Bristol. *Labour Leader* coverage of the campaign during March 1895 includes description of Gore.

115   For the range of support, see Atkinson, *Thesis*, p. 341 and *Bristol Times and Mirror*, 21 March 1895. The latter contains Whitefield's explanation for his support despite his differences with the candidate on Home Rule. The decision of the Labour and socialist bodies to remain neutral is in *Bristol Mercury*, 19 March 1895.

116   It remained a question of support by leading ILP individuals. Although a local branch was formed by those backing Gore — see *Western Daily Press*, 20 March 1895 — the national party took no decision in support of Gore.

117   *Bristol Times and Mirror*, 21 March 1895.

118   See Atkinson, *Thesis*, pp. 344—6 for the fade-out, NAC Minutes of 3 July 1897 for Bristol problems, and Glasier Diaries, 28 September 1897 for one attempt to resolve them.

119   On this see Atkinson, *Thesis*, p. 338; and Spencer to Hardie, 24 March 1895, ILP Archive, 1895/66.

120   Spencer to Hardie, 18 March 1895, ILP Archive, 1895/59.

121   R. Gilliard to Hardie (postcard), 19 March 1895, ILP Archive, 1895/60.

122   For Wills's claims that Gore was a Tory or a Tory socialist, see *Bristol Times and Mirror*, 19 and 20 March 1895.

123   Copy in Fabian Papers.

124   *Bristol Times and Mirror*, 22 March 1895.

125   For Gore's views, see *ibid.*, 19—21 March 1895.

126   For this post-mortem, see *Labour Leader*, 30 March 1895; Brocklehurst had gone as Hardie's representative to a joint meeting of the Bristol organisations, to back Gore's claims. When they refused to support him, the ILP leaders backed Gore anyway, compounding the 'Tory' controversy with accusations of broken faith.

127   Gore to Hardie, 7 March 1895, ILP Archive, 1895/41.

128   Spencer to Hardie, 21 March 1895, ILP Archive, 1895/64.

Chapter 17: Some thoughts on alternatives

1   For a discussion of this problem, see Barrington Moore Jr, *Injustice: The Social Bases of Obedience and Revolt* (Macmillan, London, 1978), chapter 11.

Appendix 1

Summary of major events occurring during the period covered by this study

Year	General political events	Trade union developments	Labour and socialist politics
To 1885	Gladstone's second administration elected **1880**. Its life dominated by Irish affairs. Third Reform, Act **October 1884**. Extends household suffrage to county seats.	**Early 1880s**, trade union membership very restricted. Craftsmen, some cotton workers, some miners.	**1874** Thomas Burt and Alexander MacDonald elected as first miners' MPs. **1881** Foundation of Democratic Federation. **1883** Democratic Federation becomes Social Democratic Federation, proclaiming adherence to marxism under dominance of H. M. Hyndman. **1884** Formation of Scottish Land and Labour League. **December** SDF splits — Socialist League formed. **1883—4** Fabian Society formed.
1885	Gladstone Government falls. Replaced by Salisbury's first Conservative Government. **November—December** General Election; Result, Liberals 335, Conservatives 249, Irish Nationalists 86, Liberals include Crofters' MPs from Scottish Highlands. Irish officially recommending Conservative vote.	**16 January** *Cotton Factory Times* begins publication.	General election sees election of 5 miners' MPs in addition to Burt. Result of expansion of electorate in county seats dominated by miners. Also success of 5 Lib-Labs elsewhere. SDF run three candidates. Derisory polls in Hampstead and Kennington. John Burns 598 votes in West Nottingham. London contests produce accusations of Tory gold.

1886	January Salisbury Government defeated by Liberal—Irish alliance. February Gladstone takes office. 26 March Chamberlain resigns over proposal to introduce Irish Home Rule Bill. 8 April Home Rule Bill introduced. 8 June Home Rule bill defeated on 2nd reading. 93 Liberals oppose Government. July General election result, Conservatives 317, Liberal Unionists 77, Liberals 191, Irish Nationalists 85. Salisbury takes office with Liberal Unionist support. 20 November Launching of Irish 'plan of campaign' on payment of fair rents.	February Henry Broadhurst appointed Under-Secretary at Home Office. First working-class Government Minister. August Ayrshire Miners' Union formed – Keir Hardie, Secretary. September TUC decision to set up Labour Representation Committee. October Scottish Miners' Federation formed.	7 and 21 February Unemployed riots in Trafalgar Square and Hyde Park. Arrest of some SDF leaders.
1887	Spring Abortive 'round table' discussion on Liberal reunion. 9 September Mitchelstown, County Tipperary, 3 killed by troops at political meeting.	January—February Lanarkshire coal strike. A major setback for Scottish mining unionism. Spring Northumberland coal strike. September TUC first confrontation between Hardie and TUC 'old guard'. Formation of Labour Electoral Association Economic depression tending to lift. Giving more chance to organise semi- and unskilled.	January Hardie founds 'The Miner: A paper for underground workers' at Cumnock. Socialist propagandists active in both Lanarkshire and Northumberland coal strikes. July Hardie and Chisholm Robertson publish Labour programme in The Miner. November Bolton engineering dispute leads to election of slate of Labour candidates to Town Council. 13 November 'Bloody Sunday' – violent dispersal of Trafalgar Square meeting of Socialists, Radicals and Irish.

1888	Local Government Act creates county councils. Commission formed to consider allegations about links between Irish Nationalists and crimes.	Amalgamated Society of Railway Servants first attempt to develop a national programme 'The Darlington Programme'.	**27 April** Mid Lanark by-election. Keir Hardie 617 votes as Independent Labour candidate. **19 May** Groups that backed Hardie hold preliminary meeting to consider forming Scottish Labour Party. **June** H. H. Champion's *Labour Elector* begins publication. **June—July** Ayr Burghs by-election. Attempts to organise Labour vote. **25 August** Scottish Labour party formed. Glasgow includes Cunninghame Graham elected as Liberal MP 1886.
1889	**January 17** Progressives victorious in first London County Council elections. **February** Pigott's exposure before Irish Crimes Commission.	**February** National Union of Dock Labourers formed Glasgow. **March** Gasworkers and General Labourers formed at meeting in Canning Town. Will Thorne a leading figure. **June** Scottish Seamens' strike. **5 July** *Yorkshire Factory Times* begins publication. **August** London dock strike. **Autumn** Formation of Ben Tillett's Dock, Wharf, Riverside and General Workers' Union. **November** Miners' Federation of Great Britain formed at Newport.	**June—July** Miners fail to capture Liberal nomination in West Fife. **July** Formation of Second International, Paris. **25 September** Liberal candidate returned, unopposed for Dundee after rumoured candidature of John Burns fails to materialise. **December** Fabian Essays published.
1890	**4 December** Irish Nationalists split after Parnell cited in O'Shea's divorce action.	**June—July** Leeds Gas Strike 'The Battle of Wortley Bridge'. **September** Founding of Shipping	**February** Abortive negotiations between Liberals and SLP centering around Partick by-election.

	2 October Gladstone endorses 'Newcastle Programme' at meeting of National Liberal Federation. 6 October Death of Parnell, leaving bitterly divided party.	Federation — a response to New Unionism. TUC Eight Hours resolution passed. John Burns elected to parliamentary committee. Broadhurst resigns as Secretary and replaced by Charles Fenwick. December—January 1891 Scots Rail strike. December—April 1891 Manningham Mills strike in Bradford.	March Hardie enters field at West Ham South. April Labour Elector ceases publication. May London Labour Movement hold their first May Day celebration. 29 August Workmans Times founded, edited by Joseph Burgess.
1891		Tom Mann stands unsuccessfully against John Anderson for Secretaryship of Amalgamated Society of Engineers. National Union of Boot and Shoe Operatives begins to show interest in Labour representation. Membership of New Unions starts to decline in face of employer counter-attack.	May Formation of Bradford Labour Union in aftermath of Manningham Mills. 21 July Formation of Colne Valley Labour Union. August—March 1892 Meetings producing Scottish United Trades Council Labour Party. 12 December Robert Blatchford's Clarion begins publication in Manchester.
1892	July General Election; result, Conservatives 268, Liberal Unionists 46, Liberals 272, Irish Nationalists 81, Independent Labour 3. August Gladstone takes office with Irish support, and John Morley responsible for Irish affairs.	March—May Durham Miners' Association on strike. July DMA joins MFGB and followed by Northumberland Miners. Gasworkers adopt Socialist preamble to rules. Amalgamated Society of Railway	April Burgess opens Workman's Times list of Independent Labour sympathisers. 14 May Formation of Manchester and Salford Independent Labour Party with 'Fourth Clause' forbidding support for non-socialist parties.

1893

8 September Second Home rule Bill defeated in Lords.

Formation of National Free Labour Association.

Temperton v. *Russell*, adversely affecting trade union position on contracts.

10 April Start of Hull dock strike.

Servants decide to run General Secretary, Harford as Parliamentary candidate. Leeds delegate meeting of ASE modernises union structure and adopts resolution on Labour representation. TUC accepts Hardie resolution on Independent Labour representation.

November Cotton spinners start twenty-week lock out terminated by Brooklands agreement.

July General Election — Hardie (West Ham South), Burns (Battersea), Havelock Wilson (Middlesbrough) elected as Independent Labour MPs — only Wilson has a Liberal opponent. SLP and SUTCLP candidates poll badly. SLP severs final ties with Liberals. Tillett polls well as Independent Labour candidate for West Bradford.

Summer Attempts to form London ILP.

August Halifax Labour Union formed.

25 August Newcastle by-election. Hardie and other oppose Morley on Eight Hours question and provoke Irish hostility.

22 September Leeds South by-election; J. L. Mahon withdraws as candidate after disorders at meetings following Championite attacks on Liberals.

November Fred Jowett elected to Bradford Town council.

Autumn Negotiation for ILP Conference.

January *Labour Elector* resumes publication.

14—16 January Inaugural ILP Conference at Bradford agrees on structure and programme. Lister Treasurer and Shaw Maxwell Secretary.

1894

3 March Gladstone resigns premiership; Rosebery emerges as successor. Budget — Harcourt introduces death duties.

Local Government Act introduces Parish Councils.

July First news of Armenian massacres.

Major onslaught on a surviving stronghold of New Unionism.
Spring Strong opposition within NUBSO to arbitration.
Summer NUBSO presidential election. Lib-Lab Hornidge defeats Socialist Votier.
July—November MFGB lockout. A successful demonstration of inter-coalfield solidarity, although Durham and Northumberland Miners' leave the Federation.

TUC scheme for Labour Representation amended in collectivist direction. Fenwick defeats Hardie in contest for secretaryship.

March Scottish Miners' Federation formed, affiliates to MFGB.
Spring NUBSO adopts socialist objective. Secretary, Liberal, Thomas Inskip resigns as Parliamentary Agent.
Summer Scottish miners' lockout shows advance in solidarity.
July Harford of ASRS adopted as Lib-Lab candidate for Northampton.
TUC adopts collectivist resolution. Sam Wood elected Secretary to Parliamentary Committee defeating Fenwick and Mann.

---

4 February Huddersfield by-election. Liberals lose seat. Local ILP urge abstention.
9 February 1st ILP contest in by-election. John Lister at Halifax third but 3028 votes.
6 March Broadhurst defeated in Grimsby by-election. Attacked by Hardie and Champion.
Hardie emerges as the one Independent Labour MP.
Estrangement from Burns and disputes with Champion.
October Championite attempt to revive SUTCLP fails.
November Joint Weavers—SDF ticket for Council elections in Nelson.
9 November Publication of Blatchford's *Merrie England*.

February 2nd ILP Conference at Manchester streamlines National Administrative Council. Tom Mann elected Secretary and Hardie President.
17 March *Workman's Times* ceases publication.
31 March Hardie's *Labour Leader* published monthly since 1893 becomes a weekly.
5 April Mid Lanark by-election. Robert Smillie stands for SLP, 3rd place, after Irish hostility.

1895

21 June Rosebery Government defeated on snap vote. Resigns next day.

July Election; result, Conservatives 340, Liberal Unionists 71, Liberals 177, Irish Nationalists 82. Salisbury takes office with Chamberlain as Colonial Secretary.

Spring NUBSO lockout. Union defeated.

May George Barnes unsuccessfully challenges Anderson for ASE Secretaryship. ASE ballot favourable to Labour Representation. Cotton unions press during election for ending of Indian cotton duties. Liberal losses in cotton towns. TUC standing orders reformed to introduce voting weighted by affiliated membership, exclusion of trades councils and of delegates neither officials of unions nor working at their trade. A blow to Socialists.

Autumn ASE involved in disputes on Clydeside and in Belfast.

Autumn Cotton workers ballot very narrowly in favour of Labour representation.

Spring Champion leaves for Australia — *Labour Elector* wound up.

3 July Sheffield Attercliffe by-election. Frank Smith stands for ILP after Liberals reject local trade unionist. This incident leads Ramsay MacDonald to join the ILP.

29 August Burgess contests Leicester for ILP. 2 MPs to be chosen. Burgess shows sympathy for one of the Liberals, Broadhurst.

Winter 1894–5 Hardie heavily involved in agitating for unemployed.

January SLP finally absorbed into ILP.

21 March East Bristol by-election. H. H. Gore, Independent Socialist 130 votes short of victory in straight fight with Liberal. Some ILP support for Gore.

April ILP Conference revises party programme.

June Glasgow Workers' Municipal elections Committee formed, bringing together trade unionists and socialists. An increasingly common pattern.

July All 28 ILP and 4 SDF candidates defeated in General Election, incl. Hardie who is displaced in straight fight with Conservative. Harford ASRS Lib-Lab defeated at Northampton.

1896	8 October Rosebery resigns as Liberal leader. Succeeded by Kimberley/Harcourt joint leadership.	June Employers' Federation of Engineering Association formed. August ASE Executive make serious personal charges against Anderson, who is challenged by Barnes for Secretaryship and defeated. October Scottish Miners' Federation Executive support socialist objective. 1896—7 Growing ILP influence on ASRS Executive. 1896 (and 1898) *Lyons v. Wilkins* limiting union right to picket.	April ILP conference removes Federations from official party structure. Presidency becomes chairmanship. 1 May North Aberdeen by-election. Tom Mann stands for ILP and loses to Liberal employer by 430 votes in straight fight. May—July Boggart Hole Clough meetings. ILPs speakers jailed. October *Progressive Review*. Product of Rainbow Circle — Radicals and Socialists, discontinued September 1897. 10 November Bradford East by-election, Hardie 3rd in three-cornered fight.
1897	Workmens Compensation Act	January MFGB Conference rejects Scottish resolution on socialist objective but accepts one for specific items of public ownership. March Foundation of Scottish TUC. July ASE Lockout begins. Autumn Culmination of ASRS 'All Grades' campaign. October Harford sacked as ASRS General Secretary. November Lib-Lab Fred Maddison quits as editor of ASRS *Railway Review* having expressed scepticism about ASRS industrial strength.	3 March Halifax by-election. Tom Mann third. April ILP Conference agrees short political statement. *ILP News* inaugurated. July Start of fusion discussions with SDF. 6 August Sheffield Brightside by-election. Fred Maddison wins for Liberals having faced strong ILP criticism. 28 October Barnsley by-election. Pete Curran a bad third for ILP. Liberal coal-owner wins, backed by Yorkshire Miners'. The peak of ILP-Lib/Lab acrimony.

1898

19 May Death of Gladstone.
Autumn Fashoda crisis.
December Resignation of Harcourt.

January ASE Lockout ends.
March George Wardle of ILP appointed editor of *Railway Review.*
1 April Start of five-month-long South Wales coal dispute.
June Richard Bell defeats Walter Hudson in contest for ASRS General Secretaryship.
October ASRS Annual General Meeting decides General Secretary should stand for Parliament on politically independent platform. NUBSO ballot chooses T. F. Richards of the ILP as parliamentary candidate.
Winter 1898—99 South Wales Miners' Federation formed in aftermath of lockout.

13 January York by-election. ILP advise Tory vote as punishment for alleged Liberal rowdyism and Liberal candidate support of engineering employers.
April ILP Conference; confused debate on fusion; Mann succeeded as Secretary by John Penny.
Summer Socialist propagandists active in South Wales during coal dispute.
July Decision by NAC to restrict parliamentary candidates at next election to 25.
November Coalition of socialists and trade unionists win control of West Ham Borough Council.

1899

6 February Campbell-Bannerman becomes Leader of the Liberal Party.
12 October South African War begins.

March ASRS Executive supports resolution from Doncaster favouring broad conference to discuss methods for increasing Labour representation. STUC supports similar proposal for Scotland.
May NUBSO Secretary, Inskip, dies. In the succeeding ballot Lib-Lab Hornidge defeats ILPer Richards.
ASE ballot backs levy for parliamentary purposes.
July General Federation of Trade Unions formed.
September TUC accepts ASRS resolution on Labour representation.

ILP leaders anxious about falling membership and financial problems.
January Article by Hardie and MacDonald in *The Nineteenth Century* emphasising ILP candidatures would be limited at next election and noting points of agreement with Radicals.
April ILP Conference passes resolution licensing participation in Labour representation conference.
June—July James Mawdsley of Cotton Spinners stands unsuccessfully as Conservative candidate in Oldham by-election.

1900

January—February Irish Nationalists reunited under John Redmond. September—October Khakhi election with Liberals divided over War. Result, Conservatives 334, Liberal Unionists 68, Liberals 184, Irish Nationalists 82, Labour Representation Committee 2.

March First Trade Union affiliations to Labour Representation committee, including Gasworkers, ASRS and Steel Smelters. Spring ASE ballot on affiliation — result in favour but not acted on due to very low turnout. March—June Lancashire and Cheshire Miners' Federation, having sent delegates to LRC foundation conference decide not to affiliate. August Taff Vale Railway dispute. NUBSO ballot on affiliation. Turnout low but accepted as ground for affiliation.

August Bell adopted as Independent candidate by Derby Trades Council. October—November Blatchford supports South African War and attacks ILP views through the *Clarion*.

6 January Scottish Workers Parliamentary Elections Committee formed at Edinburgh meeting. 27—28 February Labour Representation Committee formed at Memorial Hall Conference — Ramsay MacDonald appointed Secretary. April Glasier ILP Chairman. 25 May South Manchester by-election. Liberal backed by local ILP heavily defeated following news of relief of Mafeking. September—October General Election. LRC run 15 candidates of which 8 are sponsored by ILP and 1 by ILP and SDF. Hardie wins second Merthyr seat faced by 2 Liberal opponents. Bell sponsored by ASRS wins second Derby seat, in tandem with a Liberal and opposed by 2 Conservatives. October Formation of National Democratic League — as basis for co-ordinating Radical and Labour initiatives. Autumn ILP/NAC decide to establish propaganda fund.

1901	Blockhouse and concentration camp system introduced into South Africa by British. **14 June** Campbell-Bannerman's 'Methods of Barbarism' speech on the war. Widespread expectation that Liberal split might become permanent with possibilities for political realignment. Budget, tax on coal exports. **November—January 1902** *Times* articles on crisis in British industry emphasising negative role of trade unions. **16 December** Lord Rosebery's Chesterfield speech on divisions in Liberal Party.	**January** Northern Counties Weavers' Amalgamation decide against affiliating to the LRC. But Colne Weavers' Association affiliate separately. **July** Taff Vale legal judgment — heavy damages for ASRS. *Quinn* v. *Leatham* decision weakens trade union capacity to boycott employers. **Summer** Blackburn Weavers' dispute leading to legal action by employer — 'The cotton workers' Taff Vale'. Development of MFGB scheme for Labour Representation without limitation on party poltical allegiance. Second ASE ballot on LRC affiliation decides in favour again with a very small turnout. But this time affiliation follows in February 1902.	**January** LRC affiliated membership 41 unions, 353,070 members. **August** Social Democratic Federation withdraws from LRC on grounds of latter's lack of a socialist commitment. **26 September** North East Lanarkshire by-election. Robert Smillie stands for SWPEC and comes third, with a Conservative victor. Smillie backed by several Liberals and by Irish on account of Liberal candidate's imperialism and coldness on Home Rule.
1902	**24 February** Liberal League formed — a further sign of Liberal disharmony. Budget introduces Corn Tax, seen by some as erosion of free trade. **31 May** Peace of Vereeniging. Education Act abolishing school boards; opposed by non-conformists as favouring denominationial schools.	**January** Northern Counties Weavers' Amalgamation support principle of Labour representation. **February** Death of Mawdsley. Powerful obstacle to cotton unions linking with political organisation removed. **Winter 1902—03** Cotton workers' ballot on Labour Representation — favourable result.	**January** LRC 65 Unions affiliated with 455,450 members. **28 January** Dewsbury by-election — Harry Quelch 1597 votes as SDF candidate with some local ILP support. Previous row between SDF and LRC over candidature. **25 March** Wakefield by-election — Phillip Snowden sponsored by ILP under LRC label and loses in straight

Liberal by-election fortunes improve. **Summer** Salisbury resigns — replaced by Balfour as Prime Minister.

1903 **May** Chamberlain launches protectionist programme. **September** Cabinet upheaval over Government policy on Free Trade.

Beginning of protracted Denaby and Cadeby dispute in Yorkshire coalfield involving evictions and legal action.

January Cotton workers affiliate to LRC through their lobbying arm — the United Textile Factory Workers Association. **1 April** Final extinction of sliding scale in South Wales coalfield. Conciliation Board established. **April–May** Lancashire and Cheshire Miners decide on affiliation to LRC. **October** NUBSO Executive favours co-operation with other parties in forwarding T. F. Richards's candidature at West Wolverhampton.

fight with Conservative. **1 August** David Shackleton of Weavers returned unopposed for Clitheroe. ILP waives claims to candidature and Liberals reluctant to offend cotton workers.

Blachford publishes *Britain for the British*; J. A. Hobson publishes *Imperialism*.

January LRC affiliation 127 unions, 847,315 members. Negotiations beginning between MacDonald and Herbert Gladstone and Jesse Herbert for the Liberals over limited understanding on candidates. **February** LRC's Newcastle Conference tightens guiding notion of independence and establishes separate political fund. **11 March** Will Crooks wins Woolwich for LRC in straight fight with Conservative. Some ILP criticism of tone of Crooks' campaign. **April** Snowden ILP Chairman. **14 May** John Hodge of Steel Smelters fails at Preston in straight fight with Conservative. ILPers not encouraged to be prominent. **24 July** Arthur Henderson of the Iron Founders captures Barnard Castle for LRC — seat for which he was formerly

Liberal agent — margin 47 votes; LRC's first victory against both parties. ILP presence again limited.

4 September Leicester Liberals decide to run just one candidate in two-member seat at next election. MacDonald in field for ILP and LRC.

6 September Final agreement at national level of Gladstone—MacDonald pact reached at Leicester.

December *ILP News* ceases publication.

15 January Norwich by-election. George Roberts, ILP-sponsored, comes third for the LRC. Liberal wins easily on Free Trade.

20 January J. Johnson wins Gateshead for Liberals standing as Durham Miners' candidate.

February *Labour Leader* becomes official ILP paper.

April ILP Conference approves appointment of Francis Johnson as Party Secretary.

10 August North East Lanarkshire by-election. This time Liberals united with Irish support; they win. John Robertson for Scottish Workers' Representation Committee third but more votes than Smillie in 1901.

3 November Tom Richards wins West Monmouth by-election, under MFGB

1904

3 February Death of Pickard, MFGB President, a Lib-Lab opponent of Independent Labour. Succeeded by Lib-Lab W. Parrott as Normanton's MP.

ASRS under criticism from LRC over Bell's readiness to support Liberal candidates.

Start of long and bitter mining dispute at Hemsworth in Yorkshire. Evictions; Local union activists attracted by ILP.

NUBSO socialist objective sharpened up.

10 February Transvaal Council approves ordinance previously sanctioned by Colonial Office authorising employment of indentured Chinese Labour on the Rand. Policy opposed by some predominantly on moral grounds and by others as denial of opportunities for British Labour.

Licensing Act offends temperance lobby.

1905

Agitation over unemployment helps to produce Unemployed Workmans Act; this acknowledges some government responsibility for unemployed.

Aliens Act — culmination of agitation for more than a decade, aimed at limiting immigration. Agitation had been backed by some trade unionists. **December** Balfour Government resigns — replaced by Liberal Government under Campbell-Bannerman. Parliament dissolved.

Summer South Wales Miners Conference supports affiliation to LRC.

J. W. Taylor of Durham Colliery Mechanics and ILP emerging as likely parliamentary candidate in Durham.

Death of W. Parrott leads to struggle within Yorkshire Miners for Normanton candidacy. Fred Hall, Liberal, defeats Herbert Smith, ILP.

scheme. Lib-Lab MP although he had courted LRC support.

January Glasier editor of *Labour Leader*. ILP Conference adopts resolution for restructuring NAC to include divisional representatives.

Ramsay MacDonald publishes *Socialism and Society*.

December John Burns, first working-class cabinet minister. President of Local Government Board.

1906 and beyond

January—February Liberals win massive victory: Liberals 400, LRC 29, Conservatives 133, Liberal Unionists 24, Irish Nationalists 83, Independent Labour 1.

Durham and Northumberland miners join MFGB 1908 and 1907 respectively.

MFGB eventually affiliate to Labour Party on 1 January 1909 following two ballots in 1906 and 1908.

In 1906 election, 29 LRC candidates successful — only three opposed by official Liberals. Also J. W. Taylor wins Chester Le Street against both older parties. The 29 include seven sponsored by the ILP and several other ILP members.

LRC subsequently becomes the Labour Party. Keir Hardie elected first Chairman of the Parliamentary Labour Party.

Appendix 2: The Bradford conference

There is some doubt about the total number of delegates present at Bradford. Pelling, *Origins*, suggests 'about 120' (p. 116). ILPCR 1893, p. 1, states 115 present at the start. *MA* agrees with this (1st day, pp. 8—9), and breaks them down as 91 ILP, 11 Fabian, 6 SDF and 7 others. (Clearly SLP delegates and perhaps SUTCLP are counted as ILP.) Later (*MA*, 2nd day, p. 22), the total number is reported as 123. This addition of eight is supported by *Workman's Times*, 21 January 1893, which lists the late arrivals as delegates for St Helens Chemical and Copper Workers, Yorkshire Fabians, Camlachie SLP, Bromley and Southport ILPs, Padiham SDF plus two of the three from the Cumberland and North Lancashire Workmen's Federation. But this account diverges from the others in listing a total of only five SDF delegates, omitting John Birch of Bury.

The published report gives two lists of delegates — one by organisation inside the front cover, presumably copied from list in *MA*; the other grouped regionally, p. 1. There are some inconsistencies of spelling and also B. Bilcliffe (West Salford) is listed erroneously as a Bradford delegate on p. 1. Some names also appear on one list only:

On p. 1 but not in frontispiece
George Smith, Nottingham; F. Smith, York
In frontispiece but not on p. 1
Walter Vickers, Hyde ILP; Fred Brocklehurst, Manchester Labour Church; T. Snaith, Yorkshire Fabian Federation

It is the first pair which raises problems. Hardie (*Labour Leader*, 9 April 1914), recalled Brocklehurst and Snaith as delegates — and Hyde is listed amongst the towns represented in the NAC voting (*MA*, 2nd day, p. 2).

There is also a discrepancy over the name of the Heywood SDF delegate. Page 1 lists Walter Vicars as 'Heywood', the frontispiece gives S. J. Bardsley as representing both Heywood SDF and Ramsbottom Fabian Society, ILPCR 1893, p. 4, gives Bardsley as moving the socialist objective. Finally, 'Walter

Vickers' is given in the frontispiece as the Hyde ILP delegate. The surviving records of the Hyde ILP do not specify the name of the Bradford delegate, but Walter Vickers was a leading figure in the Hyde ILP. Possibly someone composing p. 1 confused Heywood and Hyde.

Some delegates represented more than one organisation (apart from the Bardsley case): Edward Aveling, Bloomsbury Socialist Society and Legal Eight Hours and International Labour League; W. J. Lewington, Chatham ILP and Medway District Trades Council; Arthur Field, Bromley ILP; Leicester ILP (no initial given in frontispiece re Leicester but provided p. 1); W. J. Grierson (p. 1) or Grievson (p. 1) or Grievson (frontispiece), Bolden ILP, Hebburn ILP, Jarrow ILP; H. A. Barker, London Labour Union, Hoxton ILP.

References

Manuscript sources

Aberdare Socialist Society/ILP. Notebook, Glamorgan Record Office.
Aberdare Socialist Society/ILP. Minute Book, 1901—6, Aberdare Local Collection.

Blatchford Correspondence, Manchester Central Reference Library.
Brecon Road Liberal Association, Merthyr Correspondence, Glamorgan Record Office.
British Library of Political and Economic Science Collection of ILP material, including NAC Minutes and Reports to Head Office.
Broadhurst Papers. British Library of Political and Economic Science.
Bryce Papers. Bodleian Library, University of Oxford.
John Burns Papers. British Museum.

Colne Valley Labour Union/Labour League Minutes. Colne Valley Constituency Labour Party.

Edinburgh Central ILP Minutes. Edinburgh Public Library.

Fabian Society Papers. Nuffield College, Oxford.

Gilray, John, 'Early Days of the Socialist Movement in Edinburgh', NLS Acc 4965.
Herbert Gladstone Papers. British Museum.
Glasier Collection. Sidney Jones Library, University of Liverpool.

Hardie Correspondence with Irish National League. NLS MS 1809.
Hyde ILP Minute Book. Councillor Peter Bailey (Private Owner), Hyde.

ILP Archive. To be housed in the British Library of Political and Economic Science.

Keighley Labour Union/ILP Minute Book. Keighley Public Library.

Labour Party Letter Files. Labour Party Library.
Labour Representation Committee Executive Minutes, Correspondence Files, Labour Party Library.
Leicester Liberal Association Minutes, Leicestershire County Record Office, Leicester.
Lister Papers, Halifax Public Library.

MacDonald Papers, Public Record Office.
Manchester Central ILP Minute Books, Manchester Central Reference Library.
Manchester Guardian Archive, Scott Correspondence. John Rylands Library, University of Manchester.
Mattison Collection, Brotherton Library, University of Leeds.
Mid Lanark Correspondence, NLS Dep 176.8. Vol. 8.

Scottish Labour Party, Edinburgh Central Branch Minutes, NLS Acc 3828 (Microfilm).

Scottish TUC, MSS account of Foundation Congress, Reports 1897—99; Minutes of Joint Meeting of Representatives from the ILP, SDF and Parliamentary Committee of the STUC, NLS Acc 4682 (Microfilm).

Scottish Workers' Parliamentary Elections Committee Records, NLS, Acc 4682 (Microfilm).

W. Small Material, NLS MS Acc 3350.

Stockport ILP Minute Book, Stockport Public Library.

J. John Vaughan Papers (D/D Vau), Glamorgan Record Office.

Beatrice Webb Diaries, British Library of Political and Economic Science.

H. J. Wilson Papers, Sheffield Public Library.

Trade Union records

Aberdeen Trades Council Reports, Webb TU Collection, British Library of Political and Economic Science.

Amalgamated Society of Engineers Records, AUEW Offices, Peckham, London.

ASRS Records, National Union of Railwaymen, Unity House, London NW1.

Blackburn Trades Council Reports, Blackburn Public Library.

Cardroom Amalgamation Records, Union of Textile Workers, Rochdale.

Dock, Wharf, Riverside and General Labourers' Records, Webb TU Collection.

Durham Miners' Association, NUM Durham.

Gasworkers' and General Labourers' Records, Webb TU Collection.

General Railway Workers Union, Webb TU Collection.

Glasgow Trades Council Minute Books; Reports; Centenary Brochure 1858—1958, Mitchell Library, Glasgow.

Lancashire and Cheshire Miners' Federation Records, NUM North-western Area, Bolton.

Miners' Federation of Great Britain Records, NUM North-western Area, Bolton.

National Union of Dock Labourers Reports, Webb TU Collection.

National Union of Boot and Shoe Operatives, National Union of Footwear, Leather and Allied Trades, Earls Barton, Northants.

Nelson and District Trades Council Minutes, Nelson Weavers' Institute.

Nelson Weavers' Association Records, Nelson Weavers' Institute.

Royal Commission on Labour, Minutes of Evidence.

Scottish Miners' Federation, Minute Books, NLS Acc 4312.

Sheffield Federated Trades Council Reports, Webb Trade Union Collection.

TUC 1903 Official Souvenir, Leicester Trades Council, Leicester Public Library.

TUC Reports; Parliamentary Committee Minutes (Microfilm), Manchester Central Reference Library.

Weavers' Amalgamation Records, Union of Textile Workers, Rochdale.

Yorkshire Miners' Association Records, NUM, Yorkshire Area, Barnsley.

Unpublished theses

Atkinson, Brian, 'The Bristol Labour Movement 1868—1906', Oxford, D. Phil. 1969.
Barrow, Logie, 'The Socialism of Robert Blatchford and the Clarion Newspaper 1889—1918', London, Ph.D. 1975.
Bather, L., 'A History of the Manchester and Salford Trades Council', Manchester, Ph.D. 1956.

Clark, D. G., 'The Origins and Development of the Labour Party in Colne Valley 1891—1907', Sheffield, Ph.D. 1978.
Cox, D., 'The Rise of the Labour Party in Leicester', Leicester, M.A. 1959.
Craigen, J. M., 'The Scottish Trades Union Congress 1897—1973 — A Study of a Pressure Group', Heriot Watt, M.Litt. 1975.

Fincher, Judith, 'The Clarion Movement: A Study of a Socialist Attempt to Implement the Co-operative Commonwealth in England 1891—1914', Manchester, M.A. 1971.
Fox, K. O., 'The Emergence of the Political Labour Movement in the Eastern Section of the South Wales Coalfield', University College Wales, Aberystwyth, M.A. 1965.

Gregory, R., 'The Miners and Politics in England and Wales 1906—14', Oxford, D.Phil. 1963.
Gupta, P. S., 'History of the Amalgamated Society of Railway Servants 1871—1913', Oxford, D.Phil. 1960.

Harris, P. A., 'Class Conflict, The Trades Unions and Working Class Politics in Bolton 1875—1896', Lancaster, M.A. 1971.
Hill, J., 'Working Class Politics in Lancashire 1885—1906: A Regional Study in the Origins of the Labour Party', Keele, Ph.D. 1969.

Kellas, James, 'The Liberal Party in Scotland 1885—1895', London, Ph.D. 1962.

Metcalfe, G. H., 'A History of the Durham Miners' Association 1860—1915', Durham, M.A. 1947.

Scott, I., 'The Lancashire and Cheshire Miners' Federation 1900—14', York, Ph.D. 1977.

Taplin, Eric, 'The Origins and Development of New Unionism 1870—1910', Liverpool, M.A. 1967.
Trodd, G., 'Political Change and the Working Class in Blackburn and Burnley 1880—1914', Lancaster, Ph.D. 1978.

Weeks, B. C. M., 'The Amalgamated Society of Engineers: A Study of Trade Union Government, Politics and Industrial Politics', Warwick, Ph.D. 1976.

Young, J. D., 'Working Class and Radical Movements in Scotland and the Revolt from Liberalism 1866—1900', Stirling, Ph.D. 1974.

Printed political material

Collection of Election Literature 1895, Mitchell Library Local Collection, Glasgow.
ILP Conference Reports, John Rylands, Library, University of Manchester.
ILP Pamphlets, wide selection in ILP Archive. See also check-list in Gillian B. Woolven, *Publications of the Independent Labour Party* (Society for the Study of Labour History 1977).
Labour Representation Committee Conference Reports.
Report of South Wales ILP Conference, 29 October 1905.

Press

(i) Labour Press

Aberdeen Labour Elector
Aberdeen Standard

Barrow ILP Journal
Blackburn Labour Journal
Bolton and District Independent Labour Pioneer
Bradford Labour Echo
Bradford Labour Journal

Clarion
Colliery Workman's Times
Cotton Factory Times

The Democrat, June—November 1902
Dundee Elector (Lamb Collection, Dundee Public Library)

Halifax Free Press
Hardie's Election Herald and East Bradford Campaigner

The ILPer, the monthly record of the Liverpool Branch of the Independent Labour Party
ILP News

Justice

Keighley ILP Journal

The Labour Annual
Labour Chronicle (Edinburgh)
Labour Elector
Labour Leader
Labour Prophet
Leicester Pioneer

Manchester
Merthyr Labour Pioneer
The Miner

Progress (Gloucester ILP)

The Record, (the organ of the Halifax ILP)
Rochdale Labour News
The Scout
Seedtime
Stockport Labour Journal
Swinton and Pendlebury Pioneer

Workman's Times

Yorkshire Factory Times

(ii) General

Aberdeen Daily Free Press

Barnsley Chronicle
Blackburn Weekly Standard and Express

Blackburn Weekly Telegraph
Bolton Chronicle
Bolton Evening News
Bradford Argus
Bradford Observer/Yorkshire Daily Observer
Bristol Mercury
Bristol Times and Mirror

Cheshire County News
Colne Valley Guardian

Daily Record
Dewsbury Chronicle
Dundee Advertiser
Dundee Courier
Durham Chronicle

Glasgow Herald
Glasgow Observer
Gorton Reporter

Halifax Courier
Halifax Courier and Guardian
Halifax Guardian
Hamilton Advertiser
Huddersfield Examiner
Huddersfield Weekly Chronicle
Hull Daily News

Lancashire Daily Post
Leicester Daily Post

Manchester Guardian
Merthyr Express
Midland Free Press
Motherwell Times

Nelson Chronicle
The Nineteenth Century
North British Daily Mail
Northern Daily Telegraph

Preston Guardian
Preston Herald

Rochdale Observer
Rochdale Times

Sheffield Daily Telegraph
Sheffield Independent
Southampton Times
South Wales Daily News

The Times

Western Daily Press
West Ham Guardian
West Ham Herald
West Ham and Stratford Express

Books

Anderson, Perry, *Considerations on Western Marxism* (New Left Books, London, 1980).

Armytage, W. H. G., *A. J. Mundella: 1825—1897: The Liberal Background to the Labour Movement* (Benn, London, 1951).

Arnot, R. P., *A History of the Scottish Miners* (Allen and Unwin, London, 1955).

Atherley-Jones, L., *Looking Back* (Witherby, London, 1925).

Bagwell, P., *The Railwaymen* (Allen and Unwin, London, 1963).

Barker, B. (ed.), *Ramsay MacDonald's Political Writings* (Allen Lane, London, 1972).

Barker, C. A., *Henry George* (Oxford University Press, New York, 1955).

Barnes, George, *From Workshop to War Cabinet* (Herbert Jenkins, London, 1923).

Bealey, F. and Pelling, H., *Labour and Politics 1900—1906* (Macmillan, London, 1958).

Benson, J. and Neville, R. G. (eds.), *Studies in the Yorkshire Coal Industry* (Manchester University Press, Manchester, 1976).

Blatchford, Robert, *Merrie England* (3rd edition), (Clarion Press, London, 1895).

Blatchford, Robert, *Britain for the British* (Clarion Press, London, 1902).

Blatchford, Robert, *My Eighty Years* (Cassell, London, 1931).

Brockway, A. F., *Socialism Over Sixty Years: The Life of Jowett of Bradford 1864—1944* (Allen and Unwin, London, 1946).

Brown, B. H., *The Tariff Reform Movement in Britain 1881—1895* (Columbia University Press, New York, 1943).

Brown, Kenneth, O., *John Burns* (Royal Historical Society, London, 1977).

Brown, Kenneth, O., *Labour and Unemployment 1900—14* (David and Charles, Newton Abbot, 1971).

Brown, Raymond, *Waterfront Organisation in Hull 1870—1900* (Occasional Papers in Economic and Social History, No. 5, University of Hull, 1972).

Buckley, K. D., *Trade Unionism in Aberdeen 1878—1900* (Oliver and Boyd, Edinburgh, 1955).

Bullock, Alan, *The Life and Times of Ernest Bevin*, vol. 1 (Heinemann, London, 1960).

Challinor, R., *The Lancashire and Cheshire Miners* (Frank Graham, Newcastle, 1972).

Channing, F. A., *Memories of Midland Politics* (Constable, London, 1918).

Checkland, J. G., *The Upas Tree: Glasgow 1875—1975* (Glasgow University Press, Glasgow, 1976).

Clark, David, *Colne Valley: Radicalism to Socialism* (Longman, London, 1981).

Clarke, Peter, *Lancashire and the New Liberalism* (Cambridge University Press, Cambridge 1971).

Clarke, Peter, *Liberals and Social Democrats* (Cambridge University Press, Cambridge, 1978).

Clegg, H., Fox, A. and Thompson, A. F., *A History of British Trades Unions Since 1889*, vol. 1 (Clarendon Press, Oxford, 1963).

Clinton, Alan, *The Trade Union Rank and File: Trades Councils in Britain 1900—40* (Manchester University Press, Manchester, 1977).

Clynes, J. R., *Autobiography*, vol. 1 (Hutchinson, London, 1937).

Collison, W., *The Apostle of Free Labour* (Hurst and Blackett, London, 1913).

Cross, Colin, *Philip Snowden* (Barrie and Rockliff, London, 1966).

Curtis, L. P., *Anglo-Saxon and Celt: A Study of Anti-Irish Prejudice in Victorian England* (University of Bridgeport, Conn., 1968).

Denvir, J. E., *The Irish in Britain* (Kegan Paul, London, 1892).

Dictionary of Labour Biography (Macmillan: Dates Various).

Duncan, Bob, *James Leatham 1865—1945: Portrait of a Socialist Pioneer* People's Press, Aberdeen, 1978).

Elliott, Malcolm, *Victorian Leicester* (Phillmore, Chichester, 1979).

Emy, H. V., *Liberals, Radicals and Social Politics 1892—1914* (Cambridge University Press, Cambridge, 1973).

Engels, F., *The Condition of the Working Class in England* (Panther, St Albans, 1976).

Foot, Michael, *Aneurin Bevan 1897—1945* (Paladin, St Albans, 1975).

Fox, Alan, *A History of the National Union of Boot and Shoe Operatives 1874—1957* (Blackwell, Oxford, 1958).

Francis, Hywel and Smith, David, *The Fed* (Lawrence and Wishart, London, 1980).

Gammie, Alexander, *From Pit to Parliament* (James Clarke, London, 1931).

Garrard, J., *The English and Immigration 1880—1910* (Cambridge University Press, Cambridge, 1971).

Garside, W. R., *The Durham Miners 1919—1960* (Allen and Unwin, London, 1971).

Glasier, J. Bruce, *Keir Hardie: The Man and His Message* (ILP, London, 1919).

Glasier, J. Bruce, *William Morris and the Early Days of the Socialist Movement* (Longmans, London, 1921).

Greaves, C. Desmond, *The Life and Times of James Connolly* (Lawrence and Wishart, London, 1976).

Gregory, R., *The Miners in British Politics 1906—14* (Clarendon Press, Oxford, 1968).

Griffin, A. R., *The Miners of Nottinghamshire 1881—1914* (NUM, Notts Area, Mansfield, 1955).

Grigg, John, *The Young Lloyd George* (Methuen, London, 1973).

Grigg, John, *Lloyd George: The People's Champion* (Methuen, London, 1978).

Haddow, W. M., *My Seventy Years* (Robert Gibson, Glasgow, 1943).

Handley, J. E., *The Irish in Modern Scotland* (Cork University Press, Cork, 1947).

Hanham, H. J., *Elections and Party Management: Politics in the Age of Gladstone and Disraeli* Longmans, London, 1959).

Hardie, J. K., *Address to the Aberdare Trades and Labour Council on Labour Representation on Public Bodies* (1901), Aberdare Local Collection, P43/1.

Hardie, Keir, *From Serfdom to Socialism* (George Allen, London, 1907).

Harris, Jose, Unemployment and Politics 1886—1914 (Clarendon Press, Oxford, 1972).

Harris, Sir Peter, *Forty Years In and Out of Parliament* (Melrose, London, 1947).

Hobsbawm, E., *Labour's Turning Point 1880—1900* (Lawrence and Wishart, London, 1948).

Hobsbawm, E. J., *Primitive Rebels* (Manchester University Press, Manchester, 1959).

Hobson, S. G., *Pilgrim to the Left* (Longmans, London, 1938).

Hopwood, E., *The Lancashire Weavers' Story* (Amalgamated Weavers Association, Manchester, 1969).

Hyman, R., *The Workers' Union* (Clarendon, Oxford, 1971).

Irving, R. J., *The North Eastern Railway Company 1870—1914* (Leicester University Press, Leicester, 1976).

James, Christopher, *MP for Dewsbury* (The Author, Brighouse, 1970).

Jeffreys, J. B., The Story of the Engineers 1800—1945 (Lawrence and Wishart, London, 1945).

Jeyes, Samuel and How, Frederick, *The Life of Sir Howard Vincent* (George Allen, London, 1912).

Joyce, Patrick, *Work, Society and Politics — the Culture of the Factory in Later Victorian England* (Harvester, Brighton, 1980).

Kapp, Yvonne, *Eleanor Marx*, vol. 2, *The Crowded Years* (Virago, London, 1979).

Keith-Lucas, B., *The English Local Government Franchise — A Short History* (Blackwell, Oxford, 1952).

Kent, W., *John Burns: Labour's Lost Leader* (Williams and Norgate, London, 1950).

Lawson, Jack, *A Man's Life* (Hodder, London, 1944).

Lawson, Jack, *The Man in the Cloth Cap* (Methuen, London, 1941).

Liddington, Jill and Norris, Jill, *One Hand Tied Behind Us: The Rise of the Women's Suffrage Movement* (Virago, London, 1978).

Lowe, David, *From Pit to Parliament: The Story of the Early Life of Keir Hardie* (Labour Publishing Co., London, 1923).

Lowe, David, *Souvenirs of Scottish Labour* (Holmes, Glasgow, 1919).

Lowenson, Harry, *In England Now — Vagrom Essays by a Vagrom Man* (C. Arthur Dewis, Stoke-on-Trent, No Date, probably 1898).

Lyons, F. S. L., *Charles Stewart Parnell* (Fontana, London, 1978).

Lyons, F. S. L., *Ireland Since the Famine* (Weidenfeld, London, 1978).

Lyons, F. S. L., *The Irish Parliamentary Party 1890—1910* (Faber and Faber, London, 1951).

Laurence, Dan H., *The Collected Letters of George Bernard Shaw*, vol. 1 (Max Reinhardt, London, 1965).

Macartney, R. J. and Sexton, J., *Debate on Socialism* (Young England Patriotic Association, Salford, 1895).

McBriar, A. W., *Fabian Socialism and English Politics 1884—1918* (Cambridge University Press, Cambridge, 1962).

Macintyre, Stuart, *Proletarian Science: Marxism in Britain 1917—1933* (Cambridge University Press, Cambridge, 1980).

McKenna, Frank, *The Railway workers 1840—1970* (Faber and Faber, London, 1980).

McKibbin, Ross, *The Evolution of the Labour Party 1910—1924* (Oxford University Press, London, 1974).

McLean, I., *Keir Hardie* (Allen Lane, London, 1975).

Mann, Tom, *Memoirs* (Labour Publishing Co., London, 1923).

Mann, Tom, *Why I Joined the National Democratic League* (1901).

Marquand, David, *Ramsay MacDonald* (Cape, London, 1977).

Martin, R., *Communism and the British Trade Unions 1924—1933* (Clarendon Press, Oxford, 1969).

Marwick, W. H., *A Short History of Labour in Scotland* (Chambers, Edinburgh, 1967).

Marx, Karl, *Surveys from Exile* (Penguin, Harmondsworth, 1973).

Mason, Tony, *Association Football and English Society 1863—1915* (Harvester, Hassocks, 1980).

Mavor, James, *The Scottish Railway Strike 1891: History and Criticism* (William Brown, Edinburgh, 1891).

Moore, Barrington Jnr., *Injustice: The Social Bases of Obedience and Revolt* (Macmillan, London, 1978).

Morgan, K. O., *Keir Hardie, Radical and Socialist* (Weidenfeld, London, 1975).

Morgan, K. O., *Wales in British Politics 1868—1922* (University of Wales Press, Cardiff, 1963).

Morris, William, *Signs of Change* (Reeves and Turner, London, 1888).

Morris, William, *Three Works*, edited by A. L. Morton (Lawrence and Wishart, London, 1977).

Moore, Robert, *Pitmen, Preachers and Politics: The Effects of Methodism in a Durham Mining Community* (Cambridge University Press, Cambridge 1974).

Nairn, Tom, *The Break-Up of Britain: Crisis and Neo-Nationalism* (New Left Books, London, 1977).

O'Brien, Conor Cruise, *Parnell and His Party 1880—1890* (Oxford University Press, London, 1957).

Olson, Mancur, *The Logic of Collective Action* (Schocken, New York, 1971).

Page Arnot, R., *The Miners 1889—1910* (Allen and Unwin, London, 1949).

Page Arnot, R., *The South Wales Miners 1898—1914* Allen and Unwin, London, 1967).

Pankhurst, Sylvia, *The Suffragette Movement* (Virago, London, 1977).

Pearce, Cyril, *The Manningham Mills Strike in Bradford: December 1890—April 1891* (University of Hull Occasional Papers in Economic and Social History, No. 7, 1975).

Pelling, Henry, *Social Geography of British Elections 1885—1910* (Macmillan, London, 1967).

Pelling, Henry, *The Origins of the Labour Party 1880—1900*, 2nd edn (Clarendon Press, Oxford, 1966).

Poirier, P., *The Advent of the Labour Party* (Allen and Unwin, London, 1958).

Pollard, Sidney, *A History of Labour in Sheffield* (Liverpool University Press, Liverpool, 1959).

Postgate, R., *The Life of George Lansbury* (Longmans, London, 1951).

Radice, G. and L., *Will Thorne: Constructive Militant* (Allen and Unwin, London, 1974).

Reid, A., *The New Party* (Hodder, London, 1894).

Reid, Fred, *Keir Hardie: The Making of a Socialist* (Croom Helm, London, 1978).

Roberts, B. C., *The Trades Union Congress 1868—1921* (Allen and Unwin, London, 1958).

Salvidge, Stanley, *Salvidge of Liverpool* (Hodder, London, 1934).

Semmel, Bernard, *Imperialism and Social Reform: English Social Imperial Thought 1895—1914* (Allen and Unwin, London, 1960).

Sexton, J., *Sir James Sexton: Agitator* (Faber and Faber, London, 1936).

Smillie, Robert, *My Life for Labour* (Mills and Boon, London, 1924).

Snowden, Lord, *Autobiography* (Nicholson and Watson, London, 1934).

Souvenir — 20th Annual Conference of ILP (Merthyr, 1912).

Stedman-Jones, Gareth, *Outcast London* (Clarendon Press, Oxford, 1971).

Stewart, William, *J. Keir Hardie* (ILP, London, 1921).

Stonelake, Edmund, JP, *Aberdare Trades and Labour Council Jubilee Souvenir 1900—1950* (Aberdare, 1950).

Thompson, E. P., *William Morris: From Romantic to Revolutionary*, 2nd edn, (Merlin Press, London, 1977).

Thompson, Laurence, *Robert Blatchford: Portrait of an Englishman* (Gollancz, London, 1951).

Thompson, L., *The Enthusiasts* (Gollancz, London, 1971).

Thompson, Paul, *Socialists, Liberals and Labour: The Struggle for London 1885—1914* (Routledge, London, 1967).

Thorne, W., *My Life's Battles* (Newnes, London, 1925).

Tillett, Ben, *Memories and Reflections* (Long, London, 1931).

Torr, Dona, *Tom Mann and His Times*, vol. 1, *1856—1890* (Lawrence and Wishart, London, 1956).

Tsuziki, G., *H. M. Hyndman and British Socialism* (Heinemann and Oxford University Press, London, 1961).

Turner, Ben, *About Myself* (Toulmin, London, 1930).

Turner, H. A., *Trade Union Growth Structure and Policy: A Comparative Study of the Cotton Unions* (Allen and Unwin, London, 1962).

Watts, C. and Davies, L., *Cunninghame Graham: A Critical Biography* (Cambridge University Press, Cambridge, 1979).

Webb, S. and B., *History of Trade Unionism* (Longman, London, 1907).

Webb, S. and B., *Industrial Democracy* (Longman, London, 1920).

Welbourne, E., *The Miners' Unions of Northumberland and Durham* (Cambridge Univesity Press, Cambridge, 1923).

White, Joseph L., *The Limits of Trade Union Militancy: The Lancashire Textile Workers 1910—1914* (Greenwood Press, Westport, Conn., 1978).

Williams, Glanmor (ed.), *Merthyr Politics: the Making of A Working Class Tradition* (University of Wales Press, Cardiff, 1966).

Williams, Gwyn, *The Merthyr Rising* (Croom Helm, London, 1978).

Williams, J. E., *The Derbyshire Miners* (Allen and Unwin, London, 1962).

Williams, Raymond, *Culture and Society 1780—1950* (Chatto and Windus, London, 1958).

Williams, Raymond, *Politics and Letters* (New Left Books, London, 1979).

Williams, Raymond, *The Country and the City* (Chatto and Windus, London, 1973).

Wilson, John, *A History of the Durham Miners Association 1870—1904* (J. H. Veitch, Durham, 1907).

Wilson, John, *Memories of a Labour Leader* (T. Fisher Unwin, London, 1910).

Wrigley, Chris, *David Lloyd George and the British Labour Movement* (Harvester, Hassocks, 1976).

Young, J. D., *The Rousing of the Scottish Working Class* (Croom Helm, London, 1979).

Articles

Aves, Ernest, 'The Dispute in the Engineering Trades', *Economic Journal*, March 1898, pp. 116—24.

Bealey, Frank, 'Negotiations between the Liberal Party and the Labour Representation Committee before the General Election of 1906', *Bulletin of the Institute of Historical Research*, 1956.

Blewett, N., 'The Franchise in the United Kingdom 1885—1918', *Past and Present*, December 1965, pp. 27—56.

Brown, Joyce, 'Attercliffe 1894 — How One Local Liberal Party Failed to Meet the Challenge of Labour', *Journal of British Studies*, May 1975, pp. 48—77.

Campbell, Alan, 'Honourable Men and Degraded Slaves: A Comparative Study of Trade Unionism in Two Lanarkshire Mining Communities', in Royden Harrison (ed.), *The Independent Collier* (Harvester, Hassocks, 1978).

Campbell, Alan and Reid, Fred, 'The Independent Collier', in Royden Harrison (ed.), *The Independent Collier* (Harvester, Hassocks, 1978).

Carter, Ian, 'The Changing Image of the Scottish Peasantry', in Raphael Samuel, *People's History and Socialist Theory* (Routledge, London, 1981).

Carter, S., 'The ILP in Ashton Under Lyne 1893—1900', *North-West Group for the Study of Labour History, Bulletin*, No. 4.

Chapman, S. J., 'Some Policies of the Cotton Spinners' Trade Unions', *Economic Journal*, 1900, pp. 467—73.

Clarke, Peter, 'British Politics and Blackburn Politics 1900—1910', *Historical Journal*, 1969, pp. 302—27.

Clarke, R. O., 'The Dispute in the British Engineering Industry 1897—8: An Evaluation', *Economica*, May 1957, pp. 127—37.

Collins, Henry, 'The Marxism of the Social Democratic Federation', in A. Briggs and J. Saville (eds.), *Essays in Labour History 1886—1923* (Macmillan, London, 1976).

Crowley, D. W., 'The Crofters' Party 1885—1892', *Scottish Historical Review*, 1956, pp. 110—26.

Davies, Sam, 'The Liverpool Labour Party and the Liverpool Working Class', in *North-West Group for the Study of Labour History Bulletin*, No. 6, 1979—80.

Duffy, A. E., 'New Unionism in Britain 1889—1890: A Re-Appraisal', *Economic History Review*, 1961, pp. 306—19.

Edwards, Clem, 'The Hull Shipping Dispute', *Economic Journal*, 1893, pp. 345—51.

Fowler, Alan, 'Lancashire and the New Liberalism', *North-West Group for the Study of Labour History Bulletin*, No. 4, pp. 36—62.

Fox, K. O., 'Labour and Merthyr's Khakhi Election of 1900', *Welsh History Review*, 1964—5, pp. 351—66.

Fraser, W. Hamish, 'Trades Councils in the Labour Movement in Nineteenth Century Scotland', in Ian MacDougall (ed.), *Essays in Scottish Labour History* (John Donald, Edinburgh, W.O.).

Garvin, J. L., 'A Party with a Future', *Fortnightly Review*, 1 September 1895, pp. 325—39.

Gupta, P. S., 'Railway Trade Unionism in Britain *c.* 1880—1900', *Economic History Review*, 1966, pp. 124—53.

Hardie, J. K., 'The Pioneer of the ILP', *Socialist Review*, April 1914, pp. 113—17.

Hirst, F. W., 'The Policy of the Engineers', *Economic Journal*, March 1898, pp. 124—7.

Hobsbawm, Eric, 'General Labour Unions in Britain 1889—1914', *Economic History Review*, 1949, pp. 123—42.

Hopkin, Deian, 'The Membership of the Independent Labour Party 1904—10: A Spatial and Occupational Analysis', *International Review of Social History*, 1975, pp. 175—197.

Howard, Christopher, 'Reactionary Radicalism: The Mid Glamorgan By-Election March 1910', *Glamorgan Historian* (9), pp. 24—42.

Howarth, Janet, 'The Liberal Revival in Northamptonshire 1880—1895', *Historical Journal*, 1969, pp. 78—118.

Joyce, Patrick, 'The Factory Politics of Lancashire in the Later Nineteenth Century', *Historical Journal*, 1975, pp. 525—53.

Kellas, James, 'The Liberal Party and the Scottish Church Disestablishment Crisis', *English Historical Review*, 1964, pp. 31—46.

Kellas, James, 'The Mid Lanark By-Election (1888) and the Scottish Labour Party', *Parliamentary Affairs*, 1964—5, pp. 318—29.

McCaffrey, John F., 'The Origins of Liberal Unionism in the West of Scotland', *Scottish Historical Review*, 1971, pp. 47—71.

McKenna, Frank, 'Victorian Railwaymen', *History Workshop* (1), 1976, pp. 26—73.

Martin, David, 'The Instrument of the People? The 1906 Parliamentary Labour Party' in D. Rubinstein and D. Martin, *Ideology and the Labour Movement* (Croom Helm, London, 1978), pp. 125—144.

Mathew, H. C. G., McKibbin, R. and Kay, J. A., 'The Franchise Factor in the Rise of the Labour Party', *English Historical Review*, 1976, pp. 723—52.

Mertinez, Paul, 'The People's Charter and the Enigmatic Mr. Maltman Barry', *Bulletin of the Society for the Study of Labour History*, Autumn 1980, pp. 34—45.

Moody, T. W., 'Michael Davitt', in J. W. Boyle (ed.), *Leaders and Workers* (Mercier Press, Cork, 1978), pp. 47—55.

Moody, T. W., 'Michael Davitt and the British Labour Movement', *Transactions of the Royal Historical Society*, 1953, pp. 55—77.
Morgan, K. O., 'D. A. Thomas: Industrialist as Politician', *Glamorgan Historian* (3), pp. 33—51.
Morgan, K. O., 'The New Liberalism and the Challenge of Labour: The Welsh Experience 1885—1929', in K. O. Brown, *Essays in Anti-Labour History* (Macmillan, London, 1974), pp. 159—82.
Neville, R. G., 'The Yorkshire Miners and the 1893 Lockout — the Featherstone Massacre', *International Review of Social History*, 1976, pp. 337—57.

Pelling, Henry, 'H. H. Champion: Pioneer of Labour Representation', *Cambridge Journal*, 1953, pp. 222—38.

Reid, Fred, 'Keir Hardie's Conversion to Socialism' in A. Briggs and J. Saville (eds.), *Essays in Labour History 1886—1923* (Macmillan, London, 1970).
Reynolds, J. and Laybourn, K., 'The Emergence of the Independent Labour Party in Bradford', *International Review of Social History*, 1975, pp. 313—46.
Rubinstein, David, 'The Independent Labour Party and the Yorkshire Miners — the Barnsley By-Election of 1897', *International Review of Social History*, 1978, pp. 102—34.

Savage, D. C., 'Scottish Politics 1885—6', *Scottish Historical Review*, 1961, pp. 118—35.
Saville, John, 'Henry George and the British Labour Movement', *Bulletin of the Society for the Study of Labour History*, 1962.
Saville, John, 'Trade Unions and Free Labour: The Background to the Taff Vale Decision', in A. Briggs and John Saville (eds.), *Essays in Labour History* (Macmillan, London, 1960).
Shallice, A., 'Orange and Green and Militancy: Sectarianism and Working Class Politics in Liverpool 1900—14', in *North West Labour History Society Bulletin*, **6**, 1979—80.
Spaven, Pat, 'Main Gates of Protest: Contrasts in Rank and File Activity amongst the South Yorks Miners 1885—94', in R. Harrison (ed.), *The Independent Collier* (Harvester, Hassocks, 1978).
Stead, Peter, 'The Language of Edwardian Politics' in D. Smith (ed.), *A People and a Proletariat* (Pluto Press, London, 1980).
Stead, W. T., 'The Labour Party and the Books that helped to make it', *Review of Reviews*, June 1906, pp. 568—82.
Stedman-Jones, Gareth, 'Working Class Culture and Working Class Politics in London 1870—1900: Notes on the Remaking of a Working Class', *Journal of Social History*, 1973—4, pp. 460—508.

Thompson, E. P., 'Homage to Tom Maguire' in Briggs and Saville (eds.), *Essays in Labour History* (Macmillan, London, 1960).
Thompson, E. P., 'On History, Sociology and Historical Relevance', *British Journal of Sociology*, 1976, pp. 387—402.

Walker, W. M., 'Irish Immigrants in Scotland: Their Priests, Politics and Parochial Life', *Historical Journal*, 1972, pp. 649—67.
Walker, W. M., *Juteopolis: Dundee and its textile workers 1885—1923* (Scottish Academic Press, 1979).
Williams, Gwyn, 'Dic Penderyn', *Llafur*, 1978, pp. 110—120.

Williams, Norman, 'Evan Roberts and the 1904—5 Revival', *Glamorgan Historian* (3), pp. 28—37.

Williams, Raymond, 'The Social Significance of 1926', *Llafur*, 1977, pp. 5—8.

Wilson, Gordon, 'The Strike Policy of the Miners of the West of Scotland 1842—74', in Ian MacDougall (ed.), *Essays in Scottish Labour History* (John Donald, Edinburgh, ND).

Wood, Ian, 'Irish Immigrants and Scottish Radicalism 1880—1906', in Ian MacDougall (ed.), *Essays in Scottish Labour History*.

Yeo, Stephen, 'A New Life: The Religion of Socialism in Britain 1883—1896', *History Workshop* (4), Autumn 1977, pp. 5—56.

Index